THE SUPREME COURT
AND
THE FIRST AMENDMENT

Joseph J. Hemmer, Jr.

PRAEGER SPECIAL STUDIES • PRAEGER SCIENTIFIC

New York • Westport, Connecticut • London

Library of Congress Cataloging-in-Publication Data

Hemmer, Joseph J.
  The Supreme Court and the First Amendment.

  "Praeger special studies. Praeger scientific."
  Bibliography: p.
  Includes index.
  1. Freedom of the press—United States.   2. Press
law—United States.   3. Freedom of speech—United
States.   I. Title.
  KF4774.H46   1986   342.73'0853   85-31173
  ISBN 0-275-92008-9 (alk. paper) 347.302853

Library of Congress Catalog Card Number: 85-31173
ISBN: 0-275-92008-9

First published in 1986

Praeger Publishers, 521 Fifth Avenue, New York, NY 10175
A division of Greenwood Press, Inc.

Printed in the United States of America

The paper used in this book complies with the Permanent
Paper Standard issued by the National Information Standards
Organization (Z39.48-1984).

10   9   8   7   6   5   4   3   2   1

To the memory of my mentor
ORDEAN G. NESS

PREFACE

The field of communication law—the subject matter of this book—influences our lives on a daily basis. A cursory glance at the various news media makes one cognizant of the many First Amendment questions that face our legislatures and courts. To what extent can dissatisfied citizens protest against the foreign and domestic policies of the government? In what ways can municipalities restrict the assembly and petition rights of socially conscious groups? Can school boards or parent groups ban books from our school libraries? Should we have different obscenity and pornography guidelines for children than for adults? When may a person refuse to be communicated with? Are celebrities entitled to control their own publicity? How can celebrities protect themselves from the defamatory remarks of their critics? Do the courts adequately balance the rights of criminals with the rights of a free press? Under what conditions may the government refuse to release information to the news media? Are the airwaves sufficiently regulated? How can society protect itself from deceptive advertising? These questions, and many others, are the focus of this book. Clearly, an understanding of how legislatures and courts have grappled with these First Amendment issues is a vital concern for our students and, in fact, for all of our citizens.

This work deals with First Amendment issues that affect the general public, academic institutions, business enterprises, journalistic professionals, government agencies, and the broadcast industry. Accordingly, the book contains chapters entitled Dissent, Association, Academic Freedom, Obscenity, Silence, Libel, Privacy, Copyright, News, Fair Trial, Broadcasting, and Advertising.

The book is designed as an introductory textbook for communication-law courses in journalism, communication, and political science departments. The work considers Supreme Court cases relevant to a variety of free-speech and free-press issues. The focus is on recent and precedent-setting cases, though others are considered as well, including some important lower-court cases. The method involves a description of the communication act under challenge, analysis of the issue facing the Court justices, and explication of the reasons behind the majority and dissenting opinions. Some concern is given to the impact of the decision on case law and societal behavior. The cut-off date for the material discussed is the Supreme Court's decisions through July 1985.

My gratitude is extended to the individuals who provided valuable assistance in the research and writing of *The Supreme Court and the First Amendment*. In particular, I am thankful to Sharon Hart and Bob Beitz. I am also grateful to Cindy Hoeft for allowing her artwork to be included in this book. And my appreciation goes to Vicki Buinowski, Jane Mikolajczak, and Audrey Lenroot, who typed the manuscript. I am endebted to the Carroll College Faculty Development Committee for providing funds to help finance the project. Finally, I want to thank my family for putting up with me while I was engrossed in this work. To Joy, Joe, and Andy go my heartfelt thanks.

CONTENTS

PREFACE   vii

1   INTRODUCTION   1
     Sources of Free Expression   1
     Tests of the First Amendment   2
         Clear and Present Danger   2
         Bad Tendency   4
         Balancing   6
         Preferred Position   7
         Absolutism   8
     Conclusion   9
     Notes   9
     Recommended Reading   10

2   DISSENT   12
     Tests of Dissent   12
         Schenck Test   12
         Gitlow Test   13
         Dennis Test   15
         Bond Test   18
         Summary   19
     Regulating Dissent   20
         Provocative Words   20
         Fighting Words   22
         Threatening Words   24
         Offensive Words   25
         Summary   26
     Symbolic Speech   26
         Symbol Desecration   26
         Display Symbols   31
         Summary   34
     Notes   34
     Recommended Reading   35
     Key Decisions   35
     Summary—Law of Dissent   36

3   ASSOCIATION   38
       Assembly   38
             Freedom to Associate   38
             Right to Solicit Members   41
             Right to Meet Publicly   42
             Controlling Associations   45
             Summary   49
       Petition   49
             Right to Picket and Boycott   50
             Picket and Boycott Guidelines   51
             Right to Demonstrate   56
             Demonstration Guidelines   59
             Summary   64
       Notes   65
       Recommended Reading   66
       Key Decisions   67
       Summary—Law of Association   67

4   ACADEMIC FREEDOM   69
       Administration Rights   69
             Curriculum   69
             School Rituals   70
             Teacher Fitness   73
             Campus Speakers   77
             Banned Books   78
             Summary   81
       Faculty Rights   82
             Teaching Methods   82
             Expression of Views   84
             Due Process   88
             Summary   90
       Student Rights   91
             Protest   91
             School Press   94
             Organization   95
             Due Process   96
             Summary   97
       Notes   98
       Recommended Reading   99
       Key Decisions   100
       Summary—Law of Academic Freedom   100

5   OBSCENITY   102
       Tests of Obscenity   102
           Hicklin Test   102
           Roth Test   104
           Miller Test   107
           Summary   110
       Guidelines   111
           Prior Restraint   111
           Mailings   112
           Film   114
           Scienter   115
           Pandering   115
           Youth   116
           Privacy   118
           Zoning   120
           Summary   121
       Notes   121
       Recommended Reading   122
       Key Decisions   123
       Summary—Obscenity Law   124

6   SILENCE   125
       Freedom Not to Communicate   125
           Loyalty Oaths   125
           Investigative Committees   127
           Anonymous Publication   128
           Surveillance   129
           Summary   129
       Freedom Not to Be Communicated With   130
           Sound Amplification   130
           Forced Listening   132
           Summary   132
       Freedom to Be Let Alone   132
           Solicitation and Distribution   132
           Travel   143
           Summary   146
       Notes   147
       Recommended Reading   148
       Key Decisions   148
       Summary—Law of Silence   149

7   LIBEL   150
      Procedures   150
         Types   150
         Elements   152
         Damages   157
         Defenses   160
         Summary   167
      Doctrines   168
         Individuals   168
         Groups   186
         Corporations   187
         Criminal Libel   188
         Summary   189
      Notes   190
      Recommended Reading   191
      Key Decisions   192
      Summary—Libel Law   192

8   PRIVACY   194
      Intrusion   194
         Harassment   194
         Hidden Electronic Devices   198
         Physical Entry   199
         Summary   201
      Public Disclosure   201
         Tragedy   201
         Embarrassment   202
         Intimacy   205
         Summary   207
      False Light   207
         Fictionalization   207
         Actual Malice   209
         Summary   211
      Appropriation   212
         Advertising   212
         Right of Publicity   215
         Summary   218
      Notes   218
      Recommended Reading   219
      Key Decisions   220
      Summary—Law of Privacy   220

9   COPYRIGHT   222
      History of Copyright Law   222
          Common-Law Copyright   222
          Statutory Copyright   224
          Summary   226
      Procedural Requirements   226
          Notice   226
          Deposit and Registration   228
          Summary   229
      Tests of Infringement   229
          Originality   229
          Copying   233
          Substantiality   236
          Access   240
          Damages   241
          Summary   242
      Guidelines for Fair Use   242
          Scholarly versus Commercial Gain   243
          Characters   245
          Musical Composition   246
          Speeches   246
          Unpublished Presidential Memoirs   247
          Cable Television   248
          Radio   249
          Sound Recordings   250
          Photocopying   250
          Videotaping   251
          Summary   252
      Notes   253
      Recommended Reading   254
      Key Decisions   255
      Summary—Copyright Law   255

10 NEWS   257
      News Gathering   258
          News Reporter's Privilege   258
          Shield Laws   265
          Executive Privilege   269
          Freedom of Information   273
          Banning News Reporters   284
          Third-Party Privacy   289
          Summary   290

Publishing News 290
  Prior Restraint 291
  Taxation 294
  Post-Office Control 295
  Antitrust Laws 296
  Failing-Company Doctrine 299
  Politically Oriented Information 301
  Right to Reply 302
  Prepublication Review 304
  Summary 304
Notes 305
Recommended Reading 306
Key Decisions 307
Summary—Law of News 308

11 FAIR TRIAL 310
Contempt 310
  "So Near Thereto" 310
  Bridges Principle 312
  Gag Orders 316
  Summary 319
Trial by Media 319
  Pretrial Publicity 320
  Implied Bias 325
  Summary 328
Notes 328
Recommended Reading 329
Key Decisions 330
Summary—Fair Trial 330

12 BROADCASTING 332
History of Regulation 332
  Federal Radio Commission 332
  Federal Communications Commission 336
  Summary 343
Licensing-Decision Guidelines 344
  Economic Guidelines 344
  Programming Guidelines 347
  Procedural Guidelines 367
  Summary 371
Notes 372
Recommended Reading 374
Key Decisions 375
Summary—Broadcast Law 376

13	ADVERTISING	377
	Tests of Advertising	377
	Commercial Speech	377
	Commercial Information	379
	Summary	385
	Regulation of Advertising	385
	Deception	385
	Access	392
	Summary	397
	Notes	398
	Recommended Reading	399
	Key Decisions	399
	Summary—Law of Advertising	400
14	EPILOGUE	402
	Theory	402
	Marketplace of Ideas	402
	Social Exchange	403
	Social Utility	404
	Self-Government	405
	Expression/Action Dichotomy	405
	Media Access	406
	Communication Context	407
	Practice	408
	Two-Tiered Approach	409
	Situation-Bound Approach	409
	Notes	410
INDEX OF CASES		411
GENERAL INDEX		431
ABOUT THE AUTHOR		434

1

INTRODUCTION

Freedom of expression has been encouraged in the United States since the foundation of the country. In both legal theory and social practice, the freedoms of speech, press, petition, and assembly have been treated in a manner that promotes openness and discourages restraint. Yet, within a general climate favorable to free expression, jurists and legislators have continually debated about which freedoms should be guaranteed and which restraints should be imposed on expression in a democratic society. This debate has existed since the inception of the U.S. government.

SOURCES OF FREE EXPRESSION

The delegates at the Constitutional Convention in 1789 adopted the Constitution of the United States, a document that organized a strong national government for the North American states. While the Constitution delineated such governmental powers as the right to collect taxes, declare war, and regulate trade, it provided few personal guarantees. The delegates, however, also penned the Bill of Rights—ten amendments to the Constitution. In so doing, the framers of the government responded to the influence of John Locke, John Milton, John Stuart Mill, Thomas Jefferson, Thomas Paine, and James Madison, and acknowledged that citizens possess certain inborn rights that the federal government may not violate. The Bill of Rights forbids the government to abuse the fundamental rights and liberties of the people.

Since December 15, 1791, the day the bill went into effect, the First Amendment has been the basic safeguard of freedom of expression. In part, the First Amendment provides that "Congress shall make no law...abridging the freedom of speech, or the press; or the right of the people peaceably to assemble and to petition the government for a redress of grievances." While the language of the amendment seems clear and precise, the scope and function of its meaning have been subject to dispute. Throughout the nineteenth century, the individual states guaranteed freedom of expression when they adopted their own constitutions. Yet, numerous differences existed among state provisions regarding what constituted an abuse of free expression. In 1868 Congress passed the Fourteenth Amendment, which declares that no state shall "deprive any person of life, liberty, or property, without due process of law." For the following several decades, however, states continued to apply their own divergent concepts of free expression. Finally, in the 1925 *Gitlow* case, the Supreme Court cited the Fourteenth Amendment in declaring that freedom of expression was protected from abuse by the states.

> We may and do assume that freedom of speech and the press—which are protected by the First Amendment from abridgement by Congress—are among the fundamental personal rights and "liberties" protected by the due process clause of the Fourteenth Amendment from impairment by the States.[1]

As affirmed in *Gitlow*, the First and Fourteenth Amendments provide a "national" legal basis for the freedoms associated with expression.

Over the century and a half in which Congress adopted the First Amendment, passed the Fourteenth Amendment, and during which the Supreme Court applied the Fourteenth Amendment to the states, a consitutionally protected right to free expression evolved in the United States. The interpretation of what that right actually means, however, has been left to the Supreme Court.

TESTS OF THE FIRST AMENDMENT

Even though the Supreme Court has generally upheld the free and unimpaired dissemination of information and ideas, various justices have held divergent views regarding the nature and scope of the First Amendment. Accordingly, they have applied diverse rationale in an effort to reconcile the conflict between freedom of expression and other values sought in a democratic society. As a result, the justices have established competing ways of interpreting the First Amendment. The principal tests are "clear and present danger," "bad tendency," "balancing," "preferred position," and "absolutism."

Clear and Present Danger

In the 1919 *Schenck* case, Justice Oliver Wendell Holmes, while upholding convictions for violation of the Espionage Act, introduced the "clear and present danger" test.

The most stringent protection of free speech would not protect a man in falsely shouting fire in a theatre and causing a panic.... The question in every case is whether the words used are in such a nature as to create a clear and present danger that they will bring about the substantive evils that Congress has the right to prevent.[2]

Later that year, in *Abrams,* Holmes clarified the nature of the test: The government may punish expression "that produces or is intending to produce a clear and imminent danger that it will bring about forthwith certain substantive evils." Holmes emphasized that "the power is greater in time of war than in time of peace because war opens dangers that do not exist at other times."[3] Eight years later, in *Whitney,* Justice Louis Brandeis elaborated the doctrine:

Fear of serious injury cannot alone justify suppression of free speech and assembly....To justify suppression of free speech there must be reasonable ground to fear that serious evil will result if free speech is practiced. There must be reasonable ground to believe that the danger apprehended is imminent. There must be reasonable ground to believe that the evil to be prevented is a serious one.... In order to support a finding of clear and present danger it must be shown either that immediate serious violence was to be expected or was advocated, or that the past conduct furnished reason to believe that such advocacy was then contemplated.[4]

In 1941, in the *Bridges* case, the Court stressed three essential elements that had to exist in order to find a "clear and present danger": (1) the circumstances must involve a "substantial evil," (2) the anticipated result must be "extremely serious," and (3) the "degree of imminence" of the danger must be "extremely high."[5]

The "clear and present danger" test provided guidance in a variety of cases throughout the next couple of decades. It was used by either a majority or minority of justices in deciding the constitutionality of convictions under espionage acts in *Schneck*[6] and *Abrams,*[7] under criminal syndicalism statutes in *Gitlow*[8] and *Whitney,*[9] under an anti-insurrection act in *Herndon,*[10] under an antipicketing law in *Thornhill,*[11] and under breach-of-the-peace ordinances in *Cantwell*[12] and *Terminiello.*[13] In *Terminiello* Justice William Douglas stressed the role of the First Amendment in guaranteeing public debate, subject to the constraints of the "clear and present danger" test.

A function of free speech under our system of government is to invite dispute. It may indeed best serve its high purpose when it induces a condition of unrest, creates dissatisfaction with conditions as they are, or even stirs people to anger. Speech is often provocative and challenging. It may strike at prejudices and preconceptions and have profound unsettling effects as it presses for acceptance of an idea. That is why freedom of speech, though not absolute...is nevertheless protected against censorship or punishment, unless shown likely to produce a clear and present danger of a serious substantive evil that arises far above the public inconvenience, annoyance, or unrest.[14]

In 1951, in *Dennis,* the Court further clarified the meaning of "clear and present danger." Facing heightened apprehension over the Communist movement, the Court granted the government increased authority to restrict expression.

> Overthrow of the Government by force and violence is certainly a substantial enough interest for the Government to limit speech. . . . If then, this interest may be protected, the literal problem which is presented is what has been meant by the use of the phrase "clear and present danger" of the utterances bringing about the evil within the power of Congress to punish. . . . If Government is aware that a group aiming at its overthrow is attempting to indoctrinate its members and to commit them to a course whereby they will strike when the leaders feel the circumstances permit, action by the Government is required.[15]

In *Dennis,* Chief Justice Fred Vinson accepted the thinking of lower-court Judge Learned Hand: "In each case they [courts] must ask whether the gravity of the 'evil' discounted by its improbability, justifies such invasion of free speech as is necessary to avoid the danger."[16] The "gravity of the evil" became an important element of the "clear and present danger" test. In *Dennis,* "the gravity of the evil" enabled the Court to uphold the convictions of individuals charged with conspiracy to overthrow the government, even though the case lacked a showing of imminence. The *Dennis* opinion altered the "clear and present danger" test by placing less weight on freedom of expression.

In the 1950s, the Court generally stopped applying the "clear and present danger" test. Still, the test has had some durability, appearing from time to time in such cases as *Craig,*[17] *Garner,*[18] *Wood,*[19] *Cox,*[20] and *Brandenburg.*[21]

Bad Tendency

In 1925, in *Gitlow,* Justice Edward Sanford espoused the "bad tendency" test—a standard that conferred low priority to freedom of expression. A legislature, Sanford argued, was entitled to "extinguish the spark without waiting until it has enkindled the flame or blazed into a conflagration."

> It cannot reasonably be required to defer the adoption of measures for its own peace and safety until the revolutionary utterances lead to actual disturbances of the public peace or imminent and immediate danger of its own destruction; but it may, in the exercise of its judgment, suppress the threatened danger in its incipiency.[22]

According to this test, any expression that had a tendency to lead to substantial evil could be banned. Under the ''bad tendency'' test, questionable speech or advocacy was effectively ''nipped in the bud.''

More than a decade later, in the *Herndon* and *Bridges* cases, the Supreme Court rejected the ''bad tendency'' doctrine. In *Herndon*, Justice Owen Roberts argued that power to abridge expression should be used only where there was a reasonable fear of danger.

> The power of a State to abridge freedom of expression and of assembly is the exception rather than the rule, and the penalizing even of utterances of a defined character must find its justification in a reasonable apprehension of danger to organized government.[23]

In *Bridges,* Justice Hugo Black wrote: ''In accordance with what we have said on the 'clear and present danger' cases, neither 'inherent tendency' nor 'reasona-

ble tendency' is enough to justify a restriction of free expression."[24] In *Herndon* and *Bridges,* the Court returned to the "clear and present danger" test and set aside the notion that speech could be banned if it engendered a "bad tendency."

Balancing

The "balancing" test is based on the principle that when other rights conflict with the First Amendment—for example, the right to fair trial, right to privacy, right to peace and order—the competing rights are balanced to determine which has priority. In 1950, Chief Justice Vinson fashioned the "balancing" test, and noted that the issue in the *Douds* case lent itself to the "balancing" concept.

> When particular conduct is regulated in the interest of public order, and the regulation results in an indirect, conditional, partial abridgement of speech, the duty of the Courts is to determine which of these two conflicting interests demands the greater protection under the particular circumstances presented.[25]

The "balancing" test appeared again in Justice Felix Frankfurter's opinion in *Dennis:*

> The demands of free speech in a democratic society, as well as the interest in national security are better served by candid and informed weighing of the competing interests, within the confines of the judicial process.[26]

The test was used throughout the 1950s and 1960s in such cases as *Barenblatt, Konigsberg,* and *Robel.* In *Barenblatt,* Justice John Harlan noted that when First Amendment rights are asserted to prevent governmental inquiry, "resolution of the issues always involves a balancing by the courts of the competing private and public interests at stake in the particular circumstances shown."[27] In *Konigsberg,* Harlan claimed that when constitutional protections conflict with the exercise of valid governmental power, "a reconciliation must be effected, and that perforce requires an appropriate weighing of the respective interests involved."[28] In *Robel,* Chief Justice Earl Warren acknowledged the "delicate and difficult task" facing the Court when "Congress' exercise of one of its enumerated powers clashes with those individual liberties protected by the Bill of Rights."[29] In such instances, a balancing of interests must be undertaken.

The Court has applied two variations of the test—definitional and situational balancing. The Court used definitional balancing to identify certain forms of expression that fall within constitutional protection, as well as other forms that are outside such protection. For example, in *Roth,* the Court defined the boundaries of "obscenity,"[30] and in *N.Y. Times,* the Court outlined the limits of "libel."[31]

Expression that falls within such definitions has been judged, on balance, to violate the right to personal morality and dignity.

Situational balancing involves judging each case on its particular merits. For example, in *Douds,* the Court noted that recognition of a labor union could be conditioned on the filing of affidavits by its officers that they do not belong to the Communist party and do not believe in overthrow of the government by force. Such a ruling was "a permissible one in this case."[32] In *Spence* the Court accepted the unique, mitigating factors behind an individual's display of a U.S. flag.[33] In *Lehman* the Court held that a city transit system could refuse to sell space on its buses for political advertising, because under the circumstances, the buses were not a "public forum."[34] With situational balancing, the opinions offer little guidance for future cases, because they apply only to the specifics of the particular case.

Preferred Position

The "preferred position" test resembles "balancing"—except that the test is balanced in favor of the First Amendment. In 1943, in *Murdock,* Justice Douglas noted that "freedom of press, freedom of speech...are in a preferred position."[35] Justice Wiley Rutledge strengthened the test two years later in the *Thomas* case.

> The case confronts us again with the duty our system places on this Court to say where the individual's freedom ends and the State's power begins. Choice on that border, now as always delicate, is perhaps more so where the usual presumption supporting legislation is balanced by the preferred place given in our scheme to the great, the indispensable democratic freedoms secured by the First Amendment. That priority gives these liberties a sanctity and a sanction not permitting dubious intrusions.[36]

In 1946, in *Marsh,* Justice Black noted that in balancing the rights of property owners against the rights of the people to enjoy freedom of expression, the Court must "remain mindful of the fact that the latter occupy a preferred position."[37]

A few years later, in *Kovacs,* Justices Felix Frankfurter and Stanley Reed reassessed the "preferred position" doctrine. Frankfurter considered it "a mischievous phrase, if it carries the thought, which it may subtly imply, that any law touching communication is infected with presumptive validity." He suggested that "various forms of modern so-called 'mass communications' raise issues that were not implied in the means of communication known or contemplated by Franklin and Jefferson and Madison." In *Kovacs,* Frankfurter upheld the regulation of sound trucks: "Only a disregard of vital differences between natural speech...and the noise of sound trucks would give sound trucks the constitutional rights accorded to the unaided human voice.''[38] Justice Reed also supported the regulation.

> The preferred position of freedom of speech in a society that cherishes liberty for all does not require legislators to be insensible to claims by citizens to comfort and convenience. To enforce freedom of speech in disregard of the rights of others would be harsh and arbitrary in itself.[39]

According to Reed, even though expression enjoys a preferred position, it is not immune from regulation when such control is justified.

Absolutism

During the 1950s Justices Douglas and Black argued that the First Amendment denied the government *any* power to abridge expression; that any law that restricted free speech and press was unconstitutional on its face. The "absolutist" test was designed to enlarge the scope of expression protected by the Constitution. The position was described in Black's dissenting opinion in *Konigsberg.* Black did not believe that constitutionally protected rights could ever be balanced away.

> I believe that the First Amendment's unequivocal command that there shall be no abridgement of the rights of free speech and assembly shows that the men who drafted our Bill of Rights did all the "balancing" that was to be done in this field.[40]

Black contended that since the "balancing" test denies that any expression has an "absolute" right to First Amendment protection, strict adherence to "balancing" means that there is "only a conditional right, not a complete right, for any American to express his views to his neighbors—or for his neighbors to hear those views." According to Black,

> In my judgment, such a sweeping denial of the existence of any inalienable right to speak undermines the very foundation upon which the First Amendment, the Bill of Rights, and indeed, our entire structure of government rest.[41]

Five years later Black reiterated his belief in "absolutism" in *Ginzburg:* "I think the Founders of our Nation in adopting the First Amendment meant precisely that the Federal Government should pass 'no law' regulating speech and press."[42] In 1971 Black again stressed "absolutism" in *New York Times Company,* when he discussed the test from a historical perspective.

> The Bill of Rights changed the original Constitution into a new charter under which no branch of government could abridge the people's freedoms of press,

speech, religon, and assembly. Yet the Solicitor General argues and some members of the Court appear to agree that the general powers of the Government adopted in the original Constitution should be interpreted to limit and restrict the specific and emphatic guarantees of the Bill of Rights adopted later. I can imagine no greater perversion of history. Madison and the other Framers of the First Amendment, able men that they were, wrote in language they earnestly believed could never be misunderstood: "Congress shall make no law...abridging the freedom...of the press...." Both the history and language of the First Amendment support the view that the press must be left free to publish news, whatever the source, without censorship, injunctions, or prior restraints.[43]

The "absolutist" test received support from Justice Douglas, who, in *Ginzburg*, claimed that "the First Amendment allows all ideas to be expressed—whether orthodox, popular, offbeat, or repulsive." He did not think it was permissible for the Court "to draw lines between the 'good' and the 'bad' and be true to the constitutional mandate to let all ideas alone." Under the U.S. Constitution, "all regulation of control of expression is barred."[44]

The "absolutist" test, however, has found few proponents. In fact, the "absolutist" view never received support from a majority of U.S. Supreme Court justices.

CONCLUSION

Throughout history, Supreme Court justices have applied a variety of tests while interpreting First Amendment freedoms. The specific tests—"clear and present danger," "bad tendency," "balancing," "preferred position," "absolutism"—have varied with the issue facing the Court, the historical climate of the times, and the predispositions of individual justices. This book examines significant and recent First Amendment cases in terms of how Supreme Court reasoning has shaped communication law.

NOTES

1. *Gitlow v. New York*, 45 S.Ct. 625 (1925).
2. *Schenck v. United States*, 39 S.Ct. 247 (1919).
3. *Abrams v. United States*, 40 S.Ct. 17 (1919).
4. *Whitney v. California*, 47 S.Ct. 641 (1927).
5. *Bridges v. California*, 62 S.Ct. 190 (1941).
6. *Schenck.*
7. *Abrams.*
8. *Gitlow.*
9. *Whitney.*
10. *Herndon v. Lowry*, 57 S.Ct. 732 (1937).

11. *Thornhill v. Alabama*, 60 S.Ct. 736 (1940).
12. *Cantwell v. Connecticut*, 60 S.Ct. 900 (1940).
13. *Terminiello v. Chicago*, 69 S.Ct. 894 (1949).
14. *Terminiello.*
15. *Dennis v. United States*, 71 S.Ct. 857 (1951).
16. *United States v. Dennis*, 183 F.2d 212 (1950).
17. *Craig v. Harney*, 67 S.Ct. 1249 (1947).
18. *Garner v. Louisiana*, 82 S.Ct. 248 (1961).
19. *Wood v. Georgia*, 82 S.Ct. 1364 (1962).
20. *Cox v. Louisiana*, 85 S.Ct. 476 (1965).
21. *Brandenburg v. Ohio*, 89 S.Ct. 1827 (1969).
22. *Gitlow.*
23. *Herndon.*
24. *Bridges.*
25. *American Communications Association, C.I.O. v. Douds*, 70 S.Ct. 674 (1950).
26. *Dennis.*
27. *Barenblatt v. United States*, 79 S.Ct. 1081 (1959).
28. *Konigsberg v. State Bar of California*, 81 S.Ct. 997 (1961).
29. *United States v. Robel*, 88 S.Ct. 419 (1967).
30. *Roth v. United States*, 77 S.Ct. 1304 (1957).
31. *New York Times Company v. Sullivan*, 84 S.Ct. 710 (1964).
32. *Douds.*
33. *Spence v. Washington*, 94 S.Ct. 2727 (1974).
34. *Lehman v. Shaker Heights*, 94 S.Ct. 2714 (1974).
35. *Murdock v. Pennsylvania*, 63 S. Ct. 870 (1943).
36. *Thomas v. Collins*, 65 S.Ct. 315 (1945).
37. *Marsh v. Alabama*, 66 S.Ct. 276 (1946).
38. *Kovacs v. Cooper*, 69 S.Ct. 448 (1949).
39. *Kovacs.*
40. *Konigsberg.*
41. *Konigsberg.*
42. *Ginzburg v. United States; Mishkin v. New York*, 86 S.Ct. 942 (1966).
43. *New York Times Company v. United States*, 91 S.Ct. 2140 (1971).
44. *Ginzburg.*

RECOMMENDED READING

Barron, Jerome A., and C. Thomas Dienes, *Handbook of Free Speech and Free Press.* Boston: Little, Brown, 1979.

Emerson, Thomas I., *The System of Freedom of Expression.* New York: Random House, 1970.

Francois, William E., *Mass Media Law and Regulation.* Columbus, Ohio: Grid, Inc., 3rd Ed., 1982.

Franklin, Marc A., *The First Amendment and the Fourth Estate: Communications Law for Undergraduates.* Mineola, N.Y.: Foundation Press, 2nd Ed., 1981.

Gard, Stephen W., "The Absoluteness of the First Amendment," *Nebraska Law Review* 58 (1979), 1053-86.

Gillmor, Donald M., and Jerome A. Barron, *Mass Communication Law: Cases and Comment.* St. Paul, Minn.: West Publishing Company, 4th Ed., 1984.

Haiman, Franklyn S., *Speech and Law in a Free Society.* Chicago: University of Chicago Press, 1981.

Higdon, Philip R., "The Burger Court and the Media: A Ten-Year Perspective," *Western New England Law Review* 2 (Spring, 1980), 593-680.

Overbeck, Wayne, and Rick D. Pullen, *Major Principles of Media Law.* New York: Holt, Rinehart, and Winston, 2nd Ed., 1985.

Pember, Don R., *Mass Media Law.* Dubuque, Iowa: Wm. C. Brown, 3rd Ed., 1984.

Schauer, Frederick, *Free Speech: Philosophical Enquiry.* Cambridge: Cambridge University Press, 1982.

Stevens, John D., *Shaping the First Amendment: The Development of Free Expression.* Beverly Hills, CA.: Sage, 1982.

Stonecipher, Harry W., "Safeguarding Speech and Press Guarantees: Preferred Position Postulate Reexamined," in *The First Amendment Reconsidered: New Perspectives on the Meaning of Freedom of Speech and Press,* Bill F. Chamberlin and Charlene J. Brown, (eds.), New York: Longman, 1982, 89-128.

Strong, Frank R., "Fifty Years of 'Clear and Present Danger': From *Schenck* to *Brandenburg*—and Beyond," *The Supreme Court Review* (1969), 41-80.

Tedford, Thomas L., *Freedom of Speech in the United States.* New York: Random House, 1985.

Torke, James W., "Some Notes on the Uses of the Clear and Present Danger Test," *Brigham Young University Law Review* (1978), 1-37.

2

DISSENT

Contradictory tendencies have permeated the history of dissent in the United States. During certain periods, a strong zest for dissent characterized citizens' behavior. When the country was established, colonial patriots voiced opposition to an oppressive English monarchy. Prior to the Civil War, abolitionists expressed dissatisfaction with the institution of slavery. During the 1960s and 1970s, student activists protested against U.S. involvement in the Vietnam War. At times, the government has limited freedom of expression and punished extremism in dissent. Especially during times of war and national crisis, the government has restricted forms of dissent that might disturb public order or that might endanger national security. The clash of these conflicting standards—the zeal for dissent versus the maintenance of security and order—presents a significant area of study for students interested in freedom of expression.

TESTS OF DISSENT

During the twentieth century, laws have been directed at those dissenters who obstruct the military operations of the country or who advocate the overthrow of the government by force or violence. The constitutionality of such laws has been a concern of the U.S. Supreme Court. Depending upon the specifics of the case and the justices on the Court, the decisions have tended to be contradictory. During various periods the Court has formulated four tests of dissent.

Schenck Test (Clear and Present Danger)

In 1917, shortly after Congress declared war against Germany, it enacted the Selective Service Act in order to raise an army. Subsequently, as part of the Espionage Act of 1917, Congress prohibited anyone from using false statements to interfere with the military success of the United States, promote the success of America's enemies, or obstruct the recruiting effort of the armed services. Violators were subject to a fine of up to $10,000 and/or imprisonment for not more than 20 years. A 1918 amendment, the Sedition Act, extended criminal prosecution to any person who said anything detrimental about the sale of government bonds, or who expressed anything that subjected the U.S. form of government, the Constitution, the flag, or the military uniform to disrepute. Shortly after the passage of these statutes, the Supreme Court was asked to consider the extent to which political dissent could be regulated.

Charles Schenck, general secretary of the Socialist party, had printed 15,000 leaflets criticizing the military draft. The document viewed conscription as despotism in its worst form, designed to benefit the interests of Wall Street's select few. It urged draftees to "assert your rights." When Schenck distributed the leaflets to military draftees, he was convicted under the Espionage Act. In *Schenck,* Supreme Court Justice Oliver Wendell Holmes introduced the "clear and present danger" test. Holmes acknowledged that in ordinary times Schenck would have been within his constitutional rights in expressing the ideas contained in the leaflet; but the circumstances of this situation rendered the expression outside the boundaries of protected communication. Holmes thought that expression designed to obstruct recruiting during a time when the country was at war constituted a "clear and present danger."[1] The case established that dissent was not absolutely guaranteed, but rather depended upon the circumstances of the case.

During 1919 the Supreme Court upheld other convictions based upon violations of the Espionage Act. It upheld the conviction of Jacob Frohwerk for publishing newspaper articles designed to cause disloyalty, mutiny, and refusal to serve in the military service.[2] The Court affirmed the conviction of Eugene Debs, who, at a convention of Socialists, had expressed opposition to U.S. entry into the war and had approved the behavior of individuals who obstructed military recruitment. Even though Debs had not urged his audience to resist the draft, he was convicted of attempting to obstruct the draft and was sentenced to ten years in prison.[3] The Court also upheld the conviction of Jacob Abrams and five associates who had published and distributed in New York City circulars that called for a general strike of munitions workers. Even though there was no evidence that a single person actually stopped any kind of war work or that the leaflets actually reached a single munitions worker, the defendants were convicted and sentenced to 20 years in prison.[4] The majority of the Supreme Court in *Abrams,* as in *Frohwerk* and *Debs,* upheld the *Schenck* test by affirming that, during wartime, certain forms of dissent were not protected by the First Amendment.

Gitlow Test (Bad Tendency)

Shortly after the assassination of President William McKinley, New York passed the Anarchy Act of 1902. This statute forbade the publication or distribution of material advocating "the duty, necessity or propriety of overthrowing or overturning organized government by force or violence.'' In 1925 the Supreme Court decided the constitutionality of this act.

Benjamin Gitlow and three other members of the left wing of the Socialist party were indicted for publishing a radical "manifesto" in the pamphlet *The Revolutionary Age*. The manifesto predicted that "the mass struggle of the proletariat is coming into being," urged "mass strikes" by the proletariat, and repudiated the policy of the moderate Socialists. The trial court convicted Gitlow and his colleagues under the New York statute and sentenced them to from five to ten years of hard labor. The Supreme Court affirmed the convictions. Through the opinion of Justice Edward Sanford, the Court adopted the "bad tendency" test and rejected "clear and present danger." Sanford concluded that words that advocate the overthrow of organized government may be punished, regardless of whether there is any imminent danger.

> Such utterances, by their very nature, involve danger to the public peace and to the security of the State. They threaten breaches of the peace and ultimate revolution. And the immediate danger is none the less real and substantial, because the effect of a given utterance cannot be accurately foreseen.[5]

Justices Oliver Wendell Holmes and Louis Brandeis disagreed. They applied the "clear and present danger" test, which had been established in *Schenck*. In a minority opinion, they argued:

> If the publication of this document had been laid as an attempt to induce an uprising against the government at once and not at some indefinite time in the future, it would have presented a different question....But the indictment alleges the publication and nothing more.

Holmes and Brandeis argued that Gitlow was entitled to disseminate the manifesto, because it advocated uprising only at some vague future time. Nonetheless, the majority upheld the conviction on the ground of "bad tendency."

Two years later, the Court heard a case involving the constitutionality of the California Criminal Syndicalism Act. This unique statute was not directed against the practice of criminal syndicalism, but rather at the preaching of it, and especially at association with persons who advocate it. In the five years following the enactment of the law, 504 persons were arrested and 264 were brought to trial. Anita Whitney, a woman nearing 60 years of age, had attended a convention that established the Communist Labor Party of California. She was convicted on the ground that the party was set up to teach criminal syndicalism, and by becoming a member, she had committed a crime. Justice Sanford cited *Gitlow* in affirming that California could punish utterances "tending" to produce crime or disturb the peace. Furthermore, concerted action involved a more significant threat than isolated words or acts of individuals. Assembling a political party designed to advocate proletarian revolution by mass action at some future date was outside constitutional protection. The Court upheld Whitney's conviction because of the "bad tendency" of her act.[6] Within a few months, however, Governor C. C. Young pardoned Whitney, acknowledging that "clear and present danger" should be a vital concern, and that the Communist Labor party no longer posed any threat of criminal syndicalism.

In 1937 the Court heard a case involving a similar state law, but this time arrived at a different conclusion. The case involved Dirk DeJonge, who, in a speech to Communist party members, criticized the way city police handled the maritime strike that was then in progress. DeJonge claimed that raids on the Communist headquarters and workers' halls were the result of efforts on the part of steamship and stevedoring companies to break the longshoremen's and seamen's strike. He said that the companies hoped to break the strike by pitting the longshoremen and seamen against the Communist movement. DeJonge also urged his audience to recruit members for the Communist party and to purchase Communist literature, which was sold at the meeting. DeJonge was convicted under the Oregon criminal syndicalism law for participating at a meeting of the Communist party, an organization that advocated criminal syndicalism. The Supreme Court unanimously found the Oregon statute unconstitutional. Oregon could not seize upon mere participation in a peaceable assembly as a basis for a criminal charge. Whatever the objectives of the Communist party, DeJonge was still "entitled to discuss the public issues of the day, and in a lawful manner without incitement to violence or crime, to seek redress of alleged grievances. That was the essence of his guaranteed personal liberty."[7] In *DeJonge,* the Court required more than a mere "tendency" toward criminal action as the basis for punishing advocacy.

Dennis Test (Advocacy of Action)

In a series of cases—*Dennis, Yates, Scales, Noto,* and *Brandenburg*—the Supreme Court debated whether mere advocacy of ideas or whether advocacy of action was essential in order to convict an individual for illegal dissent. During this controversy the justices established and then redefined the *Dennis* test.

In 1940 Congress passed the Alien Registration Act, which made it a crime to advocate the violent overthrow of the government or to knowingly organize or belong to a group advocating it. This act, known as the Smith Act, was designed to control subversive groups, particularly Nazis and Communists. During the 1950s, the *Dennis* and *Yates* cases tested the conspiracy provisions of the Smith Act; in 1961 *Scales* and *Noto* tested convictions under the membership clause of the act.

Eugene Dennis, secretary of the Communist party, was convicted of violating the conspiracy provisions of the Smith Act. The prosecution charged Dennis with knowingly conspiring to organize the Communist party as a group that advocated the overthrow of the government by violence. Dennis claimed that he advocated that violence was necessary to attain a Communist form of government in an existing democracy, only because the ruling classes would not permit the transformation to be accomplished peacefully, but would use force to defeat any peaceful political and economic gains the Communists might achieve. Dennis appealed his conviction. The Supreme Court, per Chief Justice Fred Vinson, noted that the Smith Act was directed at advocacy, not discussion. When the government became aware that a group dedicated to its overthrow was committing its members to strike when the leaders felt the circumstances permitted, action by the government was required. Vinson concluded:

> Petitioners intended to overthrow the government of the United States as speedily as the circumstances would permit. Their conspiracy to organize the Communist Party and to teach and advocate the overthrow of the Government of the United States by force and violence created a "clear and present danger" of an attempt to overthrow the government by force and violence. They were properly and constitutionally convicted for violation of the Smith Act. The judgments of conviction are affirmed.[8]

In *Dennis, conspiracy* to overthrow the government, rather than *overthrow* itself, was considered adequate to justify suppression of communication directed toward that effect. In all, 29 persons served prison terms for conviction under the conspiracy provisions of the Smith Act.

In *Yates* the court provided a different interpretation of the conspiracy section of the Smith Act. Oleta Yates was convicted for conspiring to organize the Communist party for the purpose of overthrowing the government by force and violence as soon as circumstances could permit. The Supreme Court reversed the lower-court decision. Justice John Harlan, writing for the majority, quoted Vinson's point in *Dennis* that the Smith Act "is directed at advocacy, not discussion." Harlan continued:

> but it is clear that the reference was to advocacy of action, not ideas, for in the very next sentence the opinion emphasizes . . . that there could be nonconviction for "advocacy in the realm of ideas." The two concurring opinions in that case likewise emphasize the distinction with which we are concerned.[9]

Advocacy of forcible overthrow as mere abstract doctrine was within the free-speech protection of the First Amendment. Harlan stressed that "those to whom the advocacy is addressed must be urged to do something, now or in the future, rather than merely to believe in something." The trial court had unconstitutionally applied the Smith Act by convicting for mere advocacy, unrelated to the potential for producing forcible action. In *Yates* the Supreme Court distinguished between "advocacy of abstract doctrine," which was permissible, and "advocacy of action," which was not.

The Court further developed the distinction between advocacy of ideas and advocacy of action in *Scales*. Janius Scales, the chairperson of the North and South Carolina districts of the Communist party, criticized U.S. aggression in Korea and claimed that revolution would come within a generation. Scales was convicted under the membership clause of the Smith Act for holding membership in an organization that advocated the overthrow of the government by force or violence and sentenced to six years in prison. In *Scales,* the Court acknowledged that *Dennis* and *Yates* had "definitely laid at rest any doubt that present advocacy of future action for violent overthrow" meets constitutional requirements "equally with advocacy of immediate action to that end." The Court confirmed Scale's conviction. Evidence supported a finding of advocacy of revolutionary action, rather than advocacy of mere abstract revolutionary doctrine. Justice Harlan wrote:

> Since the evidence amply showed that Party leaders were continually preaching during the indictment period the inevitability of eventual forcible overthrow, the first and basic question is a narrow one: whether the jury could permissibly infer that such preaching, in whole or in part, "was aimed at building up a seditious group and maintaining it in readiness for action at a propitious time...the kind of indoctrination preparatory to action which was condemned in *Dennis.* . . . On this score, we think that the jury, under instructions which fully satisfied the requirements of *Yates,* was entitled to infer...that advocacy of action" was engaged in.[10]

A companion case, *Noto,* also tested the membership clause. The key point in John Noto's case was insufficiency of evidence. The Supreme Court noted that a Smith Act conviction required rigorous standards of proof. At Noto's trial, much of the evidence came from excerpts in the "Communist classics." This literature reflected the Party's teaching through abstract doctrine that revolution was inevitable to achieve communism in a capitalist society, but testimony that suggested advocacy of action to accomplish that goal was sparse. In *Noto* the evidence of illegal advocacy lacked the compelling quality that in *Scales* was supplied by the defendant's own statements. In *Noto* the evidence was insufficient to show that the Communist party advocated the forcible overthrow of the government.[11] Following Noto's reversal, the government discontinued pending prosecutions under the membership clause. As a result, Janius Scales was the only person to serve a prison sentence under the membership provision of the Smith Act.

In 1969, the Supreme Court reexamined the *Dennis* principle. The case involved Clarence Brandenburg, a leader of the Ohio Ku Klux Klan. Brandenburg invited a Cincinnati television newsman to attend a rally. The event was filmed and portions were later broadcast on local and national television. One film showed 12 hooded figures, some of whom carried firearms, gathered around a large wooden cross. The film contained statements about blacks and Jews that were derogatory. One of the scenes on the film showed Brandenburg, in Klan regalia, deliver the following statement:

> The Klan has more members in the State of Ohio than does any other organization, but if our President, our Congress, our Supreme Court, continues to suppress the white, Caucasian race, it's possible that there might have to be some revenge taken. We are marching on Congress, July the Fourth, four hundred thousand strong.

In a second film Brandenburg said, "Personally, I believe the nigger should be returned to Africa, the Jew returned to Israel." Brandenburg was convicted under the Ohio criminal syndicalism statute; he was fined $1,000 and sentenced to from one to ten years' imprisonment. The Supreme Court noted that the guarantee of free expression does not allow a state to forbid advocacy, "except where such advocacy is directed to inciting or producing imminent lawless action and is likely to incite or produce such action." Measured by this test, Ohio's statute could not be sustained, because it punished mere advocacy and assembly with others who merely advocated action. The Ohio statute was unconstitutional. In *Brandenburg* the Court redefined the *Dennis* test in such a way that any advocacy that does not call for illegal action is protected under the First Amendment.

> More important, speech which calls for illegal action but does not seek immediate action is protected. In addition, speech which calls for immediate illegal action but where there is reason to believe that the audience will not commit the action is also protected. [12]

Bond Test (Widest Latitude)

During the 1960s numerous groups protested U.S. military involvement in Vietnam. One such group, the Student Nonviolent Coordinating Committee, issued a statement that said in part:

> We are in sympathy with, and support, the men in this country who are unwilling to respond to a military draft which would compel them to contribute their lives to United States aggression in Viet Nam in the name of the "freedom" we find so false in this country.

Julian Bond, member of the Georgia House of Representatives, publicly endorsed the SNCC statement. Subsequently, members of the Georgia House challenged Bond's right to be seated in the legislature. At a hearing Bond claimed that he "admired the courage" of people "who felt strongly enough about their convictions" to burn their draft cards, "knowing the consequences that they will face," but pointed out that he had his own draft card in his pocket and had "never suggested or counseled or advocated" that anyone burn his draft card. A House committee concluded that Bond's remarks indicated that he "does not and will not" support the Constitution, that he aided and comforted enemies of the United States, that his statement violated the Selective Service Act, and that his remarks "are reprehensible and tend to bring discredit to the House." Accordingly, the Georgia House voted not to allow Bond to take the oath of office or be seated.

A unanimous Supreme Court held that the Georgia legislature had violated Bond's right of free speech. The Court acknowledged that "there can be no question but that the First Amendment protects expression in opposition to national foreign policy in Vietnam and to the Selective Service System." The state of Georgia argued that it was justified in demanding a higher standard of loyalty from public officials than from its citizens. The Court, however, decided that even though a state may require from its legislators an oath to support the Constitution, which it does not require of its private citizens, a state does not have the power to limit its legislators in expressing their views of local, state, and national policies.

> The manifest function of the First Amendment in a representative government requires that legislators be given the widest latitude to express their views on issues of policy. . . . Legislators have an obligation to take positions so that their constituents can be fully informed by them, and be better able to assess their qualifications for office; also so they may be represented in governmental debates by the person they have elected to represent them.[13]

When one compares the statement upheld by the Supreme Court in *Bond* with those remarks denied protection in *Schenck, Debs,* and *Gitlow,* it seems apparent that the range of protected dissent has widened during the twentieth century.

Summary

The right to dissent in matters of governmental policies has long been acknowledged as a fundamental freedom. The Supreme Court, however, has applied different tests of advocacy throughout the twentieth century. In *Schenck,* Justice Oliver Wendell Holmes enunciated the "clear and present danger" test—government could punish expression that produced, or intended to produce, a significant and imminent danger. In *Gitlow,* Justice Edward Sanford adopted the "bad tendency" test—the government could punish expression that tended to produce criminal actions. In *Dennis* the Supreme Court laid the groundwork for a new test—advocacy of abstract doctrine was permissible, but "advocacy of action" was prohibited. In cases involving application of these various tests, the Supreme Court consistently extended First Amendment protection to expression involving peacetime dissent, but limited protection in times of war. In *Bond,* however, the Court applied a liberal interpretation of the First Amendment by granting the "widest latitude" to a legislator during wartime dissent.

REGULATING DISSENT

Few dissenters actually advocate the overthrow of the government by either violent or peaceful means. Numerous speakers, however, attempt to arouse audiences to support or oppose the government's policies on local, state, and national issues. Occasionally, during such public discussion, audience members may be provoked into a breach of peace or some other form of disturbance. In such cases, authorities must decide upon the appropriate course of action for dealing with the situation. Several free-speech battles in the Supreme Court have developed over this issue. The cases have involved alleged provocative, fighting, threatening, and/or offensive words.

Provocative Words

A situation that is especially perplexing for police officers occurs when a speaker expresses ideas to an audience that becomes unruly and unmanageable. What is the police officer's duty? Should the speaker be instructed to stop speaking because the unruly crowd represents a threat to public order? Should the speaker's right to communicate be protected by police officers who attempt to manage the unruly crowd? In 1949 the Supreme Court considered these questions in the *Terminiello* case.

Father Arthur Terminiello, a Catholic priest under suspension by his bishop, delivered a speech in a Chicago auditorium that was filled to capacity; more than 8,000 persons attended. The meeting was called to consider the issue, "Christian Nationalism or World Communism—Which?" Outside, a crowd of 1,000 protested the meeting. Policemen were present to maintain order, but they were unable to prevent disturbances, because the large crowd outside was turbulent. The crowd interfered with access to the front door. Members of the crowd called Terminiello and his followers "God-damned Fascists," "Hitlers," and "Nazis." Bottles, stink bombs, and bricks were tossed inside, breaking about 30 windows. The crowd broke the front door partially open. At the outset of his speech, Terminiello, realizing that some of the protesters had got inside, claimed, "And nothing I could say tonight could begin to express the contempt I have for the slimy scum that got in by mistake." In the main body of the speech, Terminiello referred to some of the elements that were "going to destroy America by revolution." He stated that "we have fifty-seven varieties of pinks and reds and pastel shades in this country; and all of it can be traced back to the twelve years we spent under the New Deal, because that was the build-up for what is going on in the world today." He specifically attacked the "communist Zionistic Jew, and those are not American Jews. We don't want them here; we want them to go back where they came from.'' The speech provoked vehement responses from some members of the audience inside the auditorium. One person claimed, ''Yes, the Jews are all killers, murderers. If we don't kill them first, they will kill us.'' Others said, ''Yes, send the Jews back to Russia,'' ''Kill the Jews,'' and ''Dirty kikes.'' Terminiello was arrested and charged with ''breach of peace.'' When he was convicted and fined \$100, Terminiello appealed. The Supreme Court noted that Terminiello was not convicted for creating a danger to public disorder, but rather for causing a breach of peace by delivering a speech that stirred the public to anger, invited dispute, or brought about a condition of unrest. The Court, per Justice William Douglas, noted that a purpose of free speech, perhaps its highest function, was to invite dispute, induce a situation of unrest, create dissatisfaction with undesirable conditions, or even stir people to anger.[14] For this kind of public speech, Terminiello could not be punished.

Two years after *Terminiello*, the Court examined the remarks of a college student, Irving Feiner, who had addressed a crowd of about 80 persons on a street corner in Syracuse, New York. Feiner stood on a large wooden box on the sidewalk and spoke through a loud-speaker system attached to an automobile. The primary purpose of his speech was to urge audience members to attend a meeting, sponsored by the Young Progressives, to be held that evening in the Syracuse Hotel. Feiner, however, also made derogatory remarks about President Truman, the American Legion, the mayor of Syracuse, and other local political officials. The Young Progressives had been given a permit to meet in a public-school auditorium, but later the permit had been cancelled; so the meeting was shifted to the Hotel Syracuse. The change in meeting plans sparked Feiner's remarks against city officials. Police officers were sent to the scene; they noticed that the crowd was restless and that traffic was affected. When Feiner urged that blacks in the audience ''should rise up in arms and fight for their rights,'' a white person told the policemen that if they did not get that ''son of a bitch'' off the soapbox, he would. The police officers feared that a fight would begin, so they told Feiner to stop speaking, but he continued. The crowd became more restless. Feiner was arrested for disorderly conduct, convicted, and sentenced to 30 days in jail. He appealed. The Supreme Court decided that the police were not acting to stifle Feiner's views, but were attempting to preserve order and the general welfare of the public. Feiner had not been arrested because of the content of his message, but rather for the reaction to it that Feiner's own behavior had provoked. Chief Justice Vinson claimed:

> We are well aware that the ordinary murmurings and objections of a hostile audience cannot be allowed to silence a speaker, and are also mindful of the possible danger of giving overzealous police officials complete discretion to break up otherwise lawful public meetings.... But we are not faced here with such a situation. It is one thing to say that the police cannot be used as an instru-

ment for the suppression of unpopular views, and another to say that, when as here the speaker passes the bounds of argument or persuasion and undertakes incitement to riot, they are powerless to prevent a breach of peace.[15]

Justice Douglas disagreed. In his dissenting opinion, he argued:

> When unpopular causes are sponsored from the public platform there will commonly be mutterings and unrest and heckling from a crowd. When a speaker mounts a platform it is not unusual to find him resorting to exaggeration, to vilification of ideas and men, to the making of false charges. But those extravagances...do not justify penalizing the speaker by depriving him of his platform or by punishing him for his conduct.

The majority of the Court, however, found a clear and present danger created by Feiner's provocative speech.

Certain factors differentiate the situations in *Feiner* and *Terminiello*. Terminiello addressed an audience in a hired hall, thereby having no "captive audience" as did Feiner, whose speech was conveyed through an amplifying system to people walking down the street, who unavoidably heard the remarks. Terminiello was not convicted of creating any clear and present danger to public disorder; Feiner was. The key distinction was that in *Feiner*, the speaker contributed significantly to the public disorder, while in *Terminiello*, the audience, rather than the speaker, contributed substantially to the chaos. When the speaker provoked disorder, the expression was not protected, but when the audience was primarily responsible, the speech fell within First Amendment guarantees.

Fighting Words

An utterance that stirs another to anger but has little if any social utility may be considered "fighting words." This doctrine was outlined by the courts in 1942, in *Chaplinsky*. Walter Chaplinsky, a Jehovah's Witness, was passing out literature in Rochester, New Hampshire, when citizens complained to the police chief that Chaplinsky was denouncing all religion as a "racket." The chief warned Chaplinsky that the crowd was getting unruly. Chaplinsky then said to the chief: "You are a God-damned racketeer" and "a damned Fascist and the whole government of Rochester are Fascists or agents of Fascists." Chaplinsky was convicted for violating a law that banned "addressing any offensive, derisive or annoying word to any other person who is lawfully in any street or other public place." When the case reached the New Hampshire Supreme Court, the justices created the "fighting words" doctrine. In their opinion,

> the test is what men of common intelligence could understand to be words likely to cause an average adressee to fight.... The English language has a number

of words and expressions which by general consent are 'fighting words' when said without a disarming smile. . . . Such words, as ordinary men know, are likely to cause a fight.

The United States Supreme Court agreed. The words used by Chaplinsky ''are epithets likely to provoke the average person to retaliation and thereby cause a breach of the peace.'' Furthermore, the words possess low social usefulness; ''such utterances are no essential part of any exposition of ideas, and are of such slight social value as a step to truth that any benefit that may be derived from them is clearly outweighed by social interest in order and morality.''[16] The words did not warrant First Amendment protection.

Since *Chaplinsky,* the Court has heard other cases involving allegations of ''fighting words.'' In both *Wilson* and *Lewis,* the Court threw out state statutes because of vagueness and overbreadth. *Wilson* involved the alleged ''fighting words'' of Johnney Wilson, who picketed a U.S. Army headquarters building in protest against the Vietnam War. He blocked the entrance, so that arriving inductees were unable to enter. When a policeman attempted to remove him, he called the officer a ''white son-of-a-bitch.'' ''I'll kill you''; ''You son-of-a-bitch, I'll choke you to death''; and ''You son-of-a-bitch, if you ever put your hands on me again, I'll cut you all to pieces.'' Wilson was convicted under a Georgia statute for using opprobrious words and abusive language. The Supreme Court ruled that the Georgia law was vague and overbroad. In comparison with *Chaplinsky,* in which the Court had defined ''fighting words'' with narrow specificity, the Georgia statute lacked such exactness. The New Hampshire statute had defined ''fighting words'' as language that was ''offensive, derisive, or annoying.'' In the Georgia case no meaningful attempt was made to properly define the terms. The dictionary definitions of ''opprobrious'' and ''abusive'' give them greater reach than ''fighting words.'' *Webster's Third New International Dictionary* of 1961 defined ''opprobrious'' as ''conveying or intended to convey disgrace,'' and ''abusive'' as ''harsh insulting language.'' Such definitions cover incidents in which words convey disgrace or insult, but fall short of ''fighting words.''[17]

In 1974 the Supreme Court struck down a Louisiana statute in another test of ''fighting words.'' Mrs. Mallie Lewis, while her son was being arrested, allegedly called the police officers ''god-damn, mother-fucking police.'' Mrs. Lewis was convicted for violating an ordinance making it unlawful ''to curse or revile or to use obscene or opprobrious language toward or with reference'' to a police officer in the performance of his duties. The Supreme Court, per Justice William Brennan, declared the ordinance to be equally applicable ''to speech, although vulgar or offensive, that is protected'' by the Constitution as it is applicable to speech that is not protected. Justice Lewis Powell, in a concurring opinion, noted:

Quite apart from the ambiguity inherent in the term "opprobrious," words may or may not be "fighting words" depending upon the circumstances of their utterance. It is unlikely, for example, that the words said to have been used here would have precipitated a physical confrontation between the middle-aged woman who spoke them and the police officer in whose presence they were uttered. The words may well have conveyed anger and frustration without provoking a violent reaction from the officer.[18]

In *Chaplinsky,* the Court established that "fighting words" were outside the scope of First Amendment protection. In *Wilson* and *Lewis,* the Court threw out instances of alleged "fighting words," because the state statutes were vague and overbroad. Nonetheless, these decisions clarify the concept of "fighting words."

Threatening Words

In addition to "fighting words," certain speech that can be construed as "threatening" is illegal. For example, a 1917 law makes it a crime to knowingly and willfully threaten to take the life of the president of the United States. A violator can be fined up to $1,000 and/or imprisoned not more than five years. The Supreme Court considered this form of "threatening words" in *Watts.*

On August 27, 1966, at a public rally on the Washington Monument grounds, 18-year-old Robert Watts and several other people participated in small group discussions about various subjects. When a member of the group suggested that U.S. youth should get more education, Watts replied: "They always holler at us to get an education. And now I have already received my draft classification as I-A and I have got to report for my physical this Monday coming. I am not going." Then Watts said: "If they ever make me carry a rifle the first man I want to get in my sights is L.B.J. They are not going to make me kill my black brothers." Watts was convicted of threatening the president. He appealed. The Supreme Court noted that Watts made the statement in the heat of political debate, his statement was made under pressure of induction into the armed forces, the remark would never become reality, and the crowd laughed along with Watts after the statement. The Court did "not believe that the kind of political hyperbole indulged in" by Watts fits within the statutory term "willfulness." The Court also noted that "the language of the political arena...is often vituperative, abusive, and inexact." Watts's statement had to be examined in context; the remark was "a kind of very crude offensive method of stating a political opposition to the President." Watts's "threatening words" were entitled to First Amendment protection because, taken in context, the words were "political hyperbole" rather than a threat upon President Lyndon Johnson's life.[19]

The *Kelner* case involved another instance of "threatening speech." The Jewish Defense League held a press conference in November 1974 to protest the appearance of Yasir Arafat, leader of the Palestine Liberation Organization, at the United Nations. During the interview, Russell Kelner announced that the Defense League was planning to assassinate Arafat. A television station broadcast Kelner's statement on an evening news program. At his trial Kelner argued that his statement was "political hyperbole" and not a threat. The court rejected this argument and convicted Kelner because he apparently intended to inflict injury. On appeal, the Second Circuit upheld the conviction. The justices concluded that Kelner could be convicted without a showing that he intended to harm Arafat, so long as he clearly stated that intention. The United States Supreme Court denied certiorari.[20]

In *Watts* the Court protected words that apparently intended to threaten President Johnson, because no actual intent to injure was shown. In *Kelner,* however, the Court punished words that apparently intended to threaten Yasir Arafat, even though no actual intent to injure was demonstrated. The Court's position on "threatening words" is unclear.

Offensive Words

Another type of questionable expression involves words that might be perceived as offensive to certain listeners. In the early 1970s the Supreme Court heard two cases that involved potentially "offensive words." Both cases concerned protests against the Vietnam War.

On April 26, 1968, Paul Cohen appeared in the corridor of the Los Angeles County Courthouse wearing a jacket bearing the words, "Fuck the Draft." When arrested by police officers, Cohen said that he wore the jacket as a means of informing the public of his feelings against the Vietnam War and the draft. Cohen was convicted for disturbing the peace "by loud or unusual noise, or by tumultuous or offensive conduct." The court believed that Cohen's behavior had a tendency to provoke others to acts of violence. Observers might become angered and attempt to remove Cohen's jacket. Cohen was sentenced to 30 days' imprisonment. The Supreme Court overturned the conviction. According to Justice Harlan, offended persons could avoid contact with the crude message simply by turning their eyes away from the jacket. Harlan pointed out that words are not perceived in the same way by all people; a word that is vulgar to one person may have an acceptable meaning for another. Harlan also noted that the Supreme Court cannot "forbid particular words without running a substantial risk of suppressing ideas in the process."[21] Government officials might censor a particular word as a convenient method of banning the expression of unpopular views.

The second case involved an antiwar demonstration on the campus of Indiana University. When a police officer heard Gregory Hess say in a loud voice, "We'll take the fucking street later," he immediately arrested Hess on a disorderly conduct charge. Witnesses claimed that Hess's remark was not addressed to any particular individual or group, and that his tone, although loud, was no louder than that of the other people in the area. Nevertheless, Hess was convicted. Upon appeal, the Supreme Court ruled that Hess's words did not fall into any of the classes of words that were denied First Amendment protection. Hess's remark could not be punished as obscene or offensive under the ruling in *Cohen*. Any suggestion that Hess's speech amounted to "fighting words" could not withstand scrutiny. The remark could not be regarded as a personal insult, since the statement was not directed at any specific person. Since Hess's remark was not aimed at any particular person, it could not be claimed that he was advocating any action. And, without evidence that his words were intended and likely to produce imminent disorder, Hess could not be punished for using words that had a "tendency to lead to violence."[22] The conviction was overturned. In *Hess*, as in *Cohen*, the Court refused to punish "offensive words."

Summary

The Supreme Court has established guidelines for regulating dissent. Provocative, fighting, threatening, and offensive words are only provisionally protected. When a speaker provokes disorder, as in *Feiner*, the expression is not protected. When the audience itself erupts, as in *Terminiello*, the authorities cannot ban the speech. *Chaplinsky* established that "fighting words" are prohibited; First Amendment claims are outweighed by the public interest in maintaining order. "Threatening words" must be judged in the context of their utterance. In *Watts*, the Court protected speech that apparently intended to threaten; in *Kelner*, it did not. "Offensive words," considered in *Cohen* and *Hess*, cannot be automatically banned; such action risks suppression of ideas.

SYMBOLIC SPEECH

During the 1960s and 1970s dissenters relied heavily on the use of "symbolic speech." In such instances the meaning was less obvious than with pure speech and print. In several cases the Supreme Court considered whether "symbolic speech" falls under the umbrella of First Amendment protection.

Symbol Desecration

The Vietnam War divided the United States as much as any event of the preceding century. Many citizens had to choose between loyalty to government policy and dedication to the soldiers who were fighting in support of that policy, and their own personal belief that the policy was immoral and likely to fail. Some outspoken opponents of the war recorded their opposition by burning their draft cards. Others chose to alter or destroy the U.S. flag. These forms of symbolic communication, through desecration of a symbol, posed a significant question for the Supreme Court—was "symbolic speech" subject to First Amendment protection, and if so, to what extent?

Draft Cards

The Universal Military Training and Service Act stipulated that U.S. men, upon reaching 18 years of age, had to register with a local draft board and be issued a registration certificate. In 1965 Congress made it a crime to mutilate the certificate. On March 31, 1966, David O'Brien and three colleagues burned their draft cards on the steps of the South Boston Courthouse. A crowd, including several FBI agents, witnessed the event. At his trial O'Brien said that he burned his certificate publicly in an effort to influence others to adopt his antiwar beliefs. O'Brien also claimed that the law prohibiting the destruction of draft cards was unconstitutional, because it violated freedom of speech. He was convicted. Before the Supreme Court, O'Brien argued that the act of burning his draft card was protected "symbolic speech" within the First Amendment. The Court disagreed; the justices rejected the notion that a limitless variety of conduct could be labeled "speech" whenever a person intended to express an idea. The justices noted that even if a communication element in O'Brien's action justified the application of the First Amendment, it did not necessarily follow that the destruction of a draft card was constitutionally protected. When "speech" and "nonspeech" elements were combined in the same conduct, important governmental interest in regulating the "nonspeech" element justified incidental limitations on First Amendment freedoms. The power of Congress to classify and conscript manpower for military service was an important governmental interest "beyond question." It was essential for the United States to have a system for raising armies that functioned with maximum efficiency. The requirement that each registrant have access to his card furthered the smooth functioning of the system. In *O'Brien* the Supreme Court ruled that Congress could establish a system of registration and could require individuals to cooperate in the system.[23]

During the next few years the Court heard other cases involving the destruction of draft cards. A nationwide draft-card turn-in was held on October 16, 1967. Thousands of persons attended a rally on the Boston Common, followed by a march to the Arlington Street Church, where more than 300 young men either burned their draft cards at the altar candle or deposited them in the collection plate. Among these men was a divinity student named James Oestereich. Meanwhile, in the midwest, 20 protestors turned in their cards to the authorities in Minneapolis; when the U.S. marshal refused to accept them, the protesters dropped the cards at his feet. One of the 20 was a full-time activist named David Gutknecht. One month later 40 young men participated in a turn-in sponsored by the Boston Resistance at the Old West Methodist Church. Among them was an undergraduate music student named Timothy Breen. As a result of their actions, Oestereich, Gutknecht, and Breen were either reclassified or moved up in the draft-call list by their local draft boards. All sued on the grounds that their freedom of speech had been violated and that the punitive use of the draft was unconstitutional. In *Oestereich* the U.S. Supreme Court, in the opinion written by Justice Douglas, decided:

> Once a person registers and qualifies for a statutory exemption we find no legislative authority to deprive him of that exemption because of conduct or activities unrelated to the merits of granting or continuing that exemption.

In this case, the "conduct of a local board...is basically lawless."[24] The local draft board rulings in *Gutknecht*[25] and *Breen*[26] were likewise vacated. It should be noted, however, that the Court did not absolve draft resisters. Possession of both the registration certificate and the notice of classification remained responsibilities required by the Selective Service regulations, and failure to comply with those responsibilities remained punishable under the Universal Training Act.

In 1970, following extensive protest against the draft during the previous decade, a presidential commission recommended that the United States establish all-voluntary military forces. In Janurary 1973, following the signing of a cease-fire agreement terminating U.S. involvement in Vietnam, the United States adopted an all-volunteer system.

The U.S. Flag

During the civil rights and Vietnam War protests, the U.S. flag was the most prominent national symbol that was subjected to desecration. These situations again raised the issue of whether "symbolic speech" warrants the protection of the First Amendment. The Supreme Court had an opportunity to grapple with this issue in *Street.* On June 6, 1966, upon hearing that civil-rights leader James Meredith had been shot by a sniper in Mississippi, Sidney Street burned a U.S. flag on a street corner. A police officer stopped his patrol car and approached Street, who was talking to a small group of people. He heard Street say, "We don't need no damn flag," and when the officer asked Street if he burned the flag, Street replied, "Yes, that is my flag; I burned it. If they let that happen to Meredith, we don't need an American flag." Street was convicted for violating a New York statute that prohibited the defiling of a U.S. flag. When the case reached the Supreme Court, a majority of the justices felt that Street might have been punished for his words rather than the act of burning the flag. According to the opinion written by Justice Harlan, Street's words offered no justification for a conviction. First, Street was not inciting the public to commit unlawful acts. Street simply recommended that the country should, at least temporarily, abandon one of its national symbols. The Fourteenth Amendment precludes states from punishing anybody who publicly advocates peaceful change in societal institutions. Second, Street's words were not so inflammatory as to provoke others to retaliate physically against him. Even though the words might excite some people, they are not "fighting words," that is, words that are "likely to provoke the average person to retaliation, and thereby cause a breach of peace." Third, Street's words were not offensive; they did not necessitate protecting the sensibilities of passersby. Any shock effect of the expression stemmed from the ideas and not the words. The Constitution forbids outlawing "the ideas themselves," even if they may be offensive to their hearers. Fourth, Street's speech was within the constitutionally protected freedom to disagree with the existing order. His remarks about the flag were not punishable for showing improper respect for the national emblem. Overall, the majority refused to uphold the conviction, because it could have been based upon a form of expression, which, even though distasteful, was guaranteed by the Constitution.[27]

The minority justices decided the case on a different basis. In their view, Street was convicted for his act of burning the flag, not for his words. Chief Justice Earl Warren said: "I believe that the States and the Federal government do have the power to protect the flag from acts of desecration and disgrace." Justice Abe Fortas wrote:

> One may not justify the burning of a house, even if it is his own, on the ground, however sincere, that he does so as a protest. One may not justify breaking the windows of a government building on that basis. Protest does not exonerate lawlessness. And the prohibition against flag burning on the public thoroughfare being valid, the misdemeanor is not excused merely because it is an act of flamboyant protest.

In *Street* the minority viewed the act for which Street was convicted—burning the flag—as not protected by the First Amendment. The majority held that the conviction may have been based on Street's words, which were protected. The majority did not, however, consider whether the act of flag burning deserved First Amendment protection.

A year after *Street,* the courts considered another instance of flag desecration. Stephen Radich, the proprietor of an art gallery, offered for sale several pieces of sculpture that expressed opposition to the Vietnam war. The sculptures prominently displayed the U.S. flag in the form of the male sexual organ, erect and protruding from the upright portion of a cross, and in the form of a human body hanging from a noose. Radich called the sculpture "protest art." He was convicted of violating the New York flag-desecration statute. The trial court ruled that the sculptures cast the flag into dishonor. The court compared Radich's treatment of the flag with that in *Street.*

> Here, the expression, if less dramatic, was given far wider circulation and, in consequence, perhaps, a measureable enhancement of the likelihood of incitement to disorder, by the placement of one of the constructions in a street display window of defendant's gallery on Madison Avenue in the City of New

"JUST KIDDING!"

York, and the exhibition and exposure for sale of the companion pieces in the public gallery and mercantile establishment within. Implicit in the invitation to view was the opportunity thereby afforded to join in the protest, or in counter-protest, with the consequent potential of public disorder.[28]

The court concluded that the public interest, which the New York law protected, was threatened by Radich's "protest art." His conviction was upheld. In 1972 the U.S. Supreme Court denied a petition to hear the case.

Two years later, the Court further developed its position regarding flag desecration. Valorie Goguen wore a small flag sewn on the seat of his blue jeans. He was convicted of violating the Massachusetts flag-misuse statute. The Supreme Court noted:

Flag wearing in a day of relaxed clothing styles may be simply for adornment or a ploy to attract attention. However, careless uses of the flag constitute unceremonial treatment that many people may regard as contemptuous.[29]

In *Goguen* the Court found the Massachusetts law to be unconstitutionally vague and overbroad, because it failed "to draw reasonably clear lines between the kinds of unceremonial treatment that are criminal and those that are not." Justice William Rehnquist, speaking for the minority, claimed that "symbolic speech," in the form of Goguen's display of the flag, was not protected expression. Forbidding desecration of a unique national symbol was a legitimate right of Massachusetts and took precedence over "abstract, scholastic interpretations" of the First Amendment. The majority protected an unusual usage of the flag.

In another case Harold Spence displayed a U.S. flag from his apartment window in Seattle. A large peace symbol was attached to both sides of the flag with removable tape. Spence was arrested under a Washington law that prohibited improper display of the flag. Spence admitted that he displayed the flag as a protest against the invasion of Cambodia and the Kent State University killings. He intended to associate the flag with peace rather than war. He was convicted. The Supreme Court reversed the conviction. The context in which this "symbol" was used constituted legitimate expression. The flag was owned privately, displayed on private property, and displayed without breach of the peace. The majority concluded that "given the protected character of his [Spence's] expression and in light of the fact that no interest the State may have in preserving the physical integrity of the privately owned flag was significantly impaired on these facts, the conviction must be invalidated."[30] Rehnquist's dissent stressed that the First Amendment allows a state to restrict expression when such restriction furthers an important interest. In this case, the interest was preserving the "physical integrity of the flag" and "preserving the flag as an important symbol of nationhood and unity." Again, Rehnquist acknowledged the presence of "symbolic speech," but denied such activity First Amendment protection.

In some instances—*Street, Goguen, Spence*—the Supreme Court overturned convictions based upon acts of "symbolic speech." In others—*O'Brien* and *Radich*—the Court refused to extend constitutional protection to actions such as draft-card burning or flag desecration. The Court is more willing to protect "pure speech" than "symbolic speech."

Display Symbols

Dissent can involve displaying a "symbol" in some prominent location, thereby calling attention to the point of the protest. A red flag, arm bands, uniforms, and a license plate have been among the "symbols" of dissent used to protest various causes. The Supreme Court has defined regulations that control the display of such symbols.

In 1931 the Supreme Court decided that California could not ban a group from flying a red flag as a symbol of opposition to organized government. Yetta Stromberg, a 19-year-old member of the Young Communist League, supervised a summer camp for 10- to 15-year-old children in the San Bernadino Mountains.

She directed a daily ritual that involved raising a red flag and pledging allegiance "to the worker's red flag, and the cause for which it stands; one aim throughout our lives, freedom for the working class." A library at the camp contained Communist literature that urged incitements to violence and armed uprising, though Stromberg claimed that none of the material was brought to the attention of the children and that no word of violence, anarchism, or sedition was used in her teaching. Stromberg was convicted under a California law, which banned the display of a flag in a public place as a symbol of opposition to organized government, as an invitation to anarchistic action, or as an aid to propaganda of a seditious character. At trial, the judge indicated that Stromberg should be convicted if the flag was displayed for any of the three reasons. The Supreme Court reversed the conviction, because it was unclear which of the reasons had been the basis for conviction. If Stromberg had been convicted for flying the flag as a symbol of opposition to organized government, her First Amendment freedom of speech had been violated.[31]

Thirty-eight years later, the Supreme Court decided a case involving the display of armbands by students. Some children of the Des Moines school district, encouraged by their parents, decided to wear black armbands to school to protest U.S. involvement in Vietnam. School administrators announced that any student wearing armbands to school would be suspended until they returned without the armband. When children from the Tinker and Eckhardt families refused to remove their armbands, they were suspended. The fathers of the students brought suit and the case reached the Supreme Court. The justices decided that wearing an armband to express views is an act of symbolic communication, which is protected by the First Amendment. According to Justice Fortas, the act of wearing an armband is closely akin to "pure speech." A school administration cannot ban an act of pure speech simply because it might cause discomfort or unpleasantness. Fortas noted that the wearing of armbands was entirely divorced from any disruptive behavior by the students engaging in the protest.

> Their deviation consisted only in wearing on their sleeve a band of black cloth, not more than two inches wide. They wore it to exhibit their disapproval of the Vietnam hostilities and their advocacy of a truce, to make their views known, and, by their example, to influence others to adopt them. They neither interrupted school activities nor sought to intrude in the school affairs or the lives of others. They caused discussion outside of the classrooms, but no interference with work and no disorder.[32]

The school administration sought to punish a few students for passive expression of their opposition to the war. There was no evidence of any disruption; the students never interfered with the work of the school or with the rights of other students. Fortas also noted that no other symbols were excluded; students were allowed to wear political buttons. School officials prohibited only one symbol, and without any indication that it was necessary to avoid disruption of school activities. Such a ban was not constitutionally permissible.

In *Schacht* the Court continued its liberal interpretation of symbol display. Daniel Schacht and his colleagues participated in a skit as part of a peaceful antiwar demonstration at the Houston Armed Forces Induction Center. The skit was designed to show undesirable aspects of U.S. presence in Vietnam. Schacht and another person were dressed in military uniforms. A third person was outfitted in typical Viet Cong apparel. The first two men carried water pistols. They would yell, "Be an able American," and then they would shoot the Viet Cong. The pistols expelled a red liquid which, when it hit the victim, gave the impression that the person was bleeding. Once the victim fell down, the other two walked up and exclaimed, "My God, this is a pregnant woman." Schacht was indicted for wearing the uniform of the armed forces without authority. Schacht claimed that he was authorized to wear the uniform under a law that provides that "while portraying a member of the Army, Navy, Air Force, or Marine Corps, an actor in a theatrical or motion picture production may wear the uniform of that armed force if the portrayal does not tend to discredit that armed force." Schacht argued that he wore the army uniform as an actor in a theatrical production. Nevertheless, he was convicted. He appealed. In a unanimous decision, the Supreme Court, per Justice Hugo Black, held that the part of the law stipulating that dramatic portrayal is lawful only if it "does not tend to discredit that armed force" was an unconstitutional abridgement of freedom of speech.[33] The Court overturned Schacht's conviction. Three justices, however, in a concurring opinion pointed out that a "theatrical production" in which a military uniform is permitted must be restricted to a setting where viewers realize that they are "watching a make-believe performance." If this thinking had been supported by the majority, Schacht would not have been engaged in a "theatrical production" and could have been found guilty.

Maynard presented a unique twist on display. Rather than dissenting through the act of showing a symbol, the Maynards dissented by partially covering their license plates. George Maynard and his wife covered the portion of their automobile license plates stamped with the New Hampshire state motto, "Live Free, or Die." The couple found the motto repugnant to their moral and religious beliefs as Jehovah's Witnesses. Maynard was convicted for knowingly obscuring the license plate. The Supreme Court, per Chief Justice Warren Burger, sided with Maynard. First, the Court noted that First Amendment protection includes the right to speak freely as well as the right to refrain from speaking at all.

A system which secures the right to proselytize religious, political, and ideological causes must also guarantee the concomitant right to decline to foster such concepts. The right to speak and the right to refrain from speaking are complementary components of the broader concept of "individual freedom of mind."

Second, the Court considered the interests claimed by New Hampshire in requiring people to display the motto. New Hampshire claimed that display of the motto facilitated the identification of passenger vehicles. The Court decided that the license plates contained "a specific configuration of letters and numbers, which makes them readily distinguishable from other types of plates, even without reference to state motto." New Hampshire also argued that requiring the display of the state motto promoted appreciation of history and state pride. The Court reasoned that a state's interest in disseminating an ideology "cannot outweigh an individual's First Amendment right to avoid becoming the courier for such messages."[34] New Hampshire could not require Maynard and his wife to display the state motto upon their license plates.

Summary

The lesson of *Maynard, Schacht, Tinker,* and *Stromberg* is that "display" is a form of "symbolic speech," which is entitled to First Amendment protection. *O'Brien, Street,* and *Radich* indicate that the level of protection given to "desecration" as a form of "symbolic speech" remains limited. The Supreme Court has recognized the right to "display" symbols of dissent, while remaining reluctant to award "desecration" the same status. Furthermore, the Court grants greater First Amendment protection to "pure speech" compared with "symbolic speech."

NOTES

1. *Schenck v. United States,* 39 S.Ct. 247 (1919).
2. *Frohwerk v. United States,* 39 S.Ct. 249 (1919).
3. *Debs v. United States,* 39 S.Ct. 252 (1919).
4. *Abrams v. United States,* 40 S.Ct. 17 (1919).
5. *Gitlow v. New York,* 45 S.Ct. 625 (1925).
6. *Whitney v. California,* 47 S.Ct. 641 (1927).
7. *DeJonge v. Oregon,* 57 S.Ct. 255 (1937).
8. *Dennis v. United States,* 71 S.Ct. 857 (1951).
9. *Yates v. United States,* 77 S.Ct. 1064 (1957).
10. *Scales v. United States,* 81 S.Ct. 1469 (1961).
11. *Noto v. United States,* 81 S.Ct. 1517 (1961).
12. *Brandenburg v. Ohio,* 89 S.Ct. 1827 (1969).
13. *Bond v. Floyd,* 87 S.Ct. 339 (1966).
14. *Terminiello v. Chicago,* 69 S.Ct. 894 (1949).
15. *Feiner v. New York,* 71 S.Ct. 303 (1951).
16. *Chaplinsky v. New Hampshire,* 62 S.Ct. 766 (1942).
17. *Gooding v. Wilson,* 92 S.Ct. 1103 (1972).
18. *Lewis v. New Orleans,* 94 S.Ct. 970 (1974).
19. *Watts v. United States,* 89 S.Ct. 1399 (1969).
20. *Kelner v. United States,* 534 F.2d 1020 (1976); 97 S.Ct. 639 (1976).

21. *Cohen v. California,* 91 S.Ct. 1780 (1971).
22. *Hess v. Indiana,* 94 S.Ct. 326 (1973).
23. *United States v. O'Brien,* 88 S.Ct. 1673 (1968).
24. *Oestereich v. Selective Service Board No. 11,* 89 S.Ct. 414 (1968).
25. *Gutknecht v. United States,* 90 S.Ct. 506 (1970).
26. *Breen v. Selective Service Local Board No. 16,* 90 S.Ct. 661 (1970).
27. *Street v. New York,* 89 S.Ct. 1354 (1969).
28. *Radich v. New York,* 459 F.2d 745 (1972); *Ross v. Radich,* 92 S.Ct. 2415 (1972).
29. *Smith v. Goguen,* 94 S.Ct. 1242 (1974).
30. *Spence v. Washington,* 94 S.Ct. 2727 (1974).
31. *Stromberg v. California,* 51 S.Ct. 532 (1931).
32. *Tinker v. Des Moines Independent Community School District,* 89 S.Ct. 733 (1969).
33. *Schacht v. United States,* 90 S.Ct. 1555 (1970).
34. *Wooley v. Maynard,* 97 S.Ct. 1428 (1977).

RECOMMENDED READING

Ferro, Gaetamo G., "First Amendment Problems in Punishing Political Threats," *Connecticut Law Review* 9 (Winter, 1977), 304-10.

Hicks, Kenneth A., "*Spence v. Washington: Smith v. Goguen:* Symbolic Speech and Flag Desecration," *Columbia Human Rights Law Review* 6 (Fall/Winter, 1974-75), 535-50.

Pearlstein, Mark, "The 'Fighting Words Doctrine' as applied to Abusive Language Toward Policemen," *DePaul Law Review* 22 (Spring, 1973), 725-36.

Shea, Thomas F., "Don't Bother to Smile When you Call me That—Fighting Words and the First Amendment," *Kentucky Law Journal* 63 (1974-75), 1-22.

Siegel, Paul, "Protecting Political Speech: *Brandenburg vs. Ohio* Updated," *Quarterly Journal of Speech* 67 (February, 1981), 69-80.

Suffet, Stephen, "The Resistance and the Court: The Punitive Draft Cases," *Free Speech Yearbook* (1971), 50-63.

Thayer, Ted J., "Freedom of Speech and Symbolic Conduct: The Crime of Flag Desecration," *Arizona Law Review* 12 (Spring, 1970), 71-88.

KEY DECISIONS

1919—*SCHENCK*—established "clear and present danger" test of First Amendment.

1925—*GITLOW*—established "bad tendency" test.

1942—*CHAPLINSKY*—established "fighting words" doctrine.

1949—*TERMINIELLO*—noted that when audience provokes public disorder, speaker's words are protected.

1951—*FEINER*—noted that when speaker provokes public disorder, speaker's words are not protected.

1951—*DENNIS*—initiated idea that "advocacy of abstract ideas" is permissible, while "advocacy of action" is punishable.

1968—*O'BRIEN*—suggests that the Supreme Court is more willing to protect "pure speech" than "symbolic speech."

1969—*TINKER*—indicates that the Supreme Court is more willing to protect symbolic speech of "display" than that of "desecration."

1969—*WATTS*—held that "threatening words" are punishable, while "political hyperbole" is permissible.

SUMMARY—LAW OF DISSENT

Definition

The law of dissent seeks to regulate the activities of those who protest against the government. Dissent may take the form of "pure" speech or "symbolic" expression.

Proof

In order to establish that a dissenter has violated the law, the prosecution might demonstrate that the dissenter's communication fell into one of the following classes:
1. Advocating the overthrow of the government by force or violence.
2. Inflammatory utterances
   a. Provocative words
   b. Fighting words
   c. Threatening words
   d. Offensive words
3. Desecration of national symbol
   a. U.S. flag
   b. Draft registration card

Defenses

A defendent might successfully support the right to dissent by establishing that:

1. Dissent involved an abstract idea rather than a specific action.
2. Dissent occurred in peacetime, thus creating minimal danger to the national security.
3. Public disorder was caused by unruly crowd rather than the dissenter's words.
4. Display of national symbols, without desecration, is a First Amendment freedom.

3

ASSOCIATION

In no country in the world has the principle of association been more successfully used or applied to a greater multitude of objects than in America. Besides
the permanent associations which are established by law under the names of
townships, cities, and counties, a vast number of others are formed and maintained by the agency of private individuals.[1]

Despite this observation of Alexis De Tocqueville during his visit to the
United States, the right of association is not mentioned in the Bill of Rights. The
freedom to form organizations was omitted by the founders of the government,
because they viewed associations as harmful to the country's well-being. The
framers did, however, recognize the more specific rights of assembly and petition. These rights acknowledged that citizens could gather peaceably (assembly)
and make grievances known to others (petition).

ASSEMBLY

What De Tocqueville observed about Americans of the nineteenth century
is certainly true today. The United States is a nation of joiners. Everywhere, people gather together to achieve political, religious, social, and economic goals.
In fact, contemporary Americans view the right of assembly as a necessary freedom. Specific tenets of the right of assembly have, however, developed over
several years, and the Supreme Court has played an influential role in shaping
those tenets.

Freedom to Associate

In 1958 the Supreme Court recognized association as a constitutional freedom. The case involved the National Association for the Advancement of Col-

ored People, an organization chartered in 1909 as a nonprofit corporation designed to eliminate racial barriers. It opened local branches in Alabama in 1918 and had 58 branches and a membership of almost 15,000 in that state by 1956. During the 1950s, the NAACP achieved several accomplishments on behalf of the civil rights of black citizens. In 1954, for example, the organization achieved a major victory in school desegregation.[2] In 1955-56 the association played a vital role in the Montgomery bus boycott. In response, southern politicians developed strategies designed to cripple the NAACP.

Alabama and several other southern states required foreign corporations to qualify prior to conducting business in the state. This necessitated filing a charter with the secretary of state. The Alabama NAACP never complied with the requirement because it considered itself exempt. In 1956 the attorney general claimed that the NAACP did business in Alabama without complying with the qualification statute. He sought to prohibit the organization from conducting further activities within the state. During court proceedings, the NAACP was ordered to produce records, including the names and addresses of the members of the association. The NAACP produced all the records, but refused to release the membership lists, claiming that Alabama could not require the surrender of the lists. The association was held in contempt and fined $100,000. The NAACP appealed. The Supreme Court unanimously ruled that the NAACP had the right to protect the membership lists on behalf of the private interests of its members. According to Justice John Harlan,

Petitioner has made an uncontroverted showing that on past occasions revelation of the identity of its rank-and-file members has exposed these members to economic reprisal, loss of employment, threat of physical coercion, and other manifestations of public hostility. Under these circumstances, we think it apparent that compelled disclosure of petitioner's Alabama membership is likely to . . . induce members to withdraw from the Association and dissuade others from joining it because of fear of exposure of their beliefs shown through their associations and of the consequences of this exposure.[3]

In *NAACP* the Court ruled that compelled disclosure of membership lists would hamper the association in pursuing its lawful goals. It constituted a restraint on freedom of association.

Four years later the Court reaffirmed the right of association. The case involved an Arkansas law that authorized localities to levy a license tax on any corporation engaging in business within city limits. Little Rock had for several years imposed license taxes on a variety of businesses, but charitable organizations were exempt. In 1957 Little Rock amended the occupation-license-tax ordinance so that upon request, any organization had to produce its official records, including the names of members and contributors. Upon such request, Daisy Bates, the custodian of records of the Little Rock NAACP, supplied some of the required information. She refused, however, to divulge the names of the organization's members and contributors. She claimed that because of anti-NAACP sentiments, disclosure of the names would lead to harassment and perhaps even bodily harm. Bates was convicted for refusing to provide the list of names. Upon appeal, the Supreme Court unanimously ruled that "it is now beyond dispute that freedom of association for the purpose of advancing ideas and airing grievances is protected by the Due Process Clause of the Fourteenth Amendment from invasion by the States."[4] In *Bates,* as in *NAACP,* the Court noted that "compulsory disclosure of the membership lists of the local branches of the National Association for the Advancement of Colored People would work a significant interference with the freedom of association of the members." According to the Court, encroachment upon personal freedom can be justified only when a state can prove a compelling interest. Such an interest was lacking in this case. There was no correlation between the city's power to impose license taxes and the compulsory disclosure of membership lists.

A similar case, which further strengthened the right to associate, involved litigation between the Florida Legislative Investigation Committee and the Miami branch of the NAACP. In 1956, when the Florida legislature began investigating the NAACP for possible connections with Communist activities, a subpoena was issued to obtain the membership list of the Miami branch. When Reverend Theodore Gibson refused to produce the list, he was sentenced to six months in prison and fined $1,200. He appealed. The Supreme Court, per Justice Arthur Goldberg, noted that "the evidence discloses the utter failure to demonstrate the existence of any substantial relationship between the NAACP and subversive or Communist activities." Furthermore, no claim was made "that the NAACP or its Miami branch was engaged in any subversive activities or that its legitimate activities have been dominated or influenced by Communists." Goldberg argued that groups that "are neither engaged in subversive or other illegal or improper activities, nor demonstrated to have any substantial connections with such activities, are to be protected in their rights of free and private association." He viewed such protection as especially vital in this instance.

> While, of course, all legitimate organizations are the beneficiaries of these protections, they are all the more essential here, where the challenged privacy is that of persons espousing beliefs already unpopular with their neighbors and the deterrent and "chilling" effect on the free exercise of constitutionally enshrined rights of free speech, expression, and association is consequently the more immediate and substantial.[5]

In *Gibson,* as in *NAACP* and *Bates,* the Court accepted the First Amendment argument of the NAACP and upheld the right of association.

Right to Solicit Members

The right to solicit members for an organization is essential to the freedom of association. Yet, unrestrained solicitation can lead to door-to-door canvassing on behalf of fraudulent causes at almost any time. In order to protect the public from such invasion of individual privacy, cities have passed laws restricting the right to solicit. In some cases—*Cantwell, Thomas, Staub*—the Supreme Court weighed the right to solicit members against the right to be left undisturbed.

Newton Cantwell and his two sons were arrested for conducting door-to-door religious solicitation on behalf of Jehovah's Witnesses, in a predominantly Catholic neighborhood in New Haven, Connecticut. The Cantwells had ignored a statute that required any person soliciting for a religious cause to apply for a certificate of approval with the welfare secretary, who then decided whether the cause conformed to "reasonable standards of efficiency and integrity." The penalty for violating the law was a $100 fine or 30 days' imprisonment, or both. The Supreme Court unanimously overturned the convictions on the ground that the statute was prohibitory, not regulatory. It allowed an official to ban religious solicitation from the streets of Connecticut entirely. If approval were issued by the welfare secretary, solicitation could proceed without any restriction whatsoever. If a certificate were denied, solicitation would then be prohibited. According to the Court, the statute established a prior restraint on First Amendment freedoms. If a state wanted to protect its citizens against door-to-door solicitation for fraudulent "religious" or "charity" causes, it could enact a regulation directed at that problem. For example, a state could grant a householder the right to terminate the solicitation by demanding that the visitor leave the premises. In addition, a state could regulate the time and manner of solicitation. The state may not, however, force people to submit to licensing of religious speech.[6] In *Cantwell* the Court found fault with the broad sweep of the Connecticut law.

Five years later, in *Thomas*, the Court strengthened the right to solicit members. A Texas statute prohibited labor-union organizers from soliciting members, unless they first obtained an identification card from a state official. R. J. Thomas, an officer of the United Automobile Workers, traveled to Pelly, Texas, to deliver a union organizing speech. The attorney general obtained a restraining order enjoining Thomas from soliciting any union memberships. When Thomas appeared as scheduled and solicited the entire audience, he was convicted of contempt of court. He appealed. The Supreme Court reversed the conviction on the ground that solicitation could not effectively be separated from general speechmaking. The Court noted that when a union organizer went beyond mere speech and advocacy to the solicitation of monies, "he enters a realm where a reasonable registration or identification requirement may be imposed," because a state has an interest in protecting its citizens against fraud and financial loss. In this case, however, Thomas had not engaged in fund raising. The Texas law infringed on Thomas's freedom to express his beliefs and to urge others to join the union.[7]

In 1958 the issue was raised once more in the *Staub* case. The International Ladies Garment Workers Union was trying to organize the employees of a manufacturing company located near Baxley, Georgia. A city ordinance required that a permit had to be obtained prior to soliciting members for any organization that required the payment of dues. Rose Staub, an employee of the union, without applying for a permit, attended a meeting at the house of a worker, where she detailed the benefits of joining the union. She urged the women to get other workers to join; blank membership cards were distributed for that purpose. Staub was charged with soliciting members for an organization without a permit. She was convicted and sentenced to spend 30 days in prison or pay a fine of $300. She appealed. The Supreme Court reversed the decision. The Baxley ordinance made freedom of association contingent upon the discretion of the mayor and the city council, thus constituting a prior restraint. The Baxley statute provided no definitive standards governing the action of city officials regarding the granting or withholding of a permit. The city officials were free to act as they wished. The Baxley ordinance was unconstitutional.[8] In *Staub*, as in *Cantwell* and *Thomas*, the Court supported the right to solicit members for an association.

Right to Meet Publicly

Most localities have statutes that specify the conditions under which public meetings may be held. Over the years some of these ordinances have been upheld, while others have been overturned by the courts. Such a case, *Hague*, reached the Supreme Court in 1939.

A Jersey City, New Jersey, statute authorized the director of public safety to process applications for parades and public assemblies. A permit could be denied "for the purpose of preventing riots, disturbances or disorderly assemblage." The Congress of Industrial Organizations was repeatedly refused permits on the ground that the individuals making the requests were Communists. The same persons were denied the right to distribute pamphlets and to rent a hall for a public meeting. Policemen stopped CIO representatives as they entered Jersey City, seized literature in their possession, and in some cases, arrested them. The CIO members denied that they were Communists and claimed that their only purpose was to describe for workers their rights under the National Labor Relations Act and to urge the workers to join the CIO. The union initiated court proceedings in order to stop enforcement of the city ordinance. Before the Supreme Court, Mayor Frank Hague argued that Jersey City's ownership of streets and parks was as absolute as an individual's ownership of a home. So, the city had power to exclude persons from the use of such places. The Court, per Justice Owen Roberts, noted that streets and parks have always been used for public assembly, communicating ideas between citizens, and discussing public issues. Yet, the right of assembly is not absolute; it may be regulated in the public interest. Assembly must not interfere with general comfort, convenience, peace, and order. Uncontrolled suppression of the right of assembly cannot, however, be substituted for the city's duty to maintain order. The New Jersey ordinance allowed city officials to arbitrarily consent to or withhold permission for public meetings. The ordinance was therefore unconstitutional. In *Hague,* the Court determined that freedom to assemble peaceably for discussion of the benefits offered by the union was a privilege protected against state abridgement by the Fourteenth Amendment.[9]

A state may regulate the use of streets and parks in the public interest. In *Cox,* the Court ruled that the control of parades or processions can be a legitimate state concern. On July 8, 1939, about 100 members of Jehovah's Witnesses met at a hall in Manchester, New Hampshire, in order to participate in an information march. The people were divided into four or five groups, which proceeded to different parts of the city's business district. The groups marched, single file, along the sidewalks; marchers carried banners and handed out leaflets announcing a meeting to be held at a later time. Most were arrested and convicted for violating a New Hampshire statute prohibiting a "parade or procession" upon a public street without a special permit. During the trial, the state pointed out that 26,000 people normally pass by one of the intersections where the defendants marched every hour on a typical Saturday night. The state claimed that the marchers had interfered with normal sidewalk travel. The Supreme Court unanimously upheld the New Hampshire statute on the ground that a state may prevent interference with normal usage of streets and parks.

> The authority of a municipality to impose regulations in order to assure the safety and convenience of the people in the use of public highways has never been regarded as inconsistent with civil liberties but rather as one of the means of safeguarding the good order upon which they ultimately depend.[10]

The court noted that the obvious advantage of a permit system was to encourage proper policing of the event. The New Hampshire statute fixed time and place, thereby avoiding confusion with overlapping processions and minimizing the risk of disorder. More important, the statute did not grant the permit board arbitrary "power"; its discretion had to be exercised with uniformity of method and treatment. With respect to the meeting held by Jehovah's Witnesses, a change in time, place, and manner was necessary to avoid a public disturbance.

A decade later the Court sharpened its position on the issue. A New York City ordinance made it illegal for an individual to hold a public worship meeting on the streets without obtaining a permit from the city police commissioner. In 1946 Carl Jacob Kunz, an ordained Baptist minister who spoke under the auspices of the Outdoor Gospel Work, obtained a permit to preach in New York City. Later that year, however, his permit was revoked, because Kunz had ridiculed Catholics and Jews at his worship meetings. Kunz applied for a permit in 1947 and again in 1948, but both times his request was rejected. On September 11, 1948, Kunz was arrested for speaking at Columbus Circle in New York City without a permit. He was convicted and fined $10. Kunz appealed. The Supreme Court held the ordinance invalid—a prior restraint on First Amendment rights. The police commissioner had refused to issue the permit on the ground that a permit had been previously revoked "for good reasons." Yet, there was no mention in the ordinance of conditions under which a permit application could be refused. The ordinance lacked standards to guide the action of the commissioner—he had discretionary power to control the right of persons to speak on religious matters in New York City.[11] In *Kunz,* the Court declared the ordinance unconstitutional.

In 1951 the Court decided another case involving the regulation of public meetings. The Jehovah's Witnesses scheduled Bible talks in the public park in Havre de Grace, Maryland. Although no ordinance regulated the use of this park, it had been customary for organizations to obtain a permit from the park commissioner. The Jehovah's Witnesses requested permission to use the park on four consecutive Sundays. Permission was refused. The petitioners were told that an Elk's Day ceremony would take place on the first Sunday, but were given no explanation for refusal on the other three Sundays. They held their meeting anyway. Daniel Niemotko, who opened the meeting, was convicted on a disorderly-conduct charge. He appealed. The Supreme Court noted that use of the park was denied because the city council disagreed with the opinions of the Jehovah's Witnesses. The city allowed other religious groups to use the park. To allow expression of religious beliefs by some and to deny the same privilege to others, merely because their views are unpopular, is a denial of equal protection of the law. The freedoms of speech and religion are entitled to firmer protection than that which depends upon the personal whims of local officials. According to Chief Justice Fred Vinson, it "thus becomes apparent that the lack of standards in the license issuing 'practice' renders that 'practice' a prior restraint in contravention of the Fourteenth Amendment, and that the completely arbitrary and discriminatory refusal to grant the permits was a denial of equal protection."[12] In *Niemotko,* the conviction was overturned.

Two years later the Court stipulated the procedure a person must follow when challenging a regulatory statute. A Portsmouth, New Hampshire, ordinance banned any "theatrical, or dramatic presentation," "parade or procession upon any public street or way," or "open air public meetings," unless a license was obtained from the city council. William Poulos, a Jehovah's Witness, was refused a permit for a religious meeting. Poulos and his colleagues held the meeting in a public park without a license. He was convicted and fined $20. On appeal, the New Hampshire Supreme Court decided that the ordinance was valid. The ordinance gave local authorities no discretion in refusing permits. Rather, the ordinance instructed them to process all applications and to regulate the issuance of licenses only when necessary to avert congestion in the public parks. Poulos's legal remedy against any discriminatory refusal by city officials to grant the permit was to obtain a judicial order to force issuance of the permit. Poulos had violated the law when he ignored the denial of the license and held the gathering anyway. The U.S. Supreme Court accepted the state court's reasoning. In the opinion of Justice Stanley Reed, Poulos had a defense only if the ordinance had been challenged and declared invalid in court. It was illegal to disobey a valid ordinance, even if it could be proven that the ordinance was implemented in a discriminatory fashion.[13] In *Poulos,* the Supreme Court affirmed the conviction.

The cases mentioned in this section support a right to meet publicly. In *Hague, Kunz,* and *Niemotko,* the Court overturned ordinances that allowed city officials to arbitrarily consent to or withhold permission for a public meeting. Specific guidelines are necessary to direct official action in determining whether permission will be granted or denied. In *Hague* and *Cox,* the Court acknowledged that a state may regulate public meetings on streets and in parks. In *Poulos,* the Court determined that a person who ignores the denial of a request for a permit to hold a public meeting, and holds the assembly anyway, has no defense unless the ordinance is later declared invalid. Proof that a valid ordinance was applied in a discriminatory fashion does not offset the crime. In general, the right to meet publicly is guaranteed, but it may be regulated to provide comfort, convenience, peace, and order.

Controlling Associations

Over the past half-century, U.S. authorities have occasionally moved to control certain groups that pose real or imagined threats to the security of the country. In 1944 the Supreme Court decided the constitutionality of an executive order that barred Japanese-American citizens from a specific geographical location. Also, during recent decades, the Court has considered the constitutionality of several laws designed to control the Communist party.

Japanese-Americans

On December 7, 1941, Japanese bombers attacked U.S. military bases at Pearl Harbor in Hawaii. President Franklin Delano Roosevelt declared war against Japan. At this time, about 112,000 persons of Japanese ancestry lived on the Pacific coast of the United States. The government, through Executive Order 9066, declared that "the successful prosecution of the war requires every possible protection against...sabotage to national-defense material." Subsequently, the government issued Civilian Exclusion Order No. 34, which directed that all Japanese-Americans should be excluded from the West Coast. Fred Toyosabubo Korematsu was convicted for defying the order by remaining in California. Korematsu was placed on probation for five years. He appealed. The

Supreme Court upheld the conviction. According to the Court, the act that permitted exclusion was necessary under the war power of Congress and the Executive. In the opinion of Justice Hugo Black, Korematsu was not excluded because of his race; rather, because military authorities feared an invasion on the West Coast and felt certain security measures were necessary.[14] In *Korematsu,* the court viewed the matter as encompassing military danger rather than social prejudice.

Communist Party

The Communist party has frequently been a target of government efforts to control "undesirable" groups. Through the years, the government has attempted to contain the growth of membership, identify persons affiliated with the organization, and control the activities of Communist party members in the United States.

In 1950, at the start of the Korean War, Congress passed the McCarran Act over President Harry Truman's veto. Under the act, Communist organizations were required to register with the attorney general, giving names of the officers and members. When the Communist party did not register, the Subversive Activities Control Board ordered it to do so. The party appealed. In June 1961, 11 years after initiation of the proceeding, the Supreme Court upheld the order. In the opinion by Justice Felix Frankfurter, the act was regulatory, not prohibitory, and the requirement to file the membership list was "demanded by rational interests high in the scale of National Concern." According to Frankfurter,

> where the mask of anonymity which an organization's members wear serves the double purpose of protecting them from popular prejudice and of enabling them to cover over a foreign-directed conspiracy, infiltrate into other groups, and enlist the support of persons who would not, if the group were revealed, lend their support...it would be a distortion of the First Amendment to hold that it prohibits Congress from revealing the mask.[15]

In *Communist Party,* the court upheld the requirement to file the membership list, whereas, in *NAACP,* such a requirement had been overturned. According to the Court, requiring disclosure of membership lists was a reasonable regulation, if the requirement were not aimed at prohibiting a particular group.

In another case heard that year, the Court again emphasized that the right to associate is not absolute. Raphael Konigsberg, a 1953 graduate of the University of Southern California Law School, refused, before the California State Committee of Bar Examiners, to answer questions relating to his membership in the Communist party. He affirmed his disbelief in the violent overthrow of the government and stated that he never knowingly had been a member of any or-

"JUST BECAUSE SHE'S SHAKING HIS HAND, DOESN'T MEAN SHE'S COMMUNIST!"

ganization that advocated such action. Konigsberg was denied admission to the California bar. He appealed. The Supreme Court weighed Konigsberg's right to free speech against California's interest in determining the fitness of applicants to the state bar.

We reject the view that freedom of speech and association, as protected by the First and Fourteenth Amendments, are "absolutes."...Throughout its history this Court has consistently recognized at least two ways in which constitutionally protected freedom of speech is narrower than an unlimited license to talk. On the one hand, certain forms of speech, or speech in certain contexts, has been considered outside the scope of constitutional protection. On the other hand, general regulatory statutes, not intended to control the content of speech but incidentally limiting its unfettered exercise, have not been regarded as the type of law the First or Fourteenth Amendment forbade Congress or the States to pass, when they have been found justified by subordinating valid governmental interests, a prerequisite to constitutionality which has necessarily involved a weighing of the governmental interest involved.[16]

Using the balancing test, the Court majority in *Konigsberg* decided that California's interest outweighed the free-speech consideration. The Court ruled against Konigsberg.

In 1971 the Court heard a case with similar facts but a different result. When taking the Arizona bar examination, Sara Baird, a 1967 graduate of the law school at Stanford University, was asked to state whether she had ever been a member of the Communist party or any organization "that advocates overthrow of the United States Government by force or violence." When she refused to answer this question, the bar committee recommended that she be denied admission. She appealed. The Supreme Court ruled that Baird did not have to answer the question. In Arizona it was perjury to answer the bar committee's question falsely, and perjury was punishable as a felony. In effect, Baird was asked to guess whether any organization to which she had ever belonged advocates the overthrow of the government by force or violence. The Court majority felt that the First Amendment protected Baird from being subjected to a question potentially hazardous to her liberty. The majority also noted that the First Amendment prohibits a state from excluding a person from a profession solely because that person is a member of a particular political organization.[17] The Court minority disagreed, basing its opinion on the *Konigsberg* reasoning. They felt that a state's insistence that a person answer questions about membership in the Communist party outweighs any deterrent effect upon freedom of speech and association. In *Baird,* however, the majority, on balance, weighted the issue in favor of First Amendment freedoms.

In the 1976 *Robel* case, the Supreme Court reduced the stigma of guilt by association with communism. The case involved Section 5 of the Subversive Activities Control Act of 1950, which prohibited members of Communist action groups from working in any defense facility. Eugene Robel, a member of the Communist party, was employed as a machinist at the Todd Shipyards Corporation. When the secretary of defense designated the shipyard as a "defense facility," an indictment was filed, charging Robel with violating the law. The case reached the Supreme Court. The Court ruled that Section 5 was an unconstitutional abridgement of the right of association. The section prohibited all members of Communist action organizations from working for the government. The law prevented employment because of guilt by mere association. According to the opinion written by Chief Justice Earl Warren, it was "precisely because that statute sweeps indiscriminately across all types of associations with communist-action groups, without regard to the quality and degree of membership, that it runs afoul of the First Amendment."[18]

Seven years later, in *Communist Party of Indiana,* the Court again upheld the freedom of association. In 1972 the Communist party of Indiana applied for a place on the Indiana ballot during the general election. The application was rejected because the party failed to submit an oath stating that it did not advocate the overthrow of the government by force or violence. The party appealed. The Supreme Court unanimously agreed that the loyalty oath violated free-speech guarantees. Indiana could not proscribe advocacy, except where such advocacy attempted to incite imminent lawless action and was likely to produce such action. For purposes of granting access to the ballot, a group advocating violent overthrow as abstract doctrine was not necessarily advocating unlawful action. The Court noted that "the right to associate with the political party of one's choice is an integral part" of protected First Amendment rights.[19]

Summary

Supreme Court decisions have established that American citizens enjoy the rights of association and assembly. Several decisions—*NAACP, Bates, Gibson*—grant groups the right to protect membership lists on behalf of the private interests of their members. Other decisions—*Cantwell, Thomas, Staub*—protect the right of organizations to recruit new members, raise funds, and inform the public of their activities and purposes. In *Hague, Kunz, and Niemotko,* the Court overturned statutes that permitted city officials to arbitrarily consent to or to deny permission for a public assembly. Specific guidelines are necessary to shape official response to such requests. The right of assembly, nonetheless, has been subjected to some regulation. According to *Hague,* and *Cox,* assembly must not interfere with public comfort, convenience, peace, and order. Parades and marches can be controlled as to time, place, and manner.

Government efforts to control groups, thereby limiting the right of association, have been interpreted rather consistently by the Supreme Court. In early cases—*Korematsu, Communist Party, Konigsberg*—the Court decided, on balance, that the nation's interests warranted the restrictions placed on association. In more recent cases—*Robel, Baird, Communist Party of Indiana*—the Court stressed that guilt by mere association contradicts First Amendment guarantees. The Court's perception of the threat that certain groups, notably the Communist party, pose for the nation has diminished over time.

PETITION

Petition is a tactic that enables citizens to bring grievances to the attention of others. During the twentieth century, groups representing diverse causes—labor, civil rights, antiwar, womens' rights, and gay liberation, to name a few—have petitioned before various audiences. Some efforts to regulate specific forms of petitioning have received attention by the Supreme Court.

Right to Picket and Boycott

The Supreme Court granted picketing First Amendment protection in 1940. The case originated when union organizer Byron Thornhill peacefully urged a group of strikebreakers not to cross a picket line. Thornhill was convicted of violating the Alabama antipicketing law. In *Thornhill* the Supreme Court, per Justice Frank Murphy, reversed the conviction and held that the right to picket enjoyed First Amendment protection. Furthermore, the Alabama antipicketing statute was deemed invalid because of two flaws—overbreadth and vagueness. First, the statute was overbroad because it proscribed activities that were constitutionally protected, as well as activities that were not. The Court noted that "the dissemination of information concerning the facts of a labor dispute must be regarded as within that area of free discussion that is guaranteed by the Constitution." Public discussion of the conditions in industry and the causes of labor disputes was indispensable in shaping "the destiny of modern industrial society." Second, the statute was vague because the term "picket" was "nowhere delineated."

> Whatever the means used to publicize the facts of a labor dispute, whether by printed sign, by pamphlet, by word of mouth or otherwise, all such activity without exception is within the inclusive prohibition of the statute.[20]

The Supreme Court acknowledged the First Amendment relationship to boycotting in 1982. The case actually began in March 1966, when black citizens in Claiborne County, Mississippi, presented white officials with a list of demands for racial equality. When the demands were generally ignored, several hundred NAACP members began boycotting white merchants in the area. In 1969 the merchants filed suit in state court to recover losses caused by the boycott and to enjoin future boycott activity. The Court held the NAACP liable for the merchants' lost earnings—it imposed damages liability and issued a permanent injunction against the boycott. The NAACP appealed. The Supreme Court, in an opinion written by Justice John Stevens, stressed the constitutionality of the boycott.

> In sum, the boycott clearly involved constitutionally protected activity. The established elements of speech, assembly, association and petition, "though not identical, are inseparable." Through exercise of these First Amendment rights, petitioners sought to bring about political, social, and economic change. Through speech, assembly, and petition—rather than through riot or revolution— petitioners sought to change a social order that had consistently treated them as second-class citizens.[21]

Stevens acknowledged that Mississippi "legitimately may impose damages for consequences of violent conduct," but it may not award compensation for the effects of "nonviolent protected activity" such as that which took place in this case. In *Claiborne Hardware,* the Court upheld the right to boycott.

Picket and Boycott Guidelines

Over the years, the Court has imposed restrictions on picketing and boycotting. At least two cases, *Hughes* and *Cameron,* involved civil-rights interests. Several other cases concerned labor disputes.

Civil-Rights Interests

In *Hughes,* the Court distinguished between the acts of picketing and speech. An organization, Progressive Citizens of America, demanded that a Lucky Stores grocery hire blacks as soon as white clerks quit, until the proportion of black to white clerks approximated the proportion of black to white customers. When store officials refused this demand, picketers began to patrol in front of the store, carrying placards that read: "Lucky Won't Hire Negro Clerks in Proportion to Negro Trade—Don't Patronize." Lucky Stores obtained an injunction restraining the group from picketing. Group members, however, continued to picket. They were convicted of contempt, sentenced to two days in jail, and fined $20 each. Upon appeal, the Supreme Court reviewed several precedents, then noted that the freedom to picket is less protected than freedom of speech.

> It has been amply recognized that picketing, not being the equivalent of speech as a matter of fact, is not its inevitable legal equivalent. Picketing is not beyond the control of a state if the manner in which the picketing is conducted or the purpose which it seeks to effectuate gives ground for its disallowance. A state is not required to tolerate in all places and circumstances, even peaceful picketing by an individual.[22]

In *Hughes,* the Court upheld California's ban on picketing.

In *Cameron,* the Court again restricted picketing. In 1964 a drive to increase voter registration of blacks was held at the courthouse in Hattiesburg, Mississippi. Blacks maintained a picket line outside the courthouse throughout the campaign. Even though the governor signed an antipicketing law, the picketing continued. When some pickets were arrested, their colleagues sought an injunction against the statute. The Supreme Court held that the statute was constitutional. First, the law was not vague—it prohibited "only picketing in such a manner as to obstruct or unreasonably interfere with free ingress or egress to and from any county courthouses." Second, the law was not overbroad—it banned "conduct subject to regulation so as to vindicate important interests in society." According to the Court, "the fact that free speech is intermingled with such conduct does not bring with it constitutional protection."[23] Third, the law was not selectively enforced—it was not designed to harass a particular group. In *Cameron*, the Court upheld the constitutionality of the Mississippi antipicketing statute.

Labor Disputes

Several cases in which the Supreme Court established picketing guidelines dealt with labor disputes. *Giboney, NLRB, International Longshoremen's Association, American Radio Association, Logan Valley Plaza, Lloyd Corporation, Hudgens,* and *PruneYard Shopping Center* fall into this category.

In the 1940s most of the retail peddlers who delivered ice door-to-door in Kansas City, Missouri, were affiliated with the American Federation of Labor. The union wanted all the peddlers to join, but most of the nonunion peddlers refused. In an attempt to break down the resistance, the AFL asked wholesale ice distributors not to sell ice to nonunion peddlers. All the distributors agreed, except for Empire Storage and Ice Company. Consequently, the union picketed the Empire building. Union truck drivers working for Empire's customers refused to deliver merchandise to and from Empire's place of business. If any of the drivers had crossed the picket line, they would have been punished by the union. This action violated Missouri antitrust law. Before the Supreme Court, AFL lawyers argued that any violation of the law was incidental to the AFL's major, legal objective—picketing to improve wages and working conditions. In *Giboney* the Supreme Court unanimously decided that labor unions did not possess "a peculiar immunity from laws against trade restraint combinations."[24] The union could not picket against a company in restraint of trade.

In the 1980 *National Labor Relations Board* case, the Court upheld a ban on picketing that encouraged consumers to boycott a secondary business. When contract negotiations between Safeco Title Insurance Company and the Retail Store Employees Union reached an impasse, company employees went on strike. The union, however, did not confine picketing to Safeco's main office, but extended its action against five local insurance companies that did business with Safeco. Upon investigation, the National Labor Relations Board determined that the five companies were neutral in the dispute. Since the picketing was "reasonably calculated to induce customers not to patronize the neutral parties," the NLRB ordered the union to cease picketing. The Supreme Court affirmed the NLRB order. A ban on "picketing that predictably encourages consumers to boycott a secondary business...imposes no impermissible restrictions upon constitutionally protected speech."[25] The ban did not violate First Amendment guarantees. Two years later the Court reinforced its position in *International Longshoremen's Association.*[26]

In *American Radio Association* the Court decided that a state, in enforcing some public policy, could constitutionally prohibit peaceful picketing. During

1971 members of the maritime unions picketed against the Liberian ship, *Aqua Glory*. The picketing publicized complaints of U.S. seamen, pertaining to the employment of foreign crewmen on foreign carriers at wages considerably lower than those paid to U.S. seamen. The picketing was effective. Longshoremen and other port workers refused to cross picket lines to load and unload the ships. Mobile Steamship Association obtained an injunction against the pickets. When the case reached the Supreme Court, the justices decided that the picketing illegally interfered with the steamship companies' business. They noted that a union official had expressed hope that the union men would refuse to cross the lines, that the port would become cluttered with ships, and that the dock would close down. According to the Court, per Justice William Rehnquist, the case involved much more than expressive conduct informing the public of injuries suffered by the seamen.

> At Mobile the picketing threatened to eliminate the 70% to 80% of the stevedores' business that depended on foreign shipping, and to cause serious losses for farmers whose agricultural crops required immediate harvesting and shipping. . . . The State may prefer these interests over petitioners' interests in conveying their "Ship American" message through the speech-plus device of dockside picketing.[27]

The justices upheld the ban on picketing—Alabama could, in the interest of a desirable public policy, seek to preserve the status quo, pending final resolution of a dispute.

In four cases decided between 1968 and 1980, the Supreme Court examined the question of whether picketing is permissible in privately owned shopping areas. The first case involved Logan Valley Plaza, a shopping-center complex located near Altoona, Pennsylvania. The shopping center was separated from adjoining roads by 12- to 15-foot wide earthen berms. In December 1965, Weis Markets opened a business in the plaza, employing only nonunion workers. Weis Markets posted a sign at the back of the building, prohibiting trespassing or soliciting by anyone other than its employees. On December 17, members of Amalgamated Food Employees Union began picketing the store. The picketers carried signs claiming that the workers were not "receiving union wages or other benefits." Logan Valley obtained a court order that enjoined the union from picketing in the storeroom, porch, parcel-pickup section, or parking areas. The order forced all picketing to be conducted along the berms beside the roads outside the shopping center. The Supreme Court overturned the order. The majority opinion, written by Justice Thurgood Marshall, noted that there was no proof that the picketing interfered with the use of the center by the general public. Furthermore, Marshall noted,

the mere fact that speech is accompanied by conduct does not mean that the
speech can be suppressed under the guise of prohibiting the conduct. Here it
is perfectly clear that the prohibition against trespass on the mall operates to
bar all speech within the shopping center.[28]

In his concurring opinion, Justice William Douglas noted: "Picketing is free
speech, *plus,* the *plus* being physical activity that may implicate traffic and related
matters. Hence, the latter aspects of picketing may be regulated." Douglas acknowledged that the provisions of the ban that prohibited picketers from inter-
fering with employees, deliverymen, and customers were proper. Those provisions, however, that make "private property a sanctuary from which some
members of the public may be excluded merely because of the ideas they es-
pouse" were illegal. In *Logan Valley* the Court concluded that trespass laws
cannot be used to exclude members of the public from exercising their First
Amendment picketing rights on premises that are freely accessible to the public.

In 1972, in *Lloyd,* the Court considered the issue again. Donald Tanner and
four colleagues distributed handbills in the mall of Lloyd Center in Portland, Oregon. The handbills announced a meeting of the "Resistance Community" to protest the draft and the Vietnam War. Since the Lloyd Center had a strict no-
handbilling regulation, security guards requested Tanner and his friends to stop.
They complied, but brought the issue before the high court. The Supreme Court's
majority opinion, written by Justice Lewis Powell, noted that Lloyd Center was
open to the public only for the purpose of doing business. The public had been
invited to shop, but there was "no open-ended invitation to the public to use the
Center for any and all purposes." Lloyd Center did not lose its private character simply because the public used the center for the purpose of carrying on business. The majority cited some distinctions to free *Lloyd* from the precedent set
by *Logan Valley.* In *Logan Valley* the picketing was directed at a specific audience and concerned the use of shopping-center property. It had been upheld
because of a lack of alternative opportunities for communicating the message to
the intended audience. The handbilling in Lloyd Center, however, was unrelated
to any activity within the center, and Tanner had adequate alternative means of
communication. The Court minority did not agree that the difference in topics—
the Vietnam War and the draft, as opposed to labor activities of a store in a shopping center—merited divergent constitutional implications. The majority, nonetheless, concluded that a privately owned shopping center had the right to prohibit
the distribution of handbills on its property, when the handbilling was unrelated
to the shopping center's operation.[29] *Lloyd* did not overrule *Logan Valley;*
rather, it stressed the differences between the two cases.

In the 1976 *Hudgens* case, the Court overruled *Logan Valley.* When strik-
ing employees of the Butler Shoe Company peacefully picketed a store in the
shopping plaza, located outside Atlanta, Georgia, the manager told them that

they could not picket within the mall or parking lot. The picketers left, but their union filed an unfair-labor-practice complaint with the National Labor Relations Board. The Supreme Court, through the opinion of Justice Potter Stewart, argued that if the young people in *Lloyd* lacked First Amendment protection to enter the shopping center to distribute handbills concerning Vietnam, then the picketers in *Hudgens* "did not have a First Amendment right to enter this shopping center for the purpose of advertising their strike against the Butler Shoe Company." The Court concluded "that under the present state of the law the constitutional guarantee of free expression has no part to play in a case such as this."[30]

In 1980 the Court heard a related case. It involved a group of high-school students who conducted a petition in the privately owned PruneYard Shopping Center in Campbell, California. The students set up a card table, from which they distributed pamphlets and asked passersby to sign a petition opposing a United Nations resolution against Zionism. A security guard informed the students that shopping-center regulations prohibited any petitioning not directly pertinent to the center's commercial purposes. The students left the premises, but initiated court action. In *PruneYard* the Supreme Court upheld a California statute that permitted citizens to exercise free speech and petition rights in a privately owned shopping center. The opinion, per Justice Rehnquist, noted key differences between *PruneYard* and *Lloyd:*

> In *Lloyd*...there was no state constitutional or statutory provision that had been construed to create rights to the use of private property by strangers, comparable to those found...here. It is, of course, well-established that a State in the exercise of its police power may adopt reasonable restrictions on private property.... *Lloyd* held that when a shopping center owner opens his private property to the public for the purpose of shopping, the First Amendment to the United States Constitution does not thereby create individual rights in expression beyond those already existing under applicable law.[31]

The California law that protected rights of expression and petition in privately owned shopping centers did not violate PruneYard's First Amendment rights.

Supreme Court cases concerned with picketing and boycotting have been reviewed in this section. *Thornhill* established the right to picket. *Claiborne Hardware Company* affirmed the right to boycott. Several subsequent cases placed rigid guidelines on that activity.

Right to Demonstrate

Throughout the 1960s mass demonstration became an effective means of petition. When the news media covered a mass demonstration, it was usually witnessed by a national audience. Such widespread coverage catapulted a grievance that affected a few people to the attention of millions. Petitioners were thus given a national forum.

In *Edwards,* a black civil-rights case, the Supreme Court recognized the right to demonstrate. On March 2, 1961, 187 black high-school and college students met at the Zion Baptist Church in Columbia, South Carolina. They walked in groups of 15 to the South Carolina statehouse grounds, where they protested current discriminatory practices against blacks. The students were met by police officers who informed the students that they could march on the grounds as long as they were peaceful. A crowd of onlookers formed, and even though the crowd did not interfere with pedestrian or vehicular traffic, the police told the students to disperse within 15 minutes, or they would be arrested. The students refused to disband. Instead, they gathered together and sang "The Star Spangled Banner" and other patriotic and religious songs, while stamping their feet and clapping their hands. After 15 minutes, they were arrested. The trial court convicted the students of disturbing the peace, and imposed sentences ranging from a $10 fine or 5 days in jail, to a $100 fine or 30 days in jail. They appealed. The Supreme Court ruled that South Carolina infringed on the rights of the protestors. First, the students had a valid complaint in what they perceived to be the discriminatory laws. Second, the students assembled peaceably. At no time was there a threat of violence on the part of the students. Police protection was always ample. Third, the students were not convicted by a precise and narrowly drawn regulatory statute. The protestors had not been arrested for violating a law regulating traffic, nor had they been arrested for violating a law defining the periods during which the statehouse grounds were open to the public. Instead, they had been arrested because "the opinions which they were peaceably expressing were sufficiently opposed to the views of the majority of the community to attract a crowd and necessitate police protection."[32] The Court concluded that a state cannot ban the peaceful expression of unpopular views. The Court reversed the convictions.

Two years later, in *Cox,* the Court reaffirmed the right to demonstrate. On December 14, 1961, 23 students from Southern University were arrested in downtown Baton Rouge for picketing stores that maintained segregated lunch counters. The next morning about 2,000 students, led by the Reverend B. Elton Cox, marched to the courthouse, where the 23 students were jailed. Police officers agreed to permit a peaceful demonstration, provided the demonstrators stayed at least 101 feet from the courthouse. The students remained across the street, an acceptable distance from the courthouse steps. They sang songs and listened to a brief speech by Cox, in which he claimed that the demonstration was a protest against the "illegal arrest" of the students. When it was lunchtime, Cox urged his audience to go out and eat, and he named the stores that had segregated lunch counters. The sheriff decided that the speech was "inflammatory," ordered the group to disperse, and used tear gas to enforce his order. Cox was arrested, charged, and convicted on three counts: "disturbing the peace," "obstructing public passages," and "court-house picketing." He appealed. The Supreme Court, first of all, considered the three offenses. The Court overturned the conviction for breach of peace. The record showed "no conduct which the State had a right to prohibit as a breach of the peace." The entire meeting was orderly and not riotous; there were no "fighting words" and there was no justifiable fear that violence was ever about to ensue. The Court also overturned the convictions for obstructing of public passages. The students had lined up across the street, thus blocking the sidewalk but not the street. The demonstration did not obstruct public passages. The Court also rejected the conviction for court-house picketing. The students had been convicted under a Louisiana statute that forbade picketing "in or near" a courthouse. In the *Cox* case, however, the students were given permission to demonstrate where they did, which was, in effect, an administrative determination that they were not "near" the courthouse. The sheriff's order to disperse could not legally revoke that determination. After rejecting the three charges, the Court examined the broader question regarding the constitutionality of the Louisiana law. The justices acknowledged that a state may vest in administrative officials the authority to regulate "the time, place, duration, or manner of use of the streets for public assemblies," if such authority is "exercised with uniformity." The Court also noted:

> It is clearly unconstitutional to enable a public official to determine which expressions of view will be permitted and which will not or to engage in invidious discrimination among persons or groups either by use of a statute providing a system of broad discretionary licensing power or, as in this case, the equivalent of such a system by selective enforcement of an extremely broad prohibitory statute.[33]

In *Cox* the Court declared the Louisiana statute to be unconstitutional.

In 1969 the right to demonstrate was reinforced in *Gregory*. Blacks in Chicago had become dissatisfied because Dr. Benjamin Willis, superintendent of Chicago's public school system, was not moving speedily enough to desegregate the public schools. A group of blacks began a march near the Chicago Loop and in an orderly fashion walked five miles to the neighborhood of Mayor Richard Daley's home. The blacks urged the mayor to remove Dr. Willis from his position. A crowd of about a thousand onlookers started shouting threats: "Goddamned nigger, get the hell out of here," and "Get out of here, niggers—go back where you belong or we will get you out of here." Cars were stopped in the streets with their horns blowing. Ku Klux Klan signs were observable, and people started singing the Alabama trooper song. Afraid that the crowd was about to erupt, the police asked march leader Dick Gregory to leave the area. Gregory refused, and was eventually convicted of breaking the Chicago disorderly-conduct law. The case reached the Supreme Court. In a brief opinion, Chief Justice Warren held that the demonstration had been orderly, and that the conduct of the marchers was protected by the First Amendment. The Chicago disorderly-conduct ordinance was too sweeping and vague. In their concurring opinion, Justices Black and Douglas reaffirmed the idea that police may not stop a peaceful demonstration simply because a hostile crowd disagrees with the protestors. Police may stop a demonstration only if there is imminent threat of violence and the police have expended all reasonable efforts to protect the demonstrators. In *Gregory* the police offered no such protection for the demonstrators. In fact, the alleged "breach of the peace" occurred when the policeman in charge determined "that the hecklers observing the march were dangerously close to rioting and that the demonstrators...were likely to be engulfed in that riot." So, he ordered Gregory to leave, and Gregory refused to do so. Black and Douglas observed: "To let a policeman's command become equivalent to a criminal statute comes dangerously near making our government one of men rather than of laws."[34] In this instance, Gregory and his followers may have been arrested simply because their behavior displeased onlookers. Such a possibility necessitated the reversal of Gregory's conviction. In *Gregory,* as in *Edwards* and *Cox,* the Court supported the right of mass demonstration.

Demonstration Guidelines

In response to the numerous demonstrations that occurred during the 1960s, cities passed new and/or invoked existing statutes in order to prevent or control mass demonstrations. These ordinances specified the conditions under which cities could resist demonstration. Several of these statutes received consideration by the Supreme Court.

In the 1966 *Adderly* case, the Court decided that the right to demonstrate did not apply when demonstrators protested against private property. About 200 students of Florida A & M University demonstrated against the prior arrest of fellow protestors. When the demonstrators blocked the jail entrance, which was used to transport prisoners from the jail to the court nearby, the sheriff notified the students that they should leave, and that any refusal to leave would result in arrest. Some students left, but the 32 demonstrators who remained were arrested and eventually convicted for trespassing upon the premises of the county jail. They appealed. The Supreme Court upheld the convictions, because the protest was lodged against a jail, traditionally closed to the public and built for security purposes. Unlike the precedent in *Edwards,* where the protest was lodged against a private building, the students in *Adderly* protested against private property, and on that ground were subject to prosecution. In a dissenting opinion, Justice Douglas argued that *Edwards* was applicable, because a jailhouse, like an executive mansion, courthouse, or statehouse, was a seat of government, "whether it be the Tower of London, the Bastille, or a small county jail. And when it houses political prisoners or those whom many think are unjustly held, it is an obvious center for protest." Douglas thought that the protest should have been viewed as a petition for the redress of grievances, rather than an incidence of trespass.[35] In *Adderly,* however, the majority upheld the convictions of students who protested against private property.

In 1972 the Court decided two cases involving demonstration in front of school buildings. The first case, *Mosley,* involved a Chicago ordinance that banned picketing within 150 feet of any elementary or secondary school, except for peaceful picketing concerning a labor dispute. Prior to the passage of the ordinance, Earl Mosley had frequently picketed Jones Commercial High School. Usually by himself, Mosley would walk on the public sidewalk next to the school, carrying a sign that read: "Jones High School practices black discrimination. Jones High School has a black quota." He was always peaceful and orderly. The day the ordinance became effective, Mosley stopped picketing, but he initiated court action, arguing that the statute punished activity protected by the First Amendment. The Supreme Court, in a unanimous opinion, held that the ordinance was unconstitutional, because it made an impermissible distinction between labor picketing and other peaceful picketing. The ordinance did not limit picketing in terms of time, place, or manner, but rather in terms of subject matter.

> The central problem with Chicago's ordinance is that it describes permissible picketing in terms of its subject matter. Peaceful picketing on the subject of a school's labor-management dispute is permitted, but all other peaceful picketing is prohibited. The operative distinction is the message on the picket sign. But, above all else, the First Amendment means that government has no power to restrict expression because of its message, its ideas, its subject matter, or its content.[36]

The Supreme Court declared the legislation unconstitutional.

The second case, *Grayned,* involved a demonstration in front of West Senior High School in Rockford, Illinois. Black students marched on the sidewalk around the school building. Many carried signs that summarized their grievances: "Black Cheerleaders to cheer too"; "Black History with black teachers"; "Equal rights, Negro counselors." There were contradictory opinions about the peacefulness of the demonstration. Officials claimed that the demonstrators baited policemen and made noise that was audible in the school, so that students were distracted from their school activities. Other witnesses claimed that the demonstrators were quiet and orderly. In any event, the demonstrators were arrested, tried, and convicted of violating two Rockford ordinances, the antipicketing and the antinoise ordinances. A $25 fine was imposed for each violation. The Supreme Court found that Rockford's antipicketing ordinance, which banned all picketing of a school building except that which related to a labor dispute, violated the equal-protection clause of the Fourteenth Amendment, for the same reasons given in *Mosley.* The conviction on this ground was reversed. The Court, however, affirmed the conviction under the antinoise ordinance, which prohibited a person from making noise that disturbed the peace or order of a school class. The Court rejected the defendant's claim that the ordinance was vague and overbroad. The Court noted that the Rockford ordinance "punishes only conduct which disrupts or is about to disrupt normal school activities." The Court also claimed:

> We recognize that the ordinance prohibits some picketing which is neither violent nor physically obstructive. Noisy demonstrations which disrupt or are incompatible with normal school activities are obviously within the ordinance's reach. Such expressive conduct may be constitutionally protected at other places or other times...but next to a school, while classes are in session, it may be

prohibited. The anti-noise ordinance imposes no such restriction on expressive activity before or after the school session, while the student/faculty "audience" enters and leaves the school.[37]

The Rockford ordinance was upheld because it restricted particular activity at a specific time and place in order to protect the school.

In 1980 the Supreme Court heard *Carey.* This case concerned an Illinois statute that prohibited picketing of residences, but exempted picketing of a place of employment involved in a labor dispute. When members of the Committee Against Racism demonstrated on the sidewalk in front of the home of Chicago Mayor Michael Bilandic, to protest his alleged failure to support school busing, they were arrested and eventually convicted. They appealed. The Court opinion, written by Justice William Brennan, pointed to the similarity between the Illinois statute and that found unconstitutional in *Mosley.*

> Nor can it be seriously disputed that in exempting from its general prohibition only the "peaceful picketing of a place of employment involved in a labor dispute," the Illinois statute discriminates between lawful and unlawful conduct based upon the content of the demonstrator's communication. On its face, the act accords preferential treatment to the expression of views on one particular subject; information about labor disputes may be freely disseminated, but discussion of all other issues is restricted. The permissibility of residential picketing under the Illinois statute is thus dependent solely on the nature of the message being conveyed. In these critical respects, then, the Illinois statute is identical to the ordinance in *Mosley,* and it suffers from the same constitutional infirmities.[38]

In the *Walker* case the Court faced another issue—were demonstrators required to obey an injunction when the ordinance upon which it was based was unconstitutional? During the spring of 1963, sit-ins and marches were conducted by the black community to protest discrimination in Birmingham, Alabama. City officials complained that the demonstrators had trespassed upon private property, picketed private places of business, congregated in mobs, and that these activities had caused an undue strain upon the police power of Birmingham. A circuit court granted a temporary injunction enjoining the leaders of the demonstrations from encouraging parades without a permit. The leaders applied for a permit, but City Commissioner Eugene "Bull" Conner categorically refused the request. Subsequently, demonstrations were held without any attempt to dissolve the injunction. Eight black ministers were arrested and held in contempt for leading the marches. They were sentenced to five days in jail and a $50 fine. They appealed, contending that the Birmingham law was unconstitutional; permission to demonstrate depended upon city administrators who had made it clear no permission would be granted. The Supreme Court affirmed the convictions, noting that initial obedience is required of an unconstitutional court decree, like the injunction in *Walker,* even though obedience is not required of an unconstitutional ordinance, as the Court had noted in *Poulos.*[39] The opinion, prepared by Justice Stewart, claimed:

> In the fair administration of justice no man can be judge in his own case, however exalted his station, however righteous his motives, and irrespective of his race, color, politics, or religon. This Court cannot hold that the petitioners were constitutionally free to ignore all the procedures of the law and carry their battle to the streets. One may sympathize with the petitioners' impatient commitment to their cause. But respect for judicial process is a small price to pay for the civilizing hand of law, which alone can give abiding meaning to constitutional freedom.[40]

The Court concluded that a court order, even if almost certain to be reversed on appeal, must be obeyed until the order is set aside by a higher court.

Eventually, in *Shuttlesworth,* the Birmingham ordinance was declared unconstitutional. On Good Friday afternoon in 1963, Reverend Fred Shuttlesworth led about 50 demonstrators along city streets to protest denial of civil rights to blacks in Birmingham. The marchers did not interfere with pedestrians, nor did the traffic suffer any inconvenience. After four blocks, the marchers were stopped and arrested by police for violating the Birmingham ordinance. Shuttlesworth was convicted and sentenced to 90 days in prison at hard labor, and an additional 48 days for failing to pay a $75 fine. He appealed. The Supreme Court stressed that picketing and parading are means of expression that are entitled to First Amendment protection. The Birmingham ordinance violated those freedoms. The ordinance subjected "the exercise of First Amendment freedoms to the prior restraint of a license, without narrow, objective, and definitive standards to guide the licensing authority." Shuttlesworth had complied with the ordinance in that he asked for a permit to picket and indicated the sidewalks where picketing would occur. The request was denied; Commissioner Conner made it clear that under no circumstances would the group be allowed to demonstrate in Birmingham. In *Shuttlesworth,* the Supreme Court found the Birmingham ordinance to be unconstitutional as a form of prior restraint that lacked ascertainable standards for granting permits.[41]

In *Carrol* the Court considered whether a city has the authority to ban a demonstration without granting a hearing to the demonstrators. On July 6, 1966, the National States Rights party, a white supremacist organization, conducted a rally near the courthouse of Princess Anne, Maryland. Public speakers, amplified so that they could be heard for several blocks, insulted blacks and Jews. State policemen were brought in when the crowd became tense. The rally eventually broke up, but another gathering was scheduled for the following evening. The Princess Anne commissioners obtained a ten-day restraining order to prevent the rally. Joseph Carroll, on behalf of the party, sought Supreme Court review of the order. The Court held the injunction unconstitutional. The proceedings that initially set up the injunction were *ex parte;* no notice was given to the States Rights party to appear. The *Carroll* decision held that *ex parte* orders restraining demonstrations are unconstitutional when it is possible to provide an opportunity for notice and hearing to the demonstrating group, but no such opportunity is provided. In this case, officials were able, but not willing, to notify Carroll of the hearing on the injunction.[42]

In *Skokie* a divided Court weighed the issue of immediacy in granting appellate review. On April 29, 1977, the Circuit Court of Cook County, Illinois, prohibited the National Socialist Party of America from performing any of the following actions within the predominantly Jewish village of Skokie: marching, walking, or parading in the uniform of the National Socialist Party of America; displaying the swastika on or off their persons; distributing pamphlets that incite or promote hatred against persons of Jewish faith or ancestry or hatred against persons of any faith or ancestry, race, or religon. The party sued. The Supreme Court decided that the injunction deprived the marchers of First Amendment rights during the period of appellate review, which could take a year or more to complete. When a state imposes a restraint of this kind, "it must provide strict procedural safeguards, including immediate appellate review."[43] In *Skokie,* the court injunction, by failing to provide for such review, was unconstitutional.

In *Community For Creative Non-Violence,* the Court considered whether a National Park Service regulation prohibiting camping in certain parks violated the First Amendment. The case arose when the Community For Creative Non-Violence conducted a demonstration in Lafayette Park in downtown Washington, D.C. The group gathered to demonstrate the plight of the homeless. It had obtained a permit authorizing the erection of two symbolic tent cities, as a means of expressing their point of view. The Park Service, however, cited the anticamping regulation in denying the group's request that demonstrators be permitted to sleep in the tents. The group initiated court action. Eventually, the Supreme Court heard the case and upheld the ban. The opinion, written by Justice Byron White, maintained:

> We have difficulty, therefore, in understanding why the prohibition against camping, with its ban on sleeping overnight, is not a reasonable time, place, and manner regulation that withstands constitutional scrutiny. Surely the regulation is not unconstitutional on its face. None of its provisions appears unrelated to the ends that it was designed to serve. Nor is it any less valid when applied to prevent camping in Memorial-core parks by those who wish to demonstrate and deliver a message to the public and the central government. Damage to the parks as well as their partial inaccessibility to other members of the public can easily result from camping by demonstrators as by non-demonstrators. In nei-

ther case must the Government tolerate it. All those who would resort to the parks must abide by otherwise valid rules for their use, just as they must observe the traffic laws, sanitation regulations, and laws to preserve the public peace. This is no more than a reaffirmation that reasonable time, place, and manner restrictions on expression are constitutionally acceptable.[44]

In *Community For Creative Non-Violence* the Court maintained that a federal regulation prohibiting camping in certain parks did not violate First Amendment rights when applied to prohibit demonstrators from sleeping in a park.

Summary

The Supreme Court has rendered numerous decisions that relate to picketing, boycotting, and demonstrations. *Thornhill* clearly established that there is a right to picket. *Claiborne Hardware Company* acknowledged a right to boycott. Subsequent cases limited those rights. In *Hughes* and *Cameron,* the Court upheld properly drawn statutes—that is, laws that were not vague, laws that regulated time, place, and manner of picketing, and laws that were not designed to harass a particular group. In *Giboney* the Court denied a union the right to picket a company in restraint of trade. *National Labor Relations Board* upheld the prohibition of picketing that encouraged consumers to boycott a secondary business; this opinion was reaffirmed in *International Longshoremen's Association.* In *American Radio Association,* the Court allowed Alabama to enjoin peaceful picketing in order to enforce a public policy. And in *Lloyd* and *Hudgens,* the Court set aside *Logan Valley* by denying public picketing in privately owned shopping centers. *PruneYard Shopping Center,* however, upheld the power of a state to protect free speech on privately owned shopping centers. Overall, the right to picket exists, but under considerable restriction.

The Court has also established guidelines concerning demonstration. In *Edwards* the Court acknowledged the right to demonstrate. In *Cox* and *Gregory* the Court affirmed the right to demonstrate, by overturning state ordinances that treated breach of peace in a broad and sweeping fashion. *Mosley* established, and *Grayned* and *Carey* affirmed, that a state may not limit picketing on the basis of subject matter. *Shuttlesworth* involved an ordinance that functioned as a prior restraint and lacked ascertainable standards for granting permits. The Court struck down the ordinance and acknowledged the right to demonstrate. In several cases, however, the Court limited the conditions under which demonstration is permissible. In *Adderley,* the Court decided that demonstrations enjoyed less protection on private property than on public property. The *Grayned* decision placed restrictions on noisy demonstrations near a school while class is in session. *Walker* stipulated that an unfairly levied injunction must be obeyed. *Carroll* confirmed the right of demonstrators to a hearing. In *Skokie* the Court ruled that when a state restrains a march, strict procedural safeguards, including immediate appellate review, must be provided. In *Community For Creative Non-Violence,* the Court upheld a federal regulation that prevented demonstrators from camping in certain national parks, even though the act of camping was intended to call attention symbolically to the point of the demonstration. The right to demonstrate is clearly established, but within limitations established by the Court.

NOTES

1. De Tocqueville, Alexis, *Democracy in America* (ed. by Phillips Bradley), New York: Vintage Books, 1945, p. 198.

2. *Brown v. Board of Education of Topeka, Shawnee County, Kansas,* 74 S.Ct. 686 (1954).

3. *National Association For The Advancement of Colored People v. Alabama,* 78 S.Ct. 1163 (1958).

4. *Bates v. City of Little Rock,* 80 S.Ct. 412 (1960).

5. *Gibson v. Florida Legislative Investigation Committee,* 83 S.Ct. 889 (1963).

6. *Cantwell v. Connecticut,* 60 S.Ct. 900 (1940).

7. *Thomas v. Collins,* 65 S.Ct. 315 (1945).

8. *Staub v. Baxley,* 78 S.Ct. 277 (1958).

9. *Hague v. Committee for Industrial Organization,* 59 S.Ct. 954 (1939).

10. *Cox v. New Hampshire,* 61 S.Ct. 762 (1941).

11. *Kunz v. New York,* 71 S.Ct. 312 (1951).

12. *Niemotko v. Maryland,* 71 S.Ct. 325 (1951).

13. *Poulos v. New Hampshire,* 73 S.Ct. 760 (1953).

14. *Korematsu v. United States,* 65 S.Ct. 193 (1944).

15. *Communist Party v. Subversive Activities Control Board,* 81 S.Ct. 1357 (1961).

16. *Konigsberg v. State Bar of California,* 81 S.Ct. 997 (1961).

17. *Baird v. State Bar of Arizona,* 91 S.Ct. 702 (1971).

18. *United States v. Robel,* 88 S.Ct. 419 (1967).

19. *Communist Party of Indiana v. Whitcomb,* 94 S.Ct. 656 (1974).

20. *Thornhill v. Alabama,* 60 S.Ct. 736 (1940).

21. *National Association For the Advancement of Colored People v. Claiborne Hardware Company,* 102 S.Ct. 3409 (1982).

22. *Hughes v. Superior Court of State of California in and for Costra County,* 70 S.Ct. 718 (1950).

23. *Cameron v. Johnson,* 88 S.Ct. 1335 (1968).

24. *Giboney v. Empire Storage and Ice Company,* 69 S.Ct. 684 (1949).

25. *National Labor Relations Board v. Retail Store Employees Union, Local 1001,* 100 S.Ct. 2372 (1980).

26. *International Longshoremen's Association, AFL-CIO v. Allied International, Inc.,* 102 S.Ct. 1656 (1982).

27. *American Radio Association, AFL-CIO v. Mobile Steamship Association,* 95 S.Ct. 409 (1974).

28. *Amalgamated Food Employees Union Local 590 v. Logan Valley Plaza,* 88 S.Ct. 1601 (1968).

29. *Lloyd Corp., Limited v. Tanner,* 92 S.Ct. 2219 (1972).

30. *Hugdens v. National Labor Relations Board,* 96 S.Ct. 1029 (1976).

31. *PruneYard Shopping Center v. Robins,* 100 S.Ct. 2035 (1980).
32. *Edwards v. South Carolina,* 83 S.Ct. 680 (1963).
33. *Cox v. Louisiana,* 85 S.Ct. 453, 466, 476 (1965).
34. *Gregory v. Chicago,* 89 S.Ct. 946 (1969).
35. *Adderley v. Florida,* 87 S.Ct. 242 (1966).
36. *Police Department of Chicago v. Mosley,* 92 S.Ct. 2286 (1972).
37. *Grayned v. City of Rockford,* 92 S.Ct. 2294 (1972).
38. *Carey v. Brown,* 100 S.Ct. 2286 (1980).
39. *Poulos.*
40. *Walker v. Birmingham,* 87 S.Ct. 1824 (1967).
41. *Shuttlesworth v. Birmingham,* 89 S.Ct. 935 (1969).
42. *Carroll v. President and Commissioners of Princess Anne County,* 89 S.Ct. 347 (1968).
43. *National Socialist Party of America v. Village of Skokie,* 97 S.Ct. 2205 (1977).
44. *Clark v. Community for Creative Non-Violence,* 104 S.Ct. 3065 (1984).

RECOMMENDED READING

Fellman, David, *The Constitutional Right of Association.* Chicago: University of Chicago Press, 1963.

Fellman, David, "Constitutional Rights of Association," *Supreme Court Review* (1961), 74-134.

Haiman, Franklyn S., "Nonverbal Communication and the First Amendment: The Rhetoric of the Streets Revisited," *Quarterly Journal of Speech* 68 (November, 1982), 371-83.

Haiman, Franklyn S., " The Rhetoric of the Streets: Some Legal and Ethical Considerations," *Quarterly Journal of Speech* 53 (April, 1967), 99-114.

Kalven, Jr., Harry, *The Negro and the First Amendment.* Chicago: University of Chicago Press, 1965.

Konvitz, Milton R., *Expanding Liberties: Freedom's Gains in Postwar America.* New York: Viking Press, 1966.

Lambeth, Evelyn J., *"Hudgens v. NLRB:* A Final Definition of the Public Forum?" *Wake Forest Law Review* 13 (Spring, 1977), 139-59.

McCauley, James M, "Transforming The Privately Owned Shopping Center into a Public Forum: *PruneYard Shopping Center v. Robins,"* *University of Richmond Law Review* 15 (Spring, 1981), 699-722.

Peterson, Hillary Anne, "Federal Courts Invalidate Attempts by Town to Restrict Nazi Demonstration through Permit and Speech Content Ordinance," *Suffolk University Law Review* 13 (Winter, 1979), 138-49.

KEY DECISIONS

1939—*HAGUE*—upheld the right of a group to assemble publicly, so long as the meeting is peaceful.

1940—*CANTWELL*—supported the right of an organization to solicit members.

1940—*THORNHILL*—determined that picketing enjoyed First Amendment protection.

1958—*NAACP*—acknowledged that an organization has the right to protect membership lists on behalf of the private interests of its members.

1963—*EDWARDS*—acknowledged the right of demonstration.

1966—*ADDERLEY*—denied demonstrations directed against private property.

1972—*MOSLEY*—overturned an ordinance that restricted picketing in terms of subject matter, rather than in terms of time, place, or manner.

1976—*HUDGENS*—denied public picketing in privately owned shopping centers.

1977—*SKOKIE*—held that when a state restrains a gathering, strict procedural safeguards, including immediate appellate review, must be provided.

1982—*CLAIBORNE HARDWARE*—acknowledged that boycotting enjoyed First Amendment protection.

SUMMARY—LAW OF ASSOCIATION

Definition

The law of association is designed to specify the freedoms and limitations surrounding such activities as assembly, petition, picketing, and demonstration.

Proof

In order to establish a violation of the law of association, a municipality must demonstrate either of the following:
1. The association violated a legally constructed ordinance.
2. The association caused a breach of the peace—that is, the association interfered with public comfort, convenience, peace, or order.

Defenses

A group may successfully contest a charge of violating the law of association by demonstrating:

1. Statutory flaws:
    a. Vagueness—law fails to define the activities that are banned.
    b. Overbreadth—law bans activities that are protected by the First Amendment.
    c. Discrimination—all groups are not provided equal protection under the law.
    d. Arbitrariness—granting or withholding of permission is left to the discretion of an official.
    e. Content orientation—law controls subject matter rather than time, place, or manner.
    f. Guilt by association—ordinance bans association without regard for the quality of the association.
2. Failure to provide alternative location for meeting—group must have a means of enjoying First Amendment rights.
3. Denial of due process—a group is entitled to:
    a. Immediate appellate review
    b. Notice of any hearing to be held concerning the denial of associational rights.

4

ACADEMIC FREEDOM

Sidney Hook defines academic freedom as "the freedom of professionally qualified persons to inquire, discover, publish, and teach the truth as they see it in the field of their competence." This freedom "is subject to no control or authority except the control or authority of the rational methods by which truths or conclusions are sought and established in these disciplines."[1] Hook's concept emphasizes the rights of faculty members. Academic freedom, however, also concerns the interests of administrators, legislators, school boards, parents, and students. At times these interests are in competition, and resolution of the conflict is left to the courts.

ADMINISTRATION RIGHTS

Over the years, various groups have attempted to influence classroom curricula, methods, materials, and activities. Such endeavors have been evaluated by the Supreme Court, and as a result, a body of case law has emerged that establishes guidelines regarding the rights and responsibilities of school administrators.

Curriculum

The curriculum includes all the subject matter offered by an educational institution. Some attempts to control the curriculum have reached the Supreme Court. Two of the earliest efforts involved the teaching of a foreign language and the use of a textbook that explained the theory of evolution.

Foreign Language

Following World War I, Nebraska passed a law banning the teaching of any elementary classroom subject in a language other than English. Robert Meyer, an instructor at Zion Parochial School, was convicted under this law for teaching his class in German. He appealed. In *Meyer* the Supreme Court determined that a state may not forbid the teaching of subjects that are not injurious to the health or morals of children. The Court ruled that mere knowledge of the German language was not harmful, that perhaps it was even desirable. The United States contained a large foreign-born population, residing in localities that routinely used foreign languages. Students could be hindered in achieving their maximum usefulness as citizens in their communities, if they were deprived of the use of a foreign language. The Court found the Nebraska law unconstitutional, since it violated the teacher's right to instruct and the parents' right to hire a teacher for their children.[2] Later that year the Court declared similar ordinances unlawful in Iowa and Ohio.[3]

Evolution

In 1925 Tennessee passed a law that forbade the teaching of Darwin's theory of evolution. The constitutionality of the act was upheld in *Scopes.*[4] In 1928 Arkansas adopted a similar law, which specified that any teacher who promoted Darwinism faced dismissal from his or her position. This law was challenged in *Epperson,* a 1968 case that concerned selection of a biology textbook. The text that had been used for decades at Little Rock Central High School did not contain a section on the Darwinian theory. Then, in 1965, acting upon the recommendation of the biology teachers, the administration adopted a text that set forth such a concept of evolution. Susan Epperson, a tenth-grade biology teacher, faced a dilemma. She was instructed to use the new book by school officials, but to do so could subject her to dismissal. Epperson instituted court action to determine whether the Arkansas statute was illegal. The Supreme Court unanimously declared the statute to be unconstitutional. According to the Court, the First Amendment's command was to protect the fundamental rights of free speech and inquiry, which are nowhere more vital than in the educational system. The Arkansas law prevented teachers from discussing the theory of evolution. It thereby hindered the quest for knowledge and restrained the freedom to teach.[5]

School Rituals

Two school rituals that were practiced frequently, in some instances daily, until the mid-twentieth century were the flag salute and prayer. During the 1940s the Supreme Court first upheld, then overturned the flag-salute ritual. Two decades later the Court declared that school-prayer exercises violated the Constitution.

Flag Salute

Lillian and William Gobitis were expelled from the Minersville, Pennsylvania, public school for refusing to pledge allegiance to the U.S. flag as part of a daily school ritual. The Gobitis children, as Jehovah's Witnesses, had been raised to believe that saluting any flag was forbidden by the Bible. Walter Gobitis, their father, initiated suit to stop the school from requiring participation in the flag salute. The Supreme Court weighed the freedom of conscience versus the power of school authorities. After deliberation, the Court upheld the authority of the administrators, who claimed that the flag salute was an effective means of promoting patriotism. The justices thought that granting to dissidents an exemption from the flag salute "might introduce elements of difficulty into the school discipline," and "might cast doubts in the minds of other children which would themselves weaken the effect of the exercise."[6] In *Gobitis* the Court approved the flag salute as a required ritual.

Three years later, in *Barnette,* the Court found a flag-salute statute to be unconstitutional. The case concerned a 1942 West Virginia Board of Education regulation that required that the flag salute become "a regular part of the program of activities in the public schools." The board declared that any student who failed to comply with the policy would be expelled, and the child's parents would be legally prosecuted. A group of Jehovah's Witnesses refused to salute the flag and was expelled from school. Their parents were prosecuted. Ultimately, the case reached the Supreme Court. The opinion, written by Justice Robert Jackson, stressed four differences between this case and *Gobitis.* First, in *Gobitis,* the Court supported the notion that a government must necessarily be stronger than the liberties of its people. In *Barnette,* the Court preferred individual freedom of mind over officially disciplined uniformity. Second, in *Gobitis,* the Court thought that to interfere with educational decisions would make the Supreme Court the school board for the nation. In *Barnette* the Court acknowledged that while boards of education have vital functions, none may be performed in violation of the Constitution. Third, in *Gobitis,* the justices reasoned that the Court had no competence in the field of education and that the controlling influence should rest with legislatures and the public. In *Barnette* the Court ruled that the rights of free speech and press are not subject to political debate or public votes. Fourth, *Gobitis* supported the view that "national unity is the basis of national security," and that school authorities have a right to decide how to attain that unity. In *Barnette* the Court did not challenge the right of officials to try to instill national unity, but they questioned whether a compulsory flag salute was an appropriate means of doing so. According to the Court, "to believe that patriotism will not flourish if patriotic ceremonies are voluntary and spontaneous instead of a compulsory routine is to make an unflattering estimate of the appeal of our institutions to free minds."[7] In *Barnette* the Court set aside the mandatory flag-salute exercise.

Prayer

The school-prayer issue came before the U.S. Supreme Court in 1962. Several parents initiated court action when the Board of Education of Union Free School District No. 9, New Hyde Park, New York, required a prayer composed by the New York Board of Regents to be said aloud at the beginning of every school day. The prayer was as follows: "Almighty God, we acknowledge our dependence upon Thee, and we beg Thy blessing upon us, our parents, our teachers, and our country." In *Engel* the Supreme Court decided that the school system's encouragement of the prayer contradicted the establishment clause of the First Amendment. Recital of a prayer was a religious activity; this prayer activity constituted an establishment. The majority of the Court, per Justice Hugo Black, ruled that it was not antireligious to order the government to refrain from writing official prayers.[8] That sort of activity should be left to the people or to their ministers.

A year later, in *Schempp* and *Murray,* the Court faced the issue again. Consistent with Pennsylvania law, Abington High School held religious exercises at the start of each school day. A student would read from the Bible ten verses that he or she had selected. This was followed by a recitation of the Lord's Prayer. Participation in the exercises was voluntary; students could leave the room if they wanted, or they could remain in the room and not participate. The Edward Schempp family, members of the Unitarian Church, brought the issue before the courts, arguing that the exercise contradicted their religious beliefs. Schempp considered having his children excused from the exercises, but decided against it, because he thought that the relationship between his children and their teachers would be adversely affected. *Schempp* came to the Supreme Court. *Murray* was a companion case. It involved a Baltimore Board of School Commissioners' rule that religious services—the reading of a chapter in the Bible and/or use of the Lord's Prayer—be held at the beginning of the school day. Madalyn Murray and her son, both atheists, brought suit. Murray argued that the exercise threatened their religious freedom "by placing a premium on belief as against nonbelief" and subjected their "freedom of conscience to the rule of the majority." Espousal of a belief in God as the basis for all moral and spiritual values rendered the Murrays' beliefs "sinister, alien, and suspect," and tended to question "their morality, good citizenship and good faith." In *Schempp* and *Murray* the Supreme Court ruled that both the establishment and the free-exercise clauses of the Constitution had been violated. In both cases the challenged law required the reading of religious prayers at the beginning of the school day. These exercises were held in a school building under the supervision of teachers. The Court decided that such an exercise was indeed a religious ceremony, and violated the establishment clause. The free-exercise clause prohibits laws that deny the right of free exercise to anyone, but it also forbids a majority to use legislative machinery to practice their beliefs.[9]

In 1981 the Court reinforced this line of thinkng in the *Stone* case. The case involved a Kentucky statute that required the posting of a copy of the Ten Commandments on the wall of each public classroom in the state. James Graham, superintendent of public instruction in Kentucky, justified the posting on two grounds. First, he claimed that the purpose of the posting was secular. The Supreme Court disagreed.

> The pre-eminent purpose for posting the Ten Commandments on schoolroom walls is plainly religious in nature. The Ten Commandments are undeniably a sacred text in the Jewish and Christian faiths, and no legislative recitation of a supposed secular purpose can blind us to that fact. The Commandments do not confine themselves to arguably secular matters, such as honoring one's parents, killing or murder, adultery, stealing, false witness, and covetousness. Rather, the first part of the Commandments concerns the religious duties of believers: worshipping the Lord God alone, avoiding idolatry, not using the Lord's name in vain, and observing the Sabbath Day.[10]

Second, Graham pointed out that the posted copies of the Ten Commandments were financed by voluntary private contributions. According to the Court, that did not justify the posting. The practice violated the establishment clause of the First Amendment. In *Stone,* as in *Schempp, Murray,* and *Engel,* the Court supported the right of each individual to choose his or her own religious exercise, free of state compulsion.

Teacher Fitness

In several states, special committees have been formed to establish standards for judging teacher fitness. In numerous cases, the Supreme Court has been called upon to evaluate punitive actions taken against teachers who have refused to testify before an investigative committee, held membership in certain organizations, or refused to take an oath of loyalty.

Refusal to Testify

In 1956 the Supreme Court heard the *Slochower* case. According to a New York City law, a city employee could be fired for invoking the Fifth Amendment privilege to avoid answering a question related to his or her employment behavior. Harry Slochower, an associate professor of German at Brooklyn College, was called to testify before the Internal Security Subcommittee of the U.S. Senate. When he refused to answer some questions about his associations on the ground that his answers might be self-incriminating, Slochower was suspended and his position declared vacant. He brought suit. The Supreme Court ruled for Slochower, noting that summary dismissal denied due process of law. The New

York law was unconstitutional, because it translated an employee's claim of Fifth Amendment privilege "into a conclusive presumption of guilt."[11] The Court acknowledged, however, that New York had broad powers in the hiring and firing of its employees. It might have been shown, after a proper inquiry, that Slochower's continued employment would impede the interests of the state. In *Slochower* no such investigation was held. Accordingly, New York's action against Slochower was overturned.

A related case, *Beilan,* involved a teacher with 22 years of service in the Philadelphia public-school system. Herman Beilan was called to the superintendent's office and asked whether he had been an officer in the Communist party; the superintendent stressed that he was investigating "a real question of the fitness of Beilan to be a teacher." When Beilan refused to answer, the school board dismissed him for "incompetency." He appealed. The Supreme Court determined that the questions asked by the superintendent were relevant to the issue of teacher fitness. When Beilan accepted the teaching position, he had agreed to be cooperative in answering questions related to his fitness to teach. The Court concluded that Beilan was removed from his job, not for his Fifth Amendment claim or his membership in the Communist party, but because his refusal to answer questions constituted evidence of unreliability and incompetency.[12] In both *Slochower* and *Beilan* the Court affirmed the power of authorities to inquire into a teacher's fitness. In *Slochower* administrative action was overturned, because dismissal occurred without a proper investigation. In both decisions, however, while the Court opposed penalizing a teacher for merely invoking the Fifth Amendment, it did not prohibit efforts to investigate teacher fitness.

Membership

Teacher fitness was also evaluated in terms of membership in certain organizations. For instance, the New York Feinberg law required that the Board of Regents prepare a list of all organizations that advocated overthrow of the government by force or violence. Membership in a listed organization constituted *prima facie* evidence for disqualification from holding a teaching position in New York schools. In *Adler* the Supreme Court considered the constitutionality of this statute. According to the Court, if teachers did not choose to work on the reasonable terms laid down by New York authorities, they were free to retain their associations, and go elsewhere. Justice Sherman Minton's opinion upheld the right of New York to oversee the associational habits of teachers.

> A teacher works in a sensitive area in a school room. There he shapes the attitude of young minds towards the society in which they live. In this, the state has a vital concern. It must preserve the integrity of the schools. That the school authorities have the right and the duty to screen the officials, teachers, and em-

ployees as to their fitness to maintain the integrity of the schools as a party of ordered society cannot be doubted.[13]

A similar case, *Wieman,* involved an Oklahoma law that required state employees to take an oath that they were not members of the Communist party or of any organization that advocated the overthrow of the government. Under the Oklahoma statute, the fact of membership alone disqualified a teacher from employment. Some faculty members at Oklahoma Agricultural and Mechanical College refused to take the oath. Paul Updegraff, a taxpaying citizen, filed suit to prevent the college from paying any faculty who had not taken the oath. The Supreme Court found the Oklahoma law unconstitutional for two reasons. First, membership could be innocent—a person might join a forbidden organization unaware of its purposes. Second, a group might be innocent at the time it was formed and might later adopt illegitimate ends. Conversely, an organization that was formerly subversive might subsequently reject such influences. The Court found the oath denied due process, because "the fact of association alone determines disloyalty and disqualification; it matters not whether association existed innocently or knowingly."[14]

The *Shelton* case involved an Arkansas law that compelled teachers to file annually a list of organizations to which they belonged during the previous five years. B. T. Shelton, a teacher in the Little Rock school district for 25 years, declined to submit the list. His contract for the next school year was not renewed. Shelton initiated court action, which ultimately reached the high court. Citing *Adler,* the Court affirmed that "there can be no doubt of the right of a state to investigate the competence and fitness of those whom it hires to teach in its schools." The Court found, however, that the Arkansas law was "unlimited and indiscriminate," in that it required a teacher to list "every conceivable kind of associational tie—social, professional, political, avocational, or religious," many of which might "have no possible bearing upon the teacher's occupational competence or fitness." In *Shelton* the Court held the law unconstitutional because its "comprehensive interference with associational freedom" went beyond what could be justified in the exercise of a state's "inquiry into the fitness and competency of its teachers."[15]

Loyalty Oaths

During the 1960s, the Supreme Court struck down several statutes that established loyalty oaths as a measure of teacher fitness. One such statute involved a Florida law requiring state employees to swear that they had never lent their "aid, support, advice, counsel or influence to the Communist Party." After David Cramp had been employed for nine years as a public-school teacher, it was discovered that he had never taken the oath. When requested to do so, he challenged the constitutionality of the oath requirement before the Supreme Court. The Court noted that those who took the oath had to swear that they had never lent their "aid," or "support," or "counsel," or "influence," to the Communist party. The Court questioned the vagueness of the terms.

> What do these phrases mean? In the not too distant past the Communist Party candidates appeared regularly and legally on the ballot in many state and local elections. Elsewhere the Communist Party has on occasion endorsed or supported candidates nominated by others. Could one who had ever cast his vote for such a candidate safely subscribe to this oath? Could a lawyer who had ever represented the Communist Party or its members swear with either confidence or honesty that he had never knowingly lent his "counsel" to the Party? Could a journalist who had ever defended the constitutional rights of the Communist Party conscientiously take an oath that he had never lent the Party his "support?": Indeed, could anyone honestly subscribe to this oath who had ever supported any cause with contemporaneous knowledge that the Communist Party also supported it?[16]

In *Cramp* the Court found the language of the act unconstitutionally vague.

A similar case, *Baggett,* came before the Court in 1964. All teachers at the University of Washington were required by the Board of Regents to swear allegiance to the laws of the United States and of the state of Washington. Teachers also had to disclaim membership in the Communist party or any other subversive organization. Lawrence Baggett and 63 other members of the faculty, staff, and student body pursued court action. In *Baggett* the Supreme Court declared the loyalty oath unconstitutional because the language of the statute was unduly vague, uncertain, and broad.[17] The statute was subject to the same type of objection posed by the Court in *Cramp*.

In the 1967 *Keyishian* case, the Court again evaluated the New York Feinberg law—a law that the Court had supported in *Adler*. The law required teachers to sign a certificate indicating that they were not Communists, and that if they had ever been, they had communicated that fact to their administrators. Harry Keyishian, an English instructor at the State University of Buffalo, refused to sign the certificate. When his contract was not renewed, Keyishian initiated action in the courts. The Supreme Court, per Justice William Brennan, found the New York law to be overly broad, since dismissal was based on mere membership without any showing of a teacher's intent to further the unlawful aims of the Communist party. Clearly, New York's intent was to keep subversives out of the teaching ranks; but the loyalty-oath procedure stifled personal liberties and posed potential harm to academic freedom.

> The classroom is peculiarly the "marketplace of ideas." The Nation's future depends upon leaders trained through wide exposure to that robust exchange of ideas which discovers truth "out of a multitude of tongues [rather] than through any kind of authoritative selection."[18]

Whitehill involved a Maryland loyalty oath. Howard Whitehill was offered a faculty position at the University of Maryland. He refused, however, to take a required oath pledging that he was "not engaged in one way or another in the attempt to overthrow the Government of the United States, or the State of Maryland, or any political subdivision of either of them, by force or violence." The question of this oath's constitutionality reached the Supreme Court. The majority opinion, per Justice William Douglas, noted the ambiguity of the act.

> Would a member of a group that was out to overthrow the Government by force or violence be engaged in that attempt 'in one way or another' within the meaning of the oath, even though he was ignorant of the real aims of the group and wholly innocent of any illicit purpose? We do not know; nor could a prospective employee know, save as he risked a prosecution for perjury.[19]

The Court decided that "the continuing surveillance which this type of law places on teachers is hostile to academic freedom," and overturned the Maryland loyalty-oath requirement.

In the cases cited in this section, the Court supported the general right of a legislature to inquire into the fitness of public-school teachers, but it has been strict concerning the procedures such tests of fitness may follow. In *Slochower* and *Beilan,* the Court opposed penalizing a teacher for merely invoking the Fifth Amendment. In *Wieman* an Oklahoma law was judged to violate due process, because it did not recognize that association with a subversive organization might be innocent. In *Shelton* an Arkansas law was declared unconstitutional, because it required a teacher to reveal associational ties that might have no bearing whatsoever upon a teacher's fitness. In *Cramp, Baggett, Keyishian,* and *Whitehill,* the Court overturned mandatory loyalty oaths because of a notable obscurity in the wording of such oaths. It seems clear, however, that the Supreme Court would uphold inquiry into teacher fitness if conducted in a legal manner—that is, without ambiguity, discrimination, or overbreadth.

Campus Speakers

During the late 1960s and early 1970s, state courts heard numerous cases that involved campus bans on outside speakers. In several cases—*Dickson,*[20] *Stacy,*[21] *Molpus,*[22] *Brooks,*[23] *Duke*[24]—courts overturned outside-speaker regulations that were vague or overbroad, stressing that any regulations must be precise. The courts rejected any system of prior restraint and any denial of speech that were not based on proof of danger to the orderly operation of the university.

Stacy provides a good example, because the court formulated specific guidelines that a university administration might follow in regulating campus speakers. The case involved a challenge of the University of Mississippi's speaker-ban policy. In *Stacy* the court emphasized that even though the freedoms of speech and assembly occupy a "preferred position" among constitutional liberties, they

"may not be exercised on public property without regard to its primary usage."
The judges acknowledged that the board of trustees had rule-making power, but
noted that the power had been improperly exercised in phrasing the speaker-ban
policy. The court then designed a set of six rules that would govern campus-
speaker policy at the University of Mississippi until such time as the board would
formulate acceptable standards: (1) any request had to be made by a bona fide
student or faculty group; (2) no invitation could be sent without prior written
permission from the head of the school; (3) any request had to include, in writing, the name of the sponsoring group, the proposed date, time, and location,
the expected size of the audience, and the topic of the speech; (4) a request could
be denied by the head of an institution only if the proposed speech would constitute a clear and present danger to orderly operation; (5) a campus review committee, composed of three faculty and two students, would hear the appeal of
an aggrieved sponsoring group—further appeal could be sought through the
courts; and (6) upon approval of the speaker, the sponsoring organization had
to submit a written report indicating whether, and when, the invitation was accepted.[25] In later state cases, the *Stacy* standards were used as a model to test
the acceptability of campus-speaker regulations.

None of the cases mentioned in this section came before the U.S. Supreme
Court. The state courts, however, by consistently overturning campus-speaker
regulations that were vague and overbroad, strengthened freedom of expression
and association at colleges and universities.

Banned Books

In recent decades, groups have attempted to prohibit certain books from
school classrooms and libraries. In the 1950s superpatriotic groups compiled lists
of "undesirable" books, which were alleged to advocate Communistic theories
or contain subversive ideas. In the 1960s civil-rights groups tried to ban books
that pictured minorities in an unfavorable light. In the 1970s parents and school
boards sought to censor "obscene" and "vulgar" books. Even though efforts
to ban "offensive" books have been commonplace, only two cases—*Presidents
Council* and *Island Trees*—received attention from the Supreme Court. These
cases shed some light on the Court's position on banning books from school
libraries.

Presidents Council involved an attempt to ban a novel entitled *Down These
Mean Streets,* written by Piri Thomas, from the libraries of three junior high
schools in Queens, New York. The book describes, in graphic detail, sexual activities and drug uses that are part of everyday life for residents of Spanish
Harlem. The book was ordered to familiarize the predominantly white, middle-
class youth of Queens with the problems of their peers who live in the Harlem
environment. Some parents complained about the book, and after a public meeting, the school board established a policy that permitted the book to remain on

"TO BAN, OR NOT TO BAN, THAT IS THE QUESTION."

the shelves, but it could be checked out only by an adult. A suit was initiated by a principal, a librarian, and some parents and children, who asked to have the board's resolution declared unconstitutional. In court the board argued that a book with such vivid accounts of sordid and perverted events was not good for junior-high students. The court upheld the board's authority to select library holdings. The judges stressed that the board action did not violate any First Amendment freedoms—the action did not prevent any teacher from discussing the book in class or from assigning it for outside reading. Parents could take the book out of the library if they wanted their child to read it. The court took the following position:

> The ensuing shouts of book burning, witch hunting, and violation of academic freedom hardly elevate this intramural strife to first amendment constitutional proportions. If it did, there would be a constant intrusion of the judiciary into the internal affairs of the school. Academic freedom is scarcely fostered by the intrusion of three or even nine federal jurists making curriculum or library choices for the community of scholars.[26]

The U.S. Supreme Court denied certiorari. In so doing, the Court affirmed the school board's authority to ban a book from a school library.

In *Island Trees* the Court reexamined its position on this issue. The case began in September 1975, when several members of the Board of Education of Island Trees Union Free School District attended a conference sponsored by a politically conservative organization concerned about educational legislation. At the conference, the board members obtained a list of books described as "objectionable" and as "improper fare for school students." The board members later learned that the Island Trees high-school library contained nine of the books, the junior high school library held one of the books, and another of the books was included in the curriculum of a twelfth-grade literature course. The board appointed a "Book Review Committee," consisting of four parents and four teachers, to read the books and to recommend whether the books should be retained. The committee recommended that five of the books should be retained, two should be removed from the school libraries, and the members could not agree on the other four books. The board rejected the committee's report and decided that only one book should be returned to the high-school library without restriction and that another be made available subject to parental approval. The remaining nine books, however, should be removed. The board gave no reasons for rejecting the recommendations of the committee it had appointed. Several students initiated court action, claiming that the board action denied them First Amendment rights. The case reached the Supreme Court.

The *Island Trees* opinion reflected the thinking of a deeply divided Supreme Court. The majority acknowledged that while local school boards have broad discretion in the management of school affairs, students do not relinquish their rights to free speech at the schoolhouse gate—school boards must discharge their duties within the limits of the First Amendment. According to the opinion of Justice Brennan, students enjoy "the right to receive information and ideas"; the school board must not violate the students' freedom "to inquire, to study and to evaluate, to gain new maturity and understanding. The school library is the principal locus of such freedom." Brennan continued:

> Petitioners [School Board] argue that they must be allowed unfettered discretion to "transmit community values" through the Island Trees schools. But that sweeping claim overlooks the unique role of the school library. It appears from the record that use of the Island Trees school libraries is completely voluntary on the part of the students. Their selection of books from these libraries affords them an opportunity at self-education and individual enrichment that is wholly optional. Petitioners might well defend their claim of absolute discretion in matters of curriculum by reliance upon their duty to inculcate community values. But we think that petitioners' reliance upon that duty is misplaced where, as here, they attempt to extend their claim of absolute discretion beyond the compulsory environment of the classroom, into the school library and the regime of voluntary inquiry that there holds sway.[27]

Brennan admitted that school boards possess significant discretion to determine the content of their school libraries; however, "that discretion may not be exercised in a narrowly partisan or political manner." In *Island Trees* the school board's decision to remove books may have "rested decisively upon disagreement with constitutionally protected ideas in those books, or upon a desire . . . to impose upon the students . . . a political orthodoxy to which petitioners and their constituents adhered." Brennan also noted that nothing in the *Island Trees* decision affects the authority of a school board to choose books to *add* to the school libraries; the decision affects only the authority to *remove* books.

> In brief, we hold that local school boards may not remove books from school library shelves simply because they dislike the ideas contained in those books and seek their removal to prescribe what shall be orthodox in politics, nationalism, religion, or other matters of opinion.

The dissenting opinion, written by Chief Justice Warren Burger, and supported by Justices Lewis Powell, William Rehnquist, and Sandra Day O'Connor, criticized the majority's reasoning.

> Today the plurality suggests that the Constitution distinguishes between school libraries and school classrooms, between removing unwanted books and acquiring books. Even more extreme, the plurality concludes that the Constitution requires school boards to justify to its teenage pupils the decision to remove a particular book from a school library. I categorically reject this notion that the Constitution dictates that judges, rather than parents, teachers, and local school boards, must determine how the standards of morality and vulgarity are to be treated in the classroom.

Nonetheless, the thrust of *Island Trees* is that while school boards have considerable authority to determine the content of school libraries, that authority may not be exercised in a narrowly partisan or political manner.

Summary

Supreme Court decisions have helped establish the rights and responsibilities of those legislators, school-board members, and parental groups that have been entrusted with the task of school administration. The Court has overturned certain efforts to control curriculum. In *Meyer* and *Epperson,* laws banning the teaching of foreign languages and evolution were declared unconstitutional. The Court has also prohibited certain school rituals. In *Barnette* the Court set aside the mandatory flag salute. In *Engel, Schempp, Murray,* and *Stone* the justices banned required prayer in the classroom. The Court has acknowledged the authority of legislators to investigate teacher fitness, but such inquiry is subject to procedural safeguards. In *Wieman* and *Shelton* the Court threw out teacher-fitness tests based on guilt by association. In *Slochower* the Court affirmed that any teacher subject to dismissal must be given a summary hearing. In *Slochower* and *Beilan* the Court prohibited administrators from equating a teacher's refusal to answer questions with an admission of incompetency. In several cases— *Cramp, Baggett, Keyishian, Whitehill*—the Court declared loyalty oaths unconstitutional. The courts have affirmed the right of administrators to formulate guidelines regarding the appearance of outside speakers on campus, but such guidelines must be clear and nondiscriminatory. *Stacy* provided model guidelines. Finally, the Court has, in *Presidents Council* and *Island Trees,* set forth general guidelines for removing books from library shelves.

FACULTY RIGHTS

In 1915 a group of scholars founded the American Association of University Professors in order to further the interests of faculty members in higher education. In its "1940 Statement of Principles on Academic Freedom and Tenure," the AAUP claimed that a teacher is entitled to (1) full freedom in research and in publication of the results, (2) freedom in the classroom in discussing his or her subject, and (3) freedom from institutional censorship or discipline when he or she communicates as a citizen.[28] While the AAUP supports academic freedom, the organization lacks legislative clout or judicial authority. Accordingly, the courts ultimately have had to shape policies affecting faculty concerns. Some specific areas involve teaching methods, expression of views, and due process.

Teaching Methods

While a Supreme Court precedent is not available, the lower courts have rendered opinions that consider the extent to which faculty members are free to select classroom materials and course assignments. In such cases, the courts have had to weigh the rights of teachers against those of school boards, principals, and parents. Three cases—*Keefe, Parducci,* and *Mailloux*—will be discussed.

High-school English teacher Robert Keefe assigned an article to be read by his students that used the word "mother-fucker" in its text. Keefe discussed the article, and the word's relevance to the article. Keefe also stated that any student who found the assignment distasteful could have an alternative one. Keefe was called before a school committee and asked to defend his use of the article. Following his explanation, the committee asked Keefe if he would agree not to use it again in the classroom. He replied that he could not, in good conscience, comply with the request. Keefe was suspended and he pursued court action. The court of appeals had to determine whether a teacher may, for educational reasons, use a "dirty" word. The judges agreed that no proper study of the article could avoid consideration of the word. The judges also noted that the word was known to many students in the senior year of high school and was used by young protesters throughout the country. In addition, the judges found that five books containing the word were housed in the school library. It was difficult "to think that any student could walk into the library and receive a book, but that his teacher could not subject the content to serious discussion in class."[29] In the light of such inconsistencies, the court supported Keefe's use of the article as a classroom assignment.

In *Parducci* a district court faced the issue of teaching method. Marilyn Parducci assigned to her English classes Kurt Vonnegut's short story, "Welcome to the Monkey House," in order that the students might acquire a better understanding of that genre of literature. Subsequently, the school board notified Parducci that she had been dismissed for assigning material that had a "disruptive" impact on the school. Parducci initiated suit, and the court considered two questions. The first question was whether the assigned story was inappropriate for high-school juniors. The court noted that it was not obscene under either the standards of *Roth*[30] or the stricter standards for minors established in *Ginsberg*.[31] The second question was whether a substantial threat of disruption existed. The court noted that only 3 of the 90 students in the class objected to the assignment. There was no evidence that the assignment caused a significant disruption. The court concluded that Parducci's dismissal violated her First Amendment right to academic freedom and ordered that she be reinstated as a teacher.[32]

In *Mailloux* another challenge to teaching method came before the courts. During one of his classes, English teacher Roger Mailloux discussed taboo words. He wrote the word "goo" on the blackboard and asked the students for a definition. No one was able to define it. Mailloux said that the word did not exist in English, but that in another culture it might be a taboo word. He then wrote "fuck" on the board, and asked the class for a definition. A student suggested that the word meant "sexual intercourse." Mailloux never used the word orally, but explained, "we have two words, sexual intercourse, and this word on the board.... One...is acceptable by society...the other is not accepted. It is a taboo word." After a short discussion of taboos, Mailloux went on to other topics. When a parent complained, the principal conducted an investigation, and after a hearing, school officials dismissed Mailloux on the charge of "conduct unbecoming a teacher." Mailloux initiated court action. The U.S. District Court noted that *Keefe* and *Parducci* had upheld two kinds of academic freedom for the teacher: the right to choose a teaching method that served an educational purpose, and the right not to be fired for using a teaching method that was not prohibited by a clearly articulated regulation. The court analyzed the particulars of *Mailloux* in the light of these criteria and made several observations: (1) The topic of taboo words is relevant to the teaching of high-school English; (2) the word "fuck" is relevant to a discussion of taboo words; (3) students in an eleventh-grade class should be able to treat the word from a serious educational view-point; (4) the class might be less disturbed by having the word written than if it had been spoken, since most students had seen the word even if they had not used it; (5) Mailloux's calling for a volunteer to define the word was a reason-able teaching technique that avoided involving anyone who did not wish to par-ticipate; and (6) the word "fuck" is in books in the school library. Then the court acknowledged that experts disagreed about the appropriateness of the teaching method Mailloux employed.

> Where, as here, a secondary school teacher chooses a teaching method that is not necessary for the proper instruction of his class, that is not shown to be regarded by the weight of opinion in his profession as permissible, that is not so transparently proper that a court can without expert testimony evaluate it as proper, but that is relevant to his subject and students and, in the opinion of experts of significant standing, serves a serious educational purpose, it is a heretofore undecided question whether the Constitution gives him any right to use the method or leaves the issue to the school authorities.[33]

The court decided that, in such cases, authorities "may suspend or discharge a teacher for using the method," but only if the teacher "was put on notice ei-ther by a regulation or otherwise that he should not use the method." In *Mail-loux* there was no regulation warning the teacher not to use the method. The court concluded that Mailloux's discharge violated due process. The *Mailloux* court conceded, however, that school authorities have considerable control of teach-ing methods.

> Nothing herein suggests that school authorities are not free after they have learned that the teacher is using a teaching method of which they disapprove, and which is not appropriate to the proper teaching of the subject, to suspend him until he agrees to cease using the method.

Overall, the cases cited in this section—*Keefe, Parducci,* and *Mailloux*—uphold a faculty member's right to determine teaching method; however, the *Mailloux* decision retains some control for school officials.

Expression of Views

The AAUP's concept of academic freedom includes a teacher's right to ex-press his or her views as a citizen. In some cases the Supreme Court has evalu-ated "unpopular" statements of teachers, in order to determine what restraints might be placed on such expressions.

In 1951 the New Hampshire legislature passed a law declaring "subversive organizations" unlawful and "subversive persons" ineligible for employment by the state government. In 1953 the legislature authorized the attorney general to investigate violations of the law. Paul Sweezy, a visiting lecturer at the University of New Hampshire, was summoned to appear. Sweezy admitted to being a "classical Marxist" and a "Socialist," but he denied that he had ever been a member of the Communist party or that he had ever been part of any effort to overthrow the government. Sweezy refused, however, to answer several questions, which he claimed were not pertinent to the inquiry and which he thought violated his First Amendment rights. Sweezy was judged in contempt and sentenced to the county jail until he cooperated. The Supreme Court overturned the verdict, because the resolution of the New Hampshire legislature had not authorized the specific questions asked of Sweezy. The Court also made a point relevant to academic freedom and the expression of unpopular views. In the opinion written by Chief Justice Earl Warren, "to impose any strait-jacket upon the intellectual leaders in our colleges and universities would imperil the future of our Nation." Warren continued,

> Scholarship cannot flourish in an atmosphere of suspicion and distrust. Teachers and students must always remain free to inquire, to study, and to evaluate, and to gain new maturity and understanding; otherwise our civilization will stagnate and die.[34]

In *Sweezy* the Court took a strong stand in favor of academic freedom.

In *Pickering* the Court strengthened the freedom of expression for teachers. Marvin Pickering, a teacher at an Illinois high school, sent a letter to the editor of a local newspaper, criticizing the manner in which the board of education and the superintendent of schools had handled proposals to raise educational funding. The letter also criticized the allocation of revenues for the school's educational and athletic programs. Pickering had neglected to comply with the "Handbook for Teachers" requirement that material submitted to local newspapers should be checked with the principal and submitted in triplicate to the publicity coordinator. The board held a hearing, at which it was charged that Pickering's letter had damaged the professional reputations of board members and of school administrators. Pickering's statements, it was claimed, could foment controversy and dissension among teachers, administrators, and the residents of the district. Also, the board charged that Pickering had made a number of false statements about the athletic budget. The board dismissed Pickering because his letter was detrimental to the efficient operation of the schools. On appeal, the Supreme Court ruled unanimously for Pickering. The justices agreed that Pickering's message was not shown "to have in any way either impeded the teacher's proper performance of his daily duties in the classroom or to have interfered with the regular operation of the schools." The opinion continued:

> In these circumstances we conclude that the interest of the school administration in limiting teachers' opportunities to contribute to public debate is not sig-

nificantly greater than its interest in limiting a similar contribution by any member of the general public.[35]

In addition, the decision was based, in part, on the "actual malice" principle established in *New York Times Company*.[36] The Court noted that the amount spent on athletics, which Pickering reported erroneously, was a matter of public record, which the board could have refuted by publishing accurate figures in the same newspaper. The Court concluded that "absent proof or false statements knowingly or recklessly made by him, a teacher's exercise of his right to speak on issues of public importance may not furnish the basis for his dismissal." Pickering's dismissal violated his constitutional right to free speech.

In *Lux* a court of appeals referred to the *Pickering* decision in restricting a faculty member's free-speech rights. The case involved William Lux, a tenured professor of history and an assistant academic dean at New Mexico Highlands University. When Lux delivered a speech to the Board of Regents, in which he engaged in "vituperation and personal vilification" against the school's administration, he was relieved of his duties as academic dean. He initiated court action. The Court of Appeals of New Mexico cited *Pickering* in noting that a statement is protected only if it deals with matters "of legitimate public concern." According to the court, Lux's "diatribe did not serve to foster rational discourse, exchange of ideas, and meaningful discussion about a matter of legitimate public interest." Accordingly, Lux's speech was not protected by the First Amendment. In 1981 the U.S. Supreme Court denied certiorari.[37]

Meinhold is another case in which a court limited the right of faculty members to express their views. Alvin Meinhold, a Nevada public-school teacher with seven years of service, was dismissed for "unprofessional conduct," because he privately stated to his own children that he did not believe in compulsory school-attendance laws. Meinhold did not state his views in the classroom, nor did he encourage his students to be truants. The Nevada Supreme Court ruled that "a teacher's right to teach cannot depend solely upon his conduct in the classroom" and upheld the firing. The U.S. Supreme Court refused to hear the case.[38] Justice Douglas, who wanted the case reviewed, cited *Pickering* in stressing that teachers may not "constitutionally be compelled to relinquish the First Amendment rights they would otherwise enjoy as citizens." Douglas asked, "May Pickering publish his criticisms in the local newspaper with impunity while the petitioner must keep his views secret from his children lest they adopt them?" Justice Douglas's question was answered six years later in *Givhan*,[39] when the Supreme Court stressed that a teacher does not relinquish First Amendment rights by expressing views privately rather than publicly.

Another case to reach the Supreme Court, *City of Madison*, involved the question of whether a teacher may speak in opposition to a union proposition at a public school-board meeting. During 1971, the Madison Board of Education and a teachers union were negotiating a collective-bargaining agreement. The union submitted several proposals, one of which called for the inclusion of a "fair-share" clause. This clause would require all teachers, whether union members or not, to pay union dues to defray the costs of collective bargaining. The negotiations became stalemated. At a school-board meeting, a portion of the time was devoted to expression of opinion by the public. First, the president of the union spoke in favor of the proposals. Then, a Madison teacher addressed the meeting. He read a petition that had been circulated among the teachers in the district, which showed that 53 percent of the teachers who had signed the petition opposed "fair-share." Later that evening, the board accepted all of the union's demands except for "fair-share." On the following morning, the union accepted the proposal and eventually a contract was signed. In January 1972, the union filed a complaint with the Wisconsin Employment Relations Commission, arguing that the board had violated proper labor practices by allowing the teacher to speak at the meeting. The union claimed that by so doing the board had engaged in negotiations with a member of the bargaining unit, other than the exclusive bargaining representative. The Supreme Court, in a unanimous opinion, ruled that the circumstances did not present a danger to labor-management relations that would justify curtailing freedom of speech. The union alone was authorized to negotiate with the board of education. The teacher's brief statement could not be considered as negotiation. The board meeting at which the teacher spoke was open to the public; the teacher spoke not merely as one of the board's employees but also as a concerned citizen, seeking to express his views on an important issue.[40] The Court noted that in *Pickering* it had held that teachers may not be "compelled to relinquish the First Amendment rights they would otherwise enjoy as citizens to comment on matters of public interest in connection with the operation of the public school in which they work."

In *Mt. Healthy* the Court heard another challenge to the right of a teacher to express his views. Beginning in 1970, Fred Doyle, an untenured teacher in Mt. Healthy, Ohio, became involved in several incidents—he argued with another teacher until the teacher slapped him, he disputed with employees of the school cafeteria over the amount of spaghetti he had received, he referred to students as "sons of bitches," and he made an obscene gesture to two girls who disobeyed him. Also, Doyle telephoned a Cincinnati radio station to report that his principal had established a dress and appearance code for teachers. The station reported the information as a news item. At the spring meeting of the board of education, Doyle's contract was not renewed because of "a notable lack of tact in handling professional matters." All of the above instances were cited. Doyle initiated court action, seeking reinstatement. The Supreme Court held unanimously that Doyle's telephone call to the radio station was protected by the First Amendment. Because it had played a "substantial part" in the decision not to rehire Doyle, he was entitled to reinstatement with back pay.[41] The Court pointed out that the district court had erred when it failed to determine whether the board of education would have reached the same decision, even in the ab-

sence of the telephone call. With such a determination, the decision not to rehire Doyle could have been upheld.

The Court heard a related case, *Givhan,* in 1979. It involved Bessie Givhan,
who had been dismissed from her junior-high-school teaching job. Givhan sought
reinstatement on the ground that nonrenewal of her contract violated her right
of free speech. In order to justify its decision to dismiss Givhan, school officials offered evidence of a series of private encounters between Givhan and the
school principal, in which Givhan allegedly made "petty and unreasonable demands" in a manner described by the principal as "insulting," "hostile,"
"loud," and "arrogant." The case reached the Supreme Court. The unanimous
decision, per Justice Rehnquist, stressed two points. First, in an effort to clear
up some misundertanding in the lower court, Rehnquist noted that a public employee, like Givhan, who arranges to communicate privately with her employer
rather than spread her views before the public, does not forfeit her freedom of
speech. In effect, the Court overturned the thrust of *Meinhold.* Second, Rehnquist
affirmed the *Mt. Healthy* standard. He noted that once an employee shows that
his or her constitutionally protected conduct played a "substantial" role in the
employer's decision to dismiss, the employer is entitled to show by a prepon-
derance of evidence that the same decision as to the employee's reemployment
would have been reached, even in the absence of protected conduct. Since, in
Givhan, the lower court found that "criticism" was the "primary" reason for
the school district's failure to rehire, the *Mt. Healthy* standard required that the
school district show that the decision to terminate Bessie Givhan would have been
made, even if her encounters with the principal had never occurred. Without such
a showing, Bessie Givhan would have to be reinstated.[42]

Generally, the Supreme Court has defended the right of teachers to express
their views. Early Court decisions, *Sweezy* and *Pickering,* supported the right
of teachers to express their personal views outside of the classroom. In *Lux,* however, the Court restricted personal expression that failed to deal with matters of
public concern. In *Meinhold,* an unusual decision, the Court refused to hear a
case involving a teacher's dismissal for comments made in the privacy of his own
home. Recently, in *City of Madison, Mt. Healthy,* and *Givhan*, the Court has
protected the right of teachers to express their views in both private and public
contexts.

Due Process

In 1972 the Supreme Court decided two cases that involved faculty claims
of due-process violation. Both cases—*Roth* and *Sindermann*—concerned nontenured members of a university faculty.

In 1968 David Roth accepted a position as assistant professor of political
science at Wisconsin State University–Oshkosh. He was hired for a fixed term
of one year. According to law, Roth was notified before February 1, 1969, that

he would not be rehired for the next year. He was given no reason for the decision and no opportunity to challenge it at any type of hearing. Roth initiated court action on the ground that the decision infringed upon his rights. First, he claimed that the real purpose was to punish him for criticizing the university administration, and that the decision violated his right to free speech. Second, he claimed that the failure to provide him with reasons for nonretention and an opportunity for a hearing violated due process. The Supreme Court's majority opinion considered only the second issue. According to Justice Potter Stewart, the terms of Roth's appointment secured absolutely no interest in reemployment for the next year.

> The respondent (Roth) surely had an abstract concern in being rehired, but he did not have a *property* interest sufficient to require the University authorities to give him a hearing when they declined to renew his contract of employment.[43]

The majority concluded that, while it might be "appropriate or wise" to provide a statement of reasons for nonretention, Roth was not constitutionally entitled to such procedure. Justice Douglas dissented on First Amendment grounds. Douglas claimed that "no more direct assault on academic freedom can be imagined than for school authorities to be allowed to discharge a teacher because of his or her philosophical, political, or ideological beliefs." Roth had publicly criticized school administrators for suspending an entire group of black students without determining individual guilt. He also criticized the administration as being authoritarian and autocratic. Douglas concluded that without a statement of the reasons for discharge and an opportunity to respond, Roth would be deprived of his constitutional rights, if nonrenewal implicated the First Amendment. In *Roth* the majority, however, decided that the nontenured professor had no claim to reemployment, and was therefore not entitled to such procedures.

A companion case involved Robert Sindermann, who between 1959 and 1969 taught in the state college system of Texas. After teaching for two years at the University of Texas and four years at San Antonio Junior College, he taught government and social science at Odessa Junior College for four years under one-year contracts. During the 1968-69 academic year, conflict developed between Sindermann and the college administration. In May 1969 the regents voted not to offer Sindermann a new contract for the next academic year. The regents issued a press release alleging insubordination, but they provided him no official statement of the reasons for nonrenewal, and they offered him no opportunity for a hearing. Sindermann initiated court action, alleging that the regents decided not to rehire him because of his criticism of the administration, and this infringed his right to free speech. He also claimed that the failure to provide him an opportunity for a hearing violated procedural due process. The Supreme Court held that the college's granting of a summary judgment against Sindermann, without full exploration of the issues, was unjustified. The Court referred to its *Roth* ruling, which established that there was no right to a hearing before the nonrenewal of a nontenured teacher's contract, unless it could be shown "that the decision not to rehire him somehow deprived him of an interest in 'liberty' or that he had a 'property' interest in continued employment, despite the lack of tenure or a formal contract." Sindermann alleged that this interest, though not secured by a contractual tenure provision, was secured by an understanding fostered by the college administration. Sindermann claimed that the college had a *de facto* tenure program, and that he had tenure under the program. He cited a provision in the college's official faculty guide.

> Teacher tenure: Odessa College has no tenure system. The administration of the college wishes the faculty member to feel that he has permanent tenure as long as his teaching services are satisfactory and as long as he displays a cooperative attitude toward his coworkers and his superiors, and as long as he is happy in his work.

Sindermann also referred to guidelines established by the Coordinating Board of the Texas College and University System, which provided that a teacher who had been employed in the state system for seven years or more has some form of job tenure. Sindermann claimed that a teacher, with his length of service, had no less a "property" interest in continued employment than a formally tenured teacher at other colleges. The Court acknowledged Sindermann's claim as a "legitimate claim of entitlement to job tenure." The Court concluded:

> Proof of such a property interest would not, of course, entitle him to reinstatement. But such proof would obligate college officials to grant a hearing at his request, where he could be informed of the grounds for nonretention and challenge their sufficiency.[44]

In *Sindermann,* as in *Roth,* the Court recognized that nontenured faculty have considerably less right to procedural safeguards than tenured members of the faculty.

Summary

The Court has accorded to teachers specific rights concerning teaching method, expression of personal views, and procedural due process. Overall, as established in *Keefe, Parducci,* and *Mailloux,* teachers have broad control over the teaching method employed in their classes. *Mailloux* does, however, retain some control for school officials. Teachers have been granted almost unbridled freedom in expressing their views. While teachers' expression was restricted in *Lux* and *Meinhold,* the right was protected in *Sweezy, Pickering, City of Madi-*

son, Mt. Healthy, and *Givhan.* The Court has also held that faculty members have procedural rights. Clearly, nontenured faculty enjoy fewer procedural safeguards than tenured faculty. In *Roth* the Court ruled that a nontenured professor who was hired for a one-year term had no right to be informed of the reasons for nonretention, nor was the faculty member entitled to a hearing at which he or she could challenge those reasons. In *Sindermann,* however, the Court acknowledged the existence of an ''informal'' tenure system that entitled a professor with considerable length of service to safeguards when facing nonrenewal.

STUDENT RIGHTS

During the second half of the 1960s, student groups attempted to convert educational institutions into agencies of social and political action. Many citizens resisted this effort to move the school away from its traditional role as an apolitical center of learning. From the student perspective, the specific issues centered around the right to engage in protest, operate an uncensored school press, form and join organizations, and enjoy due process. In several instances the Supreme Court served as the final determiner of these student rights.

Protest

In some cases the courts had to decide whether students could wear armbands or buttons at school. In others the courts had to decide when and where students could distribute leaflets. In the classic case, *Tinker,* the Supreme Court established guidelines that had an impact on later court decisions concerning students' right to protest.

Symbols

Tinker, a case discussed in Chapter 2, involved the suspension of school children who refused to remove black armbands they were wearing to protest U.S. participation in the Vietnam War. The parents sought an injunction that would restrain school officials from punishing their children. The Supreme Court, per Justice Abe Fortas, cited guidelines to help school authorities determine when expression may be restricted.

> Schools exist to carry out educational benefits at several levels one of which involves interpersonal communication among the students. Whenever a student is at school no matter what the hour or the activity that student is free to express his or her views as long as they do not materially and substantially interfere with the operation of the school.[45]

In *Tinker* the Court found no evidence "which might reasonably have led school authorities to forecast substantial disruption of or material interference with school activities." The students simply wore black armbands to protest Vietnam involvement and to influence others to adopt their views. The Court stressed that under the Constitution, students are "persons," and they cannot be treated as "closed-circuit recipients of only that which the State chooses to communicate."

One year later, in the *Guzick* case, a federal court reexamined the *Tinker* guidelines. Thomas Guzick, a student at Shaw High School, asked the principal for permission to distribute to classmates pamphlets that advocated attendance at a Chicago antiwar demonstration. Guzick was denied permission to distribute the pamphlets, and was also instructed to remove an antiwar button he was wearing. Guzick undertook court action. The court distinguished *Guzick* from *Tinker*. First of all, in *Guzick,* the principal applied a long-standing rule: The wearing of buttons, badges, scarves, or any other symbol whereby the wearers identified themselves as supporters of a particular cause, or which contained messages unrelated to education, was prohibited. The rule was established because buttons were potentially divisive in that they set a student apart from other students. In recent years, black and white students attempted to wear buttons expressing racially inflammatory messages. Because buttons contributed to the polarization of student groups, Shaw High officials enforced the antibutton rule. In *Tinker,* school authorities did not prohibit the wearing of all political symbols, only the black armbands worn in opposition to the Vietnam War. Such a policy was discriminatory. Second, the cases differed in their settings. No potential racial conflict was evident in *Tinker,* whereas the changing racial composition of Shaw High School from all-white to 70 percent black made the no-symbol rule important for maintaining order. According to the court, enforcing the symbol ban helped to achieve meaningful integration of the public schools. In *Guzick* the court concluded:

> We must be aware in these contentious times that America's classrooms and their environs will lose their usefulness as places in which to educate our young people if pupils come to school wearing the badges of their respective disagreements, and provoke confrontations with their fellows and their teachers. The buttons are claimed to be a form of speech. Unless they have some relevance to what is being considered or taught, a school classroom is no place for the untrammeled exercise of such rights.[46]

The antibutton policy at Shaw High School was upheld. In 1971 the U.S. Supreme Court refused to hear the case.

Printed Matter

During the years of protest against racial discrimination and U.S. involvement in the Vietnam War, students used leaflets, posters, pamphlets, and newspapers to proclaim their grievances. Most schools adopted regulations to cover the use of such printed matter. In *Eisner* and *Fujishima,* cases heard in the early 1970s, district courts analyzed specific school regulations in the light of the *Tinker* guidelines.

In *Eisner,* high-school students challenged the policy of the board of education of Stamford, Connecticut, which banned a person from distributing any printed material in any school building without prior approval by the school administration. The policy stated the following standards:

> No material shall be distributed, which, either by its content or by the manner of distribution itself, will interfere with the proper and orderly operation and discipline of the school, will cause violence or disorder, or will constitute an invasion of the rights of others.

The district court cited *Tinker* in acknowledging that protected expression in public secondary schools may be banned "if school authorities reasonably forecast substantial disruption of or material interference with school activities." The *Eisner* court stressed that prior restraints requiring official approval before distribution of underground student newspapers were constitutional, but requirements for prior submission of publications must be accompanied by procedural safeguards. The court declared the Stamford policy unconstitutional because of three procedural deficiencies. First, the policy failed to provide an expeditious review procedure; it prescribed no brief period of time in which school officials had to decide whether or not to permit distribution. Second, the policy failed to specify to whom and how material could be submitted for approval. Third, the ban against "distributing" material without prior consent was unconstitutionally vague. The word "distributing" might mean nothing more than one student passing to a fellow student a copy of a magazine—for example, *Time* or *Newsweek.* If students were required to obtain prior approval before exchanging magazines among themselves, "the resultant burden on speech might very likely outweigh the very remote possibility that such activities would ever cause disruption."[47] The court set aside the Stamford regulations for printed matter.

In *Fujishima* a court of appeals disagreed with the *Eisner* court's interpretation of *Tinker.* At stake was Section 6-19 of the Chicago Board of Education regulations which provided that "no person shall be permitted. . .to distribute on the school premises any books, tracts or other publications. . .unless the same shall have been approved by the General Superintendent of Schools." Because Section 6-19 required prior approval of publications, the *Fujishima* court declared the policy unconstitutional as a prior restraint in violation of the First Amendment. The judges believed that the *Eisner* court erred "in interpreting *Tinker* to allow prior restraint on publication—long a constitutionally prohibited power—as a tool of school officials in 'forecasting' substantial disruption of school activities."

Tinker in no way suggests that students may be required to announce their intentions of engaging in certain conduct beforehand so school authorities may decide whether to prohibit the conduct. Such a concept of prior restraint is even more offensive when applied to the long-protected area of publication.[48]

According to the judges in *Fujishima,* the *Tinker* "forecast rule" was designed as a formula for determining when the requirements of school discipline justify punishment of students for exercise of their First Amendment rights. It was not a rationale "for establishing a system of censorship and licensing designed to prevent the exercise of First-Amendment rights." In *Fujishima* the court declared Section 6-19 unconstitutional. The court did, however, indicate that the Chicago Board of Education could establish "reasonable, specific regulations setting forth the time, manner and place in which distribution of written materials may occur."

In *Tinker* the Court upheld the right of students to express their opinions, as long as they did not interfere with the operation of the school. Yet, because of the vagueness of the "forecast rule," state courts have applied *Tinker* somewhat inconsistently in *Guzick, Eisner,* and *Fujishima.*

School Press

In 1973 the Supreme Court considered the case of Barbara Papish, a graduate student in journalism at the University of Missouri, who was expelled for distributing a campus newspaper that contained "forms of indecent speech." The specific issue in question was objectionable in two ways. First, on the front cover the publishers had reproduced a political cartoon depicting a policeman raping the Statue of Liberty and the goddess of justice. The caption read, "With Liberty and Justice for All." Second, the issue contained an article entitled "Mother-Fucker Acquitted," which discussed the trial of a youth who was a member of an organization known as "Up Against the Wall, Mother-Fucker." Following a hearing, the Student Conduct Committee charged that Papish had violated the General Standards of Student Conduct, which specifically prohibited "indecent conduct or speech." Her dismissal was affirmed by the chancellor and the board of curators, and she was not given credit for a course in which she earned a passing grade during that semester. She claimed that her dismissal violated the First Amendment. The main issue for the Supreme Court was whether the material was obscene. In minority opinions, Justice Rehnquist held that the public use of the word "mother-fucker" is "lewd and obscene," and Chief Justice Burger argued that "to preclude a university or college from regulating the distribution of such obscene material does not protect the values inherent in the First Amendment; rather, it demeans those values." The *Papish* majority, however, in a *per curiam* opinion, felt that neither the political cartoon nor the story could be labeled as constitutionally obscene.[49] The university was ordered to award Papish any course credits she earned for the semester and to reinstate her as a student.

Organization

The ability of students to organize was essential for conducting protests during the 1960s and 1970s. In response, school administrators established regulations in order to control the membership and activities of campus associations. In *Healy,* the Supreme Court heard a challenge to a set of such regulations.

In September 1969, students at Central Connecticut State College attempted to organize a local chapter of Students for a Democratic Society. The request for official recognition as a campus organization listed three purposes of the organization: (1) to provide "a forum of discussion and self-education for students developing an analysis of American society," (2) to serve as "an agency for integrating thought with action so as to bring about constructive changes," and (3) to provide a "coordinating body for relating the problems of leftist students" with other groups on campus and in the community. The Student Affairs Committee expressed concern that the group might become associated with the national SDS organization—an active force for student activism throughout the decade. The students, however, stated that their group would remain completely independent of the national organization. The committee approved the application and recommended to Dr. F. Don James, president of the college, that the organization be awarded official recognition. President James, however, rejected the recommendation and denied campus recognition to SDS, because, in his view, the organization's philosophy was opposed to Central Connecticut State's policies. The group's survival was difficult without official recognition. Members were not allowed to announce activities in the student newspaper. They could not post notices on campus bulletin boards. They were prohibited from meeting in campus buildings. The group started court action and the case eventually reached the U.S. Supreme Court. The Court decided that First Amendment principles had been denied the group, but since the judges could not decide from the record whether the students were willing to abide by reasonable campus regulations, the case was remanded for reconsideration. By way of instruction, the Court stressed that a college administration could require "that the group seeking official recognition affirm in advance its willingness to adhere to reasonable campus law."[50] Participation in the internal life of an academic community may be refused to an organization that reserves the right to violate valid campus regulations.

In 1981, in *Widmar,* the Supreme Court affirmed its belief that the rights of free speech and association extend to university campuses. The case involved the policy of the University of Missouri at Kansas City to make its facilities available for the activities of student groups. When a student religious group was denied the use of campus buildings or grounds "for purposes of religious worship or religious teaching," the group alleged that the ban violated its First Amendment rights. The case reached the Supreme Court. The majority opinion, per Justice Powell, found fault with UMKC's exclusionary policy.

"I DON'T CARE IF I AM A STUDENT!
I STILL HAVE RIGHTS!"

> The basis for our decision is narrow. Having created a forum generally open
> to student groups, the University seeks to enforce a content-based exclusion of
> religious speech. Its exclusionary policy violates the fundamental principle that
> a state regulation of speech should be content-neutral.[51]

In *Widmar* the Court determined that UMKC had discriminated against a student group that sought to use a ''generally open forum'' to engage in speech and association behavior that is protected by the First Amendment. Such a policy is unconstitutional.

Due Process

Two cases reviewed by the Supreme Court in 1975—*Goss* and *Wood*—established the right to due process in disciplinary actions taken against students by authorities.

During a period of local unrest, several high-school students from Columbus, Ohio, were suspended from school for up to ten days without a hearing. The students argued that the statute permitting such suspensions was unconstitutional. The Supreme Court determined that the students were denied due process of law, because they were "suspended without hearing prior to suspension or within a reasonable time thereafter." The Court made it clear that students facing temporary suspension qualify for protection of the due-process clause. The student must be given notice of the charges, and, if he or she denies the validity of the charges, the student must be provided with an explanation of the evidence the officials have, as well as with an opportunity to respond. In most cases, the disciplinarian could informally discuss the charges with the student, minutes after the offense occurred. In *Goss* the Court concluded that the due-process clause "requires at least these rudimentary precautions against unfair or mistaken findings of misconduct and arbitrary exclusion from school."[52]

In *Wood* the due-process rights of students were extended by the Supreme Court. Two students at Mena Public High School, Arkansas, were expelled for the use of intoxicating beverages at school activities. The students "spiked" the punch served at a meeting of a school organization, attended by students and parents. The students admitted their involvement to a teacher and to the principal. They were suspended from school for a two-week period; but after a meeting of the school board, the students were expelled for the remainder of the semester. The students brought suit, claiming that their expulsion infringed upon their right to due process. The school board presented two arguments to the Supreme Court. First, substantial evidence had been presented. Second, board members enjoy an absolute immunity from liability. The Supreme Court unanimously agreed with the board on the first issue, since it was conclusive that there was substantial evidence supporting the charges against the students, including their own admission. Then, the Court decided, by a five-to-four vote, that a board member is not immune from liability for damages "if he knew or reasonably should have known that the action he took within his sphere of official responsibility would violate the constitutional rights" of the student, or "if he took the action with the malicious intention to cause a deprivation of constitutional rights or other injury to the student."[53] In a minority opinion, Justice Powell pondered whether the *Wood* decision, by increasing the possibility of personal liability, would discourage qualified persons from continuing "in the desired numbers to volunteer for service in public education." The *Wood* majority, however, held that a school-board member was indeed responsible for any improper behavior.

Summary

Between 1969 and 1975 the U.S. Supreme Court heard five significant cases involving student rights. In all the cases the Court upheld the academic freedom of students. In *Tinker* the Court affirmed the right of students to express their views, as long as they do not substantially disrupt school activities. In *Papish* the Court ruled that the dissemination of ideas, no matter how offensive to good taste, cannot be prohibited on a university campus simply in the name of "decency." In *Healy* the right of students to associate was upheld, even though the Court acknowledged that the university could require an organization to abide by reasonable campus rules. *Goss* held that before students could be suspended from public schools, they must be given notice of the charges and an opportunity to respond. In *Wood* the Court added that in a student suit against school administrators for violation of civil liberties, the administrators were not entitled to good-faith immunity, if they should have known that their action violated the student's constitutional rights.

NOTES

1. Hook, Sidney, *Academic Freedom and Academic Anarchy.* New York: Cowles Book Company, 1970, p. 34.

2. *Meyer v. Nebraska*, 43 S.Ct. 625 (1923).

3. *Bartlels v. Iowa; Bohning v. Ohio*, 43 S.Ct. 628 (1923).

4. *Scopes v. State*, 154 Tenn. 105; 289 S.W. 363 (1927).

5. *Epperson v. Arkansas*, 89 S.Ct. 266 (1968).

6. *Minersville School District v. Gobitis*, 60 S.Ct. 1010 (1940).

7. *West Virginia State Board of Education v. Barnette*, 63 S.Ct. 1178 (1943).

8. *Engel v. Vitale*, 82 S.Ct. 1261 (1962).

9. *School District of Abington Township v. Schempp; Murray v. Curlett*, 83 S.Ct. 1560 (1963).

10. *Stone v. Graham*, 101 S.Ct. 192 (1981).

11. *Slochower v. Board of Higher Education*, 76 S.Ct. 637 (1956).

12. *Beilan v. Board of Public Education*, 78 S.Ct. 1317 (1958).

13. *Adler v. Board of Education*, 72 S.Ct. 380 (1952).

14. *Wieman v. Updegraff*, 73 S.Ct. 215 (1952).

15. *Shelton v. Tucker; Carr v. Young*, 81 S.Ct. 247 (1960).

16. *Cramp v. Board of Public Instruction of Orange County, Florida*, 82 S.Ct. 275 (1961).

17. *Baggett v. Bullitt*, 84 S.Ct. 1316 (1964).

18. *Keyishian v. Board of Regents*, 87 S.Ct. 675 (1967).

19. *Whitehill v. Elkins*, 88 S.Ct. 184 (1967).

20. *Dickson v. Sitterson*, 415 F.2d 228 (1969).

21. *Stacy v. Williams*, 306 F. Supp 963 (1973).

22. *Molpus v. Fortune*, 311 F. Supp 240 (1970).

23. *Brooks v. Auburn University*, 296 F. Supp 188 (1969).

24. *Duke v. Texas*, 327 F. Supp 1218 (1971).

25. *Stacy.*

26. *Presidents Council, District 25 v. Community School Board No. 25*, 93 S.Ct. 308 (1972).

27. *Board of Education, Island Trees Union Free School District No. 25 v. Pico*, 102 S.Ct. 2799 (1982).

28. Joughin Louis (ed.), *Academic Freedom and Tenure: A Handbook of the American Association of University Professors.* Madison: University of Wisconsin Press, 1969, pp. 33-36.

29. *Keefe v. Geanakos*, 418 F.2d 359 (1969).

30. *Roth v. United States*, 77 S.Ct. 1304 (1957).

31. *Ginsberg v. New York*, 88 S.Ct. 1274 (1968).

32. *Parducci v. Rutland*, 316 F. Supp 352 (1970).

33. *Mailloux v. Kiley,* 323 F. Supp 1387 (1971); 448 F.2d 1242 (1971).
34. *Sweezy v. New Hampshire,* 77 S.Ct. 1203 (1957).
35. *Pickering v. Board of Education,* 88 S.Ct. 1731 (1968).
36. *New York Times Company v. Sullivan,* 84 S.Ct. 710 (1964).
37. *Lux v. Angel* cert. denied, 102 S.Ct. 92 (1981).
38. *Meinhold v. Taylor* cert. denied, 94 S.Ct. 247 (1973).
39. *Givhan v. Western Line Consolidated School District,* 99 S.Ct. 693 (1979).
40. *City of Madison, Joint School District No. 8 v. Wisconsin Employment Commission,* 97 S.Ct. 421 (1976).
41. *Mt. Healthy City School District Board of Education v. Doyle,* 97 S.Ct. 568 (1977).
42. *Givhan.*
43. *Board of Regents v. Roth,* 92 S.Ct. 2701 (1972).
44. *Perry v. Sindermann,* 92 S.Ct. 2717 (1972).
45. *Tinker v. Des Moines Independent Community School District,* 89 S.Ct. 733 (1969).
46. *Guzick v. Drebus,* 431 F.2d 594 (1970); cert. denied 91 S.Ct. 941 (1971).
47. *Eisner v. Stamford Board of Education,* 440 F.2d 803 (1971).
48. *Fujishima v. Board of Education,* 460 F.2d 1355 (1972).
49. *Papish v. Board of Curators of the University of Missouri,* 93 S.Ct. 1197 (1973).
50. *Healy v. James,* 92 S.Ct. 2338 (1972).
51. *Widmar v. Vincent,* 102 S.Ct. 269 (1981).
52. *Goss v. Lopez,* 95 S.Ct. 729 (1975).
53. *Wood v. Strickland,* 95 S.Ct. 992 (1975).

RECOMMENDED READING

Barrier, Mary L., "Restriction of the First Amendment in an Academic Environment," *University of Kansas Law Review* 22 (Summer, 1974), 597-605.

Gee, E. Gordon, "Tender Dismissal: A View From *Mount Healthy,*" *Brigham Young University Law Review* (1980), 255-73.

Huffman, John L., and Denise M. Trauth, "High School Students' Publication Rights and Prior Restraint," *Journal of Law and Education* 10 (October, 1981), 485-505.

Miller, Norman R., "Teachers' Freedom of Expression Within the Classroom: A Search For Standards," *Georgia Law Review* 8 (Summer, 1974), 837-97.

Miller, Simon A., "Teachers' Freedom of Expression Outside the Classroom: An Analysis of the Application of *Pickering* and *Tinker,*" *Georgia Law Review* 8 (Summer, 1974), 900-18.

Mooney, Brian J., "*Board of Education, Island Trees Union Free School District No. 26 v. Pico:* The Limits of Students' First Amendment Rights," *Albany Law Review* 47 (Spring, 1983), 945-74.

Reynolds, Janis L., "Free Speech Rights of Public School Teachers: A Proposed Balancing Test," *Cleveland State Law Review* 30 (Fall, 1981), 673-710.

Schulman, Carol Herrnstadt, "Employment of Nontenured Faculty: Implications of *Roth* and *Sindermann*," *Denver Law Journal* 51 (1974), 215-33.

Simpson, William Kennedy, "Constitutional Aspects of Removing Books From School Libraries," *Kentucky Law Journal* 66 (1977-78), 127-49.

KEY DECISIONS

1943—*BARNETTE*—overturned mandatory flag-salute statute.

1968—*PICKERING*—upheld a teacher's right to speak on issues of public importance.

1969—*TINKER*—affirmed the right of students to express their views, as long as they do not substantially disrupt school activities.

1972—*ROTH*—stressed that nontenured faculty members have fewer rights than tenured faculty members.

1972—*SINDERMANN*—acknowledged the existence of an "informal" tenure system, which entitled a faculty member, with considerable length of service, to procedural safeguards when facing nonrenewal.

1972—*HEALY*—acknowledged student rights of association.

1973—*PAPISH*—upheld right of students to operate uncensored school press.

1975—*GOSS*—recognized students' right to due process.

1975—*WOOD*—held that school administrators are responsible for any improper behavior. They are not entitled to good faith immunity.

1979—*GIVHAN*—acknowledged right of teachers to express views in both private and public contexts.

1982—*ISLAND TREES*—determined that while school boards have considerable authority to determine the content of school libraries, that authority may not be exercised in a partisan manner.

SUMMARY—LAW OF ACADEMIC FREEDOM

Definition

The law of academic freedom specifies the freedoms enjoyed by administrators, faculty, and students at an educational institution. Generally, the law of academic freedom facilitates open and unrestrained inquiry into the essence of a subject matter.

Proof

1. The rights of administrators include:
   a. Determination of teacher fitness
   b. Regulation of campus speakers
   c. Choosing books to add to school libraries
2. The rights of faculty members include:
   a. Selection of teaching method
   b. Expression of views on issues of public importance
   c. Due process—that is, written statement of reasons for action along with an opportunity for a hearing
3. The rights of students include:
   a. Expression of views on issues of public concern
   b. Operation of uncensored school press
   c. Forming and joining organizations
   d. Due process—that is, notice of the charges, and hearings prior to or within reasonable time after suspension

Defenses

1. An administrator might argue that restrictive action is necessary because the courts have refused to function as the school boards for the nation.
2. An administrator may contend that nontenured faculty enjoy fewer rights than tenured faculty.
3. Faculty members or students may have a strong case if they can demonstrate that an administrative policy is vague, discriminatory, or overbroad.

5

OBSCENITY

Even though numerous laws have defined obscenity as a crime, such activity was rarely prosecuted in the United States prior to the post–Civil War period. In the early 1870s, however, the situation was significantly changed, when an ardent crusader for decency, named Anthony Comstock, formed the New York Society for the Suppression of Vice. The organization sought an increase in obscenity convictions and passage of stronger federal legislation. Comstock campaigned relentlessly, and largely through his efforts, new obscenity legislation was adopted in 1873. This law provided a maximum penalty of a $5,000 fine, or a five-year prison term, or both, for anyone who was caught sending obscene material through the mail. Comstock also helped implement the new statute, as a special agent of the Post Office Department. Until his death in 1915, Comstock and his colleagues at the society seized tons of obscene materials, and prosecutions for obscenity-law violations increased steadily. "Comstockery" marked the introduction of obscenity censorship in the United States.

TESTS OF OBSCENITY

Determining exactly what "obscenity" is has proven to be a difficult problem for the courts. In fact, over the years, "obscenity" has been defined and regulated according to various criteria. The major standards have been the *Hicklin, Roth,* and *Miller* tests.

Hicklin Test

An 1868 English court case had a significant effect on the regulation of obscenity in the United States. The case began when Henry Scott, an Anglican metal broker from Wolverhampton, distributed an anti-Catholic pamphlet entitled *The Confessional Unmasked*. A local court declared the work unconstitutional because it contained explicit descriptions of statements recited in the confessional. The case was ultimately appealed to the Queen's Bench, where Lord Chief Justice Cockburn ruled the pamphlet to be obscene and offered the following test of obscenity:

> The test of obscenity is this, whether the tendency of the matter charged as obscenity is to deprave and corrupt those whose minds are open to such immoral influences and into whose hands a publication of this sort may fall.[1]

The *Hicklin* test emphasized three ideas. First, printed material did not have to offend or harm an "average person." If a work could be assumed to have a bad effect on "those whose minds are open to such immoral influences"—whether the individual was a child, an abnormal adult, or any member of the subclass of society—the work could be seized. Second, the material was not evaluated in terms of its impact as a whole; rather, if any portion of the work were found to be obscene, it was judged obscene in total. This aspect of *Hicklin* gave rise to the practice of judging a literary work by examining passages taken out of context. Third, obscenity was determined on the basis of a work's intent. Judges speculated about the thoughts induced by the reading of printed material. They banned any work that produced "thoughts of a most impure and libidinous character" without any concern whether antisocial behavior would result from exposure to the printed material.

The *Hicklin* ruling was accepted by courts in the United States and vigorously approved by Anthony Comstock. Throughout the next century, U.S. courts declared obscene such books as *Casanova's Homecoming* by Arthur Schnitzler,[2] *The Well of Loneliness* by Radclyffe Hall,[3] *An American Tragedy* by Theodore Dreiser,[4] *Lady Chatterly's Lover* by D. H. Lawrence,[5] and both *Tropic of Cancer* and *Tropic of Capricorn* by Henry Miller.[6] In these cases the "selected passages" approach of the *Hicklin* test was used to determine obscenity; the determination was based on allegedly obscene sections of the work in which the language described an illicit sexual relationship.

Objections arose to applying *Hicklin*. In 1913, in the *Kennerley* case, Judge Learned Hand questioned whether "men will regard that as obscene which is honestly relevant to the adequate expression of innocent ideas," and he suspected that "shame will long prevent us from adequate portrayal of some of the most serious and beautiful sides of human nature." Judge Hand urged that obscenity be determined by considering the "present critical point in the compromise between candor and shame at which the community may have arrived."[7] By acknowledging that societal tolerance of sexual matters varies over time, Judge Hand recognized the importance of "community standards" in a test of obscenity.

In 1933 an attempt was made to bar entry of James Joyce's *Ulysses* into the United States, on the ground that the work was obscene and therefore not importable. New York District Court Judge J. Woolsey analyzed the book and noted that the work contained explicit descriptions of sexual acts, as well as coarse language, which was commonly considered obscene. Yet, such literary techniques were necessary in order that Joyce accomplish his purpose. The words were such as would be naturally and habitually used by the types of characters Joyce described. Woolsey concluded that in spite of its unusual frankness, *Ulysses* was not obscene and could enter the United States. Even though the book tended to excite "sexual impulses or lustful thoughts," its net effect was a powerful commentary on the inner lives of men and women.[8] Woolsey departed from the practice of using excerpts to determine obscenity. He recognized the literary value of the entire work, apart from the existence of specific words or descriptions. In *Ulysses*, as in *Kennerley*, the groundwork was being laid for a new test.

Roth Test

New York businessman Samuel Roth published and sold books, photographs, and magazines, some of which authorities considered to be obscene. When Roth mailed advertisements in an effort to solicit sales, he was arrested and convicted for violating the federal obscenity statute. When this case reached the Supreme Court in 1957, a significant chapter in the history of obscenity law was written. In *Roth* the Court for the first time confronted the issue of whether obscenity is protected by the First Amendment. The justices disagreed on this issue. In a minority opinion Justices William Douglas and Hugo Black cited the wording of the First Amendment, that "Congress shall make no law. . .abridging the freedom of speech or the press." Douglas and Black thought that the broad sweep of the First Amendment should be given full support. They had "the same confidence in the ability of our people to reject noxious literature" as they had "in their capacity to sort out the true from the false in theology, economics, politics, or any other field." The majority opinion, written by William Brennan, noted "that the unconditional phrasing of the First Amendment was not intended to protect every utterance."[9] The majority concluded that obscenity was outside the protection intended for speech and press. Brennan then examined the nature of obscenity and offered a definition—obscenity involves "whether to the average person applying contemporary community standards, the dominant theme of the material taken as a whole appeals to prurient interest." The *Roth* test stressed four elements. First, the Court noted differences between sex and obscenity. Obscene material must deal with sex, but must do so in a manner that appeals to prurient interest. The portrayal of sex, in and of itself, is insufficient reason to suppress material. Second, the test applies to the average person. The printed material must be capable of affecting somebody other than a particularly susceptible individual in order to be deemed obscene. It must be applicable to "normal'' persons. Third, the material must violate "contemporary community standards." Yet, the Court did not clarify what was meant by "community." Fourth, the material must be considered as a whole. It is not judged merely by the effect of an isolated passage. Concern must be with the dominant theme of the work. Brennan noted:

> The *Hicklin* test, judging obscenity by the effect of isolated passages upon the most susceptible persons, might well encompass material legitimately with sex, and so it must be rejected as unconstitutionally restrictive of the freedoms of speech and press.

The *Roth* test set forth standards that safeguarded against the abuses associated with *Hicklin*.

During the following years the Supreme Court clarified the *Roth* test. In *Manual Enterprises* Justice John Harlan claimed that an obscenity-statute violation required proof of two elements—"patent offensiveness" and "prurient-interest appeal." In his view, both elements—"patent offensiveness and prurient-interest appeal—"must conjoin before challenged material can be found obscene."[10] In most instances, the elements tended to coalesce, but *Manual Enterprises* allowed independent consideration of the elements. The case involved magazines that contained photographs of nude male models. J. Edward Day, postmaster general of the United States, noted that the magazines were not physical-culture or body-building materials, but were read primarily by homosexuals. The magazines did not have any interest for sexually "normal" individuals. In Day's view, the magazines were obscene. Justice Harlan of the Supreme Court disagreed.

> These magazines cannot be deemed so offensive on their face as to affront current community standards of decency—a quality that we shall hereafter refer to as "patent offensiveness. . . ." Lacking that quality, the magazines cannot be deemed legally "obscene."

Even though the material was patently offensive to some, and it did have prurient appeal to a small group of homosexuals, it was not patently offensive. Even though the pictures in the magazine might be considered as unpleasant and uncouth, they were not judged as obscene in Harlan's opinion.

In *Jacobellis* the Court applied the *Roth* test in a case involving the obscenity conviction of a motion-picture-theatre manager who showed a film with an explicit love scene. Justice Brennan clarified two points of his *Roth* opinion. He indicated that an obscene work is "utterly without redeeming social importance"; the portrayal of sex in art, literature, and scientific works in not itself sufficient cause to deny constitutional protection. Brennan also noted that any suggestion that the "contemporary community standards" aspect of *Roth* involves a case-by-case determination of obscenity based on local community standards "is an incorrect reading of *Roth*." The meaning of "community standards" referred to "national standards."

> We thus reaffirm the position taken in *Roth* to the effect that the constitutional status of an allegedly obscene work must be determined on the basis of a national standard. It is, after all, a national Constitution we are expounding.[11]

The *Roth* test was further defined in two 1966 cases. In *Mishkin* the Court heard an appeal from a bookstore operator whose publishing speciality dealt with sadism and masochism. His works included several portrayals of scantily clad women being whipped, tortured, and abused. Mishkin's defense was based on the idea that the books did not appeal to the prurient interest of an average person. Mishkin argued that instead of being stimulated, the average person would be disgusted and sickened by such works. The Court rejected this argument as an unrealistic interpretation of the "prurient-appeal requirement" of *Roth*. When material is designed for and primarily disseminated to a clearly defined deviant sexual group, rather than the public at large, "the prurient-appeal requirement of the *Roth* test is satisfied if the dominant theme of the material taken as a whole appeals to the prurient interest of the members of the group" In *Mishkin*,

> No substantial claim is made that the books depicting sexually deviant practices are devoid of prurient appeal to sexually deviant groups. The evidence fully establishes that these books were specifically conceived and marketed for such groups. Mishkin instructed his authors and artists to prepare the books expressly to induce their purchase by persons who would probably be sexually stimulated by them.[12]

The Court upheld Mishkin's conviction.

In *Memoirs* Justice Brennan further clarified the *Roth* test. Three criteria must be established to determine obscenity: The dominant theme of the material taken as a whole must appeal to a prurient interest in sex; the material must be patently offensive because it affronts contemporary community standards relating to the description of sexual matters; and the material must be utterly without redeeming social value. Each of the three criteria must be applied independently; the social value of the book can neither be weighed against nor canceled by its prurient appeal or patent offensiveness.[13] In *Memoirs* the Court decided that even though John Cleland's *Fanny Hill* possessed only a modicum of social value, it could not be judged obscene. The book was not obscene because it was not "unqualifiably worthless."

Despite numerous efforts to clarify *Roth*, and the overall liberal sense of the Supreme Court, the justices could not agree about the specifics of obscenity regulation. In 1967, in *Redrup*, the Court wrote a *per curiam* opinion that summarized differences in the thinking of Court justices regarding appropriate standards for obscenity regulation.

> Two members of the Court have consistently adhered to the view that a State is utterly without power to suppress, control or punish the distribution of any writings or pictures upon the ground of their "obscenity." A third has held to the opinion that a State's power in this area is narrowly limited to a distinct and clearly identifiable class of material. Others have subscribed to a not dissimilar standard, holding that a State may not constitutionally inhibit the distribution of literary material as obscene unless "(a) the dominant theme of the material taken as a whole appeals to a prurient interest in sex; (b) the material is patently offensive because it affronts contemporary community standards relating to the description or representation of sexual matters; and (c) the material is utterly without redeeming social value," emphasizing that the "three elements must coalesce," and that no such material can "be proscribed unless it is found to be utterly without redeeming social value."[14]

In *Redrup* the Court reversed obscenity convictions in three state cases, noting that no matter which judicial thinking was applied, the convictions could not stand. Thus began a six-year policy of issuing summary reversals, without opinion, of any conviction that at least five justices, each applying his own standard, found to be under the protection of the First Amendment. From 1967 to 1973, the Court determined 31 cases in this manner. These cases became known as the "*Redrup* reversals" and marked a period of minimal regulation of obscenity.

Miller Test

The obscenity test established by the Earl Warren Court in *Roth* was overturned on June 21, 1973, when Richard Nixon appointees Lewis Powell, Harry Blackmun, William Rehnquist, and Warren Burger were joined by Byron White to constitute a five-man majority. The landmark case was *Miller*.

Marvin Miller was convicted of distributing sexually explicit advertisements to unwilling recipients. The advertising brochures depicted men and women engaging in a variety of sexual activities, often with genitals prominently displayed. In *Miller* the Supreme Court reexamined the definition of obscenity and revised its fundamental position. The majority opinion, written by Chief Justice Burger, stressed three standards. First, the Court redefined the term "community." No longer were contemporary "community" standards to be considered as "national" in scope. It was not realistic to view the First Amendment as requiring that people of one state accept conduct found tolerable in another state. People in different states vary in their tastes and attitudes. According to the Court, this "diversity is not to be strangled by the absolutism of imposed uniformity." Second, the Court retained the patent-offensiveness standard. Obscenity could be

"MAYBE THE COURTS SHOULD BE THE ONES TO DECIDE IF THIS EXHIBIT IS OBSCENE."

determined when "the work depicts or describes, in a patently offensive way, sexual conduct specifically defined by the applicable state law." The Court then identified specific examples of what might be regulated as "patently offensive": representations of normal or perverted, actual or simulated ultimate sexual acts, descriptions of masturbation and/or excretary functions, and lewd exhibition of the genitals. Third, obscenity could exist when "the work, taken as a whole, lacks serious literary, artistic, political, or scientific value." The Court thereby rejected the "utterly without redeeming social value" element of the *Roth* test and substituted the words "does not have serious literary, artistic, political or scientific value."[15]

Ensuing Court decisions clarified the provisions of the *Miller* test. The *Jenkins* and *Ward* cases clarified the meaning of the term "patently offensive." In *Jenkins* the Court evaluated the movie "Carnal Knowledge." In the unanimous opinion, Justice Rehnquist noted that the main theme of the movie is sex. There are nudity and scenes in which sexual acts are "understood" to be occurring. Yet, the camera does not focus on actors at sexually critical moments, and "ultimate sexual behavior" is only intimated. The Court emphasized that even though the film shows occasional nudity, "nudity alone does not render material obscene under *Miller's* standards." The Court also stated that even though questions of appeal to prurient interest or of patent offensiveness are "essentially questions of fact," the *Miller* test did not grant juries "unbridled discretion" in determining what constitutes sexual conduct depicted in a patently offensive way. The Court found nothing in the movie to fall within the patently-offensive standards established in *Miller*. It would be "wholly at odds" with *Miller* to affirm this obscenity conviction, "even though a properly charged jury unanimously agreed on a verdict of guilty."[16] The film simply did not depict sexual conduct in a "patently offensive" way.

The Court further expounded upon the "patently offensive" provision in *Ward*. The defendant, Wesley Ward, asserted that sado-masochistic materials may not be constitutionally proscribed, because they were not expressly included in the examples of sexually explicit materials that the Court had cited in *Miller*. Justice White noted that those specifics were offered merely as "examples" and "were not intended to be exhaustive"; they "were not intended to extend constitutional protection to the kind of flagellatory materials that were among those held obsene in *Mishkin*."[17] Ward's conviction was affirmed.

In several cases—*Jenkins, Hamling, Smith, Pinkus*— the Court clarified the meaning of "contemporary community standards." In *Jenkins* Justice Rehnquist noted that "states have considerable latitude in framing statutes under this element of the *Miller* decision." Actually, a state could define an obscenity offense in terms of "contemporary community standards" as generally defined in *Miller*, without further specification, or it could define the standards in more precise geographic terms.[18]

In *Hamling* Justice Rehnquist stressed that the *Miller* decision enabled a state, California in this case, to constitutionally proscribe obscenity in terms of a "statewide" standard, but it did not mean that any such precise geographic area is required as a matter of constitutional law. The result of *Miller* should be "to permit a juror sitting in obscenity cases to draw on knowledge of the community or vicinage from which he comes in deciding what conclusion 'the average person, applying contemporary community standards' would reach in a given case." The *Hamling* case had been tried in the Southern District of California, where presumably jurors from throughout the district were available to serve on the panel. The jurors would draw upon the standards of that "community." As the Supreme Court noted, however, a district court may admit evidence of standards existing in some other place, if such evidence would enable jurors to better resolve the issues.[19]

In *Smith* the Supreme Court had to decide whether a jury is entitled to rely on its own knowledge of community standards, or whether a state legislature may declare what the community standards shall be, and when such a declaration has been made, whether it is binding in a federal prosecution. Justice Blackmun, writing for the majority, noted that it is impossible for a state legislature to define contemporary community standards of appeal to prurient interest or patent offensiveness, largely because of that body's isolation from a particular community. The Court admitted that there was room for state legislation regarding the obscenity issue, but "the question of the community standard to apply, when appeal to prurient interest and patent offensiveness are considered, is not one that can be defined legislatively." Blackmun concluded that "though state legislatures are not completely foreclosed from setting substantive limitations for obscenity cases, they cannot declare what community standards shall be."[20] In essence, *Smith* lessened the impact of *Jenkins* and *Hamling* by indicating that the jury, not the state legislature, has "discretion to determine what appeals to prurient interest and what is patently offensive."

In *Pinkus* the Court heard the appeal of a conviction for mailing obscene materials as well as advertising brochures for such materials. William Pinkus argued that the trial court had erred by instructing the jury to include children and sensitive persons within the definition of "community," by whose standards obscenity was to be judged. Writing for the Court, Chief Justice Burger noted that "children" should not have been included.

> A jury. . .might very well reach a much lower "average" when children are part of the equation than it would if it restricted its consideration to the effect of allegedly obscene materials on adults.[21]

Inclusion of "sensitive persons" was appropriate, however. The "community" includes all adults who compose it, and a jury should consider all adults in determining community standards. Yet, the Court noted that it would be incorrect for a jury to focus "upon the most susceptible or sensitive members rather than . . .merely including them. . .along with all others in the community." In *Pinkus* the Court held that "children" are not to be included as part of the "community," but "sensitive persons" are.

Summary

The history of obscenity prosecutions has been shaped around three distinctly different tests. *Hicklin* stipulated that any printed material that was thought to have a corruptive influence on minors or sexually deviant adults was prohibited. According to *Roth*, a work was considered obscene if an average person, applying contemporary community (national) standards, would find the dominant theme of the complete material appealing to prurient interest. *Miller* gave localities responsibility for determining the obscenity of a work. And, according to *Miller*, obscene material must be "patently offensive" and lack serious literary, artistic, political, or scientific value.

GUIDELINES

Several Supreme Court decisions have established guidelines for obscenity regulation. These decisions have considered such issues as prior restraint, mailing, film, scienter, pandering, youth, privacy, and zoning.

Prior Restraint

Prior restraint involves censorship of obscene material before its appearance in print or exhibition at a theatre. This form of censorship is effective, because it prevents the obscenity from ever reaching the reading or viewing audience. In 1961 the Court approved of an instance of prior restraint. Since then, the Court has consistently struck down censorship in this form.

The 1961 case, *Times Film Corporation*, involved an attempt to show the film "Don Juan" in Chicago. The corporation applied for a permit, but a city official refused to issue the permit when the corporation declined to submit the film for prescreening. The corporation sued. The Supreme Court defined the issue as whether First Amendment protection included freedom to show, at least once, every motion picture. In arriving at its decision, the Court cited two precedents—*Roth*, which determined that obscenity is not constitutionally protected communication,[22] and *Near*, which acknowledged some "exceptional cases" regarding prior restraint in which "the primary requirements of decency may be enforced against obscene publications."[23] In *Times Film Corporation*, the Supreme Court held that even though city officials had no knowledge of the content of "Don Juan," Chicago was obligated to protect its citizens against the dangers of obscenity in the public showing of films.[24] In this instance, prior restraint was justified.

A few years later, in *Freedman*, the Court established specific standards regulating prior restraint. The case began when Ronald Freedman challenged the constitutionality of a Maryland statute by showing the film "Revenge at Daybreak" without first submitting the film to the state Board of Censors. When the case reached the Supreme Court, the justices established three specific standards that authorities must meet when censoring a film. First, the burden of proving obscenity rests on the censoring agency; the censor has the burden of initiating judicial proceedings. Second, any restraint prior to judicial review can be for only a brief period to preserve the status quo. Third, there must be assurance of a prompt judicial review.[25] In *Freedman* the Court unanimously overturned the Maryland law, because it failed to provide adequate safeguards. It constituted an invalid prior restraint.

In 1975 the Court reinforced the *Freedman* safeguards in *Southeastern Promotions*. In Chattanooga, Tennessee, promoters sought to present "Hair," a rock musical that had played for three years on Broadway and had been performed in nearly 150 cities in the United States. Even though city officials had not seen the play or read the script, they rejected the request on the ground that allowing the performance would not be "in the best interest of the community." The Supreme Court rejected this action. The justices held that refusing the use of facilities for "Hair" was decided by personal judgment about the play's content, and this constituted prior restraint. Furthermore, the restraint was final; it was not merely a temporary ban while required judicial proceedings took place. According to *Freedman*, prior restraint can be acceptable only when "it takes place under procedural safeguards designed to obviate the dangers of a censorship system." In *Southeastern Promotions* the safeguards were lacking. First, the promoter, rather than the censor, bore the burden both for obtaining judicial review and for disproving obscenity. Second, the restraint altered the status quo, because review of the request did not occur until more than five months later. The promoter was forced to schedule the performance at a later date. Third, the system failed to provide a procedure for judicial determination. Any restraint must provide prompt judicial review with minimal restriction of First Amendment rights.[26] In *Southeastern Promotions* the Court reinforced the notion that prior restraint, as a form of regulating obscenity, can be employed only when the *Freedman* criteria are met.

In 1980, in *Vance*, the Court again reinforced its thinking on prior restraint. A Texas county attorney attempted to close Carol Vance's indoor, adult motion-picture theatre in order to prevent the showing of obscene films. The action was taken under Texas "public nuisance" statutes, which approved the closing of premises on which forbidden "habitual uses" occurred. Among the prohibited uses were "commercial manufacturing. . .distribution, or. . .exhibition of obscene material." In this case, since obscene films had been shown in the past, authorities sought to close Vance's theatre in order to prevent the future exhibition of films that had not yet been determined to be obscene. Vance appealed. The Supreme Court declared the Texas laws unconstitutional; "they authorized prior restraints that are more onerous than is permissible under *Freedman* and *Southeastern.*"[27] It seems clear that the Court will tolerate prior restraint of obscene materials only when authorities comply with the *Freedman* safeguards.

Mailings

The second-class mail privilege provides a competitive advantage for a magazine publisher. With it, the publisher pays substantially lower postal rates. Congressional legislation entitles periodical publications to the second-class provision, if they are "published for the dissemination of information of a public character, or devoted to literature, the sciences, arts, or some special industry." Obscene material, however, is nonmailable and does not qualify for the second-class privilege. Over the years, Court cases have involved efforts at controlling "alleged" obscenity by restricting the use of the mails.

Hannegan reached the Court in 1946. In this case, the postmaster general revoked the second-class permit for *Esquire* magazine. The specific issues under challenge, for the months of January through November 1943, contained short stories, sports features, articles by prominent newsmakers, book and theatre reviews, and pictorial features. None of these sections were questioned. According to the postmaster general, however, the issues also contained recurrent offensive features: jokes, cartoons, pictures, articles, and poems that emphasized sex. He claimed that some "writings and pictures may be indecent, vulgar, and risqué and still not be obscene in a technical sense"; but in order to enjoy unique mail privileges, a publisher was bound to do more than refrain from disseminating obscene material. The publisher was obliged to contribute to the public welfare. It was on this ground that the postmaster general revoked the second-class privilege. In a unanimous opinion written by Justice Douglas, the Supreme Court rescinded the order.

> From the multitude of competing offerings the public will pick and choose. What seems to one to be trash may have for others fleeting or even enduring values. But to withdraw the second-class rate from this publication today because its contents seemed to one official not good for the public would sanction withdrawal of the second-class rate tomorrow from another periodical whose social or economic views seemed harmful to another official.[28]

In *Hannegan* the Court held that Congress had given the postmaster general no such power of censorship.

In *Rowan* the Court approved the right of an individual to censor his or her own mail with the help of the post office. During the 1960s public concern was aroused over the use of mail facilities to distribute unsolicited obscene advertisements. Complaints to the postmaster general about such activity had reached almost 250,000 annually, when Congress passed the Postal Revenue and Federal Salary Act of 1967. Title III of the act provides a method by which an individual may be protected from advertisements offering material that seems erotically arousing or sexually provocative. When an individual notifies the postmaster that advertisements that appear to be obscene have been received, the postmaster orders the sender to stop any future mailings of such materials to the individual. Daniel Rowan initiated a court action after receiving several prohibitory notices from the postmaster. He claimed the law violated his right of free speech. Chief Justice Burger, writing for the Court, recognized that people are inescapably captive audiences for many purposes, but a person must be free to exercise control over unwanted mail. The right of every person "to be let alone" must be measured against the right of others to communicate. In *Rowan* the Court decided that the right to communicate stops at the mailbox of an unreceptive individual. The Court "categorically" rejected the notion that a vendor has a constitutional right to send unwanted material into the home of another. The constitutionality of the federal law was upheld.[29]

The Court in *Hannegan* refused to place censorship control in the hands of a post-office official. In *Rowan*, however, the Court approved post-office regulation of obscene materials, because the receiving individual determined the control.

Film

In 1915, in *Mutual Film Corporation*, the Supreme Court held that film was a unique medium that warranted separate standards of regulation. The justices offered two reasons. First, motion pictures are "capable of evil," and are therefore in need of a censor. While films are "vivid, useful, and entertaining," they are "capable of evil, having power for it. . .because of their attractiveness and manner of exhibition." Second, film has a commercial nature. According to the Court, "the exhibition of moving pictures is a business, pure and simple, originated and conducted for profit, like other spectacles, not to be regarded, nor intended to be regarded. . .as part of the press of the country, or as organs of public opinion." The Court observed that "there are some things which should not have pictorial representation in public places and to all audiences."[30] In *Mutual Film Corporation*, the Court refused to include film in the category of First Amendment freedoms.

In the 1952 *Burstyn* case, the Court extended First Amendment protection to the film medium. This case centered around Roberto Rossellini's "The Miracle." The film received mixed reviews. It was attacked as "a sacrilegious and blasphemous mockery of Christian religious truth" by the National Legion of Decency. The National Board of Review recommended the film as "especially worth seeing." New York critics selected it as the best foreign film of 1950. After viewing the film, a committee censored it under a New York statute that permitted banning motion pictures that were "sacrilegious." When the case reached the Supreme Court, the justices considered the arguments offered in *Mutual Film Corporation* as justification for denying First Amendment protection to films. First, with regard to the claim that motion pictures "possess a greater capacity for evil" than other modes of expression, the Court held that if this is true, the capacity for evil may be relevant in determining the scope of control, but it does not authorize "unbridled censorship." Second, it had been argued that film production, distribution, and exhibition was a large-scale business conducted for profit. The Court noted:

> That books, newspapers, and magazines are published and sold for profit does not prevent them from being a form of expression whose liberty is safeguarded by the First Amendment. We fail to see why operation for profit should have any different effect in the case of motion pictures.[31]

In *Burstyn* the Court recognized film as a significant medium for the communication of ideas. And the importance of film as a vehicle of public opinion is not diminished when a film is intended to entertain, as well as to inform. Regarding the specifics of "The Miracle," the Court held that the term "sacrilegious" as used in the New York statute was vague. They concluded that a state may not bar a movie on the basis of a censor's conclusion that it is "sacrilegious." The principal significance of *Burstyn*, however, is that the justices recognized film as a medium warranting First Amendment protection.

Scienter

Scienter refers to the amount of knowledge that an individual must have in order to be held legally responsible for the consequences of his or her action. In *Smith* the Court applied the concept of scienter to obscenity. Eleazar Smith was convicted for possessing obscene material in his Los Angeles bookstore. No element of scienter, that is, knowledge by Smith of the obscene nature of the book, was considered. Thus, the ordinance imposed an "absolute" criminal liability. Smith appealed. Writing for the Court, Justice Brennan pointed out that elimination of the scienter requirement may work a substantial restriction on freedom of speech and press. A bookseller who is held liable, while unaware of any obscene contents, will probably restrict the volume of books to those that have been personally inspected. Distribution of books that are both obscene and not obscene would be impeded. Thus, a law that ignores scienter "tends to impose a severe limitation on the public's access to constitutionally protected matter."[32] In *Smith*, the Court decided that an obscenity conviction can be obtained only when the accused is aware of the obscenity.

Pandering

In *Ginzburg*, the Court upheld an obscenity conviction based largely on the activity of pandering. Bookdealer Ralph Ginzburg sold three sex-oriented publications through the mail. In order to advertise these materials, Ginzburg sought mailing privileges from the postmasters of Intercourse and Blue Ball, Pennsylvania. These towns were selected because of the value their names had for selling the publications. The postal facilities in these localities were inadequate to handle the anticipated volume of mail, so the requests were denied. Mailing privileges were then obtained from Middlesex, New Jersey. Shortly thereafter, several million circulars soliciting subscriptions for the publications were mailed from the Middlesex Post Office. The advertising boasted about the sexual candor of the publications. Ginzburg was convicted for violating the federal obscenity statute. The prosecution admitted that the materials in and of themselves might not be obscene under the *Roth*[33] test, but in the context of the advertising campaign, commercial exploitation had made them obscene. The Supreme Court agreed. Justice Brennan wrote that the question of obscenity may include consideration of the setting in which the materials are advertised. In *Ginzburg* the materials were sold as part of the sordid business of pandering, that is, "the business of purveying textual or graphic matter openly advertised to appeal to the erotic interest of their customers." Brennan noted that "where the purveyor's sole emphasis is on the sexually provocative aspects of his publications, that fact may be decisive in the determination of obscenity." Deliberate representation of the publications as erotically arousing "stimulated the reader to accept them as prurient."[34] On the basis of pandering, the Court upheld Ginzburg's conviction.

Youth

Supreme Court opinions have considered regulations that apply to youth. In *Butler* the Court declared unconstitutional a law that tended to reduce adults to

the level of youth. At issue was a Michigan statute that made it a crime to offer to the general public a book that could incite youth to violent, depraved, or immoral acts. Alfred Butler was convicted of selling such a book to a Detroit policeman. He appealed. The Supreme Court noted that the Michigan law prevented distribution of books to the general public because of the undesirable influence they might have upon youth. The adult population was reduced to reading only what was fit for children. According to the Court, the law was "not reasonably restricted to the evil with which it is said to deal."[35] The Court unanimously reversed Butler's conviction. The *Butler* decision is significant because it freed adult literature from obscenity tests that might be appropriate for children's literature.

In *Ginsberg* the Court upheld an obscenity statute that outlawed the sale to minors of material defined as specifically obscene for them. The case began in October 1965, when Sam Ginsberg was arrested for selling "girlie" magazines to a 16-year-old boy, without attempting to ascertain the youth's age. The magazines contained pictures of female nudity. A judge held that the pictures represented nudity in a manner that predominantly appeals to the prurient interest of minors, is patently offensive to prevailing standards in the adult community, and is utterly without redeeming social importance to minors. Ginsberg was tried and found guilty. The Supreme Court recognized the constitutionality of the New York statute that regulated the sale of pornography to children through special standards, broader than those designed for adults. The Court noted that the power of the state to control the conduct of children reached beyond the scope of its authority over adults. The state has an interest in protecting the "welfare of children" and seeing that they are "safeguarded from abuses." [36] The Court upheld the statute and Ginsberg's conviction.

In the 1982 *Ferber* case, the Court examined the "sexploitation" of youth in America. Throughout the 1970s the exploitive use of children in the production of pornography became a serious national problem. To combat this situation, New York passed a law that "prohibits persons from knowingly promoting a sexual performance by a child under the age of 16 by distributing material which depicts such a performance." The law defined "sexual performance" to include such conduct as actual or simulated sexual intercourse, deviate sexual intercourse, sexual bestiality, masturbation, sado-masochistic abuse, or lewd exhibition of the genitals. When Manhattan bookstore proprietor Paul Ferber was convicted for selling films depicting young boys masturbating, he appealed on the basis that the law infringed upon First Amendment rights. The Supreme Court disagreed. The opinion, per Justice White, acknowledged that "the use of children as subjects of pornographic materials is harmful to the physiological, emotional, and mental health of the child." Therefore, New York was entitled to considerable leeway in regulating pornographic depiction of children. The Court also noted that the *Miller*[37] test was not a satisfactory solution to the child pornography problem.

The *Miller* standard, like all general definitions of what may be banned as obscene, does not reflect the State's particular and more compelling interest in prosecuting those who promote the sexual exploitation of children. Thus, the question under the *Miller* test of whether a work, taken as a whole, appeals to the prurient interest of the average person bears no connection to the issue of whether a child has been physically or psychologically harmed in the production of the work. Similarly, a sexually explicit depiction need not be "patently offensive" in order to have required the sexual exploitation of a child for its production. In addition, a work which, taken on the whole, contains serious literary, artistic, political, or scientific value may nevertheless embody the hardest core of child pornography. . . . We therefore cannot conclude that the *Miller* standard is a satisfactory solution to the child pornography problem.[38]

In *Ferber*, the Court upheld the New York law, which excluded child pornography from First Amendment protection.

The cases cited in this section are significant. In *Butler* the Court rejected a statute that applied children's obscenity standards to adults. In *Ginsburg* the Court upheld a statute that defined separate obscenity standards for children, broader than those specified for adults. In *Ferber* the Court upheld a New York law that classified child pornography as an area of expression that is outside the protection of the First Amendment. In these three cases, the Court established that a state has responsibility to look after the well-being of its youth.

Privacy

The Supreme Court has explored the relationship betweeen obscenity and privacy. In 1969 the *Stanley* decision was handed down. Government agents suspected Robert Stanley of being involved in bookmaking activities. Armed with a search warrant, officers entered Stanley's home and found very little evidence of bookmaking activity, but they located three films that showed "successive orgies by nude men and women engaging in repeated acts of seduction, sodomy, and intercourse." Stanley was convicted of possessing obscene material. Before the Supreme Court, Stanley claimed the right to privacy in his own home. He demanded freedom from state inquiry into the contents of his private library. To counter, Georgia argued that Stanley did not have such rights; there are certain materials that a person may not read, or even possess. The Court unanimously supported Stanley, ruling "that a State has no business telling a man, sitting alone in his own home, what books he may read or what films he may watch." According to Justice Thurgood Marshall,

Georgia asserts the right to protect the individual's mind from the effects of obscenity. We are not certain that this argument amounts to anything more than the assertion that the State has the right to control the moral content of a per-

son's thoughts. To some, this may be a noble purpose, but it is wholly inconsistent with the philosophy of the First Amendment.[39]

The Court held that the First Amendment "prohibits making mere private possession of obscene material a crime."

In the following years, in *Thirty Seven Photographs, Reidel, Orito,* and *12
200-ft Reels,* the Court limited the scope of the *Stanley* principle. In *Thirty Seven
Photographs* the Court heard the case of Milton Luros, who, upon returning to
the United States from Europe, had in his luggage photographs that customs
agents seized as obscene. In terms of *Stanley,* the Supreme Court ruled that
Luros's situation did not involve the privacy of his own home. A port of entry
was not Luros's home. Luros's right to be let alone neither prevents the search
of his luggage, nor the seizure of obscene materials in his possession during such
a search.[40] At the same time, the Court heard the *Reidel* case. Norman Reidel
had been convicted under federal obscenity law for mailing a copy of an illustrated booklet entitled "The True Facts About Imported Pornography." Reidel
appealed. This case involved the distribution of obscene materials to willing
recipients who acknowledged being adults. The Court ruled that the *Stanley* principle was not relevant; it did not sanction the use of the channels of commerce
to disseminate obscene matter, nor did it sanction the postal service to be a party
to such activity. Obscenity, as well as its dissemination, is outside the protection of the First Amendment.[41] In *Orito* the Court further restricted the scope
of *Stanley.* Geogre Orito was convicted for knowingly transporting on Trans
World Airlines, from San Francisco to Milwaukee, 83 films, which authorities
called "lewd, lascivious, and filthy materials." In court Orito argued that the
Stanley case had established the right to possess obscene material in the privacy
of the home, and that there existed a correlative right to receive, transport, and
distribute such material. The Supreme Court, however, rejected "the idea that
some zone of constitutionally protected privacy follows such material when it
is moved outside the home area protected by *Stanley.*" Congress may regulate
interstate commerce in obscene materials.

> It is sufficient to reiterate the well-settled principle that Congress may impose
> relevant conditions and requirements on those who use the channels of inter-
> state commerce in order that those channels will not become the means of
> promoting or spreading evil, whether of a physical, moral or economic
> nature.[42]

In the *12 200-ft Reels* case, movies, photographs, color slides, and other printed
and graphic materials, being sent from Mexico to the United States, were seized
by customs officers at the Los Angeles Airport. The importer was convicted.
He appealed. The district court overturned the conviction by accepting the ar-

gument that *Stanley*, by acknowledging "the right to possess obscene material in the privacy of the home creates a right to acquire it or import it from another country." The Supreme Court, however, held that the focus in *Stanley* was on freedom of thought and mind in the privacy of the home, and a port of entry is not a traveler's home.[43] The Court disallowed the importation of obscene material for private use.

In *12 200-ft Reels*, as in *Orito, Reidel,* and *Thirty Seven Photographs*, the Court restricted the "privacy" ruling in *Stanley*. The Court upheld governmental power to regulate interstate transportation, delivery through the mails, or the importation from abroad of obscene materials for personal use.

Zoning

In many larger cities throughout the United States, obscene activity is located in a specific section of town. Police officers tend to ignore this few-block area where the dealers in pornography traffic, as long as there are no major citizen complaints or extremely gross pornographic activity. Adult theatres and adult bookstores are located in "erogenous zones" within the central city, because such areas are not very desirable for other commercial activity, but convenient for the customers of businesses offering pornography. In 1976 the Supreme Court considered whether a city could legally restrict pornography to a particular "zone."

In *Young* a divided Court supported a Detroit ordinance that restricted the geographic location of motion-picture theatres that exhibit nonobscene but sexually oriented films. According to the majority opinion written by Justice John Stevens, a "municipality may control the location of theatres as well as the location of other commercial establishments, either by confining them to certain specified commercial zones or by requiring that they be dispersed throughout the city."[44] The Court acknowledged that the content of films may be the basis for zoning restrictions. Such regulation did not violate First Amendment protection. In *Young* the Court affirmed the right of a city to determine locational requirements for adult theatres. It was the city's business to decide whether to "require adult theatres to be separated rather than concentrated in the same areas." In *Young* the Court actually upheld the regulation of protected expression that is sexually oriented, but not necessarily obscene.

Schad is a related case. In 1973 James Schad and his associates began operating an adult bookstore in the commercial zone of the Borough of Mount Ephraim, New Jersey. In 1976 Schad introduced a coin-operated machine that allowed customers to view a live, nude dancer, performing behind a glass panel. Schad was convicted of violating a local zoning ordinance that banned live entertainment within the commercial zone. Upon appeal, the Supreme Court declared the statute overbroad. By excluding live entertainment, the ordinance had prohibited a type of expression that was entitled to First Amendment protection. Justice White emphasized that the *Young* decision was not controlling in *Schad*. In *Young*

> the restriction did not affect the number of adult movie theaters that could operate in the city; it merely dispersed them. The Court did not imply that a municipality could ban all adult theaters—much less all live entertainment or all nude dancing—from its commercial districts city-wide.[45]

In *Schad* the Court recognized that the power of local governments to control land use is essential to achieving satisfactory quality of life in the community. Nonetheless, "the zoning power is not infinite and unchallengeable; it must be exercised within constitutional limits." Mount Ephraim had exceeded those limits.

Summary

Supreme Court cases have established certain guidelines for obscenity regulation. According to *Freedman*, prior restraint of expression is acceptable only in extreme circumstances. In *Hannegan* the Court refused the postmaster general power of censorship, but in *Rowan* it approved the right of an individual to censor his or her own mail with the help of the post office. The *Burstyn* decision extended First Amendment protection to the film medium. *Smith* determined that an obscenity conviction can be obtained only when the accused is aware of the obscenity. In *Ginzburg* the Court upheld a conviction based largely on pandering. *Butler* freed adult literature from obscenity tests that are appropriate for children's reading. *Ginsberg* defined separate obscenity standards for children—broader than those specified for adults. In *Stanley* the justices ruled that mere possession of obscene material in the privacy of one's home is not punishable. And the *Young* ruling upheld a locality's right to zone adult theatres that exhibit nonobscene but sexually oriented films.

NOTES

1. *Regina v. Hicklin*, L.R. 3Q.B. 360 (1868).
2. *People v. Seltzer*, 203 N.Y.S. 809 (1924).
3. *People v. Friede*, 233 N.Y.S. 565 (1929).
4. *Commonwealth v. Friede*, 171 N.E. 472 (1930).
5. *People v. Dial Press*, 182 Misc. 416 (1944).
6. *Besig v. United States*, 208 F. 2d 142 (1953).
7. *United States v. Kennerley*, 209 F. 119 (S.D.N.Y., 1913).
8. *United States v. One Book Called "Ulysses"*, 72 F. 2d 705 (1934).
9. *Roth v. United States*, 77 S.Ct. 1304 (1957).
10. *Manual Enterprises v. Day*, 82 S.Ct. 1432 (1962).

11. *Jacobellis v. Ohio,* 84 S.Ct. 1676 (1964).

12. *Mishkin v. United States,* 86 S.Ct. 958 (1966).

13. *A Book Named "John Cleland's Memoirs of a Woman of Pleasure" v. Attorney General of Massachusetts,* 86 S.Ct. 975 (1966).

14. *Redrup v. New York,* 87 S.Ct. 1414 (1967).

15. *Miller v. California,* 93 S.Ct. 2607 (1973).

16. *Jenkins v. Georgia,* 94 S.Ct. 2750 (1974).

17. *Ward v. Illinois,* 97 S.Ct. 2085 (1977).

18. *Jenkins.*

19. *Hamling v. United States,* 94 S.Ct. 2887 (1974).

20. *Smith v. United States,* 97 S.Ct. 1756 (1977).

21. *Pinkus v. United States,* 98 S.Ct. 1808 (1978).

22. *Roth.*

23.*Near v. Minnesota,* 51 S.Ct. 625 (1931).

24. *Times Film Corporation v. Chicago,* 81 S.Ct. 391 (1961).

25. *Freedman v. Maryland,* 85 S.Ct. 734 (1965).

26. *Southeastern Promotions v. Conrad,* 95 S.Ct. 1239 (1975).

27. *Vance v. Universal Amusement,* 100 S.Ct. 1156 (1980).

28. *Hannegan v. Esquire, Inc.,* 66 S.Ct. 456 (1946).

29. *Rowan v. U.S. Post Office Department,* 90 S.Ct. 1484 (1970).

30. *Mutual Film Corporation v. Industrial Commission of Ohio,* 35 S.Ct. 387 (1915).

31. *Burstyn v. Wilson,* 72 S.Ct. 777 (1952).

32. *Smith v. California,* 80 S.Ct. 215 (1959).

33. *Roth.*

34. *Ginzburg v. United States,* 86 S.Ct. 969 (1966).

35. *Butler v. Michigan,* 77 S.Ct. 524 (1957).

36. *Ginsberg v. New York,* 88 S.Ct. 1274 (1968).

37. *Miller.*

38. *New York v. Ferber,* 102 S.Ct. 3348 (1982).

39. *Stanley v. Georgia,* 89 S.Ct. 1243 (1969).

40. *United States v. Thirty Seven (37) Photographs,* 91 S.Ct. 1400 (1971).

41. *United States v. Reidel.,* 91 S.Ct. 1410 (1971).

42. *United States v. Orito,* 93 S.Ct. 2674 (1973).

43. *United States v. 12 200-ft Reels of Super 8 mm Film,* 93 S.Ct. 2665 (1973).

44. *Young v. American Mini Theatres,* 96 S.Ct. 2440 (1976).

45. *Schad v. Borough of Mount Ephraim,* 101 S.Ct. 2176 (1981).

RECOMMENDED READING

Dauber, Eric L., "Child Pornography: A New Exception to the First Amendment," *Florida State University Law Review* 10 (Winter, 1983), 684-701.

Gard, Stephen W., "Obscenity and the Right to be Let Alone: The Balancing of Constitutional Rights," *Indiana Law Review* 6 (1973), 490–508.

Haney, Roger D., "Obscenity and Pornography: Legal Arguments and Empirical Evidence," *Free Speech Yearbook* (1976), 46–59.

Hicks, Randolph S., "Federal Obscenity Prosecutions: Dirty Dealing with the First Amendment?" *Santa Clara Law Review* 18 (Summer, 1978), 720–56.

Katz, Ellen Edge, "Regulating Obscenity," *Whittier Law Review* 5 (1983), 1–35.

Ragsdale, J. Donald, "*Last Tango in Paris, et al. v. The Supreme Court*: The Current State of Obscenity Law," *Quarterly Journal of Speech* 61 (October, 1975), 279–89.

Schauer, Frederick F., "Reflections on 'Contemporary Community Standards': The Perception of an Irrelevant Concept in the Law of Obscenity," *North Carolina Law Review* 56 (January, 1978), 1–28.

Schauer, Frederick F., *The Law of Obscenity*. Washington, D.C.: Bureau of National Affairs, 1976.

Schauer, Frederick F., "The Return of Variable Obscenity?" *Hastings Law Journal* 28 (July, 1977), 1275–91.

KEY DECISIONS

1957—*ROTH*—concluded that obscenity was outside the protection of the First Amendment, and established a "liberal" definition of obscenity.

1965—*FREEDMAN*—established specific standards regulating prior restraint.

1966—*GINZBURG*—upheld obscenity conviction based on pandering.

1967—*REDRUP*—summarized differences in the thinking of Supreme Court justices regarding standards for obscenity regulation.

1969—*STANLEY*—allowed obscenity in the privacy of the home.

1970—*ROWAN*—rejected the idea that a vendor has a constitutional right to send unwanted material through the mails.

1973—*MILLER*—redefined obscenity; introduced a period of intensified regulation.

1976—*YOUNG*—upheld right of city to determine locational requirements for "adult" theatres.

1977—*SMITH*—indicated that the jury, rather than the state legislature, has responsibility for determining what is obscene.

1978—*PINKUS*—held that "children" are to be excluded as part of "community standards" for determining obscenity, yet "sensitive persons" should be included in the determination.

1982—*FERBER*—upheld a state law that excluded child pornography from First Amendment protection.

SUMMARY—OBSCENITY LAW

Definition

The Supreme Court has experienced difficulty in defining "obscenity." The current definition, set forth in *Miller*, views material as obscene if the average person, applying contemporary community standards, would find the dominant theme of the complete work appealing to the prurient interest. In addition, obscene material must be patently offensive and lack serious literary, artistic, political, or scientific value.

Proof

1. In order to win an obscenity case, the prosecution *must* show:
   a. Obscenity in the work
   b. Scienter—that is, knowledge of the obscene nature of the work
2. In order to win an obscenity case, the prosecution *might* show:
   a. Pandering—advertising material so as to appeal to the erotic interest of customers
   b. Sexploitation of youth—obscenity standards for youth are broader than for adults

Defenses

Some procedural defenses that have been applied in obscenity cases include the following:
1. Regulation constitutes prior restraint without meeting the *Freedman* safeguards:
   a. Burden of proof
   b. Brief period
   c. Prompt judicial review.
2. Ordinance is vague, overbroad, and discriminatory.
3. Materials were seized without validly obtained search warrant.

6

SILENCE

The First Amendment clearly guarantees the freedom to communicate. Does it also guarantee the freedom not to communicate? Does it guarantee the freedom not to be communicated with or the freedom to be let alone? The Supreme Court has, in several cases, answered these questions in the affirmative. Yet, while the right to silence is constitutionally protected, it is not absolute. Under certain conditions, an individual may be required to communicate, or to be communicated with, contrary to his or her will. In other situations, the individual enjoys a constitutional right to silence. This chapter reviews cases in which the Supreme Court has examined the individual's First Amendment right to remain silent, as well as the right to compel silence from others.

FREEDOM NOT TO COMMUNICATE

U.S. citizens have claimed a constitutionally protected right to refuse to communicate in a variety of situations. Some have refused to sign loyalty oaths. Others have declined to answer questions before investigative committees. Writers have sought to remain anonymous. Some individuals have objected to systems of government surveillance. The Supreme Court has been the final arbiter in many of these instances.

Loyalty Oaths

Chapter 4 considered several cases in which a loyalty oath was required as an indication of a teacher's fitness to work in the public-school system. In some of these cases—*Cramp*,[1] *Baggett*,[2] *Keyishian*,[3] and *Whitehill*[4]—the Court struck down such state requirements. The loyalty oath, however, has been required of state employees other than teachers. In some instances, these oath requirements have been tested in the courts.

In the 1966 *Elfbrandt* case, the Supreme Court was called upon to judge the constitutionality of an Arizona act that required state employees to take an oath in support of the state and national constitutions. According to the act, any employee who took the oath and "knowingly" belonged to an organization that sought to overthrow the government was subject to dismissal from his or her position. The Supreme Court found fault with the act. According to Justice William Douglas, a member who does not participate in an organization's unlawful activities poses no threat. Laws that are not restricted to members who join with the "intent" to further illegal action presume that all members share the unlawful goals of the organization. Such laws are based on the notion of "guilt by association."[5] The Arizona law was declared unconstitutional by the Court.

Five years later, in *Connell*, the Court considered a loyalty oath that was required of all Florida public employees. The oath consisted of five statements. The district court declared the following three statements unconstitutional: "I am not a member of the Communist Party"; "I have not and will not lend my aid, support, advice, counsel or influence to the Communist Party"; and "I am not a member of any organization or party which believes in or teaches, directly or indirectly, the overthrow of the Government of the United States or of Florida by force or violence." These statements rested on the assumption of "guilt by association." The Supreme Court heard an appeal regarding the remaining statements. The Court held that the provision, "I will support the Constitution of the United States and of the State of Flolrida," required no more of Florida public employees than was required of any other state or federal officer. That statement was deemed to be constitutional. The procedure surrounding the fifth statement, "I do not believe in the overthrow of the government of the United States or of the State of Florida by force or violence" was, however, held to be unconstitutional, because it provided for summary dismissal from employment. This procedure violated due process.[6]

In *Elfbrandt* and *Connell* the Court overturned loyalty oaths that were based on the assumption of "guilt by association" and that denied due process of law. In the 1972 *Richardson* case, the Court approved a Massachusetts loyalty oath that did not contain these flaws. Court action was initiated by Lucretia Richardson, who, upon refusing to take a mandatory loyalty oath, was dismissed from her job as a research sociologist at the Boston State Hospital. When the case reached the Supreme Court, the constitutionality of the oath was upheld. The oath in question contained two parts. The first required an individual to "uphold and defend" the Constitution of the United States and of the Commonwealth of Massachusetts. The justices unanimously agreed that this pledge was generally indistinguishable from oaths that had recently been approved by the Court. The second part required an individual "to oppose the overthrow of the governments" of the United States or of the Commonwealth "by force, violence or by any illegal or unconstitutional method.'' The Court determined, by a vote of four to three, that this clause sought a commitment from employees not to use illegal action to change the constitutional system. Even though the second part might be redundant, that was no ground to strike it down.[7]

Cases discussed in this section, as well as those examined in the chapter on academic freedom, suggest that the Court will not tolerate loyalty oaths that fail to meet rigid constitutional requirements. In *Cramp, Baggett, Keyishian,* and *Whitehill,* the Court rejected loyalty oaths that were ambiguous and overly broad. In *Elfbrandt* the Court overturned an oath that assumed ''guilt by association.'' In *Connell* the Court rejected a statement that provided summary dismissal from employment without a hearing. In *Richardson,* however, the Court upheld a loyalty oath that was considered to be constitutionally valid.

Investigative Committees

The *Watkins, Barenblatt,* and *Uphaus* cases involved an individual's right to refuse to answer questions before a governmental investigating committee. In these cases the Court considered whether a person has a right to silence under the First Amendment.

In April 1954, John Watkins was subpoenaed as a witness before the House Committee on Un-American Activities. In recent years, HUAC had intensified its efforts to curb Communist party activities. Before the committee, Watkins claimed that he was not then nor had he ever been a card-carrying member of the Communist party. Watkins was then confronted with the names of several people who were suspected of having been members of the Communist party. Watkins said he would answer questions about himself and about persons whom he believed to still be members of the Communist party. He would not, however, answer questions about persons who may have belonged to the Communist party in the past, but who had since terminated their membership. He did not believe that HUAC had any right to publicly expose persons because of their past activities. Watkins was found guilty of contempt and fined $100. Eventually the case reached the Supreme Court. The Court, per Chief Justice Earl Warren, declared that in congressional inquiries a witness cannot be required to testify against himself or herself, or be denied First Amendment freedoms. Warren was concerned about the compelling of an unwilling witness to testify about past beliefs and associations that are ''judged by current standards rather than those contemporary with the matters exposed.'' HUAC had ''no congressional power to expose for the sake of exposure.'' Warren emphasized that when First Amendment rights are involved, ''the delegation of power to the committee must be clearly revealed in its charter.'' In *Watkins* the investigative committee did not state the subject under inquiry and did not show the pertinence of the questions to the investigation. Because Watkins was not given a fair opportunity to decide whether he was entitled to refuse to answer, his conviction violated due process.[8] The conviction was overturned.

In *Barenblatt*, the Court upheld the conviction of Lloyd Barenblatt, who had objected to HUAC's inquiry into his "political" and "religious" beliefs, or any "other personal and private affairs" or "associational activities." Barenblatt refused to answer specific questions about his possible membership in and association with the Communist party. He was convicted of contempt, sentenced to six months' imprisonment, and fined $250. The Supreme Court upheld the conviction on three grounds. First, it was within HUAC's authority to compel testimony. Second, unlike *Watkins*, the questions asked by the committee were judged to be pertinent to the subject matter of HUAC's investigation. Third, the action of the committee did not violate the First Amendment. The Court compared the protections of the First and Fifth Amendments, noting that "the protections of the First Amendment, unlike a proper claim of the privilege against self-incrimination under the Fifth Amendment, do not afford a witness the right to resist inquiry in all circumstances."[9] In *Barenblatt* the balance between individual and governmental interests was weighted in favor of the government.

A related case, *Uphaus*, involved an effort by New Hampshire to investigate subversive activities within the state. Willard Uphaus, executive director of World Fellowship, a voluntary corporation maintaining a summer camp in New Hampshire, was asked by the New Hampshire attorney general to produce a list of the names of all the camp's employees for the two previous summer sessions and the names of all persons who attended the camp during those years. When Uphaus refused to comply with the committee's request, he was judged to be in contempt and was sent to jail until he complied with the order. The case reached the Supreme Court. The justices acknowledged that the attorney general was commissioned to determine if there were any subversive people in New Hampshire. The obvious starting point for such an inquiry was to learn what persons were in the state. Any requests for lists of persons related directly to the purpose of the probe, and thus the inquiries were "pertinent." The committee's demand for the lists was legitimate and the contempt citation for refusing to produce the lists was valid.[10] In *Uphaus* the conviction was upheld.

The cases cited in this section focus on the First Amendment right to silence enjoyed by individuals called before an investigative committee. In *Watkins, Barenblatt,* and *Uphaus* the Court noted that a witness may be required to testify about personal matters and association activities, when the questions have obvious pertinence to the purpose of the investigation.

Anonymous Publication

A Los Angeles ordinance provided that no person could distribute any leaflet that did not have printed on its face the names and addresses of the persons who had written and distributed it. When Michael Talley distributed leaflets void of the required information, he was arrested, convicted, and fined $10. He appealed. The Supreme Court decided that the law violated Talley's right to free speech and press.

> There can be no doubt that such an identification requirement would tend to restrict freedom to distribute information and thereby freedom of expression. Liberty of circulating is as essential to that freedom as liberty of publishing; indeed, without the circulation, the publication would be of little value.[11]

Justice Hugo Black noted that, throughout history, persecuted groups have been able to criticize their oppressors either by anonymous means, or not at all. According to Black, anonymity must be protected, because it had "sometimes been assumed for the most constructive of purposes." The Court supported Talley's freedom to refuse to communicate the required information.

Surveillance

In 1967 the U.S. Army was asked to assist local authorities in quelling civil disorders in Detroit, Michigan. To enhance its effort, the army developed a data-gathering system, which included the collection of information about public activities that were thought to have some potential for civil disorder. The information was then stored in a data bank at army intelligence headquarters at Fort Holabird, Maryland. Arlo Tatum, a conscientious objector who believed that he was a target for army surveillance, argued in court that the army was conducting illegal surveillance of civilian political activity. The case reached the Supreme Court. The issue was whether an individual had his or her First Amendment freedoms "chilled" by the mere existence of governmental data-gathering activity. Tatum argued that a "chilling" effect resulted from the potential abuse of power by the military and the potential later misuse of gathered data. The Court's majority opinion, prepared by Chief Justice Warren Burger, held that "allegations of a subjective 'chill' are not an adequate substitute for a claim of specific present objective harm or a threat of specific future harm." Army surveillance could be challenged in court, but only if individuals could demonstrate "actual or threatened injury."[12] Tatum had failed to demonstrate any actual injury. In effect, the *Tatum* ruling approved of the government's right to gather information that an individual did not wish to communicate.

Summary

The right not to communicate has been supported by the Supreme Court. Loyalty oaths that are vague, overly broad, based on guilt by association, or that deny due process have been declared unconstitutional. The Court has decided that an individual may be required to testify about personal matters and associational activities only when the questions have obvious pertinence to the purpose of the investigation. Moreover, the Court has protected anonymous publication as a historically significant factor in producing social change. Yet, in some cases—*Richardson, Barenblatt, Uphaus, Tatum*—the Court has upheld the government's right to require individuals to communicate. The right to silence is not absolute.

FREEDOM NOT TO BE COMMUNICATED WITH

The Supreme Court has considered the question of whether an individual enjoys a freedom to prevent incoming communication. In *Saia* and *Kovacs*, the Court considered whether restrictions could be placed on the public use of sound-amplification equipment. In *Pollak* the Court decided whether a public transportation company could broadcast a radio program over loudspeakers on its vehicles.

Sound Amplification

A Lockport, New York, ordinance prohibited the use of sound-amplification devices, except with the permission of the chief of police. Complying with this law, Samuel Saia, a minister of the Jehovah's Witnesses, obtained permission to use sound equipment, mounted atop his car, to amplify speeches on religious topics. The presentations were made in a public park on certain Sundays. When his permit expired, Saia applied for another, but his request was refused because several complaints had been received concerning the "noise." Saia then used his equipment without permission and was arrested. The case reached the Supreme Court. According to the majority opinion written by Justice Douglas, the ordinance contained several flaws. The statute provided no standards to guide the police chief in granting permission. The statute did not regulate the hours of use of loudspeakers, nor did it specify the volume of sound allowed. Douglas's opinion noted that "any abuses which loudspeakers create can be controlled by narrowly drawn statutes." The Lockport ordinance failed to satisfy this requirement. Douglas also feared the power of censorship inherent in the ordinance. Douglas noted that, in Saia's case, a permit was denied because some persons found the sound annoying. In future cases, a permit might be denied because some people found the ideas annoying. According to Douglas, "annoyance at ideas can be cloaked in annoyance at sound."[13] The Lockport ordinance allowed for prior restraint of the right of free speech. In *Saia* the Court declared the ordinance to be unconstitutional.

A year later, in *Kovacs*, the Court supported a Trenton, New Jersey, ordinance that forbade the use, on city streets, of mobile sound devices that send out loud and raucous noises. Charles Kovacs was convicted for violating this or-

"ANYTHING WRONG, OFFICER?"

dinance by speaking into an amplifier in order to comment upon a labor dispute. Kovacs appealed. The Supreme Court ruled that sound amplification in public places was subject to reasonable regulation. The majority opinion, per Justice Stanley Reed, acknowledged that "city streets are recognized as a normal place for the exchange of ideas by speech or paper. But this does not mean the freedom is beyond all control." Reed expressed concern that "such distractions would be dangerous to traffic" and that "in the residential thoroughfares the quiet and tranquility so desirable for city dwellers would likewise be at the mercy of advocates of particular religious, social or political persuaders."[14] The minority opinion, written by Justice Black, argued that an ordinance could be written that protected a community from unreasonable use of amplifying systems without absolutely denying the use of this avenue of communication. An ordinance could restrict the volume of sound or the hours during which amplification was permitted—without infringing upon free speech. The majority, however, ruled that the Trenton statute did not violate First Amendment freedoms. Under the ordinance, a person had a right not to be communicated with.

Forced Listening

In March 1948, Capital Transit Company, a privately owned transportation system that operated in the District of Columbia, initiated "music-as-you-ride" radio programs, which were played through loudspeakers in streetcars and buses. The programs consisted of about 10 percent commercial announcements on behalf of Capital Transit and 90 percent musical selections. Franklin Pollak and Guy Martin initiated court action on the ground that the radio programs interfered with their freedoms of conversation by making it necessary for them to compete against the programs in order to be heard. When the case reached the Supreme Court, the justices decided that the radio programs violated neither the right to free speech nor the right to privacy. Pollak and Martin had contended that the First Amendment guarantees a right to listen only to those points of view an individual wishes to hear. The Court found no evidence to sustain this argument, because the radio programs had not "been used for objectionable propaganda." The Court also found that the radio programs did not violate an individual's right to privacy. The Court noted that it would be incorrect to assume that a passenger on a public vehicle is entitled to privacy substantially equal to that which is available at home. No matter how complete the right to privacy is at home, it is limited by the rights of others when a person travels on public transit.[15] Under the conditions present in *Pollak*, an individual did not enjoy the right to prevent incoming communication.

Summary

In this section, cases were presented in which the Supreme Court analyzed whether an individual has the right not to be communicated with. Consideration of such cases as *Saia, Kovacs,* and *Pollak* lead to the conclusion that an individual has a limited right to this form of silence.

FREEDOM TO BE LET ALONE

The Supreme Court has contemplated several individual claims to the right to be let alone. Some of these cases involved ordinances that were designed to regulate door-to-door, community-wide, and institutional solicitation and distribution. Other cases concerned laws that were written to control an individual's freedom to travel.

Solicitation and Distribution

During the past several decades, the Supreme Court has been asked to balance the fredoms of solicitors and distributors against the right of citizens to be free from uninvited intrusions at the front doors of their homes, on the streets of their cities, or at various places throughout their communities. In such cases, the peace and quiet of both the neighborhood and the community have been at stake.

Door-to-Door

The Court has evaluated the constitutionality of various local ordinances, which, in such cases as *Lovell, Martin, Murdock, Breard, Hynes,* and *Schaumburg,* were designed to regulate door-to-door solicitation and distribution.

In *Lovell* the Court considered an ordinance that prohibited the distribution of any kind of literature in Griffin, Georgia, without the permission of the city manager. Alma Lovell was convicted for distributing, without permission, a religious pamphlet that set forth the gospel of Jehovah's Witnesses. The case was appealed. In a unanimous decision the Supreme Court declared that the ordinance was unconstitutional. It prohibited the distribution of "circulars, handbooks, advertising, or literature of any kind." It was not restricted to "literature" that was obscene or offensive to public morals, or that advocated unlawful conduct. Instead, the ordinance prevented the distribution of literature of any kind, at any place, and in any manner, without a permit. The ordinance was thus deemed to be too broad in its restrictions.[16]

In *Martin* the Court examined an ordinance that banned the distribution of literature to residences in Struthers, Ohio. When Thelma Martin distributed literature on behalf of the Jehovah's Witnesses, she was convicted of violating the ordinance and was fined $10. She appealed. The Supreme Court sided with Martin. According to the Court, a city does not have the power to prevent a person from going from residence to residence in order to distribute an announcement for a religious meeting. Even though such a distribution causes inconvenience, this is a small price to pay for the protection of free speech and press. An occupant could, however, post a notice on the door indicating his or her desire not to be disturbed by uninvited solicitors or distributors. The Struthers ordinance was overturned, because it "in effect, makes a person a criminal trespasser if he enters the property of another for an innocent purpose without an explicit command from the owners to stay away."[17] In *Martin* the Court determined that a notice to stay away is necessary to stop intrusions by "harmless" distributors.

On the same day that the Court handed down the *Martin* opinion, it decided the *Murdock* case. At stake was an ordinance prohibiting persons from soliciting in Jeanette, Pennsylvania, without first obtaining a license and paying a tax. When Robert Murdock, a member of Jehovah's Witnesses, distributed literature and solicited people to buy religious pamphlets, he was convicted and fined for violating the ordinance. When the case reached the Supreme Court, the justices faced a single issue—the constitutionality of the ordinance, which required religious colporteurs to pay a tax as a condition for the pursuit of their activities.

The Court decided, in a five-to-four vote, that the ordinance was unconstitutional, because it restrained in advance the freedoms "of press and religion and inevitably tends to suppress their exercise." The tax did not acquire validity simply because it was "nondiscriminatory." The Court majority stressed that First Amendment freedoms "are in a preferred position."[18]

In *Breard* the Court approved an ordinance that placed limitations on door-to-door solicitation. Jack Breard, a regional representative of Keystone Readers Service Company, supervised a crew of solicitors who went door-to-door in various cities seeking subscriptions for several nationally known magazines. While soliciting in Alexandria, Louisiana, Breard was arrested for violating an ordinance that required solicitors to obtain prior consent from the owners of the residences solicited. Breard was found guilty and sentenced to pay a $25 fine or spend 30 days in jail. He appealed. The Supreme Court, per Justice Reed, compared the facts in *Breard* with those in *Martin* and concluded that door-to-door solicitation for commercial purposes could be prohibited by local ordinance. The Court decided that "subscriptions may be made by anyone interested in receiving the magazines without the annoyances of house-to-house canvassing." According to Reed, "communities that have found these methods of sale obnoxious may control them by ordinance."[19]

In *Hynes* the Court considered an Oradell, New Jersey, ordinance that required any individual wishing to solicit door-to-door for a charitable or political cause to register with the police department for identification purposes. When state Assemblyman Edward Hynes wished to campaign for reelection by canvassing door-to-door and speaking with voters, he initiated suit. Hynes claimed that the ordinance restricted First Amendment freedoms. The Supreme Court noted that the ordinance lacked specific standards to be used by authorities who would apply the ordinance. There was also no clue as to what qualified as a "recognized charity" or a "political cause."[20] The ordinance was declared unconstitutional because of vagueness.

In *Schaumburg* the Court evaluated the constitutionality of an ordinance prohibiting door-to-door or on-street solicitation of contributions by charitable organizations not using at least 75 percent of their receipts for "charitable purposes." When a nonprofit, environmental-protection group, Citizens for a Better Environment, was denied a solicitation permit because it could not meet the ordinance's "75 percent requirement," the group sought relief in the courts. The Supreme Court, per Justice Byron White, decided that the requirement was illegal. Although the 75 percent requirement might be enforceable against "traditional" charities, it was not applicable to some groups. These were the organizations whose main purpose was not to provide money or services for the poor, but to gather and disseminate information about matters of public concern. Such organizations characteristically used paid employees.

> These organizations . . . pay . . . employees to obtain and process the necessary information and to arrive at and announce in suitable form the organi-

zations' preferred positions on the issues of interest to them. Organizations of this kind, although they might pay only reasonable salaries, would necessarily spend more than 25 percent of their budgets on salaries and administrative expenses and would be completely barred from solicitation.[21]

The Court held that the ordinance was unconstitutionally overbroad, in violation of the First Amendment.

The cases considered in this section indicate that the personal inconvenience that results from unsolicited distribution of literature is generally outweighed by the public interest in maintaining a free flow of information. The Court did decide, however, in *Martin*, that an individual may restrict uninvited solicitors by posting a notice to stay away. And, in *Breard*, the Court held that door-to-door solicitation for commercial purposes may be banned. In such cases, the Supreme Court recognized an individual's right to be let alone.

Community-wide

The focus of the cases described thus far has been on prohibitions against door-to-door solicitation. In other cases—*Marsh* and *Organization For A Better Austin*—the central concern has been with community-wide bans.

In *Marsh* the Supreme Court deliberated whether Alabama could forbid an individual from distributing religious literature on the premises of a company-owned town. Chickasaw, a suburb of Mobile, was owned by the Gulf Shipbuilding Corporation. There was nothing to differentiate Chickasaw from any other town, except that the title to the property belonged to a private corporation. In Chickasaw, stores were posted with a notice that declared the area private property and prohibited any distribution or solicitation without written permission. Grace Marsh, a Jehovah's Witness, was told by town officials that she could not distribute religious literature without a permit and that no permit would be issued. When Marsh proceeded to distribute leaflets, she was arrested and convicted. The case reached the Supreme Court. The majority opinion, per Justice Black, noted that people who live in company-owned towns must make decisions that affect the welfare of their community and nation. They must have access to information and the distribution of literature is vital to such access. In *Marsh*, Justice Black concluded that when the rights of property owners are balanced against First Amendment freedoms of the people, "the latter occupy a preferred position."[22]

In *Organization For A Better Austin*, the Court again evaluated a community-wide ban on distribution. Organization For A Better Austin, a racially integrated organization in the Austin neighborhood of Chicago, was formed in order to "stabilize" the racial ratio in the area. For several years the boundary of the black segregated area of Chicago had moved progressively west toward Austin. OBA, in its efforts to "stabilize" the area, opposed such real-estate tactics as "blockbusting" and "panic peddling." OBA contended that Jerome Keefe, a real-estate broker, had engaged in such activities and thereby aroused fear in white residents that blacks were moving into the area. Then, by exploiting the reactions of whites, Keefe was able to secure listings and sell homes to blacks. OBA members met with Keefe to attempt to convince him to alter his practices, but he argued that he was entitled to solicit real-estate business as he wished. Subsequently, OBA members distributed throughout Westchester, the city in which Keefe resided, leaflets that criticized Keefe's real-estate activities. Keefe obtained a lower-court injunction that prohibited OBA from distributing leaflets anywhere in Westchester. The case reached the Supreme Court. In the majority opinion, Chief Justice Warren Burger ruled that the injunction, by imposing prior restraint, constituted an impermissible restraint on First Amendment freedoms. According to Burger, the injunction operated "not to redress alleged private wrongs, but to suppress, on the basis of previous publications, distribution of literature 'of any kind' in a city [Westchester] of 18,000."[23] The injunction was vacated. In *Organization For A Better Austin*, as in *Marsh*, the Supreme Court overturned community-wide bans that violated certain free-speech rights of solicitors and distributors.

Institutional Access

In recent years several Supreme Court cases have determined the conditions, if any, under which certain traditional and respected "institutions" may facilitate solicitation and/or distribution of various types of information. In these cases the Court examined free-speech rights and responsibilities of such institutions as military bases, the postal service, corporations, state fair grounds, government property, and public posting.

Military bases.   In four cases—*Flower, Spock, Glines, Huff*—the Supreme Court pondered the issue of allowing or prohibiting petition and distribution at military facilities. In these cases the Court determined that, under certain conditions, such activities may be regulated more extensively at military installations than at other facilities.

Concerning the *Flower* case, John Flower, a member of the American Friends Service Committee, was arrested by military police while quietly distributing leaflets on New Braunfels Avenue within the limits of Fort Sam Houston. He had previously been barred from the base because he attempted to distribute "unauthorized" materials. Flower was convicted under a federal law for reentering a military base in violation of an express order not to do so. Upon appeal, the Supreme Court noted that the base commander had not barred vehicular or pedestrian traffic from the street where Flower was arrested. Therefore, New Braunfels Avenue was a public thoroughfare.

Under such circumstances the military has abandoned any claim that it has special interests in who walks, talks, or distributes leaflets on the avenue. The base commandant can no more order petitioner [Flower] off this public street because he was distributing leaflets than could the city police order any leafleteer off any public street.[24]

According to the Court, the First Amendment protected Flower under these conditions.

The *Spock* case arose when the base commander at Fort Dix denied Dr. Benjamin Spock—a candidate of the People's party for the office of president—permission to visit the post in order to distribute campaign literature and discuss election issues with servicemen and their families. Base regulations banned "demonstrations, picketing, sit-ins, protest marches, political speeches, and similar activities" and allowed the posting of handbills and the distribution of leaflets only with the prior written approval of the base commander. Spock initiated court action, contending a violation of First Amendment rights. The Supreme Court supported the Fort Dix policy "of keeping official military activities there wholly free of entanglement with partisan political campaigns of any kind." According to the Court, per Justice Potter Stewart, the policy of banning speeches was "consistent with the American Constitutional tradition of a politically neutral military establishment under civilian control." Furthermore, "it is a policy that the military authorities at Fort Dix were constitutionally free to pursue." Stewart emphasized that "the notion that federal reservations, like municipal streets and parks, have traditionally served as a place for free public assembly and communication of thoughts by private citizens is . . . historically and constitutionally false."[25] In *Spock* the Court emphasized that Fort Dix did not abandon any right to regulate the distribution of leaflets, as did the base in *Flower*. In *Flower* the street in question was a public thoroughfare and the military had abandoned any right to ban civilian traffic. In *Spock* such civilian access could be restricted.

In 1980 the Supreme Court reiterated its position in two cases—*Glines* and *Huff*. The *Glines* case involved air-force regulations that require military personnel to obtain proper authorization from their commanders prior to circulating petitions on bases. When Captain Albert Glines distributed petitions to members of Congress and to the secretary of defense, in which he complained about grooming standards, he was removed from active duty. Glines brought suit. The Supreme Court cited *Spock* in upholding the air-force regulations. According to Justice Lewis Powell, "a base commander may prevent the circulation of material that he determines to be a clear threat to the readiness of his troops."[26] In a similar case, *Huff*, the Court upheld navy and marine-corps regulations that required military personnel on overseas bases to obtain command approval before circulating petitions addressed to members of Congress.[27] Both *Glines* and *Huff* affirmed the position established in *Spock*—military regulations may lawfully require members of the armed forces to secure command approval before circulating petitions or distributing leaflets within a military base.

Postal service.   Three cases—*Procunier, Greenburgh,* and *Perry Education Association*—involved efforts to control the distribution of information through the postal service. Each case, however, took place within a different context.

In *Procunier* the Court evaluated regulations that allowed authorities to censor the mail of prison inmates. As director of the California Department of Corrections, Raymond Procunier established rules that directed inmates not to write letters in which they "unduly complain" or "magnify grievances," express "inflammatory . . . views or beliefs," describe "criminal activity," are "obscene or defamatory," include "foreign matter," or contain material that is "otherwise inappropriate." Prison employees screened both incoming and outgoing mail to determine violations of the regulations. The inmates challenged the regulations. The Supreme Court, through the opinion of Justice Powell, decided that censorship of prisoner mail is justified when two criteria are met.

> First, the regulation or practice in question must further an important or substantial governmental interest unrelated to the suppression of expression. Prison officials may not censor inmate correspondence simply to eliminate unflattering or unwelcome opinions or factually inaccurate statements. Rather, they must show that a regulation authorizing mail censorship furthers one or more of the substantial governmental interests of security, order, and rehabilitation. Second, the limitation of First Amendment freedoms must be no greater than is necessary or essential to the protection of the particular governmental interest involved. Thus a restriction on inmate correspondence that furthers an important or substantial interest of penal administration will nevertheless be invalid if its sweep is unnecessarily broad.[28]

On the basis of these criteria, the Court found that Procunier's regulations "invited prison officials and employees to apply their own personal prejudices and opinions as standards for prisoner mail censorship." The regulations allowed censorship that was "far broader than any legitimate interest in penal administration demands." In *Procunier* the Court acknowledged that censorship of prisoner mail is justifiable, but only under specific guidelines.

In *Greenburgh* the Court considered the general question of letter-box use. Council of Greenburgh Civic Associations, an umbrella organization for several civic groups in Westchester County, New York, was notified that the association's practice of delivering messages to local residents by placing unstamped notices and pamphlets in the letter boxes of private homes violated a federal ordinance. The group was advised that continuation of this practice could result in a fine. Council members filed suit in court, contending that enforcement of the ordinance would inhibit communication with residents of Greenburgh and would deny free-speech and free-press rights. The case reached the Supreme

Court. In the majority opinion, Justice William Rehnquist noted that the Court was not confronted with a regulation that in any way prohibits individuals from going door-to-door, or that prohibits individuals to use the mails to distribute their messages. The issue was solely the constitutionality of an ordinance that makes it unlawful for a person to use, without paying a fee, a letter box that has been designated as an "authorized depository" of mail by the postal service. Rehnquist argued that once a letter box becomes an "authorized depository," it does not undergo transformation into a "public forum" with First Amendment guarantees of access to all. Rehnquist pointed out that the letter box has been an essential part of a national delivery system since 1934, but there is no constitutional or historical evidence to view the letter box as a "public forum." In *Greenburgh* the Court concluded that the ordinance did not abridge First Amendment rights, because the ordinance was not geared to the content of the message sought to be placed in the letter box.[29]

Perry Education Association involved the issue of privileged access to teacher mailboxes. Perry Educational Association was the duly elected, exclusive bargaining representative for the teachers in the Perry, Indiana, school district. A collective bargaining agreement provided the association with access to the interschool mail system and to teacher mailboxes in the Perry schools. No other union was granted access. A rival union initiated court action. The issue in this case was whether the First Amendment was violated when a union that had been elected by school teachers as their exclusive bargaining representative was granted access to certain means of communication, while similar access was denied to a rival union. The Supreme Court, per Justice White, noted that an "interschool mail system is not a traditional public forum." Consequently, there is no constitutional obligation to let any organization use the school mailboxes.

> Implicit in the concept of the nonpublic forum is the right to make distinctions in access on the basis of subject matter and speaker identity. These distinctions may be impermissible in a public forum but are inherent and inescapable in the process of limiting a nonpublic forum to activities compatible with the intended purpose of the property.[30]

In White's opinion, the differential access provided to the unions was reasonable, because it enabled Perry Educational Association to perform its obligations as exclusive representative of all Perry teachers. The rival union had no similar obligations. In a dissenting opinion, Justices Brennan, Marshall, Powell, and Stevens argued that the access approved by the majority "amounts to viewpoint discrimination" and such a policy infringes on First Amendment freedoms.

In the cases cited in this section, the Supreme Court determined that, under specific conditions, individuals have differential access to the postal system as a means of distributing information. In *Procunier* the Court acknowledged that prisoner mail may be censored, if specific guidelines are met. In *Greenburgh* the Court determined that the letter box was not a public forum and that it could be restricted to those who were willing to pay a fee. In *Perry Education Association* the Court approved differential access; a labor union that was the exclusive bargaining representative for teachers could enjoy privileged access to those teachers' mailboxes.

Corporations.   In two cases—*First National Bank of Boston* and *Consolidated Edison of New York*—the Supreme Court considered the First Amendment rights of corporations. In these cases the Court examined conditions under which corporations could distribute information.

First National Bank of Boston involved a Massachusetts law that prohibited corporations from making contributions for the purpose of influencing political issues other than those "materially affecting any of the property, business or assets of the corporation." A corporation that violated the law could receive a fine of $50,000. When two national banking associations and three business corporations wanted to spend money to publicize their views on a proposed constitutional amendment, they started court action to have the law declared unconstitutional. The Supreme Court, in the opinion written by Justice Powell, rejected the notion that expression of views on public issues loses First Amendment protection when the source is a corporation that cannot prove that the issues materially affect the corporation's business.

> If the speakers here were not corporations, no one would suggest that the State could silence their proposed speech. It is the type of speech indispensable to decision-making in a democracy, and this is no less true because the speech comes from a corporation rather than an individual. The inherent worth of the speech in terms of its capacity for informing the public does not depend upon the identity of its source, whether corporation, association, union, or individual.[31]

In *First National Bank of Boston* the Court acknowledged that a corporation enjoys First Amendment rights of free expression.

In *Consolidated Edison Company of New York*, the Court once again examined corporate free-speech rights. Consolidated Edison Company of New York placed a pamphlet entitled "Independence Is Still a Goal, and Nuclear Power Is Needed to Win the Battle," in its billing envelopes. The pamphlet stated Consolidated Edison's views on "the benefits of nuclear power," saying that they "far outweigh any potential risk" and that nuclear power plants are safe, economical, and clean. Shortly thereafter, an anti-nuclear-power group requested Consolidated Edison to enclose a rebuttal, prepared by the group, in its next billing envelope. When the request was refused, the Public Service Commission of New York was asked to intervene. After deliberation, the commission prohibited "utilities from using bill inserts to discuss political matters, including the desirability of nuclear power." Consolidated Edison sought review of the order. The Supreme Court overturned the order for two reasons. First, the restriction on bill inserts could not be upheld on the ground that the company was not entitled to freedom of speech. In *First National Bank of Boston*, the Court had "rejected the contention that a State may confine corporate speech to a specified issue." Second, the order was invalidly drawn in three ways. The ban was not a valid time, place, or manner restriction; it was clearly related to subject matter. Nor was the ban a permissible subject-matter regulation.

> The First Amendment's hostility to content-based regulation extends not only to restrictions on particular viewpoints, but also to prohibition of public discussion of an entire topic. As a general matter, the First Amendment means that government has no power to restrict expression because of its message, its ideas, its subject matter, or its content.[32]

Also, the ban was not justified by a compelling state interest. It was not necessary to avoid forcing Consolidated Edison's views on a captive audience; customers could escape exposure simply by throwing the insert into a wastebasket. In *Consolidated Edison Company of New York*, as in *First National Bank of Boston*, the Supreme Court furthered the First Amendment right of corporations to distribute information.

State fair grounds.   Each year, the Minnesota Agricultural Society operates a state fair on a 125-acre, state-owned tract located in St. Paul. The fair is a major public event and attracts people from all over Minnesota, as well as from other parts of the country. One of the regulations of the fair specified that any nonprofit, charitable, or commercial organization could conduct its sales, distribution, or funds solicitation only in a rented booth, from a fixed location on the fair grounds. Representatives could walk about the grounds and promote their organization's views in face-to-face discussions, but all distribution and solicitation were to be done from the fixed locations. One day prior to the opening of the 1977 Minnesota State Fair, International Society For Krishna Consciousness filed suit in court, seeking a declaration that the regulation violated the First Amendment. Specifically, the society asserted that the regulation suppressed the practice of Sankirtan, a religious ritual that enjoins members to go into public places to distribute or sell religious literature and to solicit donations for the support of the Krishna religion. The Supreme Court, in the opinion written by Justice White, acknowledged that the oral and written dissemination of the Krishna views is protected by the First Amendment. The First Amendment does not, however, guarantee the right to communicate those views at all times and places or in any manner that may be desired. According to Justice White, the Minnesota rule was a permissible restriction on the place and manner of communicating the religious views of the Krishna group.

The Rule applies even-handedly to all who wish to distribute and sell written materials or to solicit funds. No person or organization, whether commercial or charitable, is permitted to engage in such activities except from a booth rented for those purposes.[33]

Justice White also recognized that because the fair attracted large crowds, "the State's interest in the orderly movement and control of such an assembly of persons is a substantial consideration." In *Krishna*, since the flow of the crowd and demands for safety were vital, Minnesota was justified in regulating the distribution and solicitation rights on the state fair grounds.

Government property.   In *Grace* the Court examined a federal statute that prohibited the distribution of leaflets and the display of banners on the U.S. Supreme Court grounds. The statute identified the surrounding streets and sidewalks as part of the grounds. Court action was initiated by two citizens. Thaddeus Zywicki filed a suit when he was prohibited from distributing leaflets concerning such topics as the removal of unfit judges and oppression in Central America. Mary Grace sought relief when she was not allowed to display a sign on which was inscribed the text of the First Amendment. The Supreme Court, per Justice White, decided that the section of the statute "which totally bans the specified communicative activity on the public sidewalks around the Court grounds cannot be justified as a reasonable place restriction." According to White:

Traditional public forum property occupies a special position in terms of First Amendment protection and will not lose its historically recognized character for the reason that it abuts government property that has been dedicated to a use other than as a forum for public expression. Nor may the government transform the character of the property by the expedient of including it within the statutory definition of what might be considered a non-public forum parcel of property. The public sidewalks forming the perimeter of the Supreme Court grounds, in our view, are public forums and should be treated as such for First Amendment purposes.[34]

Justice White stressed that the sidewalks at stake in this case should be regulated in the same manner as other sidewalks.

The building's perimeter sidewalks are indistinguishable from other public sidewalks in the city that are normally open to the conduct that is at issue here....
A total ban on that conduct is no more necessary for the maintenance of peace and tranquility on the public sidewalks surrounding the building than on any other sidewalks in the city.

In *Grace* the Court declared unconstitutional the section of the federal statute that applied to the sidewalks surrounding the Supreme Court grounds.

Public posting.   At issue in the 1984 *Vincent* case was a Los Angeles law that prohibited the posting of signs on public property. In 1979 Roland Vincent was a candidate for election to the Los Angeles City Council. His supporters posted signs with Vincent's name on them on utility poles at various locations. When city employees routinely removed the posters, Vincent's supporters initiated court action, seeking an injunction against enforcement of the law. The case reached the Supreme Court. The decision, per Justice John Stevens, upheld the law for three reasons. First, there was no hint of bias; the law did not seek to suppress certain ideas while favoring others. According to Stevens, the text of the law "is neutral . . . concerning any speaker's point of view." Second, Los Angeles's interest in avoiding visual clutter justified the prohibition of public postings. Third, other effective means of communication were available to Vincent's supporters.

> The Los Angeles ordinance does not affect any individual's freedom to exercise the right to speak and to distribute literature in the same place where the posting of signs on public property is prohibited. To the extent that the posting of signs on public property has advantages over these forms of expression, there is no reason to believe that these same advantages cannot be obtained through other means. To the contrary . . . there are ample alternative modes of communication in Los Angeles.[35]

In *Vincent* the Court held that Los Angeles could enforce a content-neutral, impartially administered ban against public postings.

Travel

Is there a First Amendment freedom of movement? In several cases, the Supreme Court has examined the travel rights of U.S. citizens. In *Kent, Aptheker, Zemel, Agee,* and *Wald,* the issue involved the right of U.S. citizens to travel abroad. In *Mandel,* the Court considered the right of a foreigner to enter the United States.

When Rockwell Kent wanted to attend a meeting in Helsinki, Finland, his application for a passport was denied by the secretary of state on the ground that Kent was a Communist. Kent initiated court action. The Supreme Court decided that freedom of movement was a part of the U.S. heritage.

> Freedom of movement across frontiers in either direction, and inside the country, may be as close to the heart of the individual as the choice of what he eats, or hears, or reads. Freedom of movement is basic in our scheme of values.[36]

According to the Court, the secretary of state was not entrusted with the power to grant or withhold the right to travel. In *Kent* the ban on travel was reversed.

In *Aptheker* the Court established a link between the right to travel and First

Amendment freedoms. The case involved Section Six of the Subversive Activities Control Act of 1950. The act provided that a member of a Communist organization could not apply for or use a passport. Herbert Aptheker challenged the act in court, arguing that Section Six deprived him of his constitutional right to travel. The Supreme Court, per Justice Arthur Goldberg, declared Section Six unconstitutional because its sweep was too broad and too indiscriminate. The act neglected such relevant considerations as the individual's "knowledge, activity, commitment, and purposes in and places for travel." Justice Goldberg also noted that "freedom of travel is a constitutional liberty closely related to rights of free speech and association."[37] In a concurring opinion, Justice Black viewed Section Six as unconstitutional because it denied Aptheker "the freedom of speech, press, and association which the First Amendment guarantees."

In *Zemel* the Court upheld a restriction on travel. Until 1961 no passport was required to travel anywhere in the Western Hemisphere. In that year the State Department eliminated Cuba from the list of places for which passports were not required and declared all passports invalid for travel to Cuba unless approved by the secretary of state. In 1964 Louis Zemel requested permission to travel to Cuba in order to satisfy his "curiosity about the state of affairs in Cuba" and to make him "a better informed citizen." When his request was denied, he appealed. Chief Justice Earl Warren, writing for the Court majority, upheld the secretary of state's restriction on travel. Warren contrasted the facts in *Zemel* with those in earlier decisions. The issue in *Kent* and *Aptheker* had been whether a person could be refused a passport because of political beliefs or associations. In *Zemel* the issue was whether a passport could be denied to an individual "because of foreign policy considerations affecting all citizens." In Warren's opinion, the reason for denying the right to travel in *Zemel* was justified. In *Zemel* the Court supported executive authority to impose area restrictions on travel. Warren also considered whether such a restriction violated the First Amendment. Warren admitted that the denial of travel to Cuba "renders less than wholly free the flow of information concerning that country," but pointed out that "the right to speak and publish does not carry with it the unrestrained right to gather information." Warren cited an illustration:

> For example, the prohibition of unauthorized entry into the White House diminishes the citizen's opportunities to gather information he might find relevant to his opinion of the way the country is being run, but that does not make entry into the White House a First Amendment right.[38]

In *Zemel* the Court concluded that no First Amendment freedom was violated by the ban on travel.

In *Agee* the Court again upheld a ban on travel. Court action was initiated by Philip Agee, whose passport was revoked when, though employed by the Central Intelligence Agency, he announced his intention to oppose the goals and expose the agents of the CIA. The Supreme Court, per Chief Justice Burger, claimed: "The history of passport controls since the earliest days of the Republic shows congressional recognition of Executive authority to withhold passports on the basis of substantial reasons of national security and foreign policy." Concerning Agee's specific behavior, Burger felt the revocation was justified.

> Agee's disclosures, among other things, have the declared purpose of obstructing intelligence operations and the recruiting of intelligence personnel. They are clearly not protected by the Constitution. The mere fact that Agee is also engaged in criticism of the Government does not render his conduct beyond the reach of the law.
> To the extent the revocation of his passport operates to inhibit Agee, "it is an inhibition of *action*," rather than of speech. Agee is as free to criticize the United States Government as he was when he held a passport—always subject, of course, to express limits on certain rights by virtue of his contract with the Government.[39]

In *Agee* the Supreme Court accepted the principle that the secretary of state may revoke a passport on the ground that the passport holder's activities in foreign countries caused, or were likely to cause, serious damage to the national security or foreign policy of the United States.

The 1984 *Wald* case upheld additional restrictions on travel to Cuba. In this case, Ruth Wald and other U.S. citizens who wanted to travel to Cuba challenged a federal regulation that curtailed general tourist and business travel to Cuba. The Court, per Justice William Rehnquist, decided that the regulation did not violate an individual's constitutional right to travel.

> In the opinion of the State Department, Cuba, with the political, economic, and military backing of the Soviet Union, has provided widespread support for armed violence and terrorism in the Western Hemisphere. Cuba also maintains close to 40,000 troops in various countries in Africa and the Middle East in support of objectives inimical to United States foreign policy interests. . . . We think there is an adequate basis under the Due Process Clause of the Fifth Amendment to sustain the President's decision to curtail the flow of hard currency to Cuba—currency that could then be used in support of Cuban adventurism—by restricting travel.[40]

Unlike the five previous cases, which involved the right of a U.S. citizen to travel abroad, *Mandel* examined the right of a foreign journalist to enter the United States. Ernest Mandel, a Belgian journalist and Marxist theorist, was invited to attend academic meetings in the United States. He was refused permission to enter the country under a provision of the Immigration and Nationality Act of 1952, which refuses entry to anyone who advocates "the economic, international and governmental doctrines of world communism." The attorney general could have waived ineligibility, but declined to do so on the ground that on a 1968 trip to the United States, Mandel had spoken at more universities than his visa application indicated. Thus, Mandel had engaged in behavior not stated in his visa application. In *Mandel* the Supreme Court acknowledged that Congress has absolute power to grant or deny entry to aliens. When the attorney general, for a valid reason, refused to approve Mandel's entry, the judiciary should not set the determination aside.[41] The Supreme Court majority determined not to balance the secretary of state's justification for denying entry against the First Amendment interests of those who sought communication with Mandel. Instead, the Court accepted that justification and upheld the ban on travel.

Summary

The Court has generally protected the free speech and free press rights of solicitors and distributors. In *Martin*, the Court determined that a city cannot prevent an individual from distributing religious announcements door-to-door. In *Lovell, Murdock, Hynes,* and *Schaumburg*, the Court overturned ordinances that were vague or overbroad, or that tended to suppress the exercise of First Amendment freedoms. In *Marsh* and *Organization For A Better Austin*, the Court rejected community-wide prohibitions on solicitation and distribution. The Court has, however, placed some limitations on soliciting and distributing. According to *Martin*, an individual can prevent intrusions by uninvited solicitors by posting a notice to stay away. And, in *Breard*, the Court decided that commercial solicitation could be banned by city statute. In placing these limitations, the Court has upheld the right to be let alone.

During the past decade, the Court has heard several cases that involved efforts to restrict distribution and solicitation either by institutions or on institutional premises. The Court acknowledged the free-speech rights of corporations in *First National Bank of Boston* and in *Consolidated Edison of New York*. The Court also protected individual free-speech rights in *Flower* and *Grace*. In other cases restrictions were upheld. The *Spock, Glines,* and *Huff* decisions determined that the right of distribution and solicitation may be restricted at a military installation. In *Procunier, Greenburgh,* and *Perry Education Association*, the Court approved the principle of differential access to the mailbox. In *Krishna* the Court upheld an ordinance that restricted distribution and solicitation on state fair grounds. And, in *Vincent*, the Court approved a law that prohibited posting of signs on public property.

The Supreme Court has also decided several cases involving bans on the right to travel. Though *Kent* and *Aptheker* determined that a person has a right to travel, regardless of his or her political beliefs and associations, the executive authority of the government can impose restrictions on travel for national security purposes. That was the determination in *Zemel, Agee,* and *Wald*. Finally, as determined in *Mandel*, the freedom of U.S. citizens to travel abroad does not apply similarly to foreigners wishing to enter the United States. The First Amendment interest of citizens seeking communication with an alien was secondary to the executive's authority to regulate entry.

NOTES

1. *Cramp v. Board of Public Instruction of Orange County, Florida,* 82 S.Ct. 275 (1961).
2. *Baggett v. Bullitt,* 84 S.Ct. 1316 (1964).
3. *Keyishian v. Board of Regents,* 87 S.Ct. 675 (1967).
4. *Whitehill v. Elkins,* 88 S.Ct. 184 (1967).
5. *Elfbrandt v. Russell,* 86 S.Ct. 1238 (1966).
6. *Connell v. Higginbotham,* 91 S.Ct. 1772 (1971).
7. *Cole v. Richardson,* 92 S.Ct. 1332 (1972).
8. *Watkins v. United States,* 77 S.Ct. 1173 (1957).
9. *Barenblatt v. United States,* 79 S.Ct. 1081 (1959).
10. *Uphaus v. Wyman,* 79 S.Ct. 1040 (1959).
11. *Talley v. California,* 80 S.Ct. 536 (1960).
12. *Laird v. Tatum,* 92 S.Ct. 2318 (1972).
13. *Saia v. New York,* 68 S.Ct. 1148 (1948).
14. *Kovacs v. Cooper,* 69 S.Ct. 448 (1949).
15. *Public Utilities Commission of District of Columbia v. Pollack,* 72 S.Ct. 813 (1952).
16. *Lovell v. City of Griffin,* 58 S.Ct. 666 (1938).
17. *Martin v. City of Struthers,* 63 S.Ct. 862 (1943).
18. *Murdock v. Pennsylvania,* 63 S.Ct. 870 (1943).
19. *Breard v. City of Alexandria,* 71 S.Ct. 920 (1951).
20. *Hynes v. Borough of Oradell,* 96 S.Ct. 1755 (1976).
21. *Village of Schaumburg v. Citizens For A Better Environment,* 100 S.Ct. 826 (1980).
22. *Marsh v. Alabama,* 66 S.Ct. 276 (1946).
23. *Organization For A Better Austin v. Keefe,* 91 S.Ct. 1575 (1971).
24. *Flower v. United States,* 92 S.Ct. 1842 (1972).
25. *Greer v. Spock,* 96 S.Ct. 1211 (1976).
26. *Brown v. Glines,* 100 S.Ct. 594 (1980).
27. *Secretary of the Navy v. Huff,* 100 S.Ct. 606 (1980).
28. *Procunier v. Martinez,* 94 S.Ct. 1800 (1974).
29. *United States Postal Service v. Council of Greenburgh Civic Associations,* 101 S.Ct. 2676 (1981).
30. *Perry Education Association v. Perry Local Educator's Association,* 103 S.Ct. 948 (1983).
31. *First National Bank of Boston v. Bellotti,* 98 S.Ct. 1407 (1978).
32. *Consolidated Edison Company of New York v. Public Service Commission of New York,* 100 S.Ct. 2326 (1980).
33. *Heffron v. International Society For Krishna Consciousness,* 101 S.Ct. 2559 (1981).
34. *United States v. Grace,* 103 S.Ct. 1702 (1983).
35. *Members of the City Council of the City of Los Angeles v. Taxpayers For Vincent,* 104 S.Ct. 2118 (1984).
36. *Kent v. Dulles,* 78 S.Ct. 1113 (1958).
37. *Aptheker v. Secretary of State,* 84 S.Ct. 1659 (1964).
38. *Zemel v. Rusk,* 85 S.Ct. 1271 (1965).
39. *Haig v. Agee,* 101 S.Ct. 2766 (1981).
40. *Regan v. Wald,* 104 S.Ct. 3026 (1984).
41. *Kleindienst v. Mandel,* 92 S.Ct. 2576 (1972).

RECOMMENDED READING

Byrne, Daniel H., "*Heffron v. ISKON*: The Tenuous Touchstone—A Step in the Wrong Direction," *Houston Law Review* 19 (January, 1982) 325-38.

Corvino, Robert, "*Heffron v. International Society for Krishna Consciousness, Inc.*: Reasonable Time, Place and Manner Restrictions," *John Marshall Law Review* 15 (Spring, 1982), 543-55.

Haiman, Franklyn S., "Speech v. Privacy: Is there a Right not to be Spoken to?" *Northwestern University Law Review* 67 (May-June, 1972), 153-99.

Strangeways, Erik, "Freedom of Expression in the Military: *Brown v. Glines*," *New York Law School Law Review* 26 (1981), 1135-54.

Warren, Lynn K., "*Consolidated Edison Company of New York v. Public Service Commission*: Freedom of Speech Extended to Monopolies—Is There No Escape for the Consumer?" *Pepperdine Law Review* 8 (1981), 1087-1110.

KEY DECISIONS

1943—*MARTIN*—determined that a notice to stay away is necessary to stop intrusions by "harmless" distributors and solicitors.

1946—*MARSH*—rejected a community-wide ban on solicitation and distribution.

1949—*KOVACS*—ruled that sound amplification in public places was subject to reasonable restraint.

1951—*BREARD*—concluded that door-to-door solicitation for commercial purposes may be prohibited by local ordinance.

1960—*TALLEY*—upheld the right of anonymous publication.

1964—*APTHEKER*—established a link between the right to travel and First Amendment freedoms.

1976—*SPOCK*—upheld a military installation's ban on petition and distribution of materials without prior written approval from the base commander.

1978—*FIRST NATIONAL BANK OF BOSTON*—acknowledged that a corporation enjoys First Amendment rights of free expression.

1981—*INTERNATIONAL SOCIETY FOR KRISHNA CONSCIOUSNESS*—upheld statute regulating distribution and solicitation on state fair grounds.

SUMMARY—LAW OF SILENCE

Definition

The law of silence concerns those situations in which an individual enjoys the freedom (1) not to communicate, (2) not to be communicated with, and/or (3) to be let alone.

Proof

1. Individuals have won cases involving the right to silence by showing that they have been illegally required/asked to:
   a. Sign a loyalty oath
   b. Testify before an investigative committee
   c. Listen to sound amplification devices in public places
   d. Face unwanted solicitors and distributors
   e. Refrain from travel.
2. Several laws designed to regulate silence have been declared unconstitutional. The laws had the following flaws:
   a. Ambiguous, overly broad, or discriminatory
   b. Based on "guilt by association"
   c. Violated due process by providing for summary dismissal without a hearing
   d. Allowed investigative committee to inquire into matters that were not "pertinent"
   e. Constituted a form of prior restraint
   f. Regulated subject matter, rather than time, place, and manner.

Defenses

The government may restrict an individual's right to silence in certain instances. To uphold such action, the government should:
1. Demonstrate that, on balance, violating an individual's right to silence meets a "more important" governmental interest;
2. Demonstrate that the law restricting an individual's right to silence is validly constructed.

7

LIBEL

There are certain well-defined and narrowly limited classes of speech, the prevention and punishment of which has never been thought to raise any Constitutional problem.[1]

—Justice Frank Murphy

In numerous cases the Supreme Court has identified libel as a form of expression that is outside the scope of First Amendment protection. Prosecution of this type of expression is subject to specific procedures and doctrines. This chapter contains an explanation of the procedural considerations related to a libel court action, as well as the historical development of significant libel doctrines.

PROCEDURES

Defamatory statements may have a crippling effect on an individual's ability to relate to his or her associates in personal, social, or professional ways. Appropriate legal relief is available to anyone so harmed. This section focuses on the procedural aspects of the libel court action.

Types

Libel consists of defamatory words that are either written or broadcast. Slander, by contrast, is a defamatory statement that is spoken. Slander tends to be less harmful than libel, since it is not permanently recorded and cannot be effectively transmitted to a larger audience after its utterance.

Two types of libel have been recognized by the courts—libel *per se* and libel *per quod*.

Libel per Se

Libel *per se* involves a statement that is defamatory on its face. The harm resulting from the statement is immediately apparent. Words that have been held libelous *per se* include "hog,"[2] "hypocrite,"[3] "liar,"[4] "drunkard,"[5] "Communist,"[6] "Fascist,"[7] and "criminal."[8] The 1964 *Hornby* case provides an example. Curtis Hunter initiated a suit against Harry Hornby and the *Uvalde Leader-News*. The suit alleged that Hunter had been libeled by an article claiming that a car had been stolen and that a warrant for C. H. "Curly" Hunter had been issued in connection with the theft. According to Hunter, the article implied "criminality." At trial, Hunter maintained that the 1959 Cadillac automobile referred to in the article had been in the possession of Hunter and his wife for almost a year prior to the supposed theft, that Hunter did not steal the car, and that no warrant had been issued for his arrest. The court decided that the article was not true and was defamatory. The article did "impute to Hunter the commission of a crime for which punishment by imprisonment in jail or the penitentiary may be imposed and is, therefore, libelous *per se*."[9]

Libel per Quod

Libel *per quod* is not immediately apparent. The words themselves are not defamatory, but become so when facts are associated with them. With libel *per quod*, defamation is indirect and dependent on the context in which the words are written. The *Karrigan* case illustrates this type of libel. In November 1956 the Clay Center *Dispatch* carried the following item:

> Stork-O-Grams. Ellen Marie is the name Mr. and Mrs. Phillip Karrigan of Clay Center gave to their daughter, who was born Thursday, Nov. 1, at the Clay Center Hospital. The little girl weighed nine pounds, three ounces.

In response to this news item, a certain Philip Karrigan sued, claiming the announcement, innocent on its face, was defamatory, because he was a bachelor, the only person in the vicinity with this name, and because the article made readers think that he "was married to one Betty Ellen Carpenter, a woman of ill repute and who has given birth to four children out of wedlock." The Kansas Supreme Court ruled in favor of Karrigan.

> Pecuniary loss to one's trade, profession or business should not be the sole test in a case of this kind. The article in question being nondefamatory on its face, plaintiff, in order to state a cause of action for libel *per quod*, was required to

allege explanatory extrinsic facts in connection with the subject of the article and the resulting special damage and injury to him.[10]

The court was satisfied that Karrigan met his burden of proof. The injury suffered was substantial and real, and not fictitious. It constituted libel *per quod.*

Elements

A successful libel action must include four elements: publication, identification, defamation, and fault. Without sufficient evidence proving each of these elements, the plaintiff cannot recover damages.

Publication

Of the four, publication is easiest to prove. The plaintiff need only demonstrate that a third person read or viewed the libel, and interpreted it in a defamatory sense. In the age of mass media, a statement printed in a newspaper or broadcast over the radio or television constitutes publication. In instances involving limited audiences, however, the question of what comprises publication is less clear and it is up to the courts to decide the matter. The publication issue was important in the *Arvey Corporation* case.

In September 1958 Robert Shapiro, executive vice-president of the Transo Envelope Company, answered a letter he had received from an attorney. In the letter, Shapiro provided information concerning William Peterson. Shapiro claimed that Peterson was not due any back wages; on the contrary, Peterson was indebted to the company for $1,329 for "overdraw of advances." Shapiro then wrote,

> A demand for repayment of the above has been delayed, pending completion of the investigation which is still incomplete. This involves areas of possible serious liability concerning your client. We are still awaiting the opinion of the Federal District Attorney.

Peterson initiated court action, claiming that Shapiro's letter charged him with "fraudulent acts, conversion and criminal liability." When the case reached a Pennsylvania district court, the judges focused on the publication issue. The judges considered two possible instances of publication: the dictation of the letter to a stenographer and the receipt of the letter by the attorney. Shapiro argued that the stenographer was not a third person, because the company was merely communicating through two instrumentalities—the executive and the stenographer. Thus, publication did not occur. The court, however, ruled that a secretary was a third party and dictation by an executive to his or her secretary was a publication. Shapiro also argued that the attorney was not a third party, because the letter was an answer to a request that the company pay Peterson some wages allegedly due to him. The court ruled that sending a communication to an agent of a defamed party was a publication. The judges decided that publication had occurred in both instances—to the secretary and to the attorney.[11] In *Arvey Corporation*, the court acknowledged that publication can occur when a message is communicated to a limited audience.

Identification

In regard to identification, the plaintiff must prove that the defamatory reference is to the plaintiff—whether by nickname, pseudonym, or unique circumstance. Sometimes, however, a typographical error, wrong initials, an incorrect address, or identical names may connect an innocent person to an undesirable event. In such cases, the courts must decide whether identification occurred. The *Hope* case provides an example.

Frederick Hope, a Palm Beach attorney who formerly served as a special agent for the Federal Bureau of Investigation, filed a libel action, citing a column that appeared in the Palm Beach *Times* and numerous other newspapers. The item stated: "Palm Beach is buzzing with the story that one of the resort's richest men caught his blonde wife in a compromising spot the other day with a former FBI agent." Hope claimed that he and many others easily recognized the item as referring to himself. To prove his claim of identification, Hope showed the court that he, unlike other former agents in Palm Beach, was known primarily as an ex-agent; also, that he was the only former FBI man who traveled in high-society circles. In addition to his own statements, Hope offered the testimonies of other citizens of Palm Beach. This evidence supported Hope's claim that identification had occurred. The district court awarded Hope $58,500 and the court of appeals upheld the verdict.[12]

Defamation

To demonstrate defamation, the plaintiff must show that the words in question belong to one of four classes that the courts have recognized as actionable: (1) words that lower one's public esteem, (2) words that expose one to public ridicule, scorn, or derision, (3) words that cause one to be avoided by a respectable segment of the community, and (4) words that damage one in his or her occupation or profession. These categories are exemplified by the *Roth, Zbyszko, Sally, Cowper, Blende,* and *Nichols* cases.

Of the various ways in which words may damage a person's esteem, none has brought more libel suits that a false charge of criminality. The *Roth* case involved this type of claim. The case involved a news story that was published in the September 1, 1937, issue of the *Greensboro Record*. The article identified a certain Harry Roth, who "formerly resided in Greensboro" and who "was for a time connected with the Palace Theatre in Greensboro" as the person "charged with complicity in gigantic vice operations" and "regarded as one of the higher-ups in the conspiracy." Shortly after publication, the news reporter realized that he had made an error in identification. So, the next day, the *Greensboro Record* carried a rather extensive correction. On September 11, the Harry Roth who owned the Palace Theatre wrote to the *Greensboro Record* and demanded a retraction. The paper's editor wrote to Roth, enclosing the correction, and requested that if the item did not meet with Roth's approval he should inform the *Record*. The newspaper company received no reply. Roth brought a libel suit, and won.[13] The *Roth* case indicates the importance of checking sources of information before publishing a news story. The possibility of mistaking names and addresses is ever-present, and the courts view it as libelous to publish a story that incorrectly reports a person as having been charged with a crime.

A second category of libelous words includes those that expose a person to public ridicule, scorn, or derision. *Zybszko* provides an example. The *New York American* published an article entitled "How Science Proves Its Theory of Evolution." It outlined several stages in the physical development of the human being. The body of the article claimed:

> Science does not believe that gorillas or other apes are the great-grandfathers of man. They are set down as remote cousins of mankind rather than direct ancestors. Gorilla evolution and human evolution split apart from a common ape-man parent millions of years ago. The gorilla is probably closer to man, both in body and mind, than any other species of ape now alive. The general physique of the gorilla is closely similar to an athletic man of today, and the mind of a young gorilla is much like the mind of a human body.

Accompanying the article were two illustrations, which were entitled, "Stanislaus Zbyszko, the Wrestler, Not Fundamentally Different from the Ape in Physique," and "A Mounted Specimen of the Great Kivu Gorilla in Lord Rothchild's Private Museum at Tring, Hertfordshire, England." Zbyszko sued, complaining that an impression was created in the minds of readers that he and the gorilla were fundamentally alike. He asserted that as a wrestler and businessman, he was brought into public ridicule and disgrace, and that he was shunned by relatives and friends. The court held that the tendency of the publication was to "bring him into ridicule and contempt."[14] It held the publication libelous.

A third category includes words that cause a person to be avoided by a respectable segment of the community. Most notable in this category are words that falsely attribute venereal disease, mental illness, alcoholism, and other diseases. Such unfair attribution of physical or mental illness has been held libelous in such cases as *Sally* and *Cowper*. The *Sally* case involved Shilo Sally and

Corbett Brown, who in 1926 were rivals for nomination for political office in Perry County, Kentucky. After being defeated, Sally claimed that Brown was "eat up with the clap." Brown sued for damages and was awarded $500. Sally appealed. The court noted that if Brown was in the condition Sally claimed, it would "certainly exclude him from all good society."[15] Hence, the words were actionable *per se*.

In *Cowper* the court held that the imputation of mental illness was also libelous *per se*. The case involved an alleged libel against the editor of the *Bluffs Times*. An issue of the paper contained the following as part of an account of a meeting of the local Board of School Trustees.

One board member, Cowper of Glasgow, was absent. If he is permitted to vote, (Mr. Cowper is recovering from a mental illness) we understand the voting will be delayed until all the testimony can be transcribed and digested.

George Cowper sued. After a trial, he was awarded $6,000. The Appellate Court of Illinois affirmed the decision, noting that a publication imputing impairment of mental faculties was libelous *per se*. The defamation involved in such a charge could deprive individuals of their right of social intercourse. According to the court, persons reputed to be of unsound mind were denied "the confidence and respect which all right thinking men normally accord their fellow members of society."[16]

The fourth category of libelous words includes those that may cause damage in one's occupation or profession. Mistakenly attributing a "single instance" of error to a professional person is not, however, sufficient to cause damage. There must be a claim of general incompetency. Such was the finding in the *Blende* case. When the *Seattle Post-Intelligencer* printed a story claiming that a patient died when a physician incorrectly diagnosed a broken neck as "plain drunkenness," the physician sued. In *Blende*, the court of appeals noted:

To charge a professional man with negligence or unskillfulness in the management or treatment of an individual case, is no more than to impute to him the mistakes and errors incident to fallible human nature. The most eminent and skillful physician or surgeon may mistake the symptoms of a particular case without detracting from his general professional skill or learning. To say of him, therefore, that he was mistaken in that case would not be calculated to impair the confidence of the community in his general professional competency.[17]

The "single instance" rule, however, does not protect words that impute to an individual questionable ethics in business practices. In *Nichols* the Oklahoma Supreme Court decided that a sole article accusing an individual of "shady ethics" and of operating on a "sneak basis" caused sufficient injury to a professional reputation to justify a finding of libel.[18] The *Nichols* decision indicates

"BIG DEAL, SO WE DON'T ALWAYS PRINT THE TRUTH. BUT THAT DOESN'T MAKE US GUILTY OF LIBEL···DOES IT?"

that a "single instance" defense is not applicable in cases involving claims of unethical business actions.

Fault

Fault, the fourth element in a libel action, is a relatively new requirement. It applies differently to "public" and "private" persons. A "public" person must demonstrate that the material was published with "actual malice." A "private" person, on the other hand, must show that the material was printed through "negligence." The specific cases that established the fault element are discussed in detail later in this chapter in the section on doctrines. Nonetheless, the *Demman* and *Montandon* cases are included to illustrate the fault element.

The *Demman* case involved a verbal exchange that took place on Salt Lake City radio station KSXX during the Larry Wilcox "interview" show. During the program, Wilcox invited the public to call in and ask questions of the program's guest, political candidate Fred Demman. The alleged defamatory dialogue, which took place about five hours before the polls closed on election day, involved a caller who berated Demman on his alleged qualifications for office. Demman initiated a libel suit, citing Wilcox's "infectious laugh when the caller ...suggested Demman's low-key credentials" and the station's inability to censor the comments of the caller, whose remarks appeared to delight the "malicious" Wilcox. In *Demman* the court denied the suit, however, because it could not find fault on the part of either Wilcox or the station.

> There is no evidence whatever to reflect any malice on the part of any of the station's officials.... As to Wilcox, however unthinking he may have been in failing to chop the anonymous one off the air, and no matter to what degree his risibility may have roiled the plaintiff, nonetheless, the record points up an absence of malice on his part as that term ordinarily connotes.[19]

In the *Montandon* case the evidence warranted a finding of fault. The litigation arose over a program note that was published in *TV Guide's* 1968 special "Fall Preview" issue, which was distributed throughout central California. The item read: "10:30 [2] Pat Michael-Discussion [color] 'From Party Girl to Call Girl.' Scheduled guest: TV personality Pat Montandon and author of 'How to Be a Party Girl.' " The show described in the article was to feature Pat Montandon, a public figure, who would discuss her book. In addition, unbeknownst to Miss Montandon, the host of the show decided to have another guest, an anonymous prostitute, on the show. In court, the writers for *TV Guide* justified the item on the ground that it was the ordinary procedure in talk-discussion shows not to list all guests, and the magazine did not want to use the word "prostitute" in its copy. Nonetheless, in *Montandon* the court found "actual malice" on the part of the *TV Guide* staff.

> The action by the *TV Guide* staff showed a reckless disregard of whether the statement published was true or false, because the staff was aware that the true facts, as stated in the press release, were that Pat Montandon was not a call girl but would be appearing on a show with a call girl; and a staff decision was made to leave out crucial facts in rewriting the release, thereby implying that plaintiff was a call girl. This is proof of convincing clarity to support the jury's verdict that the article was published not in good faith, but with actual malice.
>
> While this result was apparently not intentional it was one which those responsible should have foreseen and one which showed a reckless disregard for the truth or falsity of the statement. The conduct of those responsible for the publication was more than negligence, it amounted to an indifference to the impression being given to the general public.[20]

Damages

If the four elements—publication, identification, defamation, and fault—are adequately proven, the court may assess monetary damages against the offender.

Depending on the nature of the case, four types of damages may be awarded: general, actual, punitive, and nominal. The types of damages are illustrated by the *Dalton, MacLeod, United Press International,* and *Goldwater* cases.

General damages are intended to compensate for injury to one's reputation. Such compensatory damages were awarded in *Dalton.* The case involved statements by banker-businessman Howard Meister, who was charged with criminal bribery and unlawful lobbying after a grand-jury investigation was conducted by Wisconsin Assistant Attorney General LeRoy Dalton. Eventually, the charges were dismissed because the state's witness, Dorothy Effinger, was too sick to testify. Immediately following the dismissal, Meister held a press conference at which he distributed a statement that included the following paragraphs:

> Eleven months ago, I was indicted by a Grand Jury, illegally constituted, and immoral in every sense of modern day terminology conceived by gestapo leader LeRoy Dalton, who is now slithering under his rock.
>
> Today, everyone knows that any and all charges made against me were groundless and conceived in the evil minds of those who thought that through illegal means they could successfully smear me.
>
> It is now my duty to inform the public that the gestapo, the cancer in the Attorney General's office must be cut out. I for one shall lead that fight, and good men shall join me.

Meister's statement also charged Dalton with purchasing, by the offer of immunity, the "perjured testimony" of "extortionist" Dorothy Effinger, who "is no sicker today than she was seven days ago when she whistled and danced in the halls of the...District Attorney's office." Dalton initiated a libel action. A Milwaukee circuit court jury decided against Meister and awarded general damages of $75,000 to Dalton. Meister appealed. The Wisconsin Supreme Court found that the libelous statements caused Dalton's transfer from his position, disfavor with the attorney general, loss of reputation as a criminal investigator, abuse of his character as a lawyer, and public contempt, ridicule, disgrace, and humiliation.[21] The court concluded that the jury award in the *Dalton* case was not excessive.

Actual damages represent the real monetary loss suffered by the plaintiff as a result of a defamatory statement. The *MacLeod* case involved actual damages. On April 19, 1955, an article that appeared on the front page of the *Oakland Tribune* linked Dr. Grover MacLeod with the "*San Francisco People's World,* recognized throughout the state as the mouthpiece of the Communist Party." Dr. MacLeod informed the Tribune Company that the article contained false information. He demanded a correction or retraction, but none was made. MacLeod then initiated a libel suit, claiming that he had enjoyed a good reputation in his profession as a dental surgeon, and that the publication had damaged his reputation with the general public by imputing that he was a Communist sympathizer. MacLeod maintained that the implications in the article were false and malicious, that he had sustained continuing nervous strain and substantial humiliation, and that he had suffered monetary loss in his profession. The California Supreme Court acknowledged that a charge of Communist affiliation or sympathy was libelous *per se*. In addition, the court noted that a publisher was liable for what was insinuated, as well as for what was stated explicitly. In this case, readers might reasonably infer that MacLeod was unworthy of public office because of the insinuation that he was a Communist sympathizer. The court stressed that the publisher's failure to check the accuracy of the article suggested intentional falsehood. The court then turned to the issue of actual damages. MacLeod alleged that he had suffered monetary loss in his profession as a dentist because a large percentage of established patients cancelled appointments and there had been a sharp decline in the number of new patients. MacLeod contended that the loss was a continuing one and would amount to $5,000 or more. In *MacLeod* the court ruled that it was acceptable for MacLeod to estimate the amount of loss.[22] The court affirmed an award of actual damages.

Punitive damages are designed to punish past libelous behavior and to discourage similar conduct in the future. A high degree of fault is necessary to sustain an award for punitive damages. In the *United Press International* case, the Texas Court of Civil Appeals examined an award of punitive damages. The case involved a UPI news item, which reported that Bruce Mohs had been arrested for violating a local ordinance by landing his pontoon plane on a lake in Dallas. The story was published in several newspapers, including some in Madison, Wisconsin, where Mohs lived and operated an aircraft business. Mohs sued UPI for actual and punitive damages. The court found the news story to be libelous and that Mohs was harmed by the statements in the story. He was awarded $2,500 in actual damages. In addition, the jury found that publication of the story involved malice and awarded punitive damages of $5,000. UPI appealed, but complained only about the punitive damages. The court of appeals noted that even though the reporter was cognizant of possible inaccuracies in the story, neither he nor anyone else for UPI attempted to verify the story. Even though the need for more investigation was suggested, the reporter "was so pleased with a funny story holding Mohs up to ridicule that he forthwith sent it out for all to read and be amused at Mohs' expense." The court concluded that "fabrication of this libelous story was a willful and wanton act sufficient to support a finding of malice."[23] The lower court's award of punitive damages was affirmed.

Nominal damages are token damages awarded when there has been a defamation, but no serious harm to the plaintiff's reputation or financial position. Nominal damages were awarded in the *Goldwater* case. Senator Barry Goldwater brought suit against writer Ralph Ginzburg, who had written a "psychobiography" on Goldwater that claimed to alert the American people to the potential dangers of a Goldwater presidency. Ginzburg's article claimed that Goldwater suffered from "repressed homosexuality," experienced "infantile fantasies of revenge and dreams of total annihilation of his adversaries," and displayed

"paralyzing, deep-seated irrational fear." At trial, Ginzburg was unable to identify a source for the statements. The court ruled that Ginzburg was motivated
by actual malice. The seriousness of the charges called for a thorough investigation; however, Ginzburg relied on slipshod investigative techniques. The court
punished Ginzburg by awarding $75,000 in punitive damages. In addition, since
Goldwater had neither pleaded nor proved any actual damages, the jury granted
one dollar in nominal compensation.[24]

Defenses

A publisher of an alleged libel is not helpless in the face of a lawsuit. There
are four complete and six partial defenses against a libel action. In most states,
the following are complete defenses: truth, absolute privilege, qualified privilege, and fair comment. Partial defenses include use of reliable source, retraction and apology, right of reply, settlement out of court, bad reputation of plaintiff, and provocation.

Truth

Demonstrating the truth of a libelous statement is a complete defense in
several states. In some states, truth is a defense only if the statement is published
with good motives; malice destroys the defense. In establishing this defense, even
though it is unnecessary to show that every detail is accurate, substantial proof
is required in order to exonerate the defendant. The defense cited truth in *Empire Printing Company*. The case concerned an issue of the *Daily Alaska Empire*, which detailed how the Territorial Board of Road Commissioners, which
consisted of Henry Roden, Ernest Gruening, and Frank Metcalf, purchased and
operated the "Chilkoot Ferry" as part of the road system between Haines and
Juneau, Alaska. Almost the entire front page was devoted to a "special ferry
fund." The headline read "Bare 'Special' Ferry Fund." The front page also contained a photograph of a check drawn on the "special ferry fund." Beneath the
photograph was an editorial entitled "Start Talking Boys." To the right of the
page was the statement: "Gruening, Metcalf, Roden Divert 'Chilkoot' Cash to
Private Bank Account." Under this headline was the statement, "The case closely
parallels that of Oscar Olson, former Territorial Treasurer who is now serving
a prison term at McNeil Island Penitentiary for violating the law in the receipt
and disbursement of public funds." Roden, Gruening, and Metcalf initiated a
libel action. The trial jury awarded the plaintiffs one dollar in nominal damages,
and $5,000 punitive damages. Upon appeal, the defense cited truth as justifica-
tion for the story. The court, however, noted that the establishment of truth must
be as broad as the defamation. In this case, even though the defense demonstrated
the truth of the words in the article, the truth of what the reader understood was
not established. The court determined that the manner in which the front page

was set up could be regarded as a deliberate defamation by insinuation and association. Readers of the newspaper could easily infer that the members of the board had been guilty of embezzlement. According to the court, "whatever a newspaper article actually says or carries to its readers must be judged by the publication as a whole. The headlines alone may be enough to make libelous *per se* an otherwise innocuous article." In addition, "an article may become libelous by juxtaposition with other articles or photographs."[25] In *Empire Printing Company* the defense was unable to demonstrate that the board members were guilty of any dishonesty or that they made any profit for their own use. In light of the failure to establish truth as a defense, the court affirmed the jury verdict.

Absolute Privilege

The courts have extended the defense of absolute privilege to those situations in which the interests of society should prevail over the interests of an individual. The courts have recognized three types of communications that are absolutely immune from libel action: privileged communications, communications involving prior consent, and political broadcasts. The *Barr, Langford,* and *Farmers Educational and Cooperative Union of America* cases illustrate the types of absolute privilege.

Privileged communications apply to all transactions between husband and wife, attorney and client, doctor and patient, and priest and parishioner. Judges, jurors, witnesses, attorneys, and the parties in both civil and criminal cases are absolutely protected. In addition, executive and legislative officials are immune from libel that is communicated in the course of their official duties. In *Barr* the Supreme Court extended immunity to executive press releases. The case involved a proposal by Linda Matteo, chief of the personnel branch of the Office of Housing Expediter, to reallocate some funds earmarked for terminal-leave payments. This plan came under criticism from members of Congress, as well as the press. Shortly thereafter, William Barr, general manager of the agency, announced that he intended to suspend Matteo from duty, and at the same time, Barr issued a press release criticizing her plan. Matteo sued, charging that the press release defamed her and had been caused by malice on Barr's part. When the jury ruled for Matteo, Barr appealed. The Supreme Court upheld Barr's claim of absolute privilege. The majority agreed that it was important that officials

> should be free to exercise their duties unembarrassed by the fear of damage suits
> . . .which would consume time and energies which would otherwise be devoted
> to governmental service and the threat of which might appreciably inhibit the
> fearless, vigorous, and effective administration of policies of government.[26]

The Court concluded that because the action Barr took was within his line of duty, it warranted an absolute privilege. In *Barr*, four minority justices expressed concern about the advantage that government officials enjoy with the absolute privilege, while critics of government are protected by only a qualified privilege. In fact, the *Barr* decision provides an unscrupulous public official with an advantage in attacking a private person.

A person who consents to an act that subsequently libels him or her cannot collect for the suffering. Consent can be granted directly through a written release indicating prior consent. Consent can also be implied. In the *Langford* case the court recognized that when consent is implied through words or actions, the plaintiff is unable to collect in a libel suit. The case involved the May 1954 issue of *The Chase*, a student-humor magazine published at Vanderbilt University. A section of the paper poked fun at Mother's Day. The layout included four pictures with a headline that read, "Everyone Loves Mother." The upper left frame was a black space with the caption "Father Loves Mother." The upper right frame pictured a young child with the caption "Daughter Loves Mother (And wants to be one too)." The lower left frame showed a boy, his arm tattooed with a heart enclosing the word "Mother" and the caption "Sailor Boy Loves Mother." The lower right frame pictured a smiling face, partly covered by a hood, captioned "Midwife Loves Mother." None of the persons pictured were identified. Actually, the young child was Pamela Langford, whose picture had been placed in the layout by mistake. Robert Langford, Pamela's father, initiated a libel suit. Langford charged that the Mother's Day layout, through innuendo, implied that Pamela was amenable to acts of illicit sexual intercourse, that Mrs. Langford was sleeping in a darkened bedroom with a sailor, and that Mr. Langford was having sexual relations in a darkened bedroom with someone unknown. Shortly thereafter, student reporters for another Vanderbilt publication, the *Hustler*, called Langford and asked for an interview. He granted the interview, let the student journalists take some pictures, and said that he wanted publicity. The reporters went to the courthouse and read the papers filed in the suit. The students then wrote an article for the *Hustler*, which accurately summarized the suit. To help illustrate the story, the page from the Mother's Day issue was reproduced and Langford's objections were cited. Langford then filed another suit—this time against the *Hustler*. When the case reached the Tennessee Court of Appeals, the judge stressed that Langford had wanted publicity. Also, the students had made a fair and accurate statement of the proceedings.[27] In *Langford* the newspaper publication was absolutely privileged.

Another type of communication that affords the defense of absolute privilege is political broadcast. Prior to 1959 broadcast stations that granted equal time to political candidates under section 315 of the Federal Communications Act were liable for any defamation in those broadcasts. At the same time, stations were prohibited from endorsing any political viewpoint or sanctioning any political talk. The law specified:

> If any licensee shall permit any person who is a legally qualified candidate for
> any public office to use a broadcasting station, he shall afford equal opportu-

nities to all other such candidates for office in the use of the broadcasting station: provided, that such licensee shall have no power of censorship over the
material broadcast under the provision of this section. No obligation is imposed
upon any licensee to allow the use of its station by any candidate.[28]

Stations subsequently argued that if they were unable to edit libelous speeches,
they could not be held responsible for damages. In the *Farmers Educational and
Cooperative Union of America* case, the Supreme Court agreed. The case involved A. C. Townley, who in 1956 demanded equal time as an independent candidate for the U.S. Senate. Equal time was provided by station WDAY-TV in
Fargo. In the telecast Townley charged that the North Dakota Farmer's Union
was Communist-controlled. The Farmer's Union brought a $100,000 damage suit
against Townley and the station. A district court dismissed the complaint against
WDAY on the ground that Section 315 rendered the station immune from liability. The Farmer's Union appealed to the North Dakota Supreme Court, which
also ruled that radio and television stations were not liable for libelous statements
made over their facilities by political candidates. The court claimed, "We cannot believe that it was the intent of Congress to compel a station to broadcast
libelous statements and at the same time subject it to the task of defending actions for damages." The court suggested that Farmer's Union should have
brought action against Townley alone. Townley's income, however, was only
$98.50 per month, a sum that offered little satisfaction. The union appealed the
case to the U.S. Supreme Court. The justices agreed with the state courts that
Section 315 grants a licensee an immunity from liability for libelous material it
broadcasts. Since stations cannot control what candidates say over the air, they
should not be held responsible for the statements.[29] The candidates, however,
can be sued.

Qualified Privilege

The courts have also recognized the doctrine of qualified privilege. A news
medium may publish an impartial report of judicial, legislative, executive, or
other public proceedings. In the *Stice* case the court ruled that newspapers have
a qualified privilege to publish articles regarding the investigation of crime. The
Wichita Beacon had printed stories concerning charges of corruption against a
judge. Articles based largely on police statements named the judge as the leader
of a gang of burglars. The judge sued for libel, seeking $1 million in damages.
The Kansas Supreme Court noted that the news stories were based upon interviews with police officers and reports of the police department concerning the
operation of a burglary ring. Excerpts from the articles were directly attributed
to members of law-enforcement agencies—for example, "police say," "detective said," "Briggs [a detective] said," "police investigation had revealed,"
"implicated by police investigations," "detectives disclosed," "investigations
are continuing," "according to the police evidence," and "under investigation

by law enforcement officials.'' Noting the accuracy of the reports and the absence of malice, the court decided in favor of the newspaper.[30] The articles were qualifiedly privileged.

Fair Comment

Another defense is fair comment. According to this standard, reporters may fairly comment on people or institutions that offer their work for public approval or public interest. This principle was applied in the *Oswalt* case. A South Carolina newspaper had criticized police officer David Oswalt for pursuing a car at high speed. The fleeing driver crashed broadside into another car, killing two young occupants. The *State-Record* editorial claimed that there was no ''sense or justification'' for police to race with offenders on public highways to the danger of citizens' lives. The editorial concluded by calling for officials to hire qualified persons to be law-enforcement officers. Oswalt brought suit. According to the Supreme Court of South Carolina, a citizen or newspaper may criticize acts and qualifications of a public official without being liable for damages, so long as the criticism is fair and honest, and made without malice.[31]

Use of Reliable Source

In addition to the complete defenses available to defendants in a libel action, there are also partial defenses. For example, a defendant can claim reliance on an unusually trustworthy source. When a publisher can show that he or she accurately reprinted a story from a major news source, the court may be influenced to reduce damages. On August 15, 1934, the *Atlanta Constitution* published an article that claimed that Mr. Otis Wood ''and his wife'' were arrested in Mississippi and charged with violating the tariff act for having in their possession alcohol upon which no tax had been paid. Mrs. Colline Wood brought suit for libel, claiming that the article was a false and malicious defamation, which injured her reputation and exposed her to public hatred, contempt, and ridicule. In fact, at the time of the crime, Mrs. Wood was separated from her husband, because he was involved in the bootlegging business. The woman arrested with Wood was not Mrs. Wood. Wood did, however, refer to her as his wife before law enforcement officials, who reported this information to newspaper reporters. Mrs. Wood sought $50,000 in damages. The Constitution Publishing Company admitted that it published the article, but claimed that it received the story from the Associated Press, a reliable news source. In *Wood* the Georgia Court of Appeals noted that the law did not protect as privileged ''the repetition of an untruthful and libelous statement on the ground that it was communicated to the person making the statement by an authority having a reputation for truth and accuracy.'' The court decided, however, that evidence regarding the Associated Press being a reliable organization tended to show lack of malice on the part of the newspaper.[32]

Retraction and Apology

A second partial defense—a full and prompt retraction and apology—will usually mitigate the amount of damages awarded. Such a good-faith effort indicates that publication was not made with malice. Yet, retraction is not a complete defense. Some people who saw the original story may not see the retraction. There is no guarantee that the retraction will offset the harm already suffered. Nonetheless, retraction and apology usually save money for a publisher guilty of libel. The *Brush-Moore Newspapers* case provides an example. It involved a *Salisbury Times* article that erroneously reported that Sheriff Jesse Pollitt kept "incomplete" records for booking prisoners, when it should have said "complete." The article actually charged Pollitt with committing a crime. When the error was spotted, the circulation manager stopped the presses and tried to locate as many of the incorrect papers as possible. A correction was printed on the following day. Nonetheless, Pollitt sued. The court held that he had been libeled and the jury awarded the sheriff $12,000. When the case reached the Maryland Court of Appeals, the newspaper fared much better. The court agreed that the sheriff had been defamed, but it noted that the newspaper's action in trying to retrieve copies containing the error tended to mitigate damages.[33] A new trial was ordered, but the parties settled out of court for approximately $7,500. The *Times* might have done even better with a new trial.

Right of Reply

The third partial defense, the right of reply, extends to legitimate spokespersons for someone who has been defamed. This could be the defamed individual, a public relations person, an attorney, the secretary of an organization, or a family member. A victim of libel may respond with a defamatory reply, provided that the reply is in direct response to a defamatory attack and the reply does not exceed the scope of the original defamation. In addition, a newspaper may transmit libelous remarks when it supports a person replying to an attack or also when it is in a role of news gatherer. The *Dickins* case involved the right of reply. In September 1944, while attending a dance at the Statler Hotel in Washington, D.C., Navy Lieutenant Randolph Dickins, Jr. got into an argument with members of the Teamsters Union. A week later, Dickins issued a statement to the press, in which he claimed that he had been slugged by members of the union. The Teamsters soon published their side in the *International Teamster*, namely, that Dickins was drunk. Dickins sued for libel. The union argued that it had a right to reply to the earlier attacks. The jurors agreed and ruled for the Teamsters. Dickins appealed, but the court of appeals rejected his claim, explaining,

> When the author of a libel writes under the compulsion of a legal or moral duty, or for the protection of his own rights or interest, that which he writes is a privileged communication, unless the writer be actuated by malice. The appellant

testified that, before the publication of which he here complains, he himself released to the press his own charges that members of the union assaulted him and his companion. His act in so doing cast upon the union the moral duty and consequently conferred upon it the legal right to publish a reply which, even if it were false, was privileged unless the plaintiff proved the defendant knew it to be false or otherwise proved actual malice in the publication.[34]

According to *Dickins*, the right of reply is an acceptable defense unless it is motivated by "actual malice."

Settlement out of Court

A fourth way a defendant may reduce the amount of damages is to settle out of court. There are advantages to out-of-court settlement. Obviously, court costs are eliminated. Moreover, harmful publicity is avoided, and the matter is resolved quickly and comparatively painlessly. The amount of monetary damages sought by the plaintiff can be reduced through negotiation. Furthermore, the defendant usually agrees to publish an apology or allows the plaintiff an opportunity to reply. A case that was settled out of court involved the January 13, 1964, cover story in *Sports Illustrated*. The article, based on a source of questionable veracity, accused Jack Dempsey of using "loaded" gloves in his 1919 title fight with Jess Willard. Dempsey initiated a court action, but settled out of court for an undisclosed sum. *Sports Illustrated* also agreed to print Dempsey's denial that the gloves were loaded.[35] In the final analysis, the magazine saved face and finances.

Bad Reputation of Plaintiff

A fifth partial defense is proof of previous bad reputation of the plaintiff. Demonstration that the plaintiff's reputation is so bad that a new libel cannot harm it will mitigate damages. The *Nichols* case involved such a claim. The judges stressed that the relationship of the bad reputation and the defamation must be close. The defendant cannot establish the bad reputation of a plaintiff by showing misconduct at a time and place far removed from the setting of the original defamation.[36] Though the defense of bad reputation may mitigate damages, it cannot fully exonerate the defendant.

Provocation

A final partial defense requires a demonstration of provocation on the part of the plaintiff. Statements uttered in the heat of the moment or provoked by actions of the plaintiff may assist in this defense. The *Farrell* case provides an illustration. This case concerned a dispute between a nurse and a surgeon. Bernadette Farrell, a registered nurse at Cary Memorial Hospital in Caribou, Maine, criticized the postoperative treatment given to a patient who was under the care of Dr. Harry Kramer. Farrell also lodged a series of complaints with hospital officials. The complaints touched off a personal feud between Farrell and Kramer, which continued for more than a year. Later that year, Farrell was dismissed from her employment at the hospital, but the following August she was rehired. When Kramer learned that Farrell had returned, he called a hospital administrator and said, "I wanted to ask you if you would stoop so low as to hire that creep, that malignant son of a bitch, back to work for you in the hospital." He added that "she was unfit for the care of patients" and that "he could prove [it] . . .and intended to make an issue of it." When Farrell learned of the statements, she initiated a libel action. The trial jury awarded Farrell $17,500. Kramer appealed. The Supreme Judicial Court of Maine decided that the damages awarded in this case were excessive. The court noted that Farrell had begun the feud between the parties by launching an attack upon Kramer's professional competence. A nurse should know that criticism of this type will almost certainly induce anger on the part of a doctor. As a result of Farrell's attack, Kramer was forced to defend himself before a grievance committee of the medical association. The judges found it no surprise that Kramer felt persecuted by Farrell. The court concluded:

> Although the slander is not thereby excused, such provocation will substantially diminish both the public interest in the punishment of the defendant and the plaintiff's right to have severe punishment inflicted. Under these circumstances a verdict of $17,500 is patently and grossly excessive.[37]

The court decided that an award of $5,000 would compensate Farrell for any injuries stemming from the defamatory remarks.

Summary

Libel consists of defamatory words that are either written or broadcast. There are two kinds of libel. Libel *per se* is defamatory on its face. Libel *per quod* is not immediately apparent; the words are not defamatory by themselves, but become so when other facts are associated with them.

A successful libel action must demonstrate publication, identification, defamation, and fault. To show publication, a plaintiff must show that a third person read or heard the libel and interpreted it in a defamatory sense. To demonstrate identification, a plaintiff must prove that the defamatory meaning applies specifically to him or her. To prove defamation, a plaintiff must show that the words fall into one of the following classes: words that damage esteem or social standing; words that expose one to public ridicule, scorn, or derision; words that cause one to be avoided; words that damage a person in his or her occupation or profession. To show fault, a plaintiff must show negligence in the case of private persons and actual malice in the case of public persons. If these elements are demonstrated, general, actual, punitive, and/or nominal damages may be awarded.

While laws vary from state to state, the following are usually recognized as complete defenses: truth, absolute privilege, qualified privilege, and fair comment. In addition the following are recognized as partial defenses: trustworthy source, retraction and apology, right of reply, settling out of court, previous bad reputation, and provocation.

DOCTRINES

During the past few decades the Supreme Court has formulated several doctrines that relate to libel. While most of these doctrines deal with the effect of libel on individuals, the Court has recognized that groups and corporations can also be damaged by defamatory statements. In addition, the Court has expressed alarm about persons who perpetrate criminal libel. Doctrines that concern individual, group, corporation, and criminal libel are reviewed in this section.

Individuals

Recent Supreme Court decisions make it difficult for a public person to win a libel suit. In these cases, the Court has emphasized that the public has a right to be informed about the activities of its celebrities and elected officials. The Court has decided that information about topics of public interest cannot be suppressed, regardless of the effect on the public "newsmaker."

Actual Malice

In the *New York Times* case, the doctrine of "actual malice" was enunciated for the first time. On March 29, 1960, the *Times* published an advertisement entitled, "Heed Their Rising Voices." The ad stated:

> As the world knows by now, thousands of Southern Negro students are engaged in widespread nonviolent demonstrations in positive affirmation of the right to live in human dignity as guaranteed by the U.S. Constitution and the Bill of Rights.

The ad went on to charge that in their efforts to uphold these guarantees, black students "are being met by an unprecedented wave of terror by those who would deny and negate that document which the whole world looks upon as setting the pattern for modern freedom.'' The ad illustrated the ''wave of terror'' by describing specific events. For example, the third and sixth paragraphs of the ten-paragraph advertisement read:

> In Montgomery, Alabama, after students sang ''My Country, Tis of Thee'' on the State Capitol steps, their leaders were expelled from school, and truckloads of police armed with shotguns and tear-gas ringed the Alabama State College Campus. When the entire student body protested to state authorities by refusing to re-register, their dining hall was padlocked in an attempt to starve them into submission. . . .

> Again and again the Southern violators have answered Dr. King's peaceful protests with intimidation and violence. They have bombed his home almost killing his wife and child. They have assaulted his person. They have arrested him seven times—for ''speeding,'' ''loitering'' and similar ''offenses.'' And now they have charged him with ''perjury''—a felony under which they would imprison him for ten years. Obviously, their real purpose is to remove him physically as the leader to whom the students and millions of others—look for guidance and support, and thereby to intimidate all leaders who may rise in the South. . . . The defense of Martin Luther King, spiritual leader of the student sit-in movement, clearly, therefore, is an integral part of the total struggle for freedom in the South.

The ad concluded with an appeal for funds to aid the student movement, the struggle for the right to vote, and the legal defense of Dr. Martin Luther King, Jr., who at the time was under arrest in Montgomery, Alabama. The ad was signed by more than 100 people, many widely known for their work in public affairs and the performing arts. L. B. Sullivan, the supervisor of Montgomery's police department, requested that the *Times* print a retraction. When the *Times* failed to do so, Sullivan initiated a libel suit. He argued that the ad incorrectly accused the police of answering Dr. King's protests with ''intimidation and violence.'' In fact, some of the statements in the advertisement were not accurate. For example, even though black students did protest on the state capitol steps, they sang the national anthem and not ''My Country, Tis of Thee.'' Even though nine students were expelled, it was not for conducting a protest, but for demanding service at the courthouse lunch counter. Not the entire student body, but most of it, protested the expulsion—not by refusing to register, but by boycotting classes on a single day. The campus dining room had not been padlocked, and the only students barred from eating there were those who had not obtained a meal ticket. Even though the police were deployed near the campus in large numbers on three occasions, they never did ''ring'' the campus. Dr. King had been arrested only four times, not seven. Although Dr. King's home had been bombed twice, the police were acquitted of the bombings and worked to apprehend the guilty parties.

At trial, the judge submitted the case to the jury with instructions that the statements were libelous *per se* and were not privileged. The jury decided that the words were published "of and concerning" Sullivan and that his reputation had been adversely affected by statements that reflected upon the agency of which he was in charge. The *Times* and the four ministers were held liable; the jury awarded Sullivan damages of $500,000. The Supreme Court of Alabama affirmed the decision. The *Times* took the case to the U.S. Supreme Court. The Court, per Justice William Brennan, unanimously held:

> The constitutional guarantees require, we think, a federal rule that prohibits a public official from recovering damages for a defamatory falsehood relating to his official conduct unless he proves that the statement was made with "actual malice"—that is, with knowledge that it was false or with reckless disregard of whether it was false or not.[38]

In this case, the Court did not find "actual malice." First, there was no evidence that the individuals who had authorized the use of their names were aware of any erroneous statements or were "reckless" in that regard. Second, whether the statements were "substantially correct" was not relevant in deciding whether the *Times* had acted in good faith. Third, in response to Sullivan's request for a retraction, the *Times* letter to Sullivan reflected reasonable doubt that the advertisement referred to Sullivan at all. It was not a final refusal, since it asked for an explanation from Sullivan, a request that Sullivan ignored. Fourth, negligence in failing to discover misstatements is constitutionally insufficient to demonstrate the recklessness that is required for a finding of "actual malice." In *New York Times* the Court overturned the finding of the lower courts and established the doctrine of "actual malice."

Later that year the Supreme Court further developed its "actual malice" doctrine in the *Garrison* case. This libel action centered around a dispute between James Garrison, the district attorney of Orleans Parish, Louisiana, and eight justices of the Criminal District Court. The disagreement was over disbursements from the Fines and Fees Fund, which was used to defray expenses of the district attorney's office. When the judges denied Garrison use of the fund for conducting investigations of commercial vice, Garrison held a press conference at which he harshly criticized the conduct of the eight judges. Specifically, Garrison attributed the large backlog of criminal cases to the inefficiency, laziness, and excessive vacations of the judges. He also claimed that, by refusing to authorize disbursements to cover the expenses of undercover investigations, the judges had hampered his efforts to enforce the vice laws. In addition, Garrison claimed,

> the judges have now made it eloquently clear where their sympathies lie in regard to aggressive vice investigations by refusing to authorize use of the DA's

funds to pay for the cost of closing down the Canal Street clip joints. . . . This raises interesting questions about the racketeer influences on our eight vacation-minded judges.

The judges brought suit. Garrison was tried and convicted of libel under the Louisiana Criminal Defamation Statute. He appealed. The U.S. Supreme Court unanimously reversed, referring to the *Times* doctrine:

> The *New York Times* standard forbids the punishment of false statements, unless made with knowledge of their falsity or in reckless disregard of whether they are true or false. But the Louisiana statute punishes false statements without regard to that test if made with ill-will; even if ill-will is not established, a false statement concerning public officials can be punished if not made in the reasonable belief of its truth. . . . The reasonable-belief standard applied by the trial judge is not the same as the reckless-disregard-of-truth standard.[39]

The Court noted that the "reasonable belief" standard set forth in the Louisiana law did not measure up to the "actual malice" requirement.

> A reasonable belief is one which an ordinary prudent man might be able to assign a just and fair reason for; the suggestion is that under this test the immunity from criminal responsibility in the absence of ill-will disappears on proof that the exercise of ordinary care would have revealed that the statement was false.

The Court stressed that the test it set down in *New York Times* was "not keyed to ordinary care; defeasance of the privilege is conditioned, not on mere negligence, but on reckless disregard for the truth." In *Garrison* the Court rejected the concept of "reasonable belief" and insisted that public officials show "actual malice" in order to win libel suits.

In the 1967 *Beckley Newspapers Corporation* case, the Court again emphasized the "actual malice" requirement. The case arose when Harold Hanks, the clerk of courts in Raleigh County, West Virginia, initiated a libel action over three newspaper editorials that criticized his official conduct. At trial the jury was instructed that a newspaper could be found guilty if the editorials had been published "with bad or corrupt motive" or "from personal spite, ill will or a desire to injure plaintiff." The jury returned a verdict for Hanks and awarded him $5,000 damages. The U.S. Supreme Court reversed the decision, because the judge's instructions were inadequate. Nothing in the court record revealed "the high degree of awareness of probable falsity demanded by *New York Times*."[40] In *Beckley Newspapers Corporation*, as in *Garrison* and *New York Times*, the Court required the plaintiff to demonstrate a significant burden of proof—"actual malice" on the part of the defendant.

Reckless Disregard

In a series of cases during the late 1960s, the Court clarified various components of the "actual malice" doctrine. In the 1967 *Butts* and *Walker* cases, the Court offered an interpretation of "reckless disregard" and also introduced the concept of "hot news." The *Butts* case involved an article in the *Saturday Evening Post*, which reported a telephone conversation between Wally Butts, athletic director of the University of Georgia, and Paul "Bear" Bryant, head football coach at the University of Alabama, in which the two men allegedly conspired to "fix" a football game between the two schools. The source of the story was George Burnett, who, because of an electronic error, had overheard the conversation when he picked up a telephone. The *Post* story compared this "fix" to the Chicago "Black Sox" scandal of 1919, and went on to describe the presentation of Burnett's notes to University of Georgia officials, and Butts's subsequent resignation. The article concluded:

> The chances are that Wally Butts will never help any football team again. . . .
> The investigation by university and Southeastern Conference officials is continuing; motion pictures of other games are being scrutinized; where it will end no one so far can say. But careers will be ruined, that is sure.

Butts sued for $5 million in compensatory and $5 million in punitive damages. In court the *Post* argued truth as its defense, but the evidence contradicted its version of the event. Butts argued that his conversation with Bryant had been general football talk. Expert witnesses supported Butts's position, after analyzing the films of the game. The jury awarded Butts $60,000 in general damages and $3 million in punitive damages. On appeal, the U.S. Supreme Court found "reckless disregard." The opinion, written by Justice John Harlan, noted that "the evidence showed that the Butts story was in no sense 'hot' news and the editors of the magazine recognized the need for a thorough investigation of the serious charges." Necessary precautions were ignored, however. The *Post* knew that Burnett was on probation in connection with bad-check charges, but published his story without additional verification. Burnett's notes were not even analyzed by any of the magazine's personnel. An individual who was with Burnett when the phone call was overheard was not interviewed. No attempt was made to view the game film to see if Burnett's information was accurate. In short, the evidence supported a finding of "highly unreasonable conduct constituting an extreme departure from the standards of investigation and reporting ordinarily adhered to by responsible publishers."[41] The Court found "reckless disregard" and affirmed the trial court's decision.

The *Walker* case further developed the concept of "hot news." The case involved a news release about General Edwin Walker's involvement in the events surrounding the entry of James Meredith into the University of Mississippi, in September 1962. The Associated Press report stated that Walker had taken command of the violent crowd and had led a charge against federal marshals. Walker initiated court action, seeking to collect damages from newspapers and broadcasting stations that carried the AP reports. A Texas trial court awarded Walker $500,000 in general damages. The case was appealed to the Supreme Court. The Court determined that Walker was a public figure, because he had thrust his personality into an important public controversy. Moreover, in contrast to the Butts article, the Walker dispatch contained news that required immediate dissemination. AP received the information from a reporter who was present at the scene and who gave every indication of being trustworthy and competent. The story seemed reasonable to anyone familiar with Walker's previous publicized statements on the controversy. The court determined that "considering the necessity for rapid dissemination, nothing in this series of events gives the slightest hint of a severe departure from accepted publishing standards."[42] The Court did not find "reckless disregard" and concluded that Walker was not entitled to damages.

In 1968, in *St. Amant*, the Court distinguished between "negligence" and "reckless disregard." The *St. Amant* case involved a televised political broadcast in which Phil St. Amant, a candidate for public office, delivered a speech that contained numerous quotations of a second person's (J.D. Albin) opinions of St. Amant's political opponents. One of the quotations suggested that Deputy Sheriff Herman Thompson had been instrumental in hiding the records of a Teamsters Union local. Furthermore, the quotation claimed that money had "passed hands" between Thompson and the union head. Thompson initiated suit for defamation, claiming that the broadcast had "imputed...gross misconduct" and "inferred conduct of the most nefarious nature." The Louisiana Supreme Court ruled against St. Amant because he had "recklessly" broadcast false information about Thompson, though not knowingly. The court noted that St. Amant failed to verify the facts. He mistakenly believed that he had no responsibility for the broadcast, because he was merely quoting another person's words. The U.S. Supreme Court, in the opinion of Justice Byron White, reversed the decision. Justice White wrote:

> Reckless conduct is not measured by whether a reasonably prudent man would have published, or would have investigated before publishing. There must be sufficient evidence to permit the conclusion that the defendant in fact entertained serious doubts as to the truth of his publication. Publishing with such doubts shows reckless disregard for truth or falsity and demonstrates actual malice.[43]

The opinion added, however, that a defendant may not count on a favorable verdict merely by testifying that he or she published with a belief that the statements were true.

The finder of fact must determine whether the publication was indeed made in good faith. Professions of good faith will be unlikely to prove persuasive, for example, where a story is fabricated by the defendant, is the product of his imagination, or is based wholly on an unverified anonymous telephone call. Nor will they be likely to prevail when the publisher's allegations are so inherently improbable that only a reckless man would have put them in circulation. Likewise, recklessness may be found where there are obvious reasons to doubt the veracity of the informant or the accuracy of his reports.

The Supreme Court found no evidence that St. Amant was aware of the probable falsity of Albin's statement about Thompson. Albin had sworn to his statements, and St. Amant had verified some of them. Thompson's evidence had failed to demonstrate "a low community assessment of Albin's trustworthiness." The Court felt that the reasons cited by the Louisiana court fell far short of proving St. Amant's "reckless disregard" for the accuracy of the statements. Failure to investigate does not, in itself, establish bad faith. Negligence, even though undesirable, does not constitute "reckless disregard."

In *Pape* the Supreme Court examined the reportorial standards of a news magazine. The issue was whether the failure of *Time* magazine to use the word "alleged" constituted "reckless disregard." In 1961 *Time's* report of the findings of the U.S. Commission on Civil Rights claimed that 13 Chicago police officers, led by Detective Frank Pape, broke through the doors of a family's apartment, woke the parents with flashlights, and forced them at gunpoint to stand naked in the center of the living room. The report claimed that Pape struck the father with a flashlight and called him "nigger" and "blackboy" while his six children watched. After police ransacked the apartment, the report continued, the father was taken to the police station, where he was neither advised of his rights nor permitted to call an attorney. He was subsequently released without criminal charges being filed against him. The allegations in the commissioner's report had not been proven, and the *Time* article failed to make clear it was reporting mere allegations. Pape sued. The case reached the Supreme Court. The opinion of Justice Potter Stewart held that the article, at worst, reflected an error in judgment. According to Stewart, media that maintain professional standards should not be subject to financial liability for nonmalicious errors in judgment. The Court felt that if the freedoms of expression were to have "the breathing space that they need to survive, misstatements of this kind must have the protection of the First and Fourteenth Amendments."[44] In *Pape* the Court refused to punish a harmful, yet nonmalicious, statement.

The *Butts, Walker, St. Amant,* and *Pape* decisions indicate that individuals have generally free reign to publish statements about public officials, figures, or issues, as long as such publication is not made with "reckless disregard" for the truth. To prove "reckless disregard," public officials must establish more than mere negligence—they must demonstrate an uncaring and malicious disregard on the part of the publisher.

Robust Debate

Consistent with its concern for protecting freedom of expression, the Supreme Court, in *Greenbelt*, enunciated the doctrine of "robust debate." The case involved negotiations between Charles Bresler, a prominent local real-estate developer, and the Greenbelt City Council. Bresler sought to obtain zoning variances that would allow the construction of high-density housing on land that he owned. At the same time, the city was attempting to acquire a tract of land owned by Bresler for the construction of a new high school. These joint negotiations produced substantial controversy and several stormy city-council meetings. The meetings were reported at length in the news column of the *Greenbelt News Review*. The articles claimed that at the public meetings some citizens had described Bresler's negotiating position as "blackmail." Bresler brought suit. The jury awarded Bresler $5,000 in compensatory damages and $12,500 in punitive damages. Upon appeal, the Supreme Court reversed the decision on the ground that the news stories were accurate accounts of the public debates. The Court noted that by publishing the story, the *Greenbelt News Review* was performing its legitimate function as a community newspaper.

> It is simply impossible to believe that a reader who reached the word "blackmail" in either article would not have understood exactly what was meant: It was Bresler's public and wholly legal negotiating proposals that were being criticized. No reader could have thought that either the speakers at the meetings or the newspaper articles reporting their words were charging Bresler with the commission of a criminal offense. On the contrary, even the most careless reader must have perceived that the word was no more than rhetorical hyperbole, a vigorous epithet used by those who considered Bresler's negotiating position extremely unreasonable. Indeed, the record is completely devoid of evidence that anyone in the city of Greenbelt or anywhere else thought Bresler had been charged with a crime.[45]

In *Greenbelt* the Court emphasized that the societal interests in providing for "robust debate" and the discussion of subjects of substantial concern took precedence over a person's interest in maintaining his or her good name.

The doctrine of "robust debate" was reaffirmed in the 1984 *Bose Corporation* decision. The case involved an article in *Consumer Reports* that evaluated the quality of numerous brands of loudspeakers, including the Bose 901. The article presented a critical assessment of the model and claimed that "individual instruments heard through the Bose system seemed to grow to gigantic proportions and tended to wander about the room." The article urged consumers not to buy the model unless they "were sure the system would please [them] after the novelty value had worn off." The Bose corporation initiated court action on the ground that the article constituted libelous product disparagement. The district court found "actual malice," because the claim that instruments tended to wander "about the room" was false. Actually, listeners perceived "movement back and forth along the wall in front of them and between the two speakers." They did not perceive movement "about the room." The Supreme Court, per Justice John Stevens, overturned the decision. Stevens noted that the statement under question "represents the sort of inaccuracy that is commonplace in the forum of robust debate."

> Here. . . , adoption of the language chosen was "one of a number of possible rational interpretations" of an event "that bristled with ambiguities" and descriptive challenges for the writer. The choice of such language, though reflecting a misconception, does not place the speech beyond the outer limits of the First Amendment's broad protective umbrella.[46]

The *Bose Corporation* decision acknowledged that erroneous statements are inevitable in the system of free and "robust debate."

Public Official

Further clarification of the "actual malice" doctrine occurred in *Rosenblatt*, when the Court clarified the matter of libelous statements made about public officials. The case involved Alfred Rosenblatt, a columnist for the *Laconia Evening Citizen*. Rosenblatt was an outspoken proponent for change in operations at the Belkamp Recreation Area, and he was critical of the actions taken by Frank Baer, supervisor of the area. In early 1960, after Baer was fired from his position, Rosenblatt published a column that charged Baer with mismanagement. Baer sued for libel; a jury awarded him $31,500. Upon appeal, the Supreme Court overturned the decision, because the column contained no libelous statement. In fact, persons familiar with the controversy might read it as complimenting the new management for attracting increased business. In the *Rosenblatt* decision the Court, per Justice William Brennan, clarified the concept of "public official." Brennan noted that in the *New York Times* case, the Court did not determine how far down into the lower ranks of government employees the "public official" designation would extend, nor did the Court specify categories of persons who should be included. In *Rosenblatt*, the Court decided:

> Criticism of government is at the very center of the constitutionally protected area of free discussion. Criticism of those responsible for government operations must be free, lest criticism of government itself be penalized. It is clear, therefore, that the "public official" designation applies at the very least to those among the hierarchy of government employees who have, or appear to the pub-

lic to have, substantial responsibility for or control over the conduct of government affairs.[47]

In *Rosenblatt* the Court acknowledged that when interests in public discussion are strong, "the Constitution limits the protections afforded by the law of defamation."

The Court continued to apply the *New York Times* standard of "actual malice" to other cases involving "public officials" as plaintiffs. In *Monitor Patriot Company* and *Ocala Star-Banner Company*, the Court emphasized that libel actions dealing with public figures must be accompanied by proof of "actual malice." In *Monitor Patriot Company*, Alphonse Roy, a candidate for the U.S. Senate, objected to a column written by Drew Pearson. The article, which appeared in the *Concord Monitor*, described Roy as a "former small-time bootlegger." Roy lost his bid for the Senate in the Democratic primary. Roy argued that since the alleged criminal conduct had occurred in the 1920s and had involved his private life rather than his performance as a public servant, the newspaper was guilty of libel. A jury agreed and awarded damages of $10,000. The newspaper appealed. The Supreme Court unanimously disagreed. According to the opinion, per Justice Potter Stewart, the principal task of a candidate consisted of putting before the electorate every conceivable aspect of his or her public and private life that might lead the voters to form a favorable impression. A candidate, however, who vaunts a spotless record and sterling integrity before the electorate cannot cry "Foul!" when an industrious reporter attempts to demonstrate the contrary. Subsequently, the Court ruled that a charge of criminal conduct, no matter how remote in time or place, is relevant to a candidate's or official's fitness for office. Accordingly, the remarks applied to Roy as a "public official," and a showing of "actual malice" was essential for Roy to win the suit.[48] The judgment of the lower court was reversed and the case remanded.

In *Ocala Star-Banner Company*, a newspaper reported that the mayor of Crystal River, Leonard Damron, who was then a candidate for county tax assessor, had been charged with perjury in a civil-rights case. It was, however, Damron's brother who had been accused of perjury. An editor had changed the first name in the story to the mayor's. Damron lost the election, which was held two weeks after the story appeared. At trial, the judge instructed the jury that the "actual malice" rule did not apply, because the error did not involve Damron's official conduct. The jury found the newspaper guilty of libel and awarded Damron $22,000 in general damages. The Supreme Court unanimously reversed the decision. According to the opinion, written by Justice Stewart, Leonard Damron was a "public official" in two ways—as the mayor of Crystal River and as a candidate for the office of county tax assessor. The court stressed that under the *New York Times* rule a "public official" cannot recover damages for a defamatory falsehood relating to official conduct without proof that the statement was made with "actual malice." The Court was unimpressed with Damron's claim that the *Times* rule should apply only to "official conduct." Citing the *Monitor* decision, the Court reiterated that a charge of criminal conduct against an official or candidate, no matter how remote in time or place, was always "relevant to his fitness for office" for purposes of applying the *Times* rule.[49] The case was remanded.

Private Persons

Throughout the 1970s the Court clarified the law of libel, as it concerns private persons. The relevant cases include *Rosenbloom, Gertz, Firestone, Hutchinson,* and *Wolston.*

In *Rosenbloom* two separate allegations of defamation came before the Supreme Court. The events of this case began when George Rosenbloom was arrested for distributing nudist magazines in the Philadelphia area. Rosenbloom was charged with selling obscene materials. The event received coverage on the local news broadcast over radio station WIP. In the 6 P.M. newscast, the reporter stated that vice-squad officers had confiscated 1,000 "allegedly obscene" books at Rosenbloom's house and another 3,000 "obscene" books at a barn near his home. The report was rebroadcast in the same form at 6:30 P.M., but at 8 P.M. WIP changed the second reference to read "reportedly obscene." News of Rosenbloom's arrest was broadcast five more times and each report described the seized books as "allegedly" or "reportedly" obscene. Rosenbloom brought suit against police officials and against the local news media on the ground that the magazines were not obscene. A second instance of allegedly defamatory radio broadcasts related to WIP's 13 news reports of the lawsuit itself. None mentioned Rosenbloom by name. The broadcasts did mention, however, that "the girlie-book peddlers say the police crackdown and continued reference to their borderline literature as smut or filth is hurting their business." A few months later a jury acquitted Rosenbloom of the obscenity charges. Following his acquittal, Rosenbloom sought damages under Pennsylvania's libel law. He argued that WIP's unqualified characterization of the books as "obscene" in the initial broadcasts constituted libel *per se* and was proved false by Rosenbloom's acquittal. He also charged that the later broadcasts describing his court suit were also defamatory in the characterization of Rosenbloom and his associates as "smut distributors" and "girlie-book peddlers." The court awarded $25,000 in general damages and $250,000 in punitive damages. The court of appeals reversed the lower court decision. The judges emphasized that the broadcasts concerned matters of public interest and that they involved "hot news" prepared under deadline pressure. The court concluded that "the fact that plaintiff was not a public figure cannot be accorded decisive significance if the recognized important guarantees of the First Amendment are to be adequately implemented." Rosenbloom then took the case to the U.S. Supreme Court. The issue Rosenbloom raised was whether, since he was not a public official or a public figure, he had to establish "actual malice" on the part of station WIP. The Court noted:

> If a matter is a subject of public or general interest, it cannot suddenly become less so merely because a private individual is involved, or because in some sense the individual did not "voluntarily" choose to become involved. The public's primary interest is in the event; the public focus is on the conduct of the participant and the content, effect, and significance of the conduct, not the participant's prior anonymity or notoriety.
>
> In that circumstance we think the time has come forthrightly to announce that the determinant whether the First Amendment applies to state libel actions is whether the utterance involved concerns an issue of public or general concern, albeit leaving the delineation of the reach of that term to future cases.... Drawing a distinction between "public" and "private" figures makes no sense in terms of the First Amendment guarantees.[50]

In effect, the *Rosenbloom* decision held that no person—public or private—who becomes involved in an event of public interest could collect libel damages without proof of "actual malice."

Three years later the Court overturned the *Rosenbloom* rule. In the *Gertz* case, the Court ruled that private citizens have greater protection against libelous statements than do public officials or figures. The facts of this case began when Richard Nuccio, a Chicago policeman, shot and killed a young man. Authorities prosecuted Nuccio and ultimately obtained a conviction for second-degree murder. The victim's family then retained Elmer Gertz, an attorney, to represent them in civil litigation against Nuccio. Shortly thereafter, *American Opinion*, a monthly vehicle for the opinions of the conservative John Birch Society, printed a story about Nuccio's trial entitled "FRAME-UP": Richard Nuccio And The War On Police." The article contained several falsehoods. For example, the article charged that Gertz had a criminal record, that he had taken part in planning the 1968 demonstrations in Chicago, and that he was a "Leninist" and a "Communist-fronter." The editor of *American Opinion* made no effort to verify the charges against Gertz; however, he appended a statement claiming that the author had "concluded extensive research into the Richard Nuccio case." He included a photograph of Gertz and wrote the caption under it: "Elmer Gertz of the Red Guild harasses Nuccio." Gertz brought suit, claiming that the falsehoods injured his reputation. The jury awarded him $50,000. The court of appeals, referring to *Rosenbloom*, ruled that the "actual malice" standard was applicable in this case. The court noted that Gertz failed to demonstrate that the editor had acted with "actual malice." In fact, the editor knew nothing about Gertz except what he learned from the article. The court concluded that an editor's mere failure to investigate cannot establish "reckless disregard" for the truth. Gertz appealed to the U.S. Supreme Court. The primary issue was

whether a different degree of constitutional privilege applied to defamatory falsehoods about a private citizen than to those about a public official. According to
Justice Lewis Powell,

> we conclude that the state interest in compensating injury to the reputation of
> private individuals requires that a different rule should obtain with respect to
> them. . . . The first remedy of any victim of defamation is self help—using avail-
> able opportunities to contradict the lie or correct the error and thereby mini-
> mize its adverse impact on reputation. Public officials and public figures usually
> enjoy significantly greater access to the channels of effective communication
> and hence have a more realistic opportunity to counteract false statements than
> private individuals normally enjoy. Private individuals are therefore more vul-
> nerable to injury, and the state interest in protecting them is correspondingly
> greater.[51]

Powell noted that "the extension of the *New York Times* test posed by the Rosenbloom plurality would abridge this legitimate state interest to a degree that we
find unacceptable." In *Gertz* the Court decided that a libel action by a private
person required a showing of "negligence" as contrasted with a showing of "actual malice." A secondary issue was whether Gertz was a private person or a
public figure. The Court noted that Gertz was not a public figure; even though
he was "well-known in some circles, he had achieved no general fame or notoriety in the community." The Court acknowledged that the public-figure question
should be considered by looking to the extent of a person's participation in the
issue giving rise to the defamation. In this light, Gertz was not a public figure.
His involvement with the issue related only to his representation of a client. He
took no part in the criminal prosecution. He never discussed the litigation with
the press. He did not thrust himself into the center of this issue, nor did he engage the public's attention in an effort to influence its outcome. The Court concluded that the "actual malice" standard was inapplicable to Gertz, who was a
private citizen.

The Court reaffirmed this view in the *Firestone* case. After the Mary Alice
and Russell Firestone divorce proceedings, *Time* magazine printed a note in the
"Milestones" section which read:

> DIVORCED. By Russell A. Firestone Jr., 41, heir to the tire fortune: Mary
> Alice Sullivan Firestone, 32, his third wife; a one-time Palm Beach school-
> teacher; on grounds of extreme cruelty and adultery; after six years of marriage,
> one son; in West Palm Beach, Fla. The 17-month intermittent trial produced
> enough testimony of extramarital adventures on both sides, said the judge, "to
> make Dr. Freud's hair curl."

Mary Alice Firestone brought suit against *Time,* claiming that the descriptions
were "false, malicious, and defamatory." The trial court granted, and the Su-

"DARLING, YOU'LL NEVER WIN THAT LIBEL
SUIT···AFTER ALL, YOU'RE A CELEBRITY!"

preme Court of Florida affirmed, a $100,000 award of damages against the pub-
lisher. *Time* appealed, alleging that the magazine could not be liable for publishing any falsehood without proof that the publication was made with "actual
malice." According to *Time,* since Mrs. Firestone was a "public figure" and
the news item constituted a report of a judicial proceeding, the article deserved
the protection of the "actual malice" standard. The U.S. Supreme Court, in the
opinion of Justice William Rehnquist, held that the "actual malice" standard
was inapplicable in this case. Mrs. Firestone was not a public figure. In applying the *Gertz* decision, Rehnquist noted that Mrs. Firestone had not assumed a
role of "especial prominence in the affairs of society" and had not been "thrust
to the forefront of particular public controversies in order to influence the resolution of the issues involved." The Court emphasized that a private person, like
Firestone, should not forfeit protection against defamation simply by being drawn
into court.

Imposing upon the law of private defamation the rather drastic limitations worked
by *New York Times* cannot be justified by generalized references to the public

interest in reports of judicial proceedings. The details of many, if not most, courtroom battles would add almost nothing toward advancing the uninhibited debate on public issues.[52]

Rehnquist reaffirmed *Gertz,* noting that "*Gertz* provides an adequate safeguard for the constitutionally protected interests of the press and affords it a tolerable margin for error in requiring some type of fault." Rehnquist then observed that since the divorce court had not found Mrs. Firestone guilty of adultery, as reported by *Time,* the lower court had properly found the claim of accurate reporting to be invalid.

The Court reiterated its concept of "public figure" in *Hutchinson,* a case that involved an alleged defamation by a government official. William Proxmire, a U.S. senator from Wisconsin, initiated the "Golden Fleece of the Month Award" to publicize examples of wasteful governement spending. One of these awards cited several government agencies for spending half a million dollars to fund Ronald Hutchinson's research project of animals when they were exposed to aggravating, stressful stimuli. The federal agencies were interested in this research for resolving problems associated with confining humans in close quarters in space and undersea exploration. At the time of the award, Hutchinson was director of research at the Kalamazoo State Mental Hospital. He was also a professor at Western Michigan University. In presenting the award, Proxmire delivered a speech in which he declared:

> Dr. Hutchinson's studies should make the taxpayers as well as his monkeys grind their teeth. In fact, the good doctor has made a fortune from his monkeys and in the process made a monkey out of the American taxpayer.
>
> It is time for the Federal Government to get out of this "monkey business."
> In view of the transparent worthlessness of Hutchinson's study of jaw-grinding and biting by angry or hard-drinking monkeys, it is time we put a stop to the bite Hutchinson and the bureaucrats who fund him have been taking of the taxpayer.

Hutchinson filed suit, alleging that as a result of being awarded the "Golden Fleece," he suffered a loss of respect in his profession, extreme mental anguish, and a loss of ability to earn income. The case reached the U.S. Supreme Court. The Court's opinion, written by Chief Justice Warren Burger, noted that Hutchinson would not have become a public figure without Proxmire's action. In fact, Hutchinson's public profile was much like that "of countless members of his profession." His publications reached "a relatively small category of professionals concerned with research in human behavior." Hutchinson did not enjoy the access to the media that "is one of the accouterments of having become a public figure." Burger's opinion stressed that Hutchinson became a limited public figure only as a consequence of the Golden Fleece Award. Burger then argued: "Clearly, those charged with defamation cannot, by their own conduct, create their own defense by making the claimant a public figure.''[53] The Court concluded that Hutchinson was not a "public figure," and therefore a demonstration of "actual malice" was not necessary in this case.

The Court rendered a related decision in *Wolston*. The case concerned a Reader's Digest Association publication entitled *KGB, the Secret Work of Soviet Agents*. The book listed Ilya Wolston as a Soviet agent and claimed that he had been indicted for espionage. Wolston brought suit, claiming that the charges were false and defamatory. The lower courts decided that Wolston was a "public figure" and that the "First Amendment precluded recovery unless Wolston proved that the book was written with actual malice." The case reached the Supreme Court. Writing for the Court, Justice William Rehnquist summarized the Court's decisions of the previous decade.

> We identified two ways in which a person may become a public figure for purposes of the First Amendment:
>
> For the most part those who attain this status have assumed roles of especial prominence in the affairs of society. Some occupy positions of such persuasive power and influence that they are deemed public figures for all purposes. More commonly, those classed as public figures have thrust themselves to the forefront of particular public controversies in order to influence the resolution of the issues involved.

Rehnquist then argued that Wolston did not qualify as a "public figure" in either sense of the term. First, Wolston was not "one of that small group of individuals who are public figures for all purposes." Second, even though Wolston was investigated in regard to Soviet espionage in the United States, he had not "voluntarily thrust" or "injected" himself into the forefront of the public controversy. Instead, Rehnquist felt it would be more accurate to say that Wolston "was dragged unwillingly into the controversy." In *Wolston*, the Court concluded:

> A private individual is not automatically transformed into a public figure just by becoming involved in or associated with a matter that attracts public attention. To accept such reasoning would in effect re-establish the doctrine advanced by the plurality opinion in Rosenbloom . . . , which concluded that the *New York Times* standard should extend to defamatory falsehoods relating to private persons if the statements involved matters of public or general concern. We repudiated this proposition in *Gertz* and in *Firestone*, however, and we reject it again today. A libel defendant must show more than mere newsworthiness to justify application of the demanding burden of *New York Times*.[54]

Rehnquist's opinion was unequivocally clear—the liberal interpretation of the First Amendment that was set forth in *Rosenbloom* had been overturned by subsequent decisions. A "private person" did not have to demonstrate "actual malice" in order to win a libel suit.

Neutral Reportage

In 1977 a district court considered the question of whether a reporter, supplied with information from a usually reliable source that appears unreliable in this instance, can publish an account of the information without fear of punishment for "actual malice." In rendering its opinion in the *Edwards* case, the court established the doctrine of "neutral reportage." The case involved a story, written by John Devlin, which appeared in the *New York Times*. Devlin's interest in the story was first aroused when an official publication of the National Audubon Society claimed that any scientists who supported the use of DDT were "paid liars." Devlin researched the story; he requested verification from the Audubon Society and he sought response from the scientists. Even though he did not receive complete data from either side in the controversy, he published a story entitled "Pesticide Spokesmen Accused of 'Lying' on Higher Bird Count." The story accurately reported the information he had obtained from his sources. Dr. J. Gordon Edwards and other scientists filed a libel suit. The trial judge instructed the jury that the *Times* could be found guilty of "actual malice" if Devlin had serious doubts about the truth of the "paid liars" claim, even if he had no doubts that he was reporting his source's allegations faithfully. Accordingly, the jury returned a verdict against the *Times* and awarded Edwards $21,000. The district court overturned the award. Judge Irving Kaufman wrote:

> At stake in this case is a fundamental principle. Succinctly stated, when a responsible, prominent organization like the National Audubon Society makes serious charges against a public figure, the First Amendment protects the accurate and disinterested reporting of those charges, regardless of the reporter's private views regarding their validity. What is newsworthy about such accusations is that they were made. We do not believe that the press may be required under the First Amendment to suppress newsworthy statements merely because it has serious doubts regarding their truth.[55]

In *Edwards*, Kaufman formulated the doctrine of "neutral reportage." The U.S. Supreme Court denied certiorari in the *Edwards* case.

A year later, in *Dickey*, a court of appeals opposed the "neutral reportage" doctrine. In this case, a person, during a televised debate, was accused by a congressman of having accepted a bribe. The accused initiated a libel suit against the television station that presented the debate. The *Dickey* court decided that the "neutral reportage" concept violates the *St. Amant* decision. In *St. Amant* the Supreme Court ruled that an individual who publishes information, while entertaining serious doubts as to the truth of the publication, "shows reckless disregard for truth or falsity and demonstrates actual malice."[56] Influenced by this opinion, the *Dickey* court concluded: "A constitutional privilege of neutral reportage is not created...merely because an individual newspaper or television or radio station decides that a particular statement is newsworthy."[57] In any event, a determination of the constitutionality of "neutral reportage" must await a hearing by the U.S. Supreme Court.

Scope of Discovery

In *Herbert* the Supreme Court determined that a plaintiff in a libel action may probe a journalist's mind during the discovery procedure. The libel action in this case was brought by Colonel Anthony Herbert, who had received widespread media attention as a result of his bringing Vietnam war crimes to public attention. In an episode of the television program "60 Minutes," various contradictions in Herbert's story were highlighted. Shortly thereafter, Barry Lando, the producer of "60 Minutes," made the same claims in an article for *Atlantic Monthly.* Herbert's libel suit alleged that the program and article "falsely and maliciously portrayed him as a liar." Since Herbert was a "public figure," he had to show "actual malice" in order to recover damages. In order to prove his case, Herbert questioned Lando at length. Lando answered numerous questions, but refused to respond in some instances on the ground that "the First Amendment protected against inquiry into the state of mind of those who edit, produce, or publish, and into the editorial process." The district court decided that Lando's state of mind was of "central importance" to the issue of "actual malice." The court ruled that the questioning procedure was "entirely appropriate to Herbert's efforts to discover whether Lando had any reason to doubt the truth of any of his sources." When the court of appeals reversed this decision, Herbert took the case to the U.S. Supreme Court. Justice Byron White, writing for the Court, observed that previous Supreme Court decisions made it essential for recovering damages "that the plaintiff focus on the conduct and state of mind of the defendant." For example, a defamer of a public official or public figure "must know or have reason to suspect that his publication is false." In other cases, evidence "of some kind of fault, negligence perhaps, is essential to recovery." According to White, under the influence of recent cases, "the thoughts and editorial processes of the alleged defamer" are vital to the discovery process. White concluded, "According an absolute privilege to the editorial process of a media defendant in a libel case is not required, authorized, or presaged by our prior cases, and would substantially enhance the burden of proving actual malice."[58] In *Herbert* the Supreme Court determined that the First Amendment does not bar a plaintiff from inquiring into the state of mind of those responsible for publication.

Libelous Petition

In the *McDonald* case, the Court examined the meaning of the Petition Clause of the First Amendment. Robert McDonald filed a libel action against David Smith on the ground that while McDonald was being considered for the position of U.S. attorney, Smith maliciously wrote letters to President Ronald Reagan and other officials that contained "false slanderous, libelous, inflammatory and derogatory statements" concerning his qualifications for public office. McDonald claimed that the letters had their intended effect; he was not appointed and his reputation and career were injured. Smith argued that the Petition Clause of the First Amendment, which provides the right to petition the government for a redress of grievances, guarantees "absolute immunity from liability." The Supreme Court, in an opinion written by Chief Justice Burger, disagreed.

> Although the values in the right of petition as an important aspect of self government are beyond question, it does not follow that the Framers of the First Amendment believed that the Petition Clause provided absolute immunity from damages for libel.[59]

In *McDonald*, the Court determined that libelous petition was not immune from punishment.

Groups

The concept of group libel has been recognized by state courts since early in the twentieth century. In 1917 an Oklahoma appeals court noted: "The law of libel forbids the writing, publication, or circulation of libelous matter against a class as much so as against individuals."[60] The doctrine of group libel was further clarified in 1925 by the Supreme Court of Illinois. The court noted that

> a libel upon a class or group has as great a tendency to provoke a breach of the peace or to disturb society as has a libel on an individual, and such a libel is punishable, even though its application to individual members of the class or group cannot be proved.[61]

The notion of group libel, however, was first applied in the U.S. Supreme Court in the *Beauharnais* case in 1952. The libelous material was prepared by Joseph Beauharnais, the president of the White Circle League, a racist "neighborhood improvement" group. Beauharnais and his volunteers distributed in downtown Chicago leaflets that called on the mayor "to halt the further encroachment, harassment and invasion of white people, their property, neighborhoods and persons, by the Negro." The leaflets warned: "If persuasion and the need to prevent the white race from becoming mongrelized by the negro will not unite us, then the aggression...rapes, robberies, knives, guns and marijuana of the negro surely will." When Beauharnais was convicted of violating an Illinois law by distributing publications that subjected black citizens to contempt and derision, he appealed. The U.S. Supreme Court, in the opinion written by Justice Felix Frankfurter, supported the Illinois law. The Court noted that Illinois had a history of tension between races, which had often flared into violence and destruction. It seemed clear that the Illinois legislature acted within reason in attempting "to curb false or malicious defamation of racial and religious groups, made in public places and by means calculated to have a powerful emotional impact on those to whom it was presented."[62] Justices Hugo Black and William Douglas opposed the law as a form of censorship. They argued that "this act sets up a system of state censorship which is at war with the kind of free government envisioned by those who forced adoption of our Bill of Rights." The majority of the Court, however, upheld Beauharnais's conviction on the grounds of group libel. Though the doctrine has not been frequently invoked, the concept of "group libel" stands as a reminder to publishers that groups may seek retribution for libelous statements.

Corporations

Each company has a reputation to protect. The doctrine of "corporate libel" recognizes that companies enjoy the same rights to plead for damages as do individuals. The *Neiman-Marcus Company* and *Cosgrove Studio* cases provide examples.

Neiman-Marcus Company brought suit against the publishers of a book on the ground that statements made about company-employed models and sales personnel were libelous. The publication contained the following paragraphs:

> He [Stanley Marcus, president of Neiman-Marcus Company] may not know that some Neiman models are call girls—the top babes in town. The guy who escorts one feels in the same league with the playboys who took out Ziegfield's glorified. Price, a hundred bucks a night.
>
> The sales girls are good, too—pretty, and often much cheaper—twenty bucks on the average. They're more fun, too, not as snooty as the models. We got this confidential, from a Dallas wolf. . . .
>
> Houston is faced with a serious homosexual problem. It is not as evident as Dallas' because there are no expensive imported faggots in town like those in the Neiman-Marcus set.

The corporation sought $2 million in compensatory and punitive damages. The district court determined that while a corporation has no reputation in a personal sense, its prestige and position are capable of being damaged by aspersive language. A corporation could be defamed by statements directed at its employees, if they discrdit the method in which business is conducted. The court concluded that a corporation could be "damaged in a business way by a publication that it employs seriously undesirable personnel."[63]

A decade later another court affirmed the doctrine of "corporate libel." Cosgrove Studio and Camera Shop advertised that it would offer a free roll of film for every roll brought to it for developing. The next day its business competitor, Cal Pane, placed an advertisement in one of the same newspapers, which read in part: "USE COMMON SENSE—You Get Nothing for Nothing! WE WILL NOT: 1. Inflate the prices of your developing to give you a new roll free! 2. Print the blurred negatives to inflate the price of your snapshots!" Cosgrove initiated a suit for libel, alleging that Pane's advertisement suggested that Cosgrove was dishonest in business practices. The trial court said that Pane's advertisement was not libelous. The appeals court, however, reversed the judgment, claiming that Cosgrove had a cause for action. The words were libelous *per se*. Any language that "unequivocally, maliciously, and falsely imputes to an individual or corporation want of integrity in the conduct of his or its business is actionable."[64] In arriving at this decision, the court acknowledged that identification of the defamed corporation need not be by name; a party may be identified if it is pointed to by description or circumstances. In *Cosgrove Studios*, as in *Neiman-Marcus Company*, the court found a case of "corporate libel."

Criminal Libel

Though the majority of libel cases are civil matters, some instances of "criminal libel" can be cited. In cases where the defamation is so flagrant as to jeopardize the public peace, criminal prosecution may be necessary. Several states, particularly those in the South, have criminal libel statutes. Most of these statutes depend on whether the defamation causes a breach of peace. The *Ashton* case dealt with a charge of "criminal libel."

In 1963 Steve Ashton went to Hazard, Kentucky, where a bitter labor conflict was raging, to appeal for aid for unemployed miners. He distributed a pamphlet that attacked the chief of police, the sheriff, and the owner of the *Herald Citizen*. He accused these people of unethical antilabor activity. The trial court convicted Ashton of "criminal libel," arguing that such libel is defined as "any writing calculated to create disturbances of the peace, corrupt the public morals, or lead to any act, which, when done, is indictable." The court of appeals affirmed the decision. The U.S. Supreme Court, per Justice William Douglas, unanimously overturned the lower court's decision. The Court emphasized that

> since the English Common law of criminal libel is inconsistent with constitutional provisions, and since no Kentucky case has redefined the crime in understandable terms, and since the law must be made on a case to case basis, the elements of the crime are so indefinite and uncertain that it should not be enforced as a penal offense in Kentucky.[65]

According to the Court, the Kentucky law suffered from vagueness and overbreadth. Douglas also stressed that where First Amendment rights were involved, the

Court had to "look even more closely lest, under the guise of regulating conduct that is reachable by the police power, freedom of speech or of the press suffer." Because of the unclear nature of the law's target, the *Ashton* Court overturned the Kentucky "breach of peace" statute. In fact, cases of "criminal libel" are rare, because the public injury resulting from criminal defamation is usually minor or nonexistent.

Summary

Within the past two decades, the Supreme Court has formulated doctrines that make it relatively difficult for a public official to win a libel suit. According to the "actual malice" doctrine set forth in *New York Times*, a public official must demonstrate that a libelous statement was made with knowledge of falsity or with "reckless disregard" of the truth. In *Rosenblatt, Monitor Patriot,* and *Ocala Star-Banner* the Court emphasized that public officials, in particular, must prove that the libel was maliciously motivated.

In other cases the Court further clarified the doctrine of "actual malice." In *Garrison* the Court held that public officials must demonstrate more than "reasonable belief" in order to win a suit. In the *Curtis* and *Walker* cases the Court determined that "hot news" required less thorough investigation of a serious charge. The *St. Amant* decision indicated that "negligence" does not constitute "reckless disregard." *Pape* acknowledged that "minor misstatements" are protected by the First Amendment. The concept of "robust debate" was introduced in *Greenbelt*. In *Herbert* the Court approved a wide scope of discovery; the First Amendment does not prohibit a plaintiff from inquiring into the state of mind of those responsible for publication.

Since 1971 the Supreme Court has set down several rulings designed to clarify libel law as it applied to "private persons." The *Rosenbloom* opinion held that no person—public or private—who becomes involved in an event of public interest could collect libel damages without showing "actual malice." The *Gertz* case, in overturning *Rosenbloom*, conditioned a libel action by a private person on a showing of "negligence" rather than "actual malice." This doctrine was affirmed in *Firestone, Hutchinson,* and *Wolston*.

While the courts most frequently deal with defamatory statements relating to individuals, they have recognized other forms of libel as well. In *Beauharnais* the Supreme Court acknowledged that groups or classes of people can be victims of libel. The *Neiman-Marcus Company* and *Cosgrove Studio* cases acknowledged that corporations can be damaged by unfair and malicious statements. And in *Ashton* the Supreme Court considered, then overturned, a vague and overbroad state law that punished "criminal libel." In actuality, cases of "criminal libel" are uncommon, because the public damage resulting from defamation is usually difficult to determine.

NOTES

1. *Chaplinsky v. New Hampshire*, 62 S.Ct. 766 (1942).
2. *Solverson v. Peterson*, 25 N.W. 14 (1885).
3. *Overstreet v. New Nonpareil Company*, 167 N.W. 669 (1918).
4. *Smith v. Lyons*, 77 So 896 (1918).
5. *Smith v. Fielden*, 326 S.W. 2d 476 (1959).
6. *Toomey v. Farley*, 138 N.E. 2d 221 (1956).
7. *Buckley v. Littell*, 394 F. Supp. 918 (1975).
8. *Hornby v. Hunter*, 385 S.W. 2d 473 (1964).
9. *Hornby.*
10. *Karrigan v. Valentine*, 184 Kansas 783 (1957).
11. *Arvey Corporation v. Peterson*, 178 F. Supp. 132 (1959).
12. *Hope v. Hearst Consolidated Publications, Inc.*, 294 F. 2d 681 (1961).
13. *Roth v. Greensboro News Company*, 6 S.E. 2d 882 (1940).
14. *Zbyszko v. New York American, Inc.*, 228 App. Div. 277 (1930).
15. *Sally v. Brown*, 295 S.W. 890 (1927).
16. *Cowper v. Vannier*, 156 N.E. 2d 761 (1959).
17. *Blende v. Hearst Publications*, 93 P. 2d 733 (1939).
18. *Nichols v. Bristow Publishing Company*, 330 P. 2d 1044 (1957).
19. *Demman v. Star Broadcasting Company*, 497 P. 2d 1378 (1972).
20. *Montandon v. Triangle Publications, Inc.*, 120 Cal. Rptr. 186 (1975).
21. *Dalton v. Meister*, 52 Wis. 2d 173 (1971).
22. *MacLeod v. Tribune Publishing Company, Inc.*, 343 P. 2d 36 (1959).
23. *United Press International, Inc. v. Mohs*, 381 S.W. 2d 104 (1964).
24. *Goldwater v. Ginzburg*, 414 F. 2d 324 (1969); cert. denied 90 S.Ct. 1085 (1970).
25. *Empire Printing Company v. Roden*, 247 F. 2d 8 (1957).
26. *Barr v. Matteo*, 79 S.Ct. 1335 (1959).
27. *Langford v. Vanderbilt University*, 318 S.W. 2d 568 (1958).
28. 47 U.S.C. Sec. 315 (a).
29. *Farmers Educational and Cooperative Union of America v. WDAY, Inc.*, 79 S.Ct. 1302 (1959).
30. *Stice v. Beacon Newspaper Corporation, Inc.*, 340 P. 2d 396 (1959).
31. *Ostwalt v. State-Record Company*, 158 S.E. 2d 204 (1967).
32. *Wood v. Constitution Publishing Company*, 194 S.E. 760 (1937).
33. *Brush-Moore Newspapers, Inc. v. Pollit*, 151 A. 2d 530 (1959).
34. *Dickens v. International Brotherhood of Teamsters*, 171 F. 2d 21 (1948).
35. *Dempsey v. Time, Inc.*, 43 Misc. 2d 754 (1964).
36. *Nichols v. Philadelphia Tribune Company, Inc.*, 22 F.R.D. 89 (1958).
37. *Farrell v. Kramer*, 193 A. 2d 560 (1963).
38. *New York Times Company v. Sullivan*, 84 S.Ct. 710 (1964).
39. *Garrison v. Louisiana*, 85 S.Ct. 209 (1964).
40. *Beckley Newspapers Corporation v. Hanks*, 88 S.Ct. 197 (1967).
41. *Curtis Publishing Company v. Butts; Associated Press v. Walker*, 87 S.Ct. 1975 (1967).
42. *Associated Press v. Walker*, 87 S.Ct. 1975 (1967).
43. *St. Amant v. Thompson*, 88 S.Ct. 1323 (1968).
44. *Time, Inc. v. Pape*, 91 S.Ct. 633 (1971).
45. *Greenbelt Publishing Association v. Bresler*, 90 S.Ct. 1537 (1970).
46. *Bose Corporation v. Consumers Union of United States*, 104 S.Ct. 1949 (1984).
47. *Rosenblatt v. Baer*, 86 S.Ct. 669 (1966).
48. *Monitor Patriot Company v. Roy*, 91 S.Ct. 621 (1971).

49. *Ocala Star-Banner Company v. Damron*, 91 S.Ct. 628 (1971).

50. *Rosenbloom v. Metromedia*, 91 S.Ct. 1811 (1971).

51. *Gertz v. Robert Welch, Inc.*, 94 S.Ct. 2997 (1974).

52. *Time, Inc. v. Firestone*, 96 S.Ct. 958 (1976).

53. *Hutchinson v. Proxmire*, 99 S.Ct. 2675 (1979).

54. *Wolston v. Reader's Digest Association, Inc.*, 99 S.Ct. 2701 (1979).

55. *Edwards v. National Audubon Society, Inc.*, 556 F. 2d 113 (1977); cert. denied 98 S.Ct. 647 (1977).

56. *St. Amant.*

57. *Dickey v. CBS Inc.*, 583 F. 2d 1221 (1978).

58. *Herbert v. Lando*, 99 S.Ct. 1635 (1979).

59. *McDonald v. Smith*, 105 S.Ct. 2787 (1985).

60. *Crane v. State*, 166 P. 1110 (1917).

61. *People v. Spielman*, 149 N.E. 466 (1925).

62. *Beauharnais v. Illinois*, 72 S.Ct. 725 (1952).

63. *Neiman-Marcus Company v. Lait*, 107 F. Supp. 96 (1952).

64. *Cosgrove Studio and Camera Shop, Inc. v. Pane*, 182 A. 2d 751 (1962).

65. *Ashton v. Kentucky*, 86 S.Ct. 1407 (1966).

RECOMMENDED READING

Annase, Ann M., and Scott A. Milburn, "Public Figures and Malice: Recent Supreme Court Decisions Restricting the Constitutional Privilege," *University of Richmond Law Review* 14 (Summer, 1980), 737-68.

Ashdown, Gerald G., "Editorial Privilege and Freedom of the Press: *Herbert v. Lando* in Perspective," *University of Colorado Law Review* 51 (Spring, 1980), 303-39.

Boisseau, Merribeth, "*Time, Inc. vs. Firestone:* The Supreme Court's Restrictive New Libel Ruling," *San Diego Law Review* 14 (March, 1977), 435-57.

Lawhorne, Clifton O., *The Supreme Court and Libel.* Carbondale: Southern Illinois University Press, 1981.

Lindberg, Marian E., "Source Protection in Libel Suits After *Herbert v. Lando*," *Columbia Law Review* 81 (March, 1981), 338-65.

Minnick, Wayne C., "The United States Supreme Court on Libel," *Quarterly Journal of Speech* 68 (November, 1982), 384-96.

Naughton, James P., "*Gertz* and the Public Figure Doctrine Revisited," *Tulane Law Review* 54 (June, 1980), 1053-93.

Palmer, Barry J., "Editorial Privilege: *Herbert v. Lando*," *Boston College Law Review* 21 (July, 1980), 1223-48.

Sanford, Bruce W., *Synopsis of the Law of Libel and the Right of Privacy.* New York: Scripps-Howard, 1981.

KEY DECISIONS

1952—*BEAUHARNAIS*—recognized the concept of group libel.

1959—*FARMERS EDUCATIONAL AND COOPERATIVE UNION OF AMERICA*—
determined that broadcast stations are not liable for libelous statements made over
their facilities by political candidates.

1964—*NEW YORK TIMES COMPANY*—established "actual malice" doctrine.

1967—*BUTTS*—noted that when a story does not involve "hot news," reporter has adequate time for thorough investigation of the charges.

1968—*ST. AMANT*—distinguished between "negligence" and "reckless disregard."

1970—*GREENBELT*—stressed the value of "robust debate" about subjects of substantial concern.

1974—*GERTZ*—ruled that private citizens have greater protection against libelous statements than do public figures.

1979—*WOLSTON*—summarized the Court's meaning of the terms "public figure" and
"private individual."

1979—*HERBERT*—determined that a plaintiff in a libel action may inquire into the state
of mind of those responsible for publications.

SUMMARY—LIBEL LAW

Definition

Libel law seeks to compensate an individual or corporation whose reputation has been wrongfully damaged. Libel consists of defamatory words that
are either written or broadcast. Two types have been recognized by the
courts—libel *per se* and libel *per quod*. Libel *per se* involves a statement
that is defamatory on its face. Libel *per quod* involves a statement that is
not defamatory, by itself, but becomes so when certain facts are associated
with the statement. In other words, libel *per quod* is not immediately apparent.

Proof

In order to win a libel case, the plaintiff must prove all of the elements of
libel:

1 . Publication
2 . Identification
3 . Defamation
4 . Fault
    a . Malice—public person
    b . Negligence—private person

Damages

If the plaintiff proves the four elements, monetary damages may be awarded. Depending on the nature of the case, four types of damages may be awarded:
1 . General—compensating for injury to plaintiff's reputation;
2 . Actual—reimbursing the real monetary loss suffered by the plaintiff;
3 . Punitive—punishing past libelous behavior and discouraging similar conduct in the future;
4 . Nominal—token damages when there has been a libelous statement, but no serious harm to plaintiff's reputation or financial position.

Defenses

A defendant may successfully contest a libel charge by employing any of the complete and/or partial defenses:
1 . Complete defenses
    a . Truth
    b . Absolute privilege
    c . Qualified privilege
    d . Fair comment
2 . Partial defenses
    a . Reliable source
    b . Retraction and apology
    c . Right of reply
    d . Settlement out of court
    e . Bad reputation of plaintiff
    f . Provocation

8

PRIVACY

The framers of the U.S. Constitution did not provide for a "right to privacy." After all, in the 1700s, most U.S. citizens lived in their own homes, in relatively small communities, and did not feel a pressing need for securing their privacy. The legal basis for a right to privacy in the United States was initially outlined in the late nineteenth century by two law partners, Samuel Warren and Louis Brandeis. Irritated by the press coverage of parties given by his wife, Warren gathered information from numerous court decisions that dealt with defamation and trespass and, with Brandeis, published the information.[1] Since that time, the right to privacy has become generally protected and is recognized by legislatures and courts in several states.

According to the late Professor William Prosser, privacy torts include intrusion of physical solitude, public disclosure of private facts, placing an individual in a false light in the public eye, and appropriation of some element of an individual's personality for commercial use.[2]

INTRUSION

Intrusion is the act of thrusting oneself upon the peace and into the private life of another. It can occur through numerous techniques, which include harassment, hidden electronic devices, and physical entry.

Harassment

Several courts have determined that individuals suffer harassment because of intrusion into their private lives. The cases involved a variety of aspects of personal life, but especially sexual mores.

During November 1961, Estelle Griswold, executive director of the Planned Parenthood League of Connecticut, along with a physician, gave advice and supplies to married couples regarding methods of birth control. Griswold was arrested for violating a Connecticut law that prohibited any person from counseling others concerning the use of contraceptives. When she was found guilty and fined $100, Griswold appealed. The Supreme Court held that the First Amendment protects not only the right to speak and print but also the right to distribute, to receive, to read, to teach, and to associate, as well as the freedom of thought and inquiry. The Court also noted that "the First Amendment has a penumbra where privacy is protected from governmental intrusion." The Connecticut law, by restricting the use of contraceptives, intruded upon an individual's privacy surrounding the marriage relationship.[3] In *Griswold* the Court determined that married persons were entitled to access to contraceptives.

In 1972, in *Eisenstadt,* the Court approved of access to contraceptives for unmarried persons. The case involved William Baird, who was convicted under a Massachusetts law for displaying contraceptive materials during a lecture

"INTRUSION IS SUCH A **HARSH** WORD!"

to students at Boston University, as well as for giving a package of vaginal foam to a young woman at the end of his presentation. When the case reached the Supreme Court, the justices cited *Griswold* and noted that "whatever the rights of the individual to access to contraceptives may be, the rights must be the same to the unmarried and married alike." The Court stressed that a married couple is not an independent entity with one mind and heart, but an association of two persons, each with an individual intellectual and emotional makeup. Accordingly, "if the right of privacy means anything, it is the right of the individual, married or single, to be free from unwarranted governmental intrusion into matters so fundamentally affecting a person as the decision whether to bear or beget a child."[4] The Court, per Justice William Brennan, declared the Massachusetts law to be unconstitutional.

Throughout the 1970s a heated debate took place between religious groups dedicated to protecting human life and environmental organizations determined to control population growth. Several cases evolved in which the Supreme Court had to determine the constitutionality of state abortion statutes. In *Wade* an unmarried, pregnant woman challenged a Texas law that prohibited anyone from destroying a fetus except on "medical advice for the purpose of saving the life of the mother." The woman claimed that the law intruded upon her privacy by denying her the right to choose to terminate her pregnancy. Texas countered with the claim that the power to protect prenatal life constituted a compelling state interest. When the case reached the Supreme Court, the justices, though not agreeing fully with either viewpoint, concluded that "the right of personal privacy includes the abortion decision, but that this right is not unqualified and must be considered against important state interests in regulation." The Court acknowledged that, at some point, "the woman's privacy is no longer sole and any right of privacy she possesses must be measured accordingly." The "compelling" point was at approximately the end of the first trimester. From this point, a state could regulate abortion.[5] In *Wade* the Court declared the Texas law too broad, because it failed to distinguish between abortions performed early and those performed later in pregnancy, and because the law allowed abortion only in cases involving risk to the mother's life.

In *Bolton* an indigent, pregnant woman initiated court action that challenged the validity of Georgia's abortion statute. The law allowed abortion only in cases of danger to the woman's life, likelihood of a serious birth defect, or pregnancy that resulted from rape. *Bolton* reached the Supreme Court. Justice Harry Blackmun, writing for the Court, first of all reaffirmed the position taken in *Wade*, noting that a pregnant woman did not possess an absolute constitutional right to an abortion on demand. The Court overturned the Georgia law, however, because of several faulty provisions—those requiring that abortions be conducted in hospitals, that abortions be approved by a hospital committee, that two other physicians confirm the finding of the pregnant women's doctor, and that abortions be available only to Georgia residents.[6]

In the 1973 cases of *Wade* and *Bolton* the Court rejected the notion that a woman's right to abortion is absolute. According to the Court, the right "must be considered against important state interests in regulation." In 1976, in *Planned Parenthood,* the Court considered this issue as it applied to several provisions of the Missouri abortion law. A deeply divided Court upheld certain of the provisions, but overturned others. For example, the Court upheld requirements that a woman must provide informed, freely given, written consent, prior to an abortion during the first trimester of pregnancy. In addition, records must be kept by physicians and health facilities that perform abortions. On the other hand, the Court declared some provisions unconstitutional. A state cannot require written consent of the spouse of a woman seeking an abortion, nor can it require consent of the parent of an unmarried woman under 18. In these situations, the abortion decision must be left to the medical judgment of the attending physician.[7] In *Planned Parenthood* the Court specified some areas where state regulation was allowed and others where it was considered an intrusion into a woman's constitutionally protected privacy.

In another 1976 case, *Commonwealth's Attorney for City of Richmond,* the Court upheld the Virginia sodomy law. Two adult males challenged the constitutionality of the statute, as it applied to consensual homosexual relations that were conducted in private. The district court cited *Griswold* in noting that while the intimacy of husband and wife is a protected feature of the institution of marriage, it is a different matter to punish persons who establish intimacies the law forbids. Behavior such as adultery, homosexuality, fornication, and incest are not immune from criminal inquiry, even if privately practiced. The Supreme Court unanimously affirmed the district court's opinion.[8]

Cases involving harassment have dealt with personal aspects other than sexual mores. For instance, *Galella* concerned the harassment that stems from an individual's being unwillingly photographed. The case involved freelance photographer Ronald Galella, who made a living photographing celebrities. His favorite subject was Jacqueline Onassis. Galella initiated a $1.3 million damage suit on the ground that he had been roughed up by secret service and police officers whom Onassis had asked to intervene on her behalf. Galella also asked for an injunction against interference with his making a living. He claimed a right to photograph Onassis, a "camera-shy" and "uncooperative" public person. Mrs. Onassis then filed a counterclaim for $1.5 million, seeking injunctive relief against Galella's interference with secret service agents assigned to protect the former first lady and her children. According to Onassis, Galella continually stalked her, popped up everywhere, and emitted "grunting" sounds that terrified her. The court held that Galella's snooping was not protected by the First Amendment and that it violated Mrs. Onassis's right of privacy. Galella had no right under the First Amendment to trespass inside private buildings or to constantly monitor Mrs. Onassis's whereabouts.

Of course legitimate countervailing social needs may warrant some intrusion despite an individual's reasonable expectation of privacy and freedom from harassment. However, the interference allowed may be no greater than that necessary to protect the overriding public interest. Mrs. Onassis was properly found to be a public figure and thus subject to news coverage. Nonetheless, Galella's action went far beyond the reasonable bounds of news gathering.[9]

The court enjoined Galella from approaching within 300 feet of the Onassis and Kennedy homes, as well as the school attended by the children. He was required to remain 30 feet from the children and 25 feet from Mrs. Onassis at all other places. In addition, Galella was instructed not to put the family under surveillance or to attempt to communicate with them. In *Galella* the court upheld the right of freedom from harassment associated with being unwillingly photographed.

The *Johnson* case involved alleged harassment concerning an individual's personal appearance. Police officers in Suffolk County, New York, were obligated to comply with grooming regulations, which limited the length and appearance of hair, length and shape of sideburns, size and configuration of mustaches, and which prohibited beards, wigs, and hairpieces. A police officer, Edward Johnson, initiated suit against the commissioner of the police department. The suit argued that the grooming standards violated freedom of expression. The Supreme Court opinion, written by Justice William Rehnquist, noted that a state has wide latitude in imposing regulations on its employees. Law-enforcement authorities prefer similarity in the appearance of police officers. This practice makes police personnel recognizable to the public and also tends to instill an "esprit de corps" within the police force. Rehnquist concluded that hair-grooming regulations did not deprive police officers of their constitutional rights.[10] *Johnson,* as well as other cases cited in this section, indicates that freedom from harassment is not absolute. Under certain conditions, the government can intrude into an individual's personal life-style.

Hidden Electronic Devices

The *Dietemann* case involved alleged invasion of privacy through the use of a hidden camera and electronic recording equipment. A. A. Dietemann, a minimally educated, disabled veteran, practiced healing with clay, minerals, and herbs. In 1963 *Life* magazine employees Jackie Metcalf and William Ray, in collaboration with the district attorney's office, visited Dietemann in order to obtain facts and pictures concerning his activities. Dietemann, while examining Metcalf, was photographed with a hidden camera. One picture showed Dietemann with his hand on Metcalf's breast while he was holding what appeared to be a wand in his hand. Metcalf had told Dietemann that she had a lump in her breast. Dietemann concluded that she had eaten some rancid butter 11 years previously. The conversation was carried by a radio transmitter hidden in Metcalf's purse to a tape recorder in an automobile occupied by a *Life* employee and a member of the district attorney's office. Dietemann was arrested on a charge of practicing medicine without a license; he later pled no contest. Shortly thereafter, *Life* carried a story that depicted Dietemann as a quack. Pictures and information obtained by Metcalf and Ray were used to prepare the article. Dietemann initiated an invasion-of-privacy suit. He claimed that he conducted his practice in his home, which was not open to the public. *Life's* employees had gained entrance by a subterfuge. The court concluded that Metcalf and Ray had invaded Dietemann's privacy; the judge awarded $1,000 general damages for injury to Dietemann's feelings and peace of mind. Before the court of appeals, *Life* claimed that the First Amendment immunized it from liability for invading Dietemann's home with hidden devices, because its employees were gathering news. *Life* argued that such equipment constituted indispensable tools of investigative reporting. The court disagreed—the First Amendment was not a license to trespass by electronic means into another's home or office, even if the person were suspected of committing a crime.[11]

A few years later the courts heard a related case. During November 1975, Arlyn Cassidy and several other Chicago police officers acted as undercover agents in the investigation of a massage parlor for alleged solicitation and obscenities. As part of the investigation, Cassidy paid a $30 admission fee to see ''de-luxe'' lingerie modeling. He was taken to a small room by a model who changed her lingerie several times. Cassidy arrested the model for solicitation, after she established ''sufficient'' physical contact with him. At that point the door to an adjacent room opened, revealing that a camera crew had filmed the entire scene. A newsman for a local television station claimed that the news crew had reported to the massage parlor in response to a call from the manager, who had complained that his establishment was the subject of police harassment. The film crew installed a two-way mirror, which provided visual access to the activities involving Cassidy and the model. Cassidy initiated court action, alleging an invasion of privacy. The court noted that Cassidy was not a private citizen engaged in conduct that pertained only to himself. He was a public official performing a public duty.

> In our opinion, under these circumstances no right of privacy against intrusion can be said to exist with reference to the gathering and dissemination of news concerning discharge of public duties.[12]

In *Cassidy* the *Dietemann* principle was not applicable, because Dietemann was a private individual, while Cassidy was a public official.

Physical Entry

The *Pearson* and *Kunkin* cases involve accusations that a newspaper reporter and/or publisher received stolen property, which was eventually used in a published article. In both cases the courts sided with the press.

On several occasions, employees of Senator Thomas Dodd entered his office without permission and took documents from his files, made duplicates,
replaced the originals, and turned the copies over to newspapermen Drew Pearson
and Jack Anderson. The reporters knew how the copies had been obtained. Pearson and Anderson used this information in publishing articles about Dodd's alleged relationship with lobbyists for foreign interests. Dodd sued, claiming invasion of privacy. The court, however, ruled that a news medium that published
information received through physical intrusion cannot be held responsible for
the behavior of the intruders. The court stressed that injuries from intrusion and
injuries from publication should be considerd separately. According to the court,
Pearson and Anderson had not committed an act of physical intrusion. Furthermore, they had published information that was of a general public interest. The
article contained Dodd's qualifications as a U.S. senator and this type of published material was not subject to suit for invasion of privacy.[13]

In a related case Arthur Kunkin, editor of the *Los Angeles Free Press,* was
indicted for receiving a copy of a document that had been stolen from the office of the attorney general by a clerk in the office. The document was the personnel roster of the Bureau of Narcotic Enforcement. It listed the names, addresses, and telephone numbers of undercover narcotics agents throughout the
state. It was not marked "secret" or "confidential." The *Free Press* published
the roster verbatim under the headlines "Narcotics Agents Listed," "There
should be no secret police," and "Know your local Narc." When Kunkin was
convicted of receiving stolen property, he appealed. The California Supreme
Court noted that the conviction could not stand unless substantial evidence demonstrated that (1) the property was received by the accused, (2) the property had
been obtained by theft or extortion, and (3) the accused knew that the property
had been stolen. The court decided that the first two requirements were satisfied, then considered whether there was substantial evidence from which the jury
could reasonably draw an inference that Kunkin knew the roster was stolen. The
court considered five circumstances which, the attorney general argued, established Kunkin's knowledge that the roster was stolen. In each circumstance, the
court concluded that the evidence was insufficient to sustain a conviction. First,
the sensitive nature of the information, although cause for outrage at Kunkin's
gross irresponsibility in publishing it, gave no basis for presuming that he knew
the roster was stolen. Second, the list of inferences that might reasonably be
drawn about a person who hands over a list of names of undercover narcotics
agents and wishes to remain anonymous does not include the inference of theft.
Third, recognition that publication might cause trouble does not warrant an inference of theft. Fourth, Kunkin's willingness to pay for the information was
without significance, because he was willing to pay similar amounts for other
information. Fifth, knowledge of the theft could not be discerned by Kunkin's
refusal to surrender the roster after its publication. The court concluded that there
was no substantial evidence to indicate that Kunkin knew the roster was stolen.[14] The conviction was reversed.

The courts sided with the press in *Pearson* and *Kunkin*. In so doing, the courts made it difficult to obtain the conviction of a reporter who publishes information obtained through physical intrusion.

Summary

Since 1965 the courts have decided several cases involving governmental intrusion into sexual privacy. In *Griswold* the Supreme Court overturned a law that prohibited the advising of persons concerning the use of contraceptives; such a law intruded upon the privacy of the marriage relationship. *Eisenstadt* extended the same freedom to unmarried persons. In the *Wade* and *Bolton* abortion cases the Court noted that a pregnant woman did not possess an absolute constitutional right to an abortion on demand; the right had to be balanced against state interests. Then, in *Planned Parenthood*, the Court examined the specific nature of some of those state interests. The Court also heard a challenge to the Virginia sodomy law. In *Commonwealth's Attorney for City of Richmond* the Court upheld the law in the face of a challenge concerning homosexual acts performed in private.

The courts have also decided cases that arose when a newsperson thrust him- or herself into the private life of an individual. In *Pearson* and *Kunkin*, when a newspaper reporter received stolen property that was subsequently used in a published article, the courts sided with the press. Nonetheless, the *Dietemann* case acknowledged that the First Amendment is not a license to intrude by hidden electronic means into an individual's privacy. *Galella* emphasized that intrusion in the form of photographic harassment is not protected by the First Amendment.

PUBLIC DISCLOSURE

Invasion of privacy can also involve the publication of truthful, private information about a person. Such situations may involve information concerning tragedy, embarrassment, and intimacy.

Tragedy

In *Kelley* and *Costlow* the courts rejected invasion-of-privacy suits that involved publication of photographs of children who died as a result of accidents. The courts protected the newspeople, because the photographs illustrated accurate news stories about events of legitimate public interest.

The day after the 15-year-old daughter of Mr. and Mrs. James Kelley was killed in an automobile accident, a wide-circulation Boston newspaper printed an article about the accident. The story included a picture of the disfigured, dead body of the girl, referring to her as the daughter of the Kelleys. The parents sued, claiming an invasion of privacy that caused them to suffer bodily pain and mental anguish. The court noted that the parents at this time were obviously distressed and preferred to be spared the anguish of sensational publicity. If the Kelleys' claim were sustained, however, it would be difficult to fix its boundaries.

> A newspaper account or a radio broadcast setting forth in detail the harrowing cirumstances of the accident might well be as distressing to the members of the victim's family as a photograph of the sort described in the declaration. A newspaper could not safely publish the picture of a train wreck or of an airplane crash if any of the bodies of the victims were recognizable.[15]

In this instance, the only reference to the Kelleys was that the girl whose body appeared in the photograph was their daughter. The court concluded that the publication of the photograph, while probably indelicate or lacking in good taste, did not constitute an actionable invasion of the Kelleys' privacy.

Costlow is a similar case. In 1964 three-year-old Robert Costlow and his two-year-old sister Marion died by suffocation when they trapped themselves inside a refrigerator. Photographer Frederick Cusimano took pictures of the dead children and later published an article, which he illustrated with the photographs. Mr. and Mrs. Robert Costlow initiated action, alleging an invasion of privacy. They claimed that Cusimano acted maliciously, with knowledge of the grief of the parents. The Costlows argued that they suffered severe mental anguish and emotional disturbance due to the publication of the photos. The court denied the invasion-of-privacy claim. The article about the two children who suffocated by trapping themselves in a refrigerator, while necessarily unpleasant to the parents, was a matter of legitimate public interest. Furthermore, the cause of these deaths would be brought to the attention of the public, so that similar deaths might be prevented. The court found no actual malice; there was no evidence that the story falsely represented the actual occurrence. The court acknowledged that Cusimano probably exhibited his article with disregard for the emotional distress caused by the pictures, but his main purpose was to make a profit and to enhance his professional reputation.[16] The complaint was dismissed.

Embarrassment

On several occasions the courts have heard cases in which it was alleged that the publication of private information caused considerable embarrassment. *Graham, Jacova, Williams,* and *Virgil* provide examples.

Flora Graham, a middle-aged Alabama housewife, took her two sons to the county fair. Mrs. Graham accompanied the boys through the fun house, where her dress was blown up by ground-level air jets and her body was exposed from the waist down, with the exception of that portion covered by her "panties." At that moment, the photographer for the *Daily Times Democrat* snapped a picture of the situation. Four days later the picture was published on the front page of the newspaper. Mrs. Graham sued, contending that this invasion of privacy was embarrassing. The court awarded Mrs. Graham damages of $4,166. The newspaper appealed. The Supreme Court of Alabama noted that an actionable invasion of one's privacy occurred upon "the wrongful intrusion into one's private activities, in such a manner as to outrage or cause mental suffering, shame or humiliation to a person of ordinary sensibilities." An exception occurred in cases that involved the interest of the public to be informed. In *Graham* the court saw nothing of legitimate news value in the photograph. The court stressed that "not only was this photograph embarrassing to one of normal sensibilities" but it also was "offensive to modesty or decency" and expressed "something which delicacy, purity, or decency forbid to be expressed." The court also argued:

> One who is a part of a public scene may be lawfully photographed as an incidental part of that scene in his ordinary status. Where the status he expects to occupy is changed without his volition to a status embarrassing to an ordinary person of reasonable sensitivity, then he should not be deemed to have forfeited his right to be protected from an indecent and vulgar intrusion of his right of privacy merely because misfortune overtakes him in a public place.[17]

The finding of the lower court was affirmed.

The Supreme Court of Florida heard *Jacova,* a case of alleged embarrassing invasion of privacy. In a news telecast, a television station showed police raids on a restaurant and a hotel. John Jacova initiated an invasion-of-privacy suit, claiming that his picture had been shown during the news film. Jacova said he was an innocent bystander. He was in the hotel during the time of the raid, because he had stopped for a newspaper. The film showed Jacova standing against the wall with two men, presumably police officers, talking to him. While Jacova's picture was being shown an announcer said:

> [John] Tronolone's [operator of the restaurant who was arrested by police] cousin Carmen was arrested at his apartment by other officers. Then raiders visited the cigar shop of the Casablanca Hotel looking for a man reputedly accepting bets there.

Jacova claimed that his right to privacy had been invaded. The station argued that since the telecast did not falsely depict Jacova as "being arrested as a gambler," it was privileged to publish his photograph, because he became involved in a newsworthy event. The court agreed—a communication medium had a qualified privilege to use in its telecast the name or photograph of a person who had become an "actor" in a newsworthy event. In addition, the court noted:

> But certainly those of his friends and acquaintances who saw his picture on the screen would know that there was nothing sinister about his presence there. Further, the background of his picture clearly showed him to be at a newsstand and

not at some residential apartment, and that he occupied the role that, in fact, was his. If not, a simple explanation by him would make this clear. We see nothing humiliating or embarrassing in such a role—shopping at a newsstand—nor anything that would offend a person of "ordinary sensibilities."[18]

In *Jacova* the court acknowledged that since news reporters were expected to determine the facts of a controversial situation in a matter of minutes, it was only reasonable to expect that occasional errors would occur. Nevertheless, the court concluded that no unreasonable restraints should be placed upon the news reporter.

In *Williams* the Kansas City Court of Appeals heard a similar case. A Kansas City high-school student, Charles Williams, and five other youths were detained by police officers and searched with their hands against a police vehicle. News personnel for a local television station filmed the events. Williams was then booked at the police station and placed in a "line-up." He was released several hours later, when police realized that he had not committed any crime. The film was shown on the evening newscast along with the following commentary:

> Kansas City police surrounded the Jackson County Court House today, and took six young men into custody following a search of the building.
>   Three of them have since been released, but two adults and one juvenile remain in custody, and will be charged tomorrow in connection with last week's holdup of a finance company office at 219 East 12th. All six walked past that office today and three were recognized by the manager as the holdup men. He followed them to the Court House, and then alerted police. Why the six went to the Court House isn't known.

Williams sued, charging that the film showed him in a humiliating position and that even though the event was a matter of legitimate public interest, his right of privacy had been invaded. The court noted that the newsperson's right to publicize matters of general public interest applied "even though the individual publicized may have been drawn out of his seclusion and become involved in a noteworthy event involuntarily and against his will and over his protest." Matters concerning crime, police action, and apprehension of suspected criminals constitute proper public concern. Unlike *Graham,* where there was no publication of a matter of legitimate public interest, in this case Williams was involved in a newsworthy event about which the public had a right to be informed. The court found this to be true, even though Williams's involvement was purely involuntary and against his will. The court concluded that Williams, for reasons like those stated in *Jacova,* had no cause for action against the television station.[19]

In *Virgil* the courts heard another case involving alleged embarrassing invasion of privacy. The February 22, 1971, issue of *Sports Illustrated* described certain behavior of Mike Virgil—putting out cigarettes in his mouth, diving off stairs to impress women, hurting himself in order to collect unemployment insurance benefits so as to have time for body surfing during the summer, fighting in gang fights as a youngster, and eating insects. Virgil claimed an invasion of privacy that caused him embarrassment. The California District Court applied the following standard of newsworthiness:

> In determining what is a matter of legitimate public interest, account must be taken of the customs and conventions of the community; and in the last analysis what is proper becomes a matter of the community mores. The line is to be drawn when the publicity ceases to be the giving of information to which the public is entitled, and becomes a morbid and sensational prying into private lives for its own sake, with which a reasonable member of the public, with decent standards, would say that he had no concern.

The court ruled that the article was "not sufficiently offensive to reach the very high level of offensiveness necessary . . . to lose newsworthiness protection." The facts were generally unflattering and perhaps embarrassing, but they were not offensive to the degree of morbidity or sensationalism.

> In fact they connote nearly as strong a positive image as they do a negative one. On the one hand, Mr. Virgil can be seen as a juvenile exhibitionist, but on the other hand he also comes across as the tough, aggressive maverick, an archetypal character occupying a respected place in the American consciousness. Given this ambiguity as to whether or not the facts disclosed are offensive at all, no reasonable juror could conclude that they were highly offensive.[20]

The court emphasized that any reasonable person reading the article would conclude that the personal facts were included as a journalistic technique to explain Virgil's daring style of body surfing. There was "no possibility that a juror could conclude that the personal facts were included for any inherent morbid, sensational, or curiosity appeal they might have." The court concluded that public disclosure of these private facts was privileged as newsworthy under the First Amendment.

Intimacy

In the 1975 *Cohn* case, the U.S. Supreme Court heard arguments concerning the publication of private information of an intimate nature. The case involved the rape and murder of Martin Cohn's 17-year-old daughter. While covering the criminal proceedings against six youths who were indicted for the crime, a news reporter learned the victim's name by examining the indictments—public records available for inspection. He broadcast her name as part of a news report. In alleging that his privacy had been invaded, Cohn cited a Georgia law that makes it a misdemeanor to publicize the name of a rape victim. The Supreme Court, in the opinion of Justice Byron White, decided that a state could not impose sanctions on the publication of the name of a rape victim obtained from public judicial records that were open to public inspection. The news media had great responsibility to report fully and accurately the proceedings of government. Concerning judicial matters in particular, "the function of the press serves to guarantee the fairness of trials and to bring to bear the beneficial effects of public scrutiny upon the administration of justice." The Court refused to uphold a system that made public records available to the media, but at the same time forbade their publication when offensive to the sensibilities of reasonable persons. Such a policy made it very difficult for the press to inform their readers about public events. The rule invited self-censorship and would lead to the suppression of matters that should be made available to the public. According to the Court, "the prevailing law of invasion of privacy generally recognizes that the interests in privacy fade when the information involved already appears on the public record."[21]

In 1979 the *Cohn* decision was applied in *Howard,* a case involving Robbin Howard who, while a minor confined in the Jasper County Home, was sterilized against her wishes. After her release from the home, she led a quiet life and made friends who were not aware of her surgery. Sometime later Dr. Roy Sloan, the home's psychiatrist, told news reporter Margaret Engel about the sterilization. Engel eventually published this information in an article about the Jasper County Home, which appeared in the *Des Moines Sunday Register.* Howard initiated court action, charging that this article subjected her to public contempt, ridicule, humiliation, mental pain, and anguish. The court decided in favor of the newspaper on two grounds. First, the documents in question were public; the information they contained was in the public domain. As determined in *Cohn,* there is no liability when a newspaper merely gives further publicity to information that is already public. Second, the information was newsworthy. It was vital to a thorough evaluation of the administration at Jasper Home.

> In the sense of serving an appropriate news function, the disclosure contributed constructively to the impact of the article. It offered a personalized frame of reference to which the reader could relate, fostering perception and understanding. Moreover, it lent specificity and credibility to the report.
>
> In this way the disclosure served as an effective means of accomplishing the intended news function. It had positive communicative value in attracting the reader's attention to the article's subject matter and in supporting expression of the underlying theme.
>
> Examined in the light of the first amendment, we do not believe the disclosure could reasonably be held to be devoid of news value.[22]

In 1980 the Supreme Court denied certiorari in the *Howard* case.

Summary

The *Graham* case confirms that public disclosure of private information can constitute an actionable invasion of privacy. Other cases, however, indicate that the courts protect freedom of the press in invasion-of-privacy suits, when the matter is newsworthy and of public interest. In *Kelley* and *Costlow* the courts decided that publication of photographs to illustrate an article that accurately described events surrounding an accidental death constituted a matter of legitimate public interest. In *Jacova* and *Williams* the court determined that disclosure of information concerning crime and apprehension of suspected criminals comprised a matter of public concern. In *Virgil* the court ruled that even though the published information was unflattering and embarrassing, since it was not offensive to the degree of morbidity or sensationalism, the "newsworthiness" protection of the press was not lost. In *Cohn* the U.S. Supreme Court decided that a state cannot ban the disclosure of public records regarding the rape and murder of a young girl. Such a policy contradicts the freedom of the press provided by the First Amendment. In *Howard* the Court reaffirmed a newspaper's right to publish intimate information that was already public.

FALSE LIGHT

Invasion of privacy also involves the publication of false information about a person, whether the material is defamatory or not. There are two important components to false-light cases—fictionalization and actual malice.

Fictionalization

Fictionalization usually involves a writer who exaggerates while dramatizing a true happening. The courts have decided several cases of this type. *Strickler, Aquino,* and *Carlisle* illustrate this form of invasion of privacy.

A 1958 case involved Kenneth Strickler, a commander on active duty with the U.S. Navy, who was a passenger on a commercial airliner that developed engine trouble and was forced to make an emergency landing. Strickler and other passengers were rescued by a Coast Guard cutter. NBC telecast a show depicting in dramatized form Strickler's experiences. He claimed that the telecast, made without his consent, violated his right to privacy. He alleged that the program portrayed him in the highly personal act of praying during the emergency landing, that it showed him out of uniform and wearing a Hawaiian shirt, that the telecast depicted him as smoking cigarettes, and that the program did not reflect the valuable assistance he provided in the evacuation of the plane. Strickler claimed that he was placed in a false light by the telecasts and that as a result he experienced humiliation, embarrassment, and great mental pain and suffering. In *Strickler* the court ruled that the network had embellished the incident in such a way as to constitute sufficient fictionalization to warrant an invasion of privacy.[23]

Aquino is another case involving fictionalization. The case began when the daughter of Michael and Nancy Aquino secretly married a young man before a justice of the peace. The man promised the daughter that at a later date he would provide a home for her and marry her in a church. Later the man said that he did not intend to keep his promises and that he had married the daughter only to spite her parents, who had been opposed to his courting her. The news media published several stories regarding both the marriage and subsequent divorce. The Aquinos initiated an invasion-of-privacy suit. When a jury awarded them $10,000, the decision was appealed. The judges noted that the marriage and the divorce were newsworthy events; newspapers had a right to publish such information. The article in question, however, was in the form of a story not a news article. It was in a Sunday supplement and not in the news section. It was bedecked with an "illustrated" drawing covering over half of the page. The illustrated figures bore no resemblance to the daughter and young man. According to the court, the author had allowed his imagination to roam through the facts so that "newsworthy events were presented in a style used almost exclusively by writers of fiction."[24] Although the basic facts of the story were true, the author had fictionalized them. The court upheld the jury verdict.

The *Carlisle* case acknowledged that minor fictionalization did not constitute an invasion of privacy. An article in the December 1960 issue of *Motion Picture* was entitled "Janet Leigh's Own Story—'I was a Child Bride at 14!' " The article described a hasty marriage and eventual annulment. John Carlisle, the male party to the marriage, initiated action for invasion of privacy. The California District Court of Appeal noted that public figures, including actresses, have to some extent lost their right of privacy. Furthermore, people closely associated with such public figures "also to some extent lose their right to privacy that one unconnected with the famous or notorious would have." Carlisle claimed that the article contained errors, the two principal ones being that the date of the marriage was put back approximately a year to the attack at Pearl Harbor, and the age of the actress at the time of the marriage was reduced a year. These elements were altered, apparently for dramatic effect. According to the court, however, the mere fact that there were errors in the account did not constitute an invasion of privacy. Carlisle also contended that the article was fictionalized; it was not restricted to a "cold recital of the skeletal fact of the marriage and the annulment but fills in the gaps with the supposed conversations and thoughts of the participants." The court disagreed: The article contained no "so-called revelations of any intimate details that would tend to outrage public [decency]."[25] The circumstances in *Carlisle* differed considerably from those in *Strickler* and *Aquino*. In *Carlisle* the fictionalization was minor and did not constitute an invasion of privacy.

Actual Malice

In 1967 the Supreme Court handed down the *Hill* decision. In this case the Court ruled that the First Amendment shields the press from invasion-of-privacy suits involving matters of public interest, unless there is proof of "actual malice." This principle has been applied in subsequent cases.

The James Hill family became a front-page news story after being held hostage by three escaped convicts in their suburban home in Whitemarch, Pennsylvania, during September 1952. The family was eventually released unharmed. In an interview with newsmen, Hill indicated that the convicts had treated the family courteously. Hill sought to keep his family out of the public eye by declining interviews with magazine writers and appearances on television. In an attempt to preserve their privacy, the family moved to Connecticut. In 1953 Joseph Hayes published *The Desperate Hours,* a novel depicting the experience of a family of four, held hostage by three escaped convicts in the family's suburban home. Contrary to Hill's experience, however, in Hayes's story the father and son are beaten and the daughter is subjected to verbal sexual assault. The book was made into a play, which was also entitled *The Desperate Hours.* In February 1955 an article appeared in *Life* magazine, which claimed that the Hill family had experienced a "desperate ordeal" by being held prisoners by three escaped convicts. The article noted that people throughout the country

> read about it in Joseph Hayes' novel, *The Desperate Hours,* inspired by the family's experience. Now they can see the story re-enacted in Hayes' Broadway play, based on the book, and the next year will see it in his movie, which has been filmed but is being held up until the play has had a chance to pay off.

The article described the play as "a heart-stopping account of how a family rose to heroism in a crisis." *Life* claimed to transport "some of the actors to the actual house where the Hills were besieged." Pictures on the following two pages included an enactment of the son being "roughed up" by one of the convicts, a picture of the "daring daughter" biting the hand of a convict to make him drop a gun, and a picture of the father throwing his gun through the door after a "brave try" to save his family is foiled. Hill sued on the ground that the article knowingly and falsely gave the impression that the play portrayed the Hill family experience. The courts determined that even though the play was fictionalized, *Life's* article portrayed it as a reenactment of the Hills' experience in order to sell magazines. The jury awarded Hill $30,000 general damages. Before the U.S. Supreme Court, attorneys for *Life* argued that the article concerned a topic of legitimate news interest and that it was "published in good faith without any malice whatsoever." The justices sided with the press. The subject of the article—the opening of the new play—was a matter of public interest. The Court felt that sanctions against either innocent or negligent misstatements would instill in the press a fear of large verdicts in damage suits, which would inevitably cause publishers to "steer wider of the unlawful zone" and thus "create the danger that the legitimate utterance will be penalized." The Court concluded that the First Amendment shields the press from invasion-of-privacy suits involving matters of public interest, unless there is proof of actual malice, that is, proof that the material was published with deliberate falsehood or reckless disregard of the truth.[26] In *Hill* such proof was absent. In subsequent cases—*Varnish* and *Cantrell*—such proof was evident.

In 1963 Melvin Varnish's wife killed their three young children and committed suicide. A few months later an article entitled "'Happiest Mother' Kills Her Three Children and Herself" appeared in *The National Enquirer*. Varnish initiated an invasion-of-privacy suit, claiming that the portrayal of his wife and his relationship with her was fictionalized and placed him in a false and unfavorable light. He claimed that the "happy wife and mother" theme used throughout the article was fictitious and was intended, through the use or irony, to indicate Varnish's insensitivity and lack of caring for his wife. Varnish also claimed that, as a result of the article, he attempted suicide, required psychiatric attention, was unemployed, was shunned in his community, and became the victim of severe mental suffering. The case was tried before a jury, which awarded $5,000 general and $15,000 punitive damages. The case was appealed. The judges found actual malice—the article was false and it was published with knowledge that it was false or with reckless disregard for the truth. The record showed that Mrs. Varnish was a despondent, depressed, and extremely unhappy woman. A suicide note addressed to her mother expressed her extreme unhappiness.

> Just a note and explanation to let you know that I am going to put the three children and myself to sleep forever. I can't go on any longer. I see no future for the children or myself. Mitch [plaintiff] is impossible and this is the only way to get away from him. Tell Uncle Chris and Uncle Butch I'm sorry about the money they each loaned me in 1961 . . . . I owe so much I'll never have to bother anyone anymore.

The court noted that the article "presented a substantially false and distorted picture." It found sufficient evidence of recklessness, because of the author's testimony that he had no basis except his own "presumption" for labeling Mrs. Varnish a happy wife and mother. Both the suicide note and the police reports, which the author had in his possession, indicated that the Varnishes did not have a happy home life. The article "was published with knowledge that it was false, or in reckless disregard for the truth."[27] The finding of the lower court was affirmed. The Supreme Court denied certiorari in April 1969.

In *Cantrell* the U.S. Supreme Court determined that a reporter, through actual malice, had placed a family in a false light. In 1967 Margaret Cantrell's husband Melvin was killed, along with 43 other people, when a bridge collapsed.

Joseph Eszterhas, a reporter for the Cleveland *Plain Dealer,* wrote a "news feature" that focused on the funeral of Melvin Cantrell and the impact his death had on the Cantrell family. Five months later Eszterhas and a photographer returned to write a follow-up feature. Mrs. Cantrell was not at home, so the men talked with the Cantrell children and took 50 pictures. An article that stressed the family's abject poverty appeared in the Sunday magazine section of the newspaper. Mrs. Cantrell brought action for invasion of privacy; she claimed that the article placed the family in a false light through its many inaccuracies. For example, although Mrs. Cantrell was not present during the reporter's visit, Eszterhas wrote:

> Margaret Cantrell will talk neither about what happened nor about how they are doing. She wears the same mask of non-expression she wore at the funeral. She is a proud woman. She says that after it happened, the people in town offered to help them out with money but they refused to take it.

Other misrepresentations involved descriptions of the poverty in which the Cantrells were living and the dirty and dilapidated condition of the Cantrell home. Mrs. Cantrell claimed the story made the family objects of pity and ridicule and caused them to suffer outrage, mental distress, shame, and humiliation. The jury returned a verdict against the paper, the reporter, and the photographer for general monetary damages. The U.S. Supreme Court, per Justice Potter Stewart, found actual malice in the actions of the reporter. Eszterhas must have known that a number of the statements in the story were untrue. His article implied that Mrs. Cantrell had been present during his visit to her home and that Eszterhas had observed her wearing "the same mask of non-expression" she wore at her husband's funeral. These were "calculated falsehoods." The jury was correct in finding that Eszterhas had portrayed the Cantrells in a false light through knowing or reckless untruth.[28] In *Cantrell,* as in *Varnish,* the Court was willing to punish a publication that placed an individual in a false light through actual malice.

Summary

False light involves the publication of false information about an individual, whether it is defamatory or not. This type of invasion of privacy usually involves fictionalization of known facts; such exaggerations constituted the basis for decision in *Strickler* and *Aquino.* As determined in *Carlisle,* however, minor fictionalization is not actionable. In *Hill* the U.S. Supreme Court ruled that the First Amendment protects the press from invasion-of-privacy suits concerning matters of public interest, unless there is proof of actual malice. While such malice was not found in *Hill,* it was evident in *Varnish* and *Cantrell.*

APPROPRIATION

Appropriation involves taking an individual's name, picture, photograph, or likeness without that person's permission and using it for commercial gain.

Advertising

In most states, laws forbid using the name or picture of any living person for advertising purposes without obtaining consent from that person. Over the years the courts have heard several cases involving alleged violations of such laws.

In *Sarat Lahiri* a New York court set forth guidelines concerning the use of photographs in newspaper advertising. The case involved a feature article about the performance of rope tricks, especially as such acts had been performed by Hindu mystics. The article, which appeared in the magazine section of the *Sunday Mirror,* claimed that Hindu mystics, through hypnotic powers and the creation of an illusion, convinced viewers that the rope was rising into the air, when, in fact, it remained coiled upon the ground. The article was illustrated by several color photographs. One pictured Sarat Lahiri, a well-known Hindu musician, playing a musical instrument as accompaniment for a female Indian dancer. Lahiri initiated court action, claiming invasion of privacy. In *Sarat Lahiri* the court set forth specific rules applicable to unauthorized publication of photographs in a single issue of a newspaper. The court determined that it was illegal to publish, without permission, a photograph as part of an advertisement. It was also illegal to use such a photograph with a fictional article. It was, however, legal to publish a photograph in connection with an article of current news or immediate public interest. Regarding Lahiri's claim, the court noted that the article concerned a legitimate news interest. A British society had offered a substantial prize to any person who was able to perform the famous rope trick. The author explained how the trick was allegedly performed in India and discussed the possibility that the society would have to pay the prize. The only issue was whether the picture had too tenuous a connection with the article. The court decided the photograph illustrated one of the points made by the author—the mystical quality of the East. In the court's opinion, "it would be far-fetched to hold in this case that the picture was not used in an illustrative sense, but merely to promote the sale of the paper."[29]

Another New York case involved actress Shirley Booth. While Miss Booth was vacationing at a prominent resort called "Round Hill" in Jamaica, a photographer for *Holiday* magazine took photographs to use with an article concerning the resort and its guests. Booth was photographed, to her knowledge and without her objection. Booth, however, never gave written consent for publication. When the article appeared, a photograph showing Booth in the water up to her neck, wearing a brimmed, high-crowned street hat of straw, was given a prominent place in the story. This publication did not violate Booth's right of privacy, because this was reproduction for news purposes. A few months later Curtis Publishing Company reproduced the same photograph in a full-page advertisement. The ads presented Booth's photograph as a sample of the contents of *Holiday*. Booth initiated court action, claiming that the procedure invaded her privacy. The issue facing the court was whether a person's photograph, originally published in one issue of a periodical as a newsworthy subject, may be republished later as an advertisement for the periodical itself. The court differentiated between collateral and incidental advertising. Collateral advertising involves the sale of a product completely unconnected with the promotion of a news medium. Incidental advertising involves the sale and dissemination of the news medium itself. The court noted that "contemporaneous or proximate advertising of the news medium, by way of extract, cover, dust jacket, or poster, using relevant but otherwise personal matter, does not violate the statute." In *Booth* the court found "that so long as the reproduction was used to illustrate the quality and content of the periodical in which it originally appeared, the statute was not violated."[30]

The *Booth* decision was applied in *Namath*. In January 1969 *Sports Illustrated* published newsworthy photographs of Joe Namath, star quarterback of the New York Jets, the team that had defeated the Baltimore Colts in the Super Bowl. Three years later Namath initiated an invasion-of-privacy suit, charging that the magazine had used these photographs in an advertising campaign designed to promote subscriptions. Namath argued that the magazine should not be permitted to used his name or photograph without consent and without remuneration. The court cited *Booth,* noting that as far as advertising is concerned, the "incidental use of a name or likeness" is not actionable.

> It is understandable that plaintiff [Namath] desires payment for the use of his name and likeness in advertisements for the sale of publications in which he has appeared as newsworthy just as he is paid for collateral endorsement of commercial products. This he cannot accomplish under the existing law of our State and Nation. Athletic prowess is much admired and well paid in this country. It is commendable that freedom of speech and the press under the First Amendment transcends the right to privacy.[31]

A 1967 case involved action by professional golfers who objected to the use of their names for marketing the Pro-Am Golf Game. The contents of the game included 23 sheets of paper, each of which contained the name of a well-known professional golfer, accompanied by a short biography. Each of the sheets contained accurate facts concerning the golfer's professional career. Arnold Palmer, Gary Player, Doug Sanders, and Jack Nicklaus, all of whom had never given permission for the use of their profiles by the company, sought an injunction. The golfers claimed that such use constituted an invasion of their privacy.

The judges noted that the use of the names and biographies enhanced the marketability of the game. The company argued that the golfers "waived their rights of privacy because of their being well-known athletes who have deliberately invited publicity in furtherance of their careers." Since the data contained in the profiles were readily obtainable public information, the company should be allowed to reproduce it. The court disagreed:

> Although the publication of biographical data of a well-known figure does not per se constitute an invasion of privacy, the use of that same data for the purpose of a commercial project other than the dissemination of news or articles or biographies does.[32]

According to the court in *Palmer,* it was unfair for a company to commercialize, exploit, or capitalize upon a person's name, reputation, or accomplishments merely because the accomplishments had been highly publicized.

A similar case, decided in 1970, involved action by professional baseball

"TALK ABOUT INVASION OF PRIVACY!"

players, who objected to the use of their names in the marketing of games. The games used statistical information, such as batting, fielding, earned run, and other averages of some 500 to 700 major-league players, identified by team, uniform number, and playing position. The players had not given permission for the use of their names or statistics. The Association of Major League Baseball Players sought an injunction, claiming that the company was guilty of "misappropriation and use for commercial profit of the names of professional major league baseball players without the payment of royalties." The court supported the legitimate interest a celebrity has in his public personality.

> A celebrity must be considered to have invested his years of practice and competition in a public personality which eventually may reach marketable status. That identity, embodied in his name, likeness, statistics and other personal characteristics, is the fruit of his labors and is a type of property.[33]

In *Uhlaender* the court determined that the defendants violated the athletes' "rights by the unauthorized appropriation of their names and statistics for commercial use." Accordingly, the association was awarded injunctive relief.

Right of Publicity

In several cases the courts have considered whether a celebrity has the right to control his or her own publicity. *Paulsen, Man, Spahn, Lugosi, Price,* and *Zacchini* are such cases.

Pat Paulsen, a well-known television comedian, conducted a mock campaign prior to the 1968 presidential election. Claiming to be the "Put-On Presidential Candidate of 1968," Paulsen ran under the banner of the Stag party. Paulsen's satirical comments on various issues were aired with regularity on the nationally televised "Smothers Brothers" program. Paulsen received several votes in primary elections, and he participated in activities traditionally associated with political campaigning. In conjunction with this comedy routine, Paulsen granted an exclusive license to a California company in connection with all campaign buttons, stickers, and posters relating to the "Pat Paulsen for President" campaign. Without obtaining Paulsen's permission, Personality Posters, Inc. prepared for sale an enlargement of a photograph of Paulsen. In the photograph, Paulsen was dressed in beruffled cap and prim frock and held an unlit candle in one hand while his other arm cradled a rubber tire which was hoisted onto his right shoulder. A banner containing the legend "1968" was draped across Paulsen's chest. Added to the poster were the words "FOR PRESIDENT." Paulsen initiated action, claiming that distribution of the posters invaded his right of privacy. In *Paulsen* the court noted that the privacy statute was not intended to limit the dissemination of news of public interest. Even though Paulsen was "only kidding," and his presidential activities were really only a "publicity stunt," they fell within the scope of constitutionally protected matters of public interest. According to the court, "when a well-known entertainer enters the presidential ring, tongue in cheek or otherwise, it is clearly newsworthy and of public interest."[34] The poster, which reflected the spirit in which Paulsen approached the role, was a form of public-interest presentation entitled to constitutional protection. The court opinion noted that Paulsen was less concerned with the "right of privacy" than with the "right of publicity"—that is, the ability to control the financial benefits that attach to a person's name and picture. The court ruled that the right of publicity had no application in this case, which involved a matter of public interest. The use of the poster was constitutionally protected and superseded any privacy or publicity claims.

In 1970 the courts heard a similar case involving the right of publicity. Frank Man, a professional musician, mounted the stage at the Woodstock Festival in August 1969, and played "Mess Call" on his flugelhorn before 400,000 people. The festival was of wide public interest and was extensively reported in news media. Over 120 hours of sound track and motion pictures of the event were recorded and later reduced to a length suitable for exhibition as a motion picture in theatres under the title "Woodstock." Man brought action, claiming that the producers of the film included his performance in the film without his consent, thereby violating his right to privacy. According to the district court in *Man,* "there can be no question that the Woodstock Festival was and is a matter of valid public interest." Furthermore, the New York privacy statute was never intended to apply to professional entertainers who are shown giving a performance before a public audience. Man placed himself in the spotlight of a sensational event that exposed him to publicity. That fact alone made him newsworthy and deprived him of any right to complain of a violation of his privacy.[35]

The court in *Spahn* raised some questions concerning the right of publicity. Author Milton J. Shapiro and publisher Julian Messner collaborated on a biography of professional baseball pitcher Warren Spahn. The book was based on secondary sources. Shapiro never talked with Spahn, his family or friends, or even other baseball players. The book contained several inaccuracies, usually exaggerating Spahn's successes. Specific inaccuracies included attempts to make Spahn appear to be a war hero, descriptions of the influence of Spahn's father in directing him toward baseball, and accounts of the impact of a shoulder injury on Spahn's career. Overall, the writer used imaginary incidents, manufactured dialogue, and manipulated chronology. Spahn initiated judicial proceedings. In court, Shapiro and Messner admitted fictionalization, but argued that it was necessary because the book was written for children. The judges, however, decided that Messner and Shapiro were liable for invasion of privacy, and awarded Spahn $10,000 in damages.[36] A dissenting judge, Francis Bergan, raised an interesting issue. He suggested that, in light of *Hill,* the New York privacy law gave no protection against fictionalization, unless it could be shown that the book was written with actual malice. Upon appeal, the U.S. Supreme Court agreed to hear the case. The litigants, however, settled out of court, prior to a decision. The issue of how the *Hill* case applies to the control of publicity was not considered by the Supreme Court.

In two cases, *Lugosi* and *Price,* the courts considered whether the right to control publicity terminated at death. The cases involved lawsuits claiming wrongful appropriation of the names, likenesses, and characterizations of film stars Bela Lugosi, Oliver Hardy, and Stanley Laurel. The suits were initiated by the beneficiaries of the wills of these deceased actors. The courts differentiated between two concepts—the right of privacy, which terminates upon death, and the right of publicity, which does not terminate upon death. Both courts decided in favor of the beneficiaries of the wills. The *Lugosi* opinion noted: "Bella Lugosi's interest or right in his likeness and appearance as Count Dracula was a property right of such character and substance that it did not terminate with his death but descended to his heirs."[37] The *Price* decision claimed: "The present case [involving Laurel and Hardy] is easier to decide than *Lugosi* since we deal here with actors portraying themselves and developing their own characters rather than fictional characters which have been given a particular interpretation by an actor."[38] These opinions recognize a distinction between termination of a right to privacy at death and survival of a right of publicity.

In *Zacchini* the Supreme Court upheld the right of a celebrity to control his own publicity. Hugo Zacchini performed a "human cannonball" act in which he was shot from a cannon into a net some 200 feet away. In 1972 Zacchini performed his act on a regular basis at an Ohio county fair. The public was not charged a separate fee to observe his act. A television reporter videotaped the entire act, even though Zacchini had asked him not to do so. This film clip, approximately 15 seconds in length was shown on the news program that evening, along with favorable commentary. Zacchini brought action, alleging that the station "showed and commercialized the film of his act without his consent" and that such conduct constituted an "unlawful appropriation of plaintiff's professional property." The case reached the Supreme Court. Zacchini acknowledged that his appearance at the fair and his performance could be reported by the press as newsworthy items. He complained, however, that the reporter filmed and showed his entire act. This was an appropriation of his professional property. The Court noted that the broadcast of a film of Zacchini's entire performance posed a substantial threat to the economic value of that performance. Much of its economic value stemmed from the "right of exclusive control over the publicity given to his performance"; if the public could see the act free on television, they would be less willing to pay to see it performed elsewhere.

There is no doubt that entertainment, as well as news, enjoys First Amendment protection. It is also true that entertainment itself can be important news.... But it is important to note that neither the public nor respondent will be deprived of the benefit of petitioner's performance as long as his commercial stake in his act is appropriately recognized. Petitioner does not seek to enjoin the broadcast of his performance; he simply wants to be paid for it.[39]

In *Zacchini* the Court concluded that in the circumstances of this case the press was not constitutionally privileged.

In *Spahn* the court recognized the right of celebrities to control their own publicity. That right was affirmed by the U.S. Supreme Court in *Zacchini*. Yet, as was clearly demonstrated in *Paulsen* and *Man,* when a celebrity engages in an activity of legitimate public interest, that celebrity surrenders the right to control his or her own publicity regarding that activity.

Summary

In cases cited in this section the courts restricted the use of a person's name and/or photograph for advertising purposes, but upheld the right of journalists to use these items in order to illustrate news stories. *Palmer* and *Uhlaender* established that a person cannot use a celebrity's name or biographical data, even though the data are public and readily obtainable by all, as an aid in marketing a game without first obtaining that celebrity's permission. *Sarat Lahiri* specified that journalists may indeed use a person's name and/or picture in connection with an article of current news or immediate public interest. *Booth* and *Namath* held that reproducing a celebrity's picture in order to illustrate the quality and content of the magazine in which it originally appeared constituted a legitimate use of that reproduction. Such advertising was directly related to the sale and dissemination of the news medium itself.

In other cases, the courts considered the right of publicity. In *Spahn* the court recognized the right of celebrities to control their own publicity. That right was affirmed by the Supreme Court in *Zacchini*. The *Lugosi* and *Price* opinions established that the right of publicity does not terminate upon death. Yet, as was clearly demonstrated in *Paulsen* and *Man,* when a celebrity engages in an activity of legitimate public interest, that celebrity surrenders the right to control his or her own publicity regarding that activity.

NOTES

1. Warren, Samuel D. and Louis D. Brandeis, "The Right to Privacy," *Harvard Law Review* 4 (December 15, 1890), 193-200.

2. Prosser, William L., "Privacy," *California Law Review* 48 (August, 1960), 383-423.

3. *Griswold v. Connecticut,* 85 S.Ct. 1678 (1965).

4. *Eisenstadt v. Baird,* 92 S.Ct. 1029 (1972).

5. *Roe v. Wade,* 93 S.Ct. 705 (1973).

6. *Doe v. Bolton,* 93 S.Ct. 739 (1973).

7. *Planned Parenthood of Central Missouri v. Danforth, Attorney General of Missouri,* 96 S.Ct. 2831 (1976).

8. *Doe v. Commonwealth's Attorney for City of Richmond,* 403 F. Supp. 1199 (1975); 96 S.Ct. 1489 (1976).

9. *Galella v. Onassis*, 487 F.2d 986 (1973).

10. *Kelley v. Johnson*, 96 S.Ct. 1440 (1976).

11. *Dietemann v. Time, Inc.* 449 F.2d 245 (1971).

12. *Cassidy v. American Broadcasting Companies, Inc.*, 377 N.E. 2d 126 (1978).

13. *Pearson v. Dodd*, 410 F.2d 701 (1969).

14. *People v. Kunkin*, 107 Cal. Rptr. 184 (1973).

15. *Kelley v. Post Publishing Company*, 98 N.E. 2d 286 (1951).

16. *Costlow v. Cusimano*, 311 N.Y.S. 2d 92 (1970).

17. *Dailey Times Democrat v. Graham*, 162 So.2d 474 (1964).

18. *Jacova v. Southern Radio and Television Company*, 83 S.2d 34 (1955).

19. *Williams v. KCMO Broadcasting Division—Meredith Corporation*, 472 S.W. 2d 1 (1971).

20. *Virgil v. Sports Illustrated*, 424 F. Supp. 1286 (1976).

21. *Cox Broadcasting Corporation v. Cohn*, 95 S.Ct. 1029 (1975).

22. *Howard v. Des Moines Register & Tribune Company*, 283 N.W. 2d 289 (1979); cert. denied 100 S.Ct. 1081 (1980).

23. *Strickler v. National Broadcasting Company, Inc.*, 167 F. Supp. 68 (1958).

24. *Aquino v. Bulletin Company*, 190 Pa. Super 528 (1959).

25. *Carlisle v. Fawcett Publications, Inc.*, 20 Cal. Rptr. 405 (1962).

26. *Time, Inc. v. Hill*, 87 S.Ct. 534 (1967).

27. *Varnish v. Best Medium Publishing Company, Inc.*, 405 F.2d 608 (1968); cert. denied 89 S.Ct. 1465 (1969).

28. *Cantrell v. Forest City Publishing Company*, 95 S.Ct. 465 (1974).

29. *Sarat Lahiri v. Daily Mirror, Inc.*, 295 N.Y.S. 382 (1937).

30. *Booth v. Curtis Publishing Company*, 15 A.D. 2d 343 (1962).

31. *Namath v. Sports Illustrated*, 363 N.Y.S. 2d 276 (1975).

32. *Palmer v. Schonhorn Enterprises, Inc.*, 232 A. 2d 458 (1967).

33. *Uhlaender v. Henricksen*, 316 F. Supp. 1277 (1970).

34. *Paulsen v. Personality Posters, Inc.*, 299 N.Y.S. 2d 501 (1968).

35. *Man v. Warner Brothers, Inc.*, 317 F. Supp. 50 (1970).

36. *Spahn v. Julian Messner, Inc.*, 233 N.E. 2d 840 (1967).

37. *Lugosi v. Universal Pictures Company*, 172 U.S.P.Q. 541 (1972).

38. *Price v. Hal Roach Studios*, 400 F. Supp. 836 (1975).

39. *Zacchini v. Scripps-Howard Broadcasting Company*, 97 S.Ct. 2849 (1977).

RECOMMENDED READING

Emerson, Thomas I., ''The Right of Privacy and Freedom of the Press,'' *Harvard Civil Rights-Civil Liberties Law Review* 14 (Summer, 1979), 329-60.

Massengale, Roger L., ''*Zacchini v. Scripps-Howard Broadcasting Company:* The 'Entire Act' Doctrine—Economic Recognition of Intangible Property,'' *Capital University Law Review* 7 (1978), 439-51.

McKeever, Joyce, ''Right of Privacy: Publication of True Information on the Public Record,'' *Duquesne Law Review* 14 (Spring, 1976), 507-20.

Mims, Stephen S., ''*Eisenstandt v. Baird:* Massachusetts Statute Prohibiting Distribution of Contraceptives to Unmarried Persons Held Unconstitutional,'' *Southwestern Law Journal* 26 (October, 1972), 775-80.

Pember, Don R., *Privacy and the Press: The Law, the Mass Media, and the First Amendment.* Seattle: University of Washington Press, 1972.

Prosser, William L., "Privacy," *California Law Review* 48 (August, 1960), 383-423.

Sanford, Bruce W., *Synopsis of the Law of Libel and the Right of Privacy.* New York: Scripps-Howard, 1981.

KEY DECISIONS

1965—*GRISWOLD*—overturned a law that prohibited the advising of persons concerning the use of contraceptives; such a law intruded upon the privacy of the marriage relationship.

1967—*HILL*—ruled that the First Amendment shields the press from invasion of privacy suits involving matters of public interest, unless there is proof of "actual malice."

1972—*EISENSTADT*—extended the *Griswold* rule to unmarried persons.

1974—*CANTRELL*—punished a reporter who, through actual malice, placed an individual in a false light.

1975—*COHN*—acknowledged that the interests in preserving privacy fade when the information involved already appears on the public record.

1977—*ZACCHINI*—upheld the right of a celebrity to control his or her own publicity.

SUMMARY—LAW OF PRIVACY

Definition

The law of privacy is designed to protect individuals from indiscriminate snooping and prying. The statutory right to privacy is not, however, uniform throughout the states.

Proof

The courts have recognized the following types of invasion of privacy:
1. Intrusion of physical solitude
2. Public disclosure of private facts
3. Placing an individual in a false light in the public eye
4. Appropriation of some element of an individual's personality for commercial use.

Defenses

The courts have recognized the following defenses:
1. Newsworthiness or public interest
2. Consent
3. Information already on the public record
4. Lack of actual malice (applicable in limited instances).

9

COPYRIGHT

We must take care to guard against two extremes equally prejudicial; the one, that men of ability, who have employed their time for the service of the community, may not be deprived of their just merits, and the reward of their ingenuity and labour; the other, that the world may not be deprived of improvements nor the progress of the arts be retarded.[1]

Copyright law enables an author to protect his or her work against plagiarism. Copyright guarantees, however, involve conflicting issues, which have sometimes been discussed in the courts. In this chapter, the history of copyright law, procedures for obtaining a copyright, tests of infringement, and guidelines for fair use will be considered in terms of court interpretation.

HISTORY OF COPYRIGHT LAW

In 1710 the English Parliament passed the Statute of Eight Anne, a law that granted authors exclusive rights to their works and restricted unauthorized reproduction and distribution of those works. Under this system authors were encouraged to write, safe in the knowledge that their creative efforts would be protected. The first copyright law adopted in the United States closely resembled the British statute. U.S. copyright law has had two historical sources—common and statutory.

Common-Law Copyright

The 1976 Copyright Act provides for the termination of common-law copyright, which prior to that time had played a vital role in protecting an author's work. Under common-law copyright, automatic protection existed as soon as an author created a work, and it lasted as long as the work remained unpublished. It was especially useful for authors who chose not to publish their work. Common-law copyright has been recognized by the courts—*Pushman, Chamberlain,* and *Hemingway* are examples.

In 1930 Hovsep Pushman painted a color still-life, entitled "When Autumn Is Here." He sold the painting to the University of Illinois. At the time Pushman did not state that he wanted to reserve reproduction rights for this painting. Ten years later the University of Illinois sold the right to make reproductions to the New York Graphic Society. When Pushman learned of the sale, he sued in an attempt to halt the reproduction of his painting. In *Pushman* the judge recognized that a common-law copyright belongs to an artist or author until it is disposed of. The issue was whether the copyright had passed with the unconditional sale of the painting. Pushman argued that the right to reproduce his work was separate from the work itself. Since permission to reproduce did not accompany the sale, the common-law copyright did not pass from Pushman to the University of Illinois. The judge disagreed—the unconditional sale carried with it the transfer of the common-law copyright and the right to reproduce. If Pushman wished to retain the reproduction right, he should have reserved it when he sold the painting.[2]

In *Chamberlain* the focus of the alleged infringement was a story entitled "A Murder, A Mystery and a Marriage," which was written by Samuel Clemens under the pen name Mark Twain. When Twain died in 1910, the manuscript of the unpublished story was not found among his effects. In 1945 Lew Feldman bought the original manuscript at an auction. Feldman contacted Thomas Chamberlain, the owner of all Twain's property, seeking permission to publish the story. When Chamberlain refused, Feldman started court action. The judge noted that, in Twain's lifetime, the manuscript had been rejected for publication by the *Atlantic Monthly,* and it could be inferred that Twain decided that the manuscript was unsuitable and never intended it for publication. Thus, Twain never granted anyone the literary property.

> The common-law copyright, or right of first publication, is a right different from that of ownership of the physical paper; the first of those rights does not necessarily pass with the second; and the separate common law copyright or control of the right to reproduce belongs to the artist or author until disposed of by him.[3]

In *Chamberlain* the court decided that Twain had never parted with the publication rights to the story. No matter how the manuscript left Twain's possession, he apparently never intended that it be published. Therefore, Feldman had not purchased the publication rights when he bought the original manuscript.

In *Hemingway* the courts again examined the nature of common-law copyright. During the 13 years prior to his death, Ernest Hemingway formed a close friendship with a young writer, A. E. Hotchner. In conversations with Hotchner, Hemingway revealed personal reminiscences, which the young man carefully recorded on tape and on notecards. With Hemingway's approval, Hotchner wrote several articles, in which he quoted material from the conversations. After Hemingway died, Hotchner authored *Papa Hemingway,* a biography, which relied heavily on the conversations. The Hemingway family sued, alleging that *Papa Hemingway* consisted mainly of literary matter composed by Hemingway, in which he retained common-law copyright . A key issue in *Hemingway* was whether the common-law copyright extended to conversational speech. The judge decided that because speech is easily recorded with electronic devices, copyright law should not exclude protection of words a speaker might utter in private dialogue, which eventually could be published. It had, however, become a continuing practice in Hemingway's later years for Hotchner to write stories about Hemingway, approved by Hemingway, which were based largely on conversations between the two men. Under such circumstances, authority to publish was implied, thus negating any common-law copyright. The judge noted that it was possible for a speaker to reserve the common-law copyright—it could be stated in prefatory words or inferred from the circumstances in which the dialogue took place. In this case, Hemingway's words and behavior, "far from making any such reservation, left no doubt of his willingness to permit Hotchner to draw freely on their conversation in writing about him and to publish such material."[4] In *Hemingway, Chamberlain,* and *Pushman,* the court acknowledged that works of artists and authors, written and spoken, are entitled to common-law copyright. Such protection, however, is no longer available under the 1976 copyright statute.

Statutory Copyright

Article 1, Section 8, of the Constitution provides the fundamental authority for copyright law. It gives Congress power "to promote the Progress of Science and useful Arts, by securing for limited Times to Authors and Inventors the exclusive Right to their respective Writings and Discoveries." Accordingly, Congress has enacted three major copyright statutes—in 1790, 1909, and 1976.

In 1790 Congress enacted the first Copyright Act, which provided that any author of a map, chart, or book printed in the United States could control the right to print, reprint, publish, or sell the work. The term of the copyright was 14 years, plus possible renewal for another 14-year term. In order to copyright a work, a copy of the title had to be deposited and recorded in the clerk's office of the district court where the author lived, for a fee of 60 cents. The author had to publish a copy of the record in a newspaper and deposit a copy of the record with the secretary of state. Any violation was subject to penalties, which included forfeiture of all copies and a fine of 50 cents per page. Half of the fine was given to the copyright owner and the other half was retained by the government. Court action had to begin within one year of the violation. Over the next century the law was amended to provide protection to prints, musical compositions, photographs, and works of fine art. The term of protection was lengthened; the term was set at 28 years, plus a renewal period of an additional 14 years. The main aspects of the 1790 copyright law, however, remained unchanged.

In 1909 Congress revised the law. Copyrightable material included all original books, periodicals, lectures, dramas, musical compositions, maps, works of art, reproductions, scientific drawings, photographs, prints, and motion pictures. Application for copyright had to be made to the registrar of copyrights in Washington, D.C. Two copies "of the best edition" of the work had to be "promptly deposited in the copyright office" or mailed to the registrar of copyrights. The application fee for registration was $6. A published work had to contain a notice of copyright. The notice contained the symbol ©, the word "copyright," or the abbreviation "copr."; it also included the name of the copyright owner and the date of publication. The original copyright period remained 28 years, but the renewal period was increased to an additional 28 years, provided that a "proper and timely" application for renewal was made. Punitive damages for infringement were fixed; the minimum amount was $250 and the maximum was $5,000. Compensatory damages could also be awarded. In addition, the act allowed a person to use copyrighted works without obtaining permission, so long as the use constituted a "fair use." Between 1909 and 1976 technological advancements produced minor amendments to the law—radio, film, tape recorders, television, computers, photocopying, cable television, and satellite communication systems came within the scope of copyright law.

The 1976 law retained much of the content and structure of the 1909 act. There were, however, some significant revisions. The 1909 act provided that unpublished works were protected by common law; the 1976 act provides federal statutory protection from the time the work is fixed in a tangible form. A work is "fixed in a tangible medium when it is sufficiently permanent or stable to permit it to be perceived, reproduced or otherwise communicated for a period of more than transitory duration." Under this new law, unpublished works are entitled to statutory copyright. The 1976 law also established a single term of copyright, the author's lifetime plus 50 years. The fee for registration of most works was established at $10. Some provisions regarding reproduction rights of libraries and cable broadcasting systems were specified. The law clarified the doctrine of fair use, indicating that reproduction "for purposes such as criticism, comment, news reporting, teaching (including multiple copies for classroom use), scholarship, or research, is not an infringement of copyright." The act set forth the following criteria to help the courts determine whether a use is a "fair use."

> The purpose and character of the use, including whether such use is of a commercial nature or is for nonprofit educational purposes;

The nature of the copyrighted work;

The amount and substantiality of the portion used in relation to the copyrighted work as a whole;

The effect of the use upon the potential market for or value of the copyrighted work.

The 1976 law also set damages for infringement at not less than $250 and not more than $10,000. If, however, infringement was committed "willfully," the amount could be increased to as much as $50,000. And if the infringer demonstrated that he or she was unaware that the act was an infringement, the fine could be as low as $100. The courts have wide discretion on these matters.

Summary

Copyright law in America emerged from the English example and has two foundations—common and statutory. Common-law copyright provided automatic protection as soon as a work was written and remained in effect until the work was published. Common-law protection, however, has been eliminated with the passage of the 1976 Copyright Act. Statutory copyright was established by Article 1, Section 8 of the Constitution, and was clarified by legislative enactments in 1790, 1909, 1976.

PROCEDURAL REQUIREMENTS

The 1790, 1909, and 1976 laws described procedural formalities to be followed in obtaining a copyright, including notice of copyright, deposit of copies, and registration. These procedures were rigidly enforced in early cases, but rather loosely in recent court cases.

Notice

Failure to provide notice can result in loss of copyright protection. In three cases decided at the turn of the century—*Holmes* and the two *Mifflin* cases—the U.S. Supreme Court demanded strict adherence to the notice requirement.

Oliver Wendell Holmes authored "The Autocrat of the Breakfast Table," a work published without copyright protection in 12 successive issues of the *Atlantic Monthly*. Holmes then sought to publish the work as a bound book. He obtained a copyright and deposited a copy of the book in the court clerk's office in his home district. A notice of copyright was printed in all copies of every subsequent edition of the book. Several years later, another publisher printed copies of the work, taken directly from the *Atlantic Monthly* version. Holmes sued, claiming that the publication violated his copyright. The Supreme Court noted that part of the work, the bound volume, was copyrighted. The original serialized version from *Atlantic Monthly* was not. The copying did not constitute an infringement.[5]

Oliver Wendell Holmes also wrote "Professor at the Breakfast Table," which was published serially in the *Atlantic Monthly*. The first ten parts were published from January to October 1859, without a copyright being secured. The remaining two parts for November and December were copyrighted. Holmes then published the entire work in one volume, which contained a notice of copyright. When another publisher sought to publish the work, Holmes sued for violation of his copyright. The issue facing the Court was whether copyrighting only the last two parts of the work provided protection for the entire work. In *Mifflin I* the Court decided that such a procedure was inadequate—since the law set forth a specific way an author could give a reader proper notice, that was the only method the Court would accept.[6]

A similar case, *Mifflin II*, involved Harriet Beecher Stowe's "The Minister's Wooing." After the first 29 chapters of the work had appeared in the first ten issues of the *Atlantic Monthly* for 1859, Stowe published the whole work in book form and took steps to obtain a copyright. The last 13 chapters subsequently appeared in the November and December issues of the *Atlantic Monthly*. When a publishing company sought to copy the work, Stowe sued. The Supreme Court ruled that the first 29 chapters had become public property. Stowe's copyright of the last 13 chapters would have been valid, except that they appeared in the *Atlantic Monthly* without notice of copyright. The work fell into the public domain for failure to provide proper copyright notice. Regarding both *Mifflin* cases Justice Henry Brown lamented:

> It is exceedingly unfortunate that, with the pains taken by the authors of these works to protect themselves against republication, they should have failed in accomplishing their object; but the right being purely statutory, we see no escape from the conclusion that, unless the substance as well as the form of the statute be disregarded, the right has been lost in both of these cases.[7]

About 50 years later a district court was less rigid about the notice requirement. In 1948 Emily Kimbrough Wrench sold to Universal Pictures all movie rights to three of her stories, which were known collectively as "It Gives Me Great Pleasure." One of the stories, "My Heart's in My Mouth," had appeared in the *Atlantic Monthly* in June 1944. Wrench agreed to protect the copyright by seeing that the stories were published with proper notice and that the work was registered. In late 1948 a book of eight stories entitled *It Gives Me Great Pleasure* was published under a copyright notice, "Copyright, 1945, 1948 by Emily Kimbrough." There was further notation that some of the stories "originally appeared in somewhat different form as stories in the *New Yorker*." Neither 1944, the year of the *Atlantic Monthly* copyright of "My Heart's in My Mouth," nor the fact that it had appeared in that magazine, was mentioned. At the time, the copyright on the story belonged to the *Atlantic Monthly*. Because it retained no interest in the story after publication, the *Atlantic Monthly* gave the copyright to Wrench. Universal, however, thought the copyright was incorrect, and notified Wrench that they were voiding the contract. Wrench sued Universal for breach of contract. Universal claimed that because Wrench failed to preserve the copyright, the material had fallen into the public domain. The court had to decide whether the copyright on the book *It Gives Me Great Pleasure* was adequate to protect the copyright on the story "My Heart's in My Mouth." Universal claimed that the notice was faulty because 1945 was claimed as the year of the prior copyright, when the actual year was 1944, and because the copyright was not owned by Wrench, but rather by the *Atlantic Monthly*. In *Wrench* the court decided that the copyright was valid. If the story published in 1944 had been republished in 1948 with no changes, without mention of the 1944 copyright, the material would have fallen into the public domain, but revision of the story was sufficient to constitute a new work. Furthermore, it had been republished as part of a book that contained new material. The publication of a new book with its own copyright notice made it unnecessary to list any prior copyright dates. Even though publishers tend to list all prior copyrights in a republication, that practice is not necessary.[8]

Under the copyright laws operating when the Supreme Court decided *Holmes* and the *Mifflin* cases, copyright notice had to follow a specific procedure; otherwise, protection was lost. Under the 1976 law requirements for notice are not as rigid. The notice can be placed anywhere where it "can be visually perceived." Furthermore, omission of the notice does not necessarily destroy protection, if an attempt is made within five years to correct the omission.

Deposit and Registration

In 1899, in *Holmes*, the Supreme Court stressed that in order to receive protection under copyright law, an author, prior to publication, had to deposit a copy of the title of his work in the clerk's office of the district court where the author resided. The author also, within three months after publication, had to deposit a copy of the work with the clerk's office. Failure to comply with this requirement resulted in the loss of copyright protection. More recently the courts have been less rigid about copyright registration. The *Washingtonian* case provides an example.

The December 10, 1931, issue of *The Washingtonian* was published with proper copyright notice. Two years later, copies were finally deposited in the copyright office and a certificate of registration obtained. Meanwhile, in August 1932, Drew Pearson authored a book that contained material almost identical with an article contained in *The Washingtonian*. The publishing company sued. At trial, Pearson argued that "if copies were not deposited promptly after publication the opportunity to comply with the requirement of promptness was gone forever as to that particular work." In *Washingtonian* the Supreme Court had to interpret the language of the copyright law, which stated that copies should be "promptly deposited." The Court acknowledged that the Copyright Act of 1909 failed to define adequately the term "promptly," but Section Thirteen of the act authorized the register of copyrights to give notice in case of undue delay and to require deposit of copies. Upon failure to comply within three months, the copyright became void and a fine could be levied. The Court, per Justice James McReynolds concluded:

> The Congress intended that prompt deposit when deemed necessary should be enforced through actual notice by the register; also that while no action can be maintained before copies are actually deposited, mere delay will not destroy the right to sue. Such forfeitures are never to be inferred from doubtful language.[9]

Summary

During the past century, judicial and legislative bodies have eased the procedural requirements associated with copyright. In *Holmes* and the two *Mifflin* cases, the Supreme Court demanded that authors follow specific procedures in providing proper notice and in obtaining registration. In more recent cases, *Wrench* and *Washingtonian,* the court decisions allowed increased flexibility in complying with procedural formalities. According to the 1976 Copyright Act, proper notice is the only procedural requirement that an author must fulfill to protect a work.

TESTS OF INFRINGEMENT

The 1976 Copyright Act states that "anyone who violates any of the exclusive rights of the copyright owner. . .is an infringer of the copyright." The act does not specify types of infringement; that determination has been left to the courts. Some appropriate tests are originality, copying, substantiality, and access.

Originality

Originality is the fundamental requirement of copyrightable material. In a copyright-infringement trial the plaintiff seeks to show that the work in question is copied, while the defendant hopes to demonstrate originality. The exact meaning of the term "originality" has been a subject for the courts. In 1845 Judge Joseph Story provided an interpretation.

> In truth, in literature, in science and in art, there are and can be, few, if any, things, which, in an abstract sense, are strictly new and original throughout.

> Every book in literature, science, and art, borrows, and must necessarily bor-
> row, and use much which was well known and used before. No man creates
> a new language for himself, at least if he be a wise man, in writing a book.
> He contents himself with the use of language already known and used and un-
> derstood by others. No man writes exclusively from his own thoughts, unaided
> and uninstructed by the thoughts of others. The thoughts of every man are, more
> or less, a combination of what other men have thought and expressed, although
> they may be modified, exalted, or improved by his own genius or reflection.
> If no book could be the subject of copyright which was not new and original
> in the elements of which it is composed, there could be no ground for any copy-
> right in modern times, and we should be obliged to ascend very high, even in
> antiquity, to find a work entitled to such eminence.[10]

In Story's opinion, an author necessarily incorporates parts of the ideas and style
of another's work into his or her own work. Such effort constitutes sufficiently
unique treatment to warrant copyright protection. In numerous court cases the
question of infringement has centered around the issue of originality. *Bleistein,
Jewlers' Circular, Triangle, Amsterdam, Donald,* and *Lipman* provide illustrations.

In *Bleistein,* the infringement involved copying, in reduced form, three
posters that advertised a circus. The defendant argued that posters were not subject to copyright protection and could be copied. The Supreme Court noted that
the material could be copyrighted, because it met the requirement of originality. According to Justice Oliver Wendell Holmes, "these prints in their *ensem-
ble* and in all their details, in their design and particular combinations of figures,
lines, and colors, are the original work" of the designer. Holmes claimed that
"the least pretentious picture has more originality in it than directories and the
like, which may be copyrighted." In *Bleistein* the Court decided that printing
and engraving were original work, entitled to protection of copyright law. In addition, this case marked the first time the Court applied copyright law to advertising.

> A picture is none the less a picture and none the less a subject of copyright,
> that it is used for an advertisement. And if pictures may be used to advertise
> soap, or the theatre or monthly magazines, as they are, they may be used to
> advertise a circus.[11]

Another infringement involved Jewelers' Circular Publishing Company's
copyrighted 1915 edition of *Trade-Marks of the Jewelry and Kindred Trades.*
The book contained an alphabetical listing of the names and addresses of jewelers,
and opposite the jewelers' names appeared their trademarks; this information was
acquired directly from the jewelers. In 1920 Keystone Publishing Company prepared *Jewelers' Index,* a book that contained the same information. To obtain
the information, Keystone sent a letter to various jewelers, asking if enclosed

illustrations—clipped directly from *Trade-Marks of the Jewelry and Kindred Trades*—represented the appropriate trademarks. After verifying the information, Keystone published its book, which consisted of reproductions of illustrations found in *Trade-Marks of the Jewelry and Kindred Trades.* Jewelers' Circular Publishing Company sued. Keystone claimed that the Jewelers' Company book was not protected by copyright law. The court disagreed; Jewelers' book met the test of originality. It was a "directory" or "other compilation" under copyright law. It was immaterial that the trademarks themselves could not be copyrighted. Keystone also claimed that it should be entitled to research Jewelers' book, verify the accuracy of the information, and repeat that information. The court conceded that a second compiler may check his or her work against an original for compilation to verify its accuracy, but Keystone went beyond simple verification. Keystone was enjoined from publishing the trademark section of the *Index* and directed to recall all copies within 20 days.[12]

Triangle Publications is a similar case. Triangle published *Daily Racing Form* and *The Morning Telegraph,* periodicals that contained information about racehorses. Triangle paid about half a million dollars yearly to obtain information from representatives stationed at every horse track in North America. Triangle competed with New England Newspaper Publishing Company, which published daily newspapers containing data about racehorses. New England Newspaper Publishing Company did not compile race-result charts on its own; instead, it published Triangle's charts in an abbreviated form, acknowledging its copyright. Triangle sued. The Court considered two issues. First, were the Triangle periodicals copyrightable?

> To constitute a copyrightable compilation, a compendium must ordinarily result from the labor or assembling, connecting and categorizing disparate facts which in nature occurred in isolation. A compilation, in short, is a synthesis. It is rare indeed that an analysis of any one actual occurrence could be regarded as a compilation. For an account of a single event to be subject to copyright, it must have individuality of expression or must reflect peculiar skill and judgement.[13]

Yet, in this case the originality requirement was satisfied. The arrangement of charts for all races run anywhere in North America during the previous day, tables of performances for all horses scheduled to run during the day of publication, and miscellaneous information about racehorses comprised a compilation and was copyrightable. The second issue was whether an infringement occurred when New England Newspaper Publishing Company used Triangle's periodicals to prepare information for its paper. The district court concluded that no infringement took place, because none of Triangle's work was reproduced; the periodicals were used solely to secure clues concerning where horses previously ran.

The *Amsterdam* case concerned the copyrightability of maps. The focus of the case was a map that appeared in a historical article in the *Philadelphia In-*

"YOU'RE SERVING TIME FOR PLAGIARISM?"

quirer. Lewis Amsterdam, a publisher of maps, alleged that it was copied from his copyrighted map. The newspaper conceded the copying, but argued that the map was not entitled to copyright. The court stressed that "to be copyrightable a map must be the result of some original work." Then, the court considered the manner in which Amsterdam prepared the map. Amsterdam made no actual surveys of any roads, county lines, township lines, creeks, rivers, or railroad tracks; all such information had been obtained from other maps. The work of surveying, calculating, and investigating that was done by Amsterdam "was so negligible that it may be discounted entirely."[14] The court of appeals concluded that, because Amsterdam's map lacked originality, it was not copyrightable.

In *Donald* the court of appeals considered the originality of a business form. In 1961 O. W. Donald registered with the copyright office a paragraph found at the bottom of standard invoice forms, which Donald printed and sold to television dealers and repairmen. When a competitor used the same language on its forms, Donald sued. The court noted that a copyright applicant did not have to demonstrate that a work was unique or novel, only that it was original. The material could be copyrighted, even when it was based on a previously copyrighted work, if the author added "some substantial, not merely trivial, originality." The court did not find the required originality in Donald's paragragh. The word arrangement was a paraphrase of various portions of earlier forms and in copyright law paraphrasing is equivalent to outright copying. The court concluded: "The Copyright Act was not designed to protect such negligible efforts. We reward creativity and originality with a copyright but we do not accord copyright protection to a mere copycat."[15]

The *Lipman* case concerned the copyrightability of a court transcript. During the inquest into the drowning death of Mary Jo Kopechne, court stenographer Sidney Lipman was hired to record the testimony. Realizing the marketable value of the transcript, Lipman prepared several copies at his own expense. Senator Edward Kennedy, who had been driving the car in which Kopechne died, became apprehensive and instituted proceedings. The court ordered the inquest to be held *in camera* and the transcript impounded. When the order was eventually lifted, Lipman asked permission to sell the transcript. He claimed a common-law copyright in the transcript. The court of appeals noted that "since transcription is by definition a verbatim recording of other persons' statements, there can be no originality in the reporter's product."[16] Thus, the report was not copyrightable. The court rejected Lipman's scheme to make a profit from the sale of the transcript. The cases cited in this section—*Bleistein, Jeweler's Circular, Triangle, Amsterdam, Donald,* and *Lipman*—confirm the principle that originality is a requirement of copyrightability.

Copying

The concepts of copying and originality are closely related. They represent different ways of asking the same question. In an infringement trial, a court might ask, Did the defendant create the work? Was it original? A court might also inquire, Did the defendant copy the plaintiff's work? The courts have considered which parts of a work may not be copied. They have generally held that while the facts cannot be copyrighted, the style and manner in which the facts are presented can be protected. Thus, to copy an author's style or manner is an infringement. This principle has been upheld in several cases dealing with subjects ranging from news stories to art works.

News Stories

In *International News Service* the court applied this principle to news stories. Associated Press and International News Service were competitors in the gathering and distribution of news. For a fee, newspaper companies throughout the United States obtained news of current events from these services. In 1918 INS began to pirate information from AP. INS persuaded AP employees to furnish news prior to publication. In addition, INS copied parts of news stories from early newspaper editions of AP members. AP initiated court action to restrain INS from pirating news. The Supreme Court examined the question of property in news. In the Court's opinion, per Justice Mahlon Pitney, the literary style of the news story was subject to protection, but the news element itself was not.

> The news element—the information respecting current events contained in the literary production—is not the creation of the writer, but it is a report of matters that ordinarily are *publici juris,* it is the history of the day. It is not to be supposed that the framers of the Constitution...intended to confer upon one who might happen to be the first to report a historic event the exclusive right for any period to spread the knowledge of it.[17]

The Court concluded that the "pirating" of a news story was an infringement.

A few years later the courts decided a similar case. The *New York Tribune* copyrighted and printed a news story about Germany's reliance upon submarines during World War I. The Tribune Company offered the story for simultaneous publication in the *Chicago Herald,* which declined, and the *Chicago Daily News,* which purchased. Although realizing that the story was copyrighted, the *Herald* printed a condensed version. The Tribune Association initiated court action. The court affirmed that news events were not subject to copyright protection, but insofar as the story involves "literary quality and style, apart from the bare recital of the facts or statement of news, it is protected by the copyright law." The exact or substantial copying or paraphrasing of a copyrighted news story constituted an infringement. The *Herald* had presented the facts of the *Tribune* article "in the very garb wherein the author clothed them, together with some of his deductions and comments thereon in his precise words."[18]

In the *Wainright* case the court of appeals found a similar copyright violation. Wainwright Securities Company prepared in-depth analytical reports on industrial, financial, utility, and railroad corporations. The Wall Street Transcript Corporation publishes a weekly newspaper concerned with economic news. One of the paper's features is the "Wall Street Roundup," a column containing abstracts of institutional research reports. A copyright infringement action was initiated when the paper published abstracts of Wainwright's research reports. The court noted that, while the "news event" may not be copyrighted, the style or manner of a news story is entitled to protection.

> What is protected is the manner of expression, the author's analysis or interpretation of events, the way he structures his material and marshals facts, his choice of words and the emphasis he gives to particular developments. Thus, the essence of infringement lies not in taking a general theme or in coverage of the reports as events, but in appropriating the particular expression through similarities of treatment, details, scenes, events, and characterization.[19]

In *Wainwright* the court found infringement, because Wall Street Transcript copied "almost verbatim the most creative and original aspects of the reports." The paper's action "was not legitimate coverage of a news event; instead it was ...chiseling for personal profit."

Fiction

In four cases decided in the late 1970s—*Reyher, Musto, Alexander,* and *Hoehling*—courts considered the legality of copying the main idea of a story. In these cases the judges affirmed that copyright protection extends only to the style and manner of expressing an idea, never to the idea itself. Author Rebecca Reyher sued the producers of "Sesame Street," claiming that a televised skit entitled "The Most Beautiful Woman in the World" copied the story line of her children's book, *My Mother Is the Most Beautiful Woman in the World.* In *Reyher* the court of appeals decided that even though both writings present the same idea, there was no copyright infringement, because "the two stories are not similar in mood, details or characterization."[20] In the second case, David Musto alleged that a substantial portion of *The Seven Per Cent Solution,* dealing with Sherlock Holmes' addiction to cocaine, was copied from an article Musto wrote for a medical journal. The *Musto* court concluded that "the copying involved only an 'idea' and not an 'expression of an idea' and therefore is not actionable under the copyright laws."[21] In the third case, Margaret Alexander complained about similarities between her novel *Jubilee* and the book *Roots,* written by Alex Haley. Each book purports to be based on the lives of the author's ancestors. The court rejected Alexander's suit, because the similarities dealt with noncopyrightable elements—matters of historical fact, items of folk custom, *scènes à faire* (characters and settings), and clichéd language. Concerning language, the *Alexander* court observed:

> Words and metaphors are not subject to copyright protection; nor are phrases and expressions conveying an idea that can only be, or is typically, expressed in a limited number of stereotyped fashions.[22]

In the fourth case, A. A. Hoehling brought action against Universal Studios because of alleged similarities between his book *Who Destroyed the Hindenburg?* and the screenplay for a motion picture. The court noted that the idea at stake in this instance was an interpretation of an historical event, and "such interpretations are not copyrightable as a matter of law." The decision stated:

> To avoid a chilling effect on authors who contemplate tackling an historical issue or event, broad latitude must be granted to subsequent authors who make use of historical subject matter, including theories or plots.[23]

In *Hoehling,* as in *Reyher, Musto,* and *Alexander,* there was no illegal copying because the complained similarities concerned noncopyrightable elements.

Art Works

In *Franklin Mint,* the court of appeals applied the principle to a work of art. The Franklin Mint Corporation was accused of infringing on the copyright of

National Wildlife Art Exchange's painting, "Cardinals on Apple Blossom." The alleged copy was entitled "The Cardinal." Both paintings were done by artist Albert Gilbert. The court noted: "Since copyrights do not protect thematic concepts, the fact that the same subject matter may be present in two paintings does not prove copying or infringement." The judges accepted Franklin Mint Corporation's claim that the paintings were "variations on a theme."

> We do not find the phrase objectionable...because a "variation" probably is not a copy and if a "theme" is equated with an "idea," it may not be monopolized. We conceive of "variation on a theme," therefore, as another way of saying that an "idea" may not be copyrighted and only its "expression" may be protected.[24]

In *Franklin Mint* the court affirmed that while ideas cannot be copyrighted, the style and manner of expression may be protected.

Substantiality

> To constitute an invasion of copyright it is not necessary that the whole of a work should be copied, nor even a large portion of it, in form or substance, but that if so much is taken that the value of the original is sensibly diminished, or the labors of the original author are substantially, to an injurious extent, appropriated by another, that is sufficient to constitute an infringement.[25]

Few infringement suits involve total and exact copying of the copyrighted work. Consequently, the test becomes whether there is substantial similarity between the two works. In several cases the courts have had to determine the question of substantiality. Some cases—*Holt, College Entrance Book Company, Toksvig, Eisenschiml*—concerned books. Others—*Heim* and *Berlin*—dealt with musical compositions. Still others—*Columbia Pictures* and *Benny*—involved television.

Books

In 1931 Henry Holt and Company published Dr. Leon Felderman's book, *The Human Voice, Its Care and Development.* Shortly thereafter Liggett & Meyer Tobacco Company published a pamphlet entitled "Some Facts about Cigarettes," in which the following statements were copied, though not exactly, from Felderman's book.

> Statistics have it that 80 per cent of physicians are smokers.... It appears unanimous that smoking is not nearly so injurious as over-eating.... From my experience with ear, nose and throat cases, I firmly believe that tobacco, when properly used, has no ill effect upon the auditory passages.[26]

Henry Holt and Company sought an injunction, claiming that the use of Felderman's statements reflected negatively upon his professional ethics and hampered the sale of the book. The district court emphasized that the whole, or even a large portion of a book, need not be copied to constitute an infringement. It was sufficient if a "material" and "substantial" part had been copied, even though it was but a small part of the whole. In *Holt,* only three sentences had been taken from Felderman's book; however, the material made up about one-twentieth of the pamphlet. Under these circumstances, the copied matter seemed substantial. The fact that the pamphlet acknowledged the source of the information did not excuse the infringement.

The *College Entrance Book Company* case was decided on the issue of substantiality. College Entrance Books Company published two books—*High Points French: Two Years,* and *High Points French: Three Years.* These books were designed to help high-school students review for examinations. The books contained exercises in grammar and composition, copies of previous exams, lists of commonly used French words, and articles in French with English translations. College Entrance Book Company employed two high-school French teachers to compile the books. Shortly thereafter, Amsco Book Company published *French Two Years* and *French Three Years.* These books, which were offered at a lower price, had similar content and were intended for the same market as College Entrance Book Company's books. College Entrance Book Company initiated court action. In court, Amsco argued that similarities should be expected in a compilation of such stereotyped material. The court of appeals, however, found substantial similarity in several aspects of the books—omissions of words, interpretation of grammatical rules, and translations. In all, 96 percent of the items of *High Points French: Two Years* and 82 percent of the items in *High Points French: Three Years* were exactly reproduced in Amsco's books. According to the court, the "copying was unquestionably to avoid the trouble or expense of independent work."[27] The court ruled for College Entrance Book Company.

In *Toksvig* the court emphasized the importance of independent research. The case involved two books. The first, *The Life of Hans Christian Anderson* by Signe Toksvig, was written after three years of research done exclusively from Danish sources, which included the letters of Hans Christian Anderson. The second, *Flight of the Swan,* a novel by Margaret Hubbard, was based on a year's research, which was confined to English sources, including Toksvig's book. Toksvig sued for copyright violation. The court found substantial similarity—Hubbard had copied certain concepts about Anderson, his life, and his friends that were set down for the first time in Toksvig's work. In addition, Hubbard had copied 24 specific passages of the work—the copied materials were original translations made by Toksvig from Danish sources. Hubbard argued that she could have obtained the information from works originally researched by Toksvig. The court of appeals noted:

"SO WHAT IF I BORROWED ¾ OF
MY BOOK FROM SHAKESPEARE?
HE'S DEAD, ANYWAY!"

> The question is not whether Hubbard could have obtained the same informa-
> tion by going to the same sources, but rather did she go to the same sources
> and do her own independent research? In other words, the test is whether the
> one charged with the infringement has made an independent production, or made
> a substantial and unfair use of the complainant's work.[28]

Since Hubbard could not read Danish, the use of Toksvig's book facilitated completion of her book in considerably less time than would have been possible with
independent research. The book was an infringement.

In *Eisenschiml,* the court of appeals considered the similarity of writings that
contain historical facts and ideas. After extensive research, Otto Eisenschiml published two scholarly books about the death of Abraham Lincoln. In an issue of
True magazine, Joseph Millard published an article entitled "America's Greatest
Unsolved Murder." The article contained no footnotes or bibliography. Eisenschiml initiated court action, claiming that the article copied substantial portions

of his books. The judges concluded that Millard's article did not constitute copyright infringement. In historical writings such as the events surrounding Lincoln's assassination, both writers described the same persons during a limited period of time. Some similarity of treatment would unavoidably result.[29]

Music

In *Heim* the court of appeals applied the "substantiality" test to the alleged copyright infringement of a musical composition. Hungarian composer Emery Heim sued Universal Pictures for infringement of the copyright of his song "Ma Este Meg Boldog Vagyok." Heim objected to the use of a portion of the song in a motion picture. Judge Jerome N. Frank indicated that to win the lawsuit, Heim had to show two elements: that the alleged infringer copied from Heim's work and that the amount was so "material" or "substantial" as to constitute unlawful appropriation. Concerning the first element, Universal admitted that similarity existed, but claimed that their composer referred to the same source as Heim— Dvorak's "Humoresque," which had long been in the public domain. Concerning the second element, Heim's "method of dealing with the common, trite note sequence did not possess enough originality, raising it above the level of the banal, to preclude coincidence as an adequate explanation of the identity."[30] Because Heim could not demonstrate material or substantial copying, the court could not find Universal Pictures guilty of copyright infringement.

In another case, *Berlin*, the court of appeals held that musical lyrics, in the form of parody, did not constitute copyright infringement. When *Mad Magazine* published satiric parody lyrics for popular songs, the copyright holders initiated court procedures. The court noted that the theme and content of the parodies differed markedly from those of the originals. For example, "The Last Time I Saw Paris," originally written as a nostalgic ballad became "The First Time I saw Maris," a commentary upon a baseball hero. The court opinion read:

> We believe in any event that the parody lyrics involved in this appeal would be permissible under the most rigorous application of the "substantiality" requirement. The disparities in theme, content and style between the original lyrics and the alleged infringements could hardly be greater.[31]

Television

The "substantiality" criterion has also been applied to television. In 1953 NBC broadcast over its national television network a 20-minute skit entitled "From Here to Obscurity." The skit was designed as a burlesque of Columbia Picture's movie *From Here to Eternity.* There were several similarities between the film and the skit—locale, characters, and some details. Columbia Pictures initiated court action. The court noted that the use of the original work was permissible and did not constitute the taking of a substantial portion. The use of material from the motion picture

> was of only sufficient material to cause the viewer of the burlesque to recall and conjure up the motion picture, or the novel "From Here to Eternity" upon which said motion picture was based, and thus provide the necessary element of burlesque."[32]

The court concluded that since a burlesque had to use the original to conjure up the subject matter being burlesqued, the law allowed more extensive utilization of the "protectible portion of a copyrighted work in the creation of a burlesque of that work than in the creation of other fictional or dramatic works not intended as a burlesque of the original."

A similar case, *Benny,* involved Jack Benny's burlesque of Metro-Goldwyn-Mayer's film *Gas Light.* In 1945, after obtaining consent, Benny presented a 15-minute parody of *Gas Light* over a national radio network. Six years later, CBS produced a television show burlesquing *Gas Light*, with Jack Benny in the leading role. Neither Benny nor CBS had obtained permission for the telecast. In *Benny* the court of appeals found that a substantial part of the film had been copied; that

> a "parodized or burlesque" taking is to be treated no differently from any other appropriation; that is, as in all other cases of alleged taking, the issue becomes first one of fact, i.e., what was taken and how substantial was the taking; and if it is determined that there was a substantial taking, infringement exists.[33]

In *Benny* the decision granted to burlesque less protection than that allowed in *Columbia Pictures.* In 1958, in a *per curiam,* this judgment was affirmed by a divided Supreme Court.

Access

In some cases, including *MacDonald, Doran,* and *Sid & Marty Krofft Television,* a major issue was access—whether the defendant had an opportunity to copy the work. An analysis of these cases provides insight into the nature of the access criterion. In *MacDonald* the court determined that Daphne Du Maurier, in writing *Rebecca,* did not have access to either of two works written by Edwina MacDonald.

> The circumstances do not inevitably lead to the conclusion of access. . . . The denial of access made by the defendant, her proven reputation as a writer, and a reading of the three stories, have convinced me that she never saw or heard of "I Planned to Murder My Husband" or "Blind Windows" prior to the writing or publication of "Rebecca."[34]

In *Doran* the court found that the defendant had access to the plaintiff's Santa Claus plastic figure, had copied it, and thereby committed copyright infringement. The court also explained a function of the access criterion: "Infringer's access to copyrighted article is but a means of eliminating coincidence or independent effort as an explanation for likeness between copyrighted articles and infringing articles."[35] The *Sid & Marty Krofft Television* case involved McDonald Corporation commercials, which copied the H. R. PufnStuf series. The court discussed the relationship of the access criterion to copying and substantiality.

> No amount of proof of access will suffice to show copying if there are no similarities. This is not to say, however, that where clear and convincing evidence of access is presented, the quantum of proof required to show substantial similarity may not be lower than when access is shown merely by a preponderance of the evidence.[36]

The court, in finding for the plaintiff, emphasized that a high "degree of access justifies a lower standard of proof to show substantial similarity."

Damages

The 1976 Copyright Act sets the basic damages for copyright infringement to include (1) an injunction to curtail the infringing activity, (2) recovery of actual damages, (3) recovery of the infringer's profits, (4) awarding of statutory damages, and (5) recovery of attorney's fees in the court action. The nature and amount of the damages were a major issue in the *Sheldon* case.

When Metro-Goldwyn made the motion picture *Letty Lynton*, it copied Edward Sheldon's play "Dishonored Lady," in the manner of "deliberate plagiarism." Sheldon charged copyright infringement and was awarded all the profits, which amounted to $587,604.37. Metro-Goldwyn appealed, arguing that Sheldon's share of the profits should be one-fifth. If Sheldon received all the profits, he would get the benefit that stars, directors, and technicians brought to the film. The Supreme Court agreed. The Court found no justification for making "an award of profits which have been shown not to be due to the infringement. That would be not to do equity but to inflict unauthorized penalty." The Court concluded that an

> apportionment of profits can be had where it is clear that all the profits are not due to the use of the copyrighted material, and the evidence is sufficient to provide a fair basis of division so as to give to the copyright proprietor all the profits that can be deemed to have resulted from the use of what belonged to him.[37]

The Court noted that the profits from a motion picture are derived primarily from the talent and popularity of the "motion picture stars." In *Sheldon*, "the portion of the profits attributable to the use of the copyrighted play...was very small." An apportionment of 20 percent was fair.

Summary

The tests of copyright infringement are originality, copying, substantiality, and access. *Bleistein, Jewelers' Circular, Triangle, Amsterdam, Donald,* and *Lipman* affirm that originality is the fundamental requirement of copyrightable material. In *INS, Chicago Record-Herald, Wainwright, Reyher, Musto, Alexander, Hoehling,* and *Franklin Mint,* the courts decided that while ideas cannot be copyrighted, the style and manner of expression can be protected. To copy an author's style or manner is an infringement. In several cases—*Holt, College Entrance Book Company, Toksvig, Eisenschiml, Heim, Berlin, Columbia Pictures,* and *Benny*—the courts applied the substantiality criterion to evaluate alleged copyright infringement claims. Access has been an important criterion in some cases—*MacDonald, Doran,* and *Sid & Marty Krofft Television,* to name a few.

Plaintiffs in a copyright action can seek payment for damages they have suffered, plus any profits made by the infringer for pirating the protected work. In *Sheldon* the Supreme Court emphasized that any award of damages should be directly related to the act of infringement. Specific damages are explicated in the 1976 Copyright Act.

GUIDELINES FOR FAIR USE

Fair use of a copyrighted work is not an infringement. According to the 1976 Copyright Act, determining fair use involves consideration of (1) the purpose and character of the use, (2) the nature of the copyrighted work, (3) the amount used, (4) the effect of the use upon the value of the copyrighted work. The 1976 Copyright Act represents the first formal legislative statement of the fair-use doctrine.

A 1968 court case, however—*Geis*—provides an early judicial statement regarding fair use, based on the above criteria. When President John F. Kennedy was killed, Abraham Zapruder was at the scene filming the event. His film, the most important photographic evidence concerning the fatal shots, was purchased and eventually appeared in several issues of *Life*. When Josiah Thompson wrote *Six Seconds in Dallas,* a book that analyzed the assassination, he included copies of parts of Zapruder's film. *Life* had refused an offer by Bernard Geis Associates, Thompson's publisher, to pay a royalty equal to the entire profits from publication of the book in return for permission to use the film. *Life* sued, charging that certain frames of the Zapruder film were "stolen surreptitiously" by Thompson. The district court was impressed by the offer Geis Associates had made to pay all its profits for permission to use the film. Yet, Thompson was guilty of copyright infringement unless the copying was a "fair use." The court noted the criteria for determining fair use contained in legislation before Congress and found that the balance was in favor of Thompson. There was public interest in having the fullest information available about the Kennedy assassination. Thompson engaged in serious work and had a theory entitled to public consideration. While the theory could be explained with sketches, an explanation with photographic copies was easier to understand. The court stressed that Thompson's book was not purchased because it contained the Zapruder pictures; it was purchased because of Thompson's theory, illustrated by Zapruder's pictures. Also, there seemed to be little injury to *Life*. This was a case of fair use.[38] The four criteria applied by the court in *Geis* became the guidelines for fair use that were set forth in the 1976 Copyright Law.

Several questions relating to fair use have never been answered definitively by either legislative or judicial bodies. On numerous occasions the courts have offered circumstantial or partial answers. Some of those questions are considered in this section.

Scholarly versus Commercial Gain

Generally, the courts have tended to be more lenient toward copying that occurred in scholarly works than toward the use of copyrighted materials for commercial gain.

In 1917 the Supreme Court heard companion cases in which copyrighted musical compositions were performed in restaurants. In the first case, Victor Herbert's "Sweethearts" was performed by musicians who were employed to play at mealtimes. In the second case, John Church's "From Maine to Georgia" was performed in order to entertain guests during their meals. In both cases, the restaurant owners claimed that they had not violated copyright because no profit came from the music that was played to provide atmosphere in the restaurant. The Supreme Court noted that "if the rights under the copyright are infringed only by a performance where money is taken at the door, they are very imperfectly protected." The restaurants benefited financially by playing the music; it provided "a luxurious pleasure not to be had from eating a silent meal." According to the Court: "If music did not pay, it would be given up. If it pays it pays out of the public's pocket. Whether it pays or not, the purpose of employing it is profit, and that is enough."[39] In *Herbert* and *John Church Company* the Court was unsympathetic to the restaurants—the use constituted a copyright infringement.

In the 1950 *Thompson* case, the district court indicated that copying for scholarly purposes is entitled to lenient fair-use guidelines. The case involved an infringement suit initiated by psychiatrist Clara Thompson, author of an article entitled "Changing Concepts of Homosexuality in Psychoanalysis." The article appeared in *Psychiatry* magazine. Thompson sued Hugo Gernback, who published *Sexology,* a magazine advertised as a "Sex Science Magazine-Illustrated." The court noted that the doctrine of fair use "permits a writer of scientific, legal, medical and similar books or articles of learning to use even the identical words of earlier books or writings dealing with the same subject matter.''[40] In this case, however, the court found that Gernback's magazine did not qualify ''as a work of science'' and decided for Thompson. The decision recognized less restrictive guidelines for fair use where scholarly works are involved.

In the 1966 *Rosemont* case, the court of appeals blurred the relationship between scholarly purpose and commercial gain. The case involved Howard Hughes, the famous recluse who desired to remain out of the public eye. In 1954 *Look* published a series, ''The Howard Hughes Story,'' and in 1962 Random House published *Howard Hughes—A Biography by John Keats.* In 1965 Rosemont Enterprises, a Hughes-owned company, purchased the copyright to the *Look* articles. Rosemont then started a copyright infringement suit against Random House, claiming that Keats copied and paraphrased several sentences from the *Look* articles. The court, per Judge Leonard Moore, made two points. First, there was ''considerable doubt as to whether the copied and paraphrased matter constitutes a material and substantial portion of those articles.'' Second, Moore rejected any dichotomy based on whether the use was commerical or scholarly. Such a consideration was ''irrelevant to a determination of whether a particular use of copyrighted materials in a work which offers some benefit to the public constitutes a fair use.''[41] The public was entitled to learn about the life of an extraordinary man. It contradicted the public interest to allow anybody ''to buy up the copyright ownership to restrain others from publishing biographical material concerning him.'' In *Rosemont* the court decided that John Keat's biography of Howard Hughes was an instance of fair use.

In 1978, in *Meeropol,* the court of appeals invoked the scholarly-use standard. The case involved Louis Nizer's book *The Implosion Conspiracy,* an account of the events surrounding the trial of Julius and Ethel Rosenberg, spies who were convicted and executed for conspiring to give national defense secrets to the Soviet Union. Michael and Robert Meeropol, sons of the Rosenbergs, alleged that Nizer incorporated in his book substantial portions of copyrighted letters written by the Rosenbergs. The trial court accepted Nizer's claim of fair use. On appeal, however, the court remanded the case and set forth the following standard for assessing fair use.

> For a determination whether the fair use defense is applicable on the facts of this case . . . it is relevant whether or not the Rosenberg letters were used primarily for scholarly, historical reasons, or predominantly for commercial exploitation.[42]

Though the *Rosemont* case questioned the doctrine of preferred treatment for scholarly use, the *Herbert, Thompson,* and *Meeropol* cases are more representative judicial opinions. The courts have been more lenient about copying for scholarly use than for commercial gain.

Characters

In two cases—*Warner Brothers* and *Walt Disney*—the courts considered whether a writer's characters are copyrightable and whether the characters pass with the transfer of a copyright. These cases suggest that the use of another writer's characters is quite restricted.

In 1930 Dashiell Hammett sold certain defined rights to his detective story, *The Maltese Falcon,* to Warner Brothers Pictures. When Hammett continued to use one of his characters, Sam Spade, in other stories, Warner Brothers claimed infringement of copyright and initiated court action. The court concluded that even if Hammett sold the copyright to Warner Brothers, the transfer did not prevent Hammett "from using the characters...in other stories. The characters were vehicles for the story told, and the vehicles did not go with the sale of the story." Furthermore, the court found that since the use of character names was not mentioned in the agreements, "the character rights with the names cannot be held to be within the grants."[43] In *Warner Brothers* the court of appeals concluded that Hammett retained the right to use his characters.

In 1972 the district court heard another case involving copyright protection for characters. Walt Disney Productions held copyrights for several animal cartoon characters. Another company, The Air Pirates, published cartoon magazines with characters that looked similar to and used the same names as those created by Disney. The theme and plot of the publications, however, differed markedly from Disney's cartoons. Nonetheless, Walt Disney Productions claimed infringement of copyright. In court, Air Pirates admitted that Disney's copyright covered the stories. It cited *Warner Brothers,* however, in which the court ruled that "the characters were vehicles for the story told, and the vehicles did not go with the sale of the story." In the light of this decision, characters did not fall within copyright protection. The court analyzed *Warner Brothers* and concluded that in Disney's works the characters tended to constitute the story.

> The facial expressions, position and movement represented may convey far more than the words set out as dialogue in the "balloon" hovering over the character's head, or the explanatory material appended. It is not simply one particular drawing, in one isolated cartoon "panel" for which the plaintiff seeks protection, but rather it is the common features of all of the drawings of that character appearing in the copyrighted work.[44]

The main appeal of Disney's cartoons was to children, primarily through the use of "the characters and nothing else." Disney's characters were copyrightable, and Air Pirates had infringed on the copyright. By the way, the decisions in *Warner Brothers* and *Walt Disney* are consistent—a character that constitutes the story being told is entitled to copyright protection. Under such conditions, use of another writer's characters is restricted indeed.

Musical Composition

In 1978 the courts heard arguments regarding alleged copyright infringement of a musical composition. Italian Book Corporation brought action against ABC for infringement of a song titled "Dova sta Zaza." The alleged infringement occurred when an ABC television crew, covering the annual San Gennaro Festival in the Little Italy section of Manhattan, filmed portions of a band playing music and then played the strip on the evening news. ABC argued fair use. The court applied the guidelines for fair use:

> The use which defendant made of the song in question is not competitive with the commercial use plaintiff seeks to make of the song. No loss of profit or lessening of the song's value as the result of defendant's use was demonstrated; on the contrary, plaintiff has stipulated that the use complained of "did not result in any actual damage to the plaintiff, or to the market for said work."[45]

In *Italian Book Corporation* the court sustained the fair-use defense.

Speeches

During 1955 to 1958, Vice-Admiral Hyman Rickover delivered several public addresses on a variety of subjects. For most of them, he distributed advance copies to the press and sent copies to people who requested them. In 1958 Rickover began to compile texts of his speeches for publication. From that point on, he obtained copyright protection for his speeches. At the same time, a publisher asked Rickover for permission to publish some of his past speeches. Rickover refused. The publisher brought suit, seeking declaration that Rickover's previous speeches were in "the public domain." The court sided with the publisher for two reasons. First, Rickover had forfeited protection by distributing the speeches without copyright—an act that equals publication. Second, the use of government equipment and materials made the speeches uncopyrightable "government publications." The U.S. Supreme Court vacated this judgment on a technical ground and returned the case to the lower court.[46] No further proceedings were held, however, probably because the district court was deciding the *King* case.

On August 28, 1963, Dr. Martin Luther King delivered a speech in which he repeatedly used the phrase "I have a dream," during a march for civil rights in Washington, D.C. Prior to delivery, King presented copies of the speech to the press. King did not want the speech to be distributed to the public; he specifically limited it to members of the press who were covering the march. King's speech impressed the crowd and subsequently received wide coverage by the press. Shortly thereafter, Mister Maestro Company, without King's consent, prepared and sold a record entitled "The March on Washington." The record contained King's "I Have A Dream" speech. At about the same time, a record of some of King's speeches, including an abbreviated version of "I Have A Dream," was sold with King's consent by Motown Record Company. Subsequently, King charged the Mister Maestro Company with violation of his copyright. Mister Maestro argued that King's speech had been published. The court decided that King's delivering the speech did not constitute a general publication so as to place it in the public domain.

> The word "general" with respect to publication in this sense is of greatest significance. There can be a limited publication, which is a communication of the work to others under circumstances showing no dedication of the work to the public. A general publication is one which shows a dedication to the public so as to lose copyright.[47]

The delivery of this speech, no matter how vast the audience, did not amount to general publication. The court then compared *King* with *Rickover*. Rickover made a general distribution, not only to the press, but also to members of the public. King made his speech available only to the press. The court banned further use of King's speech without his permission.

Unpublished Presidential Memoirs

In 1977, former President Gerald Ford granted Harper and Row Publishers the exclusive first right to publish his memoirs. Shortly before the scheduled release of the work, *The Nation* obtained a copy of the memoirs and published an article that contained at least 300 words taken verbatim from the manuscript. Harper and Row introduced a suit, alleging violation of the Copyright Act. *The Nation* argued that the article constituted "fair use" under Section 107 because the article was published for purpose of commentary and news reporting. The U.S. Supreme Court, per Justice Sandra Day O'Connor, determined that the article violated the Copyright Law. According to O'Connor, "under ordinary circumstances, the author's right to control the first public appearance of his undisseminated expression will outweigh a claim of fair use." Furthermore, "the fact that the publication was commercial as opposed to nonprofit is a separate factor tending to weigh against a finding of fair use."

> *The Nation's* unauthorized use of the undisseminated manuscript had not merely the incidental effect but the intended purpose of supplanting the copyright holder's commercially valuable right of first publication. While there may be a greater need to disseminate works of fact than works of fiction, *The Nation's* taking of copyrighted expression exceeded that necessary to disseminate the facts and infringed the copyright holder's interests in confidentiality and creative control over the first public appearance of the work.[48]

In *Harper and Row*, the copying of unpublished presidential memoirs was not recognized as a "fair use."

Cable Television

Fortnightly Corporation operated a cable television service in the area around Clarksburg and Fairmont, West Virginia. There were two local television stations in the vicinity, but because of hilly terrain most residents could not receive the broadcasts of any additional stations through ordinary rooftop antennae. Fortnightly's system provided customers with signals from five television stations, ranging in distance from 52 to 82 miles away. United Artists held copyrights on some motion pictures that were shown on the five television stations carried by Fortnightly. United sued Fortnightly for copyright infringement, arguing that Fortnightly's cable system infringed United's exclusive right to "perform...in public for profit." Fortnightly maintained that the cable television system did not "perform" the copyrighted works. The Supreme Court, per Justice Potter Stewart, agreed.

> Essentially, a CATV system no more than enhances the viewer's capacity to receive the broadcaster's signals; it provides a well-located antenna with an efficient connection to the viewer's television set.... If an individual erected an antenna on a hill, strung a cable to his house, and installed the necessary amplifying equipment, he would not be "performing" the programs he received on his television set. The result would be no different if several people combined to erect a cooperative antenna for the same purpose. The only difference in the case of CATV is that the antenna system is erected and owned not by its users but by an entrepreneur.[49]

On the basis of this reasoning, the Court sided with Fortnightly.

Six years later the Supreme Court heard a related case. It involved a CBS copyright-infringement action against Teleprompter Corporation. The lower court distinguished between two functions of cable systems, and then compared *Fortnightly* with *Teleprompter*.

> CATV systems perform either or both of two functions. First, they may supplement broadcasting by facilitating satisfactory reception of local stations in adjacent areas in which such reception would not otherwise be possible; and second, they may transmit to subscribers the signals of distant stations entirely beyond the range of local antennae.

According to the lower court, Fortnightly performed the first function; it brought television signals to viewers who could not otherwise receive them. The signals were already in the community, but because of topographical conditions, residents could not receive the signals by usual methods. The court also noted that Teleprompter performed the second function, distributing signals beyond the range of local antennae. The system did not merely enhance the customers' chances of receiving signals that were in the area; it brought new signals into the area. Accordingly, the Teleprompter system violated copyright law. The Supreme Court, however, disagreed with the lower court. Importation of distant programs did not constitute a "performance" under the Copyright Act.

> Importation of "distant signals" from one community into another does not constitute a "performance" under the Copyright Act; thus, a community antenna television system does not lose its status as a nonbroadcaster and thus a non "performer" for copyright purposes when the signals it carries are those from distant rather than local sources.[50]

Such activity was "essentially a viewer function, irrespective of the distance between the broadcasting station and the ultimate viewer." Teleprompter, like Fortnightly, had not violated copyright protection.

Radio

One year later the question of what constitutes a "performance" reached the Supreme Court again, this time in relation to the radio medium. George Aiken, owner of a small, fast-service, food shop, which caters to "carry-out" customers who are in the restaurant for less than five minutes, had various radio stations turned on so that musical selections could be enjoyed by his employees and customers. A copyright-infringement suit was initiated by Twentieth Century Music Corporation. The complaint alleged that the radio reception in Aiken's restaurant infringed the composers' exclusive rights to "perform" their copyrighted works in public for profit. The Supreme Court cited *Fortnightly* and *Teleprompter* in noting that if, in those cable television cases, such sophisticated technological facilities "were not performing, then logic dictates that no 'performance' resulted when . . . [Aiken] merely activated his restaurant radio." The Court pointed to the impracticality of enforcement.

> The practical unenforceability of a ruling that all of those in Aiken's position are copyright infringers is self-evident. One has only to consider the countless business establishments in this country with radio or television sets on their premises—bars, beauty shops, cafeterias, car washes, dentists' offices, and drive-ins—to realize the total futility of any evenhanded effort on the part of copyright holders to license even a substantial percentage of them.[51]

The opinion of Justice Stewart concluded that a finding of infringement in this case would be inequitable for two reasons. First, a person like Aiken could guarantee freedom from liability only by keeping his radio turned off. Second, to hold that a person like Aiken "performed" these musical compositions would "authorize the sale of an untold number of licenses for what is basically a single public rendition of a copyrighted work." In *Aiken* Justice Stewart held that such a policy "would go far beyond what is required for the economic protection of copyright owners."

Sound Recordings

In 1972 Congress amended the federal copyright law to provide protection against unauthorized duplication of sound recordings. Prior to this legislation, a sound recording was presumed to fall into the public domain as soon as it was published.

In 1973 the Supreme Court heard *Goldstein,* a case that challenged the constitutionality of a state ban on sound-recording duplication. This case was initiated prior to, but decided after, the 1972 congressional amendment. The State of California charged Goldstein with violating the portion of the California Penal Code that bans "record piracy" or "tape piracy"—the unauthorized duplication of sound recordings of performances by major musical artists. Goldstein had duplicated tapes of popular musical performances and then sold the copies to the public in competition with the original tapes. Goldstein argued that the California law was unconstitutional, because it prohibited the copying of works that were not entitled to federal protection. The Supreme Court disagreed.

> The Constitution neither explicitly precludes the States from granting copyrights nor grants such authority exclusively to the Federal Government. The subject matter to which the Copyright Clause is addressed may at times be of purely local concern. No conflict will necessarily arise from a lack of uniform state regulation, nor will the interest of one State be significantly prejudiced by the actions of another. No reason exists why Congress must take affirmative action either to authorize protection of all categories of writings or to free them from all restraint. We therefore conclude that, under the Constitution, the States have not relinquished all power to grant to authors "the exclusive Right to their respective Writings."[52]

In *Goldstein* the Court upheld the California statute; California had "exercised a power which it retained under the Constitution." A few years later, Congress included national protection for sound recordings in the 1976 Copyright Act.

Photocopying

During the twentieth century, technology placed great strains on the Copyright Act of 1909. One such strain involved photocopy machines, which by 1970, were commonly used in almost every library. About this time, the National Institute of Health and the National Library of Medicine decided to provide photocopies of articles from medical and scientific periodicals, free of charge, to medical and scientific researchers. The Williams & Wilkins Company, publisher of several medical journals, initiated court action for copyright infringement. The suit complained of illegal massive photocopying. The lower court found that the "wholesale copying" was not a fair use, because the photocopies were exact duplicates of the originals, they served as substitutes for the originals, and they diminished the publisher's economic gain. The court of claims reversed, noting that the belief that copying an entire work could never be a "fair use" was "an overbroad generalization, unsupported by the decisions and rejected by years of accepted practice." The court suggested three reasons why photocopying did not constitute infringement. First, the William & Wilkins Company had not shown that it was harmed economically. On the other hand, the libraries were nonprofit institutions. Second, medical research would be injured by holding these practices to be an infringement. Scientists would not use the articles needed in their work. Third, the problem called for legislative guidance and the court should not, during the period when congressional action was forthcoming, impose upon science and medicine a risk of harm. The court stressed that no question of "vending" arose; the purpose of the copying was "scientific progress, untainted by any commercial gain." In 1975, in *Williams & Wilkins,* an equally divided Supreme Court, without opinion, affirmed the findings of the court of claims.[53]

Section 108 of the 1976 Copyright Act provided some clarity to the photocopy issue. Under the law, a library may reproduce and distribute a copy of specified types of works without the permission of the copyright owner. Under certain conditions, a library may copy an entire work. The law did not, however, approve of mass photocopying, and the rights provided in Section 108 apply only to copies prepared "without any purpose of direct or indirect commercial advantage."

Videotaping

Encyclopedia Brittanica brought suit against the Board of Cooperative Educational Services, a nonprofit corporation that provides educational services to public schools in Erie County, New York. The complaint alleged that the board videotaped several films and television programs and distributed copies to the school districts. Records indicated that the volume of copying was substantial. For example, the board duplicated approximately 10,000 tapes during a single year. It admitted that it videotaped copyrighted films without paying fees or obtaining permission. The board justified the action in terms of the fair-use doctrine, claiming that noncommercial videotaping of programs for classroom viewing was not a copyright infringement. The district court admitted that the problem of accommodating the competing interests of educators and film producers raised questions, which the legislature was better equipped to resolve than the judiciary. Congress, however, had left the issue to the courts. Accordingly, the judges found the board's activities difficult to reconcile with its claim of fair use. This case does not involve an isolated instance of a teacher copying copyrighted material for classroom use but concerns a highly organized and systematic program for reproducing video-tapes on a massive scale.[54]

In *Encyclopedia Brittanica* the court directed the board to stop videotaping educational films or television programs off the public airwaves.

In 1984 the Supreme Court heard a case involving alleged copyright infringement by the manufacturer of home videotape recorders. The case involved Sony Corporation, which manufactures videotape recorders, and Universal City Studios, which owned copyrights on several television programs aired on commercial networks. Universal Studios maintained that VTR owners had recorded copyrighted works, and that Sony contributed to copyright infringement by marketing the VTRs. Universal sought money damages, an accounting of profits, and an injunction against the manufacture and marketing of videotape recorders. When the case reached the Supreme Court, Justice John Stevens, writing for the majority, held that Sony's sale of VTRs to the general public did not constitute contributory infringement of Universal's copyright. The Court based its decision on two principal reasons. First, Sony did not control the use of the copyrighted works.

> Here, the only contact between petitioners and the users of the VTRs occurred at the moment of sale. And there is no precedent for imposing vicarious liability on the theory that petitioner sold the VTRs with constructive knowledge that their customers might use the equipment to make unauthorized copies of copyrighted material. The sale of copying equipment, like the sale of other articles of commerce, does not constitute contributory infringement if the product is widely used for legitimate, unobjectionable purposes, or, indeed, is merely capable of substantial noninfringing uses.[55]

Second, VTRs are put to numerous noninfringing uses, including time shifting of programs by private viewers. In *Sony* the Court, in a five-to-four decision, recognized that "even the unauthorized home time shifting of ...programs is legitimate fair use." Justice Stevens urged Congress to "take a fresh look at this new technology," however, in order to revise the law to compensate television producers and performers for any losses resulting from videotaping. To date, such a congressional effort has not been undertaken.

Summary

The 1976 Copyright Act stipulates that fair use of a copyrighted work is not infringement. The act notes that the determination of fair use concerns the purpose and character of the use, the nature of the copyrighted work, the amount used, and the effect of the use on the value of the work.

In several cases cited in this section, the courts have applied these guidelines to uses involving characters, musical compositions, speeches, cable television, radio, sound recordings, photocopying, and videotaping. In most of these cases, as exemplified by *Geis, Herbert, Thompson, Meeropol,* and *Williams & Wilkins,* the courts have been more tolerant of copyrighting for scholarly use than copying for economic profit. In addition, in such cases as *Fortnightly, Teleprompter, Aiken,* and *Sony,* the Supreme Court cautioned against a policy that would award too much economic protection for copyright owners.

NOTES

1. *Carey v. Longman,* 102 Eng. Rep. 138 (K.B. 1801).

2. *Pushman v. New York Graphic Society, Inc.,* 287 N.Y. 302 (1942).

3. *Chamberlain v. Feldman,* 300 N.Y. 135 (1949).

4. *Estate of Hemingway v. Random House,* 23 N.Y. 2d 341 (1968).

5. *Holmes v. Hurst,* 19 S.Ct. 606 (1899).

6. *Mifflin v. White,* 23 S.Ct. 769 (1903).

7. *Mifflin v. Dutton,* 23 S.Ct. 771 (1903).

8. *Wrench v. Universal Pictures Company, Inc.,* 104 F. Supp. 374 (1952).

9. *Washingtonian Publishing Company, Inc. v. Pearson,* 59 S.Ct. 397 (1939).

10. *Emerson v. Davies,* 8 Fed. Cas. 615 (1845).

11. *Bleistein v. Donaldson Lithographing Company,* 23 S.Ct. 298 (1903).

12. *Jewelers' Circular Publishing Company v. Keystone Publishing Company,* 281 F. 83 (1922).

13. *Triangle Publications, Inc. v. New England Newspaper Publishing Company,* 46 F. Supp. 198 (1942).

14. *Amsterdam v. Triangle Publications, Inc.,* 189 F. 2d 104 (1951).

15. *Donald v. Zack Meyer's T.V. Sales and Service,* 426 F. 2d 1027 (1970).

16. *Lipman v. Commonwealth of Massachusetts,* 475 F. 2d 565 (1973).

17. *International News Service v. Associated Press,* 39 S.Ct. 68 (1918).

18. *Chicago Record-Herald v. Tribune Association,* 275 F. 797 (1921).

19. *Wainwright Securities, Inc. v. Wall Street Transcript Corporation,* 558 F. 2d 91 (1977); cert. denied 98 S.Ct. 730 (1978).

20. *Reyher v. Children's Television Workshop,* 533 F. 2d 87 (1976); cert. denied 97 S.Ct. 492 (1976).

21. *Musto v. Meyer,* 434 F. Supp. 32 (1977).

22. *Alexander v. Haley,* 460 F. Supp. 40 (1978).

23. *Hoehling v. Universal City Studios, Inc.,* 618 F. 2d 972 (1980); cert. denied 101 S.Ct. 121 (1980).

24. *Franklin Mint Corporation v. National Wildlife Art Exchange, Inc.,* 575 F. 2d 62 (1978).

25. *West Publishing Company v. Edward Thompson Company,* 169 F. 833 (1909).

26. *Henry Holt & Company, Inc. v. Liggett & Meyers Tobacco Company,* 23 F. Supp. 302 (1938).

27. *College Entrance Book Company, Inc. v. Amsco Book Company, Inc.,* 119 F. 2d 874 (1941).

28. *Toksvig v. Bruce Publishing Company,* 181 F. 2d 664 (1950).

29. *Eisenschiml v. Fawcett Publications,* 246 F. 2d 598 (1957).

30. *Heim v. Universal Pictures Company,* 154 F. 2d 480 (1946).

31. *Berlin v. E.C. Publications, Inc.,* 329 F. 2d 541 (1964); cert. denied 85 S.Ct. 46 (1964).

32. *Columbia Pictures Corporation v. National Broadcasting Company,* 137 F. Supp. 348 (1955).

33. *Benny v. Loew's Incorporated*, 239 F. 2d 532 (1956); *Columbia Broadcasting System, Inc. v. Loew's Incorporated*, 78 S.Ct. 770 (1958).

34. *MacDonald v. DuMaurier*, 75 F. Supp. 655 (1948).

35. *Doran v. Sunset House Distributing Corp.*, 197 F. Supp. 940 (1961).

36. *Sid & Marty Krofft Television v. McDonald's Corporation*, 562 F. 2d 1157 (1977).

37. *Sheldon v. Metro-Goldwyn Pictures Corporation*, 60 S.Ct. 681 (1940).

38. *Time Inc. v. Bernard Geis Associates*, 293 F. Supp. 130 (1968).

39. *Herbert v. Shanley Company; John Church Company v. Hilliard Hotel Company*, 37 S.Ct. 232 (1917).

40. *Thompson v. Gernsback*, 94 F. Supp. 453 (1950).

41. *Rosemont Enterprises, Inc. v. Random House, Inc.*, 366 F. 2d 303 (1966).

42. *Meeropol v. Nizer*, 560 F. 2d 1061 (1977); cert. denied 98 S.Ct. 727 (1978).

43. *Warner Brothers Pictures, Inc. v. Columbia Broadcasting System, Inc.*, 216 F. 2d 945 (1954).

44. *Walt Disney Productions v. The Air Pirates*, 345 F. Supp. 108 (1972).

45. *Italian Book Corporation v. American Broadcasting Companies*, 458 F. Supp. 65 (1978).

46. *Public Affairs Associates, Inc. v. Rickover*, 82 S.Ct. 580 (1962).

47. *King v. Mister Maestro, Inc.*, 224 F. Supp. 101 (1963).

48. *Harper & Row Publishers v. Nation Enterprises*, 105 S.Ct. 2218 (1985).

49. *Fortnightly Corporation v. United Artists Television, Inc.*, 88 S.Ct. 2084 (1968).

50. *Teleprompter Corporation v. Columbia Broadcasting System, Inc.*, 94 S.Ct. 1129 (1974).

51. *Twentieth Century Music Corporation v. Aiken*, 95 S.Ct. 2040 (1975).

52. *Goldstein v. California*, 93 S.Ct. 2303 (1973).

53. *Williams & Wilkins Company v. United States*, 487 F. 2d 1345 (1973); 95 S.Ct. 1344 (1975).

54. *Encyclopedia Brittanica v. Crooks*, 447 F. Supp. 243 (1978).

55. *Sony Corporation of America v. Universal City Studios*, 104 S.Ct. 774 (1984).

RECOMMENDED READING

Brittin, Michael D., "Constitutional Fair Use," *Copyright Law Symposium* 28 (1982), 141-88.

Conine, Cary B., "Copyright: Unfair Use in Fair Competition—A Search For a Logical Rationale for the Protection of Investigative News Reporting," *Oklahoma Law Review* 30 (Winter, 1977), 214-38.

Dannay, Richard, "An Overview of *Teleprompter v. CBS* and other Recent Developments—Ominous Signals For Copyright Law," *Bulletin of the Copyright Society of the U.S.A.* 22 (October, 1974), 10-18.

Goldwag, Celia, "Copyright Infringement and the First Amendment," *Columbia Law Review* 79 (March, 1979), 320-40.

Jacobson, Jeffrey E., "Fair Use: Considerations in Written Works," *Communications and the Law* 2 (Fall, 1980), 17-38.

Johnston, Donald F., *Copyright Handbook*. New York: R. R. Bowker, 1978.

Patterson, Lyman R., "Private Copyright and Public Communication: Free Speech Endangered," *Vanderbilt Law Review* 28 (November, 1975), 1161-1211.

"Photocopying and Fair Use: An Examination of the Economic Factor in Fair Use," *Emory Law Journal* 26 (Fall, 1977), 849-84.

KEY DECISIONS

1918—*INTERNATIONAL NEWS SERVICE*—held that while facts cannot be copyrighted, the style and manner in which the facts are presented can be protected.

1940—*SHELDON*—stressed that any award of damages should be directly related to the act of infringement.

1968—*FORTNIGHTLY*—maintained that a cable television system does not "perform" copyrighted works.

1974—*TELEPROMPTER*—held that importation of distant signals did not constitute a "performance" under copyright law.

1975—*AIKEN*—cautioned against awarding too much economic protection for copyright owners.

1984—*SONY*—held that copyright law does not forbid the videotape recording of television programs for personal use.

SUMMARY—COPYRIGHT LAW

Definition

Copyright law enables an author to protect his or her work against plagiarism. To secure a copyright, an author should place a proper notice in a prominent place in the work.

Proof

Tests of copyright infringement include:
1. Originality—is the copied material the original work of the plaintiff?
2. Copying—did defendant copy plaintiff's work?
3. Substantiality—did defendant appropriate a sufficient amount of plaintiff's work?
4. Access—did defendant have the opportunity to copy the work?

Damages

The 1976 Copyright Act set damages at not less than $250 and not more than $10,000. If, however, an infringement is committed willfully, the amount can be as much as $50,000. Also, if the infringer is unaware that the act was an infringement, the fine can be as low as $100.

Defenses

1. Originality—defendant has a solid defense with a showing of originality in the work.
2. Fair Use—courts have allowed acts of copying that constitute "fair use." The criteria for determining fair use are the following:
   a. Purpose and character of the use, including whether such use is of a commercial nature or is for nonprofit educational purposes
   b Nature of the copyrighted work
   c. Amount and substantiality of the portion used in relation to the copyrighted work as a whole
   d. Effect of the use upon the potential market for or value of the copyrighted work.
3. Public Domain—copying is allowable if the material is already in the public domain.

10

NEWS

In 1643, in England, Parliament enacted a law that required licensing of the press. All printed material had to be registered with the Stationers' Company prior to publication; no printed material could be published without a license. The company had the power to search for unlicensed presses and to seize publications that violated the law. In this way, all printing was centralized in London under the direct control of the government. John Milton protested against this system in *Areopagitica*,[1] a pamphlet that defended freedom of the press. In Milton's view, truth was more likely to emerge from free discussion than from repression. Milton's work marked the beginning of the "marketplace of ideas" theory—the notion that in a free and open encounter of ideas, truth will win out against falsehood. While Milton pleaded for freedom of expression, others defied the law by actually publishing their materials without the required license. Many were brought before the courts of the Star Chamber and the High Commission, where illegal printers were sentenced to mutilation, life imprisonment, or hanging. In 1695 the licensing system in England was terminated.

Censorship took a different form in the American colonies. Prosecution for libel replaced licensing as the method through which government restrained the press. The most memorable case involved John Peter Zenger, editor of the *New York Weekly Journal*. Politicians frequently used Zenger's paper to criticize William Cosby, the colonial governor of New York. In 1734 Zenger was charged with publishing seditious libels and jailed for eight months prior to trial. When Zenger finally came to trial, the jury ignored the judge's instructions and decided that Zenger was not guilty. Winning this case was a significant achievement for Zenger's attorney, Andrew Hamilton, because under the common law truth was an irrelevant defense. The judge, not the jury, determined whether the publication had in fact printed seditious libel. The jury simply ascertained whether the defendant had published the material. During Zenger's trial, Hamilton asked the

jury to recognize truth as a defense and urged the jury to decide both issues—
the libelousness of the words and the fact of the printing. The Zenger verdict
marked a tremendous achievement for free expression in the American colonies.

The Sedition Act, which Congress passed in 1798, permitted truth as a defense, required proof of malice, and allowed the jury to pass on questions of both
law and fact. The act established as a misdemeanor the publishing of any false
or scandalous writings designed to bring the government into disrepute, excite
hostility against the government, or incite resistance to the law. Under this statute, leading Republican journalists were punished because of their criticism of
the Federalist administration. For example, Matthew Lyon was jailed for four
months and fined $1,000, when he claimed that under President John Adams the
executive branch showed "an unbounded thirst for ridiculous pomp, foolish adu-
lation, and selfish avarice" and that the public welfare was "swallowed up in
a continual grasp for power."[2] While Republicans condemned the ordinance,
the Federalists defended it as vital to the protection of the government. Nonetheless, the unpopularity of the act led to the defeat of Adams and the Federalist
party. Under Thomas Jefferson, the Sedition Act expired on March 3, 1801.

The Stationers' Company and the Sedition Act were early legislative efforts
at managing information. Through the years, other attempts to regulate the
gathering and publication of news have persisted.

NEWS GATHERING

It is the responsibility of the news media to inform citizens about their
government. The principal concerns of the news journalist involve such issues
as the efficiency level at which the government is operating and whether public
officials are behaving honestly and responsibly. The gathering of information is
essential to accomplishing such functions. Yet, news media cannot publish information if reporters lack access to it. In several cases the courts have considered various rights associated with news gathering.

News Reporter's Privilege

Several news reporters have claimed a privilege to refuse to testify before
grand juries and in courts. They argued that if reporters are required to identify confidential sources of information, the ability to use such sources in the future diminishes. Ultimately, such a policy impedes the ability to gather news.
In 1972, in the *Branzburg* case, the Supreme Court handed down an important
ruling on the matter of news reporter's privilege. The decision arose out of three
separate cases.

In November 1969 the *Louisville Courier-Journal* carried an article under
reporter Paul Branzburg's by-line, describing two young people synthesizing

hashish from marijuana, an activity that the youths claimed earned them about $5,000 in three weeks. The article noted that Branzburg had promised to keep secret the identity of the youths. A grand jury subpoenaed Branzburg, but he refused to reveal the identities of any individuals he had seen making hashish. Branzburg argued that the Kentucky reporters' privilege statute authorized his refusal to answer. The judge construed the statute as affording a reporter the privilege of refusing to divulge the identity of an informant who supplied information, but maintained that the law did not permit a reporter to refuse to testify about events or individuals the reporter had witnessed personally. In January 1971 Branzburg wrote a story that described drug use in Frankfort, Kentucky. The article claimed that in order to obtain a comprehensive view of the "drug scene," Branzburg had spent two weeks interviewing and observing drug users. Branzburg was subpoenaed to appear before a grand jury; he objected. An order was then issued that protected Branzburg from revealing confidential sources of information, but required that he answer any questions that concerned criminal acts he actually saw committed. Branzburg argued that if he were required to reveal information given to him in confidence, his effectiveness as a reporter would be severely damaged. The court rejected his argument and denied Branzburg's claim of a First Amendment privilege.

In July 1970 Paul Pappas, a television newsman-photographer, covered a Black Panther news conference at the group's headquarters in New Bedford, Massachusetts. Pappas recorded and photographed a statement presented by a Black Panther leader. Later that evening, Pappas was allowed to remain inside Panther headquarters, when he agreed not to disclose anything that transpired inside the building, except an anticipated police raid, which Pappas was free to photograph and report as he wished. Pappas remained inside the headquarters for about three hours, but there was no police raid and Pappas wrote no story concerning the incident. Two months later Pappas appeared before a grand jury and refused to answer questions about what had occurred inside the headquarters. He claimed that the First Amendment afforded him a privilege to protect confidential informants and their information. The judge, noting the absence of a statutory news reporter's privilege in Massachusetts, decided that Pappas had no constitutional right to refuse to divulge what he had seen and heard.

In February 1970 Earl Caldwell, a reporter for the *New York Times* assigned to cover black militant groups, was ordered to appear before a grand jury to testify regarding interviews given him by spokesmen of the Black Panther party, regarding the organization's aims, purposes, and activities. Caldwell objected on the ground that if he were required to appear in secret before the grand jury, it would "suppress vital First Amendment freedoms...by driving a wedge of distrust and silence between the news media and the militants." Caldwell argued that "so drastic an incursion upon First Amendment freedoms" should not be permitted "in the absence of a compelling governmental interest." In response, the government pointed out that the grand jury was investigating possible criminal violations, including threats against the president, civil disorders, interstate travel to incite a riot, and mail frauds. The court accepted Caldwell's argument to the extent of issuing a protective order, providing that even though Caldwell had to reveal whatever information he had obtained, he was not required to divulge confidential sources of information established "by him as a professional journalist." The court held that the First Amendment provided Caldwell a privilege to refuse disclosure of such information until there was "a showing by the Government of a compelling and overriding national interest." When Caldwell refused to appear before the grand jury, he was ordered committed for contempt. Caldwell appealed and the court of appeals reversed. The court ruled that the First Amendment provided a qualified privilege to news reporters, and forcing a reporter to testify deterred informants from supplying information in the future and encouraged reporters to censor reports in an effort to avoid being subpoenaed. Without compelling reasons for requiring his testimony, Caldwell was privileged to withhold it.

Eventually, all of these cases reached the Supreme Court. The argument as presented by the newsmen was

> that to gather news it is often necessary to agree either not to identify the source of information published or to publish only part of the facts revealed, or both; that if the reporter is nevertheless forced to reveal these confidences to a grand jury, the source so identified and other confidential sources of other reporters will be measurably deterred from furnishing publishable information, all to the detriment of the free flow of information protected by the First Amendment.[3]

The reporters did not claim an absolute privilege. They maintained, however, that a reporter should not be forced to testify unless sufficient grounds were shown for believing that the reporter possessed information relevant to a crime, that the information was unavailable from other sources, and that the need for the information was sufficiently compelling to override First Amendment protection. The majority opinion of the Court went against the reporters. The opinion, prepared by Justice Byron White, noted that requiring newsmen to testify before grand juries did not abridge First Amendment guarantees. White observed that news reporter's privilege enjoyed no constitutional safeguard. Accordingly, Congress had power to determine any national policy regarding that privilege. Furthermore, state legislatures were free to fashion shield laws. White claimed that the Court was "powerless to erect any bar to state courts responding in their own way and construing their own constitutions so as to recognize a newsman's privilege, either qualified or absolute."

Concerning the specific cases, the Branzburg decisions were affirmed. Branzburg had refused to answer questions that directly related to criminal conduct, which he had witnessed and written about. If what Branzburg wrote was true, "he had direct information to provide the grand jury concerning the commission of serious crimes.'' In the Pappas case, the issue was whether Pappas had to appear before the grand jury to testify—whether a reporter who had published articles about an organization could refuse to appear before a grand jury investigating possible crimes by members of the organization, when the members had been quoted in the published articles. In Massachusetts there was no statutory right to news reporter's privilege. The Supreme Court held that Pappas had to appear before the grand jury. Regarding Caldwell, the Court held that if there were no First amendment privilege to refuse to answer questions asked during a grand-jury investigation, then there was no news reporter's privilege to refuse to appear before such a grand jury until the government had demonstrated some ''compelling need'' for the reporter's testimony. By the time the Supreme Court heard these cases, the Massachusetts and California grand juries had been dismissed. Pappas and Caldwell were already free. Branzburg had moved to Detroit, and the state of Michigan refused to extradite him to Kentucky.

The minority opinion in *Branzburg*, written by Justice Potter Stewart, argued that when a reporter was asked to appear before a grand jury to reveal confidences, the government should have (1) demonstrated that the reporter had information that was clearly relevant to the probable violation of law, (2) demonstrated that the information could not be obtained by alternative means, and (3) demonstrated a compelling interest in the information. Justice Stewart cautioned that

> the sad paradox of the Court's position is that when a grand jury may exercise an unbridled subpoena power, and sources involved in sensitive matters become fearful of disclosing information, the newsman will not only cease to be a useful grand jury witness; he will cease to investigate and publish information about issues of public import.

In *Branzburg* the Court was deeply divided about the right of news reporter's privilege. The division has also been evident in the lower courts. Following *Branzburg*, some courts upheld, while others denied the right of news reporter's privilege.

In the *Baker, McCord, Morgan,* and *Orsini* cases, the lower courts recognized news reporter's privilege. The *Baker* case actually began in the early 1970s, with court action on behalf of several blacks in Chicago who had purchased homes from 60 defendants during the previous two decades. The defendants had sold homes at excessive prices by engaging in the racially discriminating practice of ''blockbusting.'' During court proceedings Alfred Balk was called as a witness. Ten years earlier, Balk had written an article entitled ''Confessions of a Block-Buster,'' which appeared in the *Saturday Evening Post*. The article was based upon information supplied to Balk by an anonymous Chicago real-estate agent, who was given the pseudonym ''Norris Vitchek.'' Balk refused to identify ''Vitchek'' in court. The U.S. Court of Appeals, Second Circuit, held that "federal law on the question of compelled disclosure by journalists of their confidential sources is at best ambiguous." The judge analyzed *Branzburg* and noted that while federal law did not recognize journalist's privilege, neither did it require disclosure of confidential sources in every case. The judge noted that there were other sources of information, which might have disclosed the real identity of "Vitcheck," that had not been exhausted. The judge also claimed that forced disclosure of confidential sources has a deterrent effect on investigative reporting and ultimately "threatens freedom of the press and the public's need to be informed."[4] Balk was not required to reveal the identity of his source.

In *McCord* the court again upheld news reporter's privilege. Several reporters were subpoenaed to appear in court and to bring with them all materials relating to the Watergate break-in. The reporters moved to quash the subpoenas. In addition, members of the Committee for the Re-election of the President, all of whom were parties in civil actions arising out of the break-in, also moved to quash the subpoenas. The U.S. District Court, District of Columbia, held that the parties were entitled to at least a qualified privilege under the First Amendment. The court could not "blind itself to the possible 'chilling effect' the enforcement of these broad subpoenas would have on the flow of information to the press, and so to the public." According to the court, there had been no showing that alternative sources of evidence had been exhausted, nor had there been any showing of the materiality of the documents sought by the subponeas. The court noted:

> The Court in no way wishes to imply that today's ruling constitutes the implicit recognition of an absolute privilege for newsmen. Such would clearly be improper under the *Branzburg* decision. It may be that at some future date, the parties will be able to demonstrate to the Court that they are unable to obtain the same information from sources other than Movants, and that they have a compelling and overriding interest in the information thus sought. Until that time, however, the Court will not require Movants to testify at the scheduled depositions or to make any of the requested materials available to the parties.[5]

The court ordered that the subpoenas be quashed.

In the *Morgan* case the court again recognized the principle of news reporter's privilege. The case began in November 1973, when the *Pasco Times* published, under the by-line of Lucy Morgan, an article about a grand-jury investigation of alleged corruption of public officials. Part of the report was based on "confidential information." The grand jury sought the source of Morgan's information. When Morgan refused to answer, she was held in contempt and sentenced to five months in jail. She appealed. The Supreme Court of Florida overturned the conviction. The court noted that the *Morgan* case "differs from *Branzburg* in that the grand jury...was not investigating a crime." Accordingly, the court weighed the competing governmental interest in preserving "secrecy in grand jury proceedings'' against the First Amendment interest in ''assuring public access to information that comes to the press from confidential informants.'' On balance, the *Morgan* court sided with the press.

> The First Amendment is clearly implicated when government moves against a member of the press because of what she has caused to be published. These contempt proceedings were not brought to punish violation of a criminal statute and were not part of an effort to obtain information needed in a criminal investigation. Their purpose was to force a newspaper reporter to disclose the source of published information, so that the authorities could silence the source. The present case falls squarely within this language in the *Branzburg* plurality opinion: ''Official harassment of the press undertaken not for purposes of law enforcement but to disrupt a reporter's relationship with his news sources would have no justification.''[6]

Orsini is another case in which the court recognized the principle. The August 16, 1976, edition of *Newsweek* contained an article written by Anthony Marro, which detailed the methods used by federal agents to gain custody of international drug dealers. Much of the information was attributed to ''confidential sources.'' Dominique Orsini, a suspected narcotics dealer, obtained a subpoena in order to compel Marro to reveal the identity of his sources. Orsini sought this information in order to demonstrate that the circumstances surrounding his arrest constituted a violation of legal due process. Marro sought to have the subpoena overturned. The district court noted that, under *Branzburg*,

> there exists no absolute rule of privilege protecting newsmen from disclosure of confidential sources. Instead, what is required is a case by case evaluation and balancing of the legitimate competing interests of the newsman's claim to First Amendment protection from forced disclosure of his confidential sources, as against the defendant's claim to a fair trial which is guaranteed by the Sixth Amendment.[7]

In *Orsini* the court decided that the information sought in the subpoena ''bears no reasonable relationship'' to the question of Orsini's due process of law. Accordingly, the subpoena was quashed. In *Orsini*, as in *Baker, McCord,* and *Morgan*, the courts ignored the main thrust of *Branzburg* and recognized the news reporter's privilege.

In several other cases, however—*Bursey, Liddy, Dow Jones, Lewis*, and *Caldero*—the courts rejected claims of news reporter's privilege. The *Bursey* case involved a speech delivered by David Hilliard, chief-of-staff of the militant Black Panther party, before a large audience in San Francisco. In the course of the address, Hilliard claimed, ''We will kill Richard Nixon.'' Hilliard's speech was printed in *The Black Panther* newspaper and was widely reported in other news media. An investigation was begun to determine whom Hilliard referred to when he said, "We will kill the President." Later the probe was expanded to include a general exploration of the affairs of the Black Panther party. Sherrie Bursey and Brenda Presley, reporters for *The Black Panther*, were called before a grand jury, but refused to answer questions relating to the internal management of the newspaper, and about the identity of persons with whom they worked on the newspaper. They were also asked whether they had any information about a plot to kill the president. Bursey answered that she had no such information. Presley refused to answer. Bursey and Presley were held in contempt. They appealed. The court maintained that freedom of the press was not guaranteed solely to shield reporters "from unwarranted governmental harassment"; the "larger purpose was to protect public access to information." The court determined that questions about the identity of persons with whom the reporters worked infringed upon the right of associational privacy and had a chilling effect on the press. Bursey and Presley did not have to answer those questions. The reporters, however, had to answer questions about Black Panther party activities, concerning possession of firearms, guerilla training, and threats against the life of the president. These questions were vital to the government's investigation, and the impact of such questions "on lawful association and protected expression" was "so slight that governmental interests would prevail."[8] The reporters were required to answer such inquiries.

The court refused to recognize journalist's privilege in *Liddy*. In its October 5, 1972, issue the *Los Angeles Times* printed four articles concerning the Watergate break-in. The stories contained information obtained from Alfred Baldwin, "in more than five hours of tape-recorded interviews with the *Times*." According to the paper, Baldwin had "monitored the telephone tap at the Democratic headquarters last May and June from a listening post in the Howard Johnson Motel across the street from the Watergate." The articles pictured Baldwin as an associate of several of the defendants in the Watergate case, the trial of which was to begin in January 1973. In October 1972 George Gordon Liddy, one of the Watergate defendants, filed a pretrial motion for a subpoena to order *Times* reporters Jack Nelson and Ron Ostrow to produce all documents related to their interview with Baldwin. The reporters objected. The district court noted that the First Amendment right to gather news afforded "no absolute privilege against the compelled revelation of news sources." Even though the public had an interest in the investigation of criminal activity, it had "an even deeper interest in assuring that every defendant receives a fair trial."[9] The court emphasized that Liddy's right to secure evidence to counter Baldwin's testimony outweighed any First Amendment considerations. The reporters were required to produce the tapes.

The courts also rejected journalist's privilege in *Dow Jones*. The case involved a *Wall Street Journal* article, written by Liz Gallese, concerning the impact on Massachusetts towns of a "anti-snob zoning law." In the article an unnamed "Stoneham official" was quoted as stating that real-estate developer

William D'Annolfo was a "bad word" in Stoneham and that he was using the law to "blackmail" town officials. D'Annolfo initiated a libel action. In court Gallese refused to identify the "Stoneham official" whom she had quoted in the article. Gallese contended that First Amendment free-press protection, while not providing an absolute privilege, "at least creates a partial shield behind which journalists may conceal their confidential sources." The plaintiff (D'Annolfo) had to exhaust alternative means of identifying the "Stoneham official" and demonstrate that the case could succeed only if the identity were revealed. The court disagreed; the First Amendment afforded no newsman's privilege, qualified or absolute.[10] The court required Gallese to reveal her source.

In the *Lewis* case the court rejected reporter's privilege. Will Lewis, general manager of a Los Angeles radio station, was convicted for contempt when he refused to comply with a federal grand jury subpoena that ordered him to produce a communiqué he had received from a group claiming responsibility for the bombing of a Los Angeles hotel. Lewis appealed on the ground that he had a First Amendment right to refuse to comply with the subpoena. The court of appeals cited *Branzburg* in ruling that Lewis had no such privilege.[11] Subsequently, the U.S. Supreme Court denied certiorari.

The court also denied news reporter's privilege in *Caldero*. The case involved an article in the *Lewiston Morning Tribune* that described an incident involving Michael Caldero, an undercover agent for the Idaho Bureau of Narcotic Enforcement. The article, written by reporter Jay Shelledly, described how Caldero fired three shots through the windshield of a suspect-driven vehicle, two of which struck and injured the suspect. The focus of the article was on the professional propriety of Caldero's behavior. In the article Shelledly attributed certain statements to an undisclosed "police expert." Caldero initiated a libel action, alleging that the article was "an unfair, false and malicious account" of the incident. The trial court found Shelledly to be in contempt when he refused to disclose the identity of the source. He appealed. The Supreme Court of Idaho, citing *Branzburg*, ruled that no "constitutional provisions in regard to freedom of speech and press afforded newsmen a privilege against such disclosure."[12] The U.S. Supreme Court denied certiorari in the *Caldero* case.

The *Branzburg* Court was deeply divided about the issue of newsman's privilege. Following *Branzburg*, the lower courts have acted with uncertainty, as indicated by the lack of consistent action. In *Baker, McCord, Morgan,* and *Orsini,* the courts recognized news reporter's privilege. In *Bursey, Liddy, Dow Jones, Lewis,* and *Caldero,* the courts denied the privilege. In the future, the matter of news reporter's privilege will probably receive more definitive action by legislatures and courts.

Shield Laws

Several state legislatures have passed laws that protect journalists who might be forced to reveal confidential sources and information. In fact, more than half the states have passed "shield laws," which set forth the conditions under which a news reporter's privilege applies. Some states—for example, New York, Alabama, and Nevada—have almost absolute laws. Other state laws are qualified and forbid use of the privilege in specific situations. In New Mexico a reporter may be compelled to reveal a source, if disclosure is "essential to prevent injustice." The Indiana law restricts protection to news reporters connected with a paper that has been published for five consecutive years in the same city and has a paid circulation of 2 percent of the population of the county in which it is published. In Arkansas the law provides that a reporter may be forced to disclose a source of information, if it can be demonstrated that the story was written or published with malice. Overall, shield laws from state to state are inconsistent regarding the information, personnel, and media protected, as well as the procedures under which the privilege may be invoked. Several shield laws have been subject to court interpretation, and in such cases the interpretation has been narrow—tending to favor disclosure. The *Lightman, Bridge, Dan, Proskin, Farr, Investigative File,* and *LeGrand* cases provide examples.

Newspaperman David Lightman, while investigating drug use and sales in Ocean City, Maryland, learned that a particular store proprietor allowed customers to smoke some marijuana before making a purchase. Lightman indicated in the story that he was a "customer" who had a conversation with the storekeeper. Lightman was summoned by a grand jury, but he refused to disclose the identity of the shopkeeper or the location of the shop. The court found Lightman in contempt for refusing to answer grand-jury inquiries. The court noted that not all information published by news reporters has as its origin a "source" protected by Maryland's shield law. When a reporter, because of his or her own investigative efforts personally observes illegal activity,

> the newsman, and not the persons observed, is the "source" of the news or information in the sense contemplated by the statute. To conclude otherwise in such circumstances would be to insulate the news itself from disclosure and not merely the source, a result plainly at odds with the Maryland law.[13]

If Lightman's information had been learned, not by personal observation, but through an informant, the identity of that informant would be protected. The court concluded that Lightman could be required to reveal the location of the shop and the identity of any persons who had engaged in illegal activities. In *Lightman* the court interpreted the Maryland shield law in a manner unfavorable to the news reporter.

The *Bridge* case involved a judicial interpretation of the New Jersey shield law. On May 2, 1972, the *Newark Evening News* carried an article written by Peter Bridge, concerning an alleged offer of a bribe. In the article Bridge wrote: "Mrs. Pearl Beatty, a commissioner of the Newark Housing Authority, said yesterday an unknown man offered to pay her $10,000 to influence her vote for the appointment of an executive director of the [Housing] authority.'' A grand jury investigated the alleged bribe offer and subpoenaed Bridge to appear. When Bridge appeared, he refused to answer any questions. The judge held Bridge in contempt and ordered that he be confined to the county jail until he answered the questions or until the grand jury was discharged. Bridge appealed. The court of appeals held that Bridge had waived his statutory news reporter's privilege by disclosing the source of his information. Thus, compelling his appearance did not abridge any rights under the First Amendment.[14]

The *Dan* case involved a court interpretation of the New York shield law. Television newscaster Stewart Dan and cameraman Roland Barnes were assigned to cover the Attica prison riots in 1972. They were subsequently called before a grand jury and asked to testify concerning what they had observed while inside Attica during the disturbances. They refused, citing the New York shield law as a defense. The appeals court noted that the shield law did not protect the reporters in this case. The questions posed by the grand jury did not require disclosure of news or the sources of news, but merely requested testimony about events Dan and Barnes had personally observed. The shield law allowed reporters to refuse to disclose the identity of any source who had supplied information, but the law ''does not permit them to refuse to testify about events which they observed personally, including the identities of the persons whom they observed.''[15]

In *Proskin* the appellate court heard another New York case. On September 17, 1971, radio station WBAI-FM received an anonymous telephone call, claiming that a letter, describing an imminent bomb threat, had been placed in a nearby phone booth. A newscaster from the station found the letter, which stated that the ''Weather Underground'' was about to bomb certain offices in the Twin Towers Office Building in Albany. The newscaster immediately notified the police. An explosion occurred as threatened, causing considerable property damage. A month later the station was subpoenaed to produce the letter. The station refused, claiming the shield law as a defense. The appellate court found that the law did not protect the station. According to the court, the statute protected a newscaster only when ''the information was received under a cloak of confidentiality.''

> The author of the letter took pains to conceal his identity by signing the letter ''Weather Underground,'' and to insure that appellant would obtain the letter without learning its author's identity. Clearly, he was not willing to rely upon appellant to shield his identity from the authorities. He refused to establish a confidential relationship with appellant but preferred to talk with anyone who answered the phone.
>
> Moreover, since the letter was left in a public telephone booth where it might have been found by anyone and turned over to the police, it is clear that the author could not have been relying upon appellant to withhold the letter itself.[16]

The court upheld the order; the station was obliged to produce the letter. It was simply not a confidential communiqué.

The *Farr* case involved the California shield law. In 1971, during the trial of Charles Manson on the charge of multiple murders, the judge prohibited any attorney, court employee, or witness from releasing the content of any testimony that might be given. Shortly thereafter the district attorney obtained a written statement from Virginia Graham, a potential witness. The statement claimed that Susan Atkins, a codefendant in the case, had confessed the crimes to Graham, and had implicated Manson. Atkins purportedly told Graham that Manson planned to murder a series of show-business personalities. William Farr, a reporter for the Los Angeles *Herald Examiner*, obtained two copies of the statement from attorneys of record. Farr told his sources that he would keep their identity confidential. Farr then wrote a story that appeared in the *Herald Examiner*. The story repeated the sensational, gory details of the planned murders, as well as the statement implicating Manson in the murders already committed. At the completion of the trial, Manson, Atkins, and other codefendants were found guilty of the murders. The court then convened to determine whether Farr's story had jeopardized a fair trial for the defendants. Farr refused to answer questions asking the identity of the persons who had furnished the Graham statement to him. The court held Farr in contempt. It ordered him incarcerated in the county jail until he answered the questions. He appealed. The court of appeals noted that the California shield law provided a newsman's privilege to "a publisher, editor, reporter, or other person connected with or employed upon a newspaper, or by a press association." Even though, however, Farr had been employed by a newspaper when he obtained the Graham statement, he was no longer a newsman when questioned by the court. He was no longer entitled to protection under the law. The court of appeals also stressed that a trial court could control prejudicial publicity only if that court could compel divulgence of the sources of such publicity. To immunize Farr from contempt would interfere with that power. The court concluded:

> Balancing, as we are required to do, the interest to be served by disclosure of source against its potential inhibition upon the free flow of information, we conclude that petitioner is not privileged by the First Amendment to refuse to answer the questions put to him in the trial court.[17]

The contempt order was affirmed. Farr went to jail. In 1974 a court of appeals ruled that continuing Farr's imprisonment would become punitive at some point. Soon thereafter Farr convinced the trial judge that more time in jail would not achieve disclosure of the sources. Farr was fined and served five additional days in jail.

The *Investigative File* case provides another example of restrictive interpretation of a shield law. The case involved the work of investigative reporter Steve

Moore. After a highway patrolman was fatally wounded, a suspect fled to a private home where he held two hostages. Moore, a reporter for the Associated Press, telephoned the home and recorded a conversation with a man who identified himself as the killer. Shortly thereafter the Montana attorney general obtained a subpoena, which demanded that the AP release the tape. The AP refused on the ground that the information was protected under the Montana shield law. The Montana District Court upheld the subpoena, noting that while the law protected the reporter (Moore) who gathered the information, it did not protect his employer (the AP). In Montana a news service could not assert reporter's privilege.[18] AP was ordered to produce the tape.

The *LeGrand* case involved the New York shield law. At issue was the status of Lee Hays, a journalist-author. Hays had received the Peabody Award for television journalism in 1967. He had published approximately 30 books, as well as several magazine articles. He had been employed by CBS News, NBC News, and Station WNET. In 1977, however, when the *LeGrand* case arose, Hays was under contract to write a book about the LeGrand "family." At the time, Navatro LeGrand was on trial, charged with committing murder. LeGrand obtained a subpoena that sought "tape recordings and notes" of conversations Hays had with witnesses for the prosecution. Hays argued that, as a "journalist," he was protected from revealing such information under the New York shield law. The New York Supreme Court disagreed, on the ground that Hays was not a "journalist." The law defined "professional journalist" as "one who, for gain or livelihood, is engaged in gathering, preparing, or editing of news for a newspaper, magazine, news agency, press association, or wire service."[19] Since the definition did not apply to an author who was under contract to write a book, Hays was required to comply with the subpoena.

In *LeGrand*, as in *Lightman, Bridge, Dan, Proskin, Farr*, and *Investigative File*, the court upheld an order requiring the news reporter to reveal the requested information. In these cases, state shield laws did not protect the news journalist. It seems that such laws provide a mere illusion of protection, rather than actual protection for the news gatherer.

Executive Privilege

In 1803 the Supreme Court recognized the concept of "executive privilege." In the *Marbury* case, Chief Justice John Marshall held that a U.S. president was not required to reveal matters communicated in confidence.

> By the Constitution of the U.S., the President is invested with certain important political powers, in the exercise of which he is to use his own discretion, and is accountable only to the country in his political character and to his own conscience.[20]

Throughout history, executive privilege has been invoked by various presidents. During the 1970s the concept was examined by the courts in several cases involving President Richard Nixon. The cases centered around tape-recorded conversations in the White House Oval Office between Nixon and his advisors. In *Sirica, Nixon, Administrator of General Services*, and *Warner Communications*, the courts clarified the concept of "executive privilege."

In July 1973 Judge John Sirica subpoenaed President Nixon to produce tape recordings of particular meetings and telephone conversations between himself and his advisors. Nixon declined. Nixon argued that Sirica lacked jurisdiction to order submission of the tapes for inspection, because executive privilege was absolute regarding presidential communications. The court of appeals rejected Nixon's argument; the president was not above the law. According to the court, the American people did not forfeit through election the right to have the law applied to any citizen—even the president. Any interference with the president's privilege depended, however, on the grand jury's ability to demonstrate the relevancy of the evidence to its investigation. The court felt that *in camera* judicial inspection constituted an appropriate method of protecting both the grand jury's purpose of obtaining relevant evidence and the president's privilege. During an *in camera* hearing, "privileged" material could be deleted, so that only "unprivileged" matter would go to the grand jury.[21] In *Sirica* the court protected the concept of executive privilege, while at the same time ruling that the privilege was not absolute. A year later the U.S. Supreme Court reached the same conclusion.

In March 1974 a federal grand jury indicted seven persons for conspiracy to defraud the government and for obstruction of justice. The charges stemmed from the cover-up of the Watergate incident. The grand jury also named President Nixon as an unindicted co-conspirator and subpoenaed him to produce specific tape recordings of conversations he had held with advisors. Nixon released edited transcripts of some conversations, but refused to release other tapes. He asserted that the court had exceeded its authority, since the material was protected by executive privilege. When the case came to the Supreme Court, the justices ruled against Nixon. The Court noted that Nixon did not claim executive privilege on the ground that the tapes involved military or diplomatic secrets. Rather, Nixon had refused to release the tapes on the claim of absolute executive privilege. The Court noted that, in the matter of criminal justice, "the very integrity of the judicial system and public confidence in the system depend on full disclosure of all the facts, within the framework of the rules of evidence." In weighing the importance of executive privilege for presidential communications against the fair administration of criminal justice, the Court concluded

> that when the ground for asserting privilege as to subpoenaed materials sought for use in a criminal trial is based only on the generalized interest in confidentiality, it cannot prevail over the fundamental demands of due process of law in

the fair administration of criminal justice. The generalized assertion of privilege must yield to the demonstrated, specific need for evidence in a pending criminal trial.[22]

The Court held that absolute privilege could be claimed when the information related to military or diplomatic secrets. When other kinds of information were involved, the privilege had to be weighed against the need for the information. In *Nixon* the Court ordered that the subpoenaed materials be submitted to the district court to determine by *in camera* examination what evidence might be relevant.

After Richard Nixon resigned as president, he made an agreement with the General Services Administration for the storage of 42 million documents and 880 tape recordings accumulated during his tenure in office. The agreement detailed conditions of access to the materials and provided for the eventual destruction of the tape recordings. Three months later Congress passed the Presidential Recordings and Materials Preservation Act, which directed the administrator of the General Services Administration to screen the materials, return to Nixon those

"THE LAST TIME A PRESIDENT TRIED TO USE EXECUTIVE PRIVILEGE AS AN EXCUSE, HE WAS ALMOST IMPEACHED."

that were personal and private in nature, preserve materials of historical value, and make available any materials that might be relevant in judicial proceedings. The administrator was also directed to formulate regulations regarding public access to the materials. Nixon initiated court action, alleging that the act violated executive privilege. The case reached the Supreme Court. Nixon argued that the potential disclosure of communications given to the president in confidence would adversely affect the ability of future presidents to obtain the candid advice necessary for effective decision making. The Court noted that this case was limited to the screening and cataloguing of specific materials by professional archivists. It also noted that any eventual public access to the materials would be governed by guidelines established by the Presidential Recordings and Materials Preservation Act—guidelines designed to protect the concept of executive privilege. According to the opinion of Justice William Brennan,

> the screening constitutes a very limited intrusion by personnel in the Executive Branch sensitive to executive concerns. These very personnel have performed the identical task in each of the Presidential libraries without any suggestion that such activity has in any way interfered with executive confidentiality.[23]

Furthermore, the legitimate purpose of the act was

> to preserve the materials for legitimate historical and governmental purposes. An incumbent President should not be dependent on happenstance or the whim of a prior President when he seeks access to records of past decisions that define or channel current governmental obligations. Nor should the American people's ability to reconstruct and come to terms with their history be truncated by an analysis of Presidential privilege that focuses only on the needs of the present.

The Court concluded that the screening process contemplated by the act would not constitute a more severe intrusion into presidential confidentiality than the *in camera* inspection approved in *Nixon*. The act's screening procedures safeguarded the president's papers from any unwarranted intrusion. In *Administrator of General Services* the Court upheld the constitutionality of the Presidential Recordings and Materials Preservation Act. In this case, as in *Sirica* and *Nixon*, the Court ruled that executive privilege was not absolute.

In *Warner Communications* the Court refused to release Nixon's tapes for commercial use. The case involved several tapes that were played during trials stemming from the Watergate break-in. After the trial had begun, Warner Communications sought permission to copy, broadcast, and sell to the public the portions of the tapes played at trial. President Nixon objected on the ground that there were no safeguards against distortion through cutting, erasing, and splicing of tapes. Nixon expressed concern that such a procedure could result in personal embarrassment and anguish. Judge John Sirica denied Warner Communications' request for access to the tapes. According to Sirica, such access might result in the manufacture of permanent phonograph records and tape recordings, perhaps with commentary by entertainers; marketing of the tapes would probably involve mass merchandising techniques designed to generate excitement in an air of ridicule to stimulate sales. [24]

Warner Communications appealed. The Supreme Court decision stressed three points. First, the right to copy judicial records is not absolute: "Every court has supervisory power over its own records, and access can be denied where court files might become a vehicle for improper purposes." According to the Court, Judge Sirica was justified when he denied the request. Second, release of the tapes might violate the law. The Court examined the procedures established by the Presidential Recordings and Materials Preservation Act and noted that the act created a custodian for the "orderly processing" of Nixon's historical materials. Immediate release of the tapes to Warner Communications would probably violate such safeguards. Third, the First Amendment did not guarantee reproduction of the tapes. Warner Communications had argued that the First Amendment assures freedom of the press—meaning the right to copy and publish the tapes. The Court stressed that the contents of the tapes were given wide publicity by all elements of the media. So, the issue was not whether the press had been denied access to information that the public had a right to know, "but whether copies of the tapes—to which the public had never had physical access— must be made available for copying." The Court concluded that the First Amendment "generally grants the press no right to information about a trial superior to that of the general public." The Supreme Court refused to release the tapes to Warner Communications. In *Warner Communications* the Court sided with Nixon.

Freedom of Information

Governmental secrecy has been a frequent barrier to information gathering by both news reporters and the general public. An example of this type of denial of access to information is the *Reynolds* case, which was decided by the Supreme Court in 1953. The case involved conflicting rights—the right of the public to know versus the right of the government to maintain secrecy in the interest of national security.

The *Reynolds* case involved the crash of a U.S. Air Force plane that was testing secret electronic equipment. The widows of some government employees who were killed in the accident suspected negligence on the part of the air force. They wanted to examine the investigatory report of the crash, as well as statements made by surviving crew members. The secretary of the air force refused to release the information on the ground that military secrets were involved. He filed a formal "Claim of Privilege." The case reached the Supreme Court. Chief Justice Frederick Vinson noted that air power was a potent weapon in the U.S. defense arsenal and that newly developed electronic devices had greatly enhanced the capabilities of air power. Such devices had to be kept secret if their military advantage was to benefit the national interest. According to Vinson, the accident investigation threatened to uncover information about secret electronic equipment. The Court upheld the air force's claim of privilege, thereby protecting the interests of governmental secrecy.[25] Such interests, however, were challenged with the passage of the Freedom of Information Act.[26]

In 1966 Congress enacted the Freedom of Information Act (FOIA). This measure was designed to make available to newsmen and other members of the public various types of information long closed to public inspection. The statute stated that all persons had access to federal records except those that fell into nine categories of exemption. The FOIA provided access to all government records except the following:

1) material authorized by executive order to be kept secret in the interest of national defense or foreign policy,
2) information related solely to internal personnel rules of an agency,
3) matters exempted from disclosure by another statute,
4) confidential trade secrets and financial data,
5) interagency and intraagency memorandums,
6) personnel and medical files,
7) investigatory records compiled for law enforcement purposes,
8) information collected for an agency responsible for the regulation of financial institutions, and
9) geological and geophysical data.

Initially, the act did not provide much improvement in obtaining information. When requests were made for records, federal agencies were reluctant to surrender them. They stalled in releasing requested information. Court action moved slowly, and often the information was no longer "news" or "relevant" by the time it was released. In 1974, and again in 1976, Congress amended FOIA in an effort to facilitate access to information. Procedural changes made records considerably more accessible. Under the amendments, federal agencies had to answer requests for records within ten days. If an appeal were filed after a denial, the agency had only 20 days to respond to the appeal. Each agency was required to publish a quarterly index of records. Agencies had to file annual reports of all records to which access was granted. Furthermore, any agency employee who denied access in an arbitrary and capricious manner could be disciplined by the Civil Service Commission. These changes facilitated access to government records. Nonetheless, several tests of the Freedom of Information Act reached the courts. The cases fell into two classifications: defining "agency records," and clarifying specific exemptions.

Defining "Agency Records"

The Freedom of Information Act defines an agency as "any executive department, military department, government corporation, government-controlled corporation or other establishment in the executive branch of government (including the Executive Office of the President), or any independent regulatory agency.'' Yet, in the *Long, Kissinger*, and *Forsham* cases, the courts were asked to clarify the definition.

The *Long* case involved a request for all the information the Internal Revenue Service had compiled in the Taxpayer Compliance Measurement Program. The program involves a continuing series of statistical studies to measure the level of compliance with federal tax laws. The requested data were in the form of check sheets and data tapes. In *Long*, the court of appeals considered two major issues. First, did computer tapes fall within the scope of FOIA? The court decided that the term "records," as used in the act, included "records maintained in computerized form."

> In view of the common, widespread use of computers by government agencies for information storage and processing, any interpretation of the FOIA which limits its application to conventional written documents contradicts the "general philosophy of full agency disclosure" which Congress intended to establish. We conclude that the FOIA applies to computer tapes to the same extent it applies to any other documents.

Second, did the FOIA require the IRS to remove identification information—names, addresses, social security numbers—from the records? The IRS argued that the process of deleting such information resulted in the creation of new records and the FOIA did "not require agencies to create records that did not previously exist." The *Long* decision, however, noted that "requiring an agency to write an opinion upon request is far different...from requiring it to excise a name or social security number from an existing record." The mere deletion of identifying information did not result in the creation of a new record.[27] In *Long*, the court determined that computer tapes are "agency records" and that the deletion of identifying information does not constitute the creation of a new record.

The *Kissinger* decision also clarified the nature of "agency records." Henry Kissinger served in the Nixon and Ford administrations as an assistant to the president for national security affairs from 1969 to 1975 and as secretary of state from 1973 to 1977. Throughout these periods, Kissinger recorded his telephone conversations—those that discussed official business as well as those that dealt with personal matters. Transcripts of the conversations were stored in Kissinger's office at the State Department until 1976, when Kissinger donated them to the Library of Congress, subject to an agreement restricting public access for a specified period—25 years, or 5 years after Kissinger's death, whichever occurred later. Shortly thereafter, a group of news reporters requested that the State Department release the transcripts. The request was denied on the ground that the transcripts were not "agency records," because their deposit with the Library of Congress terminated State Department control. The Supreme Court, per

Justice William Rehnquist, agreed. Rehnquist noted that "the FOIA is only directed at requiring agencies to disclose those 'agency records' for which they have chosen to retain possession or control." Obviously, in the *Kissinger* case, the State Department no longer controlled the transcripts. Kissinger's transcripts were no longer considered as "agency records" under the FOIA.[28]

The *Forsham* case involved further clarification of "agency records." The case concerned a group of private physicians and scientists who, in 1959, formed the University Group Diabetes Program. The group conducted a long-term study of the effectiveness of diabetes treatment. The study was funded by Department of Health, Education, and Welfare grants in the neighborhood of $15 million. The study generated more than 55 million records documenting the treatment of over 1,000 diabetic patients. The Committee on the Care of the Diabetic, a national association of physicians involved in the treatment of diabetes patients, requested access to the data in order to review the findings. When the request was denied, the committee sought to obtain the data through the courts under the FOIA. In *Forsham* the Supreme Court, per Justice Rehnquist, concluded that data generated by a private organization that had received funds from a federal agency, "but which data has not at any time been obtained by the agency, are not 'agency records' accessible under the FOIA." Rehnquist noted:

> This treatment of federal grantees under the FOIA is consistent with congressional treatment of them in other areas of federal law. Grants of federal funds generally do not create a partnership or joint venture with the recipient, nor do they serve to convert the acts of the recipient from private acts to governmental acts absent extensive, detailed, and virtually day-to-day supervision. Measured by these standards, the UGDP is not a federal instrumentality or an FOIA agency.[29]

In *Forsham*, as in *Long* and *Kissinger*, the courts clarified the meaning of "agency records."

Clarifying Specific Exemptions

Several cases have reached the courts after federal agencies invoked specific exemptions under FOIA. The *Epstein* case involved Exemption 1—material kept secret in the interest of national security. The case involved Julius Epstein, a historian who was preparing a book on forced repatriation of anticommunist Russians following World War II. He sought to examine an army file on the topic. The file had been prepared more than 20 years previously by the Allied Force Headquarters of World War II. That agency had classified the file as top secret. The classification was reviewed by the army in 1954 and 1967, and the classification was retained. In 1968 Epstein requested release of the file. The army contended that the information fell within Exemption 1 of the nine exempted categories under the FOIA. Epstein initiated court action. Before the U.S. Court of Appeals, Ninth Circuit, Epstein argued that the justices should examine the file *in camera* to determine whether the file should, after 24 years, still be classified as top secret. The court noted, however, that "the function of determining whether secrecy is required in the national interest is expressly assigned to the executive." Such a determination "is not the sort of question that courts are designed to deal with." The court claimed that "the judiciary has neither the 'aptitude, facilities, nor responsibility' to review these essentially political decisions."[30] The court decided that *in camera* examination of the file was not warranted. In *Epstein* the court concluded that, under Exemption 1, the army had justified withholding the information.

The *Mink* case involved another challenge to Exemption 1. The case involved an article that appeared in a Washington, D.C., newspaper in July 1971. The article indicated that President Richard Nixon had received conflicting reports on the advisability of the underground nuclear test scheduled for that coming fall. Two days later, Congresswoman Patsy Mink sent a telegram to Nixon urgently requesting the release of the classified reports. The request was denied. Congresswoman Mink and 32 of her colleagues in the House of Representatives initiated court action under the Freedom of Information Act. They contended that the court should examine the reports in private to determine whether they were classified properly or whether the government was simply trying to keep controversial information from the public. The Environmental Protection Agency immediately moved for summary judgment on the ground that the reports were exempted from disclosure under Exemptions 1 and 5 of the Freedom of Information Act. The EPA claimed that the documents involved highly sensitive matter vital to the national defense and foreign policy which had been classified top secret and secret. The district court ruled that the documents were exempt from compelled disclosure. The court of appeals, however, reversed, concluding that Exemption 1 permits the withholding of only the secret portions of documents. The court instructed the district judge to examine the documents *in camera*, "looking toward their possible separation for purposes of disclosure or nondisclosure." The court of appeals also concluded that the documents fell within Exemption 5, but interpreted that exemption as shielding only the "decisional processes" reflected in internal government memoranda, not "factual information," unless that information was "inextricably intertwined with policymaking processes." The court ordered the district judge to examine the documents to determine if "factual data" could be separated out and disclosed "without impinging on the policymaking decisional processes intended to be protected by this exemption." Eventually, the case reached the U.S. Supreme Court, and the justices reversed the appeals court. The Court indicated that Exemption 1 stated "with the utmost directness" that the act exempted matters "specifically required by Executive order to be kept secret." This made "wholly untenable any claim that the Act intended to subject the soundness of executive security classifications to judicial review at the insistence of any objecting citizen.'' Furthermore, it negated the idea that Exemption 1 authorized *in camera* inspection of a document so that the court could "separate the secret from the supposedly nonsecret, and order disclosure of the latter.'' In the Court's opinion, once information was classified, that classification could not be challenged. Regarding Exemption 5, the Supreme Court held that an agency should be allowed to demonstrate to a court that the information sought falls clearly outside the range of material that would be available to a private party in litigation with the agency. The burden rests with the agency and if it fails to meet that burden, the court could order *in camera* inspection.[31] In *Mink* the Court clearly upheld the government's claims based on Exemption 1—national defense and foreign policy considerations. But the Court broadened the scope of the Freedom of Information Act regarding Exemption 5 in that intraagency and interagency memos could in some circumstances be subjected to *in camera* review.

The *Mink* decision facilitated governmental abuse of power under Exemption 1, a practice that was used extensively during the Watergate investigation. The Nixon administration classified numerous documents under the national security label, thereby precluding the information from public inspection. The 1974 FOIA amendments, however, went a long way toward curbing such abuse. Under the changes, courts were able to review governmental decisions to withhold documents. Courts had the power to inspect classified documents *in camera* to determine if they were classified properly. And the executive branch had to specify the criteria used to justify a particular classification. The courts were thus able to determine whether the documents actually met the criteria.

Though the 1974 FOIA amendments specified actions courts could take, those actions were not mandatory. In the 1975 *Knopf* case, the court refused to take such action on the ground that it lacked the expertise required to make the necessary judgments. The *Knopf* case involved a former employee of the State Department who had agreed not to disclose classified information acquired during his employment. When the employee prepared a manuscript for a book that the Alfred Knopf Company planned to publish, the CIA objected to the publication, arguing that the material was classified. The Alfred Knopf Company pointed out that the FOIA amendments provided that a judge could examine the contents of agency records *in camera* to determine whether such records could be withheld under the FOIA exemptions. However, in this case the court noted:

> There is a presumption of regularity in the performance by a public official of his public duty. The presumption of regularity supports the official acts of public officers, and, in the absence of clear evidence to the contrary, courts presume that they have properly discharged their official duties.[32]

Satisfied in the "presumption of regularity," the court rejected Knopf's request that the materials be examined in private to see if they had been classified properly. Thus, in *Knopf*, the court refused to exercise power provided to it by the 1974 FOIA amendments. Such practice by the courts tends to impede the effect of FOIA, because information becomes accessible under FOIA only when court judges assume responsibility for assuring such access.

The *Vaughn* case provided a test of Exemption 2—information related to internal personnel rules. In this case the district court set forth specific guidelines for enforcement of FOIA. The case arose when Robert Vaughn, a law professor researching the Civil Service Commission, sought disclosure of evaluations of certain agencies' personnel management programs. The executive director of the Civil Service Commission refused disclosure under Exemptions 2, 5, and 6. Vaughn brought suit. In this case the district court established standards for interpreting the Freedom of Information Act. The court noted that under the current system, enforcement was hampered by two barriers. First, the method of resolving disputes actually encouraged the government to contend that large amounts of information were exempt, when part of the data was subject to disclosure. There were "no inherent incentives that would affirmatively spur government agencies to disclose information." Second, since the burden of determining the justification of a government claim of exemption ultimately fell on the court system, there was "an innate impetus that encourages agencies automatically to claim the broadest possible grounds for exemption for the greatest amount of information." In an effort to remedy these shortcomings in enforcement, the court established the following standards:

Detailed justification—Courts would no longer accept conclusionary and generalized allegations of exemptions, but would require a relatively detailed analysis of the situation.

Specificity, separation, and indexing—In a large document, the agency had to specify in detail which portions of the document were considered disclosable and which were allegedly exempt.

Adequate adversary testing—A trial court could designate a special master to examine documents and evaluate claims of exemption. This person would assume much of the burden of examining and evaluating documents that currently fell on the trial judge.[33]

The *Vaughn* decision constituted a serious effort toward eliminating barriers to effective operation of FOIA.

In 1975 a test of Exemption 3—matters exempted by another statute—reached the Supreme Court. The case involved Reuben Robertson, who requested the Federal Aviation Administration to make available analyses of the operation and maintenance performance of commercial airlines. Section 1104 of the Federal Aviation Act of 1958 permitted the FAA administrator to withhold disclosure, if it were judged to be unnecessary for the public interest. In this case the FAA administrator declined to make the reports available, on the ground that confidentiality was necessary for the effectiveness of the program. Robertson sued, claiming the records were nonexempt under the Freedom of Information Act. The Supreme Court, in an opinion prepared by Chief Justice Warren Burger, noted that Exemption 3, which prohibited the disclosure of "matters specifically exempted from disclosure by statute," was ambiguously worded and lacked clear standards for application. The Court felt that if "specifically" were meant to apply only to documents specified—either by naming them precisely or by identifying the category into which they fell—such an interpretation would require of Congress a virtually impossible task. In *Robertson* the Court recognized that the FAA administrator had the power to withhold certain information from public disclosure.[34] In this case the records were exempt from disclosure under Exemption 3. Subsequently, in 1976, Congress amended Exemption 3, stipulating that material could be exempted from disclosure when a statute required the matter to be withheld from the public, established particular criteria for withholding the matter, or referred to particular types of information to be withheld. The Court can no longer give Exemption 3, as amended, as broad an interpretation as it did in *Robertson*.

Several cases involved challenges to Exemption 5, which is also known as the executive-privilege exemption. Exemption 5 covers interagency and intraagency memoranda. The *Sears, Grumman, Grolier,* and *Weber* cases provide examples.

In July 1971 Sears, Roebuck and Company requested that the general counsel of the National Labor Relations Board release certain advice and appeals memoranda that dealt with employer/union bargaining disputes. Sears justified disclosure on the ground that the records were the only source of agency "law" on some issues. The general counsel declined Sears's request, because the materials "are exempt from disclosure . . . as intraagency memoranda." When the case reached the Supreme Court, Justice Byron White, writing for the Court, held that some of the requested memoranda were subject to disclosure, while others were not. White distinguished between predecisional communications, which are privileged, and communications made after the decision and designed to explain it, which are not.

> Those Advice and Appeals Memoranda which explain decisions by the General Counsel not to file a complaint are "final opinions" made in the adjudication of a case and fall outside the scope of Exemption 5 . . . those Advice and Appeals Memoranda which explain decisions by the General Counsel to file a complaint and commence litigation before the Board are not "final opinions" made in the adjudication of a case and do fall within the scope of Exemption 5.[35]

In *Sears* the Supreme Court, in effect, held that memoranda that are an "expression of a point of view" are not subject to disclosure, while those that are "dispositions of a charge" are not protected under Exemption 5 of the FOIA.

"LOOK, MISTER, I HAVE A DEADLINE.
CAN WE LET THE PUBLIC IN ON THIS, OR NOT?"

Grumman is a related case. The issue was whether certain documents—generated by the Renegotiation Board in deciding whether various government contractors had earned "excessive profits"— were "final opinions" explaining the reasons behind agency decisions or whether the documents were "predecisional consultative memoranda." According to the *Sears* case, the final opinions are subject to disclosure under FOIA, while predecisional opinions are protected under Exemption 5. The Supreme Court noted that only the full board has the power to decide whether excessive profits exist. Since, in *Grumman*, the documents in question were "prepared prior to that decision," the Court, per Justice White, concluded that "the reports are not final opinions and do fall within Exemption 5."[36]

The *Grolier* case, though decided in 1983, originated over a decade earlier. In 1972 the Federal Trade Commission investigated the Americana Corporation, a subsidiary of Grolier Incorporated. The investigation concerned a civil penalty action filed by the Department of Justice. In 1976 the suit was dismissed.

Two years later, Grolier Incorporated requested disclosure of all documents concerning the Americana investigation. The FTC denied the request on the basis that the records were protected under Exemption 5. The case reached the Supreme Court, where Justice White ruled that under Exemption 5, "attorney work-product is exempt from mandatory disclosure without regard for the status of the litigation for which it was prepared." In this case, the work product of FTC attorneys "would not be subject to discovery in subsequent litigation without a showing of need."[37] Until then, the information was protected under Exemption 5.

Weber involves a recent challenge to Exemption 5. On October 9, 1973, the engine of an air force plane failed in flight. Captain Richard Hoover, the pilot, was seriously injured when he ejected from the aircraft. The incident was a significant air crash, which, under air force regulations, required a "safety investigation." When Hoover filed a damages suit against Weber Aircraft Corporation—the designer and manufacturer of the plane's ejection equipment— the company sought release of the investigation reports. The air force refused to release the information. In *Weber Aircraft* the Supreme Court held that the requested documents were intraagency memoranda within the meaning of Exemption 5 of the FOIA. The opinion, written by Justice John Stevens, noted that "the legislative history of Exemption 5 . . . recognizes a need for claims of privilege when confidentiality is necessary to ensure frank and open discussion and hence efficient governmental operations."[38] In *Weber*, as in *Sears, Grumman,* and *Grolier*, the Court upheld an agency's right to refuse access to intraagency memoranda. The information was protected under Exemption 5.

The *Rose* case involved an agency's attempt to refuse access to records by invoking Exemptions 2 and 6. These exemptions involve personnel files. Michael Rose and other student editors of the *New York University Law Review*, while researching for an article about disciplinary systems at the military service academies, were denied access to case summaries of honor and ethics hearings. Even though Rose requested that all personal references or other identifying information be deleted, the U.S. Air Force Academy refused the request. When Rose initiated court action under the FOIA, the Department of the Air Force argued that refusal was justified under Exemptions 2 and 6. The Supreme Court disagreed. The *Rose* opinion, written by Justice Brennan, maintained that Exemption 2 "is not applicable to matters subject to such a genuine and significant public interest." Brennan also held that Exemption 6 did not create "a blanket exemption for personnel files." Since the case summaries contained only limited amounts of personal information, and because the files are widely disseminated for examination by fellow cadets, the documents could not be classified as a "personnel file" under Exemption 6.[39] In *Rose* the Court decided that access to the case summaries with personal, identifying references deleted met the confidentiality interests embodied in Exemption 6.

Two cases involved Exemption 7—records compiled for law-enforcement purposes. The first case, decided in 1978, was *Robbins*. Following a contested election involving employees of the Robbins Tire and Rubber Company, the National Labor Relations Board issued an unfair labor practice complaint. Prior to a hearing on the complaint, the company sought release of copies of all witnesses' statements collected during the NLRB investigation. The NLRB denied the request on the ground that the data were exempt from disclosure under Exemption 7 of the FOIA. The Supreme Court, in an opinion prepared by Justice Thurgood Marshall, decided that Exemption 7, as amended in 1974, allows nondisclosure of "investigatory records compiled for law enforcement purposes," when producing such records would "interfere with enforcement proceedings." In *Robbins* the Court noted the presence of such "interference."

> The most obvious risk of "interference" with enforcement proceedings in this context is that employers or, in some cases, unions will coerce or intimidate employees and others who have given statements, in an effort to make them change their testimony or not testify at all.... Not only can the employer fire the employee, but job assignments can be switched, hours can be adjusted, wage and salary increases held up, and other more subtle forms of influence exerted. A union can often exercise similar authority over its members and officers.[40]

In *Robbins* the Court concluded that prehearing disclosure of witnesses' statements constituted the potential level of "interference" that Exemption 7 was designed to offset.

Abramson is a related case. In 1976 journalist Howard Abramson sought to obtain copies of any FBI documents that showed the transmittal of information from the FBI to the White House or to White House aides, concerning particular individuals who had criticized the Nixon administration. Abramson was preparing an article on possible misuse of governmental information for partisan political activity. When the FBI refused to release the information, Abramson initiated court action. The FBI argued that the information was exempt from disclosure under Exemption 7 of the FOIA. In *Abramson* the Supreme Court sided with the FBI. The opinion, prepared by Justice White, acknowledged that information that is originally compiled for law-enforcement purposes retains Exemption 7 status when such information is reproduced in a new document prepared for a non-law-enforcement purpose. Justice White noted:

> We are not persuaded that Congress's undeniable concern with possible misuse of governmental information for partisan political activity is the equivalent of a mandate to release any information which might document such activity. Congress did not differentiate between the purposes for which information was requested. Rather the Act required assessment of the harm produced by disclosure of certain types of information. Once it is established that information was compiled pursuant to a legitimate law enforcement investigation and that disclosure of such information would lead to one of the listed harms, the in-

formation is exempt. Congress thus created a scheme of categorical exclusion; it did not invite a judicial weighing of the benefits and evils of disclosure on a case-by-case basis.[41]

The cases cited in this section involved efforts to define the nature of FOIA exemptions, as well as to clarify the scope of access to information under the FOIA. In most of the cases—*Epstein, Mink, Robertson, Sears, Grumman, Weber, Robbins*, and *Abramson*—the Supreme Court sided with governmental agencies and approved the exemption from disclosure.

Banning News Reporters

In recent years, court actions have arisen when news reporters were banned from specific sources and places of news. These cases involved such issues as interviewing prisoners, access to judicial proceedings, and admission to press conferences.

Prisoners

A regulation of the Bureau of Prisons states: "Press representatives will not be permitted to interview individual inmates. This rule shall apply even where the inmate requests or seeks an interview." In 1974, in the *Pell* and *Saxbe* cases, the Supreme Court heard challenges to this regulation. *Pell* involved a California Department of Corrections regulation that prohibited members of the press from conducting interviews with inmates. The policy had been established after face-to-face interviews with reporters resulted in some inmates receiving considerable notoriety. Journalist Eve Pell brought suit to prevent prison officials from enforcing the regulation. The *Saxbe* case occurred about the same time. Reporters from the *Washington Post* were denied interviews with inmates at federal prisons in Lewisburg, Pennsylvania, and Danbury, Connecticut. The regulations covering such bans were challenged in court. In *Pell* and *Saxbe*, prisoners argued that the regulations curtailed their right to free speech. Journalists contended that the rules constituted an unconstitutional obstacle to news gathering. Both cases reached the Supreme Court, where the regulations were upheld. First of all, the Court rejected the prisoners' argument. The majority believed that prisoners' free-speech rights must be balanced against the legitimate interests of the government to deter crime and protect internal security. Since alternative methods of communication were open to inmates, their free-speech rights had not been violated. The opinion noted that "the medium of written correspondence affords inmates an open and substantially unimpeded channel for communication with persons outside the prison, including representatives of the news media." Another alternative was visitation policy, which allowed prisoners to visit with their families, friends, clergy, and attorneys. Second, the Court denied the claim of the journalists. Freedom of the press was not violated, because reporters retained access to information available to the general public. In *Pell*[42] and *Saxbe*,[43] the Court held that the First Amendment did not guarantee news reporters a constitutional right of special access to information.

The Court affirmed the *Pell* and *Saxbe* decisions four years later in the *KQED* case. The case initiated when television station KQED carried a news report about the suicide of a prisoner at the jail in Santa Rita, California. The report contained a statement by a psychiatrist that the conditions at the jail were responsible for the ill health of prisoners there, and a statement from a local sheriff, which denied that prison conditions were responsible for prisoner illnesses. KQED asked permission to inspect and take pictures within the jail. After the request was refused, KQED filed suit, alleging that such refusal violated the First Amendment right of media access. The case reached the Supreme Court. In an opinion prepared by Chief Justice Burger, the Court noted that inmates may lose many rights when they are jailed, but they do not lose all civil rights.

> Inmates in jails, prisons or mental institutions retain certain fundamental rights of privacy; they are not like animals in a zoo to be filmed and photographed at will by the public or by media reporters, however "educational" the process may be for others.[44]

The Court cited *Pell* and *Saxbe* in concluding that the "news media have no constitutional right of access to a county jail, over and above that of other persons." In *KQED* the Court stressed that the First Amendment did not provide news gatherers with special access to prisons or prisoners.

Judicial Proceedings

Several cases—*Landmark Communications, Daily Mail, Gannett, Richmond Newspapers,* and *Globe Newspaper Company*—involved the issue of news-reporter access to judicial proceedings. The cases involved a variety of related concerns.

The *Landmark Communications* case involved the question of news-reporter access to the investigation of a judge. On October 4, 1975, the *Virginian Pilot*, a Landmark newspaper, published an article that reported on a pending investigation by the Virginia Judicial Inquiry and Review Commission and identified the state judge whose conduct was being investigated. A month later a grand jury indicted the Landmark Company for violating a Virginia law that prohibited such divulgence. Landmark was tried, found guilty, and fined $500 plus the costs of prosecution. On appeal, the Supreme Court, per Chief Justice Warren Burger, noted:

> The operation of the Virginia Commission, no less than the operation of the judicial system itself, is a matter of public interest, necessarily engaging the attention of the news media. The article published by Landmark provided accurate

factual information about a legislatively authorized inquiry pending before the Judicial Inquiry and Review Commission, and in so doing clearly served those interests in public scrutiny and discussion of governmental affairs which the First Amendment was adopted to protect.[45]

In *Landmark Communications* the Court sided with the press.

The *Daily Mail* case concerned the access of reporters to juvenile proceedings. On February 9, 1978, a 15-year-old student was shot and killed at Hayes Junior High School in St. Albans, West Virginia. The assailant, a 14-year-old classmate, was identified by seven eyewitnesses and was arrested by the police. The *Charleston Daily Mail* learned of the shooting by monitoring the police-band radio frequency. It immediately dispatched reporters to the school and obtained the name of the assailant. The *Daily Mail* included the juvenile's name in an article in its afternoon paper on February 10. The newspaper company was subsequently indicted for violating a law that prohibited publication of the name of a youth involved in a juvenile proceeding. The case reached the Supreme Court. Chief Justice Burger, in a unanimous decision, noted that if a newspaper lawfully obtains information about a matter of public significance, then state officials may not punish publication of the information without need to further a state interest of the highest order. In *Daily Mail* a "substantial interest" was lacking.[46] The only interest cited by officials was to protect the anonymity of juvenile offenders. The Court concluded that the specified state interest could not justify criminal sanctions against this type of publication.

The *Gannett, Richmond Newspapers,* and *Globe Newspaper Company* cases involve attempts by news gatherers to obtain access to trials. In *Gannett* the Supreme Court considered whether members of the public have a constitutional right to access to a pretrial judicial proceeding, even though the accused, the prosecutor, and the trial judge all agreed to close the proceedings in order to assure a fair trial. *Gannett* involved the pretrial hearing for two suspected murderers, who argued that adverse publicity had jeopardized their ability to receive a fair trial. When no objection was forthcoming, the judge granted the exclusionary order. Shortly thereafter a reporter sought to have the order set aside. The case reached the Supreme Court. In *Gannett* the Court, per Justice Potter Stewart, concluded that the exclusionary order was constitutional for two reasons. First, members of the public have no constitutional right under the Sixth Amendment to attend trials. Second, any First Amendment right of the press to attend trials was not violated by orders excluding members of the public and the press from a pretrial hearing in order to insure the defendants' right to a fair trial.[47]

The *Richmond Newspapers* case involved a series of trials for a murder suspect. The first trial ended in a conviction, which was eventually reversed. The second and third trials ended in mistrials. When the fourth trial began, the defendant moved that it be closed to the public. When the prosecution offered no objection, the judge ordered the proceedings closed to everybody except "witnesses when they testify." A group of news reporters appealed the order. The case eventually reached the Supreme Court. The opinion, per Chief Justice Warren Burger, distinguished *Richmond Newspapers* from *Gannett*—the former treats access to trials, while the latter concerned access to pretrial hearings. Burger then discussed the historical significance of public trials, noting that "the Bill of Rights was enacted against the backdrop of the long history of trials being presumptively open." Burger argued:

> What this means in the context of trials is that the First Amendment guarantees of speech and press, standing alone, prohibit government from summarily closing courtroom doors which had long been open to the public at the time that Amendment was adopted.... The explicit, guaranteed rights to speak and to publish concerning what takes place at a trial would lose much meaning if access to observe the trial could, as it was here, be foreclosed arbitrarily.[48]

Accordingly, the Supreme Court decided that "the right to attend criminal trials is implicit in the guarantees of the First Amendment."

The *Globe Newspaper Company* case involved the attempt by a newspaper to gain access to a rape trial. When the trial judge ordered the courtroom closed, the Globe Company moved that the order be revoked. The trial judge denied the motion and ordered the exclusion of the press and general public from the courtroom during the trial. The Globe Company appealed, and prior to the appeal being heard, the defendant in the rape case was acquitted. Nonetheless, the case reached the Supreme Court. The decision, per Justice William Brennan, noted that *Richmond Newspapers* "firmly established for the first time that the press and general public have a constitutional right of access to criminal trials." Brennan then discussed the benefits of such access.

> Second, the right of access to criminal trials plays a particularly significant role in the functioning of the judicial process and the government as a whole. Public scrutiny of a criminal trial enhances the quality and safeguards the integrity of the factfinding process, with benefits to both the defendant and to society as a whole. Moreover, public access to the criminal trial fosters an appearance of fairness, thereby heightening public respect for the judicial process. And in the broadest terms, public access to criminal trials permits the public to participate in and serve as a check upon the judicial process—an essential component in our structure of self-government. In sum, the institutional value of the open criminal trial is recognized in both logic and experience.[49]

In *Globe Newspaper* the Court ruled that the trial judge's exclusionary order violated the First Amendment. In that case, as in *Landmark Communications, Daily Mail,* and *Richmond Newspapers*, the Court overturned regulations that banned news gatherers from access to judicial proceedings. In these cases the Court sided with the press.

Press Conferences

A government official can control publicity by banning unfavorable reporters from a press conference. With such bans, the proper function of the press may be thwarted. On the other hand, a government official may ban a reporter from a press conference in order to maintain accuracy, objectivity, safety, and/or public order. In two cases, *Borreca* and *Forcade*, the courts had to balance these conflicting interests.

Richard Borreca, a news reporter for the *Honolulu Star-Bulletin*, was assigned to cover City Hall. As part of his responsibilities, Borreca attended Mayor Frank Fasi's press conferences. During 1973 the mayor decided that Borreca was "irresponsible, inaccurate, biased, and malicious in reporting on the mayor and the city administration." Fasi declared that Borreca was not welcome at City Hall and instructed his staff to keep Borreca out of the mayor's office. When Borreca appeared at the next mayor's news conference as the representative of the *Star-Bulletin*, he was not admitted. Fasi informed the *Star-Bulletin* that any other reporter would be welcome, but the paper refused to send another reporter. Borreca and the newspaper initiated court proceedings. The district court noted that First Amendment freedom of the press "includes a limited right of reasonable access to news." The right includes access to public galleries, press rooms, and press conferences dealing with government. The court stressed that any limitations on this right to access must be determined "by a balancing process in which the importance of the news gathering activity and the degree and type of the restraint sought to be imposed are balanced against the state interest to be served." The court noted that newspapers take sides, reporters are not always accurate and objective, and the press is always subject to criticism.

> But when criticism transforms into an attempt to use the powers of governmental office to intimidate or to discipline the press or one of its members because of what appears in print, a compelling governmental interest that cannot be served by less restrictive means must be shown for such use to meet Constitutional standards. No compelling governmental interest has been shown or even claimed here.[50]

In *Borreca* the court concluded that a government official could not prevent a news reporter from attending public news conferences.

The *Forcade* case involved a similar situation. Thomas Forcade was a news reporter for the Alternate Press Syndicate, an international news service that represented more than 200 subscribing newspapers. Since 1971 he had been the APS's national affairs correspondent in Washington and a member of the House and Senate Press Galleries. Another reporter, Robert Sherrill, was the Washington correspondent for *The Nation*. He had been a member of the House and Senate Periodical Press Galleries since 1966. On their arrival in Washington, Forcade and Sherrill applied for passes to attend White House press conferences and briefings. The passes for both men were denied "for reasons of security." The reporters could obtain no more specific information for the denial and were offered no opportunity to present evidence on their own behalf. They initiated court action. When the case reached the district court, FBI secret-service files were offered as evidence for the denials. The files showed that Forcade had been active in leftist student groups and that Sherrill had been involved in two cases of assault, which gave rise to charges that he was "mentally unbalanced." It was because of these activities that Forcade and Sherrill had been barred entry to the White House. Yet, in *Forcade*, the court sided with the reporters and cited two reasons for its decision. First, the White House's failure to devise specific standards for issuance or denial of press passes infringed on Forcade's and Sherrill's First Amendment right to freedom of the press. Second, the White House's failure to inform the reporters of the grounds for the denial of the pass, or to permit them an opportunity to respond, violated their Fifth Amendment right to procedural due process. The court directed the Secret Service to devise and publicize specific standards for the issuance and denial of press-pass applications, and then consider Forcade's and Sherrill's applications within the context of those standards.[51] In *Forcade*, as in *Borreca*, the court specified that a governmental official could not, without good reasons, ban a news gatherer from access to press conferences.

Third-Party Privacy

In *Stanford Daily* the Court considered the issue of "third-party privacy." The case began on April 9, 1971, when officers of the Palo Alto Police Department responded to a call from the director of the Stanford University Hospital, requesting the removal of a group of demonstrators who had seized the hospital's administrative offices. During the next few hours, physical violence occurred, involving the officers and demonstrators. Several officers were injured in the melee, but were unable to identify their assailants. On April 11 a special edition of the *Stanford Daily*, a student newspaper, printed articles and photographs about the clash. The photographs carried the by-line of a *Daily* staff member. The next day the district attorney obtained a warrant for an immediate search of the *Daily's* offices. The warrant, however, contained no allegation that members of the *Daily* staff were involved in any unlawful acts. Subsequently, the *Daily* initiated court action; the complaint alleged that the warrant violated the First and Fourth Amendments. The district court held that in "third-party searches," where the third party is a newspaper, there are "factors derived from the First Amendment" that forbid the search warrant and permit only the subpoena as a means of access to information. The main concern is that "searches of newspaper offices for evidence of crime reasonably believed to be on the premises will seriously threaten the ability of the press to gather, analyze, and disseminate news." The Supreme Court, however, per Justice Byron White, overturned the district court and upheld the issuance of a warrant.

> Properly administered, the preconditions for a warrant—probable cause, speci-
> ficity with respect to the place to be searched and the things to be seized, and
> overall reasonableness—should afford sufficient protection against the harms that
> are assertedly threatened by warrants for searching newspaper offices.[52]

In *Stanford Daily*, on balance, the Court upheld the criminal investigation procedures over the free-press interests of the First Amendment. In fact, the Court
approved the search of a newspaper's premises, even though no one on the
paper's staff was suspected of any crime. By allowing such an invasion of innocent third-party privacy, the Court dealt a potentially chilling blow to the news-
gathering process.

Summary

On the basis of cases examined in this section, it seems that the courts are
reluctant to uphold the freedom to gather news. For example, the *Branzburg* ruling rejected the notion of a national news reporter's privilege. Interpretation of
state shield laws in *Lightman, Bridge, Dan, Proskin, Farr, Investigative File*,
and *LeGrand* have tended to be narrow, requiring reporters to comply with court
rulings. Congress, by enacting and amending the Freedom of Information Act,
made information more accessible to the public. Yet, even though the courts have
considerable enforcement power under FOIA, in *Knopf* the court refused to use
that power. And in cases involving tests of FOIA exemptions, the Court has sided
with governmental agencies and approved exemption from disclosure. Such cases
include *Epstein, Mink, Robertson, Sears, Grumman, Weber, Robbins*, and
Abramson. Nonetheless, in some cases, the Court has sided with the press. During the 1970s, in three cases involving President Richard Nixon, the courts ruled
that executive privilege is not absolute, and in so doing, restricted Exemption
5 of the FOIA. In *Warner Communications*, however, the Court ruled that under the First Amendment the press has no special right to information about a
trial, superior to the rights of the general public. In *Pell, Saxbe*, and *KQED*, the
Supreme Court ruled that the press had no special right to access to prisons or
prisoners, superior to the rights of the public. Overall, the Supreme Court has
made certain information accessible to the public, but has refused to grant news
reporters the unqualified freedom to gather news.

PUBLISHING NEWS

The Supreme Court has dealt with numerous issues that have a direct impact on the publication of news. Some of the most important include prior restraint, taxation, post-office control, antitrust laws, failing company doctrine, politically oriented information, right of reply, and prepublication review.

Prior Restraint

The second-class mail privilege encouraged the dissemination of information by affording publishers low postal rates. In order to obtain the privilege, a publisher had to petition the postmaster general, who then held a hearing to determine whether the publication contained only "mailable matter." The power to revoke the privilege was exercised when the publication printed other than "mailable matter." In 1917 the second-class privilege for the *Milwaukee Leader* was revoked because the paper had become "non-mailable" under the provisions of the 1916 National Defense Law. The Milwaukee Social Democrat Publishing Company, publisher of the *Leader*, initiated a suit seeking restoration of the privilege. The matter came to the U.S. Supreme Court, where the publisher argued that the National Defense Law was unconstitutional, because it violated the right of free expression. The justices weighed the evidence. According to the postmaster general, more than 50 editorial comments appearing in the *Milwaukee Leader* during the first five months of U.S. involvement in World War I constituted the basis for the revocation. The articles claimed that it was a capitalistic war, which had been forced upon U.S. citizens by a particular class, in order to serve their selfish goals. The articles denounced the draft law as unconstitutional and oppressive, with the implication that the law should not be obeyed. The paper repeatedly condemned the U.S. government and its allies, while frequently praising its enemies. According to the opinion of Justice John Clarke, the articles in the *Leader* sought to form hostility toward and to encourage violation of the laws, thus rendering the material "non-mailable." It was reasonable to conclude that the paper would continue its unpatriotic editorial policy. It was within the power of the postmaster general to suspend the privilege until the paper corrected its editorial policy and published material that conformed to the law. When it did so, the second-class privilege could be restored.[53] The Court upheld the action of the postmaster general. In a minority opinion, Justices Louis Brandeis and Oliver Wendell Holmes opposed the decision as a form of prior restraint. They argued that the postmaster could not determine previous to publication that a specific newspaper was going to be "non-mailable." Instead, the only power the postmaster possessed was to return any "non-mailable" papers to the sender. He could not ban a paper because he thought that it would contain unpatriotic or obscene material. The minority view of Brandeis and Holmes was affirmed by the Court in 1931 in the *Near* case.

During the fall of 1927 the *Saturday Press* published articles that criticized law-enforcement officers and other public figures in Minneapolis. The paper charged the chief of police with gross neglect of duty, illicit relations with gangsters, and participation in graft. The county attorney was charged with knowing about the existing situation and failing to act to remedy the conditions. The mayor was accused of dereliction of duty. The paper called for a special grand jury to deal with the situation. Under the provisions of the 1925 Session Laws of Minnesota, the county attorney initiated an action against the paper for publishing material that was "malicious, scandalous and defamatory." He secured a temporary order restraining future publication of the periodical. J. M. Near, publisher of the *Saturday Press*, appealed the order on the ground that the Minnesota law violated freedom of the press. The U.S. Supreme Court, per Chief Justice Charles Hughes, noted that historically, during the preceding century and a half, there was almost a total absence of efforts to impose upon publications prior restraints regarding misconduct of public officials. Public officers whose behavior remained open to free discussion in the media had remedies available for dealing with false accusations under libel laws. The Court, in a five-to-four vote, decided that the First Amendment provided immunity from prior restraints. According to the Court,

> this decision rests upon the operation and effect of the statute, without regard to the question of the truth of the charges contained in the particular periodical. The fact that the public officers named in this case, and those associated with the charges of official dereliction, may be deemed to be impeccable, cannot affect the conclusion that the statute imposes an unconstitutional restraint upon publication.[54]

The Court declared the Minnesota law unconstitutional, because it provided for suppression rather than punishment of publications.

In 1971 a sharply divided Supreme Court again considered the issue of prior restraint. In this case the government sought to prevent newspapers from publishing the contents of a classified historical study of Vietnam policy. On June 13, 1971, the *New York Times* published the first article in a series dealing with the previously secret "Pentagon Papers," a study of the origins and conduct of the Vietnam War. This classified 47-volume document had been made available to the press by Dr. Daniel Ellsberg, an opponent of the war. After the *Times* published three installments, the U.S. government sought a court injunction to prevent further publication. A temporary restraining order was issued, and a hearing was ordered to determine if disclosure of any information contained in the study would "pose such grave and immediate danger to the security of the United States as to warrant their publication being enjoined." The *New York Times* asked the U.S. Supreme Court to consider the case. The government argued that releasing this information posed a threat to national security; the papers said the people had a right to know about the war and that the government simply wanted to save the Pentagon from embarrassment. The Court stayed the newspaper from further publication of the "Pentagon Papers" until a hearing on the matter could be held. Eventually, the Court wrote a brief *per curiam* decision that lifted the restraint on publication that had been issued. Each of the justices wrote a separate opinion. Three were identified as dissents—Warren Burger, John Harlan, and Harry Blackmun. The dissenters accepted the government's claim that publication would cause national harm. The majority, however, supported the newspaper's right to publish. Justice William Douglas cited the absolutist position. The First Amendment provided that "Congress should make no law...abridging the freedom of speech, or of the press." In his opinion, that left "no room for governmental restraint on the press." Justice William Brennan agreed that the Court had no right to levy prior restraint; in fact, the temporary restraint, which had been issued on the ground that it was necessary to give the Court an opportunity to examine the claim more thoroughly, should not have been issued. According to Brennan, the Constitution precluded any injunction from being issued until the government had clearly made its case. The *per curiam* opinion stressed that the government had a heavy burden to show justification for the imposition of a prior restraint.[55] In *New York Times*, as in *Near*, the government had not met that burden.

The *Progressive* case provides an example of a court's willingness to uphold prior restraint. On March 9, 1979, the government obtained a temporary restraining order enjoining *Progressive* magazine from publishing an article entitled, "The H-Bomb Secret: How We Got It. Why We're Telling It." Shortly thereafter a court hearing was held, at which both sides—government and press—aired their arguments. The government argued that national security and preservation permit the retention and classification of government secrets. It contended that publication of such information presented "immediate, direct, and irreparable harm to the interests of the United States." The *Progressive* staff argued that freedom of expression "is so central to the heart of liberty that prior restraint in any form becomes anathema." They also contended that the article contained data that were already in the public domain. Thus, it did not pose a harm to national security that justified incursion into First Amendment freedoms. In the *Progressive* case the district court sided with the government.

> Publication of the technical information on the hydrogen bomb contained in the article is analogous to publication of troop movements or locations in time of war and falls within the extremely narrow exception to the rule against prior restraint.
>
> Because of this "disparity of risk," because the government has met its heavy burden of showing justification for the imposition of a prior restraint on publication of the objected-to technical portions of the...article, and because the Court is unconvinced that suppression of the objected-to technical portions of the...article would in any plausible fashion impede the defendants in their laudable crusade to stimulate public knowledge of nuclear armament and bring about enlightened debate on national policy questions, the Court finds that the objected-to portions of the article fall within the narrow area recognized by the Court in *Near v. Minnesota* in which a prior restraint on publication is appropriate.[56]

In *Progressive* the court felt that the evidence justified "prior restraint" on publication.

Taxation

In two cases—*Grosjean* and *Minneapolis Star and Tribune Company*—the Court considered attempts by states to restrict publication through taxation. In *Grosjean* the Supreme Court turned back the attempt of the Louisiana legislature to control newspaper publication and circulation through unfair taxation. In *Minneapolis Star and Tribune Company* the Court overturned a similar tax levied by the Minnesota legislature.

In 1934 the Louisiana legislature passed a law that required any newspaper that sold advertising and had a weekly circulation in excess of 20,000 to pay a license tax of 2 percent on its gross receipts. Only 13 out of 163 state newspapers qualified for the tax, but 12 of the 13 were outspoken critics of Governor Huey Long—at whose request the law had been enacted. The act required publishers to report the receipts and pay the tax every three months. Failure to do so constituted a misdemeanor, subject to fine and/or imprisonment. Nine publishers sued to stop the enforcement of the statute. The Supreme Court determined that the Louisiana law operated as a prior restraint in two ways. First, it curtailed the amount of revenue obtained through advertising. Second, it restricted circulation. Justice George Sutherland wrote:

> The form in which the tax is imposed is in itself suspicious. It is not measured or limited by the volume of advertisements. It is measured alone by the extent of the circulation of the publication in which the advertisements are carried, with the plain purpose of penalizing the publishers and curtailing the circulation of a selected group of newspapers.[57]

Since the First Amendment forbade any form of prior restraint, the Court rejected Louisiana's attempt to control newspaper publication through unfair taxation.

Minneapolis Star and Tribune Company is a related case. While exempting periodical publications from its general sales tax, Minnesota law imposed a "use tax" on the cost of paper and ink products consumed in the production of such a publication, but exempted the first $100,000 worth of paper and ink consumed in any year. In 1975 the Minneapolis Star and Tribune Company instituted court action to seek a refund of the monies it had paid during past years, on the ground that the tax violated guarantees of freedom of the press. The Supreme Court, per Justice Sandra O'Connor, agreed.

> Minnesota's ink and paper tax violates the First Amendment not only because it singles out the press, but also because it targets a small group of newspapers. The effect of the $100,000 exemption enacted in 1974 is that only a handful of publishers pay any tax at all, and even fewer pay any significant amount of tax.... Whatever the motive of the legislature in this case, we think that recognizing a power in the State not only to single out the press but also to tailor

the tax so that it singles out a few members of the press presents such a potential for abuse that no interest suggested by Minnesota can justify the scheme.[58]

In *Minneapolis Star and Tribune Company* the Court concluded that the use tax
resembled "more a penalty for a few of the largest newspapers than an attempt
to favor struggling smaller enterprises." The practice violated the First
Amendment.

Post-Office Control

The Postal Service has a unique policy that pertains to the dissemination of
news—it distributes newspapers and other such materials at a reduced cost. As
a result of this policy, the postmaster general possesses considerable control over
the dissemination of news. The major source of such control is the second-class
mailing privilege, which is valuable for the distribution of periodicals. When this
privilege is denied, a periodical operates at a serious economic disadvantage with
competitors. The question of post-office control was central in the *Lewis Publishing Company, Hannegan,* and *Lamont* cases.

In the *Lewis Publishing Company* case, the Supreme Court upheld post-office
control. The case involved the 1912 Newspaper Publicity Law, which required
the manager of newspapers and magazines to file twice annually the names of
the editor, managing editor, publisher, and stockholders of the publication. In
addition, all advertising material had to be plainly marked. Failure to comply
with the provisions of the act could result in denial of the mails for distribution.
The Lewis Publishing Company brought suit, complaining that the law abridged
freedom of the press. The Supreme Court disagreed and unanimously upheld the
requirement that this information be filed. Placing these conditions upon the right
to enjoy second-class mail privilege was not antithetical to freedom of the
press.[59]

In *Hannegan* the Supreme Court restricted the power of the postal service.
Based on the postal department's judgment that the contents of some issues of
Esquire did not contribute to the public good, the postmaster general revoked
the magazine's second-class mailing privilege. *Esquire* appealed and the case
reached the Supreme Court. In a unanimous opinion the Court noted that the
postal laws granted the favorable second-class rates to periodicals so that the public good might be served through a "dissemination of information of a public
character, or devoted to literature, the sciences, arts or some special industry."
Congress did not intend, however, that each applicant for the second-class rate
had to convince the postmaster general that the publication contributed to the public good. Only through uncensored distribution of literature could the public use
individual tastes to choose from the multitude of competing offerings. Speaking
for the Court, Justice William Douglas noted: "Congress has left the Postmaster
General with no power to prescribe standards for the literature or the art which

a mailable periodical disseminates.''[60] In *Hannegan* the Court restricted post-office control.

In *Lamont* the Court further restricted the Postal Service, this time forbidding the department to screen political mail from abroad. The case involved a challenge to the Postal Service and Federal Employees Salary Act of 1962, which provided that unsealed mail from a foreign country that was determined by the secretary of the treasury to be "Communist political propaganda" would be detained by the postmaster general and the addressee would be notified that the mail would be delivered only upon request. To implement the law, the post office maintained about a dozen screening points, through which all unsealed mail from foreign countries was routed and checked. When a piece of mail was determined to be Communist political propaganda, a notice was sent to the addressee, advising that the mail would be destroyed unless delivery was requested by returning an attached reply card within 20 days. In 1963 the post office detained a copy of the *Peking Review #12*, which was addressed to Dr. Corliss Lamont, a publisher and distributor of pamphlets. Lamont did not respond to the notice sent to him, but instead instituted a suit to prevent enforcement of the law. The Postal Service then notified Lamont that it viewed his institution of the suit as an expression of his desire to receive Communist political propaganda and that thereafter none of his mail would be detained. The case reached the Supreme Court. The Court concluded that the law was unconstitutional, because it required an official act—returning the reply card—as a restriction on the unfettered exercise of a person's constitutional rights. Any person was likely to feel some inhibition in sending for material that federal officials had condemned as Communist political propaganda. The law violated the concept of an "uninhibited, robust, and wide-open" debate that characterized the First Amendment.[61] The Court enjoined enforcement of the law. While in *Hannegan* the Court protected the publisher's right to send material through the mails, in *Lamont* the Court affirmed an individual's right to receive information without post-office infringement or control.

Antitrust Laws

In 1890 Congress enacted the Sherman Antitrust Act. The law declared illegal all monopolistic combinations in restraint of trade. Subsequently, the Supreme Court heard several cases involving alleged combinations that restrained trade in the news industry. The *Associated Press, Lorain Journal, Times-Picayune,* and *Times-Mirror* cases provide examples.

The Associated Press, a nonprofit cooperative association of newspaper publishers, collects, assembles and distributes news. The news is distributed to the various members of the association, who pay for it under an assessment plan. The United States charged in a federal district court that AP had violated the Sherman Antitrust Act by restraining trade in news and attempting to monopolize that trade. The major charge was that AP had established a system that prohibited AP members from selling news to nonmembers and granted members power to block nonmember competitors from membership. Another charge concerned a contract between AP and the Canadian Press Agency, which obligated both organizations to furnish news exclusively to each other. The district court held that the AP by-laws violated the antitrust laws. AP appealed. The Supreme Court agreed with the district court that the

> inability to buy news from the largest news agency, or any one of its multitude
> of members, can have most serious effects on the publication of competitive
> newspapers, both those presently published and those which but for these restrictions, might be published in the future.[62]

The Court emphasized that freedom to publish is a constitutional guarantee, but freedom to combine to prevent others from publishing is not. The First Amendment did not afford any support for a combination to restrain trade in news. The Court emphasized that the decision did not restrict the AP as to what could be printed, but rather compelled AP to make the dispatches accessible to others. With more outlets, there would be more varied coverage of news events. In *Associated Press* the Court held newspapers subject to antitrust legislation.

The *Lorain Journal* case involved another antitrust violation. In 1932 the Lorain Journal Company, an Ohio corporation that published the *Journal*, purchased the *Times-Herald*, the only competing paper published in the city. After 1933, the *Journal* held a commanding position regarding news dissemination in Lorain. The paper had a daily circulation that reached 99 percent of the families in the city. In 1948 the Elyria-Lorain Broadcasting Company was licensed by the FCC to operate radio station WEOL in Elyria, eight miles south of Lorain. With the arrival of a competing medium, the Lorain Journal Company devised a plan to eliminate the threat of competition from the radio station. Under the plan, the newspaper refused to accept any advertisements for the *Journal* from any Lorain County advertiser who also advertised over WEOL. The U.S. brought suit, alleging that the company violated the Sherman Antitrust Act. The district court determined that the plan to prevent advertisers from using WEOL was designed to destroy the broadcasting company. The plan had been effective. Several Lorain merchants abandoned their plans to advertise over WEOL. The merchants maintained that advertising in the *Journal* was essential for the promotion of their sales in the area. The Supreme Court, in a unanimous decision, agreed with the district court that the newspaper publisher's conduct was an attempt to monopolize interstate commerce. The Court recognized that the plan was aimed at a larger target, the complete elimination of the radio station.[63] The Court concluded that the attempt of the Lorain Journal Company to force advertisers to boycott a competitor violated antitrust laws.

Two years later the Court heard another antitrust challenge in the *Times-*

Picayune case. In 1950 three major daily newspapers served the New Orleans area. The Item Company published the evening *Item*. The Times-Picayune Publishing Company distributed the morning *Times-Picayune* and the evening *States*. In 1950 the Times-Picayune Company instituted the unit plan for selling advertising. As a result, advertisers could not buy space in either the *Times-Picayune* or the *States* alone; parties who purchased advertising in the publications could purchase only combined insertions, which appeared in both papers and not in either separately. The United States filed suit under the Sherman Act, challenging these "unit" contracts as unreasonable restraints of trade. The district court determined that the system of unit selling caused a substantial rise in advertising placed in the *States*, enabling it to enhance its comparative standing with the *Item*. The Times-Picayune Company had instituted the system, because of the *Times-Picayune's* "dominant" or "monopoly" position, in order to "restrain general classified advertisers from making an untrammeled choice between the *States* and the *Item* in purchasing advertising space and also to substantially diminish the competitive vigor of the *Item*." The company had attempted to monopolize the afternoon newspaper advertising field by eliminating choice from "those advertisers who also required morning newspaper space and who could not because of budgetary limitations or financial inability purchase space in both afternoon newspapers." On the basis of these findings, the court decided that unit contracts violated the Sherman Act. The U.S. Supreme Court reversed the decision; it found that the paper did not enjoy a dominant position. The *Times-Picayune's* sale of advertising over the years was about 40 percent. If each of the New Orleans newspapers shared equally in the total volume of advertising, the Times-Picayune would have sold 33 1/3 percent. The small existing increment did not indicate a level of market "dominance" that would indicate a Sherman-Act violation. Furthermore, the *Item* did not suffer. The year 1950 was the *Item's* peak year for total advertising as well as circulation. The newspaper appeared "to be doing well." The court concluded that although the unit rule benefitted the *Times-Picayune*, because it expanded advertising sales, it did not disadvantage the *Item*. Since the government's case was based primarily on that supposition, the verdict of the district court was reversed.[64] In 1958 the Times-Picayune Company purchased the *Item* and thus bcame the only daily newspaper published in New Orleans. At the time of the transaction, the *Item* was experiencing a financial loss.

In *Times-Mirror* a combination was broken up because of its adverse effect on independent newspaper publishing. In 1964 the Sun Company, the largest independent publishing company in southern California, was in sound financial condition. With three newspapers—the morning *Sun*, the evening *Telegram*, and the Sunday *Sun-Telegram*—the company dominated the newspaper business in San Bernardino County. These were the only newspapers, other than Los Angeles papers, that were home delivered throughout the county. In late 1964 the Times-Mirror Company, publisher of the *Los Angeles Times*, the largest daily newspaper in southern California, began negotiations for the acquisition of the Sun Company. Shortly thereafter the purchase of the company for $15 million was completed. The government filed a complaint, however, alleging that the acquisition by the Times-Mirror Company of all the shares of stock of the Sun Company violated antitrust laws. The government argued that the acquisition could substantially lessen competition in the newspaper industry. The California District Court observed that the acquisition of the *Sun* by the Times-Mirror Company was especially anticompetitive, because it eliminated one of the few independent papers that had been able to function successfully in the morning and Sunday fields. Most newspapers in southern California were evening papers, largely because of the strength of the *Los Angeles Times*, which accounted for 70 percent of southern California's morning circulation. The court observed that

> the acquisition has raised a barrier to entry of newspapers in the San Bernardino County market that is almost impossible to overcome. The evidence discloses the market has now been closed tight and no publisher will risk the expense of unilaterally starting a new daily newspaper there.[65]

The court decided that "acquisition which enhances existing barriers to entry in the market or increases the difficulties of smaller firms already in the market is particularly anticompetitive." The court concluded that the acquisition of the stock of the Sun Company by Times-Mirror violated the Clayton Act and directed the Times-Mirror Company to divest itself of the stock and of all forms of control of the Sun Company. On appeal, this judgment was unanimously affirmed in a *per curiam* by the U.S. Supreme Court.

The cases examined in this section suggest that the Supreme Court is willing to break up monopolistic combinations in order to protect freedom of the press. In *Associated Press* the Court declared unconstitutional AP by-laws that prevented nonmember newspapers from acquiring information. In *Lorain* the Court declared that a newspaper company violated antitrust laws when it refused to accept advertising from a customer who also advertised over a particular radio station. In *Times-Mirror* the Court ruled that the acquisition of a newspaper company was illegal when the transaction eliminated one of the few independent newspapers in southern California. In these decisions the Court held newspaper publishers subject to antitrust legislation.

Failing-Company Doctrine

In 1940 the Citizen Publishing Company, the publisher of the only evening daily newspaper in Tucson, Arizona, formed a joint operating agreement with the Star Publishing Company, publisher of the only morning daily newspaper and the only Sunday newspaper in Tucson. Since 1932, the Citizen Publishing Company had operated at a substantial financial loss. Under the provisions of the agreement, the news and editorial departments of the two newspapers remained separate, but a new corporation, Tucson Newspapers, Inc. (TNI), operated all other departments as a joint project. Profits were pooled, and all competition between the two companies ceased. Under this agreement, combined profits rose from $27,531 in 1940 to $1,727,217 in 1964. In 1965 an out-of-state publisher offered to purchase the Star Company for $10 million, provided that the joint operating agreement remained in operation. According to prior agreement, however, the Citizen Company had the opportunity to purchase the *Star* at this price, which it did. The sale resulted in a merger, with the news and editorial staffs of the *Star* under the direction of the *Citizen*. The United States initiated suit, charging that the agreement constituted an unreasonable restraint of trade. The operation was held by the district court to violate the Sherman Act and the court ordered the divestiture of the evening newspaper and a modification of the joint operating agreement. On appeal, the U.S. Supreme Court affirmed the decision. According to the opinion of Justice William Douglas,

> the purpose of the agreement was to end any business or commercial competition between the two papers and to that end three types of controls were imposed. First was price fixing. The newspapers were sold and distributed by the circulation department of TNI; commercial advertising placed in the papers was sold only by the advertising department of TNI; the subscription and advertising rates were set jointly. Second was profit pooling. All profits realized were pooled and distributed to the Star and the Citizen by TNI pursuant to an agreed ratio. Third was a market control. It was agreed that neither the Star nor Citizen nor any of their stockholders, officers, and executives would engage in any other business in Pima County—the metropolitan area of Tucson—in conflict with the agreement. Thus competing publishing operations were foreclosed.[66]

Lawyers representing the Citizen Publishing Company argued the "failing company" defense as justification for the merger. Justice Douglas, however, explained why the "failing company" doctrine did not apply in this case. First, at the time the companies entered into the joint agreement, the Citizen Publishing Company was not on the verge of going out of business, nor was there a strong likelihood that the company would terminate its business if the agreement were not reached. In fact, there was "no evidence that the joint operating agreement was the last straw at which Citizen grasped. Indeed the *Citizen* continued to be a significant threat to the *Star*." Second, the failing-company doctrine could not be applied in a merger unless it was established that the company that acquired it was the only available purchaser; for, if another possible purchaser expressed interest, "a unit in the competitive system could be preserved and not lost to monopoly power." In the *Citizen Publishing* case the Court established two prerequisites to the "failing company" defense: the company must be on the verge of liquidation, and there must be no prospective buyer of the failing company other than its competitor.

The *Citizen Publishing* decision caused concern among newspaper publishers. When that case was decided, 44 daily newspapers in 22 cities operated under the terms of joint agreements similar to the Citizen-Star arrangement. In 1970, in an effort to protect such combinations, Congress passed the Newspaper Preservation Act. The statute provided an exemption from antitrust laws to newspapers in the same city that had preexisting joint operating agreements. As a result, the 44 newspapers were allowed to maintain joint advertising and subscription rates, which might otherwise have been found in violation of the antitrust laws.

In 1972 the *Bay Guardian Company* case provided a test of the new law. The case originated when Bruce Brugmann, publisher of the San Francisco *Bay Guardian*, a monthly newspaper with a circulation of 17,000, complained that the Newspaper Preservation Act had legitimized the joint advertiser and subscription rates charged by the two San Francisco daily newspapers, the *Morning Chronicle* and the evening *San Francisco Examiner.* Under the rate policy, advertisers were required to advertise in both dailies. Profits were shared by the companies on a 50-50 basis. According to Brugmann, the *Chronicle* and *Examiner* had achieved a monopoly position in the San Francisco newspaper market. Many advertisers were unable to afford to advertise in other newspapers. The result was that the *Bay Guardian* had been crippled in efforts to obtain advertisers. Brugmann initiated court action against the *Examiner* and *Chronicle*, contending that the Newspaper Preservation Act violated freedom of the press. The court upheld the act, noting that much of Brugmann's argument seemed directed at a phantom act that legitimized newspaper monopolies. The court held that

> the Act was designed to preserve independent editorial voices. Regardless of the economic or social wisdom of such a course, it does not violate freedom of the press. . . . The Act in question does not regulate or restrict publishing, rather it merely permits newspapers to merge when they might not otherwise have been able to do so because of the antitrust laws.[67]

According to the court, the Newspaper Preservation Act did not offend First Amendment freedoms.

Politically Oriented Information

Occasionally, legislation has been directed at controlling the publication of politically oriented information. In the *Mills* case, the constitutionality of such legislation was left to the Supreme Court. At issue was an Alabama law that controlled election-day editorials. In 1962 the city of Birmingham held an election to determine whether the citizens preferred to keep their city-commission form of government or replace it with a mayor-council government. On election day the Birmingham *Post-Herald* carried an editoral that strongly urged the voters to adopt the mayor-council form. The editor was arrested for violating the Alabama Corrupt Practices Act, which made it a crime to solicit votes in support of any candidates or propositions "on the day on which the election affecting such candidates or propositions is being held." When the case reached the Supreme Court, the justices had to determine whether the law abridged freedom of the press. Justice Hugo Black, writing for the Court, noted that a primary purpose of the First Amendment was to protect the free discussion of governmental affairs which "of course includes discussion of candidates, structures and forms of government, the manner in which government is operated or should be operated, and all such matters relating to political processes." The Alabama law tended to silence the press at a time when it could be most effective. The Court, in a unanimous opinion, concluded that the law was an "obvious and flagrant abridgement of the constitutionally guaranteed freedom of the press."[68] In *Mills* the Court overturned the Alabama law.

Right to Reply

The 1913 Florida Election Code provided that a political candidate had the right to publish, free of charge, a reply to a newspaper article that assailed his/her personal character or charged malfeasance in office. In *Tornillo* the Supreme Court heard a case that involved a claim for the "right to reply." In 1972 Pat Tornillo, executive director of the Classroom Teacher's Association, was a candidate for the Florida House of Representatives. The *Miami Herald* printed editorials critical of Tornillo's candidacy. The articles referred to Tornillo as a "czar" and a law breaker. The *Herald* claimed that it would be "inexcusable of the voters" if they elected Tornillo to the legislature. The reason for the paper's opposition to Tornillo stemmed from a 1960 illegal strike by Miami public-school teachers, which Tornillo had led. In light of the editorial comments, Tornillo asked for the right to reply under the Florida election code. When the *Herald* refused to print a reply, Tornillo initiated court action to secure the printing of his reply. The Supreme Court of Florida made two points in upholding the right to reply. The U.S. Supreme Court, however, reversed, disagreeing tion campaign. In order to assure fairness in campaigns, assailed candidates were entitled to an opportunity to respond—otherwise the candidates would be harmed and the public would be deprived of an opportunity to hear both sides of the controversy. First Amendment guarantees were "not for the benefit of the press so much as for the benefit of us all." Second, the Florida law promoted the flow of ideas and did not infringe upon First Amendment rights against prior restraint, since no specified newspaper content was excluded. There was nothing prohibited; rather, the law required, in the interest of full and fair discussion, additional information. For these two reasons, the Florida Supreme Court upheld the right to reply. The U.S. Supreme Court, however, reversed, disagreeing on both points. First, faced with the penalties that would accrue to any newspaper that published commentary that might warrant the "right of reply," editors might conclude that the safe course was to avoid controversy. In such instances, political coverage would be reduced. According to the Court, "government enforced right of access inescapably dampened the vigor and limits and variety of public debate." Second, the Florida statute required publishers to publish that which "reason" told them should not be published. The law operated as a command in the same sense as a law forbidding a publisher from publishing specified matter. According to the Court, "governmental restraint on publishing need not fall into familiar or traditional patterns to be subject to constitutional limitations on governmental powers."[69] The Court concluded that the statute violated the First Amendment's guarantee of a free press. In *Tornillo* the U.S. Supreme Court rejected the "right to reply."

"GO FIND OUT WHAT PEOPLE ARE SAYING ABOUT ME···ARREST THEM IF IT'S BAD!"

Prepublication Review

In 1980 the Supreme Court approved the concept of prepublication review. The case involved Frank Snepp, who had been employed with the Central Intelligence Agency. Snepp published a book about CIA activities in South Vietnam, based on his experiences as an agent. He published the information without submitting it to the CIA for prepublication review. As a condition of his employment with the CIA, Snepp had agreed not to publish any information relating to the CIA "without specific prior approval by the Agency." The CIA initiated court action. The district court found that Snepp had deliberately misled CIA officials into believing that he would submit the book for prepublication clearance. The court also determined that publication of the information had "caused the United States irreparable harm and loss." The court therefore imposed a constructive trust on Snepp's profits. Snepp appealed. The Supreme Court, in a *per curiam* decision, approved the constructive trust as a remedy that "deals fairly with both parties."

> If the agent secures prepublication clearance, he can publish with no fear of liability. If the agent publishes unreviewed material in violation of his fiduciary and contractual obligation, the trust remedy simply requires him to disgorge the benefits of his faithlessness. Since the remedy is swift and sure, it is tailored to deter those who would place sensitive information at risk. [70]

In a dissenting opinion Justice John Stevens argued that the remedy constituted "a species of prior restraint on a citizen's right to criticize his government." Stevens noted:

> Inherent in this prior restraint is the risk that the reviewing agency will misuse its authority to delay the publication of a critical work or to persuade an author to modify the contents of his work beyond the demands of secrecy.

Nonetheless, in *Snepp*, the majority supported the CIA's right of prepublication review.

Summary

Over the years, the U.S. Supreme Court has, with few exceptions, protected the right to publish news. In *Near* and *New York Times* the Court protected the press from attempts to suppress publication through prior restraint. In *Grosjean* and *Minneapolis Star and Tribune Company* the Court rejected efforts to suppress publication through unfair taxation. In *Hannegan* and *Lamont* the Court affirmed the publisher's right to send material through the mails, as well as the individual's right to receive information. In *Associated Press, Lorain Journal, Times-Picayune,* and *Times-Mirror* the Court applied antitrust laws to the newspaper industry. Any monopolistic combination aimed at the destruction of competition in publishing newspapers was declared unconstitutional. In the *Citizen Publishing* case the Court rejected the "failing company" defense, because the company was not on the verge of liquidation and there was another prospective buyer. In *Bay Guardian Company* the judges upheld the constitutionality of the Newspaper Preservation Act—a measure designed to protect independent newspaper companies from financial failure. In *Mills* the Court recognized the importance of publishing information related to political elections. In *Tornillo* the Court rejected a right to reply, because operation of this right could blunt publication regarding political campaigns. In these areas the Supreme Court consistently protected a First Amendment freedom of the press—the right to publish.

NOTES

1. Milton, John, *Areopagitica*, ed. by Edward Arber. London: English Reprints, 1868.

2. Hentoff, Nat, *The First Freedom: The Tumultuous History of Free Speech in America*. New York: Dell Publishing, 1981, pp. 79-85. See also Emerson, Thomas I., *The System of Freedom of Expression*. New York: Vintage Books, 1970, pp. 98-101; and Chafee, Zechariah, Jr., *Free Speech in the United States*. Cambridge: Harvard University Press, 1941, pp. 497-516.

3. *Branzburg v. Hayes; In the Matter of Pappas; United States v. Caldwell*, 92 S.Ct. 2646 (1972).

4. *Baker v. F. & F. Investment*, 470 F. 2d 778 (1972).

5. *Democratic National Committee v. McCord; In re Bernstein*, 356 F. Supp. 1394 (1973).

6. *Morgan v. State*, 337 So. 2d 951 (1976).

7. *United States v. Orsini*, 424 F. Supp. 229 (1976).

8. *Bursey v. United States*, 466 F. 2d 1059 (1972).

9. *United States v. Liddy*, 354 F. Supp 208 (1972).

10. *Dow Jones & Company, Inc. v. Superior Court*, 303 N.E. 2d 849 (1973).

11. *Lewis v. United States*, 517 F. 2d 236 (1975); cert. denied 95 S.Ct. 1974 (1975).

12. *Caldero v. Tribune Publishing Company*, 562 P. 2d 791 (1977); cert. denied 98 S.Ct. 418 (1978).

13. *Lightman v. Maryland*, 294 A. 2d 149 (1972); cert. denied 93 S.Ct. 1922 (1973).

14. *In re Bridge*, 295 A. 2d 3 (1972); cert. denied 93 S.Ct. 1500 (1973).

15. *People v. Dan*, 41 App. Div. 2d 687 (1973).

16. *WBAI-FM v. Proskin*, 42 App. Div. 2d 5 (1973).

17. *Farr v. Superior Court of the State of California, County of Los Angeles*, 99 Cal. Rptr. 342 (1971); *In re Farr*, 111 Cal. Rptr. 649 (1974).

18. *In re Investigative File*, 4 M.L. Rptr.1865 (1978).

19. *New York v. LeGrand* 4 M.L. Rptr. 1897 (1979).

20. *Marbury v. Madison* 5 S.Ct. 60 (1803).

21. *Nixon v. Sirica*, 487 F. 2d 700 (1973).

22. *United States v. Nixon*, 94 S.Ct. 3090 (1974).

23. *Nixon v. Administrator of General Services*, 97 S.Ct. 2777 (1977).

24. *Nixon v. Warner Communications, Inc.*, 98 S.Ct. 1306 (1978).

25. *United States v. Reynolds*, 73 S.Ct. 528 (1953).

26. Freedom of Information Act, 5 U.S.C. §552.

27. *Long v. United States Internal Revenue Service*, 596 F. 2d 362 (1979).

28. *Kissinger v. Reporters Committee For Freedom of the Press*, 100 S.Ct. 960 (1980).

29. *Forsham v. Harris*, 100 S.Ct. 978 (1980).

30. *Epstein v. Resor*, 421 F.2d 930 (1970).

31. *Environmental Protection Agency v. Mink*, 93 S.Ct. 827 (1973).

32. *Alfred A. Knopf, Inc. v. Colby*, 509 F. 2d 1362 (1975).

33. *Vaughn v. Rosen, Executive Director, United States Civil Service Commission*, 484 F. 2d 820 (1973).

34. *Administrator, Federal Aviation Administration v. Robertson*, 95 S.Ct. 2140 (1975).

35. *National Labor Relations Board v. Sears, Roebuck and Company*, 95 S.Ct. 1504 (1975).

36. *Renegotiation Board v. Grumman Aircraft Engineering Corporation*, 95 S.Ct. 1491 (1975).

37. *Federal Trade Commission v. Grolier Incorporated*, 103 S.Ct. 2209 (1983).

38. *United States v. Weber Aicraft Corporation*, 104 S.Ct. 1488 (1984).

39. *Department of the Air Force v. Rose*, 96 S.Ct. 1592 (1976).

40. *National Labor Relations Board v. Robbins Tire and Rubber Company*, 98 S.Ct. 2311 (1978).

41. *Federal Bureau of Investigation v. Abramson*, 102 S.Ct. 2054 (1982).

42. *Pell v. Procunier; Procunier v. Hillery*, 94 S.Ct. 2800 (1974).

43. *Saxbe v. Washington Post Company*, 94 S.Ct. 2811 (1974).

44. *Houchins v. KQED*, 98 S.Ct. 2588 (1978).

45. *Landmark Communications v. Virginia*, 98 S.Ct. 1535 (1978).

46. *Smith v. Daily Mail Publishing Company*, 99 S.Ct. 2667 (1979).

47. *Gannett Company v. DePasquale*, 99 S.Ct. 2898 (1979).

48. *Richmond Newspapers v. Virginia*, 100 S.Ct. 2814 (1980).

49. *Globe Newspaper Company v. Superior Court for the County of Norfolk*, 102 S.Ct. 2613 (1982).

50. *Borreca v. Fasi*, 369 F. Supp. 906 (1974).

51. *Forcade v. Knight*, 416 F. Supp. 1025 (1976).

52. *Zurcher v. Stanford Daily; Bergna v. Stanford Daily*, 98 S.Ct. 1970 (1978).

53. *Milwaukee Social Democrat Publishing Company v. Burleson*, 41 S.Ct. 352 (1921).

54. *Near v. Minnesota*, 51 S.Ct. 625 (1931).

55. *New York Times Company v. United States; United States v. Washington Post Company*, 91 S.Ct. 2140 (1971).

56. *United States v. Progressive*, 467 F. Supp 990 (1979).

57. *Grosjean v. American Press Company*, 56 S.Ct. 444 (1936).

58. *Minneapolis Star and Tribune Company v. Minnesota Commissioner of Revenue*, 103 S.Ct. 1365 (1983).

59. *Lewis Publishing Company v. Morgan; Journal of Commerce and Commercial Bulletin v. Burleson*, 33 S.Ct. 867 (1913).

60. *Hannegan v. Esquire*, 66 S. Ct. 456 (1946).

61. *Lamont v. Postmaster General; Fixa v. Heilberg*, 85 S.Ct. 1493 (1965).

62. *Associated Press v. United States; Tribune Company v. United States*, 65 S.Ct. 1416 (1945).

63. *Lorain Journal Company v. United States*, 72 S.Ct. 181 (1951).

64. *Times-Picayune Publishing Company v. United States*, 73 S.Ct. 872 (1953).

65. *Times-Mirror Company v. United States*, 88 S.Ct. 1411 (1968).

66. *Citizen Publishing Company v. United States*, 89 S.Ct. 927 (1969).

67. *Bay Guardian Company v. Chronicle Publishing Company*, 344 F. Supp. 1155 (1972).

68. *Mills v. Alabama*, 86 S.Ct. 1434 (1966).

69. *Miami Herald Publishing Company v. Tornillo*, 94 S.Ct. 2831 (1974).

70. *Snepp v. United States*, 100 S.Ct. 763 (1980).

RECOMMENDED READING

Barnett, Stephen R., ''Newspaper Monopoly and the Law,'' *Journal of Communication* 30 (Spring, 1980), 72-80.

Cappleman, Hollye E., ''Access to Judicial Proceedings: After *Gannett* and *Richmond*,''

Texas Tech Law Review 12 (1981), 663-96.

Cox, Archibald, "Freedom of the Press," *University of Illinois Law Review* (1983), 3-21.

Ferguson, Eugene, Jr., "The Freedom of Information Act: A Time For Change?" *Detroit College of Law Review* (Spring, 1983), 171-98.

Goodale, James C., "*Branzburg v. Hayes* and the Developing Qualified Privilege for Newsmen," *Hastings Law Journal* 26 (January, 1975), 709-43.

Gorski, James M., "Access to Information? Exemptions From Disclosure Under the Freedom of Information Act and the Privacy Act of 1974," *Willamette Law Journal* 13 (Winter, 1976), 135-71.

Humphrey, Kathryn Jane, "Shield Statutes: A Changing Problem in Light of *Branzburg*," *Wayne Law Review* 25 (September, 1979), 1381-403.

O'Brien, David M., "First Amendment and the Public's 'Right to Know,' " *Hastings Constitutional Law Quarterly* 7 (Spring, 1980), 579-631.

Pinkerton, Barbara A., "Freedom of the Press and a Reporter's Ability to Gather News," *Wayne Law Review* 26 (Summer, 1979), 75-95.

Reznek, Sarah G., "*Gannett v. Depasquale* and *Richmond Newspapers v. Virginia:* Reopening Courtroom Doors and Constitutional Windows," *Capital University Law Review* 10 (Fall, 1980), 101-28.

Smith, James M., *Freedom's Fetters*. Ithaca, N.Y.: Cornell University Press, 1956.

Sobel, David L., "The Freedom of Information Act: A Case Against Amendment," *Journal of Contemporary Law* 8 (1982), 47-61.

Teplitzky, Sanford V. and Kenneth A. Weiss, "Newsman's Privilege Two Years After *Branzburg v. Hayes*: The First Amendment in Jeopardy," *Tulane Law Review* 49 (January, 1975), 417-38.

KEY DECISIONS

1931—*NEAR*—acknowledged that First Amendment provides immunity from prior restraints.

1946—*HANNEGAN*—restricted post-office control of the mails; protected a publisher's right to send material through the mails.

1965—*LAMONT*—affirmed an individual's right to receive information without post-office infringement.

1971—*NEW YORK TIMES*—stressed that government has a heavy responsibility to justify the imposition of a prior restraint.

1972—*BRANZBURG*—in a deeply divided court, rejected the idea of a national news reporter's privilege.

1974—*NIXON*—determined that executive privilege is not absolute.

1974—*TORNILLO*—rejected the "right to reply," because of potential chilling effect on publishing news.

1974—*PELL*—held that the First Amendment did not guarantee news reporters any special access to information.

1975—*SEARS*—determined that final opinions are subject to disclosure under the Freedom of Information Act, while predecisional opinions are protected under exemption 5.

1978—*STANFORD DAILY*—approved the search of a newspaper's premises even though no one on the paper's staff was suspected of any crime.

1980—*RICHMOND NEWSPAPERS*—held that the public's right to attend criminal trials is protected by the Fifth Amendment.

1980—*SNEPP*—approved governmental prepublication review.

SUMMARY—LAW OF NEWS

Definition

The courts and legislatures have established laws that regulate the gathering and publishing of news. The laws stipulate the conditions under which journalists enjoy access to information.

Barriers

The government may bar access to news under certain conditions:
1. News reporter's privilege—there is *no* absolute national right protecting reporters while keeping a news source's identity confidential.
2. Freedom of Information Act—specifies federal records for which access can be denied:
   a. National defense or foreign policy
   b. Internal personnel rules
   c. Exemption by another statute

    d. Trade secrets and financial data
    e. Interagency and intraagency memoranda
    f. Personnel and medical files
    g. Records compiled for law-enforcement purposes
    h. Relation to regulation of financial institutions
    i. Geological or geophysical data.
3. Bans—news reporters usually do not enjoy any "special" access to information—that is, beyond the rights enjoyed by the general public.

Exceptions

News reporters and publishers are aided by the following doctrines:
1. Shield laws—reporter's privilege is recognized in states that have enacted shield laws, though most laws have so many exceptions that they provide little protection for the reporter.
2. Prior restraint—courts have generally turned back practices of prior restraint.

11

FAIR TRIAL

Two constitutional guarantees—freedom of expression and the right to a fair trial—come into conflict when the public clamors to know the facts of a case, but the discussion of those facts might jeopardize the defendant's right to a fair trial. In *Times-Picayune,* Justice Lewis Powell acknowledged that "the task of reconciling First Amendment rights with the defendant's right to a fair trial before an impartial jury is not an easy one."[1] In several instances the Supreme Court has been asked to balance those rights in conflict. Relevant cases may be considered under two main headings—contempt and pretrial publicity.

CONTEMPT

In 1831 federal judge James Peck suspended from legal practice an attorney who had criticized Peck's handling of some Spanish land-grant cases. A political dispute followed; Peck was impeached and tried in the U.S. Senate. The impeachment attempt failed by a one-vote margin, but the event furthered widespread resentment of the common-law method of dealing with contempt that was currently practiced. Within nine days Congress passed the Federal Contempt Act of 1831, which limited punishable contempt to disobedience of any judicial procedure and to misbehavior in the presence of the court "or so near thereto as to obstruct the administration of justice." In two subsequent cases the U.S. Supreme Court interpreted the phrase "so near thereto."

"So Near Thereto"

In 1918, in the *Toldeo Newspaper* case, the Court offered a causal rather than a geographical interpretation of the phrase. The case involved the Toledo

Railways & Light Company, which operated almost all the street railways in Toledo. When the contract under which the company controlled such local transportation expired, the city and the company engaged in a bitter dispute over the issuance of a new contract. In an effort to gain a favorable franchise with the company, the city passed legislation stipulating that the company should charge three-cent fares. This action produced considerable public agitation over the issue. The company filed suit, seeking to restrain enforcement of the city ordinance. Before any action was taken by the court, the *Toledo NewsBee* published editorials that defended the city's right to enact the ordinance and challenged any right of the court to grant relief to the company. Shortly thereafter a contempt order was issued against the editor of the newspaper. On appeal, the Supreme Court noted:

> Newspaper articles, referring to a suit in the federal court to enjoin municipal ordinances regulating street car fares, which held the federal judge up to ridicule and hatred in case he should grant an injunction, and in advance impeached his motives in so doing, and practically urged noncompliance with any such order, must be deemed acts tending to obstruct the administration of justice. . .and punishment for contempt cannot be avoided on the ground that it did not appear the judge saw the articles or that he was unaffected by them.[2]

The Court majority interpreted the Federal Contempt Act as granting power to the courts to punish a newspaper's misbehavior that showed a "reasonable tendency" to obstruct justice. In *Toledo Newspaper* the phrase "so near thereto" received a causal rather than a geographical construction. The Court affirmed the contempt citation.

In 1941, in *Nye,* the Court reversed the causative interpretation of the "so near thereto" phrase. The case involved a wrongful-death action brought by W. H. Elmore against the B. C. Remedy Company concerning the death of Elmore's son. Elmore claimed that his son died as a result of taking a medicine manufactured by the company. Shortly thereafter, R. H. Nye used alcoholic beverages and persuasive tactics to coax Elmore, a feeble, illiterate, elderly man, to drop the suit. These events took place more than 100 miles from Durham, North Carolina, where the court hearing the wrongful-death suit was located. Nye was, nonetheless, held in contempt for obstructing justice. The court held that Nye's conduct was "misbehavior so near to the presence of the court as to obstruct the administration of justice." It ordered Nye to pay the costs of the proceedings and a fine of $500. Nye appealed. In *Nye* the Supreme Court interpreted "so near thereto" to mean physical proximity. According to Justice William Douglas, the phrase connoted that the misbehavior must be in the vicinity of the court. The term "near" suggested physical proximity, not causal relevance. Nye's influence on Elmore had not been perpetrated in the "presence" of the court or "near thereto."[3] According to Douglas, the "reasonable tendency"

rule as applied in *Toledo Newspaper* contradicted the intention of the Contempt
Act of 1831. The Court reversed Nye's conviction, and by overturning *Toledo
Newspaper,* considerably limited the power of judges to punish contempt that
occurred outside of the courtroom.

Bridges Principle

In 1941 companion cases, the Supreme Court expanded the power of the press
to comment on cases and judges. In the first case, a motion for a new trial was
pending in a case involving a dispute between two labor unions. Harry Bridges,
the president of one of the unions, sent a telegram to the secretary of labor, which
described the judge's decision in the case as "outrageous," threatened a strike
by the longshoremen that would tie up the port of Los Angeles if the decision
was enforced, and announced that the CIO did "not intend to allow state courts
to override the majority vote of members." The telegram was published in Los
Angeles and San Francisco newspapers. Bridges was found guilty of contempt.
He appealed. In the second case, the Times-Mirror Company was cited for contempt for publishing editorials while the outcome of a court case was still pending. An editorial that approved the convictions of 22 sit-down strikers appeared
in the *Los Angeles Times* after the verdict, but prior to sentencing. Another
editorial approved the convictions of two labor leaders who had previously been
found guilty of assaulting nonunion truck drivers. The article urged the judge
to make examples of the labor officials: "Judge A. A. Scott will make a serious mistake if he grants probation to Matthew Shannon and Kennan Holmes. This
community needs the examples of their assignment to the jute mill." The Times-
Mirror Company appealed the conviction for contempt.

In these cases the Supreme Court applied the "clear and present danger"
rather than the "bad tendency" test. Writing for the majority, Justice Hugo Black
claimed that "the likelihood, however great that a substantive evil will result cannot alone justify a restriction upon freedom of speech or the press. The evil itself must be 'substantial.' " According to Black,

> what finally emerges from the "clear and present danger" cases is a working
> principle that the substantive evil must be extremely serious and the degree of
> imminence extremely high before the utterances can be punished.[4]

Specifically, in *Bridges,* the justices noted that the telegram threatened a strike
if the court's decision were enforced. There was no claim that the strike would
actually violate the court decision or the law. The Court found nothing that obstructed the administration of justice. In *Times-Mirror* the Court held that even
if "bad tendency" were an appropriate test, it did not justify the restriction of
free expression. The *Los Angeles Times* had a long-established policy of militancy
on labor controversies; there was no doubt that the paper would oppose proba-

tion for Shannon and Holmes. To consider such criticism a substantial influence upon the administration of justice would ''impute to judges a lack of firmness, wisdom, or honor.'' In *Bridges* and *Times-Mirror* the Court acknowledged that there were greater benefits to be derived from public discussion of pending court cases than from forced silence.

In several cases the Supreme court affirmed the *Bridges* principle. A 1946 case, *Pennekamp,* involved a newspaper that published two editorials and a cartoon accusing judges of leniency toward criminals. The paper claimed that judges used legal technicalities to subvert convictions of criminals, especially operators of gambling establishments. The newspaper's associate editor, John Pennekamp, was convicted of contempt. In *Pennekamp* the Supreme Court held that the editorials and cartoon did not constitute a ''clear and present danger to fair administration of justice,'' because the effect on juries that might eventually try alleged offenders was very remote, and the editorials criticized only court action already taken. Justice Stanley Reed noted that ''the danger under this record to fair judicial administration had not the clearness and immediacy neces-

''BUT, YOUR HONOR, IF WE CAN'T MAKE THE WITNESS OR THE SUSPECT TALK, WHO'S GOING TO TESTIFY?''

sary to close the door of permissible public comment."[5] The Supreme Court reversed Pennekamp's conviction.

One year later, in *Craig,* the Court again applied the *Bridges* principle. At the close of testimony in a Texas civil jury trial, each side moved for an instructed verdict. The judge instructed the jury to return a verdict for the plaintiff, but the jury decided in favor of the defendant. The judge refused to accept the verdict. Eventually the jury complied, noting that it acted under coercion and against its conscience. The Corpus Christi *Caller-Times* criticized the judge for taking the case away from the jury. The ruling was called "arbitrary action" and a "travesty on justice." The paper deplored the fact that a layman rather than a lawyer sat as judge. The paper also reported that a group of citizens called the judge's ruling a "gross miscarriage of justice." The *Caller-Times* claimed that the judge's behavior had properly brought down "the wrath of public opinion upon his head," that the people were aroused because the defendant "seems to be getting a raw deal," and that there was "no way of knowing whether justice was done, because the first rule of justice, giving both sides an opportunity to be heard, was repudiated." A trial court ruled that the editorials falsely represented the proceedings and that inaccurate reporting had inflamed public feeling against the court. This undercurrent of ill feeling threatened a disturbance in the courtroom, as the trial progressed. The court believed that a clear and present danger existed and found the paper in contempt. The case was appealed. Writing for the Supreme Court, Justice Douglas noted that the articles reflected inept reporting and constituted an unfair report of what transpired. But, according to Douglas, "it takes more imagination than we possess to find in this rather sketchy and one-sided report of a case any imminent or serious threat to a judge of reasonable fortitude." First of all, concerning the newspaper's attack on the judge, Douglas noted that "a judge may not hold in contempt one who ventures to publish anything that tends to make him unpopular or to belittle him." The vehemence of the language used does not, alone, constitute the measure of the power to punish for contempt. That language must spark an imminent threat to the administration of justice. The danger must not be remote or even probable; it must immediately imperil. In this case, it did not.

> Judges who stand for reelection run on their records. That may be a rugged environment. Criticism is expected. Discussion of their conduct is appropriate if not necessary. The fact that the discussion at this particular point of time was not in good taste falls far short of meeting the clear and present danger test.[6]

Second, concerning the coverage of community feelings, the paper reports events of legitimate public interest. Even if the group of citizens were guilty of contempt, "freedom of the press may not be denied a newspaper which brings their conduct to the public eye." In *Craig* the Court did not find a "clear and present danger" to the administration of justice that warranted conviction for contempt.

In the 1949 *Baltimore Radio Show* case, the courts applied the *Bridges* principle to the broadcast media. In this case Baltimore radio stations broadcast news items about a man the police suspected of killing a ten-year-old girl. The broadcasts asserted that the suspect had a long criminal record, that he had confessed to the crime, and that he had reenacted the crime when police returned him to the scene. The reports claimed that the suspect dug down into some leaves to recover the knife he had used to kill the little girl. A trial court found the broadcast media guilty of contempt. In the tradition of the *Bridges* principle, however, the Court of Appeals of Maryland reversed the conviction. The U.S. Supreme Court denied certiorari.[7]

In the cases cited thus far the *Bridges* principle has been applied to the print and broadcast media. In 1962, in the *Wood* case, the Supreme Court upheld the right of an individual citizen to criticize a court. The case began when a judge in Bibb County, Georgia, instructed a grand jury to investigate whether black bloc voting was being stimulated by illegal payments by political candidates. On the next day, with the grand jury in session, Sheriff James Wood, who was a candidate for reelection, issued a news release criticizing the judge's action. Wood also sent an open letter to the grand jury, in which he implied that the Bibb County Democratic Executive Committee was behind the corrupt purchase of votes, and that the grand jury should investigate the committee. The sheriff was convicted of contempt, on the ground that his statement presented a clear and present danger to the investigation. On appeal, the Supreme Court supported Wood's right to engage in the public dialogue. At the time of Wood's criticism, no individual was under investigation. Wood merely contributed to the public discussion at a time when public interest in the matter was at its peak. The majority of the Court noted:

> Particularly in matters of local political corruption and investigations it is important that freedom of communication be kept open and that the real issues not become obscured to the grand jury. It cannot effectively operate in a vacuum.[8]

Examination of the content of Wood's statement and the circumstances under which it was published led the Court to conclude that there was no danger to the administration of justice. Wood's conviction was reversed.

The *Goss* case provides an instance in which the court upheld a contempt citation. The case involved divorce proceedings filed by Carl Champagne against his wife, Shirley. Champagne also initiated action seeking custody of their child. Robert Risberg, a private detective employed by Carl Champagne, testified that Mrs. Champagne had stayed overnight in the apartment of Thomas Duggan Goss. At the time, Goss hosted an evening television program watched by about 200,000 people in the Chicago area. In one broadcast Goss claimed that Risberg was a "professional sneak and liar." Goss also denied that he had committed adultery with Mrs. Champagne. He stated that he had promised Mrs. Champagne

to do everything in his power "to prevent the legal kidnapping of her child."
Goss also referred to Carl Champagne, Carl's father, and his uncle as a family
"with court-admitted hoodlum connections." Contempt proceedings were initiated against Goss. He admitted making the statements with knowledge of the
pending divorce action, but claimed that his purpose was to defend himself before his television viewers against the charge of adultery. He disclaimed any intent to influence the court proceedings. Goss was found guilty because his remarks were not limited to criticism of past action. The outcome of the divorce
and custody hearings depended heavily upon testimony to be offered by witnesses
Goss attacked. His remarks were "designedly calculated to bring odium upon
the testimony of the witnesses produced by the plaintiff and to inspire distrust
in their testimony." The words were contemptuous because they were "calculated to impede, embarrass, or obstruct the court in the due administration of
justice." Goss's words interfered with judicial procedure in both the divorce and
custody cases. On appeal, the Illinois Supreme Court held that Goss's statements
"constituted a clear and present danger to the administration of justice." The
U.S. Supreme Court denied certiorari.[9]

The cases cited in this section affirm the principle established in *Bridges*—the
"clear and present danger" test rather than the "bad tendency" test should be
applied to contempt cases. Furthermore, the danger must be "substantial" and
"imminent." The principle was clearly upheld in *Pennekamp, Craig, Baltimore
Radio Show,* and *Wood.* In these cases, representatives of the media and the
general public were allowed to discuss judicial matters, court actions, and the
legal process. In *Goss,* however, when the defendant's words constituted a clear
and present danger to the judicial process, the Court upheld the contempt ruling.

Gag Orders

In order to control news coverage of court proceedings, judges may impose
gag orders regarding media coverage. For example, judges have banned newsmen from performing specific behaviors—taking photographs,[10] publishing
jurors' names,[11] reporting a verdict,[12] publishing any information about a
case,[13] printing names of witnesses,[14] making sketches of courtroom participants.[15] When the news media appealed such orders, the courts had to resolve
conflicts between the First Amendment right of free speech and the Sixth Amendment right to a fair trial.

In the 1972 *Dickinson* case, the court established a specific requirement that
reporters must follow in dealing with a gag order. In this case Baton Rouge
reporters Larry Dickinson and Gibbs Adams were cited for contempt when they
published testimony given at an open court hearing in violation of a judge's order. The hearing involved a VISTA worker who had been indicted on a charge
of conspiring to murder the mayor of Baton Rouge. At the hearing the judge ordered that no report of the testimony should be made in any news medium. The

judge acknowledged that the press could report the fact that a hearing was being held, but he outlawed reporting details of any evidence presented during the proceeding. The reporters ignored the order and wrote articles summarizing the court's testimony. They were found guilty of criminal contempt. The court of appeals noted that the public had a right to know the facts brought out in the hearing. The court also affirmed that a newspaper may not be proscribed in advance from reporting to the public events that occur during an open and public court proceeding. Nonetheless, Judge John Brown wrote:

> The conclusion that the District Court's order was constitutionally invalid does not necessarily end the matter of the validity of the contempt convictions. There remains the very formidable question of whether a person may with impunity violate an order which turns out to be invalid. We hold that in the circumstances of this case he may not.[16]

The court held that even though the judge's order was unconstitutional, the reporters should have respected the order until they had exhausted available court remedies. The U.S. Supreme Court refused to review *Dickinson*. Despite the unconstitutionality of the judge's gag order, the reporters were punished because they did not pursue available remedies through the courts.

In a 1974 case involving a gag order, the Supreme Court held that before a court can restrict free speech and press, the prohibited expression must constitute a "clear and present danger" to the administration of justice. Furthermore, there must be no doubt that the communication constitutes a serious and imminent threat. In *Times-Picayune* the Supreme Court rejected a gag order on these grounds. The case began with the rape of a young nursing student in a New Orleans public-housing project. Two suspects were arrested and charged with the crime. Immediately the case received thorough coverage. Eleven months after the crime, when the case came to trial, the judge banned reporting of any court testimony after the selection of a jury. The Times-Picayune Publishing Company sought to have the order stayed. The Supreme Court issued the stay. Justice Powell noted that the judge's decision to continue the order during all of the trial proceedings imposed "significant prior restraints on media publication." In addition, the record revealed "the absence of any showing of an imminent threat to fair trial."[17] If necessary, the court had available alternative methods for protecting the defendant's right to a fair trial.

In 1976, in *Nebraska Press Association,* the Supreme Court struck down another gag order. In October of that year Erwin Simants was charged with murdering six members of the Henry Kellie family. In the ensuing court proceedings, there was testimony that Simants had confessed to police officers. Nebraska State District Judge Hugh Stuart ordered that the Nebraska Press Association refrain from publishing or broadcasting accounts of the confession until a jury was selected. The gag order also prohibited any reporting of the contents of a note

written by Simants the night of the crime, portions of medical testimony, the identity of the victims, the nature of the assault, and the provisions of the gag order. Stuart said that "because of the nature of the crimes charged in the complaint...there is a clear and present danger that pretrial publicity could impinge
upon the defendant's right to a fair trial." Several press associations initiated
court action, asking that the restrictive order be vacated. In a unanimous opinion
the Supreme Court overturned the order. Writing for the Court, Chief Justice
Warren Burger argued that "prior restraints on speech and publication are the
most serious and least tolerable infringements on First Amendment rights."
Burger claimed that

> there was indeed a risk that pretrial news accounts, true or false, would have
> some adverse impact on the attitudes of those who might be called as jurors.
> But on the record now before us it is not clear that further publicity, unchecked,
> would so distort the views of potential jurors that 12 could not be found who
> would, under proper instructions, fulfill their sworn duty to render a just ver-
> dict exclusively on the evidence presented in open court. We cannot say on this
> record that alternatives to a prior restraint on petitoners would not have suffi-
> ciently mitigated the adverse effects of pretrial publicity so as to make prior re-
> straint unnecessary.[18]

The Court acknowledged that it was a "heavy burden to demonstrate in advance
of trial that without prior restraint a fair trial will be denied," but that kind of
evidence was necessary in order to demonstrate a "threat to fair trial rights that
would possess the requisite degree of certainty to justify restraint." Such evidence was not apparent in *Nebraska Press Association,* so the order was vacated.

The *KPNX* decision in 1982 upheld a gag order. While presiding over a murder trial in the Superior Court of Maricopa County, Arizona, the judge imposed
two specific restrictions on the press. First, the judge ordered court personnel,
counsel, witnesses, and jurors not to speak directly with the press. Instead, he
appointed a court employee as "liason with the media," to provide a "unified
and singular source for the media concerning these proceedings." Second, he
ordered that any drawings of jurors that were intended for broadcast on television had to be reviewed by the judge. The KPNX Broadcasting Company, believing that the restrictions violated First Amendment press freedoms, initiated
court action that sought to overturn the judge's order. Supreme Court Justice William Rehnquist, however, sided with the trial judge. Concerning the first order,
Rehnquist noted that "unregulated communication between trial participants and
the press at a heavily covered trial" posed a serious problem that warranted such
a restriction. Though Rehnquist found the second order "more troubling," because it "smacks...of the notion of prior restraint," he upheld the restriction.
Rehnquist decided that

of all conceivable reportorial messages that could be conveyed by reporters or artists watching such trials, one of the least necessary to appreciate the significance of the trial would be individual juror sketches.[19]

In *KPNX* Justice Rehnquist sided with the trial judge and upheld the restrictions on the press. On balance, the fair-trial rights outweighed those of the court reporters.

The cases considered in this section suggest that in order for a judge to impose a gag order, there must be an imminent, not merely a potential, threat to the administration of justice. That degree of harm was absent in *Times-Picayune* and *Nebraska Press Association,* but present in *KPNX.* The cases also suggest that reporters are subject to the *Dickinson* principle, which requires that news gatherers exhaust all available court remedies before violating an unconstitutional gag order.

Summary

The Federal Contempt Act of 1831 defined contempt as disobedience of any judicial decree in the presence of the court "or so near thereto as to obstruct the administration of justice." In *Toledo Newspaper Company* the Court offered a causal rather than a geographical interpretation of the phrase "so near thereto." In *Nye* the Court rejected the causal interpretation. "Near" meant physical proximity rather than causal relevancy. In *Bridges* the Court applied the "clear and present danger" rather than the "bad tendency" test. As a result, the Court extended the power of the press to comment on pending court cases and judges. The *Bridges* principle was reinforced in *Pennekamp, Craig, Baltimore Radio Show,* and *Wood.* Occasionally judges will impose a gag order to limit the scope of media coverage. When such orders were appealed in *Times-Picayune* and *Nebraska Press Association,* the Court gave priority to the competing First Amendment claim. In order for a judge to impose a gag order there must be imminent, not merely potential, threat to the administration of justice. The *Dickinson* principle requires reporters to exhaust all available court remedies prior to violating an unconstitutional gag order. To journalists, this rule poses a substantial barrier to thorough news coverage of courtroom proceedings.

TRIAL BY MEDIA

In an age of modern media techniques, the selection of impartial juries has become extremely difficult. Prior to jury selection, news reporters disseminate information about the crime, the victim, and the accused. News media publish the results of interviews held with police, lawyers, witnesses, even the accused.

The public is apprised of facts that will never be presented in court, because those facts are irrelevant to the issues in the case. Furthermore, the problem of prejudicial information does not end with jury selection. News reports often are available to jurors after the trial has begun. Such occurrences place in conflict the right of the accused to a fair trial and the right of the public to be informed.

Pretrial Publicity

Occasionally the news media publish potentially prejudicial information about the defendant in a criminal trial. In such instances, courts must determine the impact of such material on the conduct of the trial.

In 1949 two black men, Samuel Shepherd and Walter Irvin, were charged with the rape of a 17-year-old white girl in Florida. When a local newspaper reported that the men had confessed, a furious mob of local citizens stormed the jail in a lynch attempt, burned the house of one of the accused, and forced the other suspect's relatives to flee the community out of fear for their lives. During the trial a newspaper printed a cartoon that pictured electric chairs with the caption "No Compromise—Supreme Penalty." The suspects were sentenced to death, although their purported confessions were never introduced as evidence. On appeal to the Supreme Court, Justice Robert Jackson found it

> hard to imagine a more prejudicial influence than a press release by the officer of the court charged with defendant's custody stating that they had confessed, and here just such a statement, unsworn to, unseen, uncrossexamined, and uncontradicted, was conveyed by the press to the jury.[20]

The Court held that newspapers, in the enjoyment of their constitutional rights, may not deprive the accused of the right to a fair trial. In *Shepherd,* the crime had stirred deep feelings that were exploited to the limit by the press. During the trial the judge was helpless to provide the accused "any real protection against this out-of-court campaign to convict." The Court reversed the convictions.

In 1959 the *Marshall* case involved pretrial publicity. Howard Marshall was convicted of illegally dispensing prescription drugs. During the trial two newspapers published reports about Marshall's previous convictions for practicing medicine without a license. The defense asked for a mistrial. When questioned by the judge, seven jurors admitted reading the newspaper accounts. These jurors told the judge, however, that they would not be influenced by the articles, that they could decide the case on the basis of the evidence presented, and that they felt no prejudice against Marshall as a result of the articles. When the judge denied the motion for mistrial, Marshall appealed. In a *per curiam* decision, the Supreme Court noted that the jurors were exposed to information that the trial judge had ruled so prejudicial it could not be offered as evidence during the trial. Clearly, the prejudice to Marshall was almost certain to be as great when that evidence reached the jury through news accounts, as when it was a part of the prosecution's case.[21] Under such conditions, the Court held that a new trial should be granted.

In 1961, in *Irvin,* the Court reversed another conviction because of prejudicial pretrial publicity. The case involved Leslie Irvin, who had been arrested by Indiana state police on suspicion of burglary and writing bad checks. Within a few days, the county prosecutor and police officials released press reports announcing that ''Mad Dog'' Irvin had confessed to six killings. In the months preceding Irvin's trial, ''a barrage of newspaper headlines, articles, cartoons and pictures was unleashed against him.'' When the trial began, the press observed that ''strong feelings, often bitter and angry, rumbled to the surface,'' and noted the existence of ''a pattern of deep and bitter prejudice against the former pipefitter.'' Headlines announced that ''impartial jurors are hard to find.'' Irvin's attorney asked for and received a change of venue to a nearby county. The same media, however, were available in this location. Another request for change was denied. During *voir dire,* 370 of the 430 prospective jurors said they believed

Irvin guilty, but his lawyer had exhausted all peremptory challenges. When 12 jurors were selected, the defense attorney unsuccessfully challenged all of them for bias. The pretrial publicity appeared in newspapers that were delivered regularly to about 95 percent of the homes in the area, and local radio and television stations carried extensive newscasts covering the same incidents. Irvin was tried, found guilty, and sentenced to death. He appealed. In *Irvin* the Supreme Court concluded that because of prejudicial news reporting, Irvin had not received a fair and impartial trial.

> With his life at stake, it is not requiring too much that petitioner be tried in an atmosphere undisturbed by so huge a wave of public passion and by a jury other than one in which two-thirds of the members admit, before hearing any testimony, to possessing a belief in his guilt.[22]

The case was remanded to the district court, and Irvin was retried in a less emotional climate. He was found guilty and sentenced to life in prison.

Two years later, in *Rideau,* the Court set aside another conviction on the ground that prejudicial pretrial publicity had precluded a fair trial before an impartial jury. The case involved Wilbert Rideau, who had been arrested on suspicion of robbing a bank in Lake Charles, Louisiana, while kidnapping three and killing one of the bank's employees. The morning after his arrest, a film was made of a 20-minute "interview" in the jail between Rideau and the sheriff of Calcasieu Parish. Under interrogation Rideau admitted that he had committed the robbery, kidnapping, and murder. The film was broadcast over television station KLPC in Lake Charles. A substantial portion of the population of 150,000 persons living in Calcasieu Parish saw the film. When Rideau was charged with armed robbery, kidnapping, and murder, his lawyers filed a motion for a change of venue, on the ground that a fair trial was impossible in Calcasieu Parish. Three members of the jury admitted during *voir dire* that they had seen the television interview. In addition, two members of the jury were deputy sheriffs of Calcasieu Parish. The motion for a change of venue was denied. Rideau was convicted and sentenced to death. The Supreme Court held that Rideau was denied due process of law when the court refused to grant a change of venue "after the people of Calcasieu Parish had been exposed repeatedly and in depth to the spectacle of Rideau personally confessing in detail to the crimes with which he was later to be charged." Writing for the court, Justice Potter Stewart noted:

> For anyone who has ever watched television the conclusion cannot be avoided that this spectacle, to the tens of thousands of people who saw and heard it, in a very real sense *was* Rideau's trial—at which he pleaded guilty to murder. Any subsequent court proceedings in a community so pervasively exposed to such a spectacle could be but a hollow formality.[23]

The conviction was reversed. Rideau was later retried and convicted.

The classic case of pretrial publicity is *Sheppard*. On July 4, 1954, Marilyn Sheppard, wife of Dr. Sam Sheppard, was bludgeoned to death in the upstairs bedroom of their lake-shore home in Bay Village, a suburb of Cleveland. From the beginning, law-enforcement officials suspected Dr. Sheppard of the crime. Throughout the investigation considerable press coverage surrounded the case. Headline stories constantly stressed Sheppard's unwillingness to cooperate with the police and other officials. Newspaper articles described Sheppard's extramarital love affairs as a motive for the crime. The press sought Sheppard's arrest. A front-page editorial inquired, "Why Isn't Sam Sheppard in Jail?" It demanded, "Quit Stalling—Bring Him In." Shortly thereafter Sheppard was arrested and charged with murder. A list of the names and addresses of prospective jurors was published in all three Cleveland newspapers. Anonymous correspondence concerning the trial was subsequently received by all the prospective jurors. All but one juror admitted at *voir dire* to being exposed to the case by the media. During the trial the jurors themselves were constantly exposed to news coverage, and pictures of the jury appeared more than 40 times in Cleveland newspapers. The trial itself received enormous coverage. There were four rows of benches in the courtroom. The first row was assigned to personnel from television and radio stations, the second and third rows were occupied by reporters from newspapers and magazines, and the last row was assigned to Sam and Marilyn Sheppard's families. News personnel used all the rooms on the courtroom floor; telegraphic equipment and telephone lines were installed, so that reports could be speeded to the papers. A television station set up broadcasting facilities on the third floor, next door to the jury room. Newscasts emanated from this room throughout the trial and during jury deliberations. In the corridors outside the courtroom, photographers and television cameramen constantly flashed pictures during court recesses. Outside the building, television cameramen filmed the defendant, judge, jury, and other participants in the trial, walking to and from the courthouse. During the trial anti-Sheppard news coverage continued. One headline claimed that Marilyn had told friends that Sam was a "Dr. Jekyll and Mr. Hyde character." No such testimony was presented at the trial. Broadcaster Walter Winchell reported that Carole Beasley, who was under arrest in New York for robbery, had claimed that she had borne Sam Sheppard a child while his mistress. Two jurors admitted hearing the broadcast, but when they indicated it would have no effect on their verdict, the judge accepted their statement. Although he was not a witness at the trial, Captain Kerr of the Homicide Bureau issued a press statement denying Sheppard's claim that he had been abused by detectives after his arrest. Newspapers printed the detective's story under the headline " 'Bare-faced Liar', Kerr says of Sam." Sheppard was convicted of second degree murder. Several years later the case came to the Supreme Court. Justice Tom Clark's opinion noted that the trial judge failed to protect Sheppard from the prejudicial publicity that saturated the community and neglected to control the disruptive influences in the courtroom. Clark noted that "the carnival atmosphere at trial could easily have been avoided since the courtroom and courthouse premises are subject to the control of the court." He suggested ways in which the courtroom atmosphere could have been improved. First, the presence of the press at judicial proceedings could have been restricted, when it was clear that Sheppard could be disadvantaged. Second, the judge should have "insulated the witnesses." The media interviewed prospective witnesses at will and on numerous occasions disclosed their testimony. Third, the judge should have controlled the release of information to the press. Much of the data thus disclosed "was inaccurate, leading to groundless rumors and confusion."[24] The Court ordered that Sheppard be released, unless Ohio tried him again within a reasonable time. Ohio tried Sheppard again, but this time he was acquitted. In November 1966 Sheppard became a free man.

In cases discussed thus far—*Shepherd, Marshall, Irvin, Rideau, Sheppard*—the Supreme Court overturned convictions obtained in a trial atmosphere that was corrupted by media coverage. In 1975 the Court decision in the *Murphy* case upheld a conviction in which the jury had been exposed to press reports regarding prior convictions of the defendant. The case involved Jack Murphy, whose flamboyant life-style made him a continuing subject of press interest; he was generally referred to in the media as "Murph the Surf." Murphy's arrest in Dade County, Florida, for robbery and assault received extensive media coverage, because he had frequently been in the news before. He had been involved in the 1964 theft of the Star of India sapphire from a museum in New York. In 1968 Murphy had been convicted of murder in Broward County. In 1969 he had pleaded guilty to a federal indictment involving stolen securities. Each new case against Murphy was considered newsworthy; scores of articles reporting his activities were published during the decade. During jury selection for the robbery and assault charges, 78 jurors were questioned. Of these, 30 were excused for miscellaneous personal reasons, 20 were excused peremptorily by the defense or prosecution, 20 were excused by the court because of prejudice against Murphy, and the remaining 8 served as the jury. The defense moved to dismiss the selected jurors on the ground that they were aware of Murphy's prior convictions. The defense also requested a change of venue on the basis of alleged prejudicial pretrial publicity. Both motions were denied and Murphy was convicted. He appealed. The Supreme Court noted that unlike *Marshall*, the *voir dire* in this case indicated no such hostility to Murphy by the jurors who served in this trial "as to suggest a partiality that could not be laid aside." Some of the jurors had some knowledge of Murphy's past crimes, but none indicated any belief in the relevance of the past to the present case. Furthermore, news coverage of Murphy's past experiences was largely factual in nature. The Court's decision was that we are unable to conclude, in the circumstances presented in this case, that petitioner did not receive a fair trial. Petitioner has failed to show that the setting of the trial was inherently prejudicial or that the jury-selection process of which he complains permits an inference of actual prejudice.[25]

In *Murphy* the Court based its decision on the notion that jurors "need not...be totally ignorant of the acts and issues involved." It was sufficient that jurors be able to set aside their impressions and render a verdict based on the evidence presented in the specific case. The Court concluded that appropriate juror impartiality was evident. Nonetheless, as *Shepherd, Marshall, Irvin, Rideau*, and *Sheppard* indicate, the Court will reverse a conviction in order to offset prejudicial pretrial publicity.

Implied Bias

In 1937 the American Bar Association endorsed Canon 35, a judicial rule banning photographic and broadcast equipment in the courtroom. This policy was adopted by most states. It seemed appropriate during the following decades—a period when photography was a disruptive process. Beginning in the 1960s, several journalists complained about the regulations, arguing that modern photographic equipment rendered the ban obsolete. They also asserted that broadcasting a trial was a First Amendment freedom.

In 1962, during a Texas trial, the television ban was challenged. The case involved financier Billie Sol Estes, who was tried on charges of theft, swindling, and embezzlement. Massive pretrial publicity gave the trial national notoriety. During the two-day pretrial hearing, the courtroom was crowded to overflowing. A defense motion to prevent telecasting, radio broadcasting, and news photography was denied; so, several broadcasters carried the proceedings live. Activities of the broadcast crews often disrupted the hearing. The actual trial took place in a completely different environment. Live telecasting was restricted; only the opening and closing arguments of the prosecution and the return of the verdict to the judge were carried live with sound. Various portions of the trial were video-taped for broadcast on regularly scheduled newscasts later in the day. News commentators used the tape as a backdrop for their reports concerning the trial. After Estes was convicted, he appealed on the ground that because of the way the pretrial hearing was conducted, he had been denied a fair trial. When the case reached the Supreme Court, the justices agreed that publicity in a pretrial hearing could hamper due process in an ensuing criminal trial. Justice Clark argued the doctrine of "implied bias"—that is, prejudice is inherent in a televised trial. He offered four reasons. First, the potential impact of television on the jurors may be detrimental, because "while it is practically impossible to assess the effect of television on jury attentiveness, those of us who know juries realize the problem of jury 'distraction.' "

"NO, WE HAVEN'T REACHED A VERDICT YET, BUT WE'D ALL LIKE TO KNOW WHEN WE'LL BE ON TV."

> We are all self-conscious and uneasy when being televised. Human nature be-
> ing what it is, not only will a juror's eyes be fixed on the camera, but also his
> mind will be preoccupied with the telecasting rather than with the testimony.

Second, the quality of the testimony could be impaired. The knowledge that he
or she is being viewed by a vast audience may affect a witness. Some may be
demoralized and frightened, while others become cocky and given to overstate-
ment. Memories may falter, and accuracy of statement may be severely under-
mined. For some, "embarrassment may impede the search for the truth, as may
a natural tendency toward overdramatization." Third, the presence of television
places additional responsibilities on the judge. According to Clark, a judge's job
is to ensure that the accused receives a fair trial, but "when television comes
into the courtroom he must also supervise it." Fourth, the presence of television has an impact on the defendant; "its presence is a form of mental—if not
physical—harassment, resembling a police line up or the third degree."[26] The

Court concluded that the presence of television could only have impressed the people in the courtroom, as well as those in the community, with the notorious character of Billie Sol Estes and the significance of the trial. Televising the proceedings impaired due process. As a result of *Estes,* cameras were prohibited in courtrooms except in those states that did not subscribe to Canon 35. In a separate concurring opinion, Justice John Harlan envisioned the day "when television will have become so commonplace an affair in the daily life of the average person as to dissipate all reasonable likelihood that its use in courtrooms may disparage the judicial process." When that day comes, the opinions set forth in *Estes* will be "subject to re-examination." That reexamination and ultimate revision of Canon 35 took place in the late 1970s.

In February 1978 the American Bar Association proposed permitting courtroom coverage by the electronic media "if such coverage was carried out unobtrusively and without affecting the conduct of the trial." Later that year the Conference of State Chief Justices, by a vote of 44 to 1, approved a resolution to allow the highest court of each state to establish standards regulating radio, television, and other photographic coverage of court proceedings. Subsequently, the Florida Supreme Court established a one-year pilot program, during which electronic media were allowed to cover judicial proceedings in Florida. The Court set forth guidelines detailing the kind of electronic equipment to be used and the manner of its use.

Chandler, a case that took place under the pilot program, involved the criminal trial of former policemen Noel Chandler and Robert Granger, both of whom were charged with the burglary of a Miami Beach restaurant. A television camera recorded the testimony of the prosecution's chief witness, as well as the prosecution's closing statement. No camera was present during the presentation of any part of the case for the defense. When the jury returned a guilty verdict, the defense moved for a new trial, arguing that because of the television coverage they had been denied a fair and impartial trial. When *Chandler* reached the Supreme Court, the justices noted that the *Estes* decision did not ban electronic media coverage of all cases.

> It does not stand as an absolute ban on state experimentation with an evolving technology, which, in terms of modes of mass communication, was in its relative infancy in 1964, and is, even now, in a state of continuing change.[27]

The Court noted that several of the negative factors present in *Estes*—cumbersome equipment, distracting lighting, cables, numerous camera technicians—"are less substantial factors today than they were at that time." The justices then considered whether the very presence of television cameras in the courtroom inescapably produces an adverse psychological impact on the participants in the trial. The Court concluded:

> Whatever may be the "mischievous potentialities [of broadcast coverage] for intruding upon the detached atmosphere which should always surround the judicial process," at present no one has been able to present empirical data sufficient to establish that the mere presence of broadcast media inherently has an adverse effect on that process.

In *Chandler* the Supreme Court decided that Florida could permit electronic media to cover trials in its state courts.

When the one-year pilot program ran its course, the Florida Supreme Court evaluated the program and concluded "that on balance there was more to be gained than lost by permitting electronic media coverage of judicial proceedings subject to standards for such coverage."[28] Several other states have adopted similar laws.

Summary

In its coverage of courtroom proceedings, the press disseminates to the public information about the crime, the victim, the accused, the witnesses, and the jury. Sometimes such information can contribute to a prejudiced verdict. In *Shepherd*, *Marshall*, *Irvin*, *Rideau*, and *Sheppard*, the Court reversed convictions in order to negate "sensational" publicity. In *Murphy*, however, the Court ruled that jurors need not be completely ignorant of the facts; it is sufficient that jurors be able to set aside their impressions and render an impartial decision. The use of electronic media in the courtroom may also result in an unfair trial. In *Estes* the Court advanced the doctrine of "implied bias"—that is, that prejudice is inherent in a televised trial. That view was questioned in *Chandler*.

NOTES

1. *Times-Picayune Publishing Corporation v. Schulingkamp*, 95 S.Ct. 1 (1974).
2. *Toledo Newspaper Company v. United States*, 38 S.Ct. 560 (1918).
3. *Nye v. United States*, 61 S.Ct. 810 (1941).
4. *Bridges v. California; Time-Mirror Company v. Superior Court of State of California, In And For Los Angeles County*, 62 S.Ct. 190 (1941).

5. *Pennekamp v. Florida*, 66 S.Ct. 1029 (1946).

6. *Craig v. Harney*, 67 S.Ct. 1249 (1947).

7. *Maryland v. Baltimore Radio Show*, 67 A. 2d 497 (1949); cert. denied 70 S.Ct. 252 (1950).

8. *Wood v. Georgia*, 82 S.Ct. 1364 (1962).

9. *Goss v. Illinois*, 312 F. 2d 257 (1963); cert. denied 81 S.Ct. 1658 (1960).

10. *Seymour v. United States*, 373 F. 2d 629 (1967).

11. *Schuster v. Bowen*, 347 F. Supp. 319 (1972).

12. *Wood v. Goodson*, 485 S.W. 2d 213 (1972).

13. *Miami Herald Publishing Company v. Rose*, 271 So. 2d 483 (1972).

14. *Sun Company of San Bernadino v. Superior Court; Progress-Bulletin Publishing Company v. Superior Court*, 29 Cal. App. 3d 815 (1973).

15. *United States v. Columbia Broadcasting System, Inc.*, 497 F. 2d 102 (1974).

16. *United States v. Dickinson*, 465 F. 2d 496 (1972); cert. denied 94 S.Ct. 270 (1973).

17. *Times-Picayune Publishing Corporation.*

18. *Nebraska Press Association v. Stuart*, 96 S.Ct. 2791 (1976).

19. *KPNX Broadcasting Company v. Arizona Superior Court*, 103 S.Ct. 584 (1982).

20. *Shepherd v. Florida*, 71 S.Ct. 549 (1951).

21. *Marshall v. United States*, 79 S.Ct. 1171 (1959).

22. *Irwin v. Dowd*, 81 S.Ct. 1639 (1961).

23. *Rideau v. Louisiana*, 83 S.Ct. 1417 (1963).

24. *Sheppard v. Maxwell*, 86 S.Ct. 1507 (1966).

25. *Murphy v. Florida*, 95 S.Ct. 2031 (1975).

26. *Estes v. Texas*, 85 S.Ct. 1628 (1965).

27. *Chandler v. Florida*, 101 S.Ct. 802 (198!).

28. *Chandler.*

RECOMMENDED READING

Alberich, H. Glenn, "*Nebraska Press Association vs. Stuart:* Balancing Freedom of the Press Against the Right to Fair Trial," *New England Law Review* 12 (Winter, 1977), 763-88.

Antonelli, Carol S., "Fair Trial/Free Press—*Nebraska Press Association vs. Stuart:* Defining the Limits of Prior Restraint in the Trial by Newspaper Controversy," *Loyola University Law Journal* 8 (Winter, 1977), 417-37.

Apfel, Dou., "Gag Orders, Exclusionary Orders, and Protective Orders: Expanding the Use of Preventive Remedies to Safeguard a Criminal Defendant's Right to a Fair Trial," *American University Law Review* 29 (Spring, 1980), 439-84.

Jennings, James M., "Is *Chandler* a Final Rewrite of *Estes?*" *Journalism Quarterly* 59 (Spring, 1982), 66-73.

Stephenson, D. Grier, Jr., "Fair Trial-Free Press: Rights in Continuing Conflict," *Brooklyn Law Review* 46 (Fall, 1979), 39-66.

KEY DECISIONS

1918—*TOLEDO NEWSPAPER*—offered a causal interpretation of the phrase "so near thereto" (Federal Contempt Act).

1941—*NYE*—offered a geographical interpretation of the phrase "so near thereto" (Federal Contempt Act).

1941—*BRIDGES*—applied "clear and present danger" rather than "bad tendency" test to contempt-of-court cases, thus expanding the power of the press to comment on judges and proceedings.

1965—*ESTES*—established doctrine of "implied bias" regarding the televising of trials.

1966—*SHEPPARD*—overturned conviction obtained in a trial atmosphere that was corrupted by media coverage.

1973—*DICKINSON*—required reporters to exhaust all court remedies prior to violating an unconstitutional gag order.

1975—*MURPHY*—held that jurors need not be totally ignorant of background information regarding defendant, if they can set aside impressions and render impartial verdict.

1976—*NEBRASKA PRESS ASSOCIATION*—held that for a judge to impose a gag order there must be imminent, not merely potential, threat to the administration of justice.

1981—*CHANDLER*—challenged the doctrine of "implied bias"; noted absence of proof that television cameras in the courtroom inescapably produce an adverse impact on trial participants.

SUMMARY—FAIR TRIAL

Definition

This area of law is designed to balance the First Amendment rights of free press with the Sixth Amendment right to a fair trial.

Proof

Suspected criminals have been granted a change of venue, mistrial, or new trial in the event of potential
1. Prejudicial pretrial publicity—that is, exposure to damaging irrelevant information
2. Bias created by the presence of television medium (limited applicability).

Defenses

Judicial orders have been overturned in the case of
1. Unwarranted prior restraint—public has a right to know
2. Absence of a showing of clear and present danger to the administration of justice.

12

BROADCASTING

Society is experiencing a revolution in communication technology. Nowhere is this more evident than in the broadcasting field—radio, television, cable TV, public broadcasting. Each new advancement alters society's orientation toward information, entertainment, and promotion. The changes necessitate forms of regulation, the responsibility for which is entrusted to the Federal Communications Commission. This chapter contains an examination of both the history and significant doctrines affecting broadcast regulation.

HISTORY OF REGULATION

At the beginning of the twentieth century the principal focus of broadcast regulation was directed at the telegraph. In 1903 an international conference, held in Berlin, produced an agreement concerning cooperation in wireless communication. In 1910 Congress passed the Wireless Ship Act, which set forth specific guidelines for maritime communication. The United States had its first broadcast regulation.[1] The revolution in communication technology that has taken place during the twentieth century has spurred the passage of various forms of regulation. Each new medium brought unique problems to the area of broadcast regulation. First the Federal Radio Commission, and later the Federal Communications Commission, were assigned the tasks of regulating broadcast media and coping with problems produced by the communications revolution.

Federal Radio Commission

At the turn of the century not many people owned a radio, and only a few attempted broadcasting on their own. There was no need for government regulation. By 1912, however, electrical interference from stations using the same frequency necessitated some form of control. Congress passed the Radio Act of 1912, which placed radio licensing under the control of the secretary of commerce.[2] The law contained several guidelines for broadcast regulation. First, in order to deal with the problems resulting from electrical interference, each station was given a separate call number. Second, in applying for a license, a station had to identify its ownership, location, purpose, hours of operation, and authorized frequency. Once allowed to broadcast, a station had to be continually supervised by an authorized agent. Violators were subject to imprisonment and a fine. Third, the act provided that the president, in time of war or public peril, could close any station or authorize use of a station by the government with just compensation of the owners. Fourth, the act listed 20 regulations concerning appropriate wavelengths, broadcasting of distress signals, division of time, uses of power, secrecy of messages, and broadcasting control of vicinities.

One of the first court challenges of the act occurred in 1923, in the *Hoover* case. Intercity Radio Company was granted a license in 1920. The following year Secretary of Commerce Herbert Hoover refused to renew the license, because he was unable to assign a wavelength that would not interfere with government and private stations. Furthermore, Hoover maintained that issuing or refusing a license was left solely to his discretion. The district court disagreed. The duty of assigning a wavelength was "mandatory upon the Secretary." The only discretionary act left to the secretary was to select a wavelength that would result in the "least possible interference." According to the court, "the duty of issuing licenses to persons or corporations coming within the classification designated in the act reposed no discretion whatever in the Secretary of Commerce. The duty is mandatory."[3] In *Hoover* the court declined to grant the secretary broad discretion in radio licensing.

Another challenge to the secretary's authority occurred in the *Zenith Radio* case, which came before the district court in 1926. The case arose when the Zenith Radio Corporation operated its station on a wavelength and at times that were not authorized by the secretary. This action, according to the secretary, constituted a misdemeanor, punishable by a fine up to $500 and forfeiture of the station's apparatus. The court ruled for Zenith Radio Corporation for two reasons. First, the Radio Act of 1912 "cannot be construed to cover the acts of the defendant upon which this prosecution is based." Second, there was "no express grant of power in the act to the Secretary of Commerce to establish regulations."[4] In *Zenith Radio* the court again refused to grant discretionary powers to the secretary.

In 1927 Congress passed a new radio act.[5] The act retained many of the features of the 1912 law, including special privileges for government stations, the right of the president to authorize the use of broadcasting facilities during time of national peril, and the punishment of individuals who transmit a false signal of distress. The act, however, introduced new areas of station operation to government control. For example, the act established a type of equal-time doctrine concerning political broadcasts. According to the act,

> if any licensee shall permit any person who is a legally qualified candidate for any public office to use a broadcasting station, he shall offer equal opportunities to all other such candidates for that office.

The law also specified that any program for which money was paid had to be properly identified; the name of the sponsor had to be announced during the broadcast. And though the act gave the government significant power to regulate radio communication, it banned any form of censorship or prior restraint by the licensing authority.

The 1927 act created the Federal Radio Commission and defined its responsibilities and powers. The FRC was composed of five commissioners appointed for six-year terms by the president. Each commissioner represented a different geographical zone, and not more than three could be from the same political party. The commission was authorized to regulate broadcasting ''as public convenience, interest or necessity requires.'' The duties of the FRC included (1) classifying radio stations as to power ratings, (2) prescribing the nature of service to be rendered by each class and each station within a class, (3) assigning wavelengths to stations, (4) determining station locations, (5) regulating the apparatus to be used, (6) preventing electrical interference, (7) establishng areas to be served by each station, (8) regulating stations involved in chain (network) broadcasting, (9) establishing regulations governing records that a station must keep, and (10) holding meetings to investigate stations regarding their performance.

The Radio Act of 1927 also addressed the issue of authority. According to the act, in one year all powers vested in the FRC, except the power to revoke licenses, reverted to the secretary of commerce. Ultimate authority, however, rested with the FRC. Any party aggrieved by an action of the secretary could appeal to the FRC. And any station whose application was refused had the right to appeal to the Court of Appeals of the District of Columbia. The act also acknowleged some rights and responsibilities of applicants. All potential or incumbent licensees were afforded procedural safeguards, including the opportunity for a formal hearing. In all cases the license was granted for no longer than three years. Licenses were to be automatically denied to any station attempting to monopolize radio communication. The FRC retained discretion to revoke licenses, when a station made false statements, used profane language, or failed to operate within the limitations set forth by the license.

For the next few years the Federal Radio Commission went about its work without major incident. Its authority to license stations in the public interest, convenience, and necessity was generally unquestioned. During the 1930s, however, the authority of the FRC was tested in the *KFKB, Trinity Methodist,* and *Gregg* cases.

KFKB, a radio station located in Milford, Kansas, was first licensed by the secretary of commerce in 1923, in the name of the Brinkley-Jones Hospital Association. In 1926 it was relicensed to Dr. J. R. Brinkley. In early 1930, when the station filed for renewel of its license, the FRC decided that public interest, convenience, or necessity would not be served by granting the application. The evidence indicated that Dr. Brinkley, founder of Station KFKB, the Brinkley Hospital, and the Brinkley Pharmaceutical Association, controlled the policy of the station. Each day, Brinkley broadcast three half-hour programs, entitled the "Medical Question Box." Without ever personally diagnosing the callers, Brinkley prescribed patent medicines produced by his drug company. The FRC noted that the practice "is inimical to the public health and safety, and for that reason is not in the public interest." The FRC held that

> the testimony in this case shows conclusively that the operation of Station KFKB is conducted only in the personal interest of Dr. John R. Brinkley. While it is to be expected that a licensee of a radio broadcasting station will receive some remuneration for serving the public with radio programs, at the same time the interest of the listening public is paramount, and may not be subordinated to the interests of the station licensee.[6]

Upon appeal, the Court of Appeals, District of Columbia, unanimously affirmed the FRC's decision. The court ruled that the burden of proof was upon the applicant to show that license renewal was in the public interest, convenience, and necessity. In *KFKB* the court provided the first judicial support for the FRC's right to consider a station's programming with relation to the public interest, convenience, and necessity.

One year later the court strengthened its position. The case involved Trinity Methodist Church, South, the lessee and operator of Los Angeles radio station KGEF. The FRC determined that, though in the name of a church, the station was actually owned and operated by Reverend Doctor Shuler. In 1930 numerous citizens protested when KGEF filed an application for renewal of its license. The FRC denied the application, because the station had been used to attack the Roman Catholic Church, the broadcasts by Shuler were sensational rather than instructive, and on two occasions Shuler had been cited for using his radio talks to obstruct the administration of justice. In addition, Shuler made defamatory statements against the Board of Health, members of the judiciary, and officers in the Los Angeles Labor Temple. Appealing the decision, KGEF argued that the commission's decision was an unconstitutional violation of free speech. The court, however, affirmed the authority of the FRC to regulate broadcasting.

> Everyone interested in radio legislation approved the principle of limiting the number of broadcasting stations, or, perhaps, it would be more nearly correct to say, recognized the inevitable necessity. In these circumstances Congress intervened and asserted its paramount authority, and if it be admitted, as we think

it must be, that, in the present condition of the science with its limited facilities, the regulatory provisions of the Radio Act are a reasonable exercise by Congress of its powers, the exercise of these powers is no more restricted by the First Amendment than are the police powers of the States under the Fourteenth Amendment.[7]

The court noted that the First Amendment did not guarantee continued use of a public radio station as a forum for personal sentiments. According to the *Trinity Methodist* decision, the FRC ruling was justified.

In *Gregg* the district court expanded FRC power by ruling that even unlicensed radio operators with an intrastate signal came under federal control. The case involved a complaint against Paul Gregg, owner and operator of a radio station in Houston, Texas, known as the "Voice of Labor." The station operated without a license. The FRC complaint sought an injunction to prevent the station from operating in this fashion, on the ground that the station caused interference with other duly licensed stations in the Houston area. In court, Gregg argued that his station was justified because of the nature of his programming. The station did not operate as a commercial venture, but for education, religious, charitable, labor, and other such purposes. The court, however, found the wording of the 1927 Radio Act explicitly clear—Gregg was prohibited from operating without a license from the FRC.[8] In *Gregg,* as in *KFKB* and *Trinity Methodist,* the authority of government to license radio broadcasting in the public interest was firmly established. As a result, Federal Radio Commission rulings attained authoritative validity.

Federal Communications Commission

Faced with the complexities of new broadcast technology, especially the introduction of television, Congress enacted the Federal Communications Act of 1934.[9] The Radio Commission was replaced by a seven-member Federal Communications Commission. The commission's chairman and members were to be appointed by the president for seven-year terms. The commission, in effect, had been granted semi-autonomous status and exclusive authority to regulate the broadcasting industry. The FCC retained all of the responsibilities and powers enunciated in the 1927 act and was, in addition, provided with more effective means of enforcement. Since its formation in 1934, the FCC has faced several issues, including network broadcasting, cable television, and public broadcasting.

Network Broadcasting

According to the Communications Act of 1934, chain (network) broadcasting consisted of the "simultaneous broadcasting of an identical program by two or more connected stations.'' In 1938 the FCC initiated a study to determine whether any special regulations were applicable to chain broadcasting. In 1941 the findings were published in the commision's *Report on Chain Broadcasting,* which concluded that network control over the industry was extensive. The FCC found that at the end of 1938 there were 660 commercial radio stations in the United States and that 341 of those were affiliated with national networks: 135 exclusively with the National Broadcasting Company, 102 exclusively with the Columbia Broadcasting System, and 74 exclusively with the Mutual Broadcasting System. In addition, 25 stations were affiliated with both NBC and Mutual, and 5 with both CBS and Mutual. The report noted that the stations affiliated with the national networks utilized more than 97 percent of the total night-time broadcasting power of all the stations in the country. Nonetheless, the FCC acknowledged that network broadcasting played an ''important'' role in the development of radio.

> Chain broadcasting makes possible a wider reception for expensive entertainment and cultural programs, and also for programs of national or regional significance which would otherwise have coverage only in the locality of origin.[10]

Moreover, ''access to greatly enlarged audiences made possible by chain broadcasting has been a strong incentive to advertisers to finance the production of expensive programs.''

The FCC report focused on an area of abuse. The report argued that the networks controlled the stations and precluded the formation of competing networks. Accordingly, the FCC adopted rules to regulate such abuse. The rules were designed to prevent

- Exclusive affiliation of stations
- Lengthy term of affiliation
- ''Optional time'' clauses
- Territorial exclusivity
- Required programming
- Network ownership of stations
- Network control of station rates.

According to the FCC such practices were not in the ''public interest, convenience, or necessity.''

In 1941 the networks sought to prevent the enforcement of these rules on two grounds. First, the FCC had exceeded its authority. Second, the regulations violated the First Amendment. The case reached the Supreme Court. The opinion, written by Justice Felix Frankfurter, stressed that the FCC was empowered to provide effective use of radio in the public interest. Frankfurter claimed that with the number of radio channels limited by natural factors, the public interest demands that those who are entrusted with the available channels shall make the fullest and most effective use of them. If a licensee enters into a contract with a network organization which limits his ability to make the best use of the radio facility assigned him, he is not serving the public interest.[11]

Frankfurter also rejected the First Amendment argument. He noted that broadcasting was a limited access medium; "unlike other modes of expression, radio inherently is not available to all. That is its unique characteristic." Because it could not be used by all, "some who wish to use it must be denied." Frankfurter concluded that "since the spectrum is finite and the frequencies are not available to all who might like them, some regulation is necessary." The system of regulation established by the Federal Communications Act of 1934 clearly placed the power to grant and supervise licenses in the hands of the FCC. In *NBC* the Court upheld the FCC's authority to regulate network broadcasting.

Cable Television

Cable television systems, initially called community antenna television (CATV), began in the late 1940s. Cable systems receive signals from television broadcasting stations, then amplify and distribute the signals to subscribers who have paid for the service. Traditionally, cable systems performed two functions. First, they facilitated satisfactory reception of adjacent stations. Second, they transmitted the signals of distant stations. Importation of distant signals has increasingly become the dominant function of cable television. Since the cable industry merely redistributes signals and does not produce its own programming, it is not subject to the same FCC regulation as conventional stations. Nonetheless, the FCC established its authority over cable television in a series of cases. *Carter Mountain, Southwestern Cable, Midwest Video I, Midwest Video II,* and *Home Box Office* provide examples.

Carter Mountain Transmission Corporation applied to the FCC for permission to construct a system to transmit signals received from television stations located in several distant cities to CATV systems established in Riverton, Lander, and Thermopolie, Wyoming. The FCC denied the application. The FCC reasoned that to permit Carter Mountain to bring in outside programs would result in the "demise" of local television station KWRB-TV, and the loss of service to a substantial rural population not served by the cable system and to many other persons who did not subscribe to the system. According to the FCC, the need for the local outlet outweighed the improved service the proposed facilities would bring to those who subscribed. The FCC concluded that the cable system would not serve the public interest, convenience, and necessity. Carter Mountain brought the case before the court of appeals. In rejecting Carter Mountain's appeal, the court stressed that competition is a relevant factor in weighing the public interest.

> Federal Communications Commission, in carrying out its obligation to make such distribution of licenses, frequencies and power among the states and communities as to provide a fair, efficient and equitable distribution of service, may weigh the net effect on the community or communities to be served.[12]

The court felt that the FCC's exercise of power in this case was not capricious or arbitrary nor did it exceed the FCC's statutory jurisdiction to regulate cable systems. In 1963 the U.S. Supreme Court denied certiorari in the *Carter Mountain* case. In so doing, the Court expanded the focus of regulation into the domain of cable television.

In 1968, in *Southwestern Cable*, the Supreme Court affirmed the FCC's power to regulate the cable television industry. Midwestern Television Company claimed that Southwestern Cable Company had transmitted the signals of Los Angeles broadcasting stations into the San Diego area and thereby had adversely affected Midwestern's San Diego market. Midwestern argued that Southwestern's action had fragmented the San Diego audience, reduced the advertising revenues of local stations, and that the station would have to eventually terminate or reduce its service. Shortly thereafter, the FCC restricted Southwestern's service area. On petition for review, the court of appeals held that the FCC lacked authority under the Communications Act of 1934 to issue such an order. In an important victory for the FCC, the U.S. Supreme Court unanimously overturned the decision and upheld FCC authority.

> The Commission has been charged with broader responsibilities for the orderly development of an appropriate system of local television broadcasting. The significance of its effects can scarcely be exaggerated, for broadcasting is demonstrably a principal source of information and entertainment for a great part of the Nation's population. The Commission has reasonably found that the successful performance of these duties demands prompt and efficacious regulation of community antenna television systems. . . . We therefore hold that the Commission's authority over "all interstate . . . communication by wire or radio" permits the regulation of CATV systems.[13]

The Court also expressed concern that the cable system conflicted with the emphasis the FCC had placed on local service programming. The Court stressed that "the ability of listeners to view channels far from their homes erodes the audience of the locally based channel and therefore shrinks its appeal to local advertisers." The Court guaranteed support for incumbent license holders who, by their past performance, demonstrated concern for the public interest. In *South-*

western Cable the Court upheld the authority of the FCC to regulate cable television and also approved the local programming requirement.

In *Midwest Video Corporation I* the Supreme Court expanded the FCC's authority over cable television. In 1969 the FCC adopted a rule providing that

> no CATV system having 3,500 or more subscribers shall carry the signal of any television broadcast station unless the system also operates to a significant extent as a local outlet by cable casting and has available facilities for local production and presentation of programs other than automated services.

This ruling was designed to spur local participation in community affairs through cable television. Upon the challenge of Midwest Video Corporation, the court of appeals set aside the regulation on the ground that the FCC "is without authority to impose it." The U.S. Supreme Court, in a five-to-four decision, reversed the lower court. The Court ruled that the program-origination rule was within the FCC's authority and that the rule would promote the public interest.[14] In a dissenting opinion Justice William Douglas expressed concern "that to entrust the Commission with the power to force some, a few, or all, CATV operators into the broadcast business is to give it a forbidding authority." Nonetheless, the *Midwest Video I* majority sustained the program-origination rule, thereby approving FCC authority that was far more encompassing than that enunciated in *Southwestern Cable*.

In the late 1970s the Court decided two cases that limited FCC control over cable television. The first such case again involved Midwest Video Corporation. In 1976 the FCC set forth three rules regarding cable television systems. First, systems that have 3,500 or more subscribers were obliged to develop at least a 20-channel capacity by 1986. Second, cable systems had to make available certain channels for access by public, educational, local governmental, and leased-access users. Third, systems were required to furnish equipment and facilities for access purposes. Under these rules, cable operators were deprived of all discretion regarding who could use their access channels and what could be transmitted over such channels. On petition for review, the court of appeals set aside the FCC's rules as beyond the agency's jurisdiction. The court held that the rules imposed common-carrier obligations on cable operators, and thus ran counter to the command of the Federal Communications Act of 1934, which states that "a person engaged in. . .broadcasting shall not. . .be deemed a common carrier." The court stressed that Congress had limited the FCC's ability to provide "public access at the expense of the journalistic freedom of persons engaged in broadcasting."[15] In *Midwest Video II* the Supreme Court, in the opinion of Justice Byron White, agreed with the court of appeals. The rules exceeded the FCC's statutory authority.

The *Home Box Office* case involved a successful challenge to the FCC's "pay cable" rules. The rules restricted cablecasters from presenting certain feature films and sports programs, if a separate charge were made for the program. In addition, the rules prohibited cablecasters from devoting more than 90 percent of their broadcast hours to movie and sports programs and also banned cablecasters from showing commercial advertising. According to the FCC, the purpose of the rules was twofold. First, cable service is undesirable unless the programming is distinct from that on commercial television. Second, there is a likelihood that the revenue involved would be sufficient to allow cable operators to bid away the best programs, thus reducing the quality of conventional television. By limiting the cablecaster to material that is not otherwise shown on television, the FCC hoped to prevent such ''siphoning'' and to enhance the diversity of program offerings on broadcast television. In *Home Box Office* the court of appeals found the FCC ''pay cable'' rules to be invalid. The court had no objections to the FCC's content regulations.

> The Commission seeks only to channel movie and sports material to its intended recipients over broadcast television, rather than pay cable, whenever the economics of advertiser-supported programming permit. If the rules and their associated waiver provisions achieved no more than this...they would present no barrier: material suitable for broadcast would be broadcast; material financially viable only on cable would be on cable. Those served by pay cable would surely be served by broadcast television as well and, therefore, would have access to anything that could profitably be presented on either medium. Those without cable would at least be no worse off than at present.[16]

The court, however, found the rules in violation of the First Amendment for three reasons. First, the FCC failed to show that the 90 percent and the no-advertising rules served an ''important or substantial government interest.'' Second, the FCC failed to demonstrate that the alleged siphoning phenomenon constitutes a real threat to those not served by cable. Third, the rules were overbroad. For example, the rule applied to all films and sports programs, regardless of their suitability for broadcast. For these reasons, the court overturned the FCC's ''pay cable'' rules. In 1977 the Supreme Court denied certiorari.

Carter Mountain, Southwestern Cable, and *Midwest Video I* firmly established the authority of the FCC to regulate cable television. These cases demonstrate that all mass communication is evaluated with a concern for the public interest. In some recent cases, *Midwest Video II* and *Home Box Office,* the courts have restricted the scope of FCC power over the cable industry.

Public Broadcasting

In 1967 the Carnegie Foundation suggested the formation of a nonprofit corporation to encourage the development of noncommercial television. The Carnegie report provided much of the impetus toward government-financed public broadcasting and helped to secure passage of the Public Broadcasting Act of 1967. The act funded the development of noncommercial educational broadcasting, under the direction of the Corporation for Public Broadcasting,. To become certified by the CPB, a station had to possess a FCC noncommercial education license, facilities for local program origination, and a schedule of local programming. Certification was generally limited to one station in an area. In 1970 the CPB formed the Public Broadcasting Service, a network for public programs. At the same time the government began to reduce funding for public stations, as they became able to meet their own economic and programming needs.

Public broadcasting has been the focus of only a few court actions. One such case involved a challenge to the University of Maine's public television station. In 1970 the university broadcast a program that contained comments by State Senator Robert Stuart, an active and legally qualified candidate for the U.S. House of Representatives. The program, which lasted 40 minutes, consisted of Stuart answering questions telephoned in by the public. The station accepted the calls on a collect basis. The State of Maine initiated court action, seeking to stop the university from using its educational television system for interviews with political candidates. The state cited a law that held that

> none of the facilities, plant or personnel of any educational television system which is supported in whole or in part by state funds shall be used directly or indirectly for the promotion, advertisement or advancement of any political candidate for any municipal, county, state or federal office.... Any person convicted of a violation of any provision of this section shall be punished by a fine of not more than $5,000 or by imprisonment for not more than 11 months, or by both.

The university contended that the law conflicted with Section 315 of the Federal Communications Act of 1934. The Supreme Judicial Court of Maine agreed with the university; the "public interest" standard was as binding upon noncommercial stations as it was upon those that operated for profit. According to the court,

> the designation of their licensed activities as "educational television broadcasting" would indeed be a misnomer if state law would effectively preclude them from presenting programs which are by their very nature essential to the educational process.[17]

In *University of Maine* the court found the Maine statute to be unconstitutional.

In 1984, in *League of Women Voters of California,* the Supreme Court decided another case that affected the operation of public broadcasting. The case involved a challenge from two groups: Pacific Foundation as the owner of several public broadcasting stations, and the League of Women Voters of California as listeners and viewers of public broadcasting. The groups challenged Section 399 of the Public Broadcasting Act of 1967, which forbade any noncommercial educational station that receives funding from the CPB to "engage in editorializing." The Supreme Court, in the opinion prepared by Justice William Brennan, held that the ban violated the First Amendment. Brennan rejected the government's argument that Section 399 served "a compelling government interest in ensuring that funded noncommercial broadcasters do not become propaganda organs for the government." Brennan noted that

> the public's interest in preventing broadcasting stations from becoming forums for lopsided presentations of narrow partisan positions is already secured by a variety of other regulatory means that intrude far less drastically upon the "journalistic freedom" of noncommercial broadcasters. The requirements of the FCC's fairness doctrine, for instance, which apply to commercial and noncommercial stations alike, ensure that such editorializing would maintain a reasonably balanced and fair presentation of controversial issues. Thus, even if the management of a noncommercial educational station were inclined to seek to further only its own partisan views when editorializing, it simply could not do so.[18]

Brennan acknowledged that the FCC holds "power to regulate the content, timing, or character of speech by noncommercial educational stations." Because, however, the breadth of Section 399 "extends so far beyond what is necessary to accomplish the goals identified by the Government, it fails to satisfy First Amendment standards."

Summary

From its outset, government regulation of broadcasting has been based on the public interest, convenience, and necessity. The authority of government to regulate broadcasting was established by congressional legislation and reinforced by court opinions. The initial authority to license radio broadcasting was granted to the Federal Radio Commission by the Radio Acts of 1912 and 1927, and was reinforced in the *KFKB, Trinity Methodist,* and *Gregg* cases. Influenced by the increasing complexity of communication technology, Congress passed the Federal Communications Act of 1934. The act established the Federal Communications Commission. The power of the FCC to regulate network broadcasting was recognized by the Supreme Court in *NBC.* The FCC's power was extended to cable television in *Carter Mountain, Southwestern Cable,* and *Midwest Video I.* With the passage of the Public Broadcasting Act of 1967, the FCC became responsible for regulating public broadcasting. The courts clarified the scope of such regulation in the *University of Maine* and the *League of Women Voters of California* cases.

LICENSING-DECISION GUIDELINES

Under the regulatory scheme established by the Radio Act of 1927 and continued in the Communications Act of 1934, no radio or television station may operate without the approval of the Federal Communications Commission. The FCC regulates the broadcast industry primarily through its power to grant, renew, and revoke licenses. Several guidelines, involving economic, programming, and procedural factors, are considered by the FCC when making a licensing decision.

Economic Guidelines

The licensing decision is influenced by two economic guidelines: the effect of competition on incumbent license holders and the extent to which ownership of broadcasting facilities is diversified among different groups and individuals.

Incumbent License Holder

The *Sanders Brothers* case represents the first significant influence by the Supreme Court regarding the economic well-being of incumbent licensees. The case began in 1936, when the Telegraph Herald Company, owner of a newspaper published in Dubuque, Iowa, applied for a permit to build a broadcasting station. The incumbent license holder, Sanders Brothers radio station WKBB, sought to prevent the new station on the ground that the loss in advertising revenue would harm WKBB and that the public interest, convenience, and necessity were already being adequately served. The FCC approved of the new station, noting that two stations were necessary and that no electrical interference would result. The court of appeals reversed the decision, holding that the FCC should have investigated possible economic injury to Sanders Brothers. On appeal to the Supreme Court, the Telegraph Herald Company argued that economic injury to a competitor was not a valid ground for refusal to grant a license. The Court, per Justice Owen Roberts, agreed:

> We hold that resulting economic injury to a rival station is not, in and of itself, and apart from considerations of public convenience, interest, or necessity, an element the petitioner must weigh, and as to which it must make findings, in passing on an application for a broadcasting license.[19]

Roberts stressed that the incumbent licensee did not enjoy a vested property right to continue broadcasting. The Court noted, however, that the question of incumbent well-being was a relevant concern if it affected the public interest, convenience, and necessity. The Court noted that in the *Sanders Brothers* case the objection to the FCC ruling was not that the public interest was insufficiently protected, but that the financial interests of the incumbent had not been considered. The Supreme Court reaffirmed the FCC's decision to grant two licenses. From 1940 to 1958 the FCC interpreted the *Sanders Brothers* case to mean that potential economic injury to an incumbent was no basis for refusing to license a competitor.

In 1958 the court of appeals rejected the FCC's interpretation of the *Sanders Brothers* decision and emphasized that economic factors were relevant when potential competition seemed likely to adversely affect the public interest. The case arose when Carroll Broadcasting Company, a radio station in Carrollton, Georgia, tried to prevent West Georgia Broadcasting Company from operating in the same area. The FCC granted a license to the West Georgia Company, noting that the issue of competition was not relevant. The court of appeals reversed the FCC ruling; competition was relevant if it adversely affected the public interest.

> We hold that, when an existing licensee offers to prove that the economic effect of another station would be detrimental to the public interest, the Commission should afford an opportunity for the presentaion of such proof and, if the evidence is substantial (i.e. if the protestant does not fail entirely to meet his burden), should make a finding or findings.[20]

The court stressed that an incumbent license holder has legal standing, even though actual economic harm is not suffered. The main concern, however, is for the public interest. According to the court, "the public interest is affected when service is affected." In *Carroll* the court instructed the FCC to give appropriate consideration to the issue of economic harm to an incumbent licensee, especially with an eye toward the economic impact on the public interest.

Diversification of Ownership

In setting its licensing policies the FCC has long acted on the theory that diversification of mass-media ownership serves the public interest by promoting diversity of program and service viewpoints, as well as by preventing undue concentration of economic power. This perception of the public interest has been implemented over the years by a series of regulations imposing stringent restrictions on multiple ownership of broadcast stations. These regulations were the impetus for several court cases, including *Mansfield Journal, Greater Boston,* and *National Citizens Committee.*

In the early 1950s the city of Mansfield, Ohio, enjoyed two forms of media, the *Mansfield Journal* and radio station WMAN. These media competed for local advertising. The Mansfield Journal Company, however, attempted to coerce its advertisers to enter into exclusive contracts with the newspaper and to refrain from advertising on WMAN. It did this by refusing to permit clients who advertised on the radio to advertise in the paper. In addition, the company refused to print WMAN's program log in the paper. When the Mansfield Journal Company applied for a radio broadcasting license, the FCC denied the application. The FCC ruled that the company's previous actions were designed to suppress competition and to achieve a monopoly of news dissemination and advertising. Such practices were likely to be reinforced by the acquisition of a radio station. Granting a license would be inconsistent with the public interest. In *Mansfield Journal* the court of appeals affirmed the FCC ruling.

> This would not appear to be a consideration conceived in whimsey but rather
> a sound application of what has long been the general policy of the United States.
> Congress intended that there be competition in the radio broadcasting industry.
> It is certainly not in the public interest that a radio station be used to achieve
> monopoly.[21]

Twenty years later, in the *Greater Boston* case, the court of appeals once again took a firm stand against concentrated ownership of broadcasting facilities. The case involved WHDH Incorporated, which had broadcast over Channel 5 in Boston since 1957. In 1969, however, the FCC granted the license to the Boston Broadcasters Company instead of the other applicants—which included WHDH, Charles River Broadcasting Company, and Greater Boston T.V. Company. The Boston Broadcasters Company was awarded the license because of potential superior service due to its diversification of media control. WHDH, by contrast, was licensee of two radio stations, owner of a daily newspaper, and holder of a controlling interest in a cable television equipment manufacturing company. The FCC noted: "Diversification is a factor of first significance since it constitutes a primary objective in the Commission's licensing scheme." According to the FCC, WHDH did not deserve license renewal, because it owned and controlled a concentration of media.

> A grant to either Charles River or BBI would clearly result in a maximum diffu
> sion of control of the media of mass communications as compared with a grant
> of the renewal application of WHDH. A new voice would be brought to the Bos
> ton community as compared with continuing the service of WHDH-TV. We be
> lieve that the widest possible dissemination of information from diverse and an
> tagonistic sources is in the public interest, and this principle will be significantly
> advanced by a grant of either the Charles River or the BBI application.[22]

The commission concluded that the public interest would be served by granting the license to Boston Broadcasters Company and denying it to WHDH, Charles River Company, and Greater Boston Company. The court of appeals affirmed the FCC ruling.

In the 1978 *National Citizens Committee* case, the Supreme Court heard a challenge to FCC regulations that prohibited "co-located combinations." At issue was a 1975 FCC order that barred the licensing of newspaper-broadcast combinations where there was common ownership of a radio or television broadcast station and a daily newspaper located in the same community. The FCC ordered that divestiture of 16 existing co-located combinations had to be accomplished by January 1, 1980. In these 16 cases the combination involved the sole daily newspaper published in the community and either the sole broadcast station or the sole television station providing that community with a clear signal. Several petitions were filed, seeking review of the FCC regulations. The case reached the Supreme Court. In an opinion prepared by Justice Thurgood Marshall, the Court held that the regulations were "valid in their entirety." Specifically, the Court ruled that (1) the regulations were properly based on the "public interest" standard, and their promulgation falls within the FCC's rule-making authority; (2) the regulations did not violate the First Amendment rights of newspaper owners; (3) limiting divestiture to 16 cases of effective monopoly was not arbitrary or capricious; and (4) disregarding media sources other than newspapers and broadcast stations and differentiating between radio and television stations in setting divestiture standards was not arbitrary.[23] In *National Citizens Committee* the Court upheld FCC regulations that required diversification of mass-media ownership.

The *Mansfield Journal, Greater Boston,* and *National Citizens Committee* cases indicate that the concentration of media is looked upon with great disfavor by the courts. The greater the diversity, the better the chance that the public interest will be served. The economic "rights" of broadcasters are limited, indeed.

Programming Guidelines

Although the Communications Act of 1934 prohibits the FCC from "censoring" broadcasters, over the years the commission has adopted several regulations governing broadcast programming. While the regulation of broadcast programming is not directly tied to license renewal, the failure of a broadcaster to observe FCC regulations has been considered at the time of renewal. Some of the earliest cases that dealt with programming standards focused on the issue of local service. The *Simmons* and *Henry* cases are significant examples.

Local Service

In 1947 the FCC denied Allen Simmons's application to increase the power of station WADC in Akron, Ohio, because, if the application had been granted, WADC intended "to broadcast all programs, commercial and sustaining, offered by the CBS network." The FCC noted that

the application of WADC thus raises squarely the issue of whether the public interest, convenience and necessity would be served by a station which during

> by far the largest and most important part of the broadcast day 'plugs' into the network line and, thereafter, acts as a mere relay station of program material piped in from outside the community. We are of the opinion that such a program policy which makes no effort whatsoever to tailor the programs offered by the national network organization to the particular needs of the community served by the radio station does not meet the public service responsibilities of a radio broadcast licensee.

The FCC ruling stressed that a licensee was obliged to provide programming adapted to the interests of the local community. In agreeing with the FCC's decision, the court of appeals emphasized that the FCC could influence the content of broadcasts. The court rejected Simmons's contention that the FCC's policy amounted to censorship. According to the court, "censorship would be a curious term to apply to the requirement that licensees select their own programs by applying their own judgment to the conditions that arise from time to time."[24] The court realized that its *Simmons* decision might be viewed as a precedent for control of program content; however, the decision in no way determined which individual programs best suited the local needs of the community.

The importance of local-service programming was affirmed in 1962 in *Henry*. The case arose when Suburban Broadcasters filed an application for a permit to construct a commercial FM station in Elizabeth, New Jersey. None of Suburban's owners, however, were residents of Elizabeth, and they did not inquire into the programming needs of that community. Furthermore, Suburban's program proposals were identical with those contained in its application for FM facilities in Illinois and California. The FCC set up a hearing "to determine whether the program proposals of Suburban Broadcasters are designed to and would be expected to serve the needs of the proposed service area." On this issue the commission found that the "program proposals were not 'designed' to serve the needs of Elizabeth" and that it was not known whether the proposals could be expected to serve those needs, since no evidence was offered. In essence, the FCC refused to grant an application prepared by individuals who were without knowledge of the area they sought to serve. The commission felt that "the public deserves something more in the way of preparation for the responsibilities sought by applicant than was demonstrated on this record."[25] The court of appeals affirmed the decision, ruling that the FCC could require an applicant to demonstrate an earnest interest in serving the local community.

Quality Service

The 1970 FCC *Policy Statement on Comparative Hearings Involving Regular Renewel Applicants* made it difficult for groups to demonstrate that an existing licensee had not performed in the public interest. According to the statement, when an applicant sought the license of an incumbent licensee, the incumbent was preferred if he or she could demonstrate substantial past performance not characterized by serious deficiencies. The criterion for renewal—"substantial service to the public"—rather than choosing the applicant most likely to render the best possible service, was justified on the basis of "considerations of predictability and stability." The FCC feared that if there were no stability in the broadcast industry, it would be difficult for a station to render substantial service. Several citizen groups challenged the legality of the FCC statement. In June 1970 the U.S. Court of Appeals for the District of Columbia directed the FCC to stop applying the statement. The court cited three reasons. First, the Ashbacker rule, which required a comparative hearing for all applicants, was violated by depriving an applicant of a hearing if the incumbent made a showing of substantial service. Second, the statement violated the Administrative Procedure Act. Third, the statement chilled the exercise of First Amendment rights. In the opinion of the court, the statement had produced *rigor mortis* instead of stability. In *Citizens Communications Center* the court restored healthy competition "by repudiating a Commission policy which is unreasonably weighted in favor of the licensees it is meant to regulate, to the great detriment of the listening and viewing public."[26] The court, nonetheless, recognized the value of a worthy incumbent and established a different criterion—the public would suffer if the incumbent licensees could not expect renewal when they render superior service. Given such an incentive, "an incumbent will naturally strive to achieve a level of performance which gives him a clear edge on challengers at renewal time." Thus, *Citizens Communications Center* tended to introduce competition into a system that previously tended merely to entrench existing broadcast ownership.

A related issue involves the concept of quantitative standards. As indicated previously, the 1970 policy statement held that a renewal applicant would be preferred over challengers, if the applicant provided "substantial service" with respect to the needs and interests of its service area. A year later, in a Notice of Inquiry, the FCC instituted a proceeding to determine whether it should attempt to quantify the concept of "substantial service." In the notice, "percentage guidelines" were suggested as *prima facie* indicators of "substantial service." The guidelines were as follows: with respect to local programming, a range of 10–15 percent broadcast effort; for news, 8–10 percent for the network affiliate, 5 percent for the independent VHF station; and in the public affairs area, 3–5 percent. Six months after the notice was issued, the court of appeals invalidated the "substantial service" doctrine in the *Citizens Communication Center* case. Following this decision, another notice was issued by the FCC, urging interested parties to comment on the matter. Eventually, in 1977, after lengthy inquiry, the FCC declined to establish quantitative standards for "substantial service." The FCC expressed concern that quantitative standards would restrict licensee discretion without any guarantee as to qualitative standards. The FCC concluded that "quantitative standards would not provide significantly greater certainty as to what constituted substantial service." For the future, the commission indicated that in a comparative renewal proceeding it would review all elements of an applicant's past performance with "particular emphasis on the incumbent's responsiveness to the recognized problems, needs, and interests of the community." Shortly thereafter, the National Black Media Coalition initiated court action, seeking review of the FCC policy. The court of appeals, in upholding the FCC's position, noted: "Nothing in the Communications Act imposes any requirement that the FCC promulgate quantitative programming standards." In *National Black Media Coalition,* the court concluded that the FCC's "decision concerning quantitative program standards was reasonable and not arbitrary, capricious, or an abuse of discretion."[27]

In a somewhat related case, *Yale,* the court of appeals acknowledged the licensee's responsibility to provide quality programming consistent with the public interest. The controversy involved an order issued by the FCC regarding "drug-oriented music," which was played by some radio stations. The order required licensees to have knowledge of the content of their programming, and to evaluate the desirability of broadcasting music dealing with drug use. The FCC set up guidelines whereby a broadcaster could obtain the required knowledge: prescreening by a responsible station employee, monitoring selections while they were being played, or considering and responding to complaints made by the public. In 1973, on the ground that the licensee had failed to meet its responsibility, the FCC denied license renewal to the Yale Broadcasting Company. Yale argued that the FCC order was both unduly vague and an unconstitutional infringement of the right of free expression. The court of appeals rejected these arguments and affirmed the action of the FCC.[28] The *Yale* case reflects the concern the courts have in guaranteeing quality programming. The presumption of substantial performance by incumbent license holders is no longer adequate. Licensees have a responsibility to provide programming of superior quality, which serves the public interest, convenience, and necessity.

Format

In several cases the FCC and the courts have established guidelines that ultimately affected station programming formats. The *WEFM, WNCN, Writer's Guild,* and *Gottfried* cases provide examples.

The *WEFM* case concerned an application for transfer of station ownership, which would ultimately result in a change in program format. Since it was first licensed in 1940, Chicago radio station WEFM had offered a classical music format. In 1972 WEFM was offered for sale to a corporation that proposed to broadcast a format of contemporary music approximately 70 percent of the time. A citizens' committee contested the transfer. It argued that the classical-music format would be sorely missed by a sizable audience and that its loss would not be in the public interest. The committee pointed out that station WEFM provided a large share of the area's classical-music needs. The committee sought a hearing on the matter. The FCC, however, rejected the petition for a hearing. It ruled that programming decisions had traditionally been left to the licensee's judgment and competitive marketplace forces. In the FCC's view, abandonment of the classical format was "not a matter affected with the public interest but a business decision within the licensee's discretion." On appeal, the Circuit Court of Appeals, District of Columbia held that the committee had raised substantial questions concerning the public interest. The court questioned whether changes in program format should be left to the competitive forces of the marketplace.

> Moreover, there is no longer any room for doubt that, if the FCC is to pursue the public interest, it may not be able at the same time to pursue a policy of free competition.... There is, in the familiar sense, no free market in radio entertainment because over-the-air broadcasters do not deal directly with their listeners.[29]

The court held that the FCC had a responsibility to ensure that format changes were in the public interest. According to the court, the FCC should have held a hearing to determine the community's needs.

The Supreme Court decided a related case in 1981. The *WNCN* case arose when the FCC issued a policy statement concluding that the public interest is best served by promoting diversity in entertainment formats through market forces and competition among broadcasters. The statement also maintained that a change in entertainment programming is not a material factor that should be considered by the FCC in ruling on an application for license renewal or transfer. Soon thereafter, several citizen groups interested in preserving specific entertainment formats petitioned for review of the policy. The case reached the Supreme Court. Writing for the majority, Justice Byron White held that the policy statement (1) was consistent with the legislative history of the Federal Communications Act of 1934 and with the FCC's traditional view that the public interest is best served by promoting diversity in entertainment programming through market forces; and (2) did not conflict with the First Amendment rights of listeners, since the FCC seeks to promote "the interests of the listening public as a whole and the First Amendment does not grant individual listeners the right to have the FCC review the abandonment of their favorite entertainment programs."[30] In *WNCN* the Court upheld the FCC policy statement, thereby leaving programming-format decisions largely to market forces and competition among broadcasters.

The *Writers Guild* case involved an effort by the FCC to permit one group—the National Association of Broadcasters Television Code Review Board—to act as a national board of censors for U.S. television. As a result of FCC pressure, including threats of license denial, the three networks and the NAB adopted a programming-format policy they did not wish to adopt. The policy, known as the "family viewing policy," held that

entertainment programming inappropriate for viewing by a general family audience should not be broadcast during the first hour of network entertainment
programming in prime time and in the immediately preceding hour. In the occasional case when an entertainment program is deemed to be inappropriate for
such an audience, advisories should be used to alert viewers.[31]

The FCC imposed the family viewing policy without giving the public its right
to notice and its right to be heard. Various directors, actors, writers, and
producers of television programs challenged the validity of the policy. The court
of appeals noted that, in this case, the desirability or undesirability of the family
viewing policy was not the issue. Rather, the question was "who should have
the right to decide what shall and shall not be broadcast and how and on what
basis should these decisions be made." In *Writers Guild* the court concluded that
the adoption of the family viewing policy by the television networks violated the
First Amendment, because the FCC chairman had issued threats of government
action, should the industry refuse to adopt it. Furthermore, FCC enforcement
of the policy through the licensing process would also violate the First Amendment. In *Writers Guild* the court rejected FCC efforts to force a family viewing
policy on the three television networks.

The *Gottfried* case involved programming for handicapped persons. The Rehabilitation Act of 1973 provides that no handicapped individual shall be denied
the benefits of any program receiving federal financial assistance. Sue Gottfried
filed a petition requesting that the FCC deny renewal of a public television station's license, because the station had failed to ascertain the needs of the deaf
and hearing-impaired viewers within the service area. Gottfried filed similar objections to the renewal of seven commercial television-station licenses. Among
her objections, Gottfried alleged that the stations failed to carry enough programming with special captioning or other aids to benefit the hearing-impaired. Con-
solidating all eight proceedings, the FCC held that the public station, KCET-TV
in Los Angeles, made adequate efforts to ascertain the special needs of the community, that the Rehabilitation Act does not apply to commercial licenses, and
that the Federal Communications Act does not require the FCC to review a public
television station's license-renewal application under a different standard than
that applied to a commercial licensee's application. Eventually, the case reached
the Supreme Court. In an opinion written by Justice John Stevens, the Court
agreed with the FCC. In *Gottfried* Justice Stevens noted:

> Congress did not intend the Rehabilitation Act to impose any special enforce-
> ment obligation on the FCC. The FCC is not a funding agency and has no
> responsibility for enforcing [the Rehabilitation Act]. Moreover, there is not a
> word in the Act's legislative history suggesting that the Act was intended to alter
> the FCC's standard for reviewing the programming decisions of public televi-
> sion licensees.[32]

Therefore, "the FCC was acting within its authority when it declined to impose a greater obligation to provide special programming for the hearing impaired on a public licensee than it did on commercial licensees."

The cases discussed in this section involve efforts by the FCC and the courts to regulate program formats. In *WNCN* the court upheld a FCC policy favoring the promotion of format diversity through market forces. In *Writers Guild* the court overturned FCC efforts to force a family viewing policy on the networks. In *Gottfried* the Supreme Court approved an FCC decision that refused to provide special programming for the hearing-impaired.

Lotteries

In 1968 Congress passed a postal regulation that prohibited the use of the mails to promote lotteries. The FCC applied this regulation to the broadcast media. Violation could lead to loss of license, fines, and/or imprisonment. In 1953 the Post Office exempted some lotteries from regulation. Soon thereafter the three major networks began to broadcast give-away programs, which were based on participation by viewers and listeners at home. The FCC sought to ban the programs on the ground that they were lotteries. The networks appealed. Speaking for the Supreme Court, Chief Justice Earl Warren defined the give-away show in a permissive way.

> To be eligible for a prize on the "give away" programs involved here, not a single home contestant is required to purchase anything or pay an admission price or leave his home to visit the promoter's place of business; the only effort required for participation is listening.[33]

The Court believed "that it would be stretching the statute to the breaking point to give it an interpretation that would make such programs a crime." According to the *ABC* decision, the FCC had exceeded its rule-making power.

In 1967 the New York State Broadcasting Association challenged the FCC lottery regulations on First Amendment grounds. The principal issue concerned where to draw the line between lottery promotion and genuine news reporting. According to the FCC, broadcasting of information about lotteries was prohibited, except for "ordinary news reports concerning legislation authorizing the institution of a state lottery, or of public debate on the course state policy should take," or "any good-faith coverage which reasonably related to audiences' right and desire to know and be informed of the day-to-day happenings within the community." The New York State Broadcasting Association went to court, arguing that the FCC policy violated the right of the people to receive information. The court of appeals upheld the FCC. The judges, however, detected a flaw in the lottery law.

Petitioners contend that section 1304 is unconstitutional on its face, arguing that its broad terms improperly inhibit "lawful communication unconnected with the operating of a lottery." It is obvious that a literal reading of the statute would support petitioners' challenge, since by its terms it punishes the broadcasting of "any...information concerning any lottery."[34]

Nonetheless, the court did not believe that such a broad construction of Section 1304 was warranted. Instead, the court interpreted the phrase "information concerning any lottery" to refer only to information that directly promoted an existing lottery. Thus, even though the *New York State Broadcasting* decision upheld the regulation, it stressed that any broad construction of Section 1304 was impermissible.

In 1970 Congress amended federal lottery law by indicating that Section 1304 did not apply to advertising or reporting of newsworthy information regarding a legally conducted lottery. Both the *ABC* and *New York Broadcasting* cases illustrate that the broadcasting of lottery information is regulated, but not prohibited. Clearly, "newsworthy" lottery programming is outside the scope of FCC regulation.

Indecency and Obscenity

The federal obscenity law prohibits broadcasters from airing material that is obscene or indecent. In 1962, in the *Palmetto* case, the FCC refused to renew a license on the ground that indecent programming is not in the public interest. The case involved radio station WDKD, which devoted 25 percent of its programming to off-color jokes and statements that the FCC examiner concluded were "coarse, vulgar, suggestive, and susceptible of indecent, double meaning." On appeal, the FCC affirmed the decision and noted that though censorship was not permissible, denial of renewal could be justified, if based on public-interest grounds. In *Palmetto*, the FCC acknowledged the dangers of censorship and then stated:

> But this does not mean that the Commission has no authority to act under the public-interest standard. Rather, it means that the Commission cannot substitute its taste for that of the broadcaster or his public—that it cannot set itself up as a national arbiter of taste.... It follows that in dealing with the issue before us, we cannot act to deny renewal where the matter is a close one, susceptible to reasonable interpretation either way. We can only act where the record evidence establishes a patently offensive course of broadcasters.[35]

In *Palmetto*, the FCC denied renewal because such a large portion of broadcast time devoted to indecent material represented "an intolerable waste of the only operating broadcast facilities in the community."

Two years later the FCC modified its position regarding indecent programming. In deciding whether to grant a license to Los Angeles station KPFK, and renew the licenses of Berkeley's KPFB and KPFA-FM, and New York's WBAI-FM, all owned by Pacifica Corporation, the FCC considered programming complaints. In particular, five programs broadcast over a four-year period were considered "filthy" by a group of listeners. Pacifica Corporation argued that the programs served the interests of the listening public. The Commission upheld the programming.

> We recognize that as shown by the complaints here, such provocative programming as here involved may offend some listeners. But this does not mean that those offended have the right, through the Commission's licensing power, to rule such programming off the airwaves. Were this the case, only the wholly inoffensive, the bland, could gain access to the radio microphone or TV camera.[36]

According to the FCC, the complaints did not "pose a close question in the case: Pacifica's judgments as to the above programs clearly fall within the very great discretions which the act wisely grants to the licensee." The *Pacifica* decision signaled a philosophical shift by the FCC. It acknowledged that license holders have wide discretion in programming considerations.

In 1970 the FCC reconsidered its philosophy once again. The case involved educational radio station WUHY-FM. On January 4, 1970, Jerry Garcia of the musical group "The Grateful Dead" was interviewed as part of a weekly program. In the interivew Garcia used offensive words. His comments were frequently interspersed with the words "fuck" and "shit." The FCC subsequently fined WUHY $100. The FCC concluded that the language was obscene; it had "no redeeming social value" and was "patently offensive by contemporary community standards"—having "very serious consequences to the 'public interest in the larger and more effective use of radio.' " The FCC opinion also stressed an inherent distinction between radio and other communication media.

> Unlike a book which requires the deliberate act of purchasing and reading (or a motion picture where admission to public exhibition must be actively sought), broadcasting is disseminated generally to the public under circumstances where reception requires no activity of this nature. Thus, it comes directly into the home and frequently without any advance warning of its content.[37]

It should be noted that in *WUHY* the FCC's definition of obscenity differed significantly from the prevailing Supreme Court definition, the "*Roth* test."[38] For example, the FCC banned specific words, rather than judging the expression in its entirety. Also, the FCC failed to determine whether the expression possessed any intrinsic value, as judged by contemporary community standards. According to *WUHY,* the broadcasting of obscenity was subject to a different standard than obscenity that was communicated through other means.

In 1973, in the *Sonderling* case, the FCC compared its concept of obscenity with that set forth in *Roth.* The case centered around the programming of radio station WGLD-FM of Oak Park, Illinois. The station aired a program in which an announcer accepted calls from the audience and discussed "sex-oriented" topics. On February 23, 1973, the topic was "oral sex." The program consisted of very explicit comments, in which female callers spoke of their oral-sexual experiences. The FCC found the station guilty of obscene and indecent programming and levied a fine of $2,000. The FCC distinguished the *Sonderling* decision from *Pacifica:* "We are not dealing with works of dramatic or literary art as we were in *Pacifica.*" Two tests were applied in this case. First, the FCC applied *Roth* and concluded that the program contained explicit material that was "patently offensive to contemporary standards for broadcast matter." Special importance was placed on the fact that minors compose a significant segment of a radio audience.

> Our conclusions here are based on the pervasive and intrusive nature of broadcast radio, even if children were left completely out of the picture. However, the presence of children in the broadcast audience makes this an *a fortiori* matter. There are significant numbers of children in the audience during these afternoon hours—and not all of a pre-school age. Thus, there is always a significant percentage of school age children out of school on any given day. Many listen to radio; indeed it is almost the constant companion of the teenager.[39]

Second, the commission applied the *WUHY* decision, which set forth the FCC's interpretation of the term "indecent." As noted earlier, the "indecency" standard of *WUHY* was more restrictive than the "obscenity" standard of *Roth.*

> It is sufficient to note that to contravene the standard proscribing broadcast of indecent material, it must be shown that the matter broadcast is (a) patently offensive by contemporary community standards; and (b) is utterly without redeeming social value.

The *Sonderling* decision recognized FCC authority to ban not only obscene speech as defined in *Roth,* but indecent speech as defined in *WUHY* as well.

In the 1978 *Pacifica* decision the U.S. Supreme Court rendered an opinion on the issue of broadcasting of indecent material. The case examined the merits of a George Carlin record, aired by New York station WBAI as part of its general discussion of society's attitude toward language. The record devotes considerable time to a discussion of the use of seven "four-letter" words: shit, piss, fuck, cunt, cocksucker, motherfucker, tits. The FCC received a complaint from a father, claiming that his young son had heard the broadcast. The FCC conducted an investigation, found the seven words to be indecent for children, and sought to channel the program to a time of the day when it would be less likely that children would be present. Pacifica Foundation, the license holder of station WBAI, challenged the ruling in court. Eventually, the case reached the Supreme Court. In an opinion prepared by Justice John Stevens, the Court claimed that the content of Pacifica's broadcast was "vulgar," "offensive," and "shocking." Because content of that nature was not entitled to First Amendment protection under all circumstances, the justices had to consider its context. Stevens noted that

> patently offensive, indecent material presented over the airwaves confronts the citizen, not only in public, but also in the privacy of the home, where the individual's right to be let alone plainly outweighs the First Amendment rights of an intruder. . . .
>
> The concept requires consideration of a host of variables. The time of day was emphasized by the Commission. The content of the program in which the language is used will also affect the composition of the audience, and differences between radio, television, and perhaps closed-circuit transmissions, may also be relevant.[40]

In *Pacifica* the Supreme Court upheld the FCC's decision. The Court thus acknowledged that the FCC may regulate "indecent" as well as "obscene" expression. Also, the Court recognized that the context in which the program occurs is of vital importance.

Public Affairs

The FCC exercises control over programming through application of several doctrines that relate to the coverage of public affairs. Chief among these are the equal-time, candidate-access, fairness, personal-attack, and limited-access doctrines.

Equal-Time Rule. The equal-time rule, set forth in Section 315 of the Federal Communications Act of 1934, maintains that

> if any licensee shall permit any person who is a legally qualified candidate for any public office to use a broadcasting station, he shall afford equal opportunities to all other such candidates for that office in the use of such broadcasting station.

Such "opportunities" require equal time, equal facilities, and comparable costs for political candidates in the same election. Section 315 provides some "outs" for broadcasters, however. Though a station must provide equal "opportunities" if so requested by opposing candidates, it is under no obligation to solicit an appearance by every candidate. Furthermore, if they so choose, broadcasters do not have to allow any political candidates the use of their facilities. That would give all candidates equal time—none.

The equal-time rule contains a number of unclear and troublesome provisions. One problematic aspect concerns the meaning of the term "use." In 1959 Congress amended Section 315 to provide that an appearance by a candidate does not consititute a use when the program falls into the following categories: *bona fide* newscast; *bona fide* news interview; *bona fide* news documentary, if the appearance of the candidate is incidental to the presentation of the subject; and on-the-spot coverage of *bona fide* news events. In the years following that amendment, the FCC has been called upon to apply these exemptions to specific events. In three cases, *Goodwill Stations,*[41] *National Broadcasting Company,*[42] and *Columbia Broadcasting System,*[43] the FCC ruled that political debates failed to qualify for exemption under the four categories.

In 1975, however, the FCC decreed that "nonstudio" debates between qualified political candidates are exempt from the equal-time requirements, provided that they are covered live and there is no broadcaster favoritism.[44] Shortly thereafter the order was challenged in court by Shirley Chisholm and the Democratic National Committee. Chisholm argued that the order constituted an erroneous interpretation of Section 315. The United States Court of Appeals, District of Columbia, ruled in favor of the FCC.

> We find nothing in the Commission's Opinion inconsistent with the basic philosophy of Section 315 as amended in 1959. The 1959 amendment to Section 315 clearly limited to some extent the simple mechanistic application of that section. In creating a broad exemption to the equal time requirements in order to facilitate broadcast coverage of political news, Congress knowingly faced risks of political favoritism by broadcasters, and opted in favor of broader coverage and increased broadcaster discretion. Rather than enumerate specific exempt and nonexempt "uses," Congress opted in favor of legislative generality, preferring to assign that task to the Commission.[45]

Eventually, in 1983, the FCC ruled that broadcasters could sponsor debates directly, instead of being limited to "nonstudio" presentations. The ruling was upheld by the court of appeals one year later.[46]

A second problematic term is "legally qualified candidate." According to the FCC, a legally qualified candidate is a person who publicly announces that he or she is a candidate for nomination, meets the qualifications for the office, qualifies for a place on the ballot, and was duly nominated by a political party or makes a substantial showing that he or she is a *bona fide* candidate.

The *McCarthy* case dealt with the question of who is a legally qualified candidate. On December 19, 1967, the three major television networks carried an hour-long interview of President Lyndon Johnson. Senator Eugene McCarthy, who had prior to the broadcast announced his candidacy for the Democratic nomination, requested "equal time," on the ground that President Johnson was a legally qualified candidate. The FCC denied McCarthy's request, because President Johnson had not announced his candidacy for the nomination, and thus did

not fulfill the requirements of the definition. McCarthy argued that the definition was unreasonable, if a candidate deprived his opponents of the benefits of
the equal-time rule simply by witholding an announcement of his own candidacy.
The court of appeals, however, upheld the FCC decision,[47] and by so doing
enabled incumbents to achieve the advantage of media exposure through *bona
fide* news coverage, without allowing equal coverage of an opponent's campaign.
By delaying formal announcement of candidacy, an incumbent may still fore-
stall operation of the equal-time rule.

A third problem with the equal-time rule concerns a provision that prohibits
censorship. In establishing this provision, Congress recognized the necessity of
free and open discussion of public issues, but did not, however, fully take into
account the question of libel. Could a broadcaster be sued for libel for merely
presenting the message of a political candidate—in accord with the equal-time
rule? The issue came before the Supreme Court in 1959.

A libel suit arose regarding remarks made over station WDAY by A. C.
Townley, a legally qualified candidate in the 1956 U.S. Senate race in North
Dakota. WDAY permitted Townley to broadcast a speech, uncensored in any
respect, as a reply to previous speeches made by other senatorial candidates.
Townley accused his opponents, together with the Farmers Educational and
Cooperative Union, of conspiring to "establish a Communist Farmers Union Soviet right here in North Dakota." Farmers Union sued Townley and WDAY for
libel. The lower court dismissed the complaint against WDAY on the ground
that Section 315 rendered the station immune from liability. The Supreme Court
of North Dakota agreed.

> Section 315 imposes a mandatory duty upon broadcasting stations to permit all
> candidates for the same office to use their facilities if they have permitted one
> candidate to use them. Since power of censorship of political broadcasts is pro-
> hibited it must follow as a corollary that the mandate prohibiting censorship in-
> cludes the privilege of immunity from liability for defamatory statements made
> by the speakers.

The case reached the Supreme Court. In *WDAY,* the justices decided that any
system of broadcast censorship would undermine the purpose for which Section
315 was passed—providing unhindered discussion of political issues by legally
qualified candidates. The Court noted:

> Quite possibly, if a station were held responsible for the broadcast of libelous
> material, all remarks even faintly objectionable would be excluded out of an
> excess of caution. Moreover, if any censorship were permissible, a station so
> inclined could intentionally inhibit a candidate's legitimate presentation under
> the guise of lawful censorship in libelous matter. Because of the time limita-
> tion inherent in a political campaign, erroneous decisions by a station could not
> be corrected by the courts promptly enough to permit the candidate to bring im-

properly excluded matter before the public. It follows from all this that allowing censorship...would almost inevitably force a candidate to avoid controversial issues during political debates over radio and television, and hence restrict
the coverage of consideration relevant to intelligent political decision.[48]

In *WDAY* the Court granted broadcasters immunity from libel suits based on the
remarks of political candidates presented in accordance with Section 315.

A fourth problem with the equal-time rule is that it operates only when a
candidate uses the broadcasting facilities. A candidate has to appear in person
before Section 315 may be invoked. If a spokesperson for the candidate broadcasts a campaign message, the equal-time rule is not applicable. In order to offset the impact of such a partisan campaign broadcast, the FCC developed the
Zapple rule. The doctrine set forth in *Zapple* holds that when, during a political campaign, a broadcaster sells air time to a candidate's spokespersons or supporters, who use that time to discuss issues in the campaign, spokespersons or
supporters of the candidate's opponent are entitled to purchase comparable air
time for a reply. *Zapple* does not require free reply time, if the original broadcast was paid for. All *Zapple* stipulates is that the opposing candidate's supporters
must be sold comparable time, if they want it. Thus, *Zapple* applies the principles of the equal-time rule to a candidate's supporters and campaign committees.[49]

Candidate-Access Rule.   Section 312 of the Communications Act of
1934, as amended by the Federal Election Campaign Act of 1971, authorizes
the FCC to revoke any broadcast-station license for failure to allow reasonable
amounts of time for use by a legally qualified candidate for federal elective office. In October 1979 the Carter-Mondale Presidential Committee requested the
three major television networks to provide time for a 30-minute program early
in December. The committee intended to present, in conjunction with President
Carter's formal announcement of his candidacy, a documentary outlining the record of Carter's administration. The networks refused to make the time available. In their refusal the networks cited the large number of presidential candidates and the potential disruption of regular programming to accommodate requests
for equal treatment. The networks also noted that they had not yet determined
when they would begin selling political time for the 1980 campaign. The Carter-
Mondale committee filed a complaint with the FCC, charging that the networks
had violated their obligation to provide "reasonable access." The FCC agreed.
The networks then initiated court action, arguing that the *DNC*[50] case established that no person or group has the right to command access to the broadcast
media. The case reached the Supreme Court. The majority opinion, delivered
by Justice Warren Burger, noted that broadcasters may deny the sale of air time
prior to the start of the campaign, but once a campaign begins, they must give
reasonable attention to access requests from legally qualified candidates. Further-

more, such requests must be considered on an individual basis, and broadcasters are required to tailor their responses to accommodate a candidate's stated purposes in seeking air time. Burger noted that, in this case, the networks had employed "blanket rules concerning access." According to Burger, the FCC was justified in rejecting such a policy.

> While the adoption of uniform policies might well prove more convenient for broadcasters, such an approach would allow personal campaign strategies and the exigencies of the political process to be ignored. A broadcaster's "even-handed" response of granting only time spots of a fixed duration to candidates may be "unreasonable" where a particular candidate desires less time for an advertisement or a longer format to discuss substantive issues. In essence, petitioners seek the unilateral right to determine in advance how much time to afford all candidates. Yet [Section 312] assures a right of reasonable access to individual candidates for federal elective office, and the Commissioner's requirement that their requests be considered on an individualized basis is consistent with that guarantee.[51]

In *CBS* the Court decided that a limited right of access to the media did not violate the First Amendment rights of broadcasters by undercutting their editorial discretion, but rather, properly balanced the rights of candidates, the public, and the media.

Fairness Doctrine.   The fairness doctrine was established by the FCC in 1949, but its specific provisions developed out of the commission's decisions in earlier cases. The *Mayflower, WHKC,* and *Scott* decisions illustrate the evolution of the "fairness doctrine."

In 1938 the Yankee Network Corporation applied for renewal of its license for Boston radio station WAAB. The Mayflower Broadcasting Company challenged the renewel and applied for a construction permit. The FCC hearing revealed that Yankee Broadcasting had aired "editorials" urging the election of various candidates to public office. No pretense of impartiality was made by the station in announcing the choices. The FCC sharply condemned Yankee's partisan practices.

> Under the American system of broadcasting it is clear that responsibility for the conduct of a broadcast station must rest initially with the broadcaster. It is equally clear that with the limitations in frequencies inherent in the nature of radio, the public interest can never be served by a dedication of any broadcast facility to the support of his own partisan ends. Radio can serve as an instrument of democracy only when devoted to the communication of information and the exchange of ideas fairly and objectively presented. A truly free radio cannot be used to advocate the causes of the licensee. It cannot be used to support the candidacies of his friends. It cannot be devoted to the support of principles

he happens to regard most favorably. In brief, the broadcaster cannot be an advocate.[52]

Nevertheless, the FCC denied Mayflower's application on the ground that the company was not financially qualified to construct and operate the proposed station. The real importance of the decision, however, is that broadcasters were discouraged from editorializing. The FCC noted in *Mayflower* that "freedom of speech on the radio must be broad enough to provide full and equal opportunity for the presentation to the public of all sides of public issues."

The *WHKC* decision also recognized the importance of fairness. In a petition to deny renewal of license for station WHKC, two labor unions cited a station policy not to sell time for programs that solicited union memberships or discussed controversial subjects. While conceding that stations do not have to sell time to all who want it, the FCC noted that stations were not justified in establishing a policy of unfair coverage of controversial issues.

> The Commission recognizes that good program balance may not permit the sale or donation of time to all who may seek it for such purposes and that difficult problems calling for careful judgment on the part of station management may be involved in deciding among applicants for time when all cannot be accommodated. However, competent management should be able to meet such problems in the public interest and with fairness to all concerned. The fact that it places an arduous task on management should not be made a reason for evading the issue by a strict rule against the sale of time for any program of the type mentioned.[53]

The *Scott* case was also suggestive of the emerging doctrine of "fairness." In 1945 Robert Scott filed a petition requesting that the FCC revoke the licenses of radio stations KQW, KPO, and KFRC. Scott had been denied air time to broadcast talks on the topic of athieism, while the stations allowed the use of their facilities for arguments against atheism, as well as for various kinds of religious programs. Scott argued that the stations did not present contrasting sides of the issue and therefore did not operate in the public interest. Even though the FCC denied the petition because Scott's complaint was too broad, the commission stressed that even though a majority of the public does not accept a particular view, that was no reason to deny airing the view.

> If freedom of speech is to have meaning, it cannot be predicated on the mere popularity or public acceptance of the ideas sought to be advanced. It must be extended as readily to ideas which we disapprove or abhor as to ideas which we approve. Moreover, freedom of speech can be as effectively denied by denying access to the public means of making expression effective—whether public streets, parks, meeting halls, or the radio—as by legal restraints or punishments of the speaker.[54]

The conditions existing in the *Mayflower, WHKC,* and *Scott* cases led the FCC in 1949 to specify a broadcaster's responsibilities regarding coverage of controversial issues. The fairness doctrine involves a twofold obligation for broadcasters: First, a reasonable percentage of broadcast time must be devoted to coverage of public issues; and second, the coverage must present contrasting points of view.[55] The fairness doctrine is often confused with the equal-time rule. While the equal-time rule requires broadcasters to provide opposing political candidates with "equal" access to broadcast media, the fairness doctrine merely compels broadcasters to provide "balanced" programming of controversial public issues.

The fairness doctrine contains ambiguous terms—for example, "reasonable" and "public issues." In general, the FCC has left the interpretation of these terms to the individual broadcasters. The FCC does not monitor for violations of the doctrine, but instead depends upon viewer and listener complaints. A party seeking revocation of a license on fairness grounds, however, has a heavy burden of proof. All the broadcaster need demonstrate is a good-faith effort to abide by the doctrine's provisions.

The *Brandywine* case, which provided a particularly glaring violation of the fairness doctrine, resulted in the denial of a broadcast license. In 1965 Brandywine Main Line Radio, a company owned by the Faith Theological Seminary and presided over by right-wing preacher Carl McIntire, applied for transfer of control of radio station WXUR to Brandywine from its current owners. Community groups opposed the application, but the FCC approved the transfer after McIntire promised to provide opposing viewpoints on controversial public issues. At renewal time, citizen groups contended that WXUR had failed to provide such coverage. The renewal hearing determined that the moderator of a WXUR call-in program had encouraged and approved of the remarks of anti-Jewish callers. Furthermore, the station's programming systematically attacked celebrities of the New Left. WXUR failed to provide spokespersons to counteract its conservative, right-wing programming. In 1970 station WXUR became the first licensee in the history of broadcast regulation to lose its license because of failure to comply with the fairness doctrine. The FCC decision stated:

> We conclude upon an evaluation of all the relevant and material evidence contained in the hearing record, that renewals of the WXUR and WXUR-FM licenses should not be granted. The record demonstrates that Brandywine failed to provide reasonable opportunities for the presentation of contrasting views on controversial issues of public importance, that it ignored the personal attack principle of the Fairness Doctrine, that the applicant's representations as to the manner in which the station would be operated were not adhered to, that no adequate efforts were made to keep the station attuned to the community's or area's needs and interests, and that no showing has been made that it was, in fact, so attuned. Any one of these violations would alone be sufficient to require denying the renewals here, and the violations are rendered even more serious by the fact that we carefully drew the Seminary's attention to a licensee's responsibilities before we approved transfer of the stations to its ownership and control.[56]

In *Brandywine* the court gave notice to broadcasters that the fairness doctrine would be enforced.

Personal-Attack Rule. In 1962 the FCC declared that when a broadcast amounts to a personal attack upon an individual or group, the broadcaster has an obligation to notify the target of the attack and offer the target an opportunity to respond. In 1969 the rule was challenged in court in the *Red Lion* case.

The case began in 1964, when the Red Lion Broadcasting Company carried a program that included an attack by Reverend Billy James Hargis against Fred Cook, the author of a book entitled *Goldwater—Extremist of the Right*. Hargis cited several "shady" aspects of Cook's background, thereby hoping to discredit the book about Senator Barry Goldwater. Cook asked the radio station for an opportunity to reply to Hargis's attacks. The station, unclear as to its responsibility regarding who had to pay for the time, replied that the personal-attack rule required a licensee to make free time available only if no paid sponsorship could be located. Cook complained to the FCC. Upon hearing, the FCC held that the station was obligated to furnish free reply time. According to the FCC, the public interest required that the public be given an opportunity to hear both sides of an issue, even if the time had to be paid for by the station. The station appealed. In a companion case, the Radio Television News Directors Association brought suit for judicial review of the personal-attack rule. Suit was filed in the U.S. Court of Appeals for the Seventh Circuit, a court thought to be less sympathetic to government agencies than the Washington-based court of appeals. Subsequently, the court ruled that the personal-attack rule violated the First Amendment. Eventually both the *Red Lion* and *RTNDA* cases reached the U.S. Supreme Court. The Court, per Justice Byron White, decided that the personal-attack rule was consistent with the First Amendment. In supporting his argument, White noted that without the rule broadcasters would have "unfettered power to make time available only to the highest bidders, to communicate only their views on public issues, people, and candidates, and to permit on the air only those with whom they agreed." In laying the foundation for a doctrine of media access, White noted the inherent problems involved in allocating licenses among competing broadcasters.

> In view of the prevalence of scarcity of broadcast frequencies, the Government's role in allocating those frequencies, and the legitimate access to those frequencies for expression of their views, we hold the regulations and ruling at issue here are both authorized by statute and constitutional. The judgment of the Court of Appeals in *Red Lion* is affirmed and that in *RTNDA* reversed and the causes remanded for proceedings consistent with this opinion.[57]

Though the Court by no means broke with the traditional "limitation of the spectrum" approach, its decision set the stage for an "access doctrine." Justice White argued that

> as far as the First Amendment is concerned those who are licensed stand no better than those to whom licenses are refused. . . . It is the purpose of the First Amendment to preserve an uninhibited marketplace of ideas in which truth will ultimately prevail rather than to countenance monopolization of that market, whether it be by the Government itself or a private licensee. . . . It is the right of the public to receive suitable access to social, political, aesthetic, moral, and other ideas and experiences which is crucial here. That right may not constitutionally be abridged either by Congress or by the FCC.

In *Red Lion* the Court affirmed the constitutionality and desirability of both the personal-attack rule and the fairness doctrine.

Limited-Access Doctrine.   The broad mandate of *Red Lion* was to allow as much access to broadcast airwaves as was consistent with the First Amendment. Accordingly, the FCC maintained that if a broadcaster followed the requirements of the fairness doctrine, that broadcaster was not obligated to provide access to all who requested air time, either by selling such air time or providing it free of charge. This doctrine of limited access was supported by the Supreme Court in the *DNC* case.

In 1970 the Business Executives' Move For Vietnam Peace filed a complaint with the FCC, charging that radio station WTOP had refused to sell air time to broadcast announcements expressing views on the Vietnam War. WTOP refused to sell time to groups that wished to express views on controversial issues. It contended that since it presented full and fair coverage of public issues, including the Vietnam conflict, it was justified in refusing to accept editorial advertisements. In a separate but related case, the Democratic National Committee requested a declaratory ruling from the FCC that under the First Amendment "a broadcaster may not, as a general policy, refuse to sell time to responsible entities, such as DNC, for the solicitation of funds and for comment on public issues." Unlike BEM, DNC did not object to the policies of any specific station, but claimed that its "experiences in this area make it clear that it will encounter considerable difficulty—if not total frustration of its efforts—in carryng out its plan," if the commission declined to issue a ruling. DNC cited *Red Lion* as establishing a limited right to access of the airwaves. In dealing with both BEM and DNC, the FCC ruled that broadcasters who met their obligation to provide full and fair coverage of public issues were not required to accept editorial advertisements. The Supreme Court upheld the FCC decision.

> More profoundly, it would be anomalous for us to hold, in the name of promoting the constitutional guarantees of free expression, that the day-to-day editorial decisions of broadcast licensees are subject to the kind of restraints urged by respondents. To do so in the name of the First Amendment would be a contradiction. Journalistic discretion would in many ways be lost to the rigid limitations that the First Amendment imposes on government. Application of such standards to broadcast licensees would be antithetical to the very ideal of vigorous, challenging debate on issues of public interest. Every licensee is already held accountable for the totality of its performance of public interest obligations.[58]

The *DNC* case thus broke the momentum of the right of access suggested in *Red Lion.* The Supreme Court weighed the competing claims of licensees and those who desired access and concluded that the broadcaster had a legitimate right to deny air time to the DNC and BEM. According to the Court, "in this case, the Commission has decided that on balance the undesirable effects of the right of access urged by respondents would outweigh the asserted benefits." In effect, the *DNC* decision emphasized that the First Amendment did not require a right of access for editorial advertising, because such a right would mean an end to the editorial function in broadcast journalism.

Procedural Guidelines

Procedural questions comprise an important part of the licensing decision. Under what conditions is a complaining citizen group entitled to a hearing? Who has the burden of proof at an evidentiary hearing? Can a license be revoked for lack of candor? These procedural issues have received attention from the FCC and the courts.

Hearing and Burden of Proof

In 1955 the FCC received a complaint that charged that station WLBT had deliberately cut off a network program about racial problems. In 1957 another complaint alleged that WLBT had presented a program urging racial segregation and had refused to present the opposing viewpoint. In 1962 the FCC again received complaints that WLBT had presented only one viewpoint concerning racial integration. In 1963 the FCC requested the station to submit reports on its programs concerning racial issues. In 1964, while the FCC was investigating WLBT's programs, the station filed a license-renewal application. Enraged citizens, members of the Office of Communication of the United Church of Christ, filed a petition urging denial of WLBT's application. The group argued that WLBT had failed to serve the general public, because the station did not give a fair and balanced presentation of controversial issues—especially those concerning blacks, who comprised almost 45 percent of the population within the station's service area. The FCC concluded that "serious issues" were presented as to "whether the licensee's operations have fully met the public interest standard." Nevertheless, the commission awarded a one-year renewal in the form of a probationary grant. The conditions required WLBT to comply with the requirements of the fairness doctrine; observe strictly its representations to the commission in this area; have discussions with community leaders, including those active in the civil rights movement, as to whether its programming is meeting the needs of its area; cease discriminatory programming; and make a detailed report regarding its efforts in meeting these conditions. On appeal, the United Church group contended that since the FCC concluded that WLBT was guilty of "discriminatory programming," the commission should not renew the license, even for one year, without a hearing. The FCC argued, however, that it took all the necessary steps to insure that the discriminatory practices would cease. For this reason, the commission granted a short-term renewal in the hope that WLBT would improve. The court sided with the United Church group.

In order to safeguard the public interest in broadcasting, therefore, we hold that some "audience participation" must be allowed in license renewal proceedings. We recognize this will create problems for the Commission but it does not necessarily follow that "hosts" of protestors must be granted standing to challenge a renewal application or that the Commission need allow the administrative process to be obstructed or overwhelmed by captious or purely obstructive protests. The Commission can avoid such results by developing appropriate regulation by statutory rulemaking.[59]

In *United Church I*, the court acknowledged that the FCC must be granted "broad discretion" in setting rules for hearing—including the number and type of witnesses required and the extent of "audience participation" allowed. Accordingly, the right to a hearing is not absolute; it is granted only after weighing the claims of the various petitioners and the nature of the complaints.

Another procedural issue concerns the burden of proof. This issue was considered in the *United Church II* case. After the probationary period, the FCC conducted a hearing and then granted a three-year renewal to WLBT. Once again, the United Church of Christ took the FCC to court. The group criticized the FCC examiner's treatment of evidence and the burden of proof. The court agreed:

The Examiner seems to have regarded Appellants as "plaintiffs" and the licensee as "defendant," with burden of proof allocated accordingly. This tack, though possibly fostered by the Commission's own action, was a grave misreading of our holding on this question. We did not intend that intervenors representing a public interest be treated as interlopers. Rather, if analogues can be useful, a "Public Intervenor" who is seeking no license or private right is, in this context, more nearly like a complaining witness who presents evidence to police or a prosecutor whose duty it is to conduct an affirmative and objective investigation of all the facts and to pursue his prosecutorial or regulatory function if there is probable cause to believe a violation had occurred.[60]

The court recognized that the United Church group protested WLBT's license, not for selfish reasons, but to help determine whether the station operated in the public interest. The court noted that a neutrality that favored the incumbent licensee had guided the examiner while conducting the evidentiary hearing. In effect, the examiner had disregarded substantial evidence that showed WLBT's discriminatory programming. In *United Church II* the court revoked the license-renewal grant to WLBT and directed the FCC to invite applicants to apply for the license. In reversing the FCC's decision, the court indicated that the burden of proof rested with the incumbent licensee.

One year later, in *Hale*, the court rejected the requirement of an evidentiary hearing, except in certain cases, and reconsidered the burden-of-proof obligation. The case began when two citizens in Salt Lake City challenged the renewal application of station KSL-AM. The citizens claimed that the station had violated the fairness doctrine and applied for a hearing, which the FCC refused to grant. This FCC decision contradicted the *United Church I* decision. Subsequently, the court of appeals affirmed the FCC's determination not to grant a hearing. The court said:

> To establish a violation of this [fairness] doctrine, appellants must show that specific programs have dealt with controversial issues partially, and, if so, that other programs on the station have not balanced the coverage by presenting the alternative viewpoints. Appellants claim their inability to survey KSL-AM's general programming is due to the fact that the station does not publish a daily log of its programming in any newspaper. Such logs, however, are required to be kept by the licensee and could have been made available upon request.[61]

The court, in effect, accepted the FCC's interpretation of the 1934 Federal Communications Act, that a hearing was required only when the petition raises a new issue that requires resolution by a hearing. Furthermore, in protesting the renewal, the citizen group had to carry the burden of proof. According to the court, proof of a violation of the fairness doctrine must be based on specific facts.

> Where complaint is made to the Commission, the Commission expects a complainant to submit specific information indicating (1) the particular station involved, (2) the particular issue of a controversial nature discussed over the air, (3) the date and time when the program was carried, (4) the basis for the claim that the station has presented only one side of the question, and (5) whether the station had afforded, or has plans to afford an opportunity for the presentation of contrasting viewpoints.

In *Hale* the court established strict guidelines for meeting the burden of proof. The court made it quite difficult for citizens to obtain a hearing and to prove a violation. The *Hale* decision made renewal easier for the incumbent licensee.

In the *Stone* case the court again faced the issue of when and how a citizen group may obtain an evidentiary hearing. In 1969, 16 Washington, D.C., community leaders filed a petition to deny renewal of the television license for station WMAL-TV. The group contended that the station maintained discriminatory programming and employment policies. The FCC dismissed the petition, arguing that the group had not proven its claims. The group had failed to show that WMAL's programming exceeded the discretion afforded licensees or that WMAL used discriminatory employment practices. The court of appeals agreed with the FCC's ruling. According to the court,

> in the event, then, that a petition to deny does not make substantial and specific allegations of fact which, if true, would indicate that a grant of the application would be *prima facie* inconsistent with the public interest, the petition may be denied without hearing on the basis of a concise statement of the Commission's reasons for denial.[62]

In *Stone* the court decided that citizen groups had to clear several rigorous obstacles in order to obtain an evidentiary hearing. First, the FCC was not required to hold a hearing when no substantial and material issues existed. Second, a hearing was not required when facts necessary to resolve an issue were not disputed or when the issue turned on inferences from facts already available to the commission. In *Stone* the citizen's group did not, to the court's satisfaction, raise questions of such a nature as to require a hearing. According to the court, the objections the group had raised lacked the required specificity; they were largely conclusionary and not tied to specific programming considerations. The court noted that "such generalized criticisms run the risk of turning the FCC into a censorship board, a goal clearly not in the public interest." The court went on to rule that the plaintiff bears a substantial burden of specificity:

> In the absence of a competing broadcast application situation, where a hearing is required, plaintiffs bear a substantial burden of specificity, a burden they have not met in the case at bar.

The *Stone* decision demonstrates that in order for a citizen's group to obtain an evidentiary hearing, it must first raise substantial questions of fact and sufficiently prove specific allegations. In *Stone,* as in *Hale,* the court established procedures favorable to the incumbent licensee.

Lack of Candor

In the *RKO General* case, the court of appeals upheld a denial of license renewal based on lack of candor. The case began in 1965, when RKO petitioned to renew its license for WNAC-TV in Boston. The petition was opposed by a competing applicant, on the allegation that RKO had engaged in illegal trade practices. A comparative hearing on the two applications led to a FCC finding in favor of RKO, subject to further analysis of the trade practices. Because of strategic maneuvering by RKO competitors, however, the FCC did not reopen the proceedings until 1979. The hearing revealed several areas of misconduct by RKO, including reciprocal trade practices conducted during the mid-1960s and a lack of candor during the current proceedings. The FCC decided to deny license renewal to RKO. On appeal, the court set forth two principles related to the FCC's authority in determining license renewal. First, a finding by the FCC of anticompetitive practices that are not in the public interest cannot be applied retroactively to conduct that ceased almost 15 years before. Second, however, a licensee's lack of candor in proceedings before the FCC constitutes a valid reason for denial of license renewal.[63] In 1982 the Supreme Court declined to hear the *RKO General* case.

Summary

Under the regulatory system established by the Federal Communications Act of 1934, the Federal Communications Commission has power to grant, renew, and revoke licenses. The licensing decision usually involves economic, programming, and/or procedural considerations.

The licensing decision is influenced by economic guidelines. For example, in *Carroll*, the court instructed the FCC to consider the economic impact of competition on incumbent license holders. The *Mansfield Journal, Greater Boston,* and *National Citizens Committee* cases suggest that a concentration of media is looked upon with disfavor by the courts. In these cases the FCC sought diversification of ownership as a means of furthering the public interest.

Several programming guidelines play a part in the licensing decision. First, the *Simmons* and *Henry* cases illustrate the importance of local-service programming. Second, the *Yale* case reflects the FCC's concern for assuring superior quality programming. Third, the *WEFM* case acknowledged the FCC's responsibility for making program-format changes that are in the public interest. The *WNCN* decision, however, held that programming-format decisions should be influenced by market forces and competition among broadcasters. Fourth, the *ABC* and *New York State Broadcasting* cases illustrate that broadcasting of lottery information is regulated, but not prohibited. "Newsworthy" lottery programming is outside the scope of FCC regulation. Fifth, in *Pacifica,* the Supreme Court acknowledged that the FCC may regulate "indecent" as well as "obscene" expression. Sixth, numerous FCC opinions have established guidelines for public-affairs programming. The equal-time rule provides "equal" broadcast opportunities for legally qualified political candidates. The candidate-access rule, reinforced by the *CBS* case, holds that broadcasters may deny the sale of air time prior to the start of a campaign, but once a campaign begins, broadcasters must give reasonable attention to access requests from legally qualified candidates. The fairness doctrine, which grew out of the *Mayflower, WHKC,* and *Scott* decisions, requires broadcasters to provide fair and balanced coverage of controversial issues. The personal-attack rule, unsuccessfully challenged in the *Red Lion* case, grants the target of a personal attack in the broadcast media an opportunity to respond. The *Red Lion* decision seemed to set the stage for a right to media access. A few years later, however, the *DNC* case broke the momentum and supported a doctrine of limited access to the media. In effect, the *DNC* decision recognized the importance of the editorial function in broadcast journalism.

Procedural questions also affect the licensing decision. The *United Church* cases, as well as *Hale* and *Stone,* specify the procedures surrounding an evidentiary hearing and burden-of-proof obligations. These decisions suggest that in order for a citizens' group to obtain an evidentiary hearing, it must raise substantial issues and prove specific charges. These guidelines grant favorable procedures to the incumbent licensee. In *RKO General* the court of appeals upheld a FCC decision to deny renewal of license, because of lack of candor. These procedural guidelines, as well as the economic and programming guidelines reviewed in this chapter, influence the FCC as it considers the licensing decisions for broadcast stations.

NOTES

1. Wireless Ship Act of 1910, Public Law 262, 61st Congress, June 24, 1910.
2. Radio Act of 1912, Public Law 264, 62nd Congress, August 13, 1912.
3. *Hoover v. Intercity Radio Company*, 286 F. 1003 (1923).
4. *United States v. Zenith Radio Corporation*, 12 F. 2d 614 (1926).
5. Radio Act of 1927, Public Law 632, 69th Congress, February 23, 1927.
6. *KFKB Broadcasting Association v. Federal Radio Commission*, 47 F. 2d 670 (1931).
7. *Trinity Methodist Church, South v. Federal Radio Commission*, 62 F. 2d 850 (1932).
8. *United States v. Gregg*, 5 F. Supp 848 (1934).
9. Communications Act of 1934, Public Law 416, 73rd Congress, June 19, 1934.
10. *Report on Chain Broadcasting*, Commission Order No. 37, Docket No. 5060, May, 1941.
11. *National Broadcasting Company v. United States; Columbia Broadcasting System v. United States*, 63 S.Ct. 997 (1943).
12. *Carter Mountain Transmission Corporation v. Federal Communications Commission*, 321 F. 2d 359 (1963); cert. denied 84 S.Ct. 442 (1963).
13. *United States v. Southwestern Cable Company; Midwestern Television v. Southwestern Cable Company*, 88 S.Ct. 1994 (1968).
14. *United States v. Midwest Video Corporation*, 92 S.Ct. 1860 (1972).
15. *Federal Communications Commission v. Midwest Video Corporation; American Civil Liberties Union v. Federal Communications Commission; National Black Media Coalition v. Midwest Video Corporation*, 99 S.Ct. 1435 (1979).
16. *Home Box Office v. Federal Communications Commission*, 567 F. 2d 9 (1977); cert. denied 98 S.Ct. 111 (1977).
17. *Maine v. University of Maine*, 266 A. 2d 863 (1970).
18. *Federal Communications Commission v. League of Women Voters of California*, 104 S.Ct. 3106 (1984).
19. *Federal Communications Commission v. Sanders Brothers Radio Station*, 60 S.Ct. 693 (1940).
20. *Carroll Broadcasting Company v. Federal Communications Commission*, 258 F. 2d 440 (1958).
21. *Mansfield Journal Company v. Federal Communications Commission; Lorain Journal Company v. Federal Communications Commission*, 180 F. 2d 28 (1950).
22. *Greater Boston Television Corporation v. Federal Communications Commission*, 444 F. 2d 841 (1970).
23. *Federal Communications Commission v. National Citizens Committee for Broadcasting; Channel Two Television Company v. National Citizens Committee for Broadcasting; National Association of Broadcasters v. Federal Communications Commission; American Newspaper Publishers Association v. National Citizens Committee For Broadcasting; Illinois Broadcasting Company v. National Citizens Committee for Broadcasting; Post Company v. National Citizens Committee for Broadcasting*, 98 S.Ct. 2096 (1978).

24. *Simmons v. Federal Communications Commission*, 169 F. 2d 670 (1948).

25. *Henry v. Federal Communications Commission*, 302 F. 2d 191 (1962).

26. *Citizens Communications Center v. Federal Communication Commission; Hampton Roads Television Corporation v. Federal Communications Commission; Citizens Communications Center v. Burch;* 447 F. 2d 1201 (1971).

27. *National Black Media Coalition v. Federal Communications Commission*, 589 F. 2d 578 (1978).

28. *Yale Broadcasting Company v. Federal Communications Commission*, 478 F. 2d 594 (1973).

29. *Citizens Committee to Save WEFM v. Federal Communications Commission*, 506 F. 2d 246 (1974).

30. *Federal Communications Commission v. WNCN Listeners Guild; Insilco Broadcasting Corporation v. WNCN Listeners Guild; American Broadcasting Companies v. WNCN Listeners Guild; National Association of Broadcasters v. WNCN Listeners Guild;* 101 S.Ct. 1266 (1981).

31. *Writers Guild of America, West v. Federal Communications Commission; Tandem Productions v. Columbia Broadcasting System*, 423 F. Supp 1064 (1976).

32. *Community Television of Southern California v. Gottfried; Federal Communications Commission v. Gottfried*, 103 S.Ct. 885 (1983).

33. *Federal Communications Commission v. American Broadcasting Company; Federal Communications Commission v. National Broadcasting Company; Federal Communications Commission v. Columbia Broadcasting System;* 74 S.Ct. 593 (1954).

34. *New York State Broadcasters Association v. United States* 414 F. 2d 990 (1969).

35. *In re Palmetto Broadcasting Company*, 33 FCC 250 (1962).

36. *In re Pacifica Foundation*, 36 FCC 147 (1964).

37. *In re WUHY-FM, Eastern Educational Radio*, 24 FCC 2d 408 (1970).

38. *Roth v. United States*, 77 S.Ct. 1304 (1957).

39. *Sonderling Broadcasting Corporation, WGLD-FM*, 27 P. & F. Rad. Regs. 2d 285 (1973).

40. *Federal Communications Commission v. Pacifica Foundation*, 98 S.Ct. 3026 (1978).

41. *The Goodwill Stations, Inc.*, 40 FCC 362 (1962).

42. *National Broadcasting Company*, 40 FCC 370 (1962).

43. *Columbia Broadcasting System*, 40 FCC 395 (1964).

44. *In re Aspen Institute and CBS*, 55 FCC 2d 697 (1975).

45. *Chisholm v. Federal Communications Commission; Democratic National Committee v. Federal Communications Commission*, 538 F. 2d 349 (1976).

46. *League of Women Voters v. Federal Communications Commission*, 731 F. 2d 995 (1984).

47. *McCarthy v. Federal Communications Commission*, 390 F. 2d 471 (1968).

48. *Farmers Educational & Cooperative Union of America, North Dakota Division v. WDAY*, 79 S.Ct. 1302 (1959).

49. *Letter to Nicholas Zapple*, 23 FCC 2d 707 (1970).

50. *Columbia Broadcasting System v. Democratic National Committee; Federal Communications Commission v. Business Executives Move for Vietnam Peace; Post-Newsweek Stations, Capital Area v. Business Executives Move for Vietnam Peace; American Broadcasting Companies v. Democratic National Committee;* 93 S.Ct. 2080 (1973).

51. *Columbia Broadcasting System v. Federal Communications Commission; American Broadcasting Companies v. Federal Communications Commission; National Broadcasting Company v. Federal Communications Commission;* 101 S.Ct. 2813 (1981).

52. *In the Matter of the Mayflower Broadcasting Corporation and the Yankee Network, Inc. (WAAB)*, 8 FCC 333 (1941).

53. *In re United Broadcasting Company (WHKC)*, 10 FCC 515 (1945).

54. *In re Petition of Robert Harold Scott for Revocation of Licenses of Radio Stations KQW, KPO, and KFRC*, 11 FCC 372 (1946).

55. *In the Matter of Editorializing by Broadcast Licensees*, 13 FCC 1246 (1949).

56. *Brandywine-Main Line Radio v. Federal Communications Commission*, 473 F. 2d 16 (1972).

57. *Red Lion Broadcasting Company v. Federal Communications Commission; United States v. Radio Television News Directors Association,* 89 S.Ct. 1794 (1969).

58. *Columbia Broadcasting System v. Democratic National Committee.*

59. *Office of Communication of the United Church of Christ v. Federal Communications Commission,* 359 F. 2d 994 (1966).

60. *Office of Communication of the United Church of Christ v. Federal Communications Commission,* 425 F. 2d 543 (1969).

61. *Hale v. Federal Communications Commission,* 425 F. 2d 556 (1970).

62. *Stone v. Federal Communications Commission,* 466 F. 2d 316 (1972).

63. *RKO General v. Federal Communications Commission,* 670 F. 2d 215 (1981); cert. denied 102 S.Ct. 1974 (1982).

RECOMMENDED READING

Bittner, John R., *Broadcast Law and Regulation.* Englewood Cliffs, N.J.: Prentice-Hall, 1982.

Cole, Barry, and Mal Oettinger, *Reluctant Regulators: The FCC and the Broadcast Audience.* Reading, Mass.: Addison-Wesley, 1978.

Ellmore, R. Terry, *Broadcasting Law and Regulation.* Blue Ridge Summit, Pa.: TAB Books, 1982.

Friendly, Fred W., *The Good Guys, The Bad Guys, and the First Amendment: Free Speech v. Fairness in Broadcasting.* New York: Random House, 1976.

Kahn, Frank J., *Documents of American Broadcasting.* Englewood Cliffs, N.J.: Prentice-Hall, 3rd ed., 1978.

Krasnow, Erwin, Lawrence Longley, and Herbert Terry, *The Politics of Broadcast Regulation.* New York: St. Martin's Press, 3rd ed., 1982.

Labunski, Richard E., *The First Amendment Under Siege: The Politics of Broadcast Regulation.* Westport, Conn.: Greenwood Press, 1981.

Lane, James M., "*Pacifica Foundation v. FCC:* First Amendment Limitations on FCC Regulation of Offensive Broadcasts," *North Carolina Law Review* 56 (April, 1978), 584-601.

Miller, Nicholas P., and Alan Beals, "Regulating Cable Television," *Washington Law Review* 57 (December, 1981), 85-118.

Rowan, Ford, *Broadcast Fairness: Doctrine, Practice, Prospects.* New York: Longman, 1984.

Shapiro, Andrew O., *Media Access: Your Right to Express Your Views on Radio and Television.* Boston: Little, Brown, 1976.

Shapiro, George H., Philip B. Kurland, and James P. Mercurio, *"Cablespeech": The Case For First Amendment Protection.* New York: Harcourt, Brace, Jovanovich, 1983.

Simmons, Steven J., "The Fairness Doctrine: The Early History," *Federal Communications Bar Journal* 29 (1976), 207-300.

KEY DECISIONS

1943—*NATIONAL BROADCASTING COMPANY*—upheld the FCC's authority to regulate network broadcasting.

1959—*WDAY*—granted broadcasters immunity from libel suits based on the remarks of political candidates presented in accordance with the equal-time rule.

1968—*SOUTHWESTERN CABLE*—affirmed the FCC's power to regulate the cable-television industry.

1969—*RED LION*—affirmed the constitutionality and desirability of both the personal-attack rule and the fairness doctrine.

1973—*DEMOCRATIC NATIONAL COMMITTEE*—maintained that broadcasters who met fairness doctrine requirements were not obligated to accept editorial advertisements.

1978—*PACIFICA*—acknowledged that the FCC may regulate "indecent" programming, and recognized that the context in which the program occurs is of vital importance.

1978—*NATIONAL CITIZENS COMMITTEE*—upheld FCC regulations that required diversification of mass-media ownership.

1981—*COLUMBIA BROADCASTING SYSTEM*—noted that once a political campaign begins, broadcasters must give reasonable attention to access requests from legally qualified candidates.

1981—*WNCN*—upheld FCC policy statement that maintained that the public interest is best served by promoting diversity in formats through market forces and competition among broadcasters.

1984—*LEAGUE OF WOMEN VOTERS OF CALIFORNIA*—overturned a law that forbade any federally funded noncommercial educational station from "editorializing."

SUMMARY—BROADCAST LAW

Definition

The Federal Communications Act of 1934 established the Federal Communications Commission and entrusted that body with the task of regulating the broadcast media in the "public interest, convenience, and necessity." The FCC regulates the broadcast industry primarily through its power to grant, renew, and revoke licenses.

Proof

The FCC has refused to grant or renew licenses under certain conditions. The FCC believes that
1. Diversification of mass-media ownership serves the public interest by promoting diversity of program and service viewpoints, as well as by preventing undue concentration of economic power;
2. Regulation of "indecent" as well as "obscene" expression is consistent with the public interest; and
3. Lack of candor in investigative proceedings warrants denial of license.

Defenses

The FCC has enthusiastically granted or renewed licenses under certain circumstances: The FCC is impressed by applicants that
1. Demonstrate an interest in serving the local community;
2. Provide programming of superior quality;
3. Offer a programming format that is in the public interest, though the FCC acknowledges that formats are largely influenced by economic competition among broadcasters;
4. Meet fairness-doctrine obligations by providing fair and balanced coverage of controversial public issues;
5. Are *merely* the incumbents. In order for citizen groups to obtain an evidentiary hearing, they must raise substantial issues and sufficiently prove specific allegations.

13

ADVERTISING

The public has been bombarded in recent decades with advertising strategies and messages. During these years the amount spent annually on advertising has increased and the array of new products introduced to consumers has multiplied. The mass media—television, radio, print, billboards, transit, mails—have been employed in increasingly sophisticated ways to reach potential consumers. Concomitantly, the use of advertising techniques has produced a heightened concern about fairness and honesty in advertising. This concern, however, is not new. An inquiry into the history of advertising reveals that legislatures, consumer groups, and the courts have all applied various tests and guidelines in an effort to police the claims of advertisers.

TESTS OF ADVERTISING

Over the years, the Supreme Court has examined the relationship between advertising and the First Amendment. In the 1942 *Chrestensen* case, the Court determined that purely "commercial speech" enjoyed less constitutional protection than other forms of communication. In that case the Court granted greater protection to editorial than to commercial forms of advertising. In later cases, however, the Court expanded First Amendment protection for commercial advertising.

Commercial Speech

In 1942, in *Chrestensen*, the Supreme Court adopted the "commercial speech" doctrine. The case began when F. J. Chrestensen decided to charge a fee to people who visited a submarine that he had moored at a pier on the East

River in New York City. When he distributed a printed commercial advertisement on city streets, police officers advised him that he was violating a law that limited handbill distribution to "information of a public protest." Chrestensen subsequently prepared a double-faced handbill—on one side a revised commercial advertisement and on the other side a protest against the city Dock Department for refusing Chrestensen the use of wharfage facilities at a city pier where he intended to display his submarine. No commercial advertising appeared on this side of the handbill. Nonetheless, the police informed Chrestensen that distribution of the double-faced bill was prohibited. Chrestensen brought suit, and the case reached the Supreme Court. In *Chrestensen* the Court had to determine whether the New York law unconstitutionally abridged Chrestensen's freedom of expression. The Court acknowledged that the streets were proper places for communicating information and disseminating opinion, and that cities may not unduly restrict such communication. The Court noted, however, that the Constitution imposed no restraint on government concerning purely commercial advertising. New York could prohibit its citizens from distributing commercial advertising on the streets. The Court recognized that Chrestensen's protest was attached to the handbill solely to evade the state prohibition. If such an evasion were permitted, any merchant could advertise through leaflets in the streets, merely by appending a civic appeal or moral protest to the leaflet. The law would be rendered ineffective. The Court concluded that "states can prohibit the use of the streets for the distribution of purely commercial leaflets, even though such leaflets may have a 'civic appeal, or a moral platitude' appended."[1] In voting against Chrestensen, the Court extended a preferred position to political rather than commercial expression.

The Court affirmed this position in the 1973 *Pittsburgh Press Company* case. The National Organization for Women filed a complaint with the Pittsburgh Commission on Human Relations, claiming that the Pittsburgh Press Company was violating a local ordinance by allowing employers to place classified advertisements in sex-designated columns. The company had used the captions "Jobs—Male Interest," "Jobs—Female Interest," and "Male-Female." Advertisements were placed in the respective columns according to the advertiser's wishes. The commission ordered the Pittsburgh Press Company to cease and desist from such illegal practice and demanded that the company use a classification system with no reference to sex. The case reached the Supreme Court. The Court, per Justice Lewis Powell, decided that regulation was permissible because the advertisement, an example of commercial speech, was less protected by the Constitution than other forms of expression. The Court claimed:

> In the crucial respects, the advertisements in the present record resemble the *Chrestensen* rather than the *Sullivan* [*New York Times v. Sullivan*] advertisements. None expresses a position on whether, as a matter of social policy, certain positions ought to be filled by members of one or the other sex, nor does any

of them criticize the Ordinance or the Commission's enforcement practices. Each is no more than a proposal of possible employment. The advertisements are thus classic examples of commercial speech.[2]

The Court reaffirmed the protection afforded the press regarding the expression of views on controversial issues. Pittsburgh Press could publish advertisements commenting on the ordinance, the enforcement practices of the commission, or the propriety of sex preferences in employment. The Court held, however, that the commission's order prohibiting placement of commercial ads in sex-designated columns did not violate the First Amendment rights of the Pittsburgh newspaper. In *Pittsburgh Press Company* the Court reaffirmed the commercial-speech doctrine.

Commercial Information

During the 1970s the Supreme Court altered the commercial-speech doctrine in cases involving the advertising of abortions, prescription drug prices, lawyers' fees, real estate, contraceptives, and public utilities.

In 1975, in *Bigelow*, the Court extended First Amendment protection to an advertisement concerning abortion. Jeffrey Bigelow, the editor of the Charlottesville *Virginia Weekly*, published an advertisement on behalf of a New York organization that assisted women with unwanted pregnancies in obtaining an abortion in an accredited hospital or clinic. According to Virginia law, it was a misdemeanor to circulate any publication that encouraged abortion. When Bigelow was convicted for violating the statute, he appealed, claiming that the Virginia law violated the First Amendment. The Supreme Court, through the opinion of Justice Harry Blackmun, ruled that because a particular advertisement had commercial aspects, that did not negate all First Amendment guarantees. In this instance, the advertisement did more than simply propose a commercial transaction. It contained factual material of "public interest." Portions of the message—especially the lines "Abortions are now legal in New York" and "There are no residency requirements"—conveyed information of potential interest to a diverse public, not only to readers in need of abortions but also to those with an interest in the abortion controversy or the development of the law. In this case the Court claimed that "the relationship of speech to the marketplace of products or of services does not make it valueless in the marketplace of ideas."[3] In *Bigelow* the Court concluded that Virginia could not punish the publisher of a newspaper for printing an abortion referral agency's paid advertisement, which not only promoted the agency's services but also contained information about the availability of abortions.

One year later, in *Virginia State Board of Pharmacy*, the Court eroded the commercial-speech doctrine in a case involving drug-price advertising. Virginia law banned as unprofessional conduct any advertising by pharmacists of the prices on prescription drugs. The Virginia Citizens Consumer Council brought suit to have the statute declared unconstitutional and to enjoin the Virginia State Board of Pharmacy from enforcing it. The consumer group argued that the First Amendment entitled a user of prescription drugs to receive information that pharmacists wished to communicate concerning drug prices. The Board of Pharmacy contended that the advertisement of drug prices was outside the protection of the First Amendment because it was commercial speech. The Court, per Justice Blackmun, held that commercial speech was not "wholly outside the protection of the First Amendment."

> So long as we preserve a predominantly free enterprise economy, the alloca-
> tion of our resources in large measure will be made through numerous private
> economic decisions. It is a matter of public interest that those decisions, in the
> aggregate, be intelligent and well informed. To this end, the free flow of com-
> mercial information is indispensable.[4]

Virginia could not keep "the public in ignorance of the lawful terms that competing pharmacists are offering." The Court acknowledged that some forms of commercial-speech regulation are permissible. In the *Virginina State Board of Pharmacy* case, however, the Court found that any time, place, and manner restrictions on commercial speech contained in the Virginia law were exceeded by those provisions that singled out speech of a particular content—drug-price advertising—and sought to prevent its dissemination completely.

A year later the Supreme Court heard a related case—this time involving lawyers' fees and services. John Bates and Van O'Steen, members of the Arizona State Bar Association, placed an ad in the *Arizona Republic*. The ad offered "legal services at very reasonable fees" and listed fees for such services as divorces, adoptions, bankruptcies, and name changes. The Board of Governors of the Arizona State Bar Association complained that attorneys were prohibited from advertising in the media and imposed a one-week suspension on both Bates and O'Steen. The lawyers appealed, arguing that the bar association regulations violated the First Amendment. In *Bates* the Supreme Court acknowledged that false, deceptive, or misleading attorney advertising could be regulated.

> In fact, because the public lacks sophistication concerning legal services, mis-
> statements that might be overlooked or deemed unimportant in other advertis-
> ing may be found quite inappropriate in legal advertising. For example, adver-
> tising claims as to the quality of services . . . may be so likely to be misleading
> as to warrant restriction. Similar objections might justify restraints on in-person
> solicitation.[5]

The issue before the Court in this case, however, was whether Arizona could prevent publication of a *truthful* advertisement concerning legal services. The

Court held that "the flow of such information could not be restrained," and that the state-bar disciplinary action violated the First Amendment.

In *Ohralik* the Court clarified the commercial-information doctrine, as it applied to advertising by attorneys. The case involved lawyer Albert Ohralik, who, upon learning about an automobile accident in which a young woman had been injured, went to the hospital and offered to represent the woman in any court actions. Ohralik had the woman sign a contract, which provided that he would receive one-third of any recovery. Shortly thereafter the woman informed Ohralik that she did not want to have Ohralik represent her. Ohralik insisted that the woman had entered into a binding agreement. Even though another lawyer represented her in concluding a settlement with the insurance company, the young woman paid Ohralik one-third of her recovery, in settlement of his lawsuit against her for breach of contract. The woman then filed a complaint against Ohralik with the Ohio Bar Association. After a hearing, the bar found Ohralik had violated the Ohio Code of Professional Responsibility. The case reached the Supreme Court. The Court noted that "the solicitation of business by a lawyer through direct, in-person communication with the prospective client has long been viewed as inconsistent with the profession's ideal(s)." Such behavior posed a significant potential harm to the prospective client. The Court concluded that the bar association "acting with state authorization constitutionally may discipline a lawyer for soliciting clients in person for pecuniary gain under circumstances likely to pose dangers that the State has a right to prevent." The Court upheld the ruling; Ohralik's transaction was commercial speech.

> To require a parity of constitutional protection for commerical and noncommercial speech alike could invite dilution. . . . Rather than subject the First Amendment to such a devitalization, we instead have afforded commercial speech a limited measure of protection, commensurate with its subordinate position in the scale of First Amendment values, while allowing modes of regulation that might be impermissible in the realm of noncommercial expression.[6]

In *Bates* the Court had extended First Amendment protection to the advertising of commercial information concerning legal fees and services; in *Ohralik* the Court denied protection to direct personal solicitation of a potential client—such activity was considered commercial speech.

In the *Matter of R. M. J.*, a 1982 case, the Court again clarified the commercial-information doctrine as it applies to advertising by attorneys. As with many states, prior to the *Bates* decision Missouri prohibited advertising by lawyers. After *Bates*, the Committee on Professional Ethics and Responsibility of the Supreme Court of Missouri revised the ban. Advertising by lawyers was permitted, but it was restricted to certain categories of information and to certain specified language. When a young lawyer (R. M. J.) decided to announce the opening of his private practice, he distributed advertisements that included prohibited information. The ads contained the fact that R. M. J. was licensed in Missouri and Illinois, and that he was admitted to practice before the U.S. Supreme Court. The ads also contained a listing of areas of practice in words that deviated from the language prescribed by the advisory committee—for example, "personal injury" and "real estate" instead of "tort law" and "property law." Subsequently, the advisory committee charged R. M. J. with unprofessional conduct. In a disbarment proceeding, the Supreme Court of Missouri upheld the constitutionality of the advertising regulations and issued a reprimand to R. M. J. The case reached the U.S. Supreme Court. Justice Powell, writing for a unanimous Court, discussed the issues in the case.

> Truthful advertising related to lawful activities is entitled to the protection of the First Amendment. . . . Misleading advertising may be prohibited entirely. But the states may not place an absolute prohibition on certain types of potentially misleading information, e.g., a listing of areas of practice, if the information also may be presented in a way that is not deceptive.

Powell acknowledged that the potential for deception was "particularly strong in the context of advertising professional services," but he pointed out that "restrictions upon such advertising may be no broader than reasonably necessary to prevent the deception."[7] In the *Matter of R. M. J.* the Court decided that the restrictions were overly broad. Accordingly, the decision of the Supreme Court of Missouri was reversed.

In 1977 the Court decided *Linmark Associates*, a case concerning real-estate advertisements. In an attempt to stop "panic selling" by whites who feared that the community was becoming all black and that property values would decline, Willingboro Council banned the placing of for-sale signs on all but model homes. Linmark Associates, a real-estate agency that wanted to advertise certain property by placing such a sign on the lawn, initiated court action. The Supreme Court, per Justice Thurgood Marshall, noted that the Willingboro statute prevented residents from obtaining certain information of "vital interest." The statute affected one of the most important decisions citizens had a right to make—where to live and raise their families. The Willingboro Council restricted the free flow of this information, because it feared that homeowners would leave town. The council's concern was not with any commercial aspect of for-sale signs, but with the substance of the information communicated to the citizens.

> If dissemination of this information can be restricted, then every locality in the country can suppress any facts that reflect poorly on the locality, so long as a plausible claim can be made that disclosure would cause the recipients of the information to act irrationally.[8]

The Court concluded that even though the law was designed to promote an important governmental objective—integrated housing—the Willingboro ordinance violated the First Amendment.

Another 1977 case, *Carey*, involved the advertising of contraceptives. Population Planning Associates advertised in periodicals published in New York the mail-order sale of contraceptive devices. State officials advised PPA that the ads violated an ordinance that prohibited sales of contraceptives to minors and outlawed sales by nonpharmacists. The company challenged the statute in court. The Supreme Court opinion, written by Justice William Brennan, first of all examined the matter on privacy grounds. Brennan noted that the decision whether or not to have a child was a constitutionally protected choice that held "a particularly important place in the history of the right of privacy." Furthermore, the right to privacy concerning decisions affecting procreation extended to minors as well as to adults. Second, Brennan examined the matter of advertising and noted that the statute sought "to suppress completely any information about the availability and price of contraceptives." The law banned "the free flow of commercial information" that reflected "substantial individual and societal interests." The information suppressed by the law "related to activity with which, at least in some respects, the State could not interfere."[9] New York argued that the advertisements were offensive and embarrassing to many who were exposed to them, and that permitting them would legitimize sexual activity of young people. In *Carey* the Court concluded that the fact that protected speech may be offensive to some did not justify its suppression.

A 1980 commercial-information case dealt with advertising by public utilities. The Central Hudson Gas and Electric Corporation initiated suit in New York state court to challenge the constitutionality of a New York Public Service Commission policy statement that banned certain advertising by utilities. The policy statement divided advertising into two categories: promotional—advertising intended to stimulate the purchase of utility services; and informational—all advertising not designed to promote sales. The commission banned promotional but permitted informational advertising. The ban was intended as a vehicle for conserving energy. Writing for the Supreme Court, Justice Powell stressed that the First Amendment's relevance for commercial speech is based on the informational function of advertising—commercial messages that do not accurately inform the public about lawful activity may be suppressed. Powell acknowledged that a four-stage analysis is appropriate in determining the constitutionality of such expression.

> In commercial speech cases, then, a four-part analysis has developed. At the outset, we must determine whether the expression is protected by the First Amendment. For commercial speech to come within that provision, it at least

must concern lawful activity and not be misleading. Next, we ask whether the
asserted governmental interest is substantial. If both inquiries yield positive answers, we must determine whether the regulation directly advances the governmental interest asserted, and whether it is not more extensive than is necessary
to serve that interest.[10]

The Court then used these four stages to analyze the expression at issue in *Central Hudson Gas*. Powell noted that the advertising was neither inaccurate nor
did it relate to unlawful activity; the expression warranted First Amendment protection. Powell also noted that there was a direct link between New York's interest in energy conservation and the commission's ban on advertising. The
Court, however, declared the ban to be ''more extensive than necessary to further the State's interest in energy conservation.''

> The Commission's order reaches all promotional advertising, regardless of the
> impact of the touted service on overall energy use. But the energy conserva-
> tion rationale, as important as it is, cannot justify suppressing information about
> electric devices or services that would cause no net increase in total energy use.
> In addition, no showing has been made that a more limited restriction on the
> content of promotional advertising would not serve adequately the State's in-
> terests.

The Court concluded that because the commission's order was overbroad, the
ban violated the First Amendment.

In the 1983 *Bolger* case the Court heard a controversy involving commercial speech. A drug-products company challenged a federal law that prohibited
the mailing of unsolicited advertisements for contraceptives. The company,
Youngs Drug Products Corporation, manufactured and sold contraceptives to
wholesale distributors. The company promoted its products by various methods,
including unsolicited mass mailings to members of the public. When this promotional effort was banned by the Postal Service, Youngs Drug Products Company
contested the ban on the ground that it violated the First Amendment. The case
reached the Supreme Court. The Court's opinion, prepared by Justice Thurgood
Marshall, acknowledged that most of the mailings ''fall within the core notion
of commercial speech—speech which does no more than propose a commercial
transaction.'' Marshall stressed, however, that ''all of the mailings . . . are entitled to the qualified but nonetheless substantial protection accorded to commercial speech.'' Marshall then assessed the level of protection available to the mailings in the light of two criteria. First, Marshall examined whether the mailings
covered unlawful activity or were misleading. He found no deception; thus, the
mailings were entitled to First Amendment protection under criterion one. Second, Marshall considered whether any substantial governmental interest would
be served by banning the mailings. The government argued that the ban served
two interests: shielding recipients of the mailings from materials that are poten-

tially offensive, and aiding parents' efforts to control the manner in which their children become informed about birth control. The Supreme Court decided that these reasons did not justify the ban. Marshall noted that simply because "protected speech may be offensive to some does not justify its suppression."[11] Furthermore, the government is not justified in "purging all mailboxes of unsolicited material that is entirely suitable for adults." In *Bolger* the Court concluded that the government failed to justify its sweeping prohibition on mailings of unsolicited contraceptive advertisements. In so doing, the Court identified criteria applicable to the protection of commercial speech.

During the 1970s the Supreme Court extended limited First Amendment protection to commercial speech. An examination of relevant cases—*Bigelow, Virginia State Board of Pharmacy, Bates, Ohralik, R. M. J., Linmark, Carey, Central Hudson Gas*, and *Bolger*—reveals that the Court still distinguishes between commercial and informative communication. In these cases, however, the justices clarified the relationship between commercial and informative speech—namely, the Court will protect the free flow of commercial information, even though it is less willing to protect purely commercial messages.

Summary

Historically, the Supreme Court has defined the relationship between advertising and the First Amendment. In *Chrestensen* the Court granted greater protection to noncommercial than to commercial forms of expression. The commercial-speech test has been significantly eroded, however, in *Bigelow, Virginia State Board of Pharmacy, Bates, R. M. J., Linmark, Carey, Central Hudson Gas*, and *Bolger*. These cases indicate that an advertisement does not relinquish all First Amendment guarantees simply because it contains commercial aspects. Indeed, the free flow of commercial information is constitutionally protected.

REGULATION OF ADVERTISING

Toward the end of the nineteenth century, the United States experienced a decided shift in the public attitude toward business. The notion that the public benefits the most in an environment that allows free competition to function without restriction was replaced by an attitude that favored governmental regulation of certain business activities. Advertising is such an activity.

Deception

Until the beginning of the twentieth century, advertising was regulated principally by the doctrine of *caveat emptor*—"let the buyer beware." A more restrictive regulatory policy was introduced with the passage of the Pure Food and Drug Act in 1906 and the creation of the Federal Trade Commission in 1914. During the initial years of FTC regulation, the courts protected competitors against false and deceptive advertisements; consumer rights were secondary and at times ignored entirely. Eventually, consumer interests came under the umbrella of FTC protection.

Competitor Interests

In 1922 the Supreme Court heard *Winsted Hosiery*, a case that involved deceptive labeling. The Winsted Hosiery Company labeled the cartons in which their underwear was sold as "Natural Merino," "Natural Wool," and "Natural Worsted," even though much of the product contained as little as 10 percent wool. The Federal Trade Commission decided that the labels were false and deceptive. The FTC ordered the company to "cease and desist" from using as labels on goods not composed wholly of wool, the words "Merino," "Wool," or "Worsted," unless the labels also listed any other material that went into the

garments, or unless the labels indicated that the underwear was not made wholly of wool. The company brought suit against the FTC. The Supreme Court, per Justice Louis Brandeis, decided that a substantial part of the consuming public understood the words "Natural Merino," "Natural Wool," and "Natural Worsted" to mean that the underwear was all wool. The labels were literally false, calculated to deceive the purchasing public. The practice constituted an unfair method of competition against manufacturers of all-wool knit underwear and against those manufacturers of mixed wool and cotton underwear who labeled their products truthfully.[12] The Court upheld the FTC ruling.

The Federal Trade Commission's power to regulate deception came under attack in 1931. Raladam Company, manufacturer of an "obesity cure," advertised that the preparation was safe and effective. One of the ingredients, however—"desiccated thyroid"—impaired the health of a substantial portion of the product's users. The FTC, concluding that the advertising constituted an unfair method of competition, issued a cease-and-desist order. When the case reached the Supreme Court, the justices noted that the statute that gave the Federal Trade Commission the power to issue a cease-and-desist order required evidence that the methods complained of were *unfair*, that they were methods of *competition* in commerce, and that a proceeding by the commission to prevent the use of the methods appeared to be in the *interest of the public*. The Court acknowledged that the first and third requirements were met, then considered the second. The word "competition" in the act required the existence of present or potential competitors and injury to the business of these competitors through the deceptive methods. In *Raladam* the Court found no evidence that the advertisements were injurious. No competitor demonstrated what effect, if any, the misleading ads had upon his or her business.[13] The Court ruled that the FTC could not, by assuming the existence of competition, give itself jurisdiction to issue an order. The order was set aside.

In 1935 the FTC instituted another action against Raladam. This time considerable evidence was presented that indicated that the misleading advertisements induced consumers to purchase Raladam's medicine in preference to the products of competitors. The FTC issued another cease-and-desist order, which Raladam again appealed. In *Raladam II* the Supreme Court sided with the FTC—when the commission found that Raladam's deceptive statements referred to the quality of its competitor's merchandise, it was authorized to infer that trade would be diverted from competitors who did not engage in such "unfair methods."[14] In 1942, in *Raladam II*, the Court overruled the finding in the first *Raladam* case.

Consumer Interests

In 1937 the Supreme Court took a strong stand against the doctrine of *caveat emptor*. At that time the Federal Trade Commission became aware that the Standard Education Society was using deceptive advertising to sell the Standard

Reference Work and New Standard Encyclopedia. As part of its sales promotion, the society claimed to give certain individuals a free set of books, and maintained that the only return desired for the gift was permission to use the individual's name as a reference for advertising purposes. The only cost to the individual was $69.50 for a loose-leaf extension service; the individual was told that the regular price of the books and the extension service was between $150 and $200. These statements were false, as $69.50 was the standard price for both the encyclopedia and the loose-leaf extension. The FTC issued a cease-and-desist order. The case reached the Supreme Court. Justice Hugo Black prepared the unanimous opinion of the Court, citing some shortcomings of the rule of *caveat emptor*.

> The fact that a false statement may be obviously false to those who are trained and experienced does not change its character, nor take away its power to deceive others less experienced. There is no duty resting upon a citizen to suspect the honesty of those with whom he transacts business. Laws are made to protect the trusting as well as the suspicious. The best element of business has long since decided that honesty should govern competitive enterprises, and that the rule of caveat emptor should not be relied upon to reward fraud and deception.[15]

Promising free books and deceiving unwary purchasers about the price of the books were practices contrary to decent business standards. If the Court failed to prohibit such practices, deception in business would be elevated to the standing and dignity of truth. In *Standard Education Society* the Court upheld the FTC order.

A year later Congress amended the Federal Trade Commission Act to include the following: "Unfair methods of competition in commerce, and unfair or deceptive acts or practices in commerce are declared unlawful." Congress also prohibited "false advertisements" designed "to induce purchase of food, drugs, devices or cosmetics." This legislation, known as the Wheeler-Lea Amendments, signaled the demise of the doctrine of *caveat emptor*.

In 1965 the Supreme Court heard *Colgate-Palmolive*, a case involving deceptive demonstration on television. Colgate-Palmolive Company presented a 60-second commercial for Rapid Shave aerosol shaving cream. The commercial showed professional football player Frank Gifford, whom the announcer described as having "a beard as tough as sandpaper...a beard that needs Palmolive Rapid Shave...supermoisturized for the fastest, smoothest shave possible." The Rapid Shave lather was then spread on sandpaper and a hand appeared with a razor and shaved a clear path through the gritty surface. "To prove Rapid Shave's supermoisturizing power," the announcer concluded, "we put it right from the can onto this tough dry sandpaper. It was apply—soak—and off in a stroke." Research conducted by the FTC showed that sandpaper could not be shaved immediately following application of Rapid Shave, but required a soaking period of approximately 80 minutes. In the commercial, the substance resembling sandpaper was actually plexiglass, to which sand had been applied. If real sandpaper had been used, it would have appeared to viewers to be plain colored paper. In support of a cease-and-desist order against Colgate-Palmolive, the FTC argued that the limitations of the television medium may challenge "the creative ingenuity and resourcefulness of copy writers; but surely they could not constitute lawful justification for resort to falsehoods and deception of the public." The FTC stressed that if a company did not "choose to advertise truthfully, they could, and should discontinue advertising." The Supreme Court upheld the FTC's order. The Court determined that the commercials contained three representations to the public: that sandpaper could be shaved by Rapid Shave, that an experiment had been conducted that verified this claim, and that the viewer was actually viewing this experiment. According to the Court, the Federal Trade Commission Act prohibited the intentional misrepresentation of any fact that would constitute a material factor in a purchaser's decision to buy. In *Colgate-Palmolive* "the undisclosed use of plexiglass in the present commercials, was a material deceptive practice, independent and separate from the other misrepresentation found." The Court was unsympathetic with Colgate-Palmolive's contention that it would be impractical to inform the viewing public that it was not seeing an actual demonstration.

> If. . .it becomes impossible or impractical to show simulated demonstrations on television in a truthful manner, this indicates that television is not a medium that lends itself to this type of commercial, not that the commercial must survive at all costs. . . . If the inherent limitations of a method do not permit its use in the way a seller desires, the seller cannot by material misrepresentation compensate for those limitations.[16]

In *Colgate-Palmolive* the Court decided that simulated demonstrations in television advertising must be done in a truthful manner.

The FTC faces numerous procedural and enforcement problems in regulating deceptive advertising. This aspect of regulation is clearly illustrated by the *J. B. Williams* case. In 1959 the Federal Trade Commission determined that advertisements that promoted Geritol for the relief of iron-deficiency anemia were deceptive. The FTC issued a complaint in 1962 and a cease-and-desist order in 1964. J. B. Williams, the producer of Geritol, appealed. In 1967 the court of appeals upheld the FTC order. The court noted that

> the evidence is clear that Geritol is of no benefit in the treatment of tiredness except in those cases where tiredness has been caused by a deficiency of the ingredients contained in Geritol. The fact that the great majority of people who experience tiredness symptoms do not suffer from any deficiency of the ingre-

dients in Geritol is a "material fact" under the meaning of that term as used
in Section 15 of the Federal Trade Commission Act and Petitioners' failure to
reveal this fact in this day when the consumer is influenced by mass advertising utilizing highly developed arts of persuasion, renders it difficult for the typical consumer to know whether the product will in fact meet his needs unless
he is told what the product will or will not do.

When Geritol's commercials did not comply with the order, the FTC turned the
case over to the Department of Justice, which on April 20, 1970, filed a $1 mil-
lion suit against the company and its advertising agency. In January 1973, Geritol
and its agency were fined at total of $812,000. In 1974 a court of appeals dis-
missed the fine and sent the case back to district court for a jury trial.[17] Finally,
in 1976, the FTC won a $280,000 judgment against the company. During those
17 years, however, millions of dollars were spent on television commercials for
Geritol, and the company had been able to solidify its control of the tonic market. Clearly, enforcement can be a significant problem for the FTC.

Corrective Advertising

During the 1970s, the FTC required corrective advertising in several instances of deception. Sometimes merely stopping an ad is insufficient. When a
deceptive advertising campaign has been effective over a long period of time,
the effect of the misleading information remains in the public's mind, even after the ad is discontinued. In such instances, the FTC may impose corrective dis-
closures. Some examples are *Continental Baking* and *Ocean Spray Cranberries*.

In 1971 the FTC issued a corrective advertising order concerning Profile
bread, a product of the Continental Baking Company. Profile had been promoted
as lower in calories than ordinary bread, and of significant value for use in
weight-control diets. The ads implied that eating two slices of Profile bread before lunch and dinner would result in a loss of body weight, without any rigorous adherence to a reduced calorie diet. These advertising claims were not true.
After an investigation, the FTC ordered that the company cease and desist from
making false advertising claims. The FTC also required that corrective advertisements constitute 25 percent of the advertising for Profile bread during the
following year.[18] As a result, one ad that appeared on television had Julia Meade
make the following statement:

> I'm Julia Meade for Profile bread. And like all mothers I'm concerned about
> nutrition and balanced meals. So I'd like to clear up any misunderstanding you
> may have about Profile bread from its advertising or even its name. Does Pro-
> file have fewer calories than other breads? No, Profile has about the same per
> ounce as other breads. To be exact Profile has seven fewer calories per slice.
> But that's because it's sliced thinner. But eating bread will not cause you to

lose weight. A reduction of seven calories is insignificant. It's total calories and balanced nutrition that counts. And Profile can help you achieve a balanced meal. Because it provides protein and B vitamins as well as other nutrients.

The ad was so well received by the public that the company considered spending more than the 25 percent required by the FTC. The corrective ad actually enhanced the company's credibility.

One year later the FTC ordered corrective advertising for Ocean Spray cranberry juice. In its advertising Ocean Spray claimed that their cranberry juice was more nutritious and had more "food energy" than orange or tomato juices. The FTC determined that Ocean Spray's claims were deceptive, so the commission issued a cease-and-desist order. In addition, the commission ordered that corrective advertising constitute 25 percent of the promotion for Ocean Spray cranberry-juice cocktail during the ensuing year.[19] Accordingly, Ocean Spray presented a commercial in which the announcer made the following statement:

If you've wondered what some of our earlier advertising meant when we said Ocean Spray cranberry-juice cocktail has more food energy than orange juice

or tomato juice, let us make it clear: we didn't mean vitamins and minerals. Food energy means calories. Nothing more.

Food energy is important at breakfast since many of us may not get enough calories, or food energy, to get off to a good start. Ocean Spray cranberry-juice cocktail helps because it contains more food energy than most other breakfast drinks.

And Ocean Spray cranberry-juice cocktail gives you and your family Vitamin C plus a great wake-up taste. It's the other breakfast drink.

In *Ocean Spray* and *Continental*, as well as *Payless Drug*[20] and *Amstar*,[21] the FTC ordered corrective advertising in an attempt to curb the impact deceptive advertising had on the consumer. In some of these cases the corrective ad actually improved the image of the offending company.

In *Warner-Lambert* the corrective-advertising practice was challenged in court. Warner-Lambert Company asked the courts to determine whether the Federal Trade Commission had authority to order corrective advertising for Listerine antiseptic mouthwash. According to FTC research, Listerine's advertising claim that the mouthwash cured colds and sore throats was false. The FTC ordered corrective advertising. In circuit court, Warner-Lambert argued that the FTC order requiring corrective advertising exceeded the commission's statutory power. The company claimed that the Federal Trade Commission Act authorized the commission to issue cease-and-desist orders and did not mention any other remedies. The FTC claimed that, in this case, corrective advertising was "absolutely necessary," because "a hundred years of false cold claims have built up a large reservoir of erroneous consumer belief which would persist, unless corrected, long after petitioner ceased making the claims." The court agreed:

Listerine has built up over a period of many years a widespread reputation. When it was ascertained that that reputation no longer applied to the product, it was necessary to take action to correct it.... It is the accumulated impact of past advertising that necessitates disclosure in future advertising. To allow consumers to continue to buy the product on the strength of the impression built up by prior advertising—an impression which is now known to be false—would be unfair and deceptive.[22]

In *Warner-Lambert* the circuit court decided that the FTC has authority to order corrective advertising in appropriate cases. In 1978 the U.S. Supreme Court refused to hear the case.

Access

During the past decade or so, the issue of access has played a substantial role in developing a body of law regarding the regulation of advertising. Two specific questions faced the Supreme Court: (1) Can a communication medium deny access to a particular advertiser, while at the same time accepting ads from other advertisers? (2) Under what conditions does the fairness doctrine grant an individual the right to counteradvertise?

Rejection by Media

In 1974 the Supreme Court grappled with the question of whether the rapid transit medium can reject a specific advertisement, while at the same time accepting other ads. In *Lehman* the Court held that the medium is not bound to accept the advertising of all who apply for it. Harry Lehman, a candidate for the office of state representative to the Ohio General Assembly, wanted to advertise his candidacy on the Shaker Heights rapid transit system. He was informed that although space was available, political advertising was not permitted. Lehman sued, arguing that the transit displays constituted a public forum protected by the First Amendment and that there was a guarantee of non-discriminatory access to such publicly owned areas of communication. In a sharply divided opinion, the U.S. Supreme Court majority noted:

> Here, we have no open spaces, no meeting hall, park, street corner, or other public thoroughfare. Instead, the city is engaged in commerce. It must provide rapid, convenient, pleasant, and inexpensive service to the commuters of Shaker Heights. The car card space, although incidental to the provision of public transportation, is a part of the commercial venture. In much the same way that a newspaper or periodical, or even a radio or television station, need not accept every proffer of advertising from the general public, a city transit system has discretion to develop and make reasonable choices concerning the type of advertising that may be displayed in its vehicles.[23]

Justice Harry Blackmun's majority opinion stressed that "revenue earned from long-term commercial advertising could be jeopardized by a requirement that short-term candidacy or issue-oriented advertisements be displayed." Blackmun was joined in the opinion by Chief Justice Warren Burger and Justices Byron White and William Rehnquist. Justice William Douglas supplied the fifth vote on the ground that a political candidate had no right to force his message on a "captive audience" of commuters—the customer's privacy rights should shield him or her from exposure to all advertising. The dissenting justices viewed the city's actions as unconstitutional; Shaker Heights had preferred commercial advertising on its buses to the exclusion of political advertising. According to the minority, the city had opened up advertising space on its buses as a "public forum" and should not be able to exclude the category of political advertising. In *Lehman* the majority, however, upheld the right of transit media to select which specific types of advertising they will display. *Lehman* seemed to provide greater protection for commercial than for noncommercial messages.

In 1981, in *Metromedia*, the Supreme Court weighed the constitutionality of a city ordinance that afforded greater protection to commercial than to non-commercial outdoor billboard advertising. The San Diego statute permitted on-site commercial advertising—a sign promoting goods or services available on the property where the sign is located—but forbade other commercial and much non-commercial advertising. The stated goals of the statute were to promote traffic safety and to improve the appearance of the city. Several outdoor advertising companies initiated court action to enjoin enforcement of the law. The Court, per Justice White, acknowledged that San Diego could favor one kind of commercial advertising over another. The city, however, could not favor commercial over noncommercial messages. The San Diego law allowed an exception for all on-site commercial advertising, but failed to provide a similar exception for noncommercial messages.

> The city does not explain how or why noncommercial billboards located in places where commercial billboards are permitted would be more threatening to safe driving or would detract more from the beauty of the city. Insofar as the city tolerates billboards at all, it cannot choose to limit their content to commercial messages; the city may not conclude that the communication of commercial information concerning goods and services connected with a particular site is of greater value than the communication of noncommercial messages.[24]

Furthermore, the city could not favor one kind of noncommercial advertising over another. The Court stressed that although San Diego could distinguish between the relative value of different categories of commercial speech, the city "does not have the same range of choice in the area of noncommercial speech." Concerning noncommercial expression, the city may not choose the appropriate subjects for public debate: to do so would "allow that government control over the search for political truth." In *Metromedia* the Supreme Court judged the San Diego statute to be unconstitutional and reaffirmed that noncommercial speech enjoys greater First Amendment protection than commercial speech.

Fairness Doctrine

In 1968 the courts applied the fairness doctrine to advertising. The case began when John Banzhaf asked WCBS-TV in New York for free reply time for antismokers to respond to the prosmoking views implicit in cigarette commercials. WCBS rejected Banzhaf's request. The station claimed that it had broadcast several news and information programs about the smoking-health controversy. In addition, WCBS had aired American Cancer Society public-service announcements free of charge. The station was confident that its "coverage of the health ramifications of smoking has been fully consistent with the fairness doctrine." When Banzhaf complained to the FCC, the commission decided that reply time should be provided, because the issue of whether or not cigarettes were harmful to health was a controversial one. The Court of Appeals, District of Columbia, affirmed the commission's order on three grounds: the fairness doctrine, the public-interest standard, and the First Amendment. In terms of the fairness doctrine, cigarette smoking's effect on health was viewed as a controversial public issue. The commission's ruling aimed to provide fair and balanced coverage of this issue. With respect to the public-interest standard, a dialogue between cigarette advertisers, whose ads comprised a sizable portion of all broadcast revenues, and opponents of cigarette smoking, with no such financial clout, appeared to be in the public interest. Concerning the First Amendment, the court ruled that governmental intervention in the form of compulsory reply time was permissible, when it served as a "countervailing" force where meaningful broadcast debate would otherwise be impossible.

> Where, as here, one party to a debate has a financial clout and a compelling economic interest in the presentation of one side unmatched by its opponent, and where the public stake in the argument is no less than life itself—we think the purpose of rugged debate is served, not hindered by an attempt to redress the balance.[25]

In *Banzhaf* the court upheld the FCC ruling that required stations that carry cigarette advertising to devote a significant amount of broadcast time to airing the case against cigarette smoking.

A few years later Congress banned cigarette commercials from the airwaves completely. The Public Health Cigarette Smoking Act stipulated that after January 1, 1971, it was illegal to advertise cigarettes on broadcast media. Capital Broadcasting Company sued, alleging that the ban prohibited the "dissemination of information with respect to a lawfully sold product" in violation of the First Amendment, and that it violated due process because print media were not prohibited from publishing cigarette ads. Only electronic media were restricted, and such a distinction was "arbitrary and invidious." The district court rejected both of Capital Broadcasting Company's allegations. First, the statute restricted only the airing of commercial messages—it did not prohibit disseminating information about cigarettes. The act did not conflict with First Amendment guarantees. Second, Congress could regulate one medium at a time, if there were a rational reason for such regulation. The court noted that

> substantial evidence showed that the most persuasive advertising was being conducted on radio and television, and that these broadcasts were particularly effective in reaching a very large audience of young people.[26]

The court decided that the unique characteristics of broadcast communication made it especially subject to regulation in the public interest. The court upheld the ban. In 1972 the Supreme Court affirmed the decision without opinion.[27]

During the early 1970s the courts considered other attempts to apply the fairness doctrine to advertising. In *Green* the court of appeals turned down an effort by peace groups to respond to military recruitment advertising. According to the court, broadcast stations were justified in interpreting such ads as involving only the issue of military manpower recruitment by voluntary means. That was not a "controversial issue of public importance." The draft issue and the Vietnam War question had been "ventilated in extenso for years on (probably) every television and radio station in the land." According to the court, "no individual member of the public had the right of access to the air."[28]

In *Friends of the Earth* the court considered an environmental protection group's effort to reply to automobile company ads. The group claimed that the companies contributed significantly to air pollution and that the broadcast media had not met their fairness-doctrine responsibility of informing the public of the other side of the antipollution controversy. The Federal Communication Commission decided that no action was warranted against the media. The commission acknowledged that automobile air pollution contributed to many deaths each year, but that was true of numerous other products. According to the commission, cigarettes were distinguishable from such products; government officials had urged the public to quit smoking, but they did not urge discontinuance of the use of automobiles. The commission refused to extend the *Banzhaf* ruling "generally to the field of product advertising." The court of appeals, however, disagreed with the FCC; *Friends of the Earth* was indistinguishable from *Banzhaf* in the reach of the fairness doctrine.[29] The case was remanded to the FCC for reconsideration.

Clearly, the *Banzhaf* case expanded the scope of the fairness doctrine. *Green* and *Friends of the Earth* represented attempts to extend the *Banzhaf* principle to other areas. The movement lost momentum, however, because of two key court decisions. In 1973 the Supreme Court ruled in *DNC* that a medium that provided full and fair coverage of public issues was not obligated to accept any editorial advertisements. The case involved the efforts of a peace group and of a national political party to gain access to the broadcast media, in order to expound their views on controversial issues. In this case, the Supreme Court agreed with the FCC that providing access to the marketplace of "ideas and experiences" would not be served "by a system so heavily weighted in favor of the financially affluent, or those with access to wealth." If broadcasters were required to accept editorial advertisements, the ideas of the wealthy could well prevail, because they had the financial capability to purchase time more frequently. As a result, the time a station "allotted for editorial advertising could be monopolized by those of one political persuasion." The ultimate effect might be the

> erosion of the journalistic discretion of broadcasters in the coverage of public issues, and a transfer of control over the treatment of public issues from the

licensees who are accountable for broadcast performance to private individuals who are not. The public interest would no longer be "paramount" but, rather, subordinate to private whim, especially since...a broadcaster would be largely precluded from rejecting editorial advertisements that dealt with matters trivial or insignificant or already fairly covered by the broadcaster.[30]

The Court concluded that if the fairness doctrine were applied to editorial advertising, there would be a "substantial danger that the effective operation of that doctrine would be jeopardized." Though the *DNC* decision dealt with editorial advertising, it tended to thwart attempts to apply the fairness doctrine to areas of product advertising.

The movement was further stifled by the *National Citizens Committee for Broadcasting* decision. The case involved a challenge to the FCC's 1974 *Fairness Report*, a document that was issued after an extensive review of the fairness doctrine in general, as well as the application of that doctrine to the broadcast of commercial advertisements, discussion of public issues, and political broadcasts. The main conclusion of the report denied application of the fairness doctrine to broadcast communications promoting the sale of commercial products. This policy was challenged by several groups. The court of appeals, however, upheld the FCC's findings.

> The Fairness Report concludes that the fairness doctrine should not be applied to broadcast advertisements promoting the sale of a commercial product. This decision was made with a conscious awareness that it represents a marked shift from previous FCC policy. That previous policy, which was developed in a series of ad hoc decisions by the Commission and the courts, was never subject to precise articulation or definition, leading to uncertainty and difficulties in achieving full and fair enforcement. While we are under no illusion that the new policy...will solve all or perhaps even most of the implementation problems encountered heretofore, we believe that we are without warrant to deny the Commission the opportunity to attempt a new resolution of those difficulties.[31]

In 1978 the Supreme Court refused to review the *National Citizens for Broadcasting* case.

Summary

Misrepresentation in advertising came under heavy attack in the early 1900s. Since then, governmental agencies and the courts have enjoyed varying degrees of success in regulating advertising. The Supreme Court has frequently acted to curtail deceptive practices. In several cases—*Winsted, Raladam, Standard Education, Colgate-Palmolive*—the Court reinforced FTC power to regulate advertising. *J.B. Williams*, however, illustrates that the Federal Trade Commission can experience difficulty in enforcing those regulations. *Warner-Lambert* upheld the authority of the FTC to order corrective advertising.

In recent decades the Supreme Court has considered the issue of access. In *Lehman* the Court held that the transit media could deny access to political advertising, while at the same time accepting commercial ads. *Metromedia* determined that while a local statute could favor one kind of commercial advertising over another, it could neither favor commercial over noncommercial messages, nor could it favor one kind of noncommercial advertising over another. Beginning with *Banzhaf*, and continuing in *Green* and *Friends of the Earth*, groups sought to apply the fairness doctrine to editorial advertising. The 1973 *DNC* case, however, dampened that effort. The Supreme Court ruled that a medium that meets its obligation to provide full and fair coverage of public issues is not required to accept any editorial advertising. The movement was further stifled the *National Citizens Committee for Broadcasting* decision, in which the Court upheld the FCC opinion that withheld application of the fairness doctrine to product advertising.

NOTES

1. *Valentine v. Chrestensen*, 62 S.Ct. 920 (1942).
2. *Pittsburg Press Company v. Pittsburgh Commission on Human Relations*, 93 S.Ct. 2553 (1973).
3. *Bigelow v. Virginia*, 95 S.Ct. 2222 (1975).
4. *Virginia State Board of Pharmacy v. Virginia Citizens Consumer Council*, 96 S.Ct. 1817 (1976).
5. *Bates v. State Bar of Arizona*, 97 S.Ct. 2691 (1977).
6. *Ohralik v. Ohio State Bar Association*, 98 S.Ct. 1912 (1978).
7. *In the Matter of R. M. J.*, 102 S.Ct. 929 (1982).
8. *Linmark Associates, Inc. v. Township of Willingboro*, 97 S.Ct. 1614 (1977).
9. *Carey v. Population Services International*, 97 S.Ct. 2010 (1977).
10. *Central Hudson Gas and Electric Corporation v. Public Service Commission of New York*, 100 S.Ct. 2343 (1980).
11. *Bolger v. Youngs Drug Products Corporation*, 103 S.Ct. 2875 (1983).
12. *Federal Trade Commission v. Winsted Hosiery Company*, 42 S.Ct. 384 (1922).
13. *Federal Trade Commission v. Raladam Company*, 51 S.Ct. 587 (1931).
14. *Federal Trade Commission v. Raladam Company*, 62 S.Ct. 966 (1942).
15. *Federal Trade Commission v. Standard Education Society*, 58 S.Ct. 113 (1937).
16. *Federal Trade Commission v. Colgate-Palmolive Company*, 85 S.Ct. 1035 (1965).
17. *United States v. J. B. Williams Company, Inc.*, 498 F. 2d 414 (1974).
18. *In re ITT Continental Baking Company, Inc.*, 79 FTC 248 (1971).
19. *In re Ocean Spray Cranberries, Inc.*, 70 FTC 975 (1972).
20. *In re Payless Drug Stores Northwest, Inc.*, 82 FTC 1473 (1973).
21. *In re Amstar, Inc.*, 83 FTC 659 (1973).
22. *Warner-Lambert v. Federal Trade Commission*, 562 F. 2nd 749 (1977); cert. denied 98 S.Ct. 1576 (1978).
23. *Lehman v. Shaker Heights*, 94 S.Ct. 2714 (1974).
24. *Metromedia, Inc. v. City of San Diego*, 101 S.Ct. 2882 (1981).
25. *Banzhaf v. Federal Communications Commission: WTRF-TV, Inc. v. Federal Communica-*

tions Commission; Tobacco Institute, Inc. v. Federal Communications Commission, 405 F. 2d 1082 (1968).

26. *Capital Broadcasting Company v. Mitchell*, 333 F. Supp., 582 (1971).

27. *Capital Broadcasting Company v. Kleindienst*, 92 S.Ct. 1289 (1972).

28. *Green v. Federal Communications Commission: G.I. Association v. Federal Communications Commission*, 447 F. 2d 323 (1971).

29. *Friends of the Earth v. Federal Communications Commission*, 449 F. 2d 1164 (1971).

30. *Columbia Broadcasting System, Inc. v. Democratic National Committee; Federal Communications Commission v. Business Executives Move for Vietnam Peace; Post Newsweek Stations, Capital Area, Inc. v. Business Executives Move for Vietnam Peace; American Broadcasting Companies, Inc. v. Democratic National Committee*; 93 S.Ct. 2080 (1973).

31. *National Citizens Committee for Broadcasting v. Federal Communications Commission; Committee for Open Media v. Federal Communications Commission; Council on Economic Priorities v. Federal Communications Commission;* 567 F 2d 1095 (1977); cert. denied 99 S.Ct. 557 (1978).

RECOMMENDED READING

Denbow, Stefania A., "Commercial Speech and the First Amendment—Continuing Uncertainty After Six Years," *Capital University Law Review* 12 (Fall, 1982), 115-41.

Meiklejohn, Donald, "Commercial Speech and the First Amendment," *California Western Law Review* 13 (1977), 430-55.

Merrill, Thomas W., "First Amendment Protection for Commercial Advertising: The New Constitutional Doctrine," *University of Chicago Law Review* 44 (Fall, 1976), 205-54.

Scammon, Debra L., and Richard J. Semenik, "Corrective Advertising: Evolution of the Legal Theory and Application of the Remedy," *Journal of Advertising* 11 (No. 1, 1982), 10-19.

Scharlott, Bradford W., "The First Amendment Protection of Advertising in the Mass Media," *Communications and the Law* 2 (Summer, 1980), 43-58.

Schiro, Richard, "Commercial Speech: The Demise of a Chimera," *Supreme Court Review* (1976), 45-98.

Sunderland, John T., "*Metromedia, Inc. v. San Diego*: Billboard Advertising Still Up In The Air," *Capital University Law Review* 11 (Summer, 1982), 855-73.

KEY DECISIONS

1937—*STANDARD EDUCATION SOCIETY*—took a strong stand against the doctrine of "*caveat emptor*."

1942—*CHRESTENSEN*—determined that purely "commercial speech" enjoyed less constitutional protection than other forms of communication.

1965—*COLGATE-PALMOLIVE*—decided that simulated demonstrations in television advertising must be done in a truthful manner.

1972—*CAPITAL BROADCASTING COMPANY*—decided that the unique characteristics of broadcast media make them especially subject to regulation in the public interest.

1973—*DEMOCRATIC NATIONAL COMMITTEE*—ruled that a medium that provides full and fair coverage of public issues is not obligated to accept any editorial advertisements.

1974—*LEHMAN*—upheld, in a deeply divided Court, the right of transit media to select which types of advertising they will display.

1975—*BIGELOW*—significantly eroded the "commercial speech" doctrine; the free flow of "commercial information" is constitutionally protected.

1978—*NATIONAL CITIZENS FOR BROADCASTING*—upheld FCC order that denied application of the fairness doctrine to broadcast communications that promote the sale of products.

1978—*WARNER-LAMBERT*—decided that the FTC has authority to order corrective advertising in appropriate cases.

1980—*CENTRAL HUDSON GAS*—established four-stage analysis for determining the constitutionality of commercial expression.

1981—*METROMEDIA*—determined that while a law could favor one kind of commercial advertising over another, it could not favor commercial over noncommercial messages, nor could it favor one kind of noncommercial advertising over another.

SUMMARY—LAW OF ADVERTISING

Definition

The principal regulatory agency for advertising is the Federal Trade Commission. The FTC monitors advertisements in an effort to protect the consumer from false and/or deceptive messages.

Proof

Some key considerations include the following:
1. FTC operates in the consumer's interest by regulating false and/or deceptive advertisements.

2. Supreme Court protects the free flow of "commercial information," though it is less willing to protect "purely commercial" messages.
3. Advertisers do not enjoy a right of access to the media.
4. Fairness doctrine is generally not applicable to broadcast communications promoting the sale of commercial products.

Actions

The FTC may employ the following actions in its effort to regulate deceptive advertising:
1. Letter of compliance
2. Consent order
3. Cease-and-desist decree
4. Corrective advertising

Defenses

1. Demonstrate that advertisement is not deceptive—that is, show that ad contains no
   a. Omissions of material fact
   b. Unsupported scientific claim
   c. Manipulated statistical substantiation
   d. Unsupported claim regarding "secret ingredients"
   e. False comparison
   f. Phony demonstration.
2. Demonstrate compliance with policies of regulatory agencies, including the advertising industry's self-regulation procedures.

14

EPILOGUE

What is the meaning of the First Amendment? Specifically, who in a society should be allowed to communicate and who should be silenced? Do special circumstances alter the answers to these questions, which have confronted philosophers, judges, legislators, and citizens since the birth of our nation? This final chapter makes an attempt to ascertain the meaning of the First Amendment. Consideration is given to theoretical positions expressed by learned scholars and to practical positions adopted by the Supreme Court in specific cases.

THEORY

Scholars have approached freedom-of-expression issues from a variety of philosophical bases. The resulting body of theory provides meaningful insight into the essence of the First Amendment. The most influential theories include marketplace of ideas, social exchange, social utility, self-government, expression/action dichotomy, media access, and communication context.

Marketplace of Ideas

During the early decades of the seventeenth century, censorship was practiced extensively by the Star Chamber in England. That body, operating with Parliament's approval, exercised considerable power over the licensing of printed material. In 1644, against this background, John Milton published a call for liberty in unlicensed printing. In *Areopagitica* he introduced the rationale behind the marketplace-of-ideas theory.

> And though all the winds of doctrine were let loose to play upon the earth, so
> Truth be in the field, we do injuriously by licensing and prohibiting to misdoubt

her strength. Let her and Falsehood grapple; who ever knew Truth put to the worse in a free and open encounter?[1]

Almost three centuries later, the theory was supported and clarified by Justice Oliver Wendell Holmes.

But when men have realized that time has upset many fighting faiths, they may come to believe even more than they believe the very foundations of their own conduct that the ultimate good desired is better reached by free trade in ideas— that the best test of truth is the power of the thought to get itself accepted in the competition of the market, and that truth is the only ground upon which their wishes safely can be carried out. That at any rate is the theory of our Constitution.[2]

The marketplace-of-ideas notion holds that the First Amendment was designed to allow ideas to enter the marketplace freely, where the public can pick and choose from among contrasting views. Out of such competition, truth hopefully will emerge and win out over error. Proponents of this theory argue that the First Amendment rests on the assumption that the widest possible dissemination of information from diverse sources is essential to the welfare of society. And it is the purpose and function of the First Amendment to preserve an uninhibited marketplace of ideas in which truth will ultimately prevail.

Social Exchange

The nineteenth-century philosopher John Stuart Mill described a related concept of free expression. He stressed the importance of social exchange. According to Mill, citizens can trade false ideas for true ones only if they can hear the true ones. An open exchange of ideas guarantees that both false and true ideas are expressed.

If all mankind minus one were of one opinion, and only one person were of the contrary opinion, mankind would be no more justified in silencing that one person, than he, if he had the power, would be justified in silencing mankind. . . . But the peculiar evil of silencing the expression of an opinion is, that it is robbing the human race: posterity as well as the existing generation; those who dissent from the opinion, still more than those who hold it. If the opinion is right, they are deprived of the opportunity of exchanging error for truth; if wrong, they lose, what is almost as great a benefit, the clearer perception and livelier impression of truth, produced by its collision with error.[3]

The social-exchange theory recognizes the importance of providing the public with a variety of political, moral, and esthetic ideas. Fundamental to this end is a free flow of information. Proponents of the theory argue that the First Amendment must provide a national commitment to the principle that debate on public issues should be uninhibited, robust, and wide open.

Social Utility

In 1941 Zechariah Chafee, Jr., Langdell Professor of Law at Harvard University, set forth a social-utility view of the First Amendment. Chafee recognized two types of expression—that which serves the individual interest and that which serves the social interest. Of the two, expression related to the social interest is by far the most important. Such expression should be restrained only when the public safety is imperiled. Chafee viewed the First Amendment as functioning to balance the societal interest in public expression against the societal interest in public order. For Chafee, the balance clearly fell on the side of the First Amendment.

> The true meaning of freedom of speech seems to be this. One of the most important purposes of society and government is the discovery and spread of truth on subjects of general concern. . . . Nevertheless, there are other purposes of government, such as order, the training of the young, protection against external aggression. Unlimited discussion sometimes interferes with these purposes, which must then be balanced against freedom of speech, but freedom of speech ought to weigh very heavily in the scale. The First Amendment gives binding force to this principle of political wisdom.[4]

According to Chafee, it was useless to define the First Amendment in terms of rights. Instead, the facts of the specific situation play heavily in each case. For example, in times of war, the dissenter asserts a constitutional right to be heard, while the government asserts a constitutional right to wage war. The deadlock must be resolved. Chafee recommends a process of balancing the competing social interests.

> The true boundary line of the First Amendment can be fixed only when Congress and the courts realize that the principle on which speech is classified as lawful or unlawful involves the balancing against each other of two very important social interests, in public safety and in the search for truth. Every reasonable attempt should be made to maintain both interests unimpaired, and the great interest in free speech should be sacrificed only when the interest in public safety is really imperiled, and not. . .when it is barely conceivable that it may be slightly affected.[5]

For example, in wartime, expression should be unrestricted "unless it is clearly liable to cause direct and dangerous interference with the conduct of the war." Chafee thus suggests the point at which the social-utility theory places the boundary line for freedom of expression—it is established close to the point where expression gives rise to unlawful acts.

Self-Government

Alexander Meiklejohn, former president of Amherst College and professor of philosophy at the University of Wisconsin, recognized two types of expression: private and public. Private expression was not within the scope of the First Amendment and could be regulated. Public expression enhanced self-government and was entitled to absolute protection. According to Meiklejohn, the primary function of the First Amendment was to guarantee absolute freedom for expression that furthers self-government. The First Amendment must help provide citizens with the greatest possible opportunity to discuss society's problems. Only then are citizens exposed to the information that is necessary to make the informed judgments on which self-government depends. Meiklejohn described four types of expression from which the voter derives the capacity for sound judgment:

1. Education, in all its phases, is the attempt to so inform and cultivate the mind and will of a citizen that he shall have the wisdom, the independence, and, therefore, the dignity of a governing citizen. Freedom of education is, thus, as we all recognize, a basic postulate in the planning of a free society.

2. The achievements of philosophy and the sciences in creating knowledge and understanding of men and their world must be made available, without abridgement, to every citizen.

3. Literature and the arts must be protected by the First Amendment. They lead the way toward sensitive and informed appreciation and response to the values out of which the riches of the general welfare are created.

4. Public discussions of public issues, together with the spreading of information and opinion bearing on those issues, must have a freedom unabridged by our agents. Though they govern us, we, in a deeper sense govern them. Over our governing, they have no power. Over their governing we have sovereign power.[6]

Meiklejohn recognized two types of expression, but he maintained that their constitutional status differed radically. Private expression, such as the advertisement of a vendor selling a product, was subject to regulation. On the other hand, public expression, such as the utterance of a citizen who is intent upon self-government, enjoyed the absolute protection of the First Amendment.

Expression/Action Dichotomy

Thomas Emerson, Lines Professor Emeritus of Law at Yale University, enunciated a First Amendment theory that is based on the distinction between expression and action. As a starting point, Emerson believed that the First

Amendment should help maintain four social values: assuring individual self-fulfillment, attaining the truth, securing participation in decision making, and providing balance between stability and change.[7] According to Emerson, these social values can be realized only if expression receives full protection under the First Amendment. Emerson's theory distinguishes between expression and action.

> The central idea of a system of expression is that a fundamental distinction must be drawn between conduct which consists of "expression" and conduct which consists of "action." "Expression" must be freely allowed and encouraged "Action" can be controlled, subject to other constitutional requirements, but not by controlling expression.[8]

Emerson demands that expression be safeguarded against curtailment at all points, even when expression conflicts with social interests that the government is charged with protecting. The government may protect such interests—for example, public safety and order—through suppressing action, but not by regulating expression.

Media Access

Jerome Barron, professor of law at George Washington University, supports a media-access theory of the First Amendment. Barron claims that inequality exists among the members of society in terms of their power to communicate ideas. Changes in the communications industry, especially the technological development and growth of media, have altered the "equilibrium" in the marketplace of ideas. The commercial nature of the mass-media industry makes it difficult to give full expression to a wide spectrum of public opinion. Barron argues that when commercial considerations lead the media to suppress ideas, the function of the First Amendment is being thwarted.

> The "marketplace of ideas" has rested on the assumption that protecting the right of expression is equivalent to providing for it. But changes in the communications industry have destroyed the equilibrium in that marketplace. . . .
> A realistic view of the first amendment requires recognition that a right of expression is somewhat thin if it can be exercised only at the sufferance of the managers of mass communication.[9]

Barron calls for a right-of-access statute that would forbid the mass media from arbitrarily denying space in print media or time on broadcast media. Such legislation would guarantee an effective forum for the expression of divergent opinions. Barron notes that a right-of-access statute would only broaden the opportunity for expression and would not involve any prior restraint or punishment of communication. This type of governmental regulation of media would promote vigorous debate and expression at a level consistent with the meaning of the First Amendment.

Communication Context

Franklyn Haiman, professor of communication studies at Northwestern University, introduced a communication-context theory of the First Amendment. Haiman rejects the notion that there are specific categories of expression, which, by definition, are always unlawful. Instead, he argues that the particular context in which expression occurs provides the basis for limitation or freedom. Haiman identifies four specific contexts and offers a basic principle that applies in each context:

1. Communication about Other People—Unless the harm done by an act of communication is direct, immediate, irreparable, and of a serious material nature, the remedy in a free society should be more speech. The law is an inappropriate tool for dealing with expression which produces mental distress or whose targets are the beliefs and values of an audience.

2. Communication to Other People—Unless deprived of free choice by deception, physical coercion, or an impairment of normal capacities, individuals in a free society are responsible for their own behavior. They are not objects which can be triggered into action by symbolic stimuli but human beings who decide how they will respond to the communication they see and hear.

3. Communication and Social Order—So long as there is a free marketplace of ideas, where the widest possible range of information and alternatives is available, individuals will be the best judges of their own interests. The law is properly used to enrich and expand the communications marketplace and to insure that it remains an open system.

4. Government Involvement in the Communication Marketplace—Government in a free society is the servant of the people and its power should not be used to inhibit, distort, or dominate public discourse. There must be a compelling justification whenever the government requires unwilling communication of its people or withholds information in its possession from them.[10]

Haiman concludes that the implementation of these principles requires "a strong and vigilant citizenry." Safeguarding the function of the First Amendment rests, to no small degree, in the hands of the citizens.

The theories discussed in this section, though derived from a varied base of assumptions, tend to recognize five basic principles:

1. The First Amendment and its guarantee of free expression are essential for the preservation of U.S. society.

2. A liberal interpretation of the First Amendment, one that favors free expression over competing interests, is in the best interest of society.

3. The First Amendment should provide for robust debate—the free and open exchange of varied views.

4. Public expression (social interests) enjoys more freedom than private expression (individual interests).

5. Government regulation of the First Amendment may seek to suppress action, but not expression.

PRACTICE

In practice, the Supreme Court has considerable responsibility for determining the meaning of the First Amendment. Yet the Court has failed to adopt a comprehensive theory of what the First Amendment means or how it should be applied in specific cases. Instead, it has developed a two-tiered, situation-bound approach to First Amendment cases.

"WHICH ONE SHOULD I WEAR TODAY?"

Two-Tiered Approach

The Supreme Court has consistently supported a two-tiered approach to expression. Tier one covers worthless expression, that which has little, if any, social value. Tier two consists of worthwhile expression, that which has social value. Specific types of expression may be classified as follows:

Tier One—Worthless (Unprotected)

Dissent—advocacy of the imminent overthrow of the government by force or violence.
Provocation—fighting words
Obscenity—appeal to the prurient interest in sex
Libel—defamatory statements
Commercial speech—deceptive advertisements

Tier Two—Worthwhile (Protected)

News—data essential to an informed citizenry
Political—expression vital to the conduct of meaningful campaigns
Dissent—expression vital to a socially conscious general public
Assembly—associational expression
Petition—expression related to a redress of grievances.

Situation-Bound Approach

The Supreme Court's approach to the First Amendment also stresses a situation-bound component. At least four factors affect the definition of each case situation. First, the situation is influenced by the nature of the communication act itself. For example, the Court has applied less restriction to political than to commercial expression. In addition, the Court has been more protective of newsworthy than nonnewsworthy expression. Second, the situation is influenced by the media that are used. The Court has generally upheld the right of mass media to deny access. Also, broadcast media are subject to more extensive regulation than print. Third, the situation is influenced by the times. Courts have responded to the fluctuating pressures of war, social consciousness, and moral concern. Fourth, and most significant, the case situation is influenced by the makeup of the Court. Different justices apply different standards to similar case situations. As a result, the Court has evolved a variety of tests of the First Amendment. The tests span a broad continuum between restriction and freedom.

Bad Tendency	Balancing	Clear and Present Danger	Preferred Position	Absolutism

Restriction　　　　　　　　　　　　　　　　　　　　　Freedom

Overall, it has been the practice of the Supreme Court to apply a two-tiered approach (some expression is afforded full protection while some expression receives no protection) in a situation-bound context (certain variables— communication act, media, times, and court makeup—influence the definition of the case situation). This has been the approach of the Supreme Court to the First Amendment. The approach leads to a generally inconsistent treatment of free expression. That is the legacy of the Court's relation to the First Amendment—and it doubtless will continue in the future.

NOTES

1. Milton, John, *Areopagitica*, ed. by Edward Arber. London: English Reprints, 1868, p. 74.

2. *Abrams v. United States*, 40 S.Ct. 17 (1919).

3. Mill, John Stuart, *On Liberty*, ed. by David Spitz. New York: Norton, 1975.

4. Chafee, Zechariah, Jr., *Free Speech in the United States*. Cambridge: Harvard University Press, 1941, p. 31.

5. *Ibid.*, p. 35.

6. Meiklejohn, Alexander, "The First Amendment is an Absolute," *Supreme Court Review* (1961), 256-57. See also *Free Speech and Its Relation to Self Government*. New York: Harper and Brothers, 1948; and *Political Freedom: The Constitutional Powers of the People*. New York: Harper, 1960.

7. Emerson, Thomas I., *Toward a General Theory of the First Amendment*. New York: Vintage Books, 1966, pp. 3-15.

8. Emerson, Thomas I., *The System of Freedom of Expression*. New York: Vintage Books, 1970, p. 17.

9. Barron, Jerome A., "Access to the Press—A New First Amendment Right," *Harvard Law Review* 80 (June, 1967), 1647-48. See also *Freedom of the Press for Whom? The Right of Access to Mass Media*. Bloomington: Indiana University Press, 1973.

10. Haiman, Franklyn S., *Speech and Law in a Free Society*. Chicago: University of Chicago Press, 1981, pp. 425-26.

INDEX OF CASES

ABC; Cassidy v., 199

ABC; FCC v., 353–54, 371

ABC; Italian Book Corporation v., 246

ABC v. Democratic National Committee, 360–61, 366–67

ABC v. FCC, 361

ABC v. WNCN Listeners Guild, 350–52

Abramson; FBI v., 283–84, 290

Abrams v. United States, 3, 13

ACLU v. FCC, 339–41

Adderley v. Florida, 59, 64, 67

Adler v. Board of Education, 74–76

Administrator, Federal Aviation Administration v. Robertson, 279–80, 284, 290

Administrator of General Services; Nixon v., 270–72

Agee; Haig v., 143–46

Aiken; Twentieth Century Music Corporation v., 249–50, 253, 255

The Air Pirates; Walt Disney Productions v., 245

Alabama; Marsh v., 7, 135–36, 146, 149

Alabama; Mills v., 301–2, 305

Alabama; NAACP v., 38–40, 46, 49, 67

Alabama; Thornhill v., 3, 50, 56, 64, 67

Alexander v. Haley, 235, 242

Alexandria; Breard v., 133–35, 146, 149

Alfred A. Knopf v. Colby, 278–79, 290

Allied International; International Longshoremen's Association v., 52, 64

Amalgamated Food Employees Union v. Logan Valley Plaza, 53–54, 64

American Communications Association, C.I.O. v. Douds, 6–7

American Mini Theatres; Young v., 120–21, 123

American Newspaper Publishers Association v. National Citizens Committee For Broadcasting, 346–47

American Press Company; Grosjean v., 294, 304

American Radio Association v. Mobile Steamship Association, 52, 64

Amsco Book Company; College Entrance Book Company v. 236–37, 242

Amstar; In re, 392

Amsterdam v. Triangle Publications, 230–33, 242

Angel; Lux v., 86, 88, 90

Aptheker v. Secretary of State, 143–44, 146, 149

Aquino v. Bulletin Company, 207–8, 211

Arizona Superior Court; KPNX Broadcasting Company v., 318–19

Arkansas; Epperson v., 70–71, 81

Arvey Corporation v. Peterson, 152

Ashton v. Kentucky, 188–89

Aspen Institute and CBS; In re, 478

Associated Press; International News Service v., 233–34, 242, 255

Associated Press v. United States, 296–97, 299, 304

Associated Press v. Walker, 172–74, 189

Attorney General of Massachusetts; A Book Named "John Cleland's Memoirs of a Woman of Pleasure" v., 106

Auburn University; Brooks v., 77

Baer; Rosenblatt v., 176–77, 189

Baggett v. Bullitt, 76–77, 82, 125–26

Baird; Eisenstadt v., 195–96, 201, 220

Baird v. State Bar of Arizona, 48–49

Baker v. F. & F. Investment, 261–63, 265

Baltimore Radio Show; Maryland v., 315–16, 319

Banzhaf v. FCC, 394–98

Barenblatt v. United States, 6, 127–29

Barnette; West Virginia State Board of Education v., 71, 81, 100

Barr v. Matteo, 161–62
Bartels v. Iowa, 69–70
Bates v. Little Rock, 40, 49
Bates v. State Bar of Arizona, 380–81,
   385
Baxley; Staub v., 42, 49
Bay Guardian Company v. Chronicle
   Publishing Company, 301, 305
Beacon Newspaper Corporation; Stice
   v., 163
Beauharnais v. Illinois, 186–87, 189,
   192
Beckley Newspapers Corporation v.
   Hanks, 171
Beilan v. Board of Public Education, 74,
   77, 82
Bellotti; First National Bank of Boston
   v., 140–41, 146, 149
Benny v. Loew's Incorporated, 236, 240,
   242
Bergna v. Stanford Daily, 289–90
Berlin v. E. C. Publications, 236, 239,
   242
Bernard Geis Associates; Time v., 242–
   43, 253
Bernstein; In re, 262
Besig v. United States, 103
Best Medium Publishing Company;
   Varnish v., 210–11
Bigelow v. Virginia, 379, 385, 400
Birmingham; Shuttlesworth v., 62, 64
Birmingham; Walker v., 61–62, 64
Bleistein v. Donaldson Lithographing
   Company, 230, 233, 242
Blende v. Hearst Publications, 153, 155
Board of Curators of the University of
   Missouri; Papish v., 94, 97–98, 100
Board of Education; Adler v., 74–76
Board of Education; Fujishima v., 92–94
Board of Education; Island Trees Union
   Free School v. Pico, 80–82, 100
Board of Education of Topeka; Brown
   v., 39n
Board of Education; Pickering v., 85–
   88, 90, 100
Board of Higher Education; Slochower
   v., 73–74, 77, 82

Board of Public Education; Beilan v.,
   74, 77, 82
Board of Public Instruction; Cramp v.,
   75–77, 82, 125, 127
Board of Regents; Keyishian v., 76–77,
   82, 125, 127
Board of Regents v. Roth, 88–91, 100
Bohning v. Ohio, 69–70
Bolger v. Youngs Drug Products
   Corporation, 384–85
Bolton; Doe v., 196–97, 201
Bond v. Floyd, 18–20
A Book Named "John Cleland's
   Memoirs of a Woman of Pleasure" v.
   Attorney General of Massachusetts,
   106
Booth v. Curtis Publishing Company,
   212–13, 218
Borough of Mount Ephraim; Schad v.,
   120–21
Borough of Oradell; Hynes v., 133–34,
   146
Borreca v. Fasi, 288–89
Bose Corporation v. Consumers Union
   of United States, 175–76
Bowen; Schuster v., 316n
Brandenburg v. Ohio, 4, 15, 17–18
Brandywine-Main Line Radio v. FCC,
   364
Branzburg v. Hayes, 258–65, 290, 308
Breard v. City of Alexandria, 133–35,
   146, 149
Breen v. Selective Service Local Board,
   28
Bresler; Greenbelt Publishing
   Association v., 175, 189, 192
Bridge; In re, 266–67, 269, 290
Bridges v. California, 3, 5–6, 312–16,
   319, 330
Bristow Publishing Company; Nichols v.,
   153, 155–56
Brooks v. Auburn University, 77
Brown; Carey v., 61, 64
Brown; Sally v., 153–55
Brown v. Board of Education of Topeka,
   39n
Brown v. Glines, 136–38, 146

Bruce Publishing Company; Toksvig v., 236–38, 242
Brush-Moore Newspapers v. Pollitt, 165
Buckley v. Littell, 151
Bulletin Company; Aquino v., 207–8, 211
Bullitt; Baggett v., 76–77, 82, 125–26
Burch; Citizens Communications Center v., 349–50
Burleson; Journal of Commerce and Commercial Bulletin v., 295
Burleson; Milwaukee Social Democrat Publishing Company v., 291
Bursey v. United States, 263–65
Burstyn v. Wilson, 114–15, 121
Business Executives Move For Vietnam Peace; FCC v., 360–61, 366
Business Executives Move For Vietnam Peace; Post-Newsweek Stations, Capital Area v., 360–61, 366
Butler v. Michigan, 116–18, 121
Butts; Curtis Publishing Company v., 172–74, 189, 192

Caldero v. Tribune Publishing Company, 263–65
Caldwell; United States v., 259–61
California; Bridges v., 3, 5–6, 312–16, 319, 330
California; Cohen v., 25–26
California; Goldstein v., 250
California; Miller v., 102, 107–10, 117–18, 123–24
California; Smith v., 115, 121
California; Stromberg v., 29, 34
California; Talley v., 128–29, 149
California; Whitney v., 3, 14–15
Cameron v. Johnson, 51–52, 64
Cantrell v. Forest City Publishing Company, 210–11, 220
Cantwell v. Connecticut, 3, 41–42, 49, 67
Capital Broadcasting Company v. Kleindienst, 396, 400
Capital Broadcasting Company v. Mitchell, 395–96
Carey v. Brown, 61, 64

Carey v. Longman, 222n
Carey v. Population Services International, 383, 385
Carlisle v. Fawcett Publications, 207–8, 211
Carroll Broadcasting Company v. FCC, 345, 371
Carroll v. President and Commissioners of Princess Anne County, 62–64
Carr v. Young, 75
Carter Mountain Transmission Corporation v. FCC, 338–39, 341, 343
Cassidy v. ABC, 199
CBS; Dickey v., 184
CBS; FCC v., 353–54
CBS; Tandem Productions v., 350–53
CBS; Teleprompter Corporation v., 248–49, 253, 255
CBS; United States v., 316n
CBS; Warner Brothers Pictures v., 245
CBS v. Democratic National Committee, 360–61, 366–67, 371, 375, 396–98, 400
CBS v. FCC, 361, 371, 375
CBS v. Loew's Incorporated, 236, 240, 242
CBS v. United States, 337–38
Central Hudson Gas and Electric Corporation v. Public Service Commission of New York, 383–85, 400
Chamberlain v. Feldman, 223–24
Chandler v. Florida, 328–30
Channel Two Television Company v. National Citizens Committee For Broadcasting, 346–47
Chaplinsky v. New Hampshire, 22–24, 26, 35
Chicago; Gregory v., 58–59, 64
Chicago; Terminiello v., 3, 20–22, 26, 36
Chicago; Times Film Corporation v., 111
Chicago Record-Herald v. Tribune Association, 234, 242
Children's Television Workshop; Reyher v., 235, 242

Chisholm v. FCC, 358

Chrestensen; Valentine v., 377–78, 385, 400

Chronicle Publishing Company; Bay Guardian Company v., 301, 305

CIO; Hague v., 42–43, 45, 49, 67

Citizen Publishing Company v. United States, 299–301, 305

Citizens Committee to Save WEFM v. FCC, 330–31, 371

Citizens Communications Center v. Burch, 349–50

Citizens Communications Center v. FCC, 348–50

Citizens For A Better Environment; Village of Schaumburg v., 133–35, 146

City of Madison, Joint School District v. Wisconsin Employment Commission, 86–88, 90–91

Claiborne Hardware; NAACP v., 50–51, 56, 64, 67

Clark v. Community For Creative Non-Violence, 63–65

Cohen v. California, 25–26

Cohn; Cox Broadcasting Corporation v., 205–7, 220

Colby; Alfred A. Knopf v., 278–79, 290

Cole v. Richardson, 126–27, 130

Colgate-Palmolive Company; FTC v., 388–89, 397, 400

College Entrance Book Company v. Amsco Book Company, 230–33, 242

Collins; Thomas v., 7, 41–42, 49

Columbia Broadcasting System, 358

Columbia Pictures Corporation v. NBC, 236, 240, 242

Committee For Open Media v. FCC, 397

Commonwealth's Attorney for City of Richmond; Doe v., 197, 201

Commonwealth v. Friede, 103

Communist Party Of Indiana v. Whitcomb, 48–49

Communist Party v. Subversive Activities Control Board, 46, 49

Community For Creative Non-Violence; Clark v., 63–65

Community School Board No. 25; Presidents Council v., 78–79, 82

Community Television of Southern California v. Gottfried, 350, 352–53

Connecticut; Cantwell v., 3, 41–42, 49, 67

Connecticut; Griswold v., 195–97, 201, 220

Connell v. Higginbotham, 126–27

Conrad; Southeastern Promotions v., 111–12

Consolidated Edison Company of New York v. Public Service Commission of New York, 140–41, 146

Constitution Publishing Company; Wood v., 164

Consumers Union of United States; Bose Corporation v., 175–76

Cooper; Kovacs v., 7–8, 130–32, 149

Cosgrove Studio and Camera Shop v. Pane, 187–89

Costlow v. Cusimano, 201–2, 207

Council of Greenburgh Civic Associations; United States Postal Service v., 138–40, 146

Council on Economic Priorities v. FCC, 397

Cowper v. Vannier, 153, 155

Cox Broadcasting Corporation v. Cohn, 205–7, 220

Cox v. Louisiana, 4, 57–59, 64

Cox v. New Hampshire, 43–45, 49

Craig v. Harney, 4, 314–16, 319

Cramp v. Board of Public Instruction, 75–77, 82, 125, 127

Crane v. State, 185n

Crooks; Encyclopedia Brittanica v., 251–52

Curlett; Murray v., 72–73, 81

Curtis Publishing Company; Booth v., 212–13, 218

Curtis Publishing Company v. Butts, 172–74, 189, 192

Cusimano; Costlow v., 201–2, 207

Daily Mail Publishing Company; Smith v., 285–87

Daily Mirror; Sarat Lahiri v., 212, 218

Daily Times Democrat v. Graham, 202–4, 207

Dalton v. Meister, 158

Damron; Ocala Star-Banner Company v., 177, 189

Dan; People v., 266–67, 269, 290

Danforth; Planned Parenthood of Central Missouri v., 197, 201

Davies; Emerson v., 229–30

Day; Manual Enterprises v., 105

Debs v. United States, 13, 19

DeJonge v. Oregon, 15

Demman v. Star Broadcasting Company, 156–57

Democratic National Committee; ABC v., 360–61, 366–67

Democratic National Committee; CBS v., 360–61, 366–67, 371, 375, 396–98, 400

Democratic National Committee v. FCC, 358

Democratic National Committee v. McCord, 261–63, 265

Dempsey v. Time, 166

Dennis v. United States, 4, 6, 15–19, 36

Department of the Air Force v. Rose, 282

DePasquale; Gannett Company v., 285–86

Des Moines Independent Community School District; Tinker v., 32–34, 36, 91–94, 97, 100

Des Moines Register and Tribune Company; Howard v., 206–7

Dial Press; People v., 103

Dickens v. International Brotherhood of Teamsters, 165–66

Dickey v. CBS, 184

Dickinson; United States v., 316–17, 319, 330

Dickson v. Sitterson, 77

Dietemann v. Time, 198–99, 201

Dodd; Pearson v., 199–201

Doe v. Bolton, 196–97, 201

Doe v. Commonwealth's Attorney for City of Richmond, 197, 201

Donaldson Lithographing Company; Bleistein v., 230, 233, 242

Donald v. Zack Meyer's T.V. Sales and Service, 230, 232–33, 242

Doran v. Sunset House Distributing Corp., 240, 242

Douds, American Communications Association, C.I.O. v., 6–7

Dowd; Irvin v., 321–22, 324–25, 328

Dow Jones and Company v. Superior Court, 263–65

Doyle; Mt. Healthy City School District Board of Education v., 87–88, 91

Drebus; Guzick v., 91–94

Duke v. Texas, 77

Dulles; Kent v., 143–44, 146

DuMaurier; MacDonald v., 240, 242

Dutton; Mifflin v., 226–29

E. C. Publications; Berlin v., 236, 239, 242

Edwards v. National Audubon Society, 184

Edwards v. South Carolina, 56–59, 64, 67

Edward Thompson Company; West Publishing Company v., 236n

Eisenschiml v. Fawcett Publications, 236–37, 242

Eisenstadt v. Baird, 195–96, 201, 220

Eisner v. Stamford Board of Education, 93–94

Elfbrandt v. Russell, 126–27

Elkins; Whitehill v., 77, 82, 125–27

Emerson v. Davies, 229–30

Empire Printing Company v. Roden, 160–61

Empire Storage and Ice Company; Giboney v., 52, 64

Encyclopedia Brittanica v. Crooks, 251–52

Engel v. Vitale, 71–73, 81

Environmental Protection Agency v. Mink, 277–78, 284, 290

Epperson v. Arkansas, 70–71, 81

Epstein v. Resor, 276–77, 284, 290

Esquire; Hannegan v., 113–14, 121,
    295–97, 304, 307
Estate of Hemingway v. Random House,
    223–24
Estes v. Texas, 325–30

F. & F. Investment; Baker v., 261–63,
    265
Farley; Toomey v., 151
*Farmers Educational and Cooperative
    Union v. WDAY*, 161–63, 192, 359–
    60, 375
Farrell v. Kramer, 166
Farr, In re, 266, 268–69
*Farr v. Superior Court of the State of
    California, County of Los Angeles*,
    266–69, 290
Fasi; Borreca v., 288–89
Fawcett Publications; Carlisle v., 207–8,
    211
Fawcett Publications; Eisenschiml v.,
    236–37, 242
FBI v. Abramson, 283–84, 290
FCC; ABC v., 361
FCC; ACLU v., 339–41
FCC; Banzhaf v., 394–98
FCC; Brandywine-Main Line Radio v.,
    364
FCC; Carroll Broadcasting Company v.,
    345, 371
*FCC; Carter Mountain Transmission
    Corporation v.*, 338–39, 341, 343
FCC; CBS v., 361, 371, 375
FCC; Chisholm v., 358
*FCC; Citizens Committee to Save WEFM
    v.*, 330–31, 371
*FCC; Citizens Communications Center
    v.*, 348–50
FCC; Committee For Open Media v.,
    397
FCC; Council on Economic Priorities v.,
    397
*FCC; Democratic National Committee
    v.*, 358
FCC; Friends of the Earth v., 396–98
FCC; G.I. Association v., 396–98

*FCC; Greater Boston Television
    Corporation v.*, 345–47, 371
FCC; Green v., 396–98
FCC; Hale v., 368–71
*FCC; Hampton Roads Television
    Corporation v.*, 348–50
FCC; Henry v., 347–48, 371
FCC; Home Box Office v., 338, 340–41
FCC; League of Women Voters v.,
    358–59
FCC; Lorain Journal Company v.,
    345–46
FCC; Mansfield Journal Company v.,
    345–47, 371
FCC; McCarthy v., 358–59
*FCC; National Association of
    Broadcasters v.*, 346–47
FCC; National Black Media Coalition v.,
    349–50
*FCC; National Citizens Committee for
    Broadcasting v.*, 397–98, 400
FCC; NBC v., 361n
*FCC; Office of Communication of the
    United Church of Christ v.*, 367–69,
    371
*FCC; Red Lion Broadcasting Company
    v.*, 364–66, 371, 375
FCC; RKO General v., 370, 372
FCC; Simmons v., 347–48, 371
FCC; Stone v., 369–71
FCC; Tobacco Institute v., 394–95
FCC; Writers Guild of America v.,
    350–53
FCC; WTRF-TV v., 394–95
FCC; Yale Broadcasting Company v.,
    350, 371
FCC v. ABC, 353–54, 371
*FCC v. Business Executives Move For
    Vietnam Peace*, 360–61, 366
FCC v. CBS, 353–54
FCC v. Gottfried, 350, 352–53
*FCC v. League of Women Voters of
    California*, 342–43, 375
FCC v. Midwest Video Corporation,
    338, 340–41
FCC v. National Citizens Committee For

Broadcasting, 345–47, 371, 375
FCC v. NBC, 353–54
FCC v. Pacifica Foundation , 356–57,
   371, 375
FCC v. Sanders Brothers Radio Station,
   344–45
FCC v. WNCN Listener's Guild, 350–53,
   371, 375
Federal Radio Commission; KFKB
   Broadcasting Association v., 334–36,
   343
Federal Radio Commission; Trinity
   Methodist Church, South v., 334–36,
   343
Feiner v. New York, 21–22, 26, 36
Feldman; Chamberlain v., 223–24
Ferber; New York v., 117–18, 123
Fielden; Smith v., 151
Firestone; Time v., 178, 180–83, 189
First National Bank of Boston v. Bellotti,
   140–41, 146, 149
Fixa v. Heilberg, 296
Florida; Adderley v., 59, 64, 67
Florida; Chandler v., 328–30
Florida; Murphy v., 324–25, 329–30
Florida; Pennekamp v., 313–14, 316,
   319
Florida; Shepherd v., 320, 324–25, 328
Florida Legislative Investigation
   Committee; Gibson v., 40, 49
Flower v. United States, 136–37, 146
Floyd; Bond v., 18–20
Forcade v. Knight, 288–89
Forest City Publishing Company;
   Cantrell v., 210–11, 220
Forsham v. Harris, 275–76
Fortnightly Corporation v. United Artists
   Television, 248, 253, 255
Fortune; Molpus v., 77
Franklin Mint Corporation v. National
   Wildlife Art Exchange, 235–36, 242
Freedman v. Maryland, 111–12, 121,
   123–24
Friede; Commonwealth v., 103
Friede; People v., 103
Friends of the Earth v. FCC, 396–98

Frohwerk v. United States, 13
FTC v. Colgate-Palmolive Company,
   388–89, 397, 400
FTC v. Grolier Incorporated, 280–82
FTC v. Raladam Company, 387, 397
FTC v. Standard Education Society,
   387–88, 397, 399
FTC v. Winsted Hosiery Company, 386–
   87, 397
FTC; Warner-Lambert v., 392, 397, 400
Fujishima v. Board of Education, 92–94

Galella v. Onassis, 197–98, 201
Gannett Company v. DePasquale,
   285–86
Garner v. Louisiana, 4
Garrison v. Louisiana, 170–71, 189
Geanakos; Keefe v., 82–84, 90
Gernsback; Thompson v., 243–44, 253
Gertz v. Robert Welch, 178–83, 189,
   192
Georgia; Jenkins v., 108–10
Georgia; Stanley v., 118–21, 123
Georgia; Wood v., 4, 315–16, 319
G.I. Association v. FCC, 396–98
Giboney v. Empire Storage and Ice
   Company, 52, 64
Gibson v. Florida Legislative
   Investigation Committee, 40, 49
Ginsberg v. New York, 83, 117, 121
Ginzburg; Goldwater v., 158–60
Ginzburg v. United States, 8–9, 115–16,
   121, 123
Gitlow v. New York, 2–4, 14, 19, 35
Givhan v. Western Line Consolidated
   School District, 86, 88, 91, 100
Glines; Brown v., 136–38, 146
Globe Newspaper Company v. Superior
   Court for the County of Norfolk, 285,
   287
Gobitis; Minersville School District v.,
   71
Goguen; Smith v., 31
Goldstein v. California, 250
Goldwater v. Ginzburg, 158–60
Gooding v. Wilson, 23–24

Goodson; Wood v., 316
Goodwill Stations, Inc., 358
Goss v. Illinois, 315–16
Goss v. Lopez, 96–98, 100
Gottfried; Community Television of
   Southern California v., 350, 352–53
Gottfried; FCC v., 350, 352–53
Grace; United States v., 142, 146
Graham; Daily Times Democrat v.,
   202–4, 207
Graham; Stone v., 73, 81
Grayned v. City of Rockford, 60–61, 64
Greater Boston Television Corporation v.
   FCC, 345–47, 371
Greenbelt Publishing Association v.
   Bresler, 175, 189, 192
Greensboro News Company; Roth v.,
   153–54
Green v. FCC, 396–98
Greer v. Spock, 136–38, 146, 149
Gregg; United States v., 334–36, 343
Gregory v. Chicago, 58–59, 64
Griffin; Lovell v., 133, 146
Griswold v. Connecticut, 195–97, 201,
   220
Grolier Incorporated; FTC v., 280–82
Grosjean v. American Press Company,
   294, 304
Grumman Aircraft Engineering
   Corporation; Renegotiation Board v.,
   280–82, 284, 290
Gutknecht v. United States, 28
Guzick v. Drebus, 91–94

Hague v. CIO, 42–43, 45, 49, 67
Haig v. Agee, 143–46
Hale v. FCC, 368–71
Haley; Alexander v., 235, 242
Hal Roach Studios; Price v. 217–18
Hamling v. United States, 109–10
Hampton Roads Television Corporation
   v. FCC, 348–50
Hanks; Beckley Newspaper Corporation
   v., 171
Hannegan v. Esquire, 113–14, 121,
   295–97, 304, 307
Harney; Craig v., 4, 314–16, 319

Harper & Row Publishers v. Nation
   Enterprises, 247
Harris; Forsham v., 275–76
Hayes; Branzburg v., 258–65, 290, 308
Healy v. James, 95, 98, 100
Hearst Consolidated Publications; Hope
   v., 153
Hearst Publications; Blende v., 153–55
Heffron v. International Society For
   Krishna Consciousness, 141–42, 146,
   149
Heilberg; Fixa v., 296
Heim v. Universal Pictures Company,
   236, 239, 242
Henricksen; Uhlaender v., 215, 218
Henry Holt & Company v. Liggett &
   Meyers Tobacco Company, 236–37,
   242
Henry v. FCC, 347–48, 371
Herbert v. Lando, 185, 189, 192
Herbert v. Shanley Company, 243, 253
Herndon v. Lowry, 3, 5
Hess v. Indiana, 25–26
Hicklin; Regina v., 102–3, 105, 110
Higginbotham; Connell v., 126–27
Hill; Time v., 209–11, 216–17, 220
Hillery; Procunier v., 284–85
Hilliard Hotel Company; John Church
   Company v., 243
Hoehling v. Universal City Studios, 235,
   242
Holmes v. Hurst, 226, 228–29
Home Box Office v. FCC, 338, 340–41
Hoover v. Intercity Radio Company, 333
Hope v. Hearst Consolidated
   Publications, 153
Hornby v. Hunter, 151
Houchins v. KQED, 284–85, 290
Howard v. Des Moines Register &
   Tribune Company, 206–7
Hudgens v. NLRB, 54–55, 64, 67
Huff; Secretary of the Navy v., 136–38,
   146
Hughes v. Superior Court of California,
   51, 64
Hunter; Hornby v., 151
Hurst; Holmes v., 226, 228–29

Hutchinson v. Proxmire, 182, 189
Hynes v. Borough of Oradell, 133–34, 146

Industrial Commission of Ohio; Mutual Film Corporation v., 114
Illinois; Beauharnais v., 186–87, 189, 192
Illinois; Goss v., 315–16
Illinois; Ward v., 108–9
Illinois Broadcasting Company v. National Citizens Committee For Broadcasting, 346–47
Indiana; Hess v., 25–26
In re Amstar, 392
In re Aspen Institute and CBS, 358
In re Bernstein, 262
In re Bridge, 266–67, 269, 290
In re Farr, 266, 268–69
In re Investigative File, 266, 268–69, 290
In re ITT Continental Baking Company, 390–92
In re Ocean Spray Cranberries, 390–92
In re Pacifica Foundation, 355–56
In re Palmetto Broadcasting Company, 354
In re Payless Drug Stores Northwest, 392
In re Petition of Robert Harold Scott for Revocation of Licenses of Radio Stations KQW, KPO, and KFRC, 361–63, 371
In re United Broadcasting Company (WHKC), 361–63, 371
In re WUHY-FM, Eastern Educational Radio, 355–56
Insilco Broadcasting Corporation v. WNCN Listeners Guild, 350–51, 353
Intercity Radio Company; Hoover v., 333
International Brotherhood of Teamsters; Dickens v., 165–66
International Longshoremen's Association v. Allied International, 52–53, 64
International News Service v. Associated Press, 233–34, 242, 255
International Society For Krishna Consciousness; Heffron v., 141–42, 146, 149
In the Matter of Pappas, 259–61
In the Matter of RMJ, 381–82, 385
In the Matter of the Mayflower Broadcasting Corporation and the Yankee Network, 361–63, 371
Investigative File; In re, 266, 268–69, 290
Iowa; Bartels v., 69–70
Irvin v. Dowd, 321–22, 324–25, 328
Italian Book Corporation v. ABC, 246
ITT Continental Baking Company; In re, 390–92

Jacobellis v. Ohio, 105–6
Jacova v. Southern Radio and Television Company, 202–4, 207
James; Healy v., 95, 98, 100
J. B. Williams Company; United States v., 389–90, 397
Jenkins v. Georgia, 108–10
Jewelers' Circular Publishing Company v. Keystone Publishing Company, 230–31, 233, 242
John Church Company v. Hilliard Hotel Company, 243
Johnson; Cameron v., 51–52, 64
Johnson; Kelley v., 198
Journal of Commerce and Commercial Bulletin v. Burleson, 295
Julian Messner; Spahn v., 215–18

Karrigan v. Valentine, 151–52
KCMO Broadcasting Division—Meredith Corporation; Williams v., 202–4, 207
Keefe; Organization For A Better Austin v., 135–36, 146
Keefe v. Geanakos, 82–84, 90
Kelley v. Johnson, 198
Kelley v. Post Publishing Company, 201–2, 207
Kelner v. United States, 24–26
Kennerley; United States v., 103–4
Kentucky; Ashton v., 188–89

Kent v. Dulles, 143–44, 146
Keyishian v. Board of Regents, 76–77,
    82, 125, 127
Keystone Publishing Company; Jewelers'
    Circular Publishing Company v.,
    230–31, 233, 242
KFKB Broadcasting Association v.
    Federal Radio Commission, 334–36,
    343
Kiley; Mailloux v., 83–84, 90
King v. Mister Maestro, 246–47
Kissinger v. Reporters Committee For
    Freedom of the Press, 275–76
Kleindienst; Capital Broadcasting
    Company v., 396, 400
Kleindienst v. Mandel, 143, 145–47
Knight; Forcade v., 288–89
Konigsberg v. State Bar of California, 6,
    8, 46–49
Korematsu v. United States, 45–46, 49
Kovacs v. Cooper, 7–8, 130–32, 149
KPNX Broadcasting Company v. Arizona
    Superior Court, 318–19
KQED; Houchins v., 284–85, 290
Kramer; Farrell v., 166
Kunkin; People v., 199–201
Kunz v. New York, 43–45, 49

Laird v. Tatum, 129–30
Lait; Neiman-Marcus Company v.,
    187–89
Lamont v. Postmaster General, 295–96,·
    304, 307
Landmark Communications v. Virginia,
    285–87
Lando; Herbert v., 185, 189, 192
Langford v. Vanderbilt University,
    161–62
League of Women Voters of California;
    FCC v., 342–43, 375
League of Women Voters v. FCC,
    358–59
LeGrand; New York v., 266, 269, 290
Lehman v. Shaker Heights, 7, 393, 398,
    400
Lewis Publishing Company v. Morgan,
    295
Lewis v. New Orleans, 23–24

Lewis v. United States, 263–65
Liddy; United States v., 263–65
Liggett and Meyers Tobacco Company;
    Henry Holt & Company v., 236–37,
    242
Lightman v. Maryland, 266, 269, 290
Linmark Associates v. Township of
    Willingboro, 382–83, 385
Lipman v. Commonwealth of
    Massachusetts, 230, 233, 242
Littell; Buckley v., 151
Little Rock; Bates v., 40, 49
Lloyd v. Tanner, 54–56, 64
Loew's Incorporated; Benny v., 236,
    240, 242
Loew's Incorporated; CBS v., 236, 240,
    242
Logan Valley Plaza; Amalgamated Food
    Employees Union v., 54–55, 64
Longman; Carey v., 222n
Long v. United States Internal Revenue
    Service, 275–76
Lopez; Goss v., 96–98, 100
Lorain Journal Company v. FCC,
    345–46
Lorain Journal Company v. United
    States, 296–99, 304
Louisiana; Cox v., 4, 57–59, 64
Louisiana; Garner v., 4
Louisiana; Garrison v., 170–71, 189
Louisiana; Rideau v., 322–25, 328
Lovell v. City of Griffin, 133, 146
Lowry; Herndon v., 3, 5
Lugosi v. Universal Pictures Company,
    217
Lux v. Angel, 86, 88, 90
Lyons; Smith v., 151

MacDonald v. DuMaurier, 240, 242
MacLeod v. Tribune Publishing
    Company, 158–59
Madison; Marbury v., 269
Mailloux v. Kiley, 83–84, 90
Maine v. University of Maine, 342–43
Mandel; Kleindienst v., 143, 145–47
Mansfield Journal Company v. FCC,
    345–47, 371
Manual Enterprises v. Day, 105

Man v. Warner Brothers, 215–18
Marbury v. Madison, 269
Marshall v. United States, 320–21, 324–25, 328
Marsh v. Alabama, 7, 135–36, 146, 149
Martinez; Procunier v., 138–39, 146
Martin v. City of Struthers, 133–35, 145–46, 149
Maryland; Freedman v., 111–12, 121, 123–24
Maryland; Lightman v., 266, 269, 290
Maryland; Niemotko v., 44–45, 49
Maryland v. Baltimore Radio Show, 315–16, 319
Massachusetts; Lipman v., 230, 233, 242
Matteo; Barr v., 161–62
Maxwell; Sheppard v., 323–25, 328, 330
Mayflower Broadcasting Corporation and the Yankee Network; In the Matter of the, 361–63, 371
Maynard; Wooley v., 33–34
McCarthy v. FCC, 358–59
McCord; Democratic National Committee v., 261–63, 265
McDonald's Corporation; Sid & Marty Krofft Television v., 241–42
McDonald v. Smith, 185–86
Meeropol v. Nizer, 244, 253
Meinhold v. Taylor, 86–88, 90
Meister; Dalton v., 158
Members of the City Council of the City of Los Angeles v. Taxpayers For Vincent, 143, 146
Metro-Goldwyn Pictures Corporation; Sheldon v., 241–42, 255
Metromedia; Rosenbloom v., 178–79, 183, 189
Metromedia v. City of San Diego, 394, 398, 400
Meyer; Musto v., 235, 242
Meyer v. Nebraska, 69, 81
Miami Herald Publishing Company v. Rose, 316n
Miami Herald Publishing Company v. Tornillo, 302–3, 305, 308
Michigan; Butler v., 116–18, 121
Midwestern Television v. Southwestern

Cable Company, 338–41
Midwest Video Corporation; FCC v., 338, 340–41
Midwest Video Corporation; National Black Media Coalition v., 338, 340–41
Midwest Video Corporation; United States v., 338–41, 343
Mifflin v. Dutton, 226–29
Mifflin v. White, 226–29
Miller v. California, 102, 107–10, 117–18, 123–24
Mills v. Alabama, 301–2, 305
Milwaukee Social Democrat Publishing Company v. Burleson, 291
Minersville School District v. Gobitis, 71
Mink; Environmental Protection Agency v., 277–78, 284, 290
Minneapolis Star & Tribune Company v. Minnesota Commissioner of Revenue, 294–95, 304
Minnesota Commissioner of Revenue; Minneapolis Star & Tribune Company v., 294–95, 304
Minnesota; Near v., 111, 291–93, 304, 307
Mishkin v. United States, 106
Mister Maestro; King v., 246–47
Mitchell; Capital Broadcasting Company v., 395–96
Mobile Steamship Association; American Radio Association v., 52, 64
Mohs; United Press International v., 158–59
Molpus v. Fortune, 77
Monitor Patriot Company v. Roy, 177, 189
Montandon v. Triangle Publications, 156–57
Morgan; Lewis Publishing Company v., 295
Morgan v. State, 261–63, 265
Mosley; Police Department of Chicago v., 59–61, 64, 67
Mt. Healthy City School District Board of Education v. Doyle, 87–88, 91
Murdock v. Pennsylvania, 7, 133–34, 146
Murphy v. Florida, 324–25, 329–30

Murray v. Curlett, 72–73, 81
Musto v. Meyer, 235, 242
Mutual Film Corporation v. Industrial Commission of Ohio, 114

NAACP v. Alabama, 38–40, 46, 49, 67
NAACP v. Claiborne Hardware, 50–51, 56, 64, 67
Namath v. Sports Illustrated, 213, 218
National Association of Broadcasters v. FCC, 346–47
National Association of Broadcasters v. WNCN Listeners Guild, 350–51, 353
National Audubon Society; Edwards v., 184
National Black Media Coalition v. FCC, 349–50
National Black Media Coalition v. Midwest Video Corporation, 338, 340–41
National Broadcasting Company, 358
National Citizens Committee For Broadcasting; American Newspaper Publishers Association v., 346–47
National Citizens Committee For Broadcasting; Channel Two Television Company v., 346–47
National Citizens Committee For Broadcasting; FCC v., 345–47, 371, 375
National Citizens Committee For Broadcasting; Illinois Broadcasting Company v., 346–47
National Citizens Committee For Broadcasting; Post Company v., 346–47
National Citizens Committee For Broadcasting v. FCC, 397–98, 400
National Socialist Party of America v. Skokie, 63–65, 67
National Wildlife Art Exchange; Franklin Mint Corporation v., 235–36, 242
Nation Enterprises; Harper & Row Publishers v., 247
NBC; Columbia Pictures Corporation v., 236, 240, 242
NBC; FCC v., 353–54

NBC; Strickler v., 207–8, 211
NBC v. FCC, 361n
NBC v. United States, 337–38, 343, 375
Near v. Minnesota, 111, 291–93, 304, 307
Nebraska; Meyer v., 69, 81
Nebraska Press Association v. Stuart, 317–19, 330
Neiman-Marcus Company v. Lait, 187–89
New England Newspaper Publishing Company; Triangle Publications v., 230–33, 242
New Hampshire; Chaplinsky v., 22–24, 26, 35
New Hampshire; Cox v., 43–45, 49
New Hampshire; Poulos v., 44–45, 62
New Hampshire; Sweezy v., 85, 88, 90
New Nonpareil Company; Overstreet v., 151
New Orleans; Lewis v., 23–24
New York; Feiner v., 21–22, 26, 36
New York; Ginsberg v., 83, 117, 121
New York; Gitlow v., 2–4, 14, 19, 35
New York; Kunz v., 43–45, 49
New York; Radich v., 29–31, 34
New York; Redrup v., 106–7, 123
New York; Saia v., 130, 132
New York; Street v., 28–31, 34
New York American; Zbyszko v., 153–54
New York Graphic Society; Pushman v., 223
New York State Broadcasters Association v. United States, 353–54, 371
New York Times Company v. United States, 8–9, 292–93, 304, 308
New York Times v. Sullivan, 6, 86, 168–71, 176–77, 180–84, 189, 192, 259, 378
New York v. Ferber, 117–18, 123
New York v. LeGrand, 266, 269, 290
Nichols v. Bristow Publishing Company, 153, 155–56
Nichols v. Philadelphia Tribune Company, 166
Niemotko v. Maryland, 44–45, 49
Nixon; United States v., 270–72, 308

Nixon v. Administrator of General
    Services, 270-72
Nixon v. Sirica, 270-73
Nixon v. Warner Communications, 270,
    272-73, 290
Nizer; Meeropol v., 244, 253
NLRB; Hudgens v., 54, 64, 67
NLRB v. Retail Store Employees Union,
    52, 64
NLRB v. Robbins Tire and Rubber
    Company, 282-84
NLRB v. Sears, Roebuck and Company,
    280-82, 284, 308
Noto v. United States, 15, 17
Nye v. United States, 311, 319, 330

O'Brien; United States v., 27, 31, 34,
    36
Ocala Star-Banner Company v. Damron,
    177, 189
Ocean Spray Cranberries; In re, 390-92
Oestereich v. Selective Service Board,
    27-28
Office of Communication of the United
    Church of Christ v. FCC, 367-69, 371
Ohio; Bohning v., 69-70
Ohio; Brandenburg v., 4, 15, 17-18
Ohio; Jacobellis v., 105-6
Ohio State Bar Association; Ohralik v.,
    381, 385
Ohralik v. Ohio State Bar Association,
    381, 385
Onassis; Galella v., 197-98, 201
One Book Called "Ulysses"; United
    States v., 104
Oregon; DeJonge v., 15
Organization For A Better Austin v.
    Keefe, 135-36, 146
Orito; United States v., 119-20
Orsini; United States v., 261-63, 265
Ostwalt v. State-Record Company, 164
Overstreet v. New Nonpareil Company,
    151

Pacifica Foundation; FCC v., 356-57,
    371, 375
Pacifica Foundation; In re, 355-56

Palmer v. Schonhorn Enterprises, 213-
    14, 218
Palmetto Broadcasting Company; In re,
    354
Pane; Cosgrove Studio and Camera
    Shop v., 187-89
Pape; Time v., 174, 189
Papish v. Board of Curators of the
    University of Missouri, 94, 97-98, 100
Pappas; In the Matter of, 259-61
Parducci v. Rutland, 82-84, 90
Paulsen v. Personality Posters, 215-16,
    218
Payless Drug Stores Northwest; In re,
    392
Pearson; Washingtonian Publishing
    Company v., 228-29
Pearson v. Dodd, 199-201
Pell v. Procunier, 284-85, 290, 308
Pennekamp v. Florida, 313-14, 316, 319
Pennsylvania; Murdock v., 7, 133-34,
    146
People v. Dan, 266-67, 269, 290
People v. Dial Press, 103
People v. Friede, 103
People v. Kunkin, 199-201
People v. Seltzer, 103
People v. Spielman, 186n
Perry Educational Association v. Perry
    Local Educator's Association, 138-40,
    146
Perry Local Educator's Association;
    Perry Educational Association v.,
    138-40, 146
Perry v. Sindermann, 88-91, 100
Personality Posters; Paulsen v., 215-16,
    218
Peterson; Arvey Corporation v., 152
Peterson; Solverson v., 151
Philadelphia Tribune Company; Nichols
    v., 166
Pickering v. Board of Education, 85-88,
    90, 100
Pico; Board of Education, Island Trees
    Union Free School v., 80-82, 100
Pinkus v. United States, 110, 123
Pittsburgh Commission on Human

Relations; Pittsburgh Press Company
  v., 378–79
Pittsburgh Press Company v. Pittsburgh
  Commission on Human Relations,
  378–79
Planned Parenthood of Central Missouri
  v. Danforth, 197, 201
Police Department of Chicago v.
  Mosley, 59–61, 64, 67
Pollak; Public Utilities Commission of
  District of Columbia v., 132
Pollitt; Brush-Moore Newspapers v., 165
Population Services International; Carey
  v., 383, 385
Post Company v. National Citizens
  Committee For Broadcasting, 346–47
Postmaster General; Lamont v., 295–96,
  304, 307
Post-Newsweek Stations, Capital Area v.
  Business Executives Move For Vietnam
  Peace, 360–61, 366
Post Publishing Company; Kelley v.,
  201–2, 207
Poulos v. New Hampshire, 44–45, 62
President and Commissioners of Princess
  Anne County; Carroll v., 62, 64
Presidents Council v. Community School
  Board No. 25, 78–79, 82
Price v. Hal Roach Studios, 217–18
Procunier; Pell v., 284–85 290, 308
Procunier v. Hillery, 284–85
Procunier v. Martinez, 138–39, 146
Progress-Bulletin Publishing Company v.
  Superior Court, 316n
Progressive; United States v., 293
Proskin; WBAI-FM v., 266–69, 290
Proxmire; Hutchinson v., 182, 189
PruneYard Shopping Center v. Robins,
  56, 64
Public Affairs Associates v. Rickover,
  246–47
Public Service Commission of New York;
  Central Hudson Gas and Electric
  Corporation v., 383–85, 400
Public Service Commission of New York;
  Consolidated Edison Company of New
  York v., 140–41, 146

Public Utilities Commission of District of
  Columbia v. Pollak, 132
Pushman v. New York Graphic Society,
  223

Radich v. New York, 29–31, 34
Radio Television News Directors
  Association; United States v., 364–66
Raladam Company; FTC v., 387, 397
Random House; Estate of Hemingway v.,
  223–24
Random House; Rosemont Enterprises
  v., 244
Reader's Digest; Wolston v., 183, 189,
  192
Red Lion Broadcasting Company v.
  FCC, 364–66, 371, 375
Redrup v. New York, 106–7, 123
Regan v. Wald, 143–46
Regina v. Hicklin, 102–3, 105, 110
Reidel; United States v., 119–20
Renegotiation Board v. Grumman
  Aircraft Engineering Corporation,
  280–82, 284, 290
Reporters Committee For Freedom of the
  Press; Kissinger v., 275–76
Resor; Epstein v., 276–77, 284, 290
Retail Store Employees Union; NLRB v.,
  52, 64
Reyher v. Children's Television
  Workshop, 234, 242
Reynolds; United States v., 273–74
Richardson; Cole v., 126–27, 130
Richmond Newspapers v. Virginia, 285–
  87, 308
Rickover; Public Affairs Associates v.,
  246–47
Rideau v. Lousiana, 322–25, 328
RKO General v. FCC, 370, 372
RMJ; In the Matter of, 381–82, 385
Robbins Tire and Rubber Company;
  NLRB v., 282–84
Robel; United States v., 6, 48–49
Robert Harold Scott for Revocation of
  Licenses of Radio Stations KQW,
  KPO, and KFRC; In re Petition of,
  361–63, 371

Robertson; Administrator, Federal
Aviation Administration v., 279–80,
284, 290
Robert Welch; Gertz v., 178–83, 189,
192
Robins; PruneYard Shopping Center v.,
56, 64
Rockford; Grayned v., 60–61, 64
Roden; Empire Printing Company v.,
160–61
Roe v. Wade, 196–97, 201
Rose; Department of the Air Force v.,
282
Rose; Miami Herald Publishing
Company v., 316n
Rosemont Enterprises v. Random House,
244
Rosen; Vaughn v., 279
Rosenblatt v. Baer, 176–77, 189
Rosenbloom v. Metromedia, 178–79,
183, 189
Roth; Board of Regents v., 88–91, 100
Roth v. Greensboro News Company
153–54
Roth v. United States, 6, 83, 102, 104–
11, 115–16, 123, 355–57
Rowan v. U.S. Post Office Department,
113–14,121, 123
Roy; Monitor Patriot Company v., 177,
189
Rusk; Zemel v., 143–44, 146
Russell; Elfbrandt v., 126–27
Rutland; Parducci v., 82–84, 90

Saia v. New York, 130, 132
St. Amant v. Thompson, 173–74, 184,
189, 192
Sally v. Brown, 153–55
Sanders Brothers Radio Station; FCC v.,
344–45
San Diego; Metromedia v., 394, 398,
400
Sarat Lahiri v. Daily Mirror, 212, 218
Saxbe v. Washington Post Company,
284–85, 290
Scales v. United States, 15–17
Schacht v. United States, 33–34

Schad v. Borough of Mount Ephraim,
120–21
Schaumburg; Citizens For A Better
Environment v., 133–35, 146
Schempp; School District of Abington
Township v., 72–73, 81
Schenck v. United States, 2–3, 13–14,
19, 35
Schonhorn Enterprises; Palmer v., 213–
14, 218
School District of Abington Township v.
Schempp, 72–73, 81
Schulingkamp; Times-Picayune
Publishing Corporation v., 310, 317,
319
Schuster v. Bowen, 316n
Scopes v. State, 69
Scripps-Howard Broadcasting Company;
Zacchini v., 217–18, 220
Sears, Roebuck and Company; NLRB v.,
280–82, 284, 308
Secretary of State; Aptheker v., 143–44,
146, 149
Secretary of the Navy v. Huff, 136–38,
146
Selective Service Board; Oestereich v.,
27–28
Selective Service Local Board; Breen v.,
27–28
Seltzer; People v., 103
Seymour v. United States, 316n
Shaker Heights; Lehman v., 7, 393, 398,
400
Shanley Company; Herbert v., 243, 253
Sheldon v. Metro-Goldwyn Pictures
Corporation, 241–42, 255
Shelton v. Tucker, 75–77, 81–82
Shepherd v. Florida, 320, 324–25, 328
Sheppard v. Maxwell, 323–25, 328, 330
Shuttlesworth v. Birmingham, 62, 64
Sid & Marty Krofft Television v.
McDonald's Corporation, 241–42
Simmons v. FCC, 347–48, 371
Sindermann; Perry v., 88–91, 100
Sirica; Nixon v., 270–73
Sitterson; Dickson v., 77
Skokie; National Socialist Party of

America v., 63–65, 67
Slochower v. Board of Higher
  Education, 73–74, 77, 82
Smith; McDonald v., 185–86
Smith v. California, 115, 121
Smith v. Daily Mail Publishing
  Company, 285–87
Smith v. Fielden, 151
Smith v. Goguen, 31
Smith v. Lyons, 151
Smith v. United States, 109, 123
Snepp V. United States, 304, 308
Solverson v. Peterson, 151
Sonderling Broadcasting Corporation,
  WGLD-FM, 356
Sony Corporation of America v.
  Universal City Studios, 252–53, 255
South Carolina; Edwards v., 56–59, 64,
  67
Southeastern Promotions v. Conrad,
  111–12
Southern Radio and Television Company;
  Jacova v., 202–4, 207
Southwestern Cable Company;
  Midwestern Television v., 338–41
Southwestern Cable Company; United
  States v., 338–41, 343, 375
Spahn v. Julian Messner, 215–18
Spence v. Washington, 7, 31
Spielman; People v., 186n
Spock; Greer v., 136–38, 146, 149
Sports Illustrated; Namath v., 213, 218
Sports Illustrated; Virgil v., 202, 204–5,
  207
Stacy v. Williams, 77–78, 82
Stamford Board of Education; Eisner v.,
  93–94
Standard Education Society; FTC v.,
  387–88, 397, 399
Stanford Daily; Bergna v., 289–90
Stanford Daily; Zurcher v., 289–90, 308
Stanley v. Georgia, 118–21, 123
Star Broadcasting Company; Demman
  v., 156–57
State; Crane v., 185n

State; Morgan v., 261–63, 265
State; Scopes v., 69
State Bar of Arizona; Baird v., 48–49
State Bar of Arizona; Bates v., 380–81,
  385
State Bar of California; Konigsberg v.,
  6, 8, 46–49
State-Record Company; Ostwalt v., 164
Staub v. Baxley, 42, 49
Stice v. Beacon Newspaper Corporation,
  163
Stone v. FCC, 369–71
Stone v. Graham, 73, 81
Street v. New York, 28–31, 34
Strickland; Wood v., 96–98, 100
Strickler v. NBC, 207–8, 211
Stromberg v. California, 29, 34
Struthers; Martin v., 133–35, 145–46,
  149
Stuart; Nebraska Press Association v.,
  317–19, 330
Subversive Activities Control Board;
  Communist Party v., 46, 49
Sullivan; New York Times v., 6, 86,
  168–71, 176–77, 180–84, 189, 192,
  259, 378
Sun Company of San Bernardino v.
  Superior Court, 316n
Sunset House Distributing Corp.; Doran
  v., 240, 242
Superior Court; Dow Jones & Company
  v., 263–65
Superior Court; Progress-Bulletin
  Publishing Company v., 316n
Superior Court; Sun Company of San
  Bernardino v., 316n
Superior Court for the County of
  Norfolk; Globe Newspaper Company
  v., 285, 287
Superior Court of California; Hughes v.,
  51, 64
Superior Court of State of California, In
  And For Los Angeles County; Times-
  Mirror Company v., 312–13
Superior Court of the State of California,

County of Los Angeles; Farr v., 266–69, 290
Sweezy v. New Hampshire, 85, 88, 90

Talley v. California, 128–29, 149
Tandem Productions v. CBS, 350–53
Tanner; Lloyd v., 53–54, 64
Tatum; Laird v. 129–30
Taxpayers For Vincent; Members of the City Council of the City of Los Angeles v., 143, 146
Taylor; Meinhold v., 86–88, 90
Teleprompter Corporation v. CBS, 248–49, 253, 255
Terminiello v. Chicago, 3, 20–22, 26, 36
Texas; Duke v., 77
Texas; Estes v., 325–30
Thirty Seven (37) Photographs; United States v., 119–20
Thomas v. Collins, 7, 41–42, 49
Thompson; St. Amant v., 173–74, 184, 189, 192
Thompson v. Gernsback, 243–44, 253
Thornhill v. Alabama, 3, 50, 56, 64, 67
Time; Dempsey v., 166
Time; Dietemann v., 198–99, 201
Times Film Corporation v. Chicago, 111
Times-Mirror Company v. Superior Court of State of California, In And For Los Angeles County, 312–13
Times-Mirror Company v. United States, 296, 298, 304
Times-Picayune Publishing Company v. Schulingkamp, 310, 317, 319
Times-Picayune Publishing Company v. United States, 296, 298, 304
Time v. Bernard Geis Associates, 242–43, 252
Time v. Firestone, 178, 180–83, 189
Time v. Hill, 209–11, 216–17, 220
Time v. Pape, 174, 189
Tinker v. Des Moines Independent Community School District, 32–34, 36, 91–94, 97, 100

Tobacco Institute v. FCC, 394–95
Toksvig v. Bruce Publishing Company, 236–38, 242
Toledo Newspaper Company v. United States, 310–12, 319, 330
Toomey v. Farley, 151
Tornillo; Miami Herald Publishing Company v., 302–3, 305, 308
Township of Willingboro; Linmark Associates v., 382–83, 385
Triangle Publications; Amsterdam v., 230–33, 242
Triangle Publications; Montandon v., 156–57
Triangle Publications v. New England Newspaper Publishing Company, 230–33, 242
Tribune Association; Chicago Record-Herald, 234, 242
Tribune Company v. United States, 297, 299
Tribune Publishing Company; Caldero v., 263–65
Tribune Publishing Company; MacLeod v., 158–59
Trinity Methodist Church South v. Federal Radio Commission, 334–36, 343
Tucker; Shelton v., 75–77, 81–82
12 200-ft Reels of Super 8 mm Film; United States v., 119–20
Twentieth Century Music Corporation v. Aiken, 249–50, 253, 255

Uhlaender v. Henricksen, 215, 218
United Artists Television; Fortnightly Corporation v., 248, 253, 255
United Broadcasting Company (WHKC); In re, 361–63, 371
United Press International v. Mohs, 158–59
United States; Abrams v., 3, 13
United States; Associated Press v., 296–97, 299, 304
United States; Barenblatt v., 6, 127–29

United States; Besig v., 103
United States; Bursey v., 263–65
United States; CBS v., 337–38
United States; Citizen Publishing
  Company v., 299–301, 305
United States; Debs v., 13, 19
United States; Dennis v., 4, 6, 15–19,
  36
United States; Flower v., 136–37, 146
United States; Frohwerk v., 13
United States; Ginzburg v., 8–9, 115–
  16, 121, 123
United States; Gutknecht v., 28
United States; Hamling v., 109–10
United States; Kelner v., 24–26
United States; Korematsu v., 45–46, 49
United States; Lewis v., 263–65
United States; Lorain Journal Company
  v., 296–99, 304
United States; Marshall v., 320–21,
  324–25, 328
United States; Mishkin v., 106
United States; NBC v., 337–38, 343,
  375
United States; New York State
  Broadcasters Association v., 353–54,
  371
United States; New York Times Company
  v., 8–9, 292–93, 304, 308
United States; Noto v., 15, 17
United States; Nye v., 311, 319, 330
United States; Pinkus v., 110, 123
United States; Roth v., 6, 83, 102,
  104–11, 115–16, 123, 355–57
United States; Scales v., 15–17
United States; Schacht v., 33–34
United States; Schenck v., 2–3, 13–14,
  19, 35
United States; Seymour v., 316n
United States; Smith v., 109, 123
United States; Snepp v., 304, 308
United States; Times-Mirror Company
  v., 296, 298–99, 304
United States; Times-Picayune Publishing
  Company v., 296, 298, 304
United States; Toledo Newspaper
  Company v., 310–12, 319, 330

United States; Tribune Company v., 234,
  242
United States; Watkins v., 127–28
United States; Watts v., 24–26, 36
United States; Williams & Wilkins
  Company v., 251, 253
United States; Yates v., 15–17
United States Internal Revenue Service;
  Long v., 275–76
United States Postal Service v. Council
  of Greenburgh Civic Associations,
  138–40, 146
United States Post Office Department;
  Rowan v., 113–14, 121, 123
United States v. Caldwell, 259–61
United States v. CBS, 316n
United States v., Dickinson, 316–17,
  319, 330
United States v. Grace, 142, 146
United States v. Gregg, 334–36, 343
United States v. J. B. Williams
  Company, 389–90, 397
United States v. Kennerley, 103–4
United States v. Liddy, 263–65
United States v. Midwest Video
  Corporation, 338–41, 343
United States v. Nixon, 270–72, 308
United States v. O'Brien, 27, 31, 34, 36
United States v. One Book Called
  "Ulysses," 104
United States v. Orito, 119–20
United States v. Orsini, 261–63, 265
United States v. Progressive, 293
United States v. Radio Television News
  Directors Association, 364–66
United States v. Reidel, 119–20
United States v. Reynolds, 273–74
United States v. Robel, 6, 48–49
United States v. Southwestern Cable
  Company, 338–41, 343, 375
United States v. Thirty Seven (37)
  Photographs, 119–20
United States v. 12 200-ft Reels of Super
  8 mm Film, 119–20
United States v. Washington Post
  Company, 292–93
United States v. Weber Aircraft

Corporation, 280–82, 284, 290
United States v. Zenith Radio
  Corporation, 333
Universal Amusement; Vance v., 112
Universal City Studios; Hoehling v.,
  235, 242
Universal City Studios; Sony Corporation
  of America v., 252–53, 255
Universal Pictures Company; Heim v.,
  236, 239, 242
Universal Pictures Company; Lugosi v.,
  217
Universal Pictures Company; Wrench v.,
  227–29
University of Maine; Maine v., 342–43
Updegraff; Wieman v., 75, 77, 81–82
Uphaus v. Wyman, 127–30

Valentine; Karrigan v., 151–52
Valentine v. Chrestensen, 377–78, 385,
  400
Vance v. Universal Amusement, 112
Vanderbilt University; Langford v.,
  161–62
Vannier; Cowper v. 153, 155
Varnish v. Best Medium Publishing
  Company, 210–11
Vaughn v. Rosen, 279
Vincent; Widmar v., 95–96
Virgil v. Sports Illustrated, 202, 204–5,
  207
Virginia; Bigelow v., 379, 385, 400
Virginia; Landmark Communications v.,
  285–87
Virginia; Richmond Newspapers v.,
  285–87, 308
Virginia Citizens Consumer Council;
  Virginia State Board of Pharmacy v.,
  379–80, 385
Virginia State Board of Pharmacy v.
  Virginia Citizens Consumer Council,
  379–80, 385
Vitale; Engel v., 71–73, 81

Wade; Roe v., 196–97, 201
Wainwright Securities v. Wall Street

Transcript Corporation, 234, 242
Wald; Regan v., 143–46
Walker; Associated Press v., 172–74,
  189
Walker v. Birmingham, 61–62, 64
Wall Street Transcript Corporation;
  Wainwright Securities v., 234, 242
Walt Disney Productions v. The Air
  Pirates, 245
Ward v. Illinois, 108–9
Warner Brothers; Man v., 215–18
Warner Brothers Pictures v. CBS, 245
Warner Communications; Nixon v., 270,
  272–73, 290
Warner-Lambert v. FTC, 392, 397, 400
Washington; Spence v., 7, 31
Washingtonian Publishing Company v.
  Pearson, 228–29
Washington Post Company; Saxbe v.,
  284–85, 290
Washington Post Company; United States
  v., 292–93
Watkins v. United States, 127–28
Watts v. United States, 24–26, 36
WBAI-FM v. Proskin, 266–69, 290
WDAY; Farmers Educational and
  Cooperative Union v., 161–62, 192,
  359–60, 375
Weber Aircraft Corporation; United
  States v., 280–82, 284, 290
Western Line Consolidated School
  District; Givhan v., 86, 88, 91, 100
West Publishing Company v. Edward
  Thompson Company, 236n
West Virginia State Board of Education
  v. Barnette, 71, 81, 100
Whitcomb; Communist Party of Indiana
  v., 48–49
White; Mifflin v., 226–29
Whitehill v. Elkins, 77, 82, 125–27
Whitney v. California, 3, 14–15
Widmar v. Vincent, 95–96
Wieman v. Updegraff, 75, 77, 81–82
Williams; Stacy v., 77–78, 82
Williams & Wilkins Company v. United
  States, 251, 253
Williams v. KCMO Broadcasting

Division—Meredith Corporation, 202–
  4, 207
Wilson; Burstyn v., 114–15, 121
Wilson; Gooding v., 23–24
Winsted Hosiery Company; FTC v.,
  386–87, 397
Wisconsin Employment Commission; City
  of Madison, Joint School District v.,
  86–88, 90–91
WNCN Listeners Guild; ABC v., 350–52
WNCN Listeners Guild; FCC v., 350–53,
  371, 375
WNCN Listeners Guild; Insilco
  Broadcasting Corporation v., 350–51,
  353
WNCN Listeners Guild; National
  Association of Broadcasters v., 350–
  51, 353
Wolston v. Reader's Digest, 183, 189,
  192
Wood v. Constitution Publishing
  Company, 164
Wood v. Georgia, 4, 315–16, 319
Wood v. Goodson, 316
Wood v. Strickland, 96–98, 100
Wooley v. Maynard, 33–34
Wrench v. Universal Pictures Company,
  227–29

Writers Guild of America v. FCC,
  350–53
WTRF-TV v. FCC, 394–95
WUHY-FM, Eastern Educational Radio;
  In re, 355–56
Wyman; Uphaus v., 127–30

Yale Broadcasting Company v. FCC,
  350, 371
Yates v. United States, 15–17
Young; Carr v., 75
Youngs Drug Products Corporation;
  Bolger v., 384–85
Young v. American Mini Theatres, 120–
  21, 123

Zacchini v. Scripps-Howard
  Broadcasting Company, 217–18, 220
Zack Meyer's T.V. Sales and Service;
  Donald v., 230, 232–33, 242
Zbyszko v. New York American, 153–54
Zemel v. Rusk, 143–44, 146
Zenith Radio Corporation; United States
  v., 333
Zurcher v. Stanford Daily, 289–90, 308

GENERAL INDEX

absolute privilege, 161–63, 193
absolutism test, 8–9, 293, 409
academic freedom, 100–1
actual malice, 86, 155–57, 168–71, 178–85, 189, 192–93, 207, 209–11, 220
advertising law, 400–1
advocacy of action, 15–19, 36
anonymous publication, 128–29, 149
antitrust laws, 290, 296–99, 304
appropriation, 212–17, 220
Areopagitica, 257, 402
association, 67–68

bad tendency test, 4–6, 13–15, 19–20, 35, 312, 319, 330, 409
balancing test, 5–8, 48, 409
Barron, Jerome, 406
Bergan, Francis, 216
Black, Hugo, 5–9, 33, 46, 58, 72, 104, 129, 131, 135, 144, 187, 302, 312, 388
Blackmun, Harry, 109–10, 196, 292, 380, 393
book banning, 78–81
Brandeis, Louis, 3, 14, 194, 291
Brennan, William, 23, 61, 76, 80–81, 104–5, 115–16, 139, 170, 196, 272, 282, 287, 293, 343
broadcast law, 376
Brown, John, 317
Burger, Warren, 33, 81, 94, 107, 113, 129, 136, 145, 182, 186, 280, 285–87, 292, 318, 360–61, 393

candidate-access rule, 360–61
"Canon 35," 325, 327
caveat emptor, 385, 387–88, 399
Chafee, Zechariah, Jr., 404
Clarke, John, 291
Clark, Tom, 323–26

clear and present danger test, 2–4, 12–14, 19, 35, 312, 316, 319, 330–31, 409
commercial information, 379–85, 400–1
commercial speech, 377–79, 385, 400–1, 408–9
common-law copyright, 222–24
communication context, 407
Communications Act of 1934, 336–37, 339, 342–44, 357, 360, 369, 371, 376
Comstockery, 102
copyright law, 255–56
Copyright Act of 1790, 224–25
Copyright Act of 1909, 224–25
Copyright Act of 1976, 222, 224–26, 229, 241–43, 247, 250–52, 256
corrective advertising, 390–92, 400–1

deception, 385–92
dissent, 36–37, 409
Douglas, William, 3, 7–9, 21–22, 28, 54, 58–59, 77, 86, 89, 104, 113, 126, 130, 187–88, 293, 295, 300, 311, 314, 340, 393

Emerson, Thomas, 405–6
equal-time rule, 357–60
executive privilege, 269–73, 280, 290, 307
expression/action dichotomy, 405–6

failing-company doctrine, 290, 299–301, 305
fair comment, 164, 193
fairness doctrine, 361–64, 375–76, 394–97, 400–1
fair trial, 331
fair use, 225, 242–53, 256
false light, 207–8, 211, 220
Federal Contempt Act of 1831, 310
fictionalization, 207–8, 211

431

fighting words, 22–24, 29, 35–36, 409
First Amendment, 1, 402–10
flag salute, 70–71
forced listening, 132
forecast rule, 91–94
Fortas, Abe, 29, 91
Frankfurter, Felix, 6–7, 46, 186, 338
Frank, Jerome, 239
Freedom of Information Act, 274–84, 290, 308–9
free speech *plus*, 54

gag orders, 316–19, 330
Goldberg, Arthur, 40, 144

Haiman, Franklyn, 407
Hand, Learned, 4, 103
Harlan, John, 6, 16–17, 25, 28, 39, 172, 292
Hicklin test, 102–3
Holmes, Oliver Wendell, 2–3, 13–14, 19, 230, 291
hot news, 172–73, 189, 192
Hughes, Charles, 292

implied bias, 325–30
intrusion, 194–201, 220

Kaufman, Irving, 184

libel, 192–93, 409
libelous petition, 185–86
libel *per quod*, 151–52, 192
libel *per se*, 151, 192
limited-access doctrine, 366–67
loyalty oath, 49, 75–77, 125–27

marketplace of ideas, 257, 402–3
Marshall, Thurgood, 53, 139, 283, 384–85
McReynolds, James, 229
media access, 406–7
Meiklejohn, Alexander, 405
Miller test, 107–10
Mill, John Stuart, 403
Milton, John, 257, 402
Minton, Sherman, 74

Moore, Leonard, 244
Murphy, Frank, 50

negligence, 180, 189, 192–93
neutral reportage, 184–85
news law, 308–9
news reporter's privilege, 254–65, 290, 308–9
newsworthiness, 204–7, 221, 371

obscenity, 124, 409
O'Conner, Sandra Day, 81, 247, 294
offensive words, 25–26, 29, 36
originality, 229–33, 242, 256
overbreadth, 50–51, 60, 68, 76

pandering, 115–16, 124
Peck, James, 310
personal-attack rule, 364–65, 375
Pitney, Mahlon, 234
political hyperbole, 24–25, 36
Powell, Lewis, 23, 54, 81, 95, 97, 137–40, 180, 310, 317, 378, 382–84
prayer, 70, 72–73
preferred position test, 7–8, 77–78, 409
prepublication review, 291, 304, 308
presumption of regularity, 278
pretrial publicity, 320–25, 331
prior restraint, 41–42, 62–63, 77–78, 111–12, 290–93, 304, 307–9, 331
privacy law, 220–21
private person, 178–83, 189
provocative words, 20–22, 36
Public Broadcasting Act of 1967, 342–43
public disclosure, 201–6, 220
public figure, 180–82, 192
Public Health Cigarette Smoking Act, 395
public official, 176–78
Pure Food and Drug Act of 1906, 386

qualified privilege, 163–64, 193

Radio Act of 1912, 333, 343
Radio Act of 1927, 333–34, 336, 343–44
reasonable belief, 170–71, 189

reckless disregard, 172–75, 189, 192
Redrup reversals, 106–7
Reed, Stanley, 7–8, 45, 131, 134, 313
Rehabilitation Act of 1973, 352
Rehnquist, William, 31, 53, 81, 94, 108–9, 139, 145, 181–83, 198, 276, 318–19, 393
right of publicity, 215–18, 220
right to reply, 291, 302, 305, 308
Roberts, Owen, 5, 42, 344
robust debate, 175–76, 189, 192
Roth test, 104–6
Rutledge, Wiley, 7

Sanford, Edward, 4, 14, 19
scienter, 115, 124
scope of discovery, 185, 189
Scott, A. A., 312
self-government, 405
shield laws, 265–69, 290, 309
silence, 149
single instance rule, 155–56
social exchange, 403–4
social utility, 404
"so near therto," 310–12, 319, 330
sound amplification, 130–32, 149
Stevens, John, 50, 139, 143, 176, 252, 282, 304, 357

Stewart, Potter, 137, 174, 177, 248–49, 261, 286, 322
Story, Joseph, 229
Stuart, Hugh, 317–18
substantiality, 236–42, 256
Sutherland, George, 294
symbolic speech, 26–34, 36

third-party privacy, 289–90
threatening words, 24–25, 36
travel, 143–46
truth, 160–61, 193
two-tiered approach, 409–10

vagueness, 50–51, 60, 68, 76–77
Vinson, Frederick, 4, 6, 16, 21, 44, 273–74

Warren, Earl, 6, 29, 48, 58, 85, 127, 144, 353
Warren, Samuel, 194
White, Byron, 63, 109, 117, 121, 134, 139, 141–42, 173, 185, 260, 280–83, 289, 340, 351, 365, 393–94
widest latitude, 18–20
Wireless Ship Act, 332
Woolsey, J., 104

Zenger, John Peter, 257–58

ABOUT THE AUTHOR

JOSEPH J. HEMMER, JR., is a Professor and Chairperson of the Communication Department at Carroll College, Waukesha, Wisconsin.

Dr. Hemmer has previously published two volumes on the subject of communication law—*Communication Under Law: Free Speech* (1979) and *Communication Under Law: Journalistic Expression* (1980). He has published widely in the area of communication studies; his articles have appeared in the *Quarterly Journal of Speech, Central States Speech Journal, Southern Speech Journal, Speaker and Gavel,* and the *Journal of the Wisconsin Communication Association.*

Dr. Hemmer holds a B.A. from Wisconsin State College (Oshkosh), an M.A. from Bradley University, and a Ph.D. from the University of Wisconsin.